THE GOSPELS EXPLAINED

By the Same Author:

JESUS OF NAZARETH: A DELUDED MESSIAH
THE END OF CHRISTIANITY
WHO, WHERE, AND WHAT IS GOD?

Albrecht Dürer: Christ Crucified (1519)

ALBERTUS PRETORIUS

THE GOSPELS EXPLAINED

A NOVEL AND RATIONAL GUIDE TO THE GOSPEL NARRATIVES

WIPF & STOCK · Eugene, Oregon

THE GOSPELS EXPLAINED

Copyright © 2024 Albertus Pretorius. All rights reserved. Except for brief quotations in critical publications or reviews, no part of this book may be reproduced in any manner without prior written permission from the publisher. Write: Permissions, Wipf and Stock Publishers, 199 W. 8th Ave., Suite 3, Eugene, OR 97401.

Wipf & Stock
An Imprint of Wipf and Stock Publishers
199 W. 8th Ave., Suite 3
Eugene, OR 97401

www.wipfandstock.com

PAPERBACK ISBN: 979-8-3852-0797-8
HARDCOVER ISBN: 979-8-3852-0798-5
EBOOK ISBN: 979-8-3852-0799-2

CONTENTS

CHAPTER	PAGE
PREFACE	vii
1. INTRODUCTION	1
2. HISTORICAL BACKGROUND	23
3. THE Q DOCUMENT	84
4. PAULINE FRAGMENTS	140
5. JOHN'S NARRATIVE	176
6. THE EPISTLE OF JAMES	254
7. MARK, MATTHEW, AND LUKE	263
8. MATTHEW'S UNIQUE MATERIAL	387
9. LUKE'S UNIQUE MATERIAL	449
10. JOHN'S SERMONS, DIALOGUES, AND DISCOURSES	536
11. THE DIDACHÉ	586
12. CLEMENS ROMANUS	611
13. THE GOSPEL OF THOMAS	621
14. THE QUR'AN	679
15. CONCLUSION: THE VALUE OF THE GOSPEL NARRATIVESS	697
BIBLIOGRAPHY	720
LIST OF ILLUSTRATIONS	736

Abbreviations Used:

Cath Enc   Catholic Encyclopedia
Enc Brit   Encyclopaedia Britannica
Enc com   Encyclopedia.com
Jewish Enc   Jewish Encyclopedia
NW Enc   New World Encyclopedia

Albrecht Dürer: Christ on the Cross (1505)

PREFACE

This book is the result of a lifetime of study and much soul searching.

I spent most of my adult life in the ministry. Because I wanted to be a disciple or apprentice/pupil of Jesus Christ in the fullest sense of the word, I kept on studying after my initial training as a minister of religion in the Dutch Reformed Church in South Africa and eventually I received two doctorates. My favorite fields of study were theology (especially New Testament studies), philosophy, psychology, and history. I believe this background helped me to deliver high-quality sermons to the congregations I served and to render effective pastoral care to my parishioners.

Towards the end of my career as minister of religion, it became increasingly difficult to deliver a satisfying sermon because my studies convinced me that the Bible cannot any longer be regarded as a divinely-inspired collection of books and documents. There are just too many contradictions, inconsistencies, nonsensical statements, and inaccuracies to be a credible and trustworthy source of spiritual insights and historical knowledge.

The result was that I wrote three books after my retirement in which I demonstrated –

- That Jesus of Nazareth was a deluded messiah who was convinced that he was chosen by God to restore the Israelite kingdom of his ancestor, King David;
- That Christianity is doomed to wither away and eventually die due to all the improbable and impossible and implausible dogmas held by believers; and
- That the traditional idea of God as an omnipotent, omnipresent, omniscient, and caring creator of the universe cannot be

maintained any longer and that this idea had to be replaced by a more rational view of the divine.

This book is in a certain sense an extension of my book on Jesus as a deluded messiah. A few passages from that book appear in this book in augmented and expanded form, especially in the second chapter of this book.

While preparing sermons while still in the ministry, I always made a point of consulting the text of the relevant biblical passage in the original Hebrew or Greek. In the case of a text from the gospels, I always compared that text with parallel texts in the other gospels, if any. In addition, I consulted at least three commentaries to get a good grasp on that text.

The time has arrived that I write my own commentaries on the gospel narratives contained in the holy scriptures and elsewhere, while utilizing the method described above. I am convinced that my studies and investigations of the biblical texts, against the background of our extensive knowledge of biblical times, will shed new light on that remarkable prophet, popular teacher, gifted healer, and charismatic Jewish rabbi and throne-pretender of the first century AD, Jesus of Nazareth.

When one gets a historically valid perspective on the ministry of this very influential figure from Antiquity, after all the mythological, legendary, and clearly fictitious elements have been exposed and removed, it is possible to explain the contents of the gospel narratives so much better and determine how much value can be placed on them for accurate information about Jesus. Certain obscure passages in the gospels may become meaningful in this manner. This book is an effort in that direction.

The intended readers are all serious students of the Bible – scholars, preachers, and inquisitive lay people who seek a better understanding of the roots of Christianity.

Albertus Pretorius, South Africa, November 2023.

Chapter 1
INTRODUCTION

Object of the Book
How reliable are the gospel narratives in the Bible? What did really happen in the life of Jesus of Nazareth?

The object of this book is to provide an answer to these questions and to give a credible explanation of the background and contents of the gospel narratives in the New Testament of the Bible, as well as some extra-biblical documents, using critical, scientific, and rational methods and techniques.

This is not yet another book about the life and significance of Jesus of Nazareth as such. It is rather an investigation of the gospel narratives to determine how far they can be regarded as credible, trustworthy, and faithful sources of knowledge about his life and message.

The word "gospel" has two meanings when used in the New Testament:

- The message or "good tidings" (εὐαγγέλιον – *euangelion*) of the New Testament, as formulated in the letters of the apostle Paul and other documents in the New Testament; and
- The name given to a book containing a description of the life, teachings, and execution of Jesus of Nazareth.

This book deals mainly with the second meaning of the word "gospel". It will be used in a somewhat wider sense because the biographical details about the message, life, and execution of Jesus contained in Paul's letters will also be considered. As an afterthought, the extra-biblical epistle of Clement, the Gospel of Thomas, the Didaché, as well as the holy book of Islam, the Qur'an, will also be discussed.

Therefore, the value of the various gospel narratives as historical sources for the life, message, crucifixion, and resurrection of the historical Jesus of Nazareth will have to be investigated and evaluated. Historians strive to reconstruct the past "as it really was" on account of available sources dealing with –

- the relevant historical events;
- all the social, religious, and political movements, cults, sects, and parties of those times; as well as
- the religious beliefs and philosophy of the role players.

In this process, these sources – documents, pictures, memories of participants or observers of those events, or archaeological findings – must be approached with caution in order to ascertain their historical value, reliability, and relevance.

The gospel narratives – in the widest sense of the word, including extra-biblical sources – have all to be scrutinized and evaluated in the same manner.

This book is, of course, not the first effort to find the "historical Jesus", in contrast with the Jesus of the traditional and conventional Christian faith. The best-known investigation in this regard was done by the so-called Jesus Seminar, a group of American academics who worked together since the eighties of the previous century. The amount of literature produced by this group and their critics would fill a whole library.[1] It would be an impossible task to give an overview of all the debated points here.

---

[1] Meier, "The Present State of the 'Third Quest' for the Historical Jesus".

INTROCUCTION

The following points may be regarded as a summary of the findings of the Jesus Seminar:

- "Jesus of Nazareth was born during the reign of Herod the Great.
- "His mother's name was Mary, and he had a human father *whose name may not have been Joseph.*
- "Jesus was born in Nazareth, not in Bethlehem.
- "Jesus was an itinerant sage who ate with social outcasts.
- "Jesus practiced faith healing *without the use of ancient medicine or magic*, relieving afflictions now modernly considered psychosomatic.
- "He did not walk on water, feed the multitude with loaves and fishes, change water into wine or raise Lazarus from the dead.
- "Jesus was arrested in Jerusalem and crucified by the Romans.
- "*He was executed as a public nuisance, not for claiming to be the Son of God.*
- "*The empty tomb is a fiction – Jesus was not raised bodily from the dead.*
- "*Belief in the resurrection is based on the visionary experiences of Paul, Peter and Mary Magdalene."*[2]

This book will demonstrate that some of these findings can be accepted. However, it will be shown that those points printed in italics above must be rejected when all the evidence is considered.

    The members of the Jesus Seminar contended that the gospels had very little historical value and that most of what they reported about Jesus was legendary and tainted by political, philosophical, and mythological influences. This book does not go

---

[2] Wikipedia, "Jesus Seminar".

so far and it will be shown that the gospels do contain much reliable information and that many seemingly obscure or nonsensical passages make perfect sense when observed from the correct angle. This book will demonstrate that not all the findings of the Jesus Seminar can be upheld when the gospels are being read from the correct perspective – which will be explored and explained in the next chapter.

A notable recent effort to determine the historical value of the gospel narratives regarding the resurrection of Jesus was published by the South African historian, Leopold Scholtz. He concluded that these reports are credible and reliable historical sources, without deciding the question whether Jesus' resurrection after having died horribly on the cross – usually regarded as a medical impossibility – really did happen.[3]

This study will follow in the footsteps of Scholtz, although it will do more by commenting on all the passages in the gospel narratives, although it will not necessarily agree with all his conclusions. He was honest enough to declare his religious position as a committed Christian and elder in his church. That, certainly, influenced his positive evaluation of the gospels as reliable historical sources regarding the resurrection stories.

This type of investigation must be performed sympathe‑tically on the one hand. That means that these sources must be allowed to speak for themselves and the researcher must endeavor to understand them within their context.

This examination must, on the other hand, also be scientific and rational. That means that improbabilities, impossibilities, inconsistencies, mythological and legendary elements, demonstra‑ble errors, and the religious or ideological positions of the sources

---

[3] Scholtz, "Jesus se Kruisiging en Opwekking" (Jesus' Crucifixion and Resurrection).

must be uncovered and pointed out.

Demythologization

The Germán theologian Rudolf Bultmann became well-known for his view that we must "demythologize" the Bible. He wrote:

> "We cannot use electric lights and radios and, in the event of illness, avail ourselves of modern medical and clinical means and at the same time believe in the spirit and wonder world of the New Testament."[4]

This process of demythologizing actually started long before the time of Bultmann, although it was not typified as such. The primitive, pre-scientific cosmology of the ancient world, which is also to be found in the Bible, has been discarded systematically since the Renaissance in the sixteenth century and the Enlightenment of the eighteenth century. Educated people did not any longer believe that the earth is a flat disk, situated upon pillars that stand in a primeval flood of waters (see, for instance, Gen 1: 6 and Ex 20: 4). It was found that the earth is not the center of the universe and that it is only one of several planets circling around the sun. The planets and stars were no longer deemed to be deities or angels and God's heaven was no longer seen as a space just beyond the clouds and the stars (see, for instance, Job 22: 12 and Ps 19: 4).

The ancients, including the Israelites and the first Christians, all believed in the power of magic. There is no real difference between the feats of magicians and the various miracles described in the Bible.[5] Educated people of our age, including Christians, have largely discarded any belief in the power of magic and sorcery. Most educated people are convinced that the universe is ruled by

---

[4] Bultmann, *New Testament and Mythology*, 4.
[5] Pretorius, *The End of Christianity*, 93–97; 194–203; 226–29.

immutable natural laws and that every phenomenon has a natural cause. Scientists have, as yet, failed to discover any instances where the laws of nature were violated and where miracles, which amount to a suspension of natural laws, were documented, and explained.[6]

Satan, Demons, and Evil Spirits
We often read of Satan, demons, and evil spirits in the Bible, especially in the four canonical gospels. The belief in these entities ought also to be discarded as part of ancient mythology.

Satan plays a minor role in the Old Testament and we only encounter him in the post-exilic book of Job.

Christians usually read Genesis 2 and 3 as if Satan is the seducer of Eve, who – in turn – seduces Adam to eat of the forbidden fruit. Shawna Dolansky, however, argued: "Introduced as 'the most clever of all of the beasts of the field that YHWH God had made,' the serpent in the Garden of Eden is portrayed as just that: a serpent. Satan does not make an appearance in Genesis 2–3, for the simple reason that when the story was written, the concept of the devil had not yet been invented."[7]

Christians usually base their identification of Satan with the snake in the story of Adam and Eve on Revelation. Dolansky counters that "although the author of Revelation describes Satan as 'the ancient serpent' (Revelation 12: 9; 20: 2), there is no clear link anywhere in the Bible between Satan and Eden's talking snake."[8]

The book of Job tells the fictitious story of a pious man who suffered many calamities since God allowed Satan to test his steadfastness. It appears that Satan had unlimited access to God and may be considered to have been a member of the heavenly court:

---

[6] Pretorius, *Who, Where, and What is God?* 133–148.
[7] Dolansky, "How the Serpent Became Satan", 4.
[8] Dolansky, "How the Serpent Became Satan", 4.

- "Now it happened on the day when the sons of God came to present themselves before YHWH, that Satan also came among them" (Job 1: 6).
- "YHWH said to Satan, 'Behold, all that he [Job] has is in your power. Only on himself don't put forth your hand.' So Satan went forth from the presence of YHWH" (Job 1: 12).

Satan is introduced as a familiar figure without any further explanation. His name in Hebrew is הַשָּׂטָן (*Ha–Shathan*) "The word *Satan* is the English transliteration of a Hebrew word for 'adversary' in the Old Testament."[9]

There is evidence that this figure was adopted into the Jewish religion from the Persian religion, which knew of two chief deities, Ahura Mazda (the creator of the cosmos, the father of the pantheon and the source of light and truth) and Ahriman (an evil spirit, the antagonist of Ahura Mazda and the source of darkness and suffering).[10]

Evil spirits are also encountered in the Old Testament. These spirits are not – as is the case in the New Testament – under the reign of Satan, but they are servants of God. We read in 1 Sam16: 14–15:

"Now the Spirit of YHWH departed from Saul, and an evil spirit from YHWH troubled him. Saul's servants said to him, 'See now, an evil spirit from God troubles you.'"

The word used for "spirit" is רוּחַ (*ruach*), which means "wind, breath, mind, spirit". It is qualified by the word רע (*ra*), which means "bad, evil". The word for "trouble" is בעת (*ba'at*) and it means "to terrify, startle, fall upon, dismay, be overtaken by sudden

---

[9] Enc. Brit., "Satan".
[10] Malandra, "Iranian religion."

terror". We read further on that David, the future king and successor of Saul, had to apply music therapy by playing on the harp for Saul in order to lift his spirits.

It may be asked: what were the symptoms of this affliction? Clues are given in 1 Sam 18: 29 and 1 Sam 19: 9–10. These two passages inform us:

- "Saul was yet the more afraid of David; and Saul was David`s enemy continually."
- "An evil spirit from YHWH was on Saul, as he sat in his house with his spear in his hand; and David was playing with his hand. Saul sought to strike David even to the wall with the spear; but he slipped away out of Saul`s presence, and he struck the spear into the wall: and David fled, and escaped that night."

The same expression for "evil spirit" is used as in the previous passages.

At this point one may ask: is it possible to diagnose Saul with paranoid schizophrenia, due to his jealousy and suspicions regarding David? That is a real possibility. According to the DSM–5 of the American Psychiatric Association, the main symptoms of this condition are delusions, hallucinations, disorganized speech, and irrational suspicions. The suicide risk of sufferers is high.[11] It is, therefore, not a surprise that Saul committed suicide in the end (1 Sam 31).

A tentative diagnosis of schizophrenia in Saul is confirmed by 1 Sam 19: 24 –

---

[11] American Psychiatric Association, *DSM-5*, 99–104.

"He also stripped off his clothes, and he also prophesied before Samuel, and lay down naked all that day and all that night. Why, they say, is Saul also among the prophets?"

In Saul's case, his mental disorder – whether it was schizophrenia or something else – was attributed to an evil spirit because people in those days had no inkling of the functioning of the human brain and the human mind and they had to find a supernatural cause for Saul's strange behavior.

It has to be stressed at this point: the evil spirit that we encounter in the case of Saul was sent by God – not by Satan. This, however, does not seem to make sense; how was it possible for God, supposedly the source of all goodness, to employ an evil spirit to torment the king of Israel, his anointed son?

According to 1 Kings 22: 21–23, God sent "a lying spirit" to cause several prophets to utter false prophecies. This text, likewise, contains the idea that evil spirits were in God's service and that they did not come from Satan. This text, anyway, seems irrational. Why would God, supposedly the source of all benevolence and truth, deliberately cause prophets to pronounce false prophecies? It just does not make sense.

The word "devil" (Greek: διάβολος – *diabolos*) occurs 35 times in the New Testament and the name "Satan" (Greek: Σατανᾶς – *Satanas*, a literal transcription of the Hebrew name) is used 36 times.

Perhaps the most well-known episode in which this figure appears is the story of Jesus' temptation in the desert after he had been baptized by John. The original story in Mark, the oldest and shortest Gospel, appears in Mark 1: 12–13. We are only briefly told that Jesus stayed forty days in the desert where he was tempted by Satan. The version of this episode in the other two Synoptic Gospels (Matt 4: 1–11 and Luke 4: 1–13) is much more detailed. This expanded story seems to be part of the Q Document, the oldest report we have regarding Jesus' actions and words.[12] The fact that both Mark and Q – independent sources – contain reports regarding Jesus' temptation, leads to the conclusion that something of this sort really must have happened.

In these stories, we are informed that Jesus stayed without food for forty days during his stay in the desert. When he became hungry, he was tempted by the devil who promised him various favors, should Jesus worship him. The only source for this story must have been Jesus himself since there were no independent eye-witnesses of these episodes. He must have related it at a later stage to his followers, from whom the authors of Mark and Q must have collected it. There is, therefore, no independent corroboration for the veracity of all the supernatural events described in Matthew and Luke.

We find the following Greek words to describe Satan:

- διάβολος (*diabolos* – a calumniator, false accuser, slanderer)
- πειράζων (*peirazon* – someone to test one maliciously, to craftily put to the proof one's feelings or judgments)

If Jesus stayed forty days in the heat of the desert without food and water, he most probably would have succumbed to heatstroke or hyperthermia. Young describes the effects of this condition as follows:

> "Initially, there is a mild impairment of cognitive function including judgment, followed by a more profound acute confusional state. This may progress to a delirium with

---

[12] Mack, *The Lost Gospel,* 82, 174–175, 179; (see also Chapter 2).

agitation, increased sympathetic nervous activity, and hallucinations."[13]

It is, therefore, most probable that Jesus became confused or hallucinated while fasting, in which time Satan seemed to appear to him. For him, it would have been a very real experience, while we know today that a heatstroke can have a profound effect on the brain and its functioning, often causing hallucinations. Although it is probable that Jesus spent some time alone in the desert where he fasted, this appearance of the devil to him would, therefore, not have been a real historical event; it would merely have been the product of a temporarily malfunctioning brain.

In Luke 10:18, Jesus is reported as saying: "I saw Satan having fallen like lightning from heaven." This is another indication that he believed in the reality of Satan, just as other people of those times.

Satan is seen in the New Testament as the adversary, one who opposes another in purpose or act, the name given to the prince of evil spirits, the inveterate adversary of God and Christ. In Matt 12: 24 we again read of the Devil: "But when the Pharisees heard it, they said, 'This man does not cast out demons, except by Beelzebul, the prince of the demons.'" It is remarkable that the Devil is given the name of *Beelzebul* (Greek: Βεελζεβούλ) in this passage, since that was the name of a pagan deity in the Old Testament (2 Kgs 1: 2, 6, 16). We are informed that he is called "the prince of the demons".

Demons and demonic possession are often mentioned in the gospels and Acts. The Greek word for "demon" is δαιμόνιον (*daimonion*), and it means a spirit, a being inferior to God, superior to men, or evil spirits or the messengers and helpers of the Devil. It

---

[13] Young, "Hypothermia", 611.

is clear from Matt 4: 24 that any disease or malady for which no explanation could be given was regarded in those days with its primitive and pre-scientific world view as a case of demonic possession:

> "The report about him went forth into all Syria. They brought to him all who were sick, afflicted with various diseases and torments, possessed with demons, epileptics, and paralytics; and he healed them."

It is necessary to explain the Greek words used in this passage:

- κακῶς (*kakos* – miserable, to be ill);
- νόσος (*nosos* – disease, sickness);
- βάσανος (*basanos* – torture, torment, acute pain)
- δαιμονίζομαι (*daimonizomai* – to be under the power of a demon)
- σεληνιάζομαι (*seleniazomai* – to be moon-struck or lunatic; to be epileptic)
- παραλυτικός (*paralytikos* – paralytic, disabled, weak of limb)

From this it is clear that in those days all sorts of diseases were seen as being caused by demons; being possessed by a demon was simply used as a synonym for being ill or suffering pain. In our time, we have enough medical knowledge to know that no disease is caused by a demon or that epilepsy is not caused by the moon or the moon goddess, Selene. There are natural explanations for all sorts of aches and pains, fever, epilepsy, paralysis *etcetera*. We do not need Satan, demons, or malicious spirits to explain medical, neurological, and psychiatric conditions. The numerous stories in the gospels about

Jesus who liberated people from evil spirits must be interpreted from this point of view.

Historical Method
On account of all the preceding, answers must be found to the following questions in order to follow tested and tried methods in the discipline of historical research:

- How were the written historical sources compiled?
- Are there any available written documents drafted by direct participants or contemporary observers and commentators?
- How much time elapsed between the events and the description thereof in the extant written reports?
- Who exactly were the authors of these sources?
- Did these authors rely on other sources – written and/or oral – or did they report their own experiences or observations?
- How reliable were the written and oral sources consulted by the authors of the extant and available sources?
- What were the religious and political convictions, nationalities, and social positions of these authors and how did these factors influence their descriptions of the events they reported on?
- What was the general social, political, economic, and military situation during the time of the described events, as well as at the time of the compilation of these written sources and reports?
- Were the beliefs, experiences, and actions of the role players influenced by their medical and psychological conditions?
- Which objectives did the authors of the available written sources wish to achieve with their letters, documents, and reports?
- The application of he razor of Occam: the most simple and least complicated explanation of a phenomenon or a text is usually the correct or most likely explanation.

These principles are similar to those used in a court of law to determine the credibility of evidence placed before it.

All this means that a distinction must be made between primary and secondary sources. Secondary sources are usually reports that quote or make use of primary sources. The four canonical gospels must be regarded as secondary sources that have been compiled several decades after the events they describe. They quote primary sources or comment on them – the memories of eye-witnesses that have been collected and put in writing or became part of a fixed tradition. In the case of the gospels, these primary sources can often be reconstructed, as will be shown later.

It is also necessary to remember that the interpretation of historical sources always happens against the religious or ideological position of the researcher. For instance, Christian and Muslim historians may create different narratives and draw different pictures about the Christian crusades during the Middle Ages. Church historians who write about the Reformation of the sixteenth century will, inevitably, present their publications from a Roman Catholic, Protestant, or Anabaptist perspective.

On account of all the preceding considerations, it must be evident that historical research cannot be an exact science, such as physics, astronomy, chemistry, geology, or any of the other natural sciences. Very often, the historian must be honest and declare that he can only reconstruct certain aspects of the past with variable degrees of certainty or probability.

Christian Suppositions Regarding the Gospels
Almost all commentaries on the four biblical gospels explain these narratives and their contents from a more or less traditional or conventional Christian point of view. This viewpoint boils down in most cases to the following:

- As part of the Bible, the Word of God, the events described and the thoughts expressed in the gospels must have been written under the guidance of the Holy Spirit and are, therefore, true and accurate in all respects and it amounts to sacrilege to question the veracity or reliability of these documents;
- Jesus of Nazareth, the Christ, the Messiah, is regarded as the second person in the Divine Trinity, namely the eternal Son of God and of the same substance as his heavenly Father and the Holy Spirit, although he also adopted a human nature; and
- Jesus is seen as the savior of the world by taking upon himself the punishment all sinners deserve in hell in the afterlife when he was executed on the cross, although he was resurrected with a glorified body after three days in a tomb.

When the veracity of the gospel narratives is being investigated, these traditional Christian suppositions and perspectives must be placed on hold and the gospels must be investigated in a rational and non-partisan way, as any other ancient documents have to be approached – and that is what this book promises to do. The present author had to, as it were, forget about his background as a Christian preacher and approach the gospel narratives purely from the perspective of an inquisitive, impartial, rational, and sceptic historian.

Most conventional commentaries analyze the contents of the gospels to find confirmation for the traditional Christian beliefs and dogmas regarding the reliability of the Bible and the nature and position of Jesus Christ as savior of the world. This book refrains from doing that and concentrates exclusively on the explanation of the background and contents of these narratives in the light of the questions posed above. It may appear that certain Christian convictions cannot be maintained when the evidence in the gospel narratives is scrutinized rationally, scientifically, impartially, and honestly.

Development of the Gospel Narratives
Experts on the New Testament have demonstrated convincingly that the four biblical gospels, as we have them today, went through a process of development and editing during which different (sometimes primary) sources were merged into a single gospel book.

It is possible to dissect various other biblical books in this manner. The first that comes to mind is the Pentateuch, the collection of the first five books of the Old Testament, which was traditionally regarded as the work of Moses. It was shown in 1886 by the German scholar, Julius Wellhausen, to be a combination of four literary sources.

Wellhausen identified these four documents that were combined to form the first five books of the Old Testament or Torah. The first three in the following list are especially characterized by the different names used for the God of Israel:

- The "J" or Yahwist source;
- The "E" or Elohist source (later combined with J to form the "JE" text);
- The "P" or Priestly source; and
- The "D" or Deuteronomist text – the whole book of Deuteronomy.

Conservative biblical scholars tend to reject this theory and maintain that Moses must have been the sole author of the whole Pentateuch. They declare that there does not exist any external evidence – apart from the current text of the Pentateuch – to support this theory.[14] Most scholars, however, accept Wellhausen's theory.

A careful analysis of the prophetic book of Isaiah in the Old Testament reveals that it contains three separate books in succession, each one from a different historical period. Because the second and third parts are anonymous, scholars named the three parts respectively Isaiah, Deutero-Isaiah, and Trito-Isaiah.[15]

The gospels of Mark, Matthew, Luke, and John also show signs of having been compiled in stages by combining different sources. We must consider that the writers of the gospels were dependent upon oral and written traditions regarding the life and work of Jesus, as Luke reminded his readers in Luke 1: 1–4. Jesus left no writings and nobody wrote down what he did or said while he was still alive. The authors of the gospels were, therefore, dependent upon the memories of people who were eye-witnesses and who passed their memories on to others who joined the early Jesus Movement. As time passed, these memories got blurred and distorted and when they were eventually written down, often decades after the events, they were colored and interpreted in the light of subsequent situations. Much of the information regarding Jesus as contained in the gospels is, therefore, legendary, and even mythological in nature.

Magee's description of the origin and growth of the gospels is certainly correct:

> "The gospels have obviously been changed frequently by deliberating editing or by copying errors since they were first written, and it is not even clear that the gospels of Mark and

---

[14] *N W Enc,* "Documentary Hypothesis"; Closson, "Did Moses Write the Pentateuch?"
[15] Boshoff *et al., Geskiedenis en Geskrifte,* 134–38, 179–83, 190–91.

Luke even existed in an agreed form at first. There is good reason for thinking that both could have existed initially as a draft form (proto–Mark and proto–Luke) and this was worked up by many hands into the books we now have. A similar scheme applies too to Matthew which was originally not at all like the gospel we now have but was a collection of sayings, perhaps a version of the document called 'Q.' This was combined with Mark, to give a fuller, richer, and more polished gospel and this was edited by many editors before it reached the modern form."[16]

That Magee has a valid point is attested by the fact that there are, for instance, three different endings to the Gospel of Mark known to us. Luke reminds us at the beginning of his gospel (1: 1) that "many have undertaken to draw up a narrative concerning those matters" dealing with the life and work of Jesus before he took this task upon himself. The report in John 8: 1–11 regarding the woman caught in adultery does not appear in the oldest manuscripts of this gospel and it was only added at a later stage. There are clear indications that the last Chapter in John, Chapter 21, is an afterthought that was added later.

The authors and editors of the gospels did not report how they gathered their information and assembled their material into coherent narratives. Their method was likely to interview people who witnessed or remembered what Jesus said and did and to write their words down. Since none of these witnesses could provide a complete chronology of Jesus' ministry, the authors of Q (the oldest source about Jesus' teachings) and Mark had to arrange their notes into some order with the object of constructing a credible and coherent gospel. Matthew and Luke merged Q with Mark, but added

---

[16] Magee, "Christianity Revealed", 38.

some material of their own. They also often rearranged Mark's chronology. John's chronology differs from that of the other three gospels.[17]

Therefore, in this book it be shown –

- That the gospels of Matthew and Luke can almost be regarded as expanded and corrected re-editions of the gospel of Mark;
- That the oldest gospel we have, the so-called Q Document, was later incorporated into the gospels of Matthew and Luke;
- That Matthew and Luke contain other older material, not included in one of the other gospels, which they gathered from other sources (called the M Source and the L Source); and
- That the gospel of John was initially a simple narrative, but was later expanded by the inclusion of a philosophical prologue and purported dialogues and sermons of Jesus, much in the same style as the philosopher Plato presented his own ideas in the form of dialogues between his teacher Socrates and other men. Similarly, ancient historians often invented speeches and dialogues of famous personages to fit a certain occasion.

It must be stressed that the New Testament gospel narratives cannot be seen as objective and factual reports about the message, life, and work of Jesus. They must be classified as religious propaganda, documents explaining the beliefs of the authors about who and what Jesus was with the goal of convincing their readers to share these beliefs.

That the gospels are primarily propaganda is evident from the following introductory phrase in the Gospel of Mark: "The beginning of the gospel of Jesus Christ, the Son of God" (Mark 1: 1). The word "gospel" (Greek: εὐαγγέλιον – *euangelion*) has a

---

[17] Pretorius, *Jesus of Nazareth*, 18–19.

specific meaning in this context, namely "good tidings". The book of Mark was, therefore, not written to give an objective or impartial account of the life and work of Jesus. It was rather written to convince people that it contained "good tidings" regarding Jesus, who is the Son of God (or a divine figure, such as many mythological figure of Antiquity). It was meant to convince people that it was worthwhile to read this book and get to gain knowledge and believe in Jesus as the Christ, the Messiah.

Towards the end of John's gospel, we read:

> "Therefore, Jesus did many other signs in the presence of his disciples, which are not written in this book; but these are written, that you may believe that Jesus is the Christ, the Son of God, and that believing you may have life in his name" (John 20: 30–31).

In other words, the author of John's gospel wrote this book with the stated purpose of convincing people to believe in Jesus and to accept that he is the Christ or Messiah and the Son of God. That was, in any case, the silent intention of all the other gospel narratives. They were meant to preserve memories of their religious teacher and Messiah, Jesus of Nazareth.

Although the evangelists do not always present their readers with factually accurate and objective information about Jesus, we may assume that they were honest in their efforts to preserve and disseminate knowledge about him and that they mostly did not deliberately distort or falsify information they had gathered. It happened, though, that they invented stories to fill up gaps in their knowledge, for instance the nativity stories of Matthew and Luke, as well as some of the reports of Jesus' trial, resurrection, and ascension, which are obviously pious inventions. Their goal was simply to convince people to believe in Jesus as the Messiah.

INTROCUCTION

It will become evident when the different gospels and other narratives are discussed that much valuable and reliable information may be found after all the mythological, legendary, and propagandistic elements have been identified and removed or rectified.

In their efforts to preserve as much information about Jesus as possible, the gospel authors often inserted seemingly insignificant details into their stories. It will be shown in the analysis of the different gospels that these snippets of information often reveal a very important, but overlooked, aspect of Jesus' life and work.

From the above, it must be apparent that this book is not a conventional commentary on the gospel narratives. The focus is on the historical reliability of these narratives. How well did they preserve information about Jesus of Nazareth?

Albrecht Dürer: Jesus with the Crown of Thorns

INTROCUCTION

A vast body of literature has been produced about the background and contents of the gospels and no single scholar is able to absorb all the information and views expressed by countless theologians since the second century AD. This book must not be seen as an effort to discuss all the possible points of view regarding the different gospel passages. Only a rather brief introduction to each gospel narrative will be given, based on contemporary research, after which the reliability and likely accuracy of the contents of these writings will be commented upon.

    Before that can be done, it is necessary to obtain a clearer description of who Jesus of Nazareth and his followers really were when seen against their historical background. The meaning of Jesus' actions and teachings will become much more intelligible when this perspective is being kept in mind.

Chapter 2
HISTORICAL BACKGROUND

Conventional View of Jesus
The conventional view regarding Jesus of Nazareth, held by most Christians and formulated in several declarations of faith, amounts to the following: Jesus –

- Is the second person in the Divine Trinity, the eternal Son of God, together with God the Father and the Holy Spirit, although there is only one, single God, differentiated into three divine persons;
- Has a dual nature, namely a divine nature and a human nature, combined in one person;
- Is the Messiah promised in the Old Testament and the savior of the world because he suffered the punishment all sinners deserve in hell by dying a horrible death by being crucified;
- Was resurrected from the grave after three days, after which he ascended into heaven; and
- Is expected to return on Judgment Day as the divine judge.

Agreed Details of Jesus' Life
Most Bible students will agree with the following details regarding Jesus' life and ministry:

- In the Greek New Testament his name is Ἰησοῦς (*Iesous*). Most languages, including English, use the Latin transcription of this name, namely Jesus. His name in Hebrew or Aramaic – the home language of the Jews at the time – was *Yehoshua* (יְהוֹשֻׁעַ), which

means: "YHWH is salvation or deliverance," the same name of Joshua, the successor of Moses as leader of the Israelites.
- The name – or rather title – of "Christ" means "anointed" and is derived from the Greek Χριστός (*Christos*). It is the Greek equivalent of the Hebrew מָשִׁיחַ (*mashiyach*), which is rendered in English as "Messiah". In the letters of Paul, the title of "Christ" is used as a proper name.
- We know next to nothing about Jesus' youth and his education or whether he was married and had children. We are informed, though, that he had brothers and sisters (Mark 6: 3; John 7: 5; Acts 1: 14). The gospels contain details of his teachings, his miracles, his trial, death, and resurrection.
- In Mark 6: 3, he is called a "carpenter" and in Matt 13: 55 he is mentioned as "the carpenter's son". The Greek word translated with "carpenter" is τέκτων (*tekton*). It may be translated as "carpenter", but may also mean "craftsman", "builder" and even "building contractor".
- Since Jesus was evidently a learned man who knew the Hebrew Scriptures, it may well be that he received a good education befitting the son of a well-to-do building contractor. Luke informs us that he was able to read, which not many people in those days were able to do (Luke 4: 17).
- As a youngster, he reportedly attracted the attention of some teachers of the Law at the temple with his knowledge of and insight in the Scriptures (Luke 2: 46–47).
- People regarded him as a learned man since he was often addressed as "Rabbi" – the title used for a Jewish teacher of the Law (Mark 9: 5; Mark 11: 21; Matt 26: 25, 49; John 1: 49; John 3: 2; John 9: 2 *etcetera*).
- As a learned Jewish rabbi, he regarded the Hebrew Scriptures as reliable and valid guides. His whole worldview was based on the

Old Testament and his life was guided by the Law of Moses and the writings of the prophets.
- His teachings never amounted to a contradiction or rejection of these Scriptures, although he sometimes gave a novel and original interpretation thereof. There are no indications that he was influenced by Greek philosophy or any pagan religion. It can be safely said that he was a Jewish nationalist.
- It is possible that he knew some Greek,[18] which may explain why he was able to converse with the Roman governor, Pontius Pilate, during his trial.
- His ancestry from King David ought also to have played a role to place him and his family amongst the Jewish gentry. He and his family must have been well-known people because the crowds in Jerusalem greeted him more than once with the words: "Hosanna to the son of David!" (Matt 21: 9, 15; see also Mark 11: 9–10; Luke 19: 38; John 12: 13).
- There cannot be the slightest doubt that he was crucified after having been sentenced to death by the Roman governor, Pontius Pilate. The sign on the cross explained his crime: "Jesus the Nazorean, the king of the Jews" (John 19: 19).

To understand the gospels, it is necessary to take note of the political, social, and military situation under which Jesus lived and under which the gospels were written some decades after his time.

The Roman Empire and Pontius Pilate
After the death of the Greek conqueror Alexander the Great in 323 BC, his empire was divided by his generals. Palestine eventually ended up under the reign of the Seleucids, the kings of Syria. A successful revolt under the leadership of the Maccabees during the

---

[18] Fredriksen, *Jesus of Nazareth*, 162–64.

second century BC led to the establishment of an independent Jewish kingdom. Strife between opposing factions that supported different pretenders to the throne led John Hyrcanus II to appeal to Rome for help. Pompey, a Roman general, intervened and Judea came under Roman control during 63 BC.

The country was initially ruled by client kings of which the most well-known was Herod the Great (ruled: 37–4 BC). After his death and the removal of his son and heir, Herod Archelaus, who proved to be incompetent, a Roman governor was appointed to administer Judea. Other parts of Palestine, Galilee and Perea, were ruled by other heirs of Herod the Great.[19]

Pontius Pilate was appointed governor or prefect of Judea by Emperor Tiberius in AD 26, during Jesus' lifetime. The depiction of his character as being weak and easily swayed by the Jewish leadership in the four gospels does not tally with a more impartial assessment by Flavius Josephus, the ancient Jewish historian. According to him, Pilate was proud, headstrong, cruel, and resolute. He harbored no love for the Jews and showed gross disrespect for their religion on more than one occasion. His task was to uphold Roman law in this far-flung province, to quell any sign of rebellion and to punish those who were found guilty of *crimen maiestatis* – an insult to the emperor or his representative, the governor – by crucifixion.[20]

A revolt against the harsh Roman rule of Palestine broke out in AD 66. After initial successes against the Roman army, the Jewish forces were totally routed and Jerusalem with its temple went up in flames during August AD 70. Although the gospels do not mention this catastrophe directly because it happened some decades after the

---

[19] Rylaarsdam *et al.*, "Biblical Literature"; Jones and Bugh, "Palestine".
[20] Flavius Josephus, *Wars*, Liber II/IX/2–4; Cohn, *The Trial and Death of Jesus,* 14–15; Enc. Brit., "Pontius Pilate".

time of Jesus, this war certainly cast a shadow over the gospel reports of Jesus' life – as will be shown when the separate gospels are being investigated and explained in detail.

The Geography of Palestine

The gospel narratives deal with events during the first half of the first century AD in Palestine and it is necessary to understand where Judea, Samaria, Galilee, and various other places mentioned in the gospels were situated.

Palestine during the first century AD covered more or less the territory governed previously by the Israelite kings David and Solomon. This kingdom was divided after Solomon's death into two kingdoms – the kingdom of Judah in the south with Jerusalem as capital and the kingdom of Samaria, the kingdom of the ten tribes, with Samaria as its capital.

Both kingdoms were conquered by the Assyrians and the Babylonians respectively. After Babylonia was conquered by the Persians, the Jewish exiles in Babylonia were allowed in 538 BC to return and rebuild their temple. They refused help from the Samaritans, the descendants of remnants of the ten tribes and pagan settlers.

This animosity between the Judeans or Jews and the Samaritans continued during the following centuries.

During Jesus' lifetime, the Jews of Palestine lived in Judea and Galilee, although many Jews were also to be found in various regions around the Mediterranean Sea, including Egypt, Asia Minor, Greece, and Rome.

Jesus grew up in Nazareth in Galilee and most of his ministry was spent in Galilee. It is unknown how many visits he brought to Jerusalem because the gospels are unclear in this respect. To travel to Jerusalem from Galilee, he had to traverse Samaria. Since there was no border control in those days, he didn't need a passport.

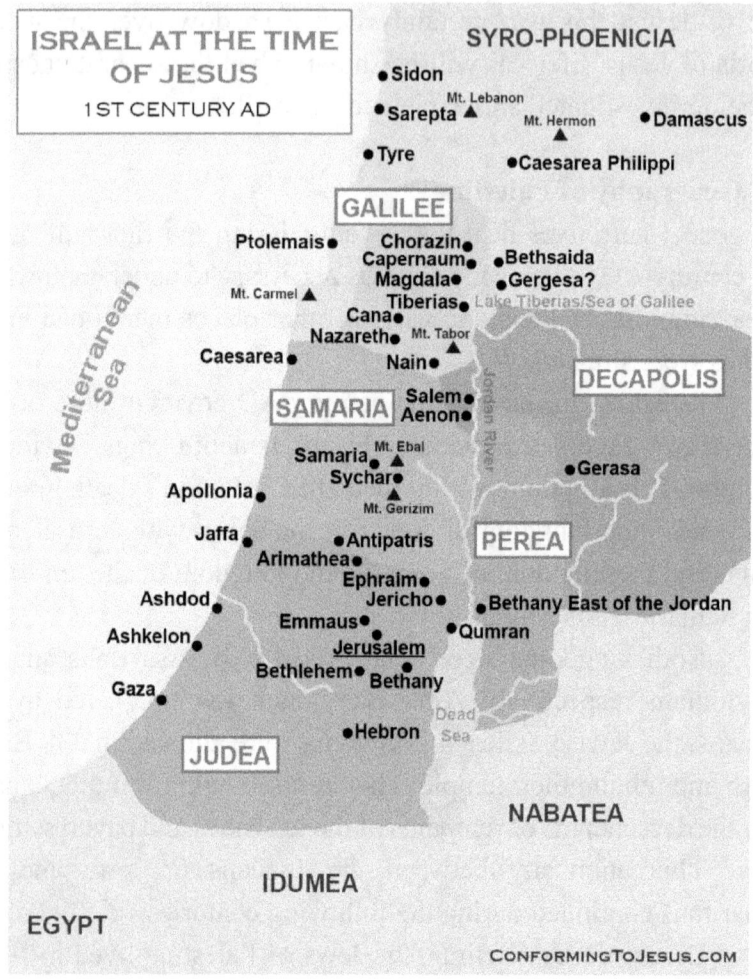

Jesus usually avoided contact with the Samaritans, but a conversation with a Samaritan woman and her fellow-villagers is recorded in John 4: 4–40. One of the best-known parables of Jesus deals with a Samaritan who helped a Jewish victim of a highway robbery (Luke 10: 25–37).

It is, furthermore, necessary to provide a brief description of the main religious and political groups at the time of Jesus, namely The Sadducees, the Pharisees, the Zealots, and the Essenes.

The High Priest, the Sanhedrin, and the Sadducees

In Roman times, the high priesthood in Jerusalem was confined to a few families who belonged to the party of the liberal and aristocratic Sadducees and who could pay for the privilege. When Jesus was tried, the high priest was Caiaphas, son-in-law of Annas, the retired former high priest.[21]

The high priest presided over the Sanhedrin, the Jewish Council, which had jurisdiction over internal Jewish political and religious matters. There were 71 members of which the majority belonged to the party of the Pharisees, a group of conservative Jews (see below). The Council was comprised of priests, Levites, lay aristocrats, and scholars or teachers of the Law.[22]

The high priest was responsible to the Roman governor who appointed him and his task was to keep law and order and to prevent any form of rebellion. He also needed the support of the Sanhedrin to execute his duties and pursue his policies, which included the smooth running of the temple complex in Jerusalem. The Sanhedrin had the power to punish people when they were found guilty of transgressing the Law of Moses. The punishment for blasphemy was death by stoning (Lev 24: 16).[23] It may be assumed that Caiaphas and the members of the council tried their best to further Jewish interests, within the constraints placed upon them by the Roman occupation of Judea.[24]

The party of the Sadducees, which is often mentioned in the gospels, usually cooperated with the Roman authorities.[25]

---

[21] Cohn, *The Trial and Death of Jesus*, 22–24.
[22] Cohn, *The Trial and Death of Jesus*, 24–26.
[23] Cohn, *The Trial and Death of Jesus*, 30–31.
[24] Cohn, *The Trial and Death of Jesus*, 27.
[25] Rylaardsdam *et.al.*, "Biblical Literature."

It appears from the gospels that the Sadducees and priests distrusted John the Baptist and Jesus, while John and Jesus criticized them often (Matt 3: 7–10; 16: 1–12; 20: 17–19; 22: 41–45; 26: 3–5; 26: 59–67; John 1: 19–28; 8L 13–30; 10: 22–41; 11: 45–53; 18: 13–14 & 19–24).

The Pharisees
The authors of the gospels did not seem to be sure about the attitude towards Jesus of the Pharisees, the members of a conservative religious movement that tried to live according to the Law of Moses. On the one hand, they were often described as Jesus' opponents:

- "The Pharisees went out, and immediately took counsel with the Herodians against him [Jesus], how they might destroy him' (Mark 3: 6).
- "The scribes and the Pharisees watched him [Jesus], to see whether he would heal on the Sabbath, that they might find an accusation against him" (Luke 6: 7).

These words suggest that the Pharisees were Jesus' enemies who wanted to get rid of him. When the gospels mention the Pharisees as Jesus' enemies, the members of the Sanhedrin are meant. Luke 13: 31, on the other hand, tells a different story:

> "… some Pharisees came, saying to him [Jesus], 'Get out of here, and go away, for Herod wants to kill you.'"

If all the Pharisees really were so hostile towards Jesus, they would never have warned him to remove himself from mortal danger. What we know of the Pharisees suggests that many of them must have been sympathetic towards Jesus since their religious views coincided in more than one respect.²⁶ Two prominent members of the party of the Pharisees, Nicodemus and Joseph of Arimathea, were known supporters of Jesus and they buried him after his crucifixion (John 3; John 19: 38–39).

A leader of the Pharisees and member of the Sanhedrin, Gamaliel, showed his sympathy with the followers of Jesus when they were tried by the Sanhedrin for purportedly teaching a false doctrine (Acts 5: 38–39). We are informed in Acts 15: 5 that some Pharisees believed in Jesus and joined the followers of Jesus in Jerusalem after his crucifixion, which would not have happened if the they really thought that Jesus was a blasphemer or a heretic.

It must be concluded that the Pharisees were pictured in the gospels as Jesus' enemies in order to vilify the Jews and to exonerate the role of the Roman rulers in Jesus' execution. The truth is, though, that at least some Pharisees were well disposed towards Jesus.

The Zealots

The party of the Zealots was an ultra-nationalist group that resisted the pagan Roman rule through acts of terrorism and the assassination of Roman soldiers and Jews who cooperated with the Romans. They despised the Sadducees who worked together with the Romans to rule the country and the Pharisees who accepted Roman rule passively as the will of God.

The leaders of this party were responsible for starting the Jewish War against the Romans in AD 66, which led to the destructtion of Jerusalem four years later.²⁷

The Essenes

The Jewish party or sect of the Essenes was a semi-ascetic and paci-

---

[26] Cohn, *The Trial and Death of Jesus*, 66.
[27] Enc Brit, "Zealots.".

fistic group that practiced celibacy in some instances. When their members did get married, they regarded these unions as unbreakable and divorce was forbidden. Several of them were priests who regarded the Jerusalem priests who belonged to the party of the Sadducees to be corrupt and false due to their cooperation with the pagan Roman overlords.

Some of the Essenes may be described as Nazarites due to their sober and ascetic lifestyle and, according to their own literature, they followed the strict rules imposed upon Nazarites in Num 6. They had strong messianic expectations and awaited royal and priestly messiahs.[28] Various researchers believe that John the Baptist had links with this sect, due to his lifestyle and message.[29]

The name "Essenes" (Hebrew: אִסִּיִּים – *Issiyim*; Greek: Ἐσσηνοί, Ἐσσαῖοι, or Ὀσσαῖοι – *Essenoi*, *Essaioi* or *Ossaioi*) does not occur in the New Testament and many scholars thought that the authors of the gospels simply ignored them and that our knowledge about them is only to be found in the writings of Flavius Josephus, Pliny the Elder, Philo of Alexandria, and other ancient authors.[30]

However, they do appear repeatedly under another name in the New Testament, namely that of the "Nazoreans" (Greek: Ναζωραῖοι – *Nazoraioi*).

According to Epiphanios, the bishop of Constantia on Cyprus, who wrote a lengthy book, the Panarion, during the last half of the fourth century AD and in which he described and criticized all the heresies of his time, the sect of the Essenes, which he called the Ὀσσαῖοι, Ὀσσηνοι or Ἰεσσαῖοι (*Ossaioi, Ossenoi* or *Jessaioi*),

---

[28] Enc Brit, "Essenes"; Rylaarsdam *et al.*, "Biblical Literature".
[29] Pixner, "Jerusalem's Essene Gateway"; Strugnell, "John the Baptist"; see also: Epiphanios, *Panarion,* Liber I, 19:1–6
[30] Duling, "The Jewish World"; Enc Brit, "Essenes".

was none other than the Nazoreans.³¹

Various modern scholars concur with him.³²

The Nazoreans

Jesus is often called a Nazorean in the gospels and Acts (Matt 2: 23; 26:71; Luke 18: 37, John 18: 5, 7; 19: 19; Acts 2: 22; 3: 6; 4: 10; 6: 14; 22: 8; and 26: 9). In other words: Jesus was a member of the sect of the Essenes.

The Greek name of "Nazorean" is probably derived from the Hebrew word for "branch" as used in Isaiah and Daniel, namely נֵצֶר (*netzer*).³³ After all, according to the dictionaries consulted, the word "Nazorean" means "one separated or a Nazarite".

Kinzig notes: "In ancient rabbinical literature, too, the Christians are occasionally referred to as נוֹצְרִים (notsrim)"³⁴ – which seems to confirm the connection of the name "Nazorean" with the Hebrew word נֵצֶר (*netzer*).

In addition, the Greek word for "Nazorean" (Ναζωραῖος – *Nazoraios*) may also have a connection with the Hebrew word for Nazarite, namely נָזִיר (*Nazir*), which means "a consecrated or devoted one."

In Matt 2: 23, we read that there was a prophecy that Jesus would be a Nazorean "that it might be fulfilled which was spoken through the prophets: 'He will be called a Nazorean.'"

---

³¹ Epiphanios, *Panarion*, Liber I/XIX:1–6, XXIX/1–5.
³² International Standard Bible Encyclopedia Online, "Essenes"; McClintock and Strong Biblical Encyclopedia, "Jessaeans"; Valois, "The old Nazoreans: A Higher Idea of God."
³³ Duling, "The Jewish World"; Kinzig, "The Nazoreans", 470.
³⁴ Kinzig, "The Nazoreans", 471.

It is difficult to identify the prophecy referred to in this text and McGrath thinks that the evangelist erroneously thought that such a prophecy was to be found in the Old Testament.[35]

This prophecy was perhaps to be found in Isa 11: 1 where it is said of the Messiah: "There shall come forth a shoot out of the stock of Jesse, and a branch out of his roots shall bear fruit."

Isaiah 62: 21 is another prophecy that may, perhaps, have been meant: "Your people also shall be all righteous; they shall inherit the land forever, the branch of my planting, the work of my hands, that I may be glorified" (see also: Dan 11: 7).

Jesus was also called a Nazorean on the inscription on his cross (John 19: 19). His followers after his death were, accordingly, called "the sect of the Nazoreans" (Acts 24: 5).

The name "Nazorean" should not be confused with the name of "Nazarene" – as happened in most Bible translations. Saint Jerome, the translator of the Bible into Latin, the Vulgate, made this mistake and he used the word "Nazarenus" every time he encountered the Greek word Ναζωραῖος (*Nazoraios*) – except for Matt 2: 23. His example was followed by other translators.

However, the authoritative Greek–English dictionary of Arndt and Gingrich explains that Ναζωραῖος (*Nazoraios* - Nazorean) and Ναζαρηνός (*Nazarenos* – Nazarene) are two totally different and unrelated words and that there is no linguistic connection between them. The word "Nazarene" is used for people from the village of Nazareth where Jesus grew up. The name "Nazarene" was often used of Jesus and he was, accordingly, sometimes called "Jesus of Nazareth" or "Jesus the Nazarene" (Mark 1: 24; Mark 10: 47; Mark 14: 67; Mark 16: 6; Luke 4: 34; and Luke 24: 19).

---

[35] McGrath, "He Shall Be Called a Nazorean".

The name "Nazorean", on the other hand, means "one separated [as a branch from the trunk, as the Essenes separated themselves from the other Jews] or a Nazarite". According to Josephus, the Essenes also kept themselves separate from other Jews while living in communities in various towns and villages.

The fact that the two words, "Nazorean" and "Nazarene", are often regarded as synonyms results from Matt 2: 23 where the name of the town "Nazareth" and the name "Nazorean" occur in the same sentence. We read there that Joseph and his family "came and lived in a city called Nazareth; that it might be fulfilled which was spoken through the prophets: 'He will be called a Nazorean.'"

This does not mean that the author of Matthew thought that the name "Nazorean" was somehow derived from the name of the village of Nazareth. He must have known that the two words have nothing in common and he only made use of a play of words with two similar-sounding words in one sentence.

The best proof that the names "Nazarene" and "Nazorean" are not synonyms or two versions of the same word, is found in Acts 24: 5 where Paul is called "a ringleader of the sect of the Nazarenes", according to most translations. This translation does not make sense. The sect in question certainly didn't consist of people from Nazareth only – they came from Jerusalem and other parts of Judea and Galilee. Paul can by no stretch of imagination be called a "Nazarene", a native of Nazareth. It makes much more sense to regard this sect to be the "Nazoreans" – in other words, Essenes – as stated explicitly in the Greek text and which is usually given a wrong translation by transforming "Nazoreans" into "Nazarenes".

It must be added that Epiphanios, who wrote his book to expose the heresies of various sects in the early church, made a clear distinction between the "Nazarenes" and the "Nazoreans".[36]

Flavius Josephus on the Essenes
It is necessary to quote some of Josephus' descriptions of this sect:

> "These men are despisers of riches… (and) that those who come to them must let what they have be common to the whole order, insomuch that among them all there is no appearance of poverty, or excess of riches, but every one's possessions are intermingled with every other's possessions, and so there is, as it were, one patrimony among all the brethren. (. . .) They have no one certain city, but many of them dwell in every city; and if any of their sect come from other places, what they have lies open for them, just as if it were their own…"

Josephus added that they "wear white always" to distinguish them from other Jews and to symbolize their purity.[37]

The aversion of the Nazoreans or Essenes of wealth and opulence stems from their antipathy against the rich Sadducees – which was also the case with John the Baptist and Jesus. John even called them the "offspring of vipers" (Matt 3: 7).

Philo of Alexandria on the Essenes
A Jewish theologian and philosopher, who was a contemporary of Jesus, Philo of Alexandria, gave a detailed description of the Essenes that agrees with Josephus' report. He described them as –

- Very pious;
- Diligent in the study of the Hebrew Scriptures;

---

[36] Epiphanios, *Panarion*, Liber 1: 19, 29.
[37] Josephus. *Wars, II(8)*.

- Sharing their belongings and wages with each other;
- Practicing hospitality to travelling members of their sect;
- Living apart from other Jews to avoid contamination;
- Punishing those who broke their rules harshly;
- Keeping no slaves;
- Prohibiting oaths;
- Washing themselves regularly to stay clean; and
- Being pacifists who refused to use any weapons.[38]

The Essene Lifestyle and Beliefs of Jesus and his Followers
It is clear the Jesus and his disciples and followers lived according to the Essene principles as explained by Josephus and Philo.

When Jesus sent his twelve disciples and later 72 of his followers to spread the news about the imminent establishment of the Kingdom of God, he advised them not to take a purse with money along but to rely on the hospitality and generosity of those where they lodged (Mark 6: 8–11; Matt 9: 9–10; Luke 9: 3–5; 10: 1–8), just as the Essenes did when they travelled and lodged with other members of their sect. When the 72 reported back to Jesus, he asked them: "'When I sent you out without purse, and wallet, and shoes, did you lack anything?' They said, 'Nothing'" (Luke 22: 35).

Jesus preached pacifism in Matt 5: 9 and 43–45 in accordance with the views of the Essenes: "

> "Blessed are the peacemakers, for they shall be called sons of God. (…) You have heard that it was said, `You shall love your neighbor, and hate your enemy.` But I tell you, love your enemies, bless those who curse you, do good to those who hate you, and pray for those who spitefully use you and

---

[38] Philo, *Every Good Man is Free*, XII, 75–87 (as quoted by Lawrence H. Schiffman, *Texts and Traditions*, 282–84).

persecute you, that you may be sons of your Father who is in heaven."

Jesus agreed with the Essenes when he condemned divorce, declaring in Matt 5: 27–28 & 31–32:

> "You have heard that it was said, `You shall not commit adultery;` but I tell you that everyone who gazes at a woman to lust after her has committed adultery with her already in his heart. (…) It was also said, `Whoever shall put away his wife, let him give her a writing of divorce,` but I tell you that whoever who puts away his wife, except for the cause of sexual immorality, makes her an adulteress; and whoever shall marry her when she is put away commits adultery."

Just as the Essenes, Jesus advocated a life of poverty –

> "Don`t lay up treasures for yourselves on the earth, where moth and rust consume, and where thieves break through and steal; but lay up for yourselves treasures in heaven, where neither moth nor rust consume, and where thieves don`t break through and steal; for where your treasure is, your heart will be there also (Matt 6: 19–21).

Jesus added:

> "Therefore don`t be anxious, saying, `What will we eat?`, `What will we drink?` or, `With what will we be clothed?` For the Gentiles seek after all these things, for your heavenly Father knows that you need all these things. But seek first God`s Kingdom, and his righteousness; and all these things will be added to you."

This was also how Jesus and his group of disciples lived. He declared that "[t]he foxes have holes, and the birds of the sky have nests, but the Son of Man has nowhere to lay his head" (Luke 9: 58). According to Luke 18: 24–25, Jesus followed the Essenes' condemnation of opulence when he taught:

> "How hard it is for those who have riches to enter into the kingdom of God! For it is easier for a camel to enter in through a needle's eye, than for a rich man to enter into the kingdom of God."

We are told in Luke 8: 2–3 of some women who followed Jesus and his band of disciples and "ministered to them from their possessions" – just as the Essenes did.

According to Jesus, following the lifestyle of the Essenes, generosity is a desirable virtue (Matt 5: 41–42):

> "Whoever compels you to go one mile, go with him two. Give to him who asks you, and don't turn away him who desires to borrow from you."

Jesus warned his followers against false prophets in Matt 7: 15 –

> "Beware of false prophets, who come to you in sheep's clothing, but inwardly are ravening wolves."

This warning is probably an echo of the Essenes' distrust of the Sadducees and the priestly class in Jerusalem.

The Essenes were against taking any vows. Jesus taught the same in Matt 5: 33–35:

> "You have heard that it was said to them of old time, 'You shall not make false vows, but shall perform to the Lord your vows. But I tell you, don't swear at all: neither by heaven, for it is the

throne of God; nor by the earth, for it is the footstool of his feet; nor by Jerusalem, for it is the city of the great King. Neither shall you swear by your head, for you can't make one hair white or black. But let your speech be, 'Yes, yes; No, no.' Whatever is more than these is of the evil one."

We read in Acts 2: 44–47 about the followers of Jesus after his death who shared their belongings with each other:

> "All who believed were together, and had all things common. They sold their possessions and goods, and distributed them to all, according as anyone had need. Day by day, continuing steadfastly with one accord in the temple, and breaking bread at home, they took their food with gladness and singleness of heart, praising God, and having favor with all the people."

We also read about the group of Jesus' followers in Jerusalem:

> "For neither was there among them any who lacked, for as many as were owners of lands or houses sold them, and brought the prices of the things that were sold, and laid them at the apostles' feet, and distribution was made to each, according as anyone had need" (Acts 4: 34–35).

According to Acts 5: 1–10, a certain Ananias and his wife, Sapphira, lied about the sale of their property, assuring Peter that they donated all the money to the community, while secretly keeping a part for themselves. Peter condemned both – just as the Essenes dealt harshly with those who broke their rules.

Qumran near the Dead Sea
The headquarters of the Essenes was at the monastery of Qumran on

the shores of the Dead Sea. Scholars agree that the so-called Dead Sea Scrolls, found in nearby caves since 1947, were the library of this sect that was hidden in safe places during the Jewish revolt against the Romans of AD 66–70. This library contained mostly Hebrew and Aramaic texts, but also a few in Greek.[39] If Jesus received his education at Qumran he would certainly have learnt some Greek as well.

That Qumran was the headquarters of the Essenes or Nazoreans is confirmed by the following remark of Pliny the Elder (Latin: Gaius Plinius Secundus) in his encyclopedic book Natural History (Latin: Naturalis Historia) in which he gave a description of the geography of Palestine:

> "On the west side of the Dead Sea, but out of range of the noxious exhalations of the coast, is the solitary tribe of the Essenes which is remarkable beyond all the other tribes of the whole world as it has no women and has renounced all sexual desire, has no money, and has only palm trees for company. Day by day the throng of refugees is recruited to an equal number by numerous accessions of persons tired of life and driven there by the waves of fortune to adopt their manners."[40]

Pliny mentioned the celibate lifestyle of some Essenes. That may be the reason why the gospels are silent about a wife of Jesus. As an Essene, he may well have stayed celibate and unmarried.

Josephus wrote that the Essenes lived in many towns and

---

[39] Pixner, "Jerusalem's Essene Gateway"; Rylaarsdam *et al.* "Biblical Literature".
[40] Pliny, Natural History, Liber V, xv; Taylor, "On Pliny, the Essene Location and Kh. Qumran".

villages in Palestine, including Jerusalem – in contrast with Pliny who was only aware of the settlement on the western bank of the Dead Sea.[41]

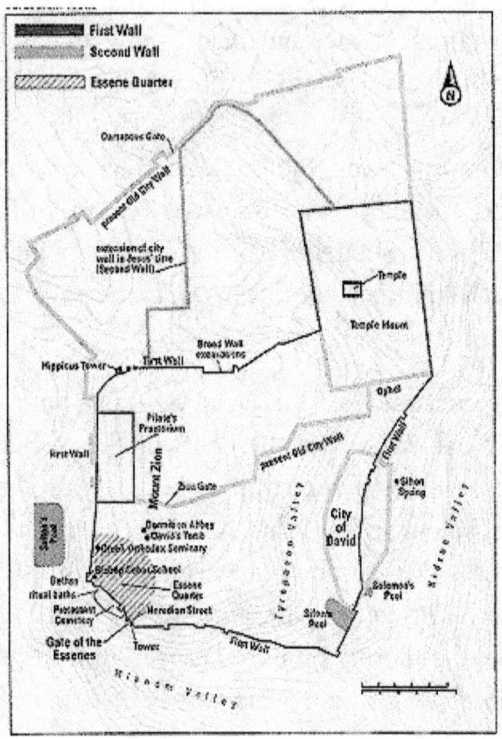

Map of Jerusalem before the destruction of the city by the Romans in AD 70. The Essene Quarter was in die south western corner (the shaded area).

Archaeologists have located the Essene Quarter in ancient Jerusalem of Jesus' time, namely in the south western corner of the city. There was a gate in the city wall next to this quarter, called by Josephus the "Gate of the Essenes". Directly outside this gate the ritual baths and ablution facilities of these Essenes were to be

---

[41] Josephus, *Wars*, Liber II, 8.

found,[42] including the pool of Siloam, mentioned in John 9: 7, 11.

The eminent Swiss Catholic theologian, Hans Küng, wrote a monumental book about Jesus: Christ Sein (On Being a Christian). He explained that one can only be a Christian by following Jesus Christ. According to him, Jesus did not belong to any of the four religious groups of his time and offered an alternative to each of them, namely the Pharisees, the Sadducees, the Zealots, and the Essenes.[43]

Unfortunately, Küng had it wrong. Despite his excellent research and scholarship, he never realized that the evidence in the gospels is very clear that Jesus was indeed a prominent member of the sect of the Essenes or Nazoreans.

A King-in-Waiting

In order to understand the contents of the gospel narratives, it is necessary to point out that Jesus is to be regarded primarily as the king-in-waiting of Israel – and certainly not as the savior of mankind. The following reasons will motivate this thesis more than adequately.

The Jews of Jesus' time experienced great hardship under the rule of Herod the Great and the Roman governors and they longed for a savior to liberate them and to restore the ancient kingdom of David. This yearning is perhaps best expressed in the Psalms of Solomon, a collection of hymns from the first century BC when Palestine came under Roman rule. Toy provides this summary of the contents of this hymn book:

> "Suffering inflicted by foreign invasion (i, viii); desecration of Jerusalem and the temple, death in Egypt of the invader

---

[42] Pixner, "Jerusalem's Essene Gateway".

[43] Küng. Christ Sein, *passim*.

(ii.); debauchery of Jewish 'men–pleasers' (iv.); recognition of God's justice in rewarding the pious and in punishing the wicked (iii., vi., ix., x., xiii., xiv., xv.); expectation of and prayer for divine intervention (vii., xi., xii., xvi.); description of the Messiah (xvii., xviii.)."[44]

The need for a messiah is best expressed in Ps 17 of this collection:

23.	"Behold, oh Lord, and raise up unto them their king, the son of David, At the time the which Thou seest, o God, that he may reign over Israel thy servant
24.	And gird him with strength, that he may shatter unrighteous rulers,
25.	And that he may purge Jerusalem from nations that trample (her) down to destruction. wisely, righteously.
26.	He shall thrust out sinners from (the) inheritance, He shall destroy the pride of the sinner as a potter's vessel. With a rod of iron, he shall break in pieces all their substance, He shall destroy the godless nations with the word of his mouth."[45]

The gospels and Acts are totally silent regarding the harshness, cruelty, and inhumanity of the Roman rule. These works were only completed after the Romans had destroyed Jerusalem to end the Jewish revolt of AD 66–70. No author of a gospel could have dared to criticize the Romans in those circumstances. All the blame for Jesus' execution was, therefore, placed upon the unpopular vanquished Jews. However, there was an urgent need for a messiah or savior to deliver the Jews from the horrible Roman yoke.

---

[44] Toy, "The Psalms of Solomon".
[45] Gray, "The Psalms of Solomon", 631–52.

Although the Old Testament mentions several messiahs, people anointed on behalf of God, such as kings, prophets, and priests, there was a strong expectation on account of several prophecies that a descendant of David would claim the throne in Jerusalem and establish a theocracy and become *the* Messiah – for instance, 2 Sam: 7: 16; Isa 9: 5–6; Ezek 37: 21–22; and Jer 23: 5–6.[46]

It will be worthwhile to quote Ezek 37: 21–22:

> "Say to them, Thus says the Lord YHWH: Behold, I will take the children of Israel from among the nations, where they are gone, and will gather them on every side, and bring them into their own land: and I will make them one nation in the land, on the mountains of Israel; and one *king* shall be *king* to them all; and they shall be no more two nations, neither shall they be divided into two *kingdoms* any more at all" (*emphasis added*).

Jesus must have been acutely aware of these prophecies and expectations and, therefore, he deliberately acted in such a manner that it amounted to a fulfillment of these prophecies.

It is highly probable and possible that Jesus saw events coinciding with his baptism by John the Baptist as God's calling to become the savior and king of Israel (Mark 1: 9–11; Matt 3: 13–17; Luke 3: 21–22). The total solar eclipse of 24 November AD 29[47] at about 10:40 local time over Galilee[48] most probably happened when

---

[46] Fredriksen, *Jesus of Nazareth*, 124–28.

[47] Gertoux, who compiled a credible chronology of Jesus' life, also places his baptism in AD 29, although he calculated that Jesus was baptized during August ("Herod the Great and Jesus", 53).

[48] Although the Gospel of Matthew states that John was baptizing at the river Jordan in the "wilderness of Judea" (Matt 3: 1), John must actually have been in Galilee to the north of Judea at that time since Herod Antipas,

Jesus was baptized and that he saw this as a sign that God called him to become *the* Messiah. The report of this event in Mark 1: 9–11, the oldest gospel, must be quoted in full:

> "It happened in those days, that Jesus came from Nazareth of Galilee, and was baptized by John in the Jordan. Immediately coming up from the water, he saw the heavens parting, and the Spirit descending on him like a dove. A voice came out of the sky, 'You are my beloved Son, in whom I am well pleased.'"

All three synoptic gospels report that the heavens were opened directly after Jesus' baptism – most probably the stars in the sky that became visible during day-time when the light of the sun was blocked by the intervening moon during the eclipse.

It must be remembered that the ancient Israelites thought that God's heaven was directly beyond the stars and that the stars were, in fact, angels (Neh 9: 6; Job 22: 12–14; Job 38: 4–8; Ps 104: 3; Ps 148: 2–3; Isa 40: 22). In other words: when the stars unexpectedly became visible during day-time it seemed as if the heaven, the abode of God and the angels, was miraculously opened.[49]

During a solar eclipse "a pronounced fall in temperature" is experienced, due to the blocking of the rays of the sun. That causes a wind to blow from the warmer areas outside the path of the moon's shadow to the cooler areas where the heat of the sun is absent.[50]

---

the ruler of Galilee, had him arrested shortly after Jesus' baptism – and that could only have happened within Herod's area of jurisdiction (Matt 14: 3; Mark 1: 14; Mark 6: 17; Luke 3: 19–20). It also appears from the chronology in the Synoptic Gospels that Jesus concentrated his ministry initially to Galilee and only appeared in Judea at a later date.

[49] Scholtz, *The Prophecies of Revelation*, 30–41.
[50] Enc Brit, "Eclipse: sun".

That must also have been the case with the eclipse of 24 November AD 29 and people would also have noticed the sudden wind – apart from the appearance of the stars in the sky.

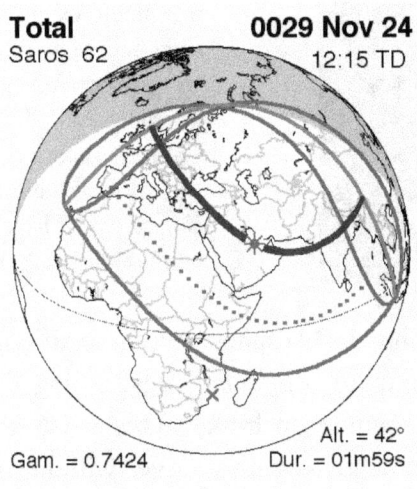

The path of the moon's shadow, where a total solar eclipse was visible, passed through the northern parts of Palestine on 24 November AD 29. The duration of totality was 2 minutes.[51]

The Greek word for "wind", πνεῦμα (*pneuma*), is also the word used for "spirit", just as the Hebrew word for "wind" is also the word for "spirit" (רוּחַ – *ruach*). For the Jews, therefore, there was no real difference between a spirit and the wind or breath and, therefore, the gospels reported that the (Holy) Spirit "descended" upon Jesus at his baptism (Mark 1: 10; Matt 3: 16; Luke 3: 22) – while it was only an unexpected but ordinary wind that blew.

Mark – the oldest gospel – merely reported that Jesus saw the Spirit (or the wind) descending on him *like* a dove or a pigeon

---

[51] NASA, Eclipse Website.

(the Greek word may mean both species of birds) – not in the *form* of a dove. Luke 3: 22, though, added that "the Holy Spirit descended in a bodily form" on Jesus.

A computerized reconstruction of the maximum extent of the almost total solar eclipse at 10: 40 local time on 24 November AD 29, as seen from Caesarea-Philippi, north of the Sea of Galilee, when almost 94% of the sun was blocked by the moon. A total eclipse would have been visible further north on the banks of the Jordan.

The Gospel of John (1: 32) states: "John testified, saying, 'I have seen the Spirit [πνεῦμα – *pneuma*] descending like a dove out of heaven, and it remained on him.'" This verse also compares the "Spirit" – or the "wind" – with a dove, without mentioning that a real dove was seen.

It is on account of Luke's description that illustrations of the event usually show a real dove or pigeon coming down upon Jesus. But that is not what the reports in Mark and John said. They only compared the Spirit or the wind with the movement of air caused by the flapping of the bird's wings as it perches upon a person's shoulder or head. If this interpretation is correct, then Jesus would have perceived the unexpected solar eclipse and the blowing of the sudden wind as a direct message from God, declaring him to be God's "beloved Son" – in other words: the king of Israel.

It must be stressed that the only people ever called the "son of God" in the Old Testament were the kings of Israel (2 Sam 7: 14; 1 Chr 17: 13; 1 Chr 22: 10; 1 Chr 28: 6; Ps 2: 6–7, 12; Ps 89: 26–28) – except for the angels (Job 1: 6; 2: 1; 38: 8) and the people of Israel (Ex 4: 22; Deut 14: 1; Jer 31: 9; Hos 11: 1). In John 1: 49, the expressions "Son of God" and "king of Israel" are used as synonyms.

The people in those days had no explanation for eclipses and they interpreted these phenomena as mysterious divine interventions.[52] The Jewish newspaper Haaretz quoted Rabbi Blitz: "In Jewish tradition, a total solar eclipse is a warning to the Gentiles and a sign of judgment on the nations."[53]

That may also be how Jesus interpreted the event and he must have seen it as a confirmation of his calling to become *the* Messiah and to liberate of the Jews from the pagan Romans.

We can speculate that Jesus and John planned this baptism specifically for that day because they, somehow or other, knew of the expected eclipse. Eshbal Ratzon of the University of Haifa has demonstrated that the so-called Astronomical Book of Enoch, part of the Dead Sea Scrolls, explained how to predict lunar and solar eclipses – something the ancient Sumerians, Babylonians, and Greeks could do.[54] It is, of course, impossible to determine whether Jesus and John knew of this book and its contents, or heard that this eclipse was predicted, but their ties with the Essene community of Qumran may have made that a possibility.

The constellations of stars that became visible around the darkened sun all proclaimed the same message to Jesus. Knowledge of the constellations was widespread in those days, as is evident from the fact that there are various allusions to Babylonian astrology in the Old Testament and that most of the visions that John of Patmos had and which he described in the book of Revelation, were actually descriptions of the night sky with its constellations and

---

[52] Stephenson, "Eclipse".
[53] Haaretz, 19.03.2015.
[54] Ratzon, "The first Jewish Astronomers".

planets during AD 96.⁵⁵ Jacobus also analyzed an astrological text from the Dead Sea Scrolls, the library of the Essene community at Qumran.⁵⁶

A computerized reconstruction of a part of the sky over Galilee during the solar eclipse of 24 November AD 29, showing the outlines of the stellar constellations.

The eclipsed sun appeared just below the constellation of Ophiuchus or Serpentarius, the Snake Catcher. Ophiuchus is traditionally depicted as a man grasping a snake, the constellation of Serpens, the Serpent.

According to Jewish stellar lore, the constellation of Serpens was a depiction of Satan, the Serpent that tempted Eve to eat from

---

[55] Scholtz, *The Prophecies of Revelation*, 27–41.
[56] Jacbus, "The Zodiac".

the forbidden fruit (Gen 3).[57] In Job 26: 12–13 we also read:

> "He stirs up the sea with his power, and by his understanding he strikes through Rahab. By his Spirit the heavens are garnished. His hand has pierced the swift serpent."

The name "Rahab" (רַהַב) denotes a mythical sea monster. The Hebrew word for "serpent" is נָחָשׁ (*Nachash*). It is clear that these two creatures are meant to be one and the same being that resided in "the heavens" – that is, between the stars.

Jesus would certainly have been conscious of these passages in the Hebrew Scriptures, as well as of the significance of the constellation of Serpens. He certainly would have connected that to his calling to become the savior of Israel who was destined to conquer the evil forces of Satan and paganism.

It is likely that Jesus alluded to this vision in Luke. 10: 18:

> "He said to them, 'I saw Satan having fallen like lightning from heaven. Behold, I give you authority to tread on serpents and scorpions, and over all the power of the enemy. Nothing will in any way hurt you.'"

In the computerized reconstruction of the sky at the time of the solar eclipse, the constellations of Serpens and Scorpius (the Scorpion) lie next to each other, just above the horizon. Both were regarded by the Jews as representations of Satan[58]. The constellations of Aquila (the Roman Eagle) and Scutum (the Roman Shield) were also

---

[57] Allen, *Star Names,* 375.
[58] [58] Allen, *Star Names,* 362; Scholtz, *The Prophecies,* 189–91.

hovering on the horizon.[59] It also appeared as if the Snake Catcher was trampling upon the Scorpion.

From the perspective of Jesus, on the banks of the Jordan, it must have appeared as if these constellations were about to fall from heaven where they lay just above the horizon. The "lightning" that Jesus mentioned must have been the tiny sliver of the sun that became visible directly after totality had ended.

Another important constellation was Capricornus, the Goat. In Jewish stellar lore from the time of Jesus and subsequent centuries, this constellation was named גדיא (*Gadiya*, the kid goat)[60]. That reminds one of the exclamation of John the Baptist after he had baptized Jesus: "Behold, the Lamb of God, who takes away the sin of the world!" (John 1: 29). The planet Venus, the bright morning star, was at that time inside Capricornus, drawing the attention of onlookers to this constellation. The Hebrew names of this planet was כוכבת (*Kokebet*, the she–star) and מְלֶכֶת הַשָּׁמַיִם (*Meleket Hasshamayim*, the Queen of Heaven).

Libra, the Scales (Hebrew: מאזנים – *moznayim*), a symbol of justice[61], lay next to Serpens and Scorpius – conveying the idea that all satanic forces were to be weighed and judged by God. Directly below the occluded sun the constellation of Corona Australis, the Southern Crown or Garland, a symbol of kingship or victory,[62] was visible. This garland was usually associated with the adjacent constellation of Sagittarius, the Archer, usually regarded as a conquering warrior[63] – another symbol of the Messiah.

---

[59] Allen, *Star Names*, 57.
[60] Jacobus, "The Zodiac", 318, 323.
[61] Allen, *Star Names*, 273.
[62] Allen, *Star Names*, 172.
[63] Allen, *Star Names*, 352.

All these celestial phenomena would have held a powerful message: Jesus, who was baptized on that day, was destined, and anointed by God to be the "beloved Son" of God, the Messiah and king of Israel, liberator of his people and conqueror of the Romans. It was, as it were, as if a voice from heaven gave him this message.

It is noteworthy that a partial lunar eclipse occurred during the early evening of 9 December AD 29 – a fortnight after the solar eclipse. Jesus was wandering through the desert, struggling with demonic forces (Matt 4: 1–11). Jesus – and those who witnessed the solar eclipse at his baptism – must have seen this partial lunar eclipse as yet another confirmation that he was *the* Messiah and that delivery from the hated pagan Romans was due.

What is remarkable about this eclipse, is that the darkened moon lay within the constellation of Gemini and next to the planet Saturn. Gemini, the Twins, with its two bright stars, Castor and Pollux, reminded the Jews of Esau and Jacob, the twin sons of Isaac.[64] Another name for Jacob was Israel (Gen 32: 28).

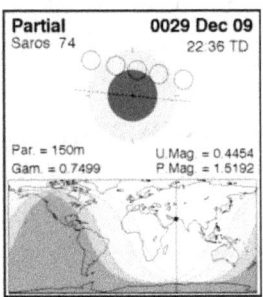

The white areas on this map show the parts of the world where the partial lunar eclipse of 9 December AD 29 was visible. The white circles in the top part of the illustration show how much of the moon was covered by the earth's shadow (the larger dark circle).

Shlomo Sela pointed out, furthermore, that "a special link [exists] between Saturn and Saturday, the holiest day of the week for the Jews". The Hebrew name for this planet is שבתאי (*Shabtai*) – a name connected to the word for "Shabbath" – just as there is a link

---

[64] Orlov, *The Atoning Dyad*, 27.

between Saturn and Saturday in the English language. Therefore, Saturn was "the planet in charge of the Jews."[65]

The eclipsed moon within Gemini and next to Saturn would have given Jesus the message that something special was due to happen to the Jews while they watched how their enemies would be darkened or vanquished with their special star protecting them.

A computerized recreation of the eclipsed moon within the constellation of Gemini with its principal stars Castor and Pollux during the early evening of 9 December AD 29. Saturn is also part of the scene.

Jesus departed for the desert after his baptism and during this time he tried to make sense of the events surrounding his baptism. He reportedly experienced temptations by Satan, but afterwards was cared for by angels (Mark 1: 9–12; Matt 3: 13–4: 11; Luke 3: 21–22; Luke 4: 1–13).

This period of forty days must be greatly exaggerated. Nobody can survive more than ten days without water, especially not in a desert environment in which Jesus experienced these temptations.[66] The period of forty days is rather a symbolic number, a reminder of the forty years the Israelites had spent in the desert after escaping from slavery in Egypt. It is also a reminder of Moses who

---

[65] Sela, "Saturn and the Jews".
[66] Craighead and Nemeroff, *The Corsini Encyclopedia of Psychology and Behavioral Science*, 1587; Swaab, *Wij zijn ons Brein*, 247; Enc Brit, "Dehydration".

reportedly stayed forty days on the mountain without eating and drinking, while receiving God's commandments (Ex 34: 28).

Anyway, if Jesus fasted for an extended period and consequently suffered from malnutrition and dehydration, it is very possible and highly probable that he would have experienced hallucinations with a religious content, in which he struggled with demonic forces, had encounters with angels and which he regarded as a confirmation of his calling from God to establish the kingdom of God in Israel.

The "angels" who cared for him after Satan had left were likely desert dwellers who found the disoriented, dehydrated, and dog-hungry Jesus in the desert and nursed him back to health.

These experiences must have been so real for Jesus that he afterwards told his friends and disciples about them – and the compilers of the gospels must have collected these stories from people who heard it from Jesus or from his friends or disciples.

If Jesus was baptized in November AD 29 and he was crucified on 3 April AD 33 (see below), then his public ministry, which started shortly after his baptism, would have spanned somewhat more than three years. During this time, he repeatedly acted as if he was the king-in-waiting of the Jews.

That Jesus was a popular figure and that many regarded him to be *the* Messiah, the savior from oppression, is clear from the gospels. It is repeatedly stated that he drew crowds when he was teaching, as well as from the following descriptions of his triumphant entry into Jerusalem when he and his disciples attended the annual Passover during April AD 33:

- They brought the colt to Jesus, and threw their garments on him, and Jesus sat on him. Many spread their garments on the way, and others were cutting down branches from the trees, and spreading them on the road. Those who went in front, and those who followed, cried, 'Hosanna! Blessed is he who comes in the name of the Lord! *Blessed is the kingdom of our father David that is coming* in the name of the Lord! Hosanna in the highest!' Jesus entered into the temple in Jerusalem." (Mark 11: 7–11 – *emphasis added*).

- On the next day a great multitude had come to the feast. When they heard that Jesus was coming to Jerusalem, they took the branches of the palm trees, and went out to meet him, and cried out, "Hosanna! Blessed is he who comes in the name of the Lord, the *King of Israel*!" Jesus, having found a young donkey, sat on it. As it is written, "Don't be afraid, daughter of Zion. Behold, your *King* comes, sitting on a donkey's colt" (John 12: 12–15 – *emphasis added*).

He entered Jerusalem in this manner on purpose to fulfill a prophecy from the Old Testament:

"Rejoice greatly, daughter of Zion; shout, daughter of Jerusalem: behold, your king comes to you; he is just, and having salvation; lowly, and riding on a donkey, even on a colt the foal of a donkey" (Zech 9: 9).

Jesus was certainly also aware of the rest of this prophetic utterance of Zechariah, which stated with regards to the king who was to enter Jerusalem on the back of a donkey:

"I will cut off the chariot from Ephraim, and the horse from Jerusalem; and the battle bow shall be cut off; and he shall speak peace to the nations: and his dominion shall be from sea to sea, and from the River to the ends of the earth" (Zech 9: 10).

This prophecy promised that the future king of Israel would rule over a huge part of the earth. Jesus clearly relied on this prophecy that God would render the chariots, horses, and battle bows of Israel's enemies useless in any struggle.

By upending the tables of the dishonest money changers and animal merchants outside the temple, Jesus followed the example of Nehemiah who threw out the furniture of a certain Tobiah who had taken up residence in a chamber in the temple complex (Neh 13: 7–9). He also referred to Jer 7: 11 to motivate his action: "Is this house, which is called by my name, become a den of robbers in your eyes?" He probably did this to legitimize his claim to be a messiah.

One of the characteristics of Jesus' preaching was that he often called God his "Father" and referred to himself as "the Son (of God)" (Matt 6: 9; Matt 11: 27; Matt 16: 27–28; Matt 23: 9; Matt 27: 54; John 3: 35; John 5: 21; John 6: 46; John 8: 18; John 8: 42 *etcetera*). No prophet of the Old Testament ever did this. Jesus' habit of calling God his Father and describing himself as the son of God was a way of telling the people that he was chosen by God to be the next king of Israel. It has already been shown that the only person in the Old Testament who was ever called a son of God was the Israelite king in Jerusalem (except for the angels and the nation of Israel) – just as the Egyptian pharaohs regarded themselves as sons of the god Osiris.[67]

Jesus also often referred to himself as the "Son of Man" (Matt 9: 6; 12: 8; 12: 40; 13: 41; 16: 13; 16:28; 24: 27–37; Luke 18: 31 *etcetera*). This expression was taken from Daniel 7: 13–14 –

> "I saw in the night–visions, and, behold, there came with the clouds of the sky one like a son of man, and he came even to the ancient of days, and they brought him near before him.

---

[67] Oakes and Gahlin, *Ancient Egypt,* 331.

> There was given him dominion, and glory, and a kingdom, that all the peoples, nations, and languages should serve him: his dominion is an everlasting dominion, which shall not pass away, and his kingdom that which shall not be destroyed."

This vision in Daniel is clearly a prophecy of the advent of *the* Messiah and Jesus applied it consciously to himself in order to convey the message that he was God's anointed and that he had been called to claim the royal throne.

For Jesus and his contemporaries, politics and religion were inextricably connected; it was not possible to treat them as separate aspects of life.[68] Jesus saw himself as the successor of his ancestor David as king of the Jews. He also thought of the coming kingdom of God as a theocracy on earth since many of his teachings and parables attest that the Jews would be ruled according to the laws of the Old Testament. It is very possible that Jesus remembered the following prophecy of Isaiah regarding this theocracy, which was to be established by *the* Messiah:

> "For to us a child is born, to us a son is given; and the government shall be on his shoulder: and his name shall be called Wonderful, Counsellor, Mighty God, Everlasting Father, Prince of Peace. Of the increase of his government and of peace there shall be no end, on the throne of David, and on his kingdom, to establish it, and to uphold it with justice and with righteousness from henceforth even forever. The zeal of YHWH of Hosts will perform this" (Isa 9: 6–7).

---

[68] Armstrong, *Fields of Blood*, 123.

He saw himself, therefore, as the earthly representative of God through whom this theocracy was miraculously to be brought about, the Romans driven away and the dynasty of David restored.

Jesus' core message was an echo of that of John the Baptist: "Repent, for the Kingdom of Heaven is at hand!" (Matt 3: 2; Matt 4: 17). Jesus proclaimed the "gospel [good news] of the Kingdom" throughout his ministry (Matt 9: 35; Matt 24: 14).

Many Christians through the ages interpreted Jesus' message regarding the Kingdom of God or of Heaven, as reported in the gospels, as pertaining to a situation in the far future after Judgment Day and to the heavenly bliss promised to the faithful in the afterlife. It was supposed to be a spiritual kingdom.

The Heidelberg Catechism declares that the Kingdom of God is also to be found wherever people submit to the authority of God through his Word and his Spirit, as well as where the works of Satan are destroyed in this world and in the world to come (Q & A 123) – which also amounts to a spiritual kingdom.

That was not how Jesus saw the Kingdom of God or of Heaven. There are various instances reported where he clearly stated that the (political) Kingdom was at hand and that those who were alive at that time would not see death before the Kingdom was re-established (Matt 16: 27–28; Matt 24: 34; Matt 26: 29, 64; Mark 9: 1; Mark 13: 20; Luke 9: 27; Luke 21: 32). His disciples and even some Pharisees had the clear expectation that he would restore the Israelite kingdom in the immediate future (Luke 17: 20; Luke 19: 11; Acts 1: 6). There were people who wanted to "take him by force, to make him king" (John 6: 15).

He taught his disciples to pray: "May your kingdom come. May your will be done, as in heaven, so on earth" (Matt 6: 10). They had, therefore, to pray for the realization of God's kingdom on earth.

Joseph of Arimathea, a member of the Jewish Council and who buried Jesus in his family tomb after the crucifixion, "was himself waiting for the kingdom of God" (Mark 15: 43; Luke 23: 51).

When Jesus recruited Nathaniel as a disciple, we read:

"Nathanael answered him, 'Rabbi, you are the Son of God! You are King of Israel!' Jesus answered him, 'Because I told you, I saw you underneath the fig tree, do you believe? You will see greater things than these.' He said to him, 'Most assuredly, I tell you, hereafter you will see heaven opened, and the angels of God ascending and descending on the Son of Man'" (John 1: 49–51).

This certainly means that Jesus expected that his experience at his baptism, when the heaven was opened and the stars – in other words, angels – miraculously appeared, to be repeated at some other time.

Jesus regarded the fact that he was able to cast out demons as a proof that the kingdom of Heaven was due to be established at any moment (Matt 12: 28).

He saw himself as the legitimate heir to the throne of David. Therefore, he entered Jerusalem a few days before his execution on the back of an ass to fulfill the prophecy of Zechariah, while enjoying the adulation of the crowds – as pointed out previously. The enthusiastic crowds greeted him as the "son of David" (Matt 21: 1–11, 15; Mark 11: 1–11; Luke 19: 29–44).

He confirmed that he was indeed the king of the Jews when questioned by Governor Pontius Pilate, according to Matt 27: 11; Mark 15: 2; Luke 23: 3; and John 18: 33. Therefore, the Roman soldiers mocked him afterwards as a quasi-royal figure by placing a crown of thorns upon his head (Mark 15: 16–18; John 19: 1–2).

Albrecht Dürer: The Man of Sorrows (ca 1511)

He told his disciples, "Most assuredly I tell you, that you who have followed me, in the regeneration when the Son of Man will sit on the throne of his glory, you also will sit on twelve thrones, judging the twelve tribes of Israel" (Matt 19: 28). In other words, they were supposed to become judges or leaders of the nation of Israel, just as the judges of whom we read in the book of Judges. They would, in effect, become Jesus' cabinet ministers or councilors.

Jesus saw it as his mission to be the liberator and king specifically of Israel, including the ten lost tribes that were exiled and thereafter disappeared after the fall of Samaria in 722 BC.

To a Canaanite woman, whom he initially refused to help, he said: "I wasn't sent to anyone but the lost sheep of the house of Israel" (Matt 15: 24). When he sent his twelve apostles to spread his message and heal the sick, he gave them the following instructions:

> "Don't go among the Gentiles, and don't enter into any city of the Samaritans. Rather, go to the lost sheep of the house of Israel. As you go, preach, saying, 'The Kingdom of Heaven is at hand'" (Matt 10: 5–7)."

Paula Fredriksen concluded: "His mission was a mission to Israel."[69]

---

[69] Fredriksen, *Jesus of Nazareth*, 238.

We read in Matt 25: 31 that he told his disciples: "But when the Son of Man comes in his glory, and all the holy angels with him, then will he sit on the throne of his glory" (see also Mark 8: 38; Mark 14: 62; Luke 9: 26; Luke 22: 69; John 1: 51). Jesus, therefore, had the sadly misguided expectation that he would be able to overthrow the might of Rome with the help of God and a host of angels and re-establish the Israelite theocracy. This expectation would turn out to be a tragic delusion.

The Romans to be Driven Away
Jesus also told his disciples that Judgment Day and the arrival of the Kingdom would happen soon with the help of an army of angels:

> "For the Son of Man will come in the glory of his Father with his angels, and then will he render to every man according to his deeds. Most assuredly I tell you, there are some standing here, who will in no way taste of death, until they see the Son of Man coming in his kingdom" (Matt 16: 27–28; see also Luke 9: 27).

Jesus, no doubt, found various examples in the Old Testament where God had sent angels to aid the Israelites in their battles (Ex 12: 29; Ex 14: 19; Judg 2: 1; Judg 6: 11; 2 Sam 24: 16; *etcetera*) and that must have given him the false confidence that the battle against the Romans was destined to succeed. Although these reports in the Old Testament must have been legendary or mythological in nature, Jesus must have taken them at face value as an accurate rendering of history and he staked his future success on them.

Jesus, certainly, must also have been inspired by the success of the Jewish revolutionaries under the leadership of Judas Maccabeus and his brothers who managed to throw off the yoke of the Seleucid kings of Syria during the fifties of the second century

BC and established an independent Jewish kingdom in Palestine.[70]

It is likely that Jesus was inspired and influenced by the so-called War Scroll, one of the Dead Sea Scrolls discovered in 1947. This scroll is catalogued under the number of 1QM, 4Q491-496 and it is badly damaged, but scholars have been able to reconstruct some of the missing parts. It consists of 19 columns, of which the first 14–19 lines of each have been preserved.

This War Scroll is on the one hand a prophetic book forecasting the victory of the "Sons of Light" over the "Sons of Darkness". On the other hand, it was also a manual on how the "Sons of Light" or the Israelites had to prepare for the war against the "Kittim" – a code name for the Romans who occupied their country.

This scroll can be summarized as follows:

> "The Kittim of Asshur come in alliance with the biblical enemies Edom, Moab, Ammon, and Philistia. Cooperating with this unholy alliance are the 'violators of the covenant': Jews who had spurned the message of the Yahad [the Essene community] and in so doing aligned themselves with the Sons of Darkness. The second stage expands the war's influence to the Kittim who dwelt in Egypt, and then finally to the Kings of the North. (…) In the seventh and final confrontation 'the great hand of God shall overcome [Belial and al]l the angels of his dominion, and all the men of [his forces shall be destroyed forever]' (lQM 1:14–15). Along the way, in true apocalyptic fashion, the scroll goes into elaborate detail concerning the battle trumpets (2:15–3:11), banners (3:12-5-2), and operational matters (5:3–9:16). Priestly prayers for the various phases of the conflict are recorded next (9:17-15:3). Finally, the seven savage

---

[70] Enc Brit, "Maccabees".

engagements of the final day of battle are detailed (15:4–18:8), culminating in a ceremony of thanksgiving on the day following the victory (18:10–19:14)."[71]

Jesus seems to have been familiar with the contents of this scroll, which he could have studied while being educated at the Essene school at Qumran. He used the expression "sons of light" from the War Scroll in Luke 16: 8 and John 12: 36. In Matt 5: 14 he told his disciples: "You are the light of the world."

The following excerpts of the War Scroll[72] could have given Jesus the assurance that an army of attacking angels would help to vanquish the Romans:

> "For You have a multitude of holy ones in the heavens and hosts of angels in Your exalted dwelling to pr[aise] Your [name]" (Column 12: 1).

> "Your covenant of peace You engraved for them with a stylus of life in order to reign o[ver them]: for all time, commissioning the hos[ts of Your [e]lect by their thousands and tens of thousands together with Your holy ones [and] Your angels, and directing them in battle [so as to condemn] the earthly adversaries by trial with Your judgments" (Column 12: 3–5).

> "No one crippled, blind, or lame, nor a man who has a permanent blemish on his skin, or a man affected with ritual uncleanness of his flesh; none of these shall go with them to battle. All of them shall be volunteers for battle, pure of spirit and flesh, and prepared for the day of

---

[71] Frontline. "The War Scroll".
[72] Wise *et al. The Dead Sea Scrolls*.

vengeance (…) for holy angels are present with their army (Column 7: 4–6).

In column 10: 5 we read of "the holy angels, whose ears are open; hearing deep things. [O God, You have created] the expanse of the skies, the host of luminaries…" In other words: the stars were seen as angels in God's service.

If Jesus was familiar with this War Scroll, it would have given him the belief that the "Sons of Light" would prevail with the aid of God's holy angels.

Jesus certainly had links with Jewish militant groups of which there were enough in his day. Two of his disciples were Simon the Zealot (or terrorist) and Judas Iscariot (or assassin).[73] Two other disciples, the brothers James and John, the sons of Zebedee, were given the nicknames of "Sons of Thunder", which typified their explosive and aggressive personalities (Mark 3: 14–19). His group of disciples were, therefore, a band of armed rowdies who acted as his bodyguard (Matt 26: 51; Luke 22: 49; *etcetera*).

Jesus' links with terrorist groups seem strange in the light of the known pacifist convictions of the Essenes. It may well be that Jesus argued that his ancestor, King David, was a great warrior and that the Israelite kingdom could only be restored by overthrowing the repressive Roman yoke by means of armed resistance, albeit it with help of the heavenly host of angels – as described in the War Scroll. For that reason, Jesus declared: "Don't think that I came to send peace on the earth. I didn't come to send peace, but a sword" (Matt 10: 34).

He also said: "I came to throw fire on the earth, I wish it were already kindled. (Luke 12: 49). Jesus instructed his followers: "But now, whoever has a purse, let him take it, and likewise a wallet.

---

[73] Enc Brit, "Simon the Apostle, Saint"; and "Judas Iscariot".

Whoever has none, let him sell his cloak, and buy a sword" (Luke 22: 36).

It seems as if Peter took this advice to heart because he tried to defend Jesus with his sword when his master was later arrested (John 18: 10).

The Jews of the time directly before and during Jesus' ministry expected the Kingdom of God to comprise a huge feast. It is probable that Jesus' last Passover meal with his disciples before his arrest was meant to be a foreshadowing of, or preparation for this feast.[74] After all, during this meal he declared, "Truly I say to you, I will take no more of the fruit of the vine till the day when I take it new in the kingdom of God" (Mark 14: 25). He had the tragic expectation that that day would arrive shortly afterwards.

During this last conversation with his disciples, Jesus gave them a long lecture regarding the coming kingdom and Judgment Day and he illustrated it with various parables (Matt 24–25). Christians usually read these parables as if they describe something in the far future after Judgment Day. When one keeps the preceding arguments in mind it becomes clear that Jesus was describing the wonderful peace and prosperity and progress that would descend upon the Jews after the Romans had miraculously been driven away and the dynasty of David had been reinstated, in the near future.

Although the authors of the gospels repeatedly put words into the mouth of Jesus to the effect that he presented himself as the savior of mankind (*e.g.,* Matt 20: 28; Matt 26: 63–64; John 10: 30, 38; John 14: 6–14), one can safely regard these utterances as fiction and a reinterpretation of Jesus' mission as seen from the perspective of decades later. These purported words of Jesus cannot be reconciled with his repeated declaration that he was only interested in liberating "the lost sheep of the house of Israel".

---

[74] Fredriksen, *Jesus of Nazareth,* 118–19.

If Jesus really did see himself as the redeemer of man, as God incarnate who had come to save sinners from hell, then he, surely, would have made sure that his message would be passed on to the rest of the world. Jesus, however, did nothing of the sort. We don't have a scrap of paper he wrote and there is no record that he dictated his message and claims to any of his followers to write down.

That Jesus did make a huge impact on his followers is clear from the fact the Paul wrote extensively about his interpretation of Jesus' message and that several gospels were written decades after his time to preserve memories about him. But Jesus himself did nothing to pass his message on to posterity – which proves that he never thought of himself as the savior of sinners and the greatest benefactor of mankind in general. It must be stressed that he more than once declared that he was only interested in liberating "the lost sheep of the house of Israel" – and not humanity in general.

One reason why we do not have anything that Jesus has written or dictated may be the fact that his movement was initially an underground organization. He worked in secret in the beginning to keep out of sight of the Roman authorities.

Only one conclusion can be drawn from all this: Jesus saw himself as the liberator and the legitimate king of the restored nation of Israel, the successor of his famous ancestor, King David. If a total solar eclipse occurred at the time of his baptism when the heavens were opened, the stars became visible and a miraculous wind blew over him, it is understandable that Jesus thought of himself as God's instrument to establish a theocracy in Israel.

The Date of the Crucifixion

It is possible to calculate the date and time when Jesus was crucified. Experts used the information given in the gospels, together with astronomical calculations, to determine when the Passover – always at a full moon – fell on a Friday during Jesus' lifetime.

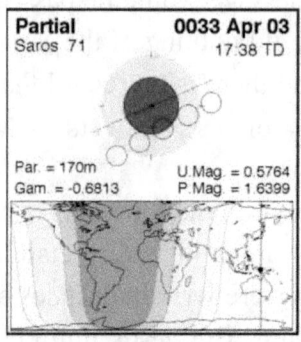

The white areas on the map of the world show where the partial lunar eclipse of 3 April AD 33 was visible. Palestine lies directly on the edge of this area and that means that the partially eclipsed full moon rose over Jerusalem shortly after sunset. The big dark circle represents the earth's shadow that covered most of the moon.

The most probable date of Jesus' execution is 3 April (14 Nisan) AD 33 at 15:00. Jesus must have been at least 37 years old at that time. What is remarkable about that date is that a partial lunar eclipse occurred when the full moon rose in the east directly after sunset.[75]

That may be the reason why Peter alluded to a moon with the color of blood during his speech on Pentecost (Acts 2: 20), seven weeks after the crucifixion.[76] During this speech. Peter quoted from Joel 2: 28–32, including these words: "The sun will be turned into darkness, and the moon into blood, before the great and glorious day of the Lord comes" (Acts 2: 20).

There are two explanations for the darkened sun on the day when Jesus was crucified (Luke 23: 45).

It could have been a volcanic outburst or seismic activity somewhere in the eastern Mediterranean – a part of the earth known for its volcanoes and earthquakes. The inhabitants of Jerusalem would have had a clear memory of such an event while Jesus was hanging on the cross. According to Matt 27: 51, an earthquake was

---

[75] NASA, Eclipse Website.
[76] Humphreys and Waddington, "The Jewish Calendar"; Akin, "7 Clues"; Young, "Lunar Eclipses Shed Light"; Gertoux, "Herod the Great", 67.

felt and fissures in the earth were torn open, releasing dust clouds and smoke at that time. Jerusalem does experience frequent earthquakes due to the movement of tectonic plates.[77] Another possibility is a dust storm, which often happens in Israel when an easterly wind blows dust clouds over the country.

Peter combined that memory with the memory of the partial lunar eclipse on the same day and many Jews may have explained these events as direct messages from God to confirm that Jesus was indeed *the* Messiah and that the kingdom of God was, after all, due to be established soon.

The Jesus Movement

The conventional Christian view is that Jesus never envisaged the founding of the Christian Church and that the church was only founded on the day of Pentecost when the Holy Spirit was poured out onto the assembled followers of Jesus in Jerusalem after his execution.

It is clear, though, that Jesus did start at least a movement or party within Judaism – parallel to other movements and parties of his time, such as the Sadducees, Pharisees, Zealots, and the followers of John the Baptist. One can characterize this party as a kingdom party or monarchist party. When Jesus sent his disciples out on a recruiting drive for his movement, he instructed them:

> "Don't go among the Gentiles, and don't enter into any city of the Samaritans. Rather, go to the lost sheep of the house of Israel. As you go, preach, saying, 'The Kingdom of Heaven is at hand.'" (Matt 10: 5–7).

---

[77] Earthquake Track, "Recent Earthquakes near Jerusalem"; Wikipedia, "List of Earthquakes in the Levant." (Wikipedia lists an earthquake during AD 33 with its epicenter in the Jordan Valley).

Jesus certainly thought of organizing his followers. For instance, we read in Matt 16: 16–19 –

> "Simon Peter answered, 'You are the Christ, the Son of the living God.' Jesus answered him, 'Blessed are you, Simon Bar–Jonah, for flesh and blood has not revealed this to you, but my Father who is in heaven. I also tell you, that you are Peter, and on this rock I will build my assembly, and the gates of Hades will not prevail against it. I will give to you the keys of the Kingdom of Heaven...'"

This passage in the Gospel of Matthew seems to preserve a memory that Jesus thought of his followers as an "assembly" and that this assembly would have as its motto or "rock" that Jesus was the son of the living God – in other words: the promised king of Israel. Peter was given the promise that he would be one of the leading figures in this movement or "assembly" and that this "assembly" would herald in the (earthly) Kingdom of Heaven, of which Peter was given the keys. That must have led to some jealousy amongst the disciples because they, on occasion, argued amongst themselves who would be the most important in Jesus' kingdom (Mark 9: 33–34).

Jesus also mentioned his "assembly", "congregation", or "gathering" in Matt 18: 17. The Greek word used is ἐκκλησία (*ekklesia*) and its most basic meaning is "an assembly of the people convened at a public place of the council for the purpose of deliberating". It is most probably a translation of the Hebrew word קָהָל (*qahal*) – which was used in the Old Testament for a gathering of the people of Israel with the object of worship, but also in a political sense, namely the whole of the chosen nation belonging to God. Jesus most probably used the word "qahal" when addressing his disciples – which word was then rendered with "ekklesia" in

Greek in the gospel. It does seem, therefore, that Jesus thought of some sort of a movement or organization comprised of his followers.

He meant this movement to be a restoration of the people of Israel with him as royal sovereign and for that reason he chose twelve disciples or apostles as symbolic representatives of the twelve patriarchs and twelve tribes of Israel.

The word "ekklesia" is used in the rest of the New Testament for the "church" or "congergation" – the gathering of Christians. This movement or party, largely composed of Essenes or Nazoreans, survived after Jesus' execution and later his brother James became the leader. The initial leadership was exercised by the twelve apostles and they were assisted by seven men (Acts 6: 1–6) – who later appeared as the body of elders of which we read in Acts 15: 4. This movement seems to have expected the return of Jesus to establish the kingdom but the revolutionary fervor of the days of Jesus seems to have evaporated.

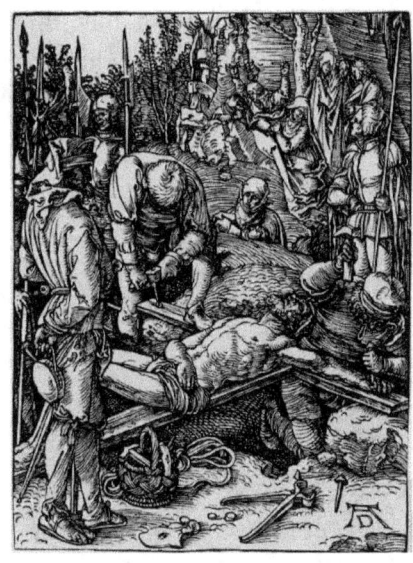

Christ Nailed to the Cross, 1511 by Albrecht Dürer

We are told that even some priests and Pharisees joined this movement, which became known as "The Way" (Acts 6: 7, 9: 2; 19: 9, 23; 24: 14, 22) or "the sect of the Nazoreans" (Acts 24: 5).

There may have been a few thousand members of this group, who were baptized "in the name of Jesus Christ" (Acts 2: 38, 41).

After Jesus' execution and disappearance from the scene, his Jewish followers continued to revere him as a messiah and they seemed to have expected his return. To keep his memory alive his teachings were collected from people who remembered them and that led eventually to the compilation a number of gospels. The fact that Jesus' followers were called the "sect of the Nazoreans" (Acts 24: 5) is an indication that a substantial number of Essenes were members of the Jesus Movement after his execution.

The Jewish Encyclopedia explains: "The silence of the New Testament about the Essenes is perhaps the best proof that they furnished the new sect [the Jesus people] with its main elements both as regards personnel and views. The similarity in many respects between Christianity and Essenism is striking."[78] The Jewish Encyclopedia adds that the Nazoreans were a "[s]ect of primitive Christianity; it appears to have embraced all those Christians who had been born Jews and who neither would nor could give up their Jewish mode of life."[79]

Abba Yesai Nasrai even described the Essenes as "[a]n ascetic group flourishing until their mass conversion to Nazorean Christianity in the first century AD."[80]

Moshe Dann posed the question: "Was Christianity the spiritual heir of the Essenes?" He answered this question in the affirmative and pointed out that many of the practices and views of the Essenes were taken over by Christianity[81] – which is no surprise, since many Essenes were followers of Jesus.

Only two early Christian authors wrote about the Nazoreans: Epiphanius (who was already referred to) and Jerome, the translator

---

[78] Kohler, "Essenes".
[79] Jewish Enc, "Nazarenes".
[80] Nasrai, "Cherubic Sword".
[81] Dann, "The Essenes".

of the Bible into Latin. Kinzig notes: "Jerome mentions the Nazoraeans only incidentally in a number of passages scattered across his huge exegetical work."[82] In the light of this, it is actually strange that Jerome consistently translated Ναζωραῖος (*Nazoraios*) in the gospels and Acts into Latin with "Nazarenus" – in other words: "Nazarenes" and not "Nazoreans", except for Matt 2: 23 where he rendered this word with "Nazareus".

The Ebionites

History knows the Jesus Movement after his death also under the name of the "Ebionites" (Ἐβιωναῖοι – *Ebionaioi*). Bishop Epiphanios wrote that the Ebionites were simply an offshoot of the Nazoreans. He, evidently, did not know the origin of the name "Ebionites" and he described them as the followers of a certain Ebion who "was of the Nazoraeans' school."[83]

According to the description given by Epiphanios of the doctrine of the Ebionites and the Nazoreans, there were no real differences and these groups may be regarded as actually one and the same.[84] These doctrines were – as it is to be expected – similar to the ideas propagated by the Essenes.[85]

Epiphanios reported that members of both these groups were to be found in his time in the area of Decapolis and Pella, where they fled during the Jewish war of AD 66–70,[86] which confirms that they were actually a single group, known by two names. Their flight from Jerusalem and Judea was totally in accordance with their known abhorrence of violence and the use of instruments of war.

---

[82] Kinzig, "The Nazoreans", 464.
[83] Epiphanios, *Panarion,* 30:1(1).
[84] Epiphanios, *Panarion,* 29 and 30; Enc Brit, "Ebionite".
[85] Enc Brit, "Ebionite".
[86] Epiphanios, *Panarion,* 29(7:7), 30(2:7).

Information about the Ebionites is scarce and we must rely on the descriptions given by their critics and opponents. Their name in Hebrew, אֶבְיוֹנִים (*Ebyonim*), describes them as "the poor". It was probably meant as a derogatory name, due to their frugal lifestyle and criticism of affluent people. Although this name only entered history during the second century AD, they may be regarded as the direct descendants of the first followers of Jesus in Palestine.[87]

It is inaccurate to call the Ebionites "Christians" since they apparently never used this name for themselves – they were merely the members of the group of Jewish followers of Jesus after his crucifixion.[88] According to Acts 9: 2, 19: 9, 23 and 24: 5, the Jewish followers of Jesus called themselves "The Way" (ἡ ὁδός – *he hodos*) or the "Nazoreans" (Ναζωραῖοι – *Nazaraioi*). In Acts 21: 16, they are simply called "disciples".

The Ebionites denied the virgin birth and divinity of Jesus. Epiphanios wrote that they taught that "Christ is the offspring of a man, that is, of Joseph." They, nevertheless, regarded Jesus as a messiah or a person anointed by God[89] – more or less as Jesus was portrayed in the Q document (see the next chapter).

The importance of this group has often been neglected by conventional Christian theologians since they just could not accept that any early followers of Jesus, Jewish or Gentile, could really deny his divine nature, virgin birth, and resurrection from the grave. It will be shown, though, that these people constituted the first Jerusalem congregation of the followers of Jesus after his execution, as well as the continuation of the Essene or Nazorean community.

It has already been mentioned that the Jews in Jesus' time yearned for a messiah, someone to deliver them from the burden of

---

[87] Jewish Enc, "Ebionites".
[88] Epiphanios, *Panarion*, 30:2(2).
[89] Epiphanios, *Panarion*, 30(3:1).

foreign domination by the pagan Romans. They found promises in the prophecies of the Old Testament that such a figure would indeed appear. It must be stressed that these prophecies nowhere taught that the Messiah would be a divine figure, God himself who would appear in human form. The Messiah – there were more than one, including King Cyrus of Persia (Isa 45: 1) – was always portrayed as an ordinary human being. The final Messiah was expected to be a king descended from David and a mighty warrior who would free his people from their enemies.[90]

The Ebionites (and Nazoreans), who were Jews and knew the Hebrew Scriptures, would therefore never have expected their Messiah, Jesus of Nazareth, to have a divine nature.

The early Christian theologian, Origen, wrote that "those Jews who have received Jesus as Christ are called by the name of Ebionites" (Ἐβιωναῖοι χρηματίζουσιν οἱ ἀπὸ Ἰουδαίων τὸν Ἰησοῦν ὡς Χριστὸν παραδεξάμενοι – *Ebionaioi chrematizousin hoi apo Ioudaion ton Iesoun hos Christon paradexamenoi*).[91] Eusebius, the first Christian historian, equated the Ebionites with the "people of the Church in Jerusalem" (λαός ἐν Ἱεροσολύμοις ἐκκλησίας – *laos en Ierosolymois ekklesias*).[92]

Eusebius also informs us that the leader of the followers of Jesus in Jerusalem after his crucifixion was James, the brother of Jesus (see Acts 15: 13; Acts 21: 18; Gal 1: 19). He was succeeded by Symeon, "a cousin of the Savior" (ἀνεψιός τοῦ σωτῆρος – *anepsios tou soteros*) and he, in turn, was succeeded by other relatives of Jesus after he had been martyred, including a nephew called Judas.[93] These leaders definitely knew Jesus during his

---

[90] König, *Die Groot Geloofswoordeboek*, 323–25.
[91] Origen: *Contra Celsum (ΚΑΤΑ ΚΕΛΣΟΥ)*, Liber II(1).
[92] Eusebius, *Historia Ecclesiastice*, Liber III/v/3 and XXVII.
[93] Eusebius, *Historia Ecclesiatica*, Liber III/XI and XXXII.

lifetime or had relatives who knew Jesus. The fact that brothers and other relatives of Jesus succeeded him as leaders of the Jesus Movement is an indication that some sort of a dynasty was established and that the followers of Jesus constituted a separate sect within Judaism – just as there were other factions, parties, or sects in Judea and Galilee, such as the Pharisees, Sadducees and Zealots (Acts 5: 17; 15: 5; 26: 5; 28: 22).

The main difference between the Jesus Movement and other Jewish religious groups was that they regarded Jesus as *the* Messiah and that he would return soon (James 5: 7–9) to free the Jews from foreign domination – a view other Jewish groups did not share. The distinction between these sects or groups was not always clear-cut. We read, for instance, in Acts 6: 7 and 15: 5 of priests and Pharisees who were also followers of Jesus.

It is reported in Acts 4: 34 that the first "Christians" in Jerusalem lived in poverty and shared their belongings with each other – a sign of their Essene background.

Another reason why the members of the Jerusalem congregation sold all their belongings and shared the proceeds was probably that they expected Jesus' return and even Judgment Day to arrive very soon and that it did not make sense to gather worldly possessions, which would prove to be worthless on Judgment Day.

Paul writes in Gal 2: 10 that he was requested during his visit to Jerusalem "to remember the poor". This may be an oblique reference to the Ebionites, the "poor" followers of Jesus in and around Jerusalem. In 1 Cor 16: 3 and 2 Cor 8: 4 we are told that Paul collected money for the poor "saints" in Jerusalem.

Acts 15: 1 and 5 relate that some followers of Jesus from Judea came to Antioch and taught that believers had to be circumcised, according to the Law of Moses. This affirms that these

Jewish followers of Jesus adhered to all the Old Testament laws and continued to live as Jews. They, no doubt, quoted Jesus:

"Whoever then goes against the smallest of these laws, teaching men to do the same, will be named least in the kingdom of heaven; but he who keeps the laws, teaching others to keep them, will be named great in the kingdom of heaven" (Matt 5: 19).

They also found support in these words of Jesus:

"But it is easier for heaven and earth to pass away, than for one tiny stroke of a pen in the law to fall" (Luke 16: 17).

They did not see themselves as belonging to a new religion and most probably came to investigate Paul's doctrines in Antioch, which seemed to differ from Jesus' teachings. We read that Paul and Barnabas disagreed with these Jewish followers of Jesus and that the congregation in Antioch resolved to send Paul, Barnabas, and others to Jerusalem to settle the issue. The people who came from Judea to Antioch must have known Jesus personally while he was still with them, while Paul and Barnabas – who thought that these people taught a heresy – never knew Jesus personally.

Paul tells his readers in Gal 2: 11–21 that he and Peter clashed publicly in Antioch about the obligation of followers of Jesus to live according to the Old Testament laws. This must be an indication that Peter was one of those who came to Antioch to investigate Paul's teachings as recorded in Acts 15: 1. That means that the Apostle Peter didn't regard himself as a Christian – he was simply a Jewish follower of Jesus, an Essene or a Nazorean.

Paul also had a meeting with James, brother of Jesus and leader of the group in Jerusalem, and the elders during his last visit to that city before his arrest. James told Paul that "many thousands there are among the Jews of those who have believed, and they are all zealous for the law" (Acts 21: 20). In other words: the Jewish followers of Jesus in Judea continued to live as Jews and they merely formed a sect or group within the Jewish religious community.

James also informed Paul that these followers of Jesus could not agree with his teachings since "you teach all the Jews who are among the Gentiles to forsake Moses, telling them not to circumcise their children neither to walk after the customs" (Acts 21: 21).

Paul was then forced to undergo the Jewish purifying rites before he could be allowed to enter the temple and bring sacrifices according to the laws of Moses (Acts 21: 24–26). The fact that Paul succumbed to these requirements is an indication that he realized that James was an influential person and that he could not afford to lose his sympathy and support – although he must have thought that these ceremonies were unnecessary and that they clashed with his view that Christ has fulfilled and abolished the obligations of the Law (Gal 3: 13).

At the outbreak of the Jewish war of AD 66–70, these Jewish followers of Jesus fled to Pella on the eastern side of the Jordan and to Syria, where they continued to practice their brand of Jewish Christianity. They also spread to Egypt and Asia Minor.

Christian theologians of the second century AD and afterwards regarded them as heretics since they denied the virgin birth and divinity of Christ.[94] Justin Martyr, the Christian apologist of the second century AD, for instance, was aware of "Christians" holding the view that Jesus was nothing but an ordinary man. In his Dialogue with Trypho he places the following words in the mouth of his oppo-

---

[94] Jewish Enc, "Ebionites"; Enc Brit, "Ebionite"; Eusebius, *Historia Ecclesiastica* Liber III/V/3 & XXVII/5–6.

nent Trypho:

> "Those who affirm him [Jesus] to have been a man, and to have been anointed by election, and then to have become Christ, appear to me to speak more plausibly than you who hold those opinions which you express. For we all expect that Christ will be a man [born] of men..."[95]

Irenaeus, another theologian of the second century AD, described the Ebionites in the following words:

> "Those who are called Ebionites agree that the world was made by God; but their opinions with respect to the Lord are similar to those of Cerinthus and Carpocrates. They use the Gospel according to Matthew only, and repudiate the Apostle Paul, maintaining that he was an apostate from the law. As to the prophetical writings, they endeavor to expound them in a somewhat singular manner: they practice circumcision, persevere in the observance of those customs which are enjoined by the law, and are so Judaic in their style of life, that they even adore Jerusalem as if it were the house of God."[96]

Several scholars agree that the early Jewish followers of Jesus in Judea and Galilee were indeed none other than the Ebionites (and the Nazoreans) who denied the virgin birth of Jesus and his divine nature. Michael Goulder concluded that this stance "was the creed of the Jerusalem Church from early times."[97] Gerd Lüdemann

---

[95] Justin Martyr, *Dialogue with Trypho*, ch 49
[96] Irenaeus, *Adversus Haereses*, Liber I/XXVI/2.
[97] Goulder, *St. Paul versus St. Peter*, 134.

thought that "the group of Ebionites should be seen as an offshoot of the Jerusalem community."[98] According to Robert Eisenman, the first leader of the Ebionites was none other than James, the brother of Jesus.[99] John Painter saw a "connection between early Jerusalem Christianity (the Hebrews) and the later Ebionites."[100]

That the Ebionites were opposed to Paul and his teaching, is no surprise. During Paul's last visit to Jerusalem and the temple, some Jews from Asia assaulted him because they said: "Men of Israel, help! This is the man who teaches all men everywhere against the people, and the law, and this place" (Acts 21: 27–28).

It is not unreasonable to surmise that the Q document had its origin amongst these Ebionites while they still resided in and around Judea. Their version of the Gospel according to Matthew could have been none other than Q.

Kinzig remarks: "[T]hey appear to have read the Gospel of Matthew in an archaic 'Hebrew,' i.e., probably Aramaic version."[101] He elaborates that "there was in principle only one Aramaic gospel, called 'according to the Hebrews,' which was used by the Nazoraeans and other groups. This gospel was written at around 100 C.E. and was considered the Ur–Matthäus."[102]

Since the Ebionites and Nazoreans were the Jewish followers of Jesus and their direct descendants in Jerusalem, Judea, and Galilee, one can expect that they retained more authentic memories of Jesus than Christians elsewhere who depended upon the four gospels and the writings of Paul for information regarding Jesus. In other words: the view of the Ebionites and Nazoreans that

---

[98] Lüdemann, *Heretics*, 52.
[99] Eisenman, *James*, 154–56.
[100] Painter, *Just James*, 229.
[101] Kinzig, "The Nazoreans", 472.
[102] Kinzig, "The Nazoreans", 473.

Jesus was an ordinary mortal, that he was the son of Joseph and Mary and not a divine figure, must be regarded as definitely more convincing than the views of other Christians who worshipped him as the eternal and divine Son of God, the equal of God the Father.

Conclusions

It is important to remember that Jesus and his followers regarded him as *the* Messiah, the king-in-waiting of the Jews, the liberator of his oppressed people. Matthew's Gospel reports the following about the beginning of Jesus' ministry:

> "From that time, Jesus began to preach, and to say, 'Repent! For the Kingdom of Heaven is at hand.' (…) Jesus went about in all Galilee, teaching in their synagogues, preaching the gospel of the kingdom, and healing every disease and every sickness among the people" (Matt 4: 17 & 23 – see also: Mark 1: 14–15 and Luke 10: 9–11).

The message regarding the imminent arrival of the Kingdom of Heaven (or of God) was not about some or other spiritual or heavenly kingdom, but about a political kingdom on earth, the restoration of the kingdom of David. Jesus promised his followers that this kingdom would be established while they were still alive.

When reading the four gospels, this aspect must be kept in mind and it will have a decisive influence on how the teachings and actions of Jesus must be understood. Should one strip away the improbable, impossible, and clearly mistaken aspects from these narratives, it will become obvious that Jesus prepared his followers for the coming of the kingdom of God, with him on the throne of David in Jerusalem. Many an obscure passage in the gospels will become clearer and make sense when read from this perspective.

In the process of propagating the kingdom, Jesus taught a religious message in accordance with his Essene or Nazorean background because he wanted his fellow-Jews to repent, mend their ways, and turn to God.

The distrust of the Sadducees and the priestly class in Jerusalem against Jesus, as reported in the gospels, may be understood in this context.

The high priest was the most important person in the Jewish community at that time and he would have protected his privileged position vehemently against anybody who threatened this position, even if it was the popular Jesus of Nazareth who was hailed by the crowd as the successor of King David. Jesus was critical of the priestly class, the teachers of the Law and the Jerusalem elite in the same vein as his predecessor as a teacher, John the Baptist, and they, of course, did not take kindly to that situation. The Jewish religious authorities also seemed to have been afraid of the success of Jesus' campaign to attract followers in an effort to restore the monarchy in Israel. According to John 11: 46–54, they argued that an insurrection by Jesus and his followers would be crushed by the Romans in a horrible and cruel way, which would result in a calamity for all the Jews. Therefore, Jesus and his campaign had to be stopped.

The animosity against and distrust of Jesus by some Pharisees may be due to Jesus' Galilean background. When the gospels mention that "the Jews" (Greek: Ἰουδαῖοι – *Ioudaioi*) conspired against Jesus, they mean the "Judeans", the people from Judea[103] – in contrast with the Jews from Galilee, in their eyes a backward region, far from Jerusalem and its temple. During Jesus' lifetime, Galilee was a different country, ruled by Herod Antipas, who had John the Baptist beheaded to please his wife and his step-daughter.

---

[103] Anderson, "The John, Jesus, and History Project", 20.

The Judeans, who lived in the city of David, Jerusalem, and the home town of David, Bethlehem, evidently, felt superior to the Galileans and they just could not believe that the Messiah would come from that region (John 7: 41–42).

* * * * *

In the pages that follow, the gospel narratives will be analyzed and commented upon from the perspective gained in this Chapter, namely that Jesus must primarily be understood as the king-in-waiting of Israel, as well as an Essene. He strived to be a religious reformer such as Moses, Elijah, Ezra, and Nehemiah in the Old Testament and who wanted to get rid of false priests and affluent religious leaders in accordance with his Essene background.

Chapter 3
THE Q DOCUMENT

The Existence of the Q Document

The very first four verses of the Gospel of Luke declare:

> "Because many have undertaken to draw up a narrative concerning those matters which have been fulfilled among us, even as they delivered them to us, who from the beginning were eyewitnesses and ministers of the word, it seemed good to me also, having traced the course of all things accurately from the first, to write to you in order, most excellent Theophilus; that you might know the certainty concerning the things in which you were instructed."

With these words, Luke informed his readers that he was not the first author to write about the life, ministry, message, and execution of Jesus and that he was aware of these previous efforts, which depended upon the memories of eye-witnesses of the ministry of Jesus. He did some research himself and he now presents this narrative to his friend and sponsor, a certain Theophilus.

The question now arises: who wrote about Jesus before Luke did? Two German scholars, Heinrich Holtzmann in 1863, and Bernhard Weiss in 1887–88, proposed an answer to this question, namely that Luke, as well as Matthew, used Mark and another written source when they compiled their respective gospels.[104]

Experts on the New Testament refined this view and found that Luke and Matthe used the following sources:

---

[104] Rylaarsdam *et al.*, "Biblical Literature".

- The Gospel of Mark, the oldest and shortest complete gospel (of which they copied large parts, often word for word);
- The so-called Q Document; and
- Some material unique to each gospel, some of which may also have been parts of the Q Document not used by either Matthew or Luke. This unique material may be designated as "M" for Matthew's material and "L" for Luke's unique source(s) [105]

The process of how Matthew and Luke were assembled may be illustrated by the following diagram:

M	Q		MARK	L
↓	↓ ↘	↙	↓	↓
↓	↓	↘↙	↓	↓
↓	↓	↙↘	↓	↓
↓	↓ ↙		↘ ↓	↓
↓→→→→MATTHEW			LUKE ←←←← ↓	

Matthew contains material from Q, Mark, and M, while Luke is composed of material taken from Q, Mark, and L.

There are those who dispute this point of view. Their main argument is that the so-called Q Document has never been found and that there is no proof from the writings of ancient authors for this hypothesis, namely that Matthew and Luke depended mainly on older sources, namely the Gospel of Mark and the Q Document. They also point out that there are no indications that Paul, who wrote his letters during the fifties and early sixties of the first century AD, was aware of such a document or quoted from it.[106]

This hypothesis of multiple sources for Matthew and Luke

---

[105] Early Christian Writings, "The Lost Sayings Gospel Q at a Glance" Rylaarsdam *et al.,* "Biblical Literature".
[106] Linnemann, "The Lost Gospel of Q—Fact or Fantasy?" McDowell. "What is the document Q supposed to be?"

of Holtzmann and Weiss, with various modifications and refinements by other scholars, is the generally accepted solution to the so-called synoptic problem, the relationship between Matthew, Mark, and Luke, the so-called Synoptic Gospels. They are called "synoptic" because they basically have the same views.[107]

The designation "Q" for one of the sources for Matthew and Luke is derived from the German word "Quelle," which means "source". The reconstructed Q Document consists of the material used by both Matthew and Luke, but not by Mark.[108]

This hypothesis is supported by the fact that almost all the contents of Mark appear in Matthew and Luke. Mark has 661 verses, of which more than 600 appear in Matthew and 350 in Luke. Only about 31 verses of Mark are absent from the other two Synoptic Gospels. In the passages common to all three these gospels, there is very seldom a verbatim agreement between Matthew and Luke against Mark. Such agreement, though, often occurs between Matthew and Mark or Luke and Mark or where all three agree.[109]

Apart from stories of the temptation of Jesus and the healing of the centurion's slave, that are usually ascribed to Q, most of the material in Q consists of sayings of Jesus. For this reason, Q is sometimes called the Sayings Gospel.[110]

The compiler(s) of Q followed the examples of the books of Proverbs and Ecclesiastes, which are for the most part collections of the sayings and wisdom of Solomon and other sages.

Several scholars have been able to reconstruct Q, using mainly the wording found in Luke, which seems to be the most au-

---

[107] Rylaarsdam *et al.* "Biblical Literature".
[108] Early Christian Writings. "The Lost Sayings Gospel Q at a Glance", Rylaarsdam *et al.* "Biblical Literature.".
[109] Early Christian Writings. "The Priority of Mark".
[110] Early Christian Writings. "The Lost Sayings Gospel Q at a Glance".

thentic version of Q.[111]

Since it was difficult to get excited about something that does not really exist, the existence of Q remained a nebulous hypothesis. But when the extra-biblical Gospel of Thomas was discovered at Nag Hammadi in Egypt in 1945, scholars saw a parallel between this document and Q. Both contain a series of teachings by Jesus. This discovery gave researchers the hope that a copy of Q may turn up in future.[112]

Burton Mack observed that the community in which Q must have originated obviously did not attach any religious connotations on Jesus' passion and resurrection. Q – as well as Thomas – are totally silent on these matters. The only reason for the compilation of these gospels by members of the Jesus Movement was to preserve the teachings of Jesus.[113]

It is also possible that Jesus was still alive somewhere at the time when Q was compiled. It will be shown in the rest of this book, especially in Chapter 5, that Jesus did not really die on the cross and that his friends nursed him back to relative health after he was taken from the cross. If he was still alive when Q was composed it may explain why his crucifixion and resurrection received no attention.

Place of Origin and Date of Q
It is difficult to locate the place or origin of the Q Document, though it has been proposed that northern Palestine or Galilee may be

---

[111] Early Christian Writings. "The Lost Sayings Gospel Q"; Klopperborg. *Q, the Earliest Gospel*, 123–144; Mack, *The Lost Gospel*; Michel, "Sayings of Jesus: the Lost Gospel of Q"; Miller, ed. *The Complete Gospels*, 249–300; Robinson *et al,. The Critical Edition of Q.*
[112] Mellowes, "More About Q and the Gospel of Thomas": Early Christuan Writings. "The Existence of Q".
[113] Mack, *The Lost Gospel,* 4–8.

considered. The only towns mentioned in Q – apart from Jerusalem – are the Galilean towns of Chorazin, Bethsaida, and Capernaum, which Jesus condemned for refusing to accept his messengers' (Luke 10: 13–15 and Matt 11: 21–23).[114]

Since Jesus seems to have spent most of his ministry in Galilee in Essene communities, one would expect that more people in these parts and communities would have been eye-witnesses who were consulted by the compiler(s) of Q than anywhere else.

If Q originated in Galilee, it explains why Paul took no notice of it. He wrote his extant letters while moving around in Asia Minor and Greece where Q was not yet known during his lifetime. It also explains why Mark made no use of Q. It will be shown in Chapter 7 that Mark was most probably written during the seventies of the first century AD in Greece, where Q was still unknown.

It is probable that Q – together with M and L – was still around during the first part of the second century AD when the Gospel of Thomas was written. It will be shown in Chapter 13 that almost three-quarters of the sayings in this apocryphal gospel are dependent upon Q, M, and L. The fact that Thomas made use of these three sources, together with a few quotations from Mark, John, and Revelation, may point to a common origin of Q and those parts of M and L used by Thomas.

It must be concluded that Q was written before the destruction of Jerusalem during the Jewish War of AD 66–70. There is no hint of this catastrophe and no reference to any military operations against Jerusalem in Q. Jesus only condemned Jerusalem with its Sadducee elite, where the prophets had been killed. Jesus, however, expected the people of Jerusalem to accept him as the king of Israel when he entered the city in triumph (Luke 13: 34–35).

---

[114] Early Christian Writings. "The Lost Sayings Gospel Q at a Glance".

It will be shown in Chapter 6 that there are at least six allusions or references to sayings in Q in the Epistle of James. If James, the leader of the Ebionites in Jerusalem, wrote his letter during the early fifties of the first century AD, then Q may well have appeared during the forties in Palestine in an Essene environment.

The existence of communities of Jewish followers of Jesus who were being persecuted by the Jerusalem elite are pre-supposed in Luke 6: 22–23, 11: 49–5, 12: 4–5, and 12: 11–12. Such persecutions did happen after the crucifixion of Jesus. James, the son of Zebedee, was executed by Herod Agrippa more or less during AD 44, when Peter was also arrested (Acts 12: 1–4). Paul mentioned in 1 Thess 2: 14–16 that the believers who "are in Judea in Christ Jesus" were being persecuted by the Jews at that time, namely during the fifties of the first century AD. All these persecutions could have prompted the compiler(s) of Q to include appropriate or relevant sayings attributed to Jesus in this document.[115]

On the other hand, there are enough indications in Q and the canonical gospels that John the Baptist and Jesus with their followers endured enough opposition from the rich priestly class in Jerusalem, whom they often criticized and condemned. These oblique references to persecutions could, therefore, also be applied to Jesus and his disciples during his lifetime.

The Text of Q

Burton Mack found that Q grew in three stages and he published his reconstruction of Q with indications of how these stages followed upon each other.[116] John Kloppenborg proposed something similar and published his text of Q with the three layers clearly distinguish-

---

[115] Early Christian Writings. "The Lost Sayings Gospel Q at a Glance".
[116] Mack, *The Lost Gospel*, 73–102.

ed from each other.[117]

It will be shown in the chapters dealing with the unique material of Matthew and Luke that certain parts of M and L were almost certainly originally part of Q but were used by only one of these two gospels. If these passages are incorporated into the reconstructed Q it may lead to a revision of the hypothesis of how Q grew in stages.

In the analysis of the text of Q in this chapter, only the full or final reconstructed text of Q as published will be used since both Matthew and Luke must have used the final version as a source when they wrote their gospels during the eighties AD. They were probably unaware of how Q may have grown in stages.

The reconstructed Q is the first gospel narrative to be discussed in this book since it is arguably the earliest, written between ten and thirty years after Jesus' execution by an author or authors who could consult various eye-witnesses of the ministry of John the Baptist and Jesus in Galilee and Judea.

It is impossible to determine how many of the sayings in Q are authentic. Some may be distortions of genuine sayings, while others may have been wrongly attributed to Jesus. Most of them seem to be a fair rendering of Jesus' teachings.

The reconstructed Q is, of course, written in Greek since it was distilled from the Greek Gospels of Luke and Matthew. There are no signs that it was translated from Hebrew or Aramaic. That it was written in Greek is no surprise. Among the Dead Sea Scrolls, , some documents and papyrus fragments in Greek were found in Cave 7 – although most of these documents were either in Hebrew or Aramaic.[118]

The text of Q, as reconstructed by Robert J. Miller, appears

---

[117] Kloppenborg, *Q, the Earliest Gospel*, 123–44.
[118] Wikipedia, "List of Dead Sea Scrolls".

below. Headings were added at appropriate places.[119]

John's Preaching
Luke 3: 7–9 (Matt 3: 7–9)

7.	John said to the crowds that came out to be baptized by him, "You brood of vipers! Who warned you to flee from the wrath to come?
8.	Bear fruits worthy of repentance. Do not begin to say to yourselves, 'We have Abraham as our ancestor'; for I tell you, God is able from these stones to raise up children to Abraham.
9.	Even now the ax is lying at the root of the trees; every tree therefore that does not bear good fruit is cut down and thrown into the fire".

These words of John the Baptist were certainly aimed at the haughty and corrupt Sadducees, the rich and liberal priestly class in Jerusalem who cooperated with the Roman authorities. John was just as critical of them as the Essenes/Nazoreans. He warned them that their ancestry from Abraham would not guarantee their survival and that Judgment Day is awaiting them.

The baptism by John was probably based on or copied from the regular ritual baths taken by the Essenes.

Luke 3: 16–17 (Matt 3: 11–12)	
16.	John answered all of them by saying, "I baptize you with water; but one who is more powerful than I is coming; I am not worthy to untie the thong of his sandals. He will baptize you with the Holy Spirit and fire.

---

[119] Miller, *The Complete Gospels*, 249–300.

> 17. His winnowing fork is in his hand, to clear his threshing floor and to gather the wheat into his granary; but the chaff he will burn with unquenchable fire."

Albrecht Dürer: John the Baptist, ca 1503

John informed his audience to expect the appearance of the Messiah who was so important that John was not even worthy to untie his sandals. It was to be foreseen that he would get rid of all the enemies of God's true people (the chaff – the Sadducees and the pagan Romans) who would be burnt with everlasting fire. The Messiah would baptize people with the Holy Spirit (God's breath/mind or a synonym for God himself – see Acts 5: 3–4) when these enemies are vanquished.

John's knowledge of the appearance of the Messiah is an indication that he and Jesus had an alliance and common loyalty to the cause of the Essenes, who regarded themselves as the only true people of the God of Israel.

The Temptation of Jesus
Luke 4: 1–13 (Matt 4: 1–4, 9–12, 5–7, 13)

> 1. Jesus, full of the Holy Spirit, returned from the Jordan and was led by the Spirit in the wilderness,

> 2. where for forty days he was tempted by the devil. He ate nothing at all during those days, and when they were over, he was famished.
> 3. The devil said to him, "If you are the Son of God, command this stone to become a loaf of bread."
> 4. Jesus answered him, "It is written, 'One does not live by bread alone.'"
> 5. Then the devil led him up and showed him in an instant all the kingdoms of the world.
> 6. And the devil said to him, "To you I will give their glory and all this authority; for it has been given over to me, and I give it to anyone I please.
> 7. If you, then, will worship me, it will all be yours."
> 8. Jesus answered him, "It is written, 'Worship the Lord your God, and serve only him.'"
> 9. Then the devil took him to Jerusalem, and placed him on the pinnacle of the temple, saying to him, "If you are the Son of God, throw yourself down from here,
> 10. for it is written, 'He will command his angels concerning you, to protect you,'
> 11. and 'On their hands they will bear you up, so that you will not dash your foot against a stone.'"
> 12. Jesus answered him, "It is said, 'Do not put the Lord your God to the test.'"
> 13. When the devil had finished every test, he departed from him until an opportune time.

The details of the story of Jesus' temptation could only have come from Jesus himself, since there were no other witnesses of these events. Jesus certainly related his experiences later to his followers, who passed their knowledge on to the compiler(s) of Q. It has been shown in the previous chapter that Jesus must have been dehydrated and starving after fasting for a protracted period, which could easily have led to hallucinations. These experiences, though, were so real to him that he regarded them as part of God's calling to become *the* Messiah and liberator of Israel.

The devil could have been a personification in Jesus' mind of the Sadducees and priests who opposed John the Baptist and him, as well as of the Roman oppressors. Belief in the devil and evil spirits was part and parcel of the ancient world view, shared by the Jews and early Christians.

The quotations from the Old Testament were taken from Deut 8: 3; Deut 6: 13 & 16; and Deut 10: 20.

Jesus' Teaching
Luke 6: 12, 17, 20–26 (Matt 5: 1–2; 5: 3, 6, 4, 11–12)

12.	Now during those days he went out to the mountain to pray; and he spent the night in prayer to God.
17.	He came down with them and stood on a level place, with a great crowd of his disciples and a great multitude of people from all Judea, Jerusalem, and the coast of Tyre and Sidon.
20.	Then he looked up at his disciples and said: "Blessed are you who are poor, for yours is the kingdom of God.
21	"Blessed are you who are hungry now, for you will be filled. "Blessed are you who weep now, for you will laugh.
22.	"Blessed are you when people hate you, and when they exclude you, revile you, and defame you on account of the Son of Man.

> 23. Rejoice in that day and leap for joy, for surely your reward is great in heaven; for that is what their ancestors did to the prophets.
> 24. "But woe to you who are rich, for you have received your consolation.
> 25. "Woe to you who are full now, for you will be hungry. "Woe to you who are laughing now, for you will mourn and weep.
> 26. "Woe to you when all speak well of you, for that is what their ancestors did to the false prophets.

This passage in Luke, which also occurs at different spots in Matthew, contains the well-known Beatitudes, as well as a condemnation of those who are the opposite of those who are to be blessed by God.

A noteworthy difference between the two versions is Matthew who changed Luke 6: 20 where real poor people are mentioned, to "blessed are the poor in spirit" [Μακάριοι οἱ πτωχοὶ τῷ πνεύματι (*Makarioi hoi ptochoi to pneumati*) – Matt 5: 3]. This expression in Matthew was sometimes interpreted as referring to those defective in intelligence, but it rather refers to those who have troubled spirits and are unhappy or downhearted.

This contrast between poor people and rich people is typical of the Essene outlook regarding social affairs in those times. After all, the Essenes, who mostly became the followers of Jesus after his lifetime, also became known as the Ebionites, the "Poor People". Jesus was clearly on the side of these paupers who would receive places of honor in the coming kingdom of God, of which he was due to be the sovereign.

Verse 22 hints at the opposition Jesus and his movement endured from the elite in Jerusalem.

Love of Enemies, Judging, and Generosity
Luke 6:27–36 (Matt 5: 44, 39–42; 7: 12; 5: 46–47, 45, 48)

27.	"But I say to you that listen, Love your enemies, do good to those who hate you,
28.	bless those who curse you, pray for those who abuse you.
29.	If anyone strikes you on the cheek, offer the other also; and from anyone who takes away your coat do not withhold even your shirt.
30.	Give to everyone who begs from you; and if anyone takes away your goods, do not ask for them again.
31.	Do to others as you would have them do to you.
32.	"If you love those who love you, what credit is that to you? For even sinners love those who love them.
33.	If you do good to those who do good to you, what credit is that to you? For even sinners do the same.
34.	If you lend to those from whom you hope to receive, what credit is that to you? Even sinners lend to sinners, to receive as much again.
35.	But love your enemies, do good, and lend, expecting nothing in return. Your reward will be great, and you will be children of the Most High; for he is kind to the ungrateful and the wicked.
36.	Be merciful, just as your Father is merciful.

Luke 6: 37–38 (Matt 7: 1–2)

37.	"Do not judge, and you will not be judged; do not condemn, and you will not be condemned. Forgive, and you will be forgiven;
38.	give, and it will be given to you. A good measure, pressed down, shaken together, running over, will be put into your

> lap; for the measure you give will be the measure you get back."

The Essenes were known for their pacifism and generosity and hospitality towards each other. That was also the sentiments Jesus advocated in these passages.

Blind Guides
Luke 6: 39–40 (Matt 15: 14; 10: 24–25)

> 39. He also told them a parable: "Can a blind person guide a blind person? Will not both fall into a pit?
> 40. A disciple is not above the teacher, but everyone who is fully qualified will be like the teacher.

The blind guides and teachers mentioned in this passage were clearly the Jewish elite in Jerusalem of Jesus' time. The Essenes accused them of distorting the Scriptures and regarded the priests at the temple as false priests and frauds.

On Pretense
Luke 6: 41–42 (Matt 7: 3–5)

> 41. Why do you see the speck in your neighbor's eye, but do not notice the log in your own eye?
> 42. Or how can you say to your neighbor, 'Friend, let me take out the speck in your eye,' when you yourself do not see the log in your own eye? You hypocrite, first take the log out of your own eye, and then you will see clearly to take the speck out of your neighbor's eye.

The hypocrites mentioned in this saying clearly refer to the Sadducees in Jerusalem who did not take kindly to the teachings of

John the Baptist and Jesus. They were so blinded by their own sense of importance that they refused to listen to John and Jesus.

This saying displays Jesus' sense of humor where he asked his audience to imagine something absurd: a log stuck in an eye!

Trees and Fruit
Luke 6: 43–45 (Matt 7: 16–20; 12: 33–35)

43.	"No good tree bears bad fruit, nor again does a bad tree bear good fruit;
44	for each tree is known by its own fruit. Figs are not gathered from thorns, nor are grapes picked from a bramble bush.
45.	The good person out of the good treasure of the heart produces good, and the evil person out of evil treasure produces evil; for it is out of the abundance of the heart that the mouth speaks.

Jesus mentioned an obvious piece of wisdom: a person's character and personality becomes visible in his actions. The evil people mentioned in this passage were obviously the Sadducees and teachers of the Law who opposed John and Jesus.

Foundations
Luke 6: 46–49 (Matt 7: 21, 24–27)

46.	"Why do you call me 'Lord, Lord,' and do not do what I tell you?
47	I will show you what someone is like who comes to me, hears my words, and acts on them.
48.	That one is like a man building a house, who dug deeply and laid the foundation on rock; when a flood arose, the river burst against that house but could not shake it, because it had been well built.

49.	But the one who hears and does not act is like a man who built a house on the ground without a foundation. When the river burst against it, immediately it fell, and great was the ruin of that house."

It is clear that the foundation upon which one ought to build one's life must be the message of Jesus. He was, though, critical of those who refused to accept him and his message, which was a call to repentance and to observe the pronouncements and ideas of Moses and the prophets.

Healing a Roman Officer's Slave
Luke 7: 1–10 (Matt 7: 28; 8: 5–10, 13)

1.	After Jesus had finished all his sayings in the hearing of the people, he entered Capernaum.
2.	A centurion there had a slave whom he valued highly, and who was ill and close to death.
3.	When he heard about Jesus, he sent some Jewish elders to him, asking him to come and heal his slave.
4.	When they came to Jesus, they appealed to him earnestly, saying, "He is worthy of having you do this for him,
5.	for he loves our people, and it is he who built our synagogue for us."
6.	And Jesus went with them, but when he was not far from the house, the centurion sent friends to say to him, "Lord, do not trouble yourself, for I am not worthy to have you come under my roof; therefore I did not presume to come to you. But only speak the word, and let my servant be healed.

> 7. For I also am a man set under authority, with soldiers under me; and I say to one, 'Go,' and he goes, and to another,
> 8. 'Come,' and he comes, and to my slave, 'Do this,' and the slave does it."
> 9. When Jesus heard this he was amazed at him, and turning to the crowd that followed him, he said, "I tell you, not even in Israel have I found such faith."
> 10. When those who had been sent returned to the house, they found the slave in good health.

Capernaum was an important town in Galilee on the shores of the Lake of Galilee during Jesus' lifetime. Although it was not known as a garrison town of the Roman Army, there seems to have been a detachment of soldiers of which this centurion or commander of a company of 100 soldiers, was the commanding officer. Zeichmann remarked: "A centurion at Capernaum (so Mt. 8: 5–13; Lk: 7.1–10) might help protect administrators and tax collectors stationed in a combination border-town/port village."[120]

It is unknown how Jesus was able to heal the slave from far away. Josephus and Philo noted that the Essenes were skilled healers (see Chapter 2) and it is possible that Jesus was taught the healing arts at the Essene school at Qumran.

Nevertheless, Jesus helped the centurion out of sympathy with the slave who was a victim of Roman oppression, although he was also impressed by the Roman officer's confidence in him as a well-known healer. It is even possible that this Roman officer converted to the Jewish faith by becoming a proselyte. That would also explain Jesus' willingness to help.

---

[120] Zeichmann, "Military Forces in Judea", 92

What Jesus and John Thought of each Other
Luke 7: 18–20, 22–23 (Matt 11: 2–6)

18.	The disciples of John reported all these things to him. So John summoned two of his disciples
19.	and sent them to the Lord to ask, "Are you the one who is to come, or are we to wait for another?"
20.	When the men had come to him, they said, "John the Baptist has sent us to you to ask, `Are you the one who is to come, or are we to wait for another?'"
21.	(...)
22.	And he answered them, "Go and tell John what you have seen and heard: the blind receive their sight, the lame walk, the lepers are cleansed, the deaf hear, the dead are raised, the poor have good news brought to them.
23.	And blessed is anyone who takes no offense at me."

It seems as if John felt less certain that Jesus was really the Messiah and he sent his disciples to make sure. Jesus cited several healing miracles – even resurrecting dead people – to serve as proof that he was, in fact, the Messiah. It must be remembered that Jesus, as a member of the sect of the Essenes, most probably had some training in the healing arts by using herbs and other medicines. Jesus also emphasizes that the poor people – none other than the Essenes – have received the good news, the gospel about the approaching kingdom of God.

Luke 7: 24–28 (Matt 11: 7–11)

24.	When John's messengers had gone, Jesus began to speak to the crowds about John: "What did you go out into the wilderness to look at? A reed shaken by the wind?

25.	What then did you go out to see? Someone dressed in soft robes? Look, those who put on fine clothing and live in luxury are in royal palaces.
26.	What then did you go out to see? A prophet? Yes, I tell you, and more than a prophet.
27.	This is the one about whom it is written, 'See, I am sending my messenger ahead of you, who will prepare your way before you.'
28.	I tell you, among those born of women no one is greater than John; yet the least in the kingdom of God is greater than he."

With these words, Jesus contrasted the rich and powerful Sadducees and the family of Herod the Great who lived in luxury with John the Baptist who lived a simple life in the wilderness. Yet, he declared that John was the greatest prophet that had ever lived and that his work – to pave the way for the Messiah – was foretold in the Scriptures (see Isa 40: 3).

On the other hand, Jesus also told his audience that the least and most unimportant official in the coming kingdom of God – of which he would become the king in Jerusalem – would be regarded as more important than John, who lived in the wilderness.

Luke 7: 31–35 (Matt 11: 16–19)

31.	"To what then will I compare the people of this generation, and what are they like?
32.	They are like children sitting in the marketplace and calling to one another, 'We played the flute for you, and you did not dance; we wailed, and you did not weep.'
33.	For John the Baptist has come eating no bread and drinking no wine, and you say, 'He has a demon';

34.	the Son of Man has come eating and drinking, and you say, 'Look, a glutton and a drunkard, a friend of tax collectors and sinners!'
35.	Nevertheless, wisdom is vindicated by all her children."

With these enigmatic sayings, Jesus vindicated John the Baptist and himself, despite being slandered by unwise people, such as the Jerusalem elite. Those who played the flute – John and Jesus – expected a positive response from their audience. Those who wept – John and Jesus – hoped that others would weep along with them about the sins of the Jews. Instead, John and Jesus were defamed and accused of being under the influence of an evil spirit or fraternizing with the dregs of society. John and Jesus were, however, children of the Lady Wisdom of the book of Proverbs (Prov 7–9) and their messages were the result of their wisdom.

Jesus calls himself "the Son of Man" – another way of saying that he was *the* Messiah as predicted by Daniel (7: 9–14).

Luke 9:57–62 (Matt 8:19–22)

57.	As they were going along the road, someone said to him, "I will follow you wherever you go."
58.	And Jesus said to him, "Foxes have holes, and birds of the air have nests; but the Son of Man has nowhere to lay his head."
59.	To another he said, "Follow me." But he said, "Lord, first let me go and bury my father."
60.	But Jesus said to him, "Let the dead bury their own dead; but as for you, go and proclaim the kingdom of God."
61.	Another said, "I will follow you, Lord; but let me first say farewell to those at my home."

62.	Jesus said to him, "No one who puts a hand to the plow and looks back is fit for the kingdom of God."

Jesus was recruiting followers for his party, the party that had to prepare the way for the approaching kingdom of God, the restored monarchy of his ancestor, King David. According to Jesus, his followers had to be totally committed to this cause.

Messengers for the Coming Kingdom
Luke 10: 2–12 (Matt 9: 37–38; 10: 7–16)

2.	He said to them, "The harvest is plentiful, but the laborers are few; therefore ask the Lord of the harvest to send out laborers into his harvest.
3.	Go on your way. See, I am sending you out like lambs into the midst of wolves.
4.	Carry no purse, no bag, no sandals; and greet no one on the road.
5.	Whatever house you enter, first say, `Peace to this house!'
6.	And if anyone is there who shares in peace, your peace will rest on that person; but if not, it will return to you.
7	Remain in the same house, eating and drinking whatever they provide, for the laborer deserves to be paid. Do not move about from house to house.
8.	Whenever you enter a town and its people welcome you, eat what is set before you;
9.	cure the sick who are there, and say to them, `The kingdom of God has come near to you.'
10.	But whenever you enter a town and they do not welcome you, go out into its streets and say,

11.	Even the dust of your town that clings to our feet, we wipe off in protest against you. Yet know this: the kingdom of God has come near.'
12.	I tell you, on that day it will be more tolerable for Sodom than for that town.

Jesus sent his disciples and followers out on a recruitment drive in order to increase the number of his followers – laborers to gather the harvest, the harvest of new recruits. They had to concentrate on other Essenes, who would provide them with lodgings and food, as the Essenes were known to do towards other members of their sect. They had to distribute the news that God's kingdom was near – in other words: the time was almost ripe to restore the Israelite monarchy.

If the inhabitants of certain towns refused to provide hospitality, the disciples were advised to shake off the dust of that town from their feet and keep on announcing that the kingdom is near.

The Fate of Galilean Towns
Luke 10: 13–15 (Matt 11: 21–24)

13.	"Woe to you, Chorazin! Woe to you, Bethsaida! For if the deeds of power done in you had been done in Tyre and Sidon, they would have repented long ago, sitting in sackcloth and ashes.
14.	But at the judgment it will be more tolerable for Tyre and Sidon than for you.
15.	And you, Capernaum, will you be exalted to heaven? No, you will be brought down to Hades.

The Galilean towns of Chorazin, Bethsaida, and Capernaum refused to provide hospitality to Jesus' messengers and to accept Jesus' teaching that the kingdom was on the point of being restored. Jesus cursed them for failing to supporting him and his helpers.

Luke 10: 16 (Matt 10: 40)

> "Whoever listens to you listens to me, and whoever rejects you rejects me, and whoever rejects me rejects the one who sent me."

Jesus was convinced that he was called by God to restore the monarchy of Israel. If people did not accept his message (such as the three towns in Galilee), it meant that they rejected God who had sent him.

Jesus' Prayer
Luke 10: 21–22 (Matt 11: 25–27)

> 21. At that same hour Jesus rejoiced in the Holy Spirit and said, "I thank you, Father, Lord of heaven and earth, because you have hidden these things from the wise and the intelligent and have revealed them to infants; yes, Father, for such was your gracious will.
> 22. All things have been handed over to me by my Father; and no one knows who the Son is except the Father, or who the Father is except the Son and anyone to whom the Son chooses to reveal him."

After the return of his messengers from their recruitment drive, Jesus was joyful and thanked God for the success of this campaign. He stated that outsiders, the clever priests in Jerusalem, did not realize who he really was, namely the son of God, the chosen king of Israel, but that those to whom he had revealed his calling, understood it.

The Privileged Disciples
Luke 10: 23–24 (Matt 13: 16–17)

23.	Then turning to the disciples, Jesus said to them privately, "Blessed are the eyes that see what you see!
24.	For I tell you that many prophets and kings desired to see what you see, but did not see it, and to hear what you hear, but did not hear it."

Jesus assured his followers that they were the privileged witnesses of a successful campaign to disseminate the news that the Israelite monarchy was to be restored soon. Prophets and kings of previous centuries were not so fortunate to witness these events.

Teaching on Prayer
Luke 11: 2–4 (Matt 6: 9–13)

2.	He said to them, "When you pray, say: Father, hallowed be your name. Your kingdom come.
3.	Give us each day our daily bread.
4.	And forgive us our sins, for we ourselves forgive everyone indebted to us. Bring us not into temptation, but deliver us from the evil one."

Jesus taught his disciples how to pray. The honor of God had to receive priority. After that, they had to pray for the speedy arrival of the Israelite monarchy on earth, their daily needs, and for forgiveness. They also had to pray for courage and patience while waiting for the kingdom to be established.

The Greek word for "the evil one" is πονηρός (*Poneros*), which usually means an annoyance, hardship, something bad or evil. In this case, it may either point to Satan, the pagan Roman Empire, or both.

Matthew added the following words after the prayer for the speedy arrival of the kingdom: "May your will be done, as in heaven, so on earth." That amounts to a description of the kngdom, the theocracy.

Some old manuscripts added the following ending: "For yours is the kingdom, the power and the glory forever. Amen."

It is notworthy that the Didache (Did 8: 2) quotes the full text of the Lord's Prayer, together with this ending (see Chapter 11).

Prayers Never in Vain
Luke 11: 9–13 (Matt 7: 7–11)

9.	"So I say to you, Ask, and it will be given you; search, and you will find; knock, and the door will be opened for you.
10.	For everyone who asks receives, and everyone who searches finds, and for everyone who knocks, the door will be opened.
11.	Is there anyone among you who, if your child asks for a fish, will give a snake instead of a fish?
12.	Or if the child asks for an egg, will give a scorpion?
13.	If you then, who are evil, know how to give good gifts to your children, how much more will the heavenly Father give the Holy Spirit to those who ask him!"

Jesus taught his disciples that one never prays to the heavenly Father in vain. He can be relied upon to look after his children.

The expression "the Holy Spirit" in Luke 11: 13 is problematic and it is possible that Luke (or a later copyist) changed the original wording of Q. Matthew 7: 11 seems to have the original phrase with "good things" instead of "the Holy Spirit". Some old manuscripts also have "good things" in Luke 11: 13. That may have been the original words in Q, but a later scribe may also have changed Luke 11: 13 in accordance with Matt 7: 11.

Getting Rid of Evil Spirits
Luke 11: 14–23 (Matt 12: 22–30)

14.	Now he was casting out a demon that was mute; when the demon had gone out, the one who had been mute spoke, and the crowds were amazed.
15.	But some of them said, "He casts out demons by Beelzebul, the ruler of the demons."
16.	(…)
17.	But he knew what they were thinking and said to them, "Every kingdom divided against itself becomes a desert, and house falls on house.
18.	If Satan also is divided against himself, how will his kingdom stand? — for you say that I cast out the demons by Beelzebul.
19.	Now if I cast out the demons by Beelzebul, by whom do your exorcists cast them out? Therefore they will be your judges.
20.	But if it is by the finger of God that I cast out the demons, then the kingdom of God has come to you.
21.	When a strong man, fully armed, guards his castle, his property is safe.
22.	But when one stronger than he attacks him and overpowers him, he takes away his armor in which he trusted and divides his plunder.
23.	Whoever is not with me is against me, and whoever does not gather with me scatters.

This is another example where Jesus was maligned, when he was accused of casting out demons with the power of Beelzebul (Greek: Βεελζεβούλ – *Beelzeboul*), the prince or ruler of the demons. Jesus easily pointed out the logical flaw in this accusation by arguing that it is impossible that Satan (Beelzebul) would be willing to get rid of his helpers, the lesser little devils. Jesus also compared himself with a strong man who overpowered another strong man (Satan) by looting his armor and his treasures.

The name Beelzebul is derived from the name of a Philistine deity, mentioned in 2 Kgs 1: 2–3, 6, and 16) where he is called Beelzebub (Baal or Lord of the Flies) (Hebrew: בַּעַל זְבוּב – *Baal–Zebub*). Those who accused Jesus of using the power of Beelzebul tried to discredit him as an imposter, somebody in an alliance with Satan or a pagan god. Jesus countered by declaring that the demons were driven out "by the finger of God" and that that was a sign that God's kingdom would be established soon. He added that those who did not gather (followers or helpers for his campaign) together with him, were against him and only scattering the people of God.

It must be noted that the presentation of demons or evil spirits in the Bible is rather confusing, due to the ancient and pre-scientific world view. In the passage discussed above, Beelzebul or Satan is described as the prince of the demons. On the other hand, in 1 Sam 16: 14–15, 1 Sam 19: 9–10 and 1 Kgs 22: 21–23 we read of evil spirits that were sent by God – not by Satan.

Luke 11: 24–26 (Matt 12: 43–45)

24.	"When the unclean spirit has gone out of a person, it wanders through waterless regions looking for a resting place, but not finding any, it says, 'I will return to my house from which I came.'
25.	When it comes, it finds it swept and put in order.
26.	Then it goes and brings seven other spirits more evil than itself, and they enter and live there; and the last state of that person is worse than the first."

Jesus must have had the experience that expelling evil spirits – regarded in those days as the cause of illness and disorders – had no lasting effects and that a person, who was seemingly healed, only became worse afterwards. This is a tacit admission that Jesus' ministry of healing did not always help sick people in the long run.

Jesus' Signs
Luke 11: 27–28

27.	While he was saying this, a woman in the crowd raised her voice and said to him, "Blessed is the womb that bore you and the breasts that nursed you!"
28.	But he said, "Blessed rather are those who hear the word of God and obey it!"

It seems that Jesus received a compliment from a woman in the crowd. He corrected her by declaring that those who obey God, those who accept his message, are the real blessed.

Luke 11: 16, 29–32 (Matt 12: 38–42)

29.	Others, to test him, kept demanding from him a sign from heaven.
30.	When the crowds were increasing, he began to say, "This generation is an evil generation; it asks for a sign, but no sign will be given to it except the sign of Jonah.
31.	For just as Jonah became a sign to the people of Nineveh, so the Son of Man will be to this generation.
32.	The queen of the South will rise at the judgment with the people of this generation and condemn them, because she came from the ends of the earth to listen to the wisdom of Solomon, and see, something greater than Solomon is here!
33.	The people of Nineveh will rise up at the judgment with this generation and condemn it, because they repented at the

> proclamation of Jonah, and see, something greater than Jonah is here!

Some Jews demanded a sign from Jesus to prove that he was really sent by God as a teacher or a prophet. The Greek word for "sign" is σημεῖον (*semeion*) and it means a sign, mark, token; but also, a miracle by which God authenticates the men sent by him, or by which men prove that the cause they are pleading is God's cause.

Jesus refused to perform any miracles on demand to show off his powers and declared that the only sign the people would get was the sign of Jonah who preached to the pagan city of Nineveh. The people of that city relented and turned to God – just as the Queen of Sheba took Solomon's wisdom to heart. Those who demanded a sign from Jesus would stand condemned on Judgment Day because they doubted his message, in contrast with the men of Nineveh and the Queen of Sheba who believed what they had heard.

Lighting a Lamp
Luke 11: 33 (Matt 5: 15)

> "No one after lighting a lamp puts it in a cellar, but on the lampstand so that those who enter may see the light.

The meaning of this short parable of Jesus is that he did not hide his message (described as the light of a lamp), but spoke openly in public, by calling the people to repent and turn to God. His followers ought to follow his example.

Against the Pharisees. Scribes and Teachers of the Law
Luke 11: 34–36 (Matt 6: 22–23)

34.	Your eye is the lamp of your body. If your eye is healthy, your whole body is full of light; but if it is not healthy, your body is full of darkness.
35.	Therefore consider whether the light in you is not darkness.
36.	If then your whole body is full of light, with no part of it in darkness, it will be as full of light as when a lamp gives you light with its rays."

This short parable is a hidden rebuke of the religious authorities and the priestly class in Jerusalem who opposed Jesus' teachings. According to Jesus, they were blind and lived in darkness – in contrast with those who have seen the validity of his message and who lived in the light as a result.

Luke 11: 42 (Matt 23: 23)

"But woe to you Pharisees! For you tithe mint and rue and herbs of all kinds, and neglect justice and the love of God; it is these you ought to have practiced, without neglecting the others.

The Pharisees were known for their strict obedience to the Law of Moses. Jesus pointed out that they even followed the smallest requirements of the Law, but neglected the most important issues, namely justice and love towards God. Matthew added mercy and faith to these important issues.

Luke 11: 39–41 (Matt 23: 25–27)

39.	Then the Lord said to him, "Now you Pharisees clean the outside of the cup and of the dish, but inside you are full of greed and wickedness.
40.	You fools! Did not the one who made the outside make the inside also?

41.	So give for alms those things that are within; and see, everything will be clean for you.

According to Jesus, the Pharisees were only interested in the outward appearance of their piety, including giving alms to the poor, while their hearts were not filled with love, mercy, and compassion towards the poor.

Luke 11: 43 (Matt 23: 6)

Woe to you Pharisees! For you love to have the seat of honor in the synagogues and to be greeted with respect in the marketplaces.

Jesus – just as the Essenes – preferred a humble and simple lifestyle – in contrast with some Pharisees, members of the Sanhedrin – who loved to occupy seats of honor at meetings to display their importance.

Luke 11: 44 (Matt 23: 27–28)

Woe to you! For you are like unmarked graves, and people walk over them without realizing it."

This saying was an insult aimed at the Pharisees who were members of the Sanhedrin who are compared with an unmarked tomb full of rotting corpses.

Luke 11: 46 (Matt 23: 4)

And he said, "Woe also to you lawyers! For you load people with burdens hard to bear, and you yourselves do not lift a finger to ease them.

Jesus had no respect for the teachers of the Law who entangled the people in clever-sounding interpretations of Moses' Law, while disregarding their own teachings.

The Tombs of the Prophets
Luke 11: 47–48 (Matt 23: 29–32)

47.	Woe to you! For you build the tombs of the prophets whom your ancestors killed.
48.	So you are witnesses and approve of the deeds of your ancestors; for they killed them, and you build their tombs.

Jesus added to the previous passage that the prophet Zechariah was killed by the ancestors of the teachers of the Law and the Pharisees. Jesus probably thought of Jer 2: 30 that mentions that the people of Israel "mocked the messengers of God, and despised his words, and scoffed at his prophets, until the wrath of the Lord arose against his people." We also read in 2 Chr 30: 16 that the people "mocked the messengers of God, and despised his words, and scoffed at his prophets, until the wrath of the Lord arose against his people." Jesus accused, in effect, the teachers of the Law and the Pharisees of condoning the sins of their ancestors by building tombs for the prophets.

Luke 11: 49–51 (Matt 23: 34–36)

49.	Therefore also the Wisdom of God said, 'I will send them prophets and apostles, some of whom they will kill and persecute,'
50.	so that this generation may be charged with the blood of all the prophets shed since the foundation of the world,

51.	from the blood of Abel to the blood of Zechariah, who perished between the altar and the sanctuary. Yes, I tell you, it will be charged against this generation.

The "Wisdom of God" is described in Prov 8–9, but Jesus may also have thought of the apocryphal book of Ecclesiasticus where "Wisdom" is personified in Chapter 24.

Wisdom is quoted as having promised to send prophets and apostles who were due to be killed. No such promise is to be found in the Old Testament or the apocrypha and it must be a case where the memories of the informants of the author(s) of Q became confused, while Jesus said something quite different.

Nevertheless, the stoning of the prophet Zechariah is described in 2 Chr 24: 20–22. Jesus emphasized his view that the wrath of God would rest upon those Jews who opposed him, just as it angered God that the prophets were mocked and killed.

Luke 11: 52 (Matt 23: 13)

Woe to you lawyers! For you have taken away the key of knowledge; you did not enter yourselves, and you hindered those who were entering."

With these words, Jesus accused the lawyers of misrepresenting the Scriptures, preventing the common folk of understanding that Jesus himself was promised in the Scriptures as *the* Messiah.

Truth and Lies
Luke 12: 2–3 (Matt 10: 26–27)

2.	Nothing is covered up that will not be uncovered, and nothing secret that will not become known.

> 3. Therefore whatever you have said in the dark will be heard in the light, and what you have whispered behind closed doors will be proclaimed from the housetops.

Jesus repeated an old piece of wisdom, namely that the truth has the habit of being discovered and that lies are due to be unmasked for what they are. Jesus also seems to have hinted that the truth about his mission, to be the Messiah, will not stay hidden.

God's Power
Luke 12: 4–7 (Matt 10: 28–31)

> 4. I tell you, my friends, do not fear those who kill the body, and after that can do nothing more.
> 5. But I will warn you whom to fear: fear him who, after he has killed, has authority to cast into hell. Yes, I tell you, fear him!
> 6. Are not five sparrows sold for two pennies? Yet not one of them is forgotten in God's sight.
> 7. But even the hairs of your head are all counted. Do not be afraid; you are of more value than many sparrows.

This passage contains two unrelated thoughts.

In the first part, Jesus mentioned those who could kill people. He probably thought of the Roman overlords who suppressed the people of Palestine. His followers rather had to fear God who has the power to send sinners to hell (Greek: γέεννα – *Geenna*, a name derived from the Hebrew/Aramaic name for the Valley of Hinnom: גֵיא־הִנֹּם – *Gē'–Hīnnōmm*, the place where all Jerusalem's trash was dumped and burnt).

In the second part, Jesus' followers are reminded that the all-knowing and all-powerful God cares for his creation, especially those who serve him.

The Angels of God
Luke 12: 8–9 (Matt 10: 32–33)

8.	And I tell you, everyone who acknowledges me before others, the Son of Man also will acknowledge before the angels of God;
9.	but whoever denies me before others will be denied before the angels of God.

This saying was traditionally interpreted as a description of Judgment Day. A more plausible explanation, though, is that Jesus expected an army of the angels of God to drive the Romans away and allow him to ascend the throne in Jerusalem as the Son of Man, the Messiah (Matt 25: 31; Mark 8: 38; Mark 14: 62; Luke 9: 26; Luke 22: 69; John 1: 49–51). That event would reveal people's support for Jesus. Those who opposed him, would be exposed to the vengeance of the angels, while those who openly sided with him would be honored in the presence of the angels from heaven.

Blasphemy against the Holy Spirit
Luke 12: 10 (Matt 12: 32)

> And everyone who speaks a word against the Son of Man will be forgiven; but whoever blasphemes against the Holy Spirit will not be forgiven.

This saying seems to contradict the previous saying.

However, it may mean that if somebody repents after having opposed Jesus, it may be forgiven. It is, though, unforgivable if somebody blasphemes against the Holy Spirit, God's spirit, his personality or mind.

Luke 12: 11–12 (Matt 10: 19)

11.	When they bring you before the synagogues, the rulers, and the authorities, do not worry about how you are to defend yourselves or what you are to say;
12.	for the Holy Spirit will teach you at that very hour what you ought to say.

Jesus expected his followers to suffer prosecution from the Jewish and Roman authorities. He was confident that God's spirit would aid them in their defense.

Parable of the Rich Man
Luke 12: 16–21

16.	Then he told them a parable: "The land of a rich man produced abundantly.
17.	And he thought to himself, 'What should I do, for I have no place to store my crops?'
18.	Then he said, 'I will do this: I will pull down my barns and build larger ones, and there I will store all my grain and my goods.
19.	And I will say to my soul, 'Soul, you have ample goods laid up for many years; relax, eat, drink, be merry.'
20.	But God said to him, 'You fool! This very night your life is being demanded of you. And the things you have prepared, whose will they be?'
21.	So it is with those who store up treasures for themselves but are not rich toward God."

This parable is a warning not to put one's trust in riches and to forget that we all are mortal. Jesus' association with Essenes gave him the view that prosperity only leads people away from God.

On Anxieties
Luke 12: 22–31 (Matt 6: 25–33)

22.	He said to his disciples, "Therefore I tell you, do not worry about your life, what you will eat, or about your body, what you will wear.
23.	For life is more than food, and the body more than clothing.
24.	Consider the ravens: they neither sow nor reap, they have neither storehouse nor barn, and yet God feeds them. Of how much more value are you than the birds!
25.	And can any of you by worrying add a single hour to your span of life?
26.	If then you are not able to do so small a thing as that, why do you worry about the rest?
27.	Consider the lilies, how they grow: they neither toil nor spin; yet I tell you, even Solomon in all his glory was not clothed like one of these.
28.	But if God so clothes the grass of the field, which is alive today and tomorrow is thrown into the oven, how much more will he clothe you— you of little faith!
29.	And do not keep striving for what you are to eat and what you are to drink, and do not keep worrying.
30.	For it is the nations of the world that strive after all these things, and your Father knows that you need them.
31.	Instead, strive for his kingdom, and these things will be given to you as well.

Jesus was seemingly an incurable optimist who believed that God would always provide and care for the faithful, just as He cares for the rest of his creation.

One must, though, take into regard Jesus' Essene background. The Essenes had the habit of sharing all their belongings with each other, with the result that nobody went hungry, unclothed, or homeless.

However, the most important thing to strive for was God's kingdom, the theocracy in Israel with Jesus, God's son, as the king.

On Possessions
Luke 12: 33–34 (Matt 6: 19–21)

34.	Sell your possessions, and give alms. Make purses for yourselves that do not wear out, an unfailing treasure in heaven, where no thief comes near and no moth destroys.
35.	For where your treasure is, there your heart will be also.

With this saying, Jesus encouraged his followers to adopt the Essene lifestyle of poverty and generosity. One's relationship with God is the most important part of life.

On Being Ready
Luke 12: 39–40 (Matt 24: 43–44)

39.	But know this: if the owner of the house had known at what hour the thief was coming, he would not have let his house be broken into.
40.	You also must be ready, for the Son of Man is coming at an unexpected hour."

This saying is usually seen as a warning that Judgment Day and the Second Coming of Christ will happen unexpectedly. It may, however, just as well be regarded as a warning directed towards

Jesus' followers that they must be always ready for the sudden coming of the Son of Man, the Messiah, the day on which the monarchy in Jerusalem will be restored with the help of God's angels.

Luke 12: 42–46 (Matt 24: 45–51)

42.	And the Lord said, "Who then is the faithful and prudent manager whom his master will put in charge of his slaves, to give them their allowance of food at the proper time?
43.	Blessed is that slave whom his master will find at work when he arrives.
44.	Truly I tell you, he will put that one in charge of all his possessions.
45.	But if that slave says to himself, `My master is delayed in coming,' and if he begins to beat the other slaves, men and women, and to eat and drink and get drunk,
46.	the master of that slave will come on a day when he does not expect him and at an hour that he does not know, and will cut him in pieces, and put him with the unfaithful.

Jesus is called "the Lord" (Greek: κύριος – *kurios*) in this passage. It is by no means an indication of a divine status; it is merely the title by which any important person was addressed or referred to in those days. It may also be translated as "Master".

With this parable, Jesus warned his followers that his accession to the throne in Jerusalem may occur unexpectedly and that they ought to work to make that event possible by recruiting more supporters for Jesus' campaign.

Divisions in Families
Luke 12: 49, 51–53 (Matt 10: 34–36)

> 49. I came to bring fire to the earth, and how I wish it were already kindled!
> 51. Do you think that I have come to bring peace to the earth? No, I tell you, but rather division!
> 52. From now on five in one household will be divided, three against two and two against three;
> 53. they will be divided: father against son and son against father, mother against daughter and daughter against mother, mother-in-law against her daughter-in-law and daughter-in-law against mother-in-law."

The only explanation for this strange saying can be that people will receive Jesus as monarch of Israel in different ways, which may cause divisions within families. On that day, there won't be peace because the host of angels from heaven will pour down fire onto the enemies of Israel and onto Jesus' opponents.

Signs of the Times
Luke 12: 54–56 (Matt 16: 2–3)

> 54. He also said to the crowds, "When you see a cloud rising in the west, you immediately say, `It is going to rain'; and so it happens.
> 55. And when you see the south wind blowing, you say, `There will be scorching heat'; and it happens.
> 56. You hypocrites! You know how to interpret the appearance of earth and sky, but why do you not know how to interpret the present time?"

According to Jesus, there were enough signs that God's kingdom with him occupying the throne, would be established soon, but the people who opposed him, the hypocrites, were too blind to notice and interpret those signs.

Settlement out of Court
Luke 12: 57–59 (Matt 5: 25–26)

57.	And why do you not judge for yourselves what is right?
58.	Thus, when you go with your accuser before a magistrate, on the way make an effort to settle the case, or you may be dragged before the judge, and the judge hand you over to the officer, and the officer throw you in prison.
59.	I tell you, you will never get out until you have paid the very last penny.

Jesus gave sound advice, namely that it is better to settle a dispute out of court because the judgment may cause serious problems for the accused or respondent in the case.

Parable of the Mustard Seed
Luke 13: 18–21 (Matt 13: 31–33)

18.	He said therefore, "What is the kingdom of God like? And to what should I compare it?
19.	It is like a mustard seed that someone took and sowed in the garden; it grew and became a tree, and the birds of the air made nests in its branches."
20.	And again he said, "To what should I compare the kingdom of God?
21.	It is like yeast that a woman took and mixed in with three measures of flour until all of it was leavened."

Jesus explained with these two parables that he was optimistic that his movement, consisting of people who wanted to restore the kingdom of God, a theocracy in Jerusalem, would continue to grow until the kingdom would be restored finally.

The Door to the Kingdom
Luke 13: 24–27 (Matt 7: 13–14, 22–23)

24.	"Strive to enter through the narrow door; for many, I tell you, will try to enter and will not be able.
25.	When once the owner of the house has got up and shut the door, and you begin to stand outside and to knock at the door, saying, `Lord, open to us,' then in reply he will say to you, `I do not know where you come from.'
26.	Then you will begin to say, `We ate and drank with you, and you taught in our streets.'
27.	But he will say, `I do not know where you come from; go away from me, all you evildoers!'

The owner of the house in this parable is, of course, Jesus himself. His house is the kingdom of God, which would soon be established. His followers are those who entered through the narrow door into this coming kingdom. Those outside who knock on the door are the Sadducees, the false priests and scribes who opposed him and who won't be allowed to enjoy the benefits of the coming kingdom.

The Banquet in the Kingdom
Luke 13: 28–30 (Matt 8: 11–12; 20: 16)

28.	There will be weeping and gnashing of teeth when you see Abraham and Isaac and Jacob and all the prophets in the kingdom of God, and you yourselves thrown out.
29.	Then people will come from east and west, from north and south, and will eat in the kingdom of God.
30.	Indeed, some are last who will be first, and some are first who will be last."

Jesus evidently expected the heavens to be opened when the kingdom of God was to be established in Jerusalem with the aid of a crowd of angels – just as the heavens were opened when he was baptized by John the Baptist. With the heavens opened, people would get a glimpse of the patriarchs and prophets of Israel. The important people of Jerusalem would be excluded, resulting in their weeping, and gnashing of teeth, but other people from the four directions of the earth would be guests of honor at a royal banquet in Jerusalem.

Lament over Jerusalem
Luke 13: 34–35 (Matt 23: 37–39)

34.	Jerusalem, Jerusalem, the city that kills the prophets and stones those who are sent to it! How often have I desired to gather your children together as a hen gathers her brood under her wings, and you were not willing!
35.	See, your house is left to you. And I tell you, you will not see me until the time comes when you say, `Blessed is the one who comes in the name of the Lord.'"

Jesus clearly felt let down that the Jerusalem elite did not take him seriously and even rejected and opposed him because Jerusalem was meant to be the capital of the restored Israelite monarchy. He promised that the day will come when he would be welcomed as *the* Messiah, sent by God.

On Humility
Luke 14: 11, 18: 14 (Matt 23: 12)

14: 11	For all who exalt themselves will be humbled, and those who humble themselves will be exalted."
18: 14	I tell you, this man went down to his home justified rather than the other; for all who exalt themselves will be humbled, but all who humble themselves will be exalted."

This saying – which occurs twice in Luke – was clearly directed against the Jerusalem elite. Jesus promised these haughty Jews that they would be humiliated when he ascends the Israelite throne, while his followers, mostly the poor Essenes, would receive honorable positions.

The Followers of Jesus
Luke 14: 16–24 (Matt 22: 1–10)

16.	Then Jesus said to him, "Someone gave a great dinner and invited many.
16.	At the time for the dinner he sent his slave to say to those who had been invited, `Come; for everything is ready now.'
17.	But they all alike began to make excuses. The first said to him, `I have bought a piece of land, and I must go out and see it; please accept my regrets.'
18.	Another said, `I have bought five yoke of oxen, and I am going to try them out; please accept my regrets.'
19.	Another said, `I have just been married, and therefore I cannot come.'
20.	So the slave returned and reported this to his master. Then the owner of the house became angry and said to his slave, `Go out at once into the streets and lanes of the town and bring in the poor, the crippled, the blind, and the lame.'
21.	And the slave said, `Sir, what you ordered has been done, and there is still room.'
22.	Then the master said to the slave, `Go out into the roads and lanes, and compel people to come in, so that my house may be filled.
23.	For I tell you, none of those who were invited will taste my dinner.'"

The host at this banquet in this parable is, of course, Jesus himself. The banquet represents the reestablishment of the monarchy in Israel. The slaves are his disciples and followers who had to recruit new followers and supporters of the monarchy. The important people who were invited to join Jesus and his movement and who did not show any interest, are clearly the false priest, Pharisees, and teachers of the Law in Jerusalem. Jesus recruited followers and members for his movement rather from the poor people, the Essenes.

Total Commitment
Luke 14: 26–27, 17: 33 (Matt 10: 37–39)

26.	Whoever comes to me and does not hate father and mother, wife and children, brothers and sisters, yes, and even life itself, cannot be my disciple.
27.	Whoever does not carry the cross and follow me cannot be my disciple.
17: 33.	Those who try to make their life secure will lose it, but those who lose their life will keep it.

One may wonder whether Jesus' words were recorded correctly. After all, the Ten Commandments require of us to honor our parents. There is nothing in the Old Testament informing us that one must hate one's family. The point of these sayings is, though, that Jesus expected total loyalty from his followers in turning to God and to support his campaign to recruit more supporters for his party or movement. They had to forget about their own interests and only live and work for the approaching kingdom of God.

Salt as a Preservative
Luke 14: 34–35 (Matt 5: 13)

34.	Salt is good; but if salt has lost its taste, how can its saltiness be restored?

> 35. It is fit neither for the soil nor for the manure pile; they throw it away. Let anyone with ears to hear listen!"

Salt was a valuable commodity in those times. The English word "salary" is even derived from the Latin word for salt, namely "sal", because soldiers and other people were often paid with blocks of salt. Salt was a necessary preservative for food in the warm weather of the Mediterranean world. It may happen, though, that a block of salt became wet, was dissolved, and disappeared.

Jesus encouraged his followers to be the salt of the earth, to help preserve that which is good and right.

Parable of the Good Shepherd
Luke 15: 4–10 (Matt 18: 12–13)

> 4. Which one of you, having a hundred sheep and losing one of them, does not leave the ninety–nine in the wilderness and go after the one that is lost until he finds it?
> 5. When he has found it, he lays it on his shoulders and rejoices.
> 6. And when he comes home, he calls together his friends and neighbors, saying to them, 'Rejoice with me, for I have found my sheep that was lost.'
> 7. Just so, I tell you, there will be more joy in heaven over one sinner who repents than over ninety–nine righteous persons who need no repentance.
> 8. Or what woman having ten silver coins, if she loses one of them, does not light a lamp, sweep the house, and search carefully until she finds it?
> 9. When she has found it, she calls together her friends and neighbors, saying, 'Rejoice with me, for I have found the coin that I had lost.'

> 10. Just so, I tell you, there is joy in the presence of the angels of God over one sinner who repents."

Jesus continuously called the Jews to repent and to serve God with their whole being. There were those, however, who did not serve God as they should have done. But if somebody repents, there will be joy in heaven, just as when a shepherd has found a lost sheep or when a woman has found her lost coin.

The Choice between God and Wealth
Luke 16: 13 (Matt 11: 12–13)

> No slave can serve two masters; for a slave will either hate the one and love the other, or be devoted to the one and despise the other. You cannot serve God and wealth."

This saying betrays Jesus' Essene background. The Essenes were known for their criticism of the rich priestly class in Jerusalem, their simple lifestyle, and their generosity towards members of their own group.

Good News about the Kingdom
Luke 16: 16 (Matt 11: 12–14)

> The law and the prophets were in effect until John came; since then the good news of the kingdom of God is proclaimed, and everyone tries to enter it by force.

Jesus evidently uttered these words in the presence of his disciples and followers. According to him, the people of Israel only had the Law of Moses and the writings of the prophets to guide them until the time when John the Baptist started his ministry, but since John's appearance the good news or gospel regarding the restoration of the kingdom of God, the Israelite monarchy, also gave them guidance and hope.

Immutability of the Law
Luke 16: 17 (Matt 5: 18)

> But it is easier for heaven and earth to pass away, than for one stroke of a letter in the law to be dropped.

Jesus was convinced that the Law of Moses was given by God and, therefore, may never be changed or abolished. That was why his followers in Jerusalem differed from Paul regarding the necessity of followers of Jesus to be circumcised (Acts 15).

On Divorce
Luke 12: 18 (Matt 5: 32).

> Anyone who divorces his wife and marries another commits adultery, and whoever marries a woman divorced from her husband commits adultery.

Jesus' condemnation of any form of divorce and remarriage as adultery can be explained from his Essene background. The Essenes were also very much against any form of divorce – in spite of Ex 21: 11; Deut 24: 1–3; and Ezra 10: 1–16 that allowed divorce and remarriage under certain circumstances.

Stumbling
Luke 17: 1–2 (Matt 18: 6–7)

> 1. Jesus said to his disciples, "Occasions for stumbling are bound to come, but woe to anyone by whom they come!

> 2. It would be better for you if a millstone were hung around your neck and you were thrown into the sea than for you to cause one of these little ones to stumble.

It is not quite clear what Jesus meant by "stumbling". The Greek word used is σκάνδαλον (*skandalon*), which may mean a trap, a stumbling block over which one may trip, or an action causing somebody else to commit a sin.

This saying has a general application: it will be a scandal if anybody lures somebody else into a situation where he does something wrong or bad.

It may, however, also be applied to the Sadducees, the priestly class in Jerusalem, and the scholars of the Law who led people astray with their skewed explanations of the Scriptures and their denial that Jesus was the Messiah.

Forgiveness
Luke 17: 3–4 (Matt 18: 15, 21–22)

> 3. Be on your guard! If another disciple sins, you must rebuke the offender, and if there is repentance, you must forgive.
> 4. And if the same person sins against you seven times a day, and turns back to you seven times and says, `I repent,' you must forgive."

With this advice to forgive continuously, Jesus taught a lesson in accordance with the Essenes' pacifism and non-violent attitude.

Faith
Luke 17: 6 (Matt 17: 20)

> The Lord replied, "If you had faith the size of a mustard seed, you could say to this mulberry tree, 'Be uprooted and planted in the sea,' and it would obey you.'"

Jesus wanted his followers to have faith in him as the future king of Israel. He relied upon his heavenly father to work miracles to put him on the throne in Jerusalem. This is the only way in which this parable makes sense – otherwise it would have boiled down to jumbled magical thinking.

The Day of the Son of Man
Luke 17:22–24, 26–30, 34–35, 37 (Matt 24: 26–28, 37, 39–41)

> 22. Then he said to the disciples, "The days are coming when you will long to see one of the days of the Son of Man, and you will not see it.
> 23. They will say to you, 'Look there!' or 'Look here!' Do not go, do not set off in pursuit.
> 24. For as the lightning flashes and lights up the sky from one side to the other, so will the Son of Man be in his day.
> 26. Just as it was in the days of Noah, so too it will be in the days of the Son of Man.
> 27. They were eating and drinking, and marrying and being given in marriage, until the day Noah entered the ark, and the flood came and destroyed all of them.
> 28. Likewise, just as it was in the days of Lot: they were eating and drinking, buying and selling, planting and building,
> 29. but on the day that Lot left Sodom, it rained fire and sulfur from heaven and destroyed all of them
> 30. — it will be like that on the day that the Son of Man is revealed.

> 34. I tell you, on that night there will be two in one bed; one will be taken and the other left.
> 35. There will be two women grinding meal together; one will be taken and the other left."
> 37. Then they asked him, "Where, Lord?" He said to them, "Where the corpse is, there the vultures will gather."

This passage is usually interpreted as a prophecy about Judgment Day and the so-called rapture when certain people will be taken up to heaven and others left behind.

It must, rather, be seen as the day on which Jesus, as the Son of Man, as the Messiah, re-establishes the kingdom of Israel with the help of a bunch of angels from heaven. It was meant to be a sudden event, not expected by the people. Some will become part of this kingdom, while others will be left out, or rather, leave this earth through death.

The corpse and the vultures mentioned in the rather enigmatic saying at the end of this passage, only makes sense when it is understood to be either the corpse of the Roman Empire, or the corpse of the corrupt Sadducees and priests in Jerusalem, which will be devoured by vultures, the hungry and angry angels from heaven.

One can only wonder whether Jesus had any knowledge about the size and strength of the Roman Empire and its military might at that stage.

Matthew added this comment at the end of this passage: "Watch therefore, for you don't know in what hour your Lord comes" (Matt 24: 38).

The Parable of the Lazy Slave
Luke 19: 12–26 (Matt 25: 14–30)

12.	So he said, "A nobleman went to a distant country to get royal power for himself and then return.
13.	He summoned ten of his slaves, and gave them ten pounds, and said to them, `Do business with these until I come back.'
14.	But the citizens of his country hated him and sent a delegation after him, saying, `We do not want this man to rule over us.'
15.	When he returned, having received royal power, he ordered these slaves, to whom he had given the money, to be summoned so that he might find out what they had gained by trading.
16.	The first came forward and said, `Lord, your pound has made ten more pounds.'
17.	He said to him, `Well done, good slave! Because you have been trustworthy in a very small thing, take charge of ten cities.'
18.	Then the second came, saying, `Lord, your pound has made five pounds.'
19.	He said to him, `And you, rule over five cities.'
20.	Then the other came, saying, `Lord, here is your pound. I wrapped it up in a piece of cloth,
21.	for I was afraid of you, because you are a harsh man; you take what you did not deposit, and reap what you did not sow.'
22.	He said to him, `I will judge you by your own words, you wicked slave! You knew, did you, that I was a harsh man,
23.	taking what I did not deposit and reaping what I did not sow?
24.	Why then did you not put my money into the bank? Then when I returned, I could have collected it with interest.'

25.	He said to the bystanders, 'Take the pound from him and give it to the one who has ten pounds.'
26.	(And they said to him, 'Lord, he has ten pounds!')
27.	'I tell you, to all those who have, more will be given; but from those who have nothing, even what they have will be taken away.

The following role players are mentioned in this parable:

- The nobleman who became king – Jesus himself;
- The people of the country who rejected him – the Sadducees and the priestly class in Jerusalem who refused to believe in him; and
- The slaves – Jesus' disciples and followers whom he had sent out to recruit other supporters.

With this parable, Jesus motivated his followers to work diligently to recruit more people to his cause. Those who neglected to do this, would have to endure his displeasure when he is proclaimed king of Israel in Jerusalem.

The Kingdom of Jesus
Luke 22: 28–30 (Matt 19: 28)

	You are those who have stood by me in my trials; and I confer on you, just as my Father has conferred on me, a kingdom,
29.	so that you may eat and drink at my table in my kingdom, and you will sit on thrones judging the twelve tribes of Israel.

Jesus appointed his disciples as his councilors in his imminent kingdom. They were to be guests at his royal table and sit on thrones to judge the tribes of Israel – just as the judges of the Old Testament did. This saying of Jesus cannot be interpreted as referring to a spiritual kingdom in heaven; it was undeniably meant to be the restoration of the Israelite monarchy in which Jesus, as God's son, would receive the kingship from his Father – just as the ancient kings of the house of David.

Matthew added (Matt 19: 28) that Jesus told his disciples that all this would happen "in the regeneration". The Greek word is παλιγγενεσία (*palingenesia*), which may also be translated as "renovation", "renewal" or "restoration" (of the Israelite kingdom).

Conclusions

The first impression one gets when working though the Q Document is that it is a loose collection of unrelated sayings. They are only held together by the fact that they were spoken by Jesus. It is clear that the compiler(s) of Q consulted with a wide range of people who remembered something about Jesus' messages and stories – probably in Essene communities in Galilee.

There is, though, a golden thread connecting all these sayings: they mostly deal with the coming kingdom of God, the restoration of the Israelite monarchy with Jesus occupying the throne of his ancestor, King David.

One must conclude that the Q Document contains much authentic memories of Jesus. It is, after all, the earliest document we have with information about his teachings and some of his deeds, written only one or two decades after his execution, in contrast with the canonical gospels that were written and/or finalized at least four decades after Jesus' time. Where these gospels used material from Q, one may assume that that material is for the most part trustworthy.

The compiler(s) of Q were confronted with a big dilemma. They reported numerous sayings of Jesus in which he announced the imminent arrival of the kingdom of God, the restoration of the

Israelite monarchy, with him occupying the throne of David. This did not happen as Jesus predicted and he was executed as a criminal by the Romans. It must be that the author(s) of Q expected him, somehow, to return and complete his campaign against the Roman oppressors and the Jerusalem elite. It may also be that they awaited a miracle from heaven, just as Jesus also expected, and therefore recorded Jesus' announcements of the imminent arrival of the kingdom.

They wanted, on the one hand, to record the sayings of Jesus as truthfully as possible, but, on the other hand, the predictions of Jesus were not (yet) realized when they wrote them down. That may have caused them to distort some of Jesus' sayings.

It must also be remembered that the memories of people are fallible. Many eye-witnesses of the ministry of Jesus, who provided information to the compiler(s) of Q, could have had skewed recollections. Much of the information in Q may even have been passed on through three or four informants before being written down. That must, also, be taken into account.

Burton Mack summarized the underlying message and background of Q as follows:

> "The remarkable thing about the people of Q is that they were not Christians. They did not think of Jesus as a messiah or the Christ. They did not take his teachings as an indictment of Judaism. They did no regard his death as a divine, tragic, or saving event. And they did not imagine that he had been raised from the dead to rule over a transformed world. Instead, they thought of him as a teacher whose teachings made it possible to live with verve in troubled times. Thus they did not gather to worship in his name, honor him as a god, or cultivate his memory through hymns, prayers, and rituals. They did not form a cult of the Christ

such as the one that emerged among Christian communities familiar to readers of the letters of Paul. The people of Q were Jesus people, not Christians."[121]

One must agree with most of Mack's assessment, although this collection of sayings in Q leaves no doubt that Jesus was regarded as *the* Messiah or Christ whose wish was to resurrect the dynasty of King David.

The most important question that must be asked at this stage is: exactly *why* was the Q Document compiled? The obviously easy answer is, of course: it was important to preserve memories about Jesus' teachings. But then one may ask: exactly *why* was it so important and necessary and valuable to preserve these recollecttions? The only possible and rational answer can be that the Jesus people believed that Jesus was still alive somewhere after his crucifixion and they believed his promise that he would return. They kept on recruiting supporters for his campaign to revive the Israelite kingdom and Q had to be used as propaganda material with this goal in mind.

---

[121] Mack, *The Lost Gospel*, 4–5.

Chapter 4
PAULINE FRAGMENTS

The most influential person mentioned in the New Testament, after Jesus of Nazareth, was certainly the Apostle Paul. He was initially known as Saul of Tarsus. His home town was a major Greek city in Asia Minor and a Roman colony, which automatically made him a Roman citizen. He grew up in a Jewish home and belonged to the tribe of Benjamin (Phil 3: 5).

As a youngster, he must have been exposed to the intellectual and mythological heritage of Greece. It will be shown in the discussion of 1 Cor 15 that he was probably familiar with some of the thoughts of the Greek philosopher Aristotle. He also quoted the Stoic philosopher Cleanthes (Κλεάνθης; c. 330 BC – c. 230 BC), in Tit 1: 12 – "One of them, a prophet of their own, said, 'Cretans are always liars, evil beasts, and idle gluttons.'"[122]

He became known under his Latin name, Paulus (Greek: Παῦλος – *Paulos*). This name, which sounds rather similar to his Jewish name of Saul, may have been a nickname . "Paulus" in Latin means "small" and that may, perhaps, be an indication that he was not a tall man. When reading about his travels in the book of Acts, as well as his letters, one gets the impression of an energetic, reso-

---

[122] Paul obviously did not grasp the real meaning of this quotation. Cleanthes formulated it to demonstrate a logical absurdity. It amounts to the following statement: "Cleanthes, a Cretan, said that all Cretans are liars." The consequence is that Cleanthes, who is a Cretan himself, must also be lying when he calls all his countrymen liars!

lute, and strong personality who wrote in good Greek.

According to Acts 22: 3, he sat as a student "at the feet of Gamaliel", a leader and teacher of the party of the Pharisees. His studies made him familiar with the contents of the Hebrew Scriptures and he often quoted from them in his letters. He was initially also a Pharisee and in his zeal for the Jewish faith, he persecuted the followers of Jesus, who regarded the Pharisees of Jerusalem as frauds and hypocrites.

As a student in Jerusalem, he must have heard stories about Jesus who was crucified by the Romans. He believed, as most Jews, that Jesus had died from his wounds on the cross.

His conversion and work as a Christian missionary are described in the second part of the book of Acts, although some of the details differ from the particulars he gave in his own letters.

Paul was a prolific writer and some of his letters were collected after his death as a martyr in Rome during the sixties of the first century AD when Emperor Nero clamped down on the Christians. His letters form a substantial part of the New Testament.

These letters were probably written in the following order during the fifties and early sixties of the first century AD:

- 1 Thessalonians;
- 1 Corinthians;
- 2 Corinthians;
- Galatians;
- Philippians; and
- Romans.

The apostle Paul (ceiling mosaic, Archiepiscopal Chapel of St. Andrew, Ravenna, Italy)

The following letters are regarded as "Deutero-Pauline" – probably written by Paul's followers on his behalf, namely Ephesians,

Colossians, and 2 Thessalonians. The so-called pastoral epistles, 1 and 2 Timothy and Titus, are "Trito-Pauline" and were probably also written by members of the Pauline school according to his directives, or a generation after his death.[123]

In the late fifties Paul returned to Jerusalem with the money he had raised for the poor followers of Jesus in Jerusalem. There he was arrested and after a series of trials he was sent to Rome. In Chapter 5 of the First Letter of Clement, a later bishop of Rome, it is stated that he and Peter died a martyr's death in Rome during the reign of Nero.[124]

Paul held views that differed substantially from those of the apostles in Jerusalem and that led to debates and even clashes. Paul taught that Christians, the followers of Jesus Christ, were freed from the obligation to live according to the Law of Moses because Christ, the eternal and divine Son of God, fulfilled all those obligations on their behalf (Acts 15; 21: 19–30; Gal 1: 22–2: 21, *etcetera*).

Paul claimed that he had received visions and revelations in which Jesus Christ appeared to him, although there were no independent witnesses to corroborate or confirm these visions and revelations (Gal 1: 11–19; 1 Cor 2: 10; 11: 23; 15: 1–9; 2 Cor 12: 1–5; Eph 3: 3; Col 1: 26–27).[125]

Paul's writings were already accepted as "Scriptures" and authoritative at an early date because 2 Pet 3: 15–16 informs us:

> "Regard the patience of our Lord as salvation; even as our beloved brother Paul also, according to the wisdom given to him, wrote to you; as also in all of his letters, speaking in

---

[123] Sanders, "Paul, the Apostle, Saint."
[124] 1 Clement, ch 5
[125] See the present author's book, *Jesus of Nazareth: a Deluded Messiah*, for a full discussion of Paul's visions and revelations, which were most probably the result of hallucinations due to epileptic fits.

them of these things. In those are some things hard to be understood, which the ignorant and unsettled twist, as they do also to the *other scriptures*, to their own destruction" (*emphasis added*).

Paul never met Jesus when he was alive and his knowledge of the life and message of Jesus was second-hand or even third-hand, obtained from the apostles in Jerusalem and other eye-witnesses or people who got their information from them (Acts 9: 26 and 15: 2; Gal 1: 17) – apart from his own subjective visions and revelations.

In the paragraphs that follow, Paul's references to Jesus will be investigated for their historical relevance and probable accuracy. These references will be presented, as far as possible, in chronological order. The letters probably written by the followers and students of Paul will be included, insofar they may also contain some relevant biographical material about Jesus.

Albrecht Dürer: Saint Paul (1514)

The Death, Resurrection, and Return of Jesus
1 Thess 1: 10

> … and to wait for his Son from heaven, whom he raised from the dead – Jesus, who delivers us from the wrath to come.

1 Thess 4: 13–18

> 13. But we don't want you to be ignorant, brothers, concerning those who have fallen asleep, so that you don't grieve like the rest, who have no hope.

30.	For if we believe that Jesus died and rose again, even so those who have fallen asleep in Jesus will God bring with him.
31.	For this we tell you by the word of the Lord, that we who are alive, who are left to the coming of the Lord, will in no way precede those who have fallen asleep.
32.	For the Lord himself will descend from heaven with a shout, with the voice of the archangel, and with God's trumpet. The dead in Christ will rise first,
33.	then we who are alive, who are left, will be caught up together with them in the clouds, to meet the Lord in the air. So we will be with the Lord forever.
34.	Therefore comfort one another with these words.

1 Thess 2: 14–15

14.	For you, brothers, became imitators of the assemblies of God which are in Judea in Christ Jesus; for you also suffered the same things from your own countrymen, even as they did from the Jews;
15.	who killed the Lord Jesus and the prophets, and drove us out, and didn't please God, and are contrary to all men;

1 Thess 5: 1–3

1.	But concerning the times and the seasons, brothers, you have no need that anything be written to you.
2.	For you yourselves know well that the day of the Lord comes like a thief in the night.

> 3. For when they are saying, "Peace and safety," then sudden destruction will come on them, like birth pains on a pregnant woman; and they will in no way escape .

If the first letter to the Thessalonians is Paul's earliest extant letter, then his references to the exalted Lord Jesus Christ, the divine Son of God, is the first we have in writing from him. Jesus is described as the savior who brought deliverance from the horrors of Judgment Day to believers.

The only biographical details about Jesus in these passages are that the Jews killed him as they also killed the prophets, that he was resurrected, and he is expected to return on Judgment Day like a conquering general, when all the deceased faithful will be resurrected and those who are still alive, will be transformed and taken up into heaven.

Divisions in Corinth
1 Cor 1: 11–12

> 11. For it has been reported to me concerning you, my brothers, by those who are from Chloe's household, that there are contentions among you.
> 12. Now I mean this, that each one of you says, "I follow Paul," "I follow Apollos," "I follow Cephas," and, "I follow Christ."

This passage shows that there were divisions among the followers of Jesus in a Greek city like Corinth during the fifties AD. There were the following groups:

- The followers of Paul – mostly converts from paganism and people who accepted his version of the gospel, namely that

Jesus' death on the cross was meant to save sinners from hell and that Jesus was the divine Son of God;
- The followers of Apollos – mostly Jews who regarded John the Baptist as the greatest prophet, greater than even Jesus, and who practiced John's type of baptism (Acts 18: 24–28; 19: 1–3);
- The followers of Cephas or Peter – they must have been mostly Essenes or Ebionites who regarded Jesus as the earthly Messiah and rejected Paul's interpretation of the mission of Jesus (Gal 2: 11–14); and
- The followers of Christ, the Messiah – probably Jewish followers of Jesus who did not belong to the party of the Essenes or Ebionites, but who believed in Jesus and continued to live as Jews.

This passage demonstrates that there were different parties in the early church. Christianity, comprising all the followers of Jesus, was never a unified movement or organization.

Jesus' Teaching about Divorce
1 Cor 7: 10–12

10.	But to the married I command – not I, but the Lord – that the wife not leave her husband
35.	(but if she departs, let her remain unmarried, or else be reconciled to her husband), and that the husband not leave his wife.
36.	But to the rest I – not the Lord – say, if any brother has an unbelieving wife, and she is content to live with him, let him not leave her.

Paul referred in this passage to the teaching of Jesus who condemned any divorce, in accordance with his Essene background. It is not clear how Paul got his information about the teachings of Jesus – perhaps from the apostles when he visited Jerusalem after his conversion. He added his own advice on how a Christian husband ought to treat his pagan wife.

Paul's Calling
1 Cor 9: 1

> Am I not free? Am I not an apostle? Haven't I seen Jesus Christ, our Lord? Aren't you my work in the Lord?

Paul defended his calling as an apostle or missionary on account of the vision he had of Jesus Christ on the Damascus Road. Reports of this incident are to be found in Acts 9: 1–7,; 22: 5–11; and 26: 12–18. It is clearly stated in Acts 22: 9 that Paul's travelling companions did not hear the voice of Jesus that he heard during this incident.

In Acts 22: 17–18, we are told that Paul fell into a trance while he was in Jerusalem and that Jesus again spoke to him. The Greek word for "trance" is ἔκστασις (*ekstasis*) – from which the English word "ecstasy" is derived. It may denote a state of bewilderment or amazement, or an altered state of consciousness – which is consistent with an epileptic fit.

One account of all this, one must conclude that Paul's experiences and visions of Jesus were purely subjective with no independent evidence about what he saw and heard.

The Eucharist
1 Cor 11: 22–28

> 22. What, don't you have houses to eat and to drink in? Or do you despise God's assembly, and put them to shame who don't have? What will I tell you? Will I praise you? In this I don't praise you.

23.	For I received from the Lord that which also I delivered to you, that the Lord Jesus on the night in which he was betrayed took bread.
24.	When he had given thanks, he broke it, and said, "Take, eat. This is my body, which is broken for you. Do this in memory of me."
25.	In the same way he also took the cup, after supper, saying, "This cup is the new covenant in my blood. Do this, as often as you drink, in memory of me."
26.	For as often as you eat this bread, and drink this cup, you proclaim the Lord's death until he comes.
27.	Therefore whoever eats this bread or drinks the Lord's cup in an unworthy manner, will be guilty of the body and the blood of the Lord.
28.	But let a man examine himself, and so let him eat of the bread, and drink of the cup.

This passage is certainly the most detailed description of what Jesus did and said in any of Paul's letters. It seems as if he obtained the information about the institution of the eucharist from a reliable source – most probably an eye-witness (or somebody who heard it from an eye-witness), namely one of the apostles whom he had met in Jerusalem (Acts 9: 26 and 15: 2; Gal 1: 17). This description of the institution of the eucharist is essentially the same as that found in Mark 14: 22–24, Matt 26: 26–29, and Luke 22: 19–20. This agreement is an indication that these texts contain reliable information.

We find the following biographical details regarding Jesus in this passage:

Albrecht Dürer: The Last Supper, 1510

- Jesus instituted the eucharist on the night when he was betrayed (by Judas);
- He knew his blood would be spilt and that his flesh would be torn apart during the expected crucifixion. According to the gospels, he predicted this fate and even prepared for it; and
- We also learn that Jesus was expected to return, but Paul was silent on when that would happen.

It is not possible that Paul received his information from a reading of Mark, because Mark was only written two decades later – as will be shown when the Gospel of Mark is discussed

Jesus' Resurrection and Appearances
1 Cor 15: 1–8

1.	Now I declare to you, brothers, the gospel which I preached to you, which also you received, in which you also stand,
2.	by which also you are saved, if you hold firmly the word which I preached to you – unless you believed in vain.
3.	For I delivered to you first of all that which also I received: that Christ died for our sins according to the scriptures,
4.	that he was buried, that he was raised on the third day according to the Scriptures,
5.	and that he appeared to Cephas, then to the twelve.

6.	Then he appeared to over five hundred brothers at once, most of whom remain until now, but some have also fallen asleep.
7.	Then he appeared to James, then to all the apostles,
8.	and last of all, as to the child born at the wrong time, he appeared to me also.

Paul provided his readers with a list of people who purportedly saw Jesus after his resurrection. It is noteworthy that he failed to mention the women who were the first to find the empty tomb, according to the gospels (Matt 28: 1–8; Luke 24: 1–10; John 20: 1–2).

This passage cannot be used as solid proof that Jesus really cheated death and was resurrected. Apart from Paul's subjective visions and revelations, he mentions other people who purportedly saw Jesus after his resurrection – as told to him by unknown informants. Paul's information was, therefore, second-hand, or even third-hand.

There are no independent reports of an occasion when Jesus was supposed to have appeared to more than five hundred men, unless this is a skewed reference to the events on Pentecost when the Holy Spirit was poured out onto a group of apostles and other people (Acts 2).

Paul's declaration that "the Scriptures" foretold the death and resurrection of Christ is not correct. The only part of the Old Testament where something of the sort is seemingly written is Isa 52: 13–15 and 53: 1–13 where a description of the suffering "servant of YHWH" is given. This passage is often mentioned in the New Testament as a prophecy of the Messiah that was fulfilled by Jesus (Luke 22: 37; 24: 26–27; Acts 3: 18; 8: 26–40; 26: 22–23; Rom 15: 21; Phil 2: 7–11; Eph 5: 2; 1 Pet 2: 22–25; 3: 18).

The most plausible explanation of this passage in Isaiah is that the "servant of YHWH" must be seen as the nation of Israel – not the promised Messiah, as Christians believe. Hirsch analyzed the whole of the Old Testament and found that this expression was applied to the patriarch Jacob and his descendants, the people of Israel as a whole, as well as other leaders of Israel like Joshua, David, or the prophets. The promised Messiah was never linked to this expression.

For example: Ezek 28: 25 contains these words:

> "Thus says the Lord YHWH: When I shall have gathered the house of Israel from the peoples among whom they are scattered, and shall be sanctified in them in the sight of the nations, then shall they dwell in their own land which I gave to *my servant Jacob*" (emphasis added).

In Isa 41: 8–9 we read:

> "But you, *Israel, my servant, Jacob* whom I have chosen, the seed of Abraham my friend, you whom I have taken hold of from the ends of the earth, and called from the corners of it, and said to you, you are *my servant*, I have chosen you and not cast you away" (emphasis added).

Isaiah 44: 1 states:

> "Yet now hear, *Jacob my servant, and Israel*, who I have chosen"[126] (emphasis added).

Professor Mordochai ben–Tziyyon of the University of Jerusalem concurs with Hirsch regarding the meaning of the expression

---

[126] Hirsch, "Servant of God".

"servant of YHWH" in Isa 52–53. He adds that the nation of Israel has, indeed, suffered much during the centuries and he reminds his readers that most Jewish scholars through the centuries held this view.

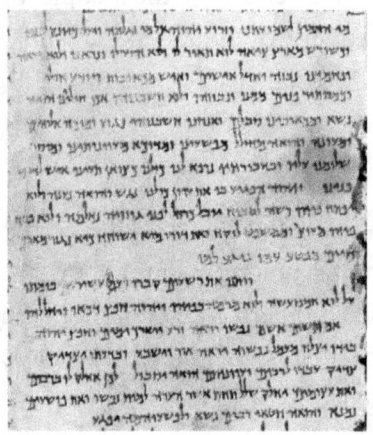

Isaiah 53 in the Great Isaiah Scroll, the best preserved of the biblical scrolls found at Qumran from the second century BC (and mostly identical to the Masoretic version).

Ben-Tziyyon accuses Christian translators of the Old Testament of making deliberate mistakes in order to create the impression that the passage in Isa 52–53 refers to "the christian man-god" (*i e* Jesus Christ). An example is Isa 53: 8 as he translated it, which contains a clear reference to Israel's exile in Babylonia –

> "Now that they have been released from detention and judgement, who could have imagined such a generation? for they were removed far from the land where they lived, and a plague came upon them through the transgression of my people."

The Hebrew word translated by "stroke" or "plague" (נֶגַע – *Nega*) actually means "leprosy" – something Jesus never suffered from. This verse also refers to the people of Israel who suffered because the verbs are in the plural, not the singular as Christian translations have it.

Professor Ben–Tziyyon wrote that Isa 52–53 may also refer to a specific pious person of that time who experienced suffering due to the sins of the people of Israel, but certainly not to the promised Messiah of the future.[127]

It must be concluded that Paul's statement that "the Scriptures" – especially Isa 52–53 – contain prophecies regarding Christ's death and resurrection cannot be maintained.

The End
1 Cor 15: 24–28

24.	Then the end comes, when he will deliver up the kingdom to God, even the Father; when he will have abolished all rule and all authority and power.
26.	For he must reign until he has put all his enemies under his feet.
26.	The last enemy that will be abolished is death.
27.	For, "He put all things in subjection under his feet." But when he says, "All things are put in subjection," it is evident that he is excepted who subjected all things to him.
28.	When all things have been subjected to him, then the Son will also himself be subjected to him who subjected all things to him, that God may be all in all.

This text states that Christ will abdicate his position after Judgment Day when he will subject himself to God.

Similar thoughts are found elsewhere in 1 Corinthians. In chapter 3: 21–22 we are told: "All are yours, and you are Christ's,

---

[127] Ben–Tziyyon, "The 'Suffering Servant' in ch.53 of *Y'shayahu*".

and Christ is God`s." 1 Cor 11: 3 says: "But I would have you know, that the head of every man is Christ, and the head of the woman is the man, and the head of Christ is God."

These passages must be seen as a contradiction of the Christian doctrine of the trinitarian God – three divine, eternal persons in one Godhead. If Christ has God (the Father) as his head and he will subject himself to God (the Father) on Judgment Day, then he cannot be God as well. He will then, at most, be a lesser deity, such as the offspring of Zeus, father of the Greeks gods.

Paul's assertion "that God may be all in all" reminds one the philosophy of pantheism, "the doctrine that the universe conceived of as a whole is God and, conversely, that there is no God but the combined substance, forces, and laws that are manifested in the existing universe.".

A similar thought of Paul is also to be found in 1 Cor 12: 6 – "There are various kinds of workings, but the same God, who works all things in all" (see also Eph 1: 23 and Col 3: 11). That means that the whole of reality will be dissolved into God and that nothing outside of God will exist at the end. It seems as if Paul borrowed this pantheism from the ancient Greek philosophy of Stoicism that taught that the All and the Soul of the World are one and the same.[128]

One looks in vain for a clear doctrine of creation in Paul's letters and when he does speak of God as creator, it is in a pantheistic manner. For instance, in 1 Cor 1: 5–6 he wrote:

> "For though there are things that are called 'gods,' whether in the heavens or on earth; as there are many 'gods' and many 'lords;' yet to us there is one God, the Father, of whom are

---

[128] Enc. Brit, "Pantheism".

all things, and we to him; and one Lord, Jesus Christ, through whom are all things [exist], and we through him."

In Col 1: 15–17, Christ is called the firstborn of creation, as well as the agent through which the whole of creation was brought about (*qv*). This boils down to the idea that Christ, as God, as it were, created himself when the universe had its origin – which is also a pantheistic notion.

With his pantheism, Paul's thoughts are at odds with the whole of the Old Testament where it is taken for granted that God, the creator, cannot be part of his creation, but is outside of it – in other words, He is transcendent, not imminent, and not to be confused with his creation.

The Resurrected Body
I Cor 15: 19–20. 35–58

19.	If we have only hoped in Christ in this life, we are of all men most pitiable.
20.	But now Christ has been raised from the dead. He became the first fruits of those who are asleep.
35.	But someone will say, "How are the dead raised?" and, "With what kind of body do they come?"
36.	You foolish one, that which you yourself sow is not made alive unless it dies.
37.	That which you sow, you don't sow the body that will be, but a bare grain, maybe of wheat, or of some other kind.
38.	But God gives it a body even as it pleased him, and to each seed a body of its own.

39. All flesh is not the same flesh, but there is one flesh of men, another flesh of animals, another of fish, and another of birds.

40. There are also celestial bodies, and terrestrial bodies; but the glory of the celestial differs from that of the terrestrial.

41. There is one glory of the sun, another glory of the moon, and another glory of the stars; for one star differs from another star in glory.

42. So also is the resurrection of the dead. It is sown in corruption; it is raised in incorruption.

43. It is sown in dishonor; it is raised in glory. It is sown in weakness; it is raised in power.

44. It is sown a natural body; it is raised a spiritual body. If there is a natural body, there is also a spiritual body.

45. So also it is written, "The first man, Adam, became a living soul." The last Adam became a life-giving spirit.

46. However that which is spiritual isn't first, but that which is natural, then that which is spiritual.

47. The first man is of the earth, made of dust. The second man is the Lord from heaven.

48. As is the one made of dust, such are those who are also made of dust; and as is the heavenly, such are they also that are heavenly.

49. As we have borne the image of those made of dust, let's also bear the image of the heavenly.

50. Now I say this, brothers, that flesh and blood can't inherit the kingdom of God; neither does corruption inherit incorruption.

51.	Behold, I tell you a mystery. We will not all sleep, but we will all be changed,
52.	in a moment, in the twinkling of an eye, at the last trumpet. For the trumpet will sound, and the dead will be raised incorruptible, and we will be changed.
53.	For this corruptible must put on incorruption, and this mortal must put on immortality.
54.	But when this corruptible will have put on incorruption, and this mortal will have put on immortality, then what is written will happen: "Death is swallowed up in victory."
55.	"Death, where is your sting? Hades, where is your victory?"
56.	The sting of death is sin, and the power of sin is the law.
57.	But thanks be to God, who gives us the victory through our Lord Jesus Christ.
58.	Therefore, my beloved brothers, be steadfast, immovable, always abounding in the Lord's work, because you know that your labor is not in vain in the Lord.

Paul wrote in this lengthy and rather messy passage that believers will be resurrected with a "heavenly body" or a "spiritual body". Since Christ is the "first fruit" of those who will be resurrected in glory, it goes without saying that he must also have left the grave with a "spiritual body". The same idea occurs in Phil 3: 20–21.

Likewise, 1 Pet 3: 18 declares that Christ was "put to death in the flesh, but made alive in the spirit" – in other words, he was resurrected only spiritually (whatever that means), and not bodily or physically.

It is probable and possible that Paul thought of this heavenly or spiritual body as composed of a fifth element, the so-called quintessence – apart from the four "ordinary" elements, namely fire, air, water, and earth – of which the celestial or astronomical bodies were supposed to be made, according to the Greek philosopher Aristotle.[129]

One can only conclude that Paul thought of the resurrected "spiritual body" of Jesus as a heavenly or "celestial body" – composed of the same stuff as the sun, moon, and stars, which differs from the "dust" of our earth and with which he could ascend into heaven, between or beyond the stars (see also Eph 4: 10).

Christ the Image of God
2 Cor 4: 4

> ... in whom the god of this world has blinded the minds of the unbelieving, that the light of the gospel of the glory of Christ, who is the image of God, should not dawn on them.

Christ is called "the image of God". In other words: Christ made the invisible God visible to earthlings when he walked the earth.

Paul's Visions of Christ
2 Cor 12: 1–7

> 1. It is doubtless not profitable for me to boast. I will come to visions and revelations of the Lord.
> 2. I know a man in Christ, fourteen years ago (whether in the body, I don't know, or whether out of the body, I don't know; God knows), such a one caught up into the third heaven.
> 3. I know such a man (whether in the body, or apart from the body, I don't know; God knows),

---

[129] Aristotle, *On the Heavens*, Book 1: 9.

4.	how he was caught up into Paradise, and heard unspeakable words, which it is not lawful for a man to utter.
5.	On behalf of such a one I will boast, but on my own behalf I will not boast, except in my weaknesses.
6.	For if I would desire to boast, I will not be foolish; for I will speak the truth. But I forbear, so that no man may account of me above that which he sees in me, or hears from me.
7.	By reason of the exceeding greatness of the revelations, that I should not be exalted excessively, there was given to me a thorn in the flesh, a messenger of Satan to buffet me, that I should not be exalted excessively.

This is the most detailed description we have of the type of visions and revelations that Paul experienced. He stated that this episode had happened fourteen years previously – probably when he fell down on the Damascus Road and where he experienced that Christ spoke to him. The "thorn in the flesh" from which he suffered may well have been embarrassing and uncomfortable epileptic fits, together with hallucinations.[130]

He based his insight that Jesus was raised from the dead on these visions he had of the risen Christ – and not from any personal experience shortly after the crucifixion of Jesus.

Paul's Revelations
Gal 1: 12

For neither did I receive it from man, nor was I taught it, but it came to me through revelation of Jesus Christ.

---

[130] Pretorius, *Jesus of Nazareth*, 122–43.

Gal 2: 1–2

1.	Then after a period of fourteen years I went up again to Jerusalem with Barnabas, taking Titus also with me.
2.	I went up by revelation, and I laid before them the gospel which I preach among the Gentiles, but privately before those who were respected, for fear that I might be running, or had run, in vain.

Paul's insights about Christ, the gospel he preached, namely that Christ was resurrected after being crucified, were based on various revelations he said he had received. These revelations were by their very nature subjective and not amenable to verification by others.

Redemption through Christ
Gal 3: 13–14

37.	Christ redeemed us from the curse of the law, having become a curse for us. For it is written, "Cursed is everyone who hangs on a tree,"
38.	that the blessing of Abraham might come on the Gentiles through Christ Jesus; that we might receive the promise of the Spirit through faith.

Gal 4: 4–5

4.	But when the fullness of the time came, God sent forth his Son, born to a woman, born under the law,
5.	that he might redeem those who were under the law, that we might receive the adoption of sons.

Paul quoted from Deut 21: 23 where it is required that a criminal's "body shall not remain all night on the tree, but you shall surely bury him the same day; for he who is hanged is accursed of God."

The point he wished to make is that Christ suffered the curse of God to free believers from that curse. We also learn that Christ was "born to a woman, born under the law" – the Law of Moses since he was a Jew. Paul seemed to be ignorant of the virgin birth of Jesus as described in the gospels of Matthew and Luke.

The Hymn on Christ
Phil 2: 5–11

5.	Have this in your mind, which was also in Christ Jesus,
6.	who, existing in the form of God, didn't consider it robbery to be equal with God,
7.	but emptied himself, taking the form of a servant, being made in the likeness of men.
8.	Being found in human form, he humbled himself, becoming obedient to death, yes, the death of the cross.
9.	Therefore God also highly exalted him, and gave to him the name which is above every name;
10.	that at the name of Jesus every knee would bow, of those in heaven, those on earth, and those under the earth,
11.	and that every tongue would confess that Jesus Christ is Lord, to the glory of God, the Father.

Paul quoted this hymn to encourage the readers of his letter to be humble, gentle, and generous – just as Christ was.

This hymn, that must have been known to his readers, may even have been composed by Paul himself. It is "a poem in three parts:

- Christ as God;

- Christ as man; and
- Christ in glory."[131]

This song is a good expression of Paul's views regarding Christ who had a pre-existence with his Father, his equal, but who humbled himself by becoming a human and being executed on a cross. He was, though, resurrected, taken up into heaven so that creation as a whole would recognize him as the Lord, as God himself.

Attention must be drawn to the primitive and prescientific world view of Paul where he mentions the three layers of creation, populated by "those in heaven, those on earth, and those under the earth" in other words: the angels and demons (stars in the sky), people on earth, and those in Hades below the surface of the earth.[132]

The Resurrected Body
Phil 3: 20–21

20.	For our citizenship is in heaven, from where we also wait for a Savior, the Lord, Jesus Christ;
21.	who will change the body of our humiliation to be conformed to the body of his glory, according to the working whereby he is able even to subject all things to himself.

According to Paul, believers will receive bodies of glory on Judgment Day – the same type of body of glory with which Christ rose from the grave. No details of this type of body are given, but one may suppose that Paul thought of a "heavenly body" or a "spiritual body", which he mentioned in 1 Cor 15.

---

[131] Bright, "Letter of Joy".
[132] Pretorius. *Who, What, and Were is God?* 5–58.

Brief Description of Jesus Christ
Rom 1: 1–5

1.	Paul, a servant of Jesus Christ, called to be an apostle, set apart for the gospel of God,
2.	which he promised before through his prophets in the holy scriptures,
3.	concerning his Son, who was born of the seed of David according to the flesh,
4.	who was declared to be the Son of God with power, according to the spirit of holiness, by the resurrection from the dead, Jesus Christ our Lord,
5.	through whom we received grace and apostleship, to obe– dience of faith among all the nations, for his name's sake.

The readers of Paul's letter to the Romans got the barest details regarding the life of Jesus Christ in the preamble to his letter. We are merely told that the prophets foretold his coming, that he was a descendant of King David, that he was declared to be the Son of God on account of his resurrection, that he is the Lord, and that Paul was called to become his apostle or missionary who had to preach the gospel.

Something strange about this passage is that Christ was only declared the Son of God after his resurrection – not during his life on earth. This is contradicted by the numerous occasions in the gospels where Jesus called God his Father and he called himself the son of God.

Rom 6: 4–7

3.	Or don't you know that all we who were baptized into Christ Jesus were baptized into his death?

4. We were buried therefore with him through baptism to death, that just like Christ was raised from the dead through the glory of the Father, so we also might walk in newness of life.

6. For if we have become united with him in the likeness of his death, we will also be part of his resurrection;

7. knowing this, that our old man was crucified with him, that the body of sin might be done away with, so that we would no longer be in bondage to sin.

Part of Paul's Epistle to the Romans in Papyrus, early 3rd century

Rom 8: 11

But if the Spirit of him who raised up Jesus from the dead dwells in you, he who raised up Christ Jesus from the dead will also give life to your mortal bodies through his Spirit who dwells in you.

The only details that can be learnt from these passages regarding Jesus' life are that he died and was resurrected.

Paul mentioned "the Spirit" twice in Rom 8: 11. It is clear that he thinks of the Holy Spirit. His teaching on the (Holy) Spirit is rather confusing. As a Jew who studied under Gamaliel, he must have known the Old Testament and he often quotes from it. His use of the expression "the Holy Spirit" or "the Spirit of God" often reminds one of the use of these expressions in the Hebrew scriptures.

The phrase רוּחַ אֱלֹהִים (*ruach Elohim* – Spirit of God) occurs often in the Old Testament and it has a wide range of meanings: the spirit, breath, power, or mind of God – or God himself. An encyclopedia explains:

> "The Old Testament clearly does not envisage God's spirit as a person, neither in the strictly philosophical sense, nor in the Semitic sense. God's spirit is simply God's power. If it is sometimes represented as being distinct from God, it is because the breath of Yahweh acts exteriorly (Isa 48: 16; 63: 11; 32: 15)".[133]

Paul often uses the words "the Spirit of God" and "the Holy Spirit", but one also encounters "the Spirit of his Son" (Gal 4: 6) or "the Spirit of Christ" (Rom 8: 9). He even writes: "Now the Lord [*i.e.,* Jesus Christ] is the Spirit and where the Spirit of the Lord is, there is liberty" (2 Cor 3: 17).

Paul thinks of the Spirit as the mind of God as well because he writes in 1 Cor 2: 11 –

> "For who among men knows the things of a man, except the spirit of the man, which is in him? Even so, no one knows

---

[133] Enc.com, "Spirit of God".

the things of God, except God's Spirit."

At times, Paul regarded the Holy Spirit is as a third divine person, apart from God (the Father) and Christ (the Son). For instance, these three persons are mentioned in the benediction at the end of 2 Corinthians (13: 14).

There is, therefore, no consistent teaching or thoughts regarding the (Holy) Spirit in Paul's writings.

Authorship of Colossians
Col 4: 10 & 18
According to Col 4: 10 & 18, Paul was a prisoner when this letter was written. The style and vocabulary of this letter differs markedly from Paul's other letters and it is likely that one of Paul's helpers wrote it on his behalf, only giving it to Paul to sign off with his own hand at the end (Col 4: 18).

A Hymn on Christ
Col 1: 13–20

13.	[The Father] who delivered us out of the power of darkness, and translated us into the kingdom of the Son of his love;
14.	in whom we have our redemption through his blood, the forgiveness of our sins.
15.	He is the image of the invisible God, the firstborn of all creation.
16.	For in him were all things created, in the heavens and on the earth, things visible and things invisible, whether thrones or dominions or principalities or powers; all things have been created through him, and to him.

> 17. He is before all things, and in him all things are held together.
> 18. He is the head of the body, the assembly, who is the beginning, the firstborn from the dead; that in all things he might have the preeminence.
> 19. For all the fullness was pleased to dwell in him;
> 20. and through him to reconcile all things to himself, having made peace through the blood of his cross.
> Through him, I say, whether things on the earth, or things in the heavens.

This passage contains an old hymn on Christ (vs 15–18), dealing with three aspects:

- Christ's relationship with God (1:15);
- His relationship with creation (1:16–17); and
- His relationship with the church (1:18).[134]

The preceding two verses mention the kingdom of Christ, which is clearly thought to be a spiritual or heavenly kingdom – not a kingdom with Jerusalem as its capital.

The hymn itself reminds one of the prologue to John's gospel where we read:

> "In the beginning was the Word, and the Word was with God, and the Word was God. The same was in the beginning with God. All things were made through him. Without him was not anything made that has been made" (John 1: 1–3).

---

[134] MacArthur, "Background to Colossians".

This passage in John harks back to Genesis 1 where God's creative word called the creation into being. The same theme appears in this hymn. Christ is introduced as the visible presentation of God who is invisible. As firstborn of the creation, he is not part of creation but the agent through which creation came about. As such, he is the head of the church. His death and resurrection are also mentioned as the act through which the believers are redeemed.[135]

Because this passage dealt with Christ on a metaphysical level, no real biographical details were given, except for his blood on the cross and that he was the firstborn from the dead. On the other hand, his divinity was emphasized. These views are consistent with the visions and revelations Paul has received and of which he convinced his converts.

It is almost as if Jesus of Nazareth was not a man of flesh and blood, but an ethereal being who briefly visited mankind on earth and who rules his church, his spiritual kingdom, from heaven.

Col 2: 8–12

8.	Be careful that you don't let anyone rob you through his philosophy and vain deceit, after the tradition of men, after the elements of the world, and not after Christ.
9.	For in him all the fullness of the Godhead dwells bodily,
10.	and in him you are made full, who is the head of all principality and power;
11.	in whom you were also circumcised with a circumcision not made with hands, in the putting off of the body of the sins of the flesh, in the circumcision of Christ;

---

[135] Pocock, "Christ has Everything you Need."

> 12. having been buried with him in baptism, in which you were also raised with him through faith in the working of God, who raised him from the dead.

This passage also introduces a metaphysical Christ. The readers of the letter were warned against strange philosophies, with which pagan religions, Greek philosophical schools, and Jewish religious ideas may have been meant. Christ, as a human being with a physical body, was actually a manifestation of God.

The Christian baptism, which replaced the Jewish circumcision, amounts to a symbolic burial together with Christ who was buried after having died, but also a symbolic resurrection from death, together with Christ.

Christ's Reign
Eph 1: 15–23

> 39. For this cause I also, having heard of the faith in the Lord Jesus which is among you, and the love which you have toward all the saints,
> 40. don't cease to give thanks for you, making mention in my prayers,
> 41. that the God of our Lord Jesus Christ, the Father of glory, may give to you a spirit of wisdom and revelation in the knowledge of him;
> 42. having the eyes of your hearts enlightened, that you may know what is the hope of his calling, what are the riches of the glory of his inheritance in the saints,
> 43. and what is the exceeding greatness of his power toward us who believe, according to that working of the strength of his might

44.	which he worked in Christ, when he raised him from the dead, and made him to sit at his right hand in the heavenly places,
45.	far above all rule, and authority, and power, and dominion, and every name that is named, not only in this world, but also in that which is to come.
46.	He put all things in subjection under his feet, and gave him to be head over all things to the assembly,
47.	which is his body, the fullness of him who fills all in all.

Paul (or his helper who wrote on his behalf) taught his readers in this long-winded and clumsy passage that Christ was exalted after his resurrection to sit with God on his throne and rule over all forces, beneficial and evil, throughout creation.

It is remarkable, though, that we read in verse 17 of "the God of our Lord Jesus Christ, the Father of glory". The implication is that Christ is supposed to be a lesser deity than his Father. After all, God gave Christ the right to join him on his throne. If Jesus was fully God, just as his Father, he would not have had a God and be subjected to some higher authority who granted him certain powers and privileges. This passage contradicts Paul's stance elsewhere that Christ is fully divine, on the same level as his Father.

Paul's Visions
Eph 3: 3–5

3.	…how that by revelation the mystery was made known to me, as I wrote before in few words,
4.	whereby, when you read, you can perceive my understanding in the mystery of Christ;

5.	which in other generations was not made known to the sons of men, as it has now been revealed to his holy apostles and prophets in the Spirit;

Paul claims that he received revelations "in the Spirit" regarding the "mystery of Christ". His knowledge about Jesus, therefore, depended primarily upon supernatural messages and not information received from eye-witnesses or own experience. These revelations were, by their very nature, subjective and could not be confirmed independently.

Eph 3: 8–12

8.	To me, the very least of all saints, was this grace given, to preach to the Gentiles the unsearchable riches of Christ,
9.	and to make all men see what is the administration of the mystery which for ages has been hidden in God, who created all things through Jesus Christ;
10.	to the intent that now through the assembly the manifold wisdom of God might be made known to the principalities and the powers in the heavenly places,
11.	according to the eternal purpose which he purposed in Christ Jesus, our Lord;
12.	in whom we have boldness and access in confidence through our faith in him.

This passage is another example of the clumsy style characteristic of Colossians and Ephesians. Although Paul calls himself "the very least of all saints", he claims the "grace" to preach to the Gentiles about the mysteries of a cosmic or metaphysical Christ through whom all creation was brought about – a mystery that was hidden until it was revealed to Paul.

Christ's Sacrifice
Eph 5: 2

> Walk in love, even as Christ also loved you, and gave himself up for us, an offering and a sacrifice to God for a sweet–smelling fragrance.

According to Paul, Jesus' death on the cross was a loving sacrifice to benefit the believers.

Descended from David
2 Tim 2: 8

> Remember Jesus Christ, risen from the dead, of the seed of David, according to my gospel...

This sentence tells us that Jesus was risen from the dead and was a descendant of King David. Paul did not disclose his source for this information, but it may have been James, the brother of Jesus.

Summary
Although Paul wrote his letters between twenty and thirty years after Jesus' crucifixion, these writings contain a minimum of biographical and historically relevant information. We are informed that Jesus was descended from King David, taught that divorce is wrong, instituted the eucharist, was crucified, was resurrected, was taken up into heaven with a glorified body and is expected to return on Judgment Day.

Paul's conviction that Jesus was resurrected from the grave and ascended into heaven is dependent upon his subjective visions and revelations – for which no corroboration or confirmation can be supplied. Believers simply had to accept that these visions and revelations had a supernatural origin, although they only had Paul's word for that conviction.

The image of Jesus Christ drawn by Paul differs fundamentally from that which can be concluded from the Q Document, where Jesus is presented as an ordinary mortal, a wise teacher, and the king-in-waiting of Israel – and certainly not the savior of mankind or the agent through which creation came to be.

Lucas van Leyden: Apostle Paul

Paul's interest lay foremost in the religious implications of Jesus life, death, and resurrection, namely that he sacrificed himself to save believers from the horrors of hell in the afterlife.

Paul saw Christ sometimes as the equal of his Father, as God himself, and the agency through which the creation was called into existence. Through his resurrection with a spiritual, glorified, or heavenly body and ascension into heaven he proved to be the victor over all evil forces.

Jesus' ascension into heaven was the logical outcome of his resurrection and appearances to Paul in his visions.

It has also been shown that there are utterances of Paul in which he contradicted himself regarding the divinity of Christ, rendering him a lesser deity than God, his Father. This Christ was expected to abdicate his position after Judgment Day.

His notions about the Holy Spirit are also confusing.

Paul's views regarding a deified Christ would have not have been so strange to his Gentile converts since the classical world was familiar with mythical figures who were demi-gods, in many cases the offspring of Zeus, the chief deity of the Greeks, who made quite a few earthly maidens pregnant. These sons, including the strong man Hercules, became mythological demi-gods.[136] The Egyptian pharaohs and the Roman emperors also regarded themselves as sons or descendants of some or other deity.

One of the founders of the movement of Gnosticism, Simon the Magician, also known as Simon Magus, of whom we read in Acts 8: 9–24, was revered by his followers as an incarnation of the Greek god Zeus.[137]

In a similar process, Paul transformed the Old Testament idea of "son of God" as applied to the kings of the house of David (Ps 2: 7, *etcetera*), into a Greek mythological concept. In other words, he ignored the use in the Old Testament of this title and declared Jesus to be the *only* Son of God (Rom 2: 2–4) – which later led to the Christian dogma of the Divine Trinity consisting of three divine persons, Father, Son, and Holy Spirit, united in one Godhead.

The description of the metaphysical and mythological Christ in Paul's epistles tells us very little about the life, ministry, teachings, and execution of Jesus – although he wrote long passages about his views regarding the religious implications of Christ's death, resurrection, and ascension.

Although he claimed that the appearance of Jesus, as the Messiah, was promised in the Old Testament, his presentation of

---

[136] Grayling, *The God Argument,* 31.
[137] Enc Brit, "Simon Magus"

Jesus differs fundamentally from the Jewish expectations of the promised Messiah.

His pantheistic notions regarding the relationship between God and his creation are also foreign to the teachings of the Old Testament.

Chapter 5
JOHN'S NARRATIVE

The Composition of the Gospel of John

It was generally assumed in the past that the Gospel of John was written in one go by a single author, John, the son of Zebedee, the brother of James, and a disciple of Jesus.

The oldest authority to attest to this view was the church father Irenaeus, who wrote during the second half of the second century AD: "Afterwards [*sc.* after the writing of the other gospels] John, the disciple of the Lord, who also reclined on his bosom, published his gospel, while staying at Ephesus in Asia".[138]

However, critical research has shown that this is probably not quite the case.

The Contribution of Bultmann

The influential German expert on the New Testament, Rudolf Bultmann, wrote much about the Gospel of John. His most influential work on this topic was a monumental commentary on this gospel, published in 1941 and reprinted many times, the last time in 1986.[139] In this commentary, he distinguished five sources for the Gospel of John as we know it, namely –

- a Signs Source (containing the narrative parts, describing *inter alia* the "signs" performed by Jesus);

---

[138] Irenaeus, *Adversus Haereses.* m, i, 1; (quoted in Euscbius, *Historia Ecclesiastica,* Liber V/VIII/4).

[139] Bultmann, *Das Evangelium des Johannes.*

- a Revelation-Sayings Source (comprised of the dialogues and discourses of Jesus);
- a Passion Source (the story of Jesus arrest, trial, and crucifixion);
- the Evangelist's work; and
- the final Redactor's contributions.[140]

Anderson criticized this approach and found that the division into these sources was rather arbitrary and random. He added:

> "It wrongly assumes that edited material was lying together, side-by-side (as on an editor's desk), rather than composed and added later. Ancient texts more likely grew by accretion than shuffling fragments into experimental sequences, and a theory of disordering involving breaks only between sentences is theoretically problematic."[141]

According to Anderson, Bultmann also wrongly assumed that the Evangelist's thinking processes were dialectical, such as that of scholars in the twentieth century.[142]

The Work of Newer Scholars

Bultmann has, nevertheless, shown convincingly that more than one author compiled the Gospel of John. There are simply too many differences in style and viewpoints between different elements of the gospel that lead to the conclusion that it is a composite work.

Rylaarsdam *et al.* observe:

---

[140] Bultmann, *Das Johannes Evangelium*.

[141] Anderson, *Christology*, 72–89.

[142] Anderson, *Christology*, 90–109 (see also: Anderson. "The John, Jesus, and History Project", 14–15).

"In John there is a mixture of long meditational discourses on definite themes and concrete events recalling the structure of Matthew (with events plus discourses); and, although the source problem is complex and research is still grappling with it, there can be little doubt that John depended on a distinct source for his seven miracles ..."[143]

The research by, for instance, Robert Fortna, seems to lead to a satisfactory explanation of how this gospel was composed. Fortna found that the "redaction-critical value of the source analysis" of the fourth gospel implies the existence of a narrative source in the style of the other gospels that provided the skeleton for the final gospel. This primitive gospel may have been reshaped and amplified by the final redactor. The oral transmission of eye-witnesses and others was later recorded in writing. Fortna finds that this "Signs Gospel" contains trustworthy historical material.[144]

Apart from this narrative element, namely the "Signs Gospel" plus the description of Jesus' passion, there are passages with discourses making up most of the rest of the gospel. Fortna finds that there is tension between these elements. The narrative sources contain stories about an earthly Jesus. These stories are told in a lively manner and in the third person, and show similarities with the style of the other three gospels, the Synoptic Gospels. The narrative material contains a "primitive Christology" and Jesus is presented as a miracle worker who manifests himself as the Messiah, and in whom people must believe.

The discourses of Jesus in John, on the other hand, display a different style: they are written in the first or second person, are rather drawn-out, repetitive, and didactic. The discourses also

---

[143] Rylaarsdam *et al.*, "Biblical Literature."
[144] Fortna, "Jesus Tradition", 201–02.

contain a "higher Christology" in which Jesus is presented as the Son who was sent by the Father and who accomplished the tasks that his Father gave him.[145]

Gilbert van Belle, who agreed with Fortna, concluded: "Even though the hypothesis [of Fortna] has a stubborn opposition, it still remains the most exquisite pearl in Johannine source-criticism."[146]

Anderson is of the opinion that the chronology of John as found in the narrative elements, with Jesus visiting Jerusalem three times, must be regarded as more plausible than the chronology of the Synoptic Gospels.[147]

The "Signs Gospel" contains narratives of the following seven "signs" or miracles:

- Turning water to wine at the wedding at Cana;
- The healing of a nobleman's son;
- The healing of a paralyzed man at the pool of Bethezda;
- The feeding of the multitude;
- Jesus walking on water;
- The cure of a man who was blind from birth; and
- The raising of Lazarus from the grave.

The descriptions of these seven signs supply the structure of the narrative parts of John – apart from the passion report. In John 20: 30–31, the purpose of these signs is explained:

> "Jesus did many other signs in the presence of the disciples, which are not written in this book; but these are written that you may believe that Jesus is the Christ, the Son of God, and

---

[145] Fortna, *The Fourth Gospel*.
[146] Van Belle, "The Signs Source", 42.
[147] Anderson, "The John, Jesus, and History Project", 33.

that believing you may have life in his name."

The concept of belief in Jesus as the Messiah is the main theme of the Proto-Gospel of John and it occurs at the end of every description of one of these seven signs, as well as elsewhere.

Authorship of the Proto-Gospel of John
Because John's Gospel is anonymous and the earliest attribution of authorship of John by Irenaeus, around AD 180, many scholars assumed that the author is unknown.

Anderson noted:

"However, an incidental detail from Acts 4: 19–20 introduces new evidence that has been totally missed from all sides of the debate. In particular, this is the only time the Apostle John is mentioned as speaking in Acts, but we have here two statements. The first, 'we must obey God rather than man,' is echoed by Peter elsewhere in Acts 5: 29 and 11: 17 – the sort of thing Peter is thought by Luke to have said. The next statement could not have been uttered in a more Johannine way: 'we cannot help but speak about what we have *seen and heard.*' The closest parallel grammatically is 1 John 1: 3, not passages found elsewhere in Luke/Acts, and this connecting of the son of Zebedee with a Johannine saying is performed a full century before Irenaeus' linking of the two. This might not prove Johannine authorship, but it challenges severely the view that John the Apostle was not associated with the Johannine tradition until Irenaeus, around 180 C.E."[148]

---

[148] Anderson, "The John, Jesus, and History Project", 25.

A good summary of the arguments of why the apostle John, and nobody else, must be regarded as the author of this gospel – or at least the narrative parts, the proto-gospel – is to be found in an essay by David Malick.[149]

According to Malick, the author must have been a Jew who often quoted from the Old Testament (John 12: 40; 13: 18; 19: 37). It seems that he knew and understood Jewish customs, including wedding feasts (John 2: 1–10), purification practices (John 3: 25; 11: 55) and the burial of the dead (John 11: 38, 44; 19: 40). He was aware of the Jews' yearning for a messiah (John 1: 9–18) and the religious differences between the Jews and the Samaritans (John 4: 9, 20).

The author must have known the country of Palestine. He tells his readers that the pool of Bethesda had five porches (John 5: 2), that Bethany was not far from Jerusalem (John 11: 18), that the village of Ephraim was near the wilderness (John 11: 54), that the Garden of Gethsemane was on the other side of the brook Kidron (John 18: 1), and that there was a paved area outside of the Praetorium where Jesus was tried (John 19: 13).

He was aware of the region of Samaria and that the deep Jacob's well was located at Sychar (John 4: 5–6, 11). He knew about the sacred mountain where the Samaritans worshipped (John 4: 20–21). He was aware of the region of Galilee (John 1: 44, 46; 2: 1, 2).

The author seems to have been an eye-witness of the events he described by providing certain details that betray his personal involvement. He knew the number of pots used at the wedding at Cana (2: 6), he knew the value of the anointing spices (John12: 5), he witnessed the crucifixion of Jesus (John 19: 33–35), and he knew the distance from the shore of the apostles' boat and the number of

---

[149] David Malick, "An Introduction to the Gospel of John": 2–4.

fish caught (John 21: 8, 11). He presents himself as an eye-witness by writing: "This is the disciple who is bearing witness to these things, and who has written these things; and we know that his testimony is true" (John 21: 24).

The author must also have been an apostle of Jesus, most probably John. He is often referred to as the disciple whom Jesus loved (John 13: 23; 19: 26; 20: 2; 21:7, 20). The identity of this beloved disciple can be narrowed down to be John through a process of elimination. From John 21: 7 this disciple may be identified as one of the seven persons mentioned in John 21: 2, namely Simon Peter, Thomas called the Twin, Nathaniel of Cana in Galilee, the sons of Zebedee, and two others. He must be one of the Twelve since only they were with the Lord at the last supper (John 13:23–24). He is not Peter because he sat next to the Lord at the Last Supper, and Peter motioned to him (John 13: 23–24). His future is distinguished from Peter's (John 21: 20ff). He is, furthermore, closely related to Peter and thus seems to be one of the inner circle of three, namely James, John, and Peter (John 20: 2–10). James, John's brother, died in A.D. 44 and, therefore, he could not have been the author (Acts 12: 2).

Accordingly, if it is true that he was an apostle, and one of the inner circle of three, this apostle was not Peter, neither James, and therefore he must have been the apostle John.

Malick also lists a long list of early Christian writers who regarded John as the author of the gospel.[150]

These witnesses should not be distrusted out of hand. There may be some truth in their identification of the author of the gospel as being the apostle John. It may be possible that his memories of Jesus' ministry and execution form the core of the narrative part of the gospel, while the philosophical dialogues and discourses were

---

[150] Malick, "An Introduction to the Gospell of John", 2.

added much later by somebody else, possibly a follower or group of followers or students of John who expanded the Proto-Gospel of John into its present form.

On the other hand, the fact that the Gospel of John omits to mention two important episodes where John was involved, seems to point to another (unknown) author. These episodes, only described in the synoptic gospels, are the transfiguration of Jesus (Mark 9: 2–10) and the request by James and John to be assigned seats next to Jesus' throne in his kingdom (Mark 10: 35–41). If the Proto-Gospel of John does contain John's memories of Jesus, it is strange that descriptions of these crucial events do not appear in his writings – unless these episodes never happened – which seems unlikely.

It should also be remembered that John does not describe himself as the author of his gospel anywhere. We read in John 19: 33 – "He who has seen has testified, and his testimony is true. He knows that he tells the truth, that you also may believe." In other words: John was merely the source of information.

The solution to the question of authorship must be that a friend or a pupil of John recorded his memories of Jesus, but exaggerated some of Jesus' signs or miracles to support and strengthen Jesus' claim to be the Messiah.

Relationship with the Author of Revelation

The first Christian church historian, Eusebius of Caesarea, who lived in the fourth century AD, stated that – according to some earlier authors – John the apostle was also the author of Revelation, that he was the leader of the churches in Asia Minor, that he was banished to the island of Patmos for being a witness for Jesus Christ during the reign of Emperor Domitian, that he was released after the death of Domitian and was buried in Ephesus after his death[151].

Although one can agree with most of what Eusebius reported, it cannot be confirmed that the author of Revelation and the apostle of Jesus were the same person. This confusion arises from the fact that there is evidence that the apostle John moved to Ephesus with Mary, Jesus' mother, and that he and the author of Revelation, who was also called John and who also lived in Ephesus, were as a result confused with each other and thought to be the same person.[152]

Eusebius adds – in contrast with his earlier statement – that, according to Papias, who knew some of the apostles personally, the author of Revelation was known as John the "presbyter" to distinguish him from the apostle.[153] Elsewhere, Eusebius wrote:[154]

> "[T]here were two persons in Asia that bore the same name [of John], and that there were two tombs in Ephesus, each of which, even to the present day, is called John's. It is important to notice this. For it is probable that it was the second, if one is not willing to admit that it was the first that saw the Revelation, which is ascribed by name to John."

The fact that there were two different graves or tombs of men called John in Ephesus seems to settle the issue that the author of Revelation and the apostle, the author of the proto-gospel, were two different persons.

Date and Place of Origin of the Proto-Gospel of John

It may be possible to date the narrative parts of the Gospel of John

---

[151] Eusebius, *Historia Ecclesiastica,* Liber III/XVIII/1-5; XX/10-11; & XXIII/5; Liber V/XXIV/3.
[152] Chadwick, "John the Apostle, Saint."
[153] Eusebius, *Historia Ecclesiatics,* Liber III/XXXIX/5 & 7.
[154] Eusebius, *Historia Ecclesiastica* Liber III/XXXXIX/6.

since there are no hints that Jerusalem and its temple were destroyed during the Jewish War of AD 66–70. This document may, therefore, be dated to the fifties or early sixties of the first century AD, more or less contemporary with Paul's letters.

John 5: 2 implies an intact Jerusalem before the war: "Now in Jerusalem by the sheep gate, there is a pool, which is called in Hebrew, 'Bethesda,' having five porches." The present tense in this sentence, namely "is" (Greek: ἔστιν – *estin*) and "having" (Greek: ἔχουσα – *echousa*) can only mean one thing, namely that that pool was situated in an undamaged Jerusalem at the time when the Proto-Gospel of John was written.

The presence of the mythological or magical elements in the Proto-Gospel's description of the "signs" or miracles may be an indication of a somewhat later date of composition, probably during the early sixties AD – three decades after Jesus' ministry. These mythological and magical elements are absent in the earlier Q Document.

According to Paul Anderson, the Signs Gospel of John seems to have originated "in pre-70 C.E. Palestine". It was meant to convince the Jewish followers of John the Baptist to believe in Jesus as the Christ. It reflects the tensions between Galileans and the Judeans or the "Jews" who are often mentioned in this gospel, (see, for instance, John 1: 19).[155]

It differs in various respects from the Q Document and the sayings in the M Document, which may be seen as the oldest pieces of Christian literature at our disposal. Q and parts of M mostly contain sayings of Jesus, while the Proto-Gospel of John is a narrative, describing episodes in the life of Jesus of Nazareth.

John was evidently not aware of Q and M and he does not quote from them in his proto-gospel. There are some parallels

---

[155] Anderson, "The John, Jesus, and History Project", 20.

between this proto-gospel and the other canonical gospels and it may be assumed that these parallels, probably taken from different sources, describe real events and words of Jesus as remembered by different followers of Jesus.

The detailed descriptions of the geography of Palestine and the customs of the Jews, indicate an intended readership of Greek-speakers who didn't know Palestine.

Commentary on Proto-John

In the pages that follow, the different episodes in Proto-John, including the so-called Signs Gospel, will be discussed against the background of the historical method described in the Introduction to this book, as well as from the perspective of Jesus as the king-in-waiting of Israel, as explained in Chapter 2.

John the Baptist's Appearance
John 1: 6, 19–27

6.	There came a man, sent from God, whose name was John.
19.	This is John's testimony, when the Jews sent priests and Levites from Jerusalem to ask him, "Who are you?"
20.	He confessed, and didn't deny, but he confessed, "I am not the Christ."
21.	They asked him, "What then? Are you Elijah?" He said, "I am not." "Are you the prophet?" He answered, "No."
22.	They said therefore to him, "Who are you? Give us an answer to take back to those who sent us. What do you say about yourself?"
23.	He said, "I am the voice of one crying in the wilderness, 'Make straight the way of the Lord,' as Isaiah the prophet said."

24.	The ones who had been sent were from the Pharisees.
25.	They asked him, "Why then do you baptize, if you are not the Christ, nor Elijah, nor the Prophet?"
26.	John answered them, "I baptize in water, but among you stands one whom you don't know,
27.	he who comes after me, whose sandal strap I'm not worthy to untie."

The "Jews" from Jerusalem, members of the Judean elite and the party of the Pharisees, did not trust this wild prophet named John, due to his connections to the Essenes and who criticized the priests at the temple for being false priests and frauds, although his father was also a priest.

John's denial that he was the Messiah and his affirmation that he only prepared the way for the Messiah, was meant to convince the disciples and followers of John after his death – probably during AD 30 – that Jesus was the real Messiah.

Calling of the Disciples
John 1: 35–51

35.	Again, on the next day, John was standing with two of his disciples,
36.	and he looked at Jesus as he walked, and said, "Behold, the Lamb of God!"
37.	The two disciples heard him speak, and they followed Jesus.
38.	Jesus turned, and saw them following, and said to them, "What are you looking for?" They said to him, "Rabbi" (which is to say, being interpreted, Teacher), "where are you staying?"

39.	He said to them, "Come, and see." They came and saw where he was staying, and they stayed with him that day. It was about the tenth hour.
40.	One of the two who heard John, and followed him, was Andrew, Simon Peter's brother.
41.	He first found his own brother, Simon, and said to him, "We have found the Messiah!" (which is, being interpreted, Christ).
42.	He brought him to Jesus. Jesus looked at him, and said, "You are Simon the son of Jonah. You shall be called Cephas" (which is by interpretation, Peter).
43.	On the next day, he was determined to go forth into Galilee, and he found Philip. Jesus said to him, "Follow me."
44.	Philip was from Bethsaida, of the city of Andrew and Peter.
45.	Philip found Nathanael, and said to him, "We have found him, of whom Moses in the law, and the prophets, wrote: Jesus of Nazareth, the son of Joseph."
46.	Nathanael said to him, "Can any good thing come out of Nazareth?" Philip said to him, "Come and see."
47.	Jesus saw Nathanael coming to him, and said about him, "Behold, an Israelite indeed, in whom is no deceit!"
48.	Nathanael says to him, "How do you know me?" Jesus answered him, "Before Philip called you, when you were under the fig tree, I saw you."
49.	Nathanael answered him, "Rabbi, you are the Son of God! You are King of Israel!"
50.	Jesus answered him, "Because I told you, 'I saw you underneath the fig tree,' do you believe? You will see greater things than these."

51.	He said to him, "Most assuredly, I tell you, hereafter you will see heaven opened, and the angels of God ascending and descending on the Son of Man."

This whole passage was meant to demonstrate that Jesus was *the* Messiah, the Son of God, the expected king of Israel. The exclamation of Nathanael demonstrates that the expressions "Son of God" and "king of Israel" are synonyms.

There is an allusion to the day of his baptism by John the Baptist when a solar eclipse most probably occurred and the angels (the stars) became visible. Jesus evidently thought that the establishment of the Israelite monarchy would happen with the aid of an army of angels from heaven (see Chapters 2 and 3).

Jesus started recruiting followers and supporters – most probably in Galilee and from among his fellow-Essenes.

The Wedding at Cana
John 2: 1–11

1.	The third day, there was a marriage in Cana of Galilee. Jesus' mother was there.
2.	Jesus also was invited, with his disciples, to the marriage.
3.	When the wine ran out, Jesus' Mother said to him, "They have no wine."
4.	Jesus said to her, "Woman, what does that have to do with you and me? My hour has not yet come."
5.	His mother said to the servants, "Whatever he says to you, do it."
6.	Now there were six water pots of stone set there after the Jews' manner of purifying, containing two or three metretes apiece.

7.	Jesus said to them, "Fill the water pots with water." They filled them up to the brim.
8.	He said to them, "Now draw some out, and take it to the ruler of the feast." They took it.
9.	When the ruler of the feast tasted the water now become wine, and didn't know where it came from (but the servants who had drawn the water knew), the ruler of the feast called the bridegroom,
10.	and said to him, "Everyone serves the good wine first, and when the guests have drunk freely, then that which is worse. You have kept the good wine until now!"
11.	This beginning of his signs Jesus did in Cana of Galilee, and revealed his glory. His disciples believed in him

Jesus' remark to his mother, "My hour has not yet come," is repeated in John 7: 6 & 30; 8: 20; 12:23; and 13:1. It is usually interpreted that the time for Jesus to be crucified and be resurrected has not yet arrived. A more plausible explanation is that he meant to make it clear that the time was not yet ripe to re-establish the monarchy in Israel and drive the Romans away.

It is told in verse 11 that this first "sign" (Greek: σημεῖον – *semeion*, meaning "sign" or "miracle") of Jesus had the result that it "revealed his glory" so that "his disciples believed in him." The theme of belief in Jesus occurs frequently in this gospel.

People of our age may accept that Jesus really attended a wedding, but that he magically turned water into wine, does seem incredible (and chemically impossible). There is, though, the possibility that the story got distorted through the decades and that Jesus somehow got hold of a new supply of wine, without performing any miracles or magic.

Cleansing of the Temple
John 2: 12–25

12.	After this, he went down to Capernaum, he, and his mother, his brothers, and his disciples; and there they stayed not many days.
13.	The Passover of the Jews was at hand, and Jesus went up to Jerusalem.
14.	He found in the temple those who sold oxen, sheep, and doves, and the changers of money sitting.
15.	He made a whip of cords, and threw all out of the temple, both the sheep and the oxen; and he poured out the changers' money, and overthrew their tables.
16.	To those who sold the doves, he said, "Take these things out of here! Don't make my Father's house a marketplace!"
17.	His disciples remembered that it was written, "Zeal for your house will eat me up."
18.	The Jews therefore answered him, "What sign do you show to us, seeing that you do these things?"
19.	Jesus answered them, "Destroy this temple, and in three days I will raise it up."
20.	The Jews therefore said, "Forty–six years was this temple in building, and will you raise it up in three days?"
21.	But he spoke of the temple of his body.
22.	When therefore he was raised from the dead, his disciples remembered that he said this, and they believed the scripture, and the word which Jesus had said.

> 23. Now when he was in Jerusalem at the Passover, during the feast, many believed in his name, observing his signs which he did.
> 24. But Jesus didn't trust himself to them, because he knew all people,
> 25. and because he didn't need for anyone to testify concerning man; for he himself knew what was in man

Jesus seemed to have made Capernaum the headquarters of his campaign of becoming the king of Israel. At this stage, he did not trust the Judeans of Jerusalem yet to support him and, therefore, he did not campaign openly there, although he became well-known on account of the "signs" he performed there. Most probably, the Essene community in Jerusalem supported him, but the temple elite did not.

The story of the throwing out of the dishonest merchants and money exchangers placed this event at the beginning of Jesus' ministry – in contrast with the other gospels, where it took place shortly before the crucifixion.

It must be noted that the temple authorities did not stop Jesus, probably because he was already a popular figure due to all his signs. These businessmen put up their stalls on the temple mount, but not inside the temple itself. The Sanhedrin had no jurisdiction there and, therefore, did not intervene.[156]

Jesus' announcement about the temple of his body that would be destroyed and restored three days later, was probably meant to prepare the readers of this gospel for the passion story. There are also signs in the Synoptic Gospels that Jesus anticipated his crucifixion by the Romans, but that he and some helpers

---

[156] Cohn, *The Trial and Death of Jesus*, 54–59.

conspired to rescue him from the cross to bolster his claim to be the Messiah (see Chapter 7).

Nicodemus Visits Jesus
John 3: 1–2, 22–24

1.	Now there was a man of the Pharisees named Nicodemus, a ruler of the Jews.
2.	The same came to him by night, and said to him, "Rabbi, we know that you are a teacher come from God, for no one can do these signs that you do, unless God is with him."
22.	After these things, Jesus came with his disciples into the land of Judea. He stayed there with them, and baptized.
23.	John also was baptizing in Enon near Salim, because there was much water there. They came, and were baptized.
24.	For John was not yet thrown into prison.

This passage makes the point that at least one prominent Jew believed that Jesus had a divine mission and consulted him during the night in secret. Thereafter, Jesus moved around in the Judean countryside, preaching and baptizing, just as John the Baptist, while recruiting followers for his campaign.

The Samaritan Woman
John 4: 1–9, 16–19, 27–30, 39–44

1.	Therefore when the Lord knew that the Pharisees had heard that Jesus was making and baptizing more disciples than John
2.	(although Jesus himself didn't baptize, but his disciples),
3.	he left Judea, and departed again into Galilee.

4.	He needed to pass through Samaria.
5.	So he came to a city of Samaria, called Sychar, near the parcel of ground that Jacob gave to his son, Joseph.
6.	Jacob's well was there. Jesus therefore, being tired from his journey, sat down by the well. It was about the sixth hour.
7.	A woman of Samaria came to draw water. Jesus said to her, "Give me a drink."
8.	For his disciples had gone away into the city to buy food.
9.	The Samaritan woman therefore said to him, "How is it that you, being a Jew, ask for a drink from me, a Samaritan woman?" (For Jews have no dealings with Samaritans.)
16.	Jesus said to her, "Go, call your husband, and come here."
17.	The woman answered, "I have no husband." Jesus said to her, "You said well, 'I have no husband,'
18.	for you have had five husbands; and he whom you now have is not your husband. This you have said truly."
19.	The woman said to him, "Sir, I perceive that you are a prophet.
27.	At this, his disciples came. They marveled that he was speaking with a woman; yet no one said, "What are you looking for?" or, "Why do you speak with her?"
28.	So the woman left her water pot, and went away into the city, and said to the people,
29.	"Come, see a man who told me everything that I did. Can this be the Christ?"
30.	They went out of the city, and were coming to him.

39.	From that city many of the Samaritans believed in him because of the word of the woman, who testified, 'He told me everything that I did."
40.	So when the Samaritans came to him, they begged him to stay with them. He stayed there two days.
41.	Many more believed because of his word.
42.	They said to the woman, "Now we believe, not because of your speaking; for we have heard for ourselves, and know that this is indeed the Christ, the Savior of the world."
43.	After the two days he went forth from there and went into Galilee.
44.	For Jesus himself testified that a prophet has no honor in his own country.

The source of this story is probably John himself, who overheard Jesus' conversation with this Samaritan woman and reported it to the author of his gospel some years later.

To reach Galilee, Jesus' heartland, he had to travel through Samaria. As pointed out in this story, the Jews did not accept the inhabitants of Samaria as fellow-Jews because they were not pure Israelites. They were the descendants of Israelites who were not deported by the Assyrians when Samaria was conquered in 722 BC and pagan immigrants, placed there by the Assyrians.[157]

Some of Jesus' disciples went into the town of Sychar to buy food since there were no Essenes where they could enjoy hospitality. Jesus struck up a conversation with a local woman who came to fetch water from the well. Jesus did not have a bucket or jug to draw water from the well and asked the woman for a drink of water.

How Jesus knew about her various marriages and affairs, is

---

[157] Enc Brit, "Samaritan".

not told. Perhaps some bystanders informed Jesus about her reputation. She concluded that Jesus was a prophet and even the Messiah and she fetched some of the townspeople who listened to Jesus who preached to them. They believed in him after he had lingered there for two days.

Jesus Heals a Nobleman's Son
John 4: 45–54

45.	So when he came into Galilee, the Galileans received him, having seen all the things that he did in Jerusalem at the feast, for they also went to the feast.
46.	He came therefore again to Cana of Galilee, where he made the water into wine. There was a certain nobleman whose son was sick at Capernaum.
47.	When he heard that Jesus had come out of Judea into Galilee, he went to him, and begged him that he would come down and heal his son, for he was at the point of death.
48.	Jesus therefore said to him, "Unless you see signs and wonders, you will in no way believe."
49.	The nobleman said to him, "Sir, come down before my child dies."
50.	Jesus said to him, "Go your way. Your son lives." The man believed the word that Jesus spoke to him, and he went his way.
51.	As he was now going down, his servants met him and reported, saying "your child lives!"
52.	So he inquired of them the hour when he began to get better. They said therefore to him, "Yesterday at the seventh hour, the fever left him."

53.	So the father knew that it was at that hour in which Jesus said to him, "Your son lives." He believed, as did his whole house.
54.	This is again the second sign that Jesus did, having come out of Judea into Galilee.

According to John's chronology, this was the second "sign" that Jesus performed in Galilee. John 2: 23 mentions other signs performed in Jerusalem after the first sign and before this one.

This incredible "sign" only makes sense if one believes in magical cures over a distance. It is quite possible that Jesus was somehow involved in the healing of this boy, but certainly not in the way described. It is possible that the boy got better on his own and that his improvement was attributed to the presence of Jesus.

Jesus' saying in vs 48 ("Unless you see signs and wonders, you will in no way believe") seems strange since Jesus performed his previous signs with the explicit goal of convincing people to believe in him as the Messiah.

The Paralyzed Man at the Pool of Bethesda
John 5: 1–16

1.	After these things, there was a feast of the Jews, and Jesus went up to Jerusalem.
2.	Now in Jerusalem by the sheep gate, there is a pool, which is called in Hebrew, "Bethesda," having five porches.
3.	In these lay a great multitude of those who were sick, blind, lame, or paralyzed, waiting for the moving of the water;
5.	A certain man was there, who had been sick for thirty-eight years.

6.	When Jesus saw him lying there, and knew that he had been sick for a long time, he asked him, "Do you want to be made well?"
7.	The sick man answered him, "Sir, I have no one to put me into the pool when the water is stirred up, but while I'm coming, another steps down before me."
8.	Jesus said to him, "Arise, take up your mat, and walk."
9.	Immediately, the man was made well, and took up his mat and walked. Now it was the Sabbath on that day.
10.	So the Jews said to him who was cured, "It is the Sabbath. It is not lawful for you to carry your mat."
11.	He answered them, "He who made me well, the same said to me, 'Take up your mat, and walk.'"
12.	Then they asked him, "Who is the man who said to you, 'Take up your mat, and walk'?"
13.	But he who was healed didn't know who it was, for Jesus had withdrawn, a crowd being in the place.
14.	Afterward Jesus found him in the temple, and said to him, "Behold, you are made well. Sin no more, so that nothing worse happens to you."
15.	The man went away, and told the Jews that it was Jesus who had made him well.
16.	For this cause the Jews persecuted Jesus, and sought to kill him, because he did these things on the Sabbath.

The use of the present tense in verse 2 ("there *is* a pool, which *is called* in Hebrew, 'Bethesda' *having* five porches") is a sign that the Proto-Gospel of John was written before the Jewish War and the destruction of Jerusalem with its temple during AD 66–70.

Certain aspects of this fantastic story may be true. Archeologists have found the remains of the pool of Bethesda in Jerusalem. It consisted of a pool that could be used for ritual baths and a reservoir with a supply of fresh water to replenish the pool if the water level sank too low. That may have accounted for the "stirring" of the water at certain times.[158]

It is rather unbelievable that this pool had magical healing properties. One may also ask: how was Jesus able to do mind reading and know that the man was ill for thirty-eight years? Who brought the man to this pool and looked after his needs, but was unable to help him into the water?

It may be possible that Jesus visited the pool and helped a man with his knowledge of the healing arts, obtained from the Essenes. That this story acquired some legendary aspects as time went on, seems probable.

That some Jewish religious leaders were dismayed that Jesus helped this man on the Sabbath, may also be true. That they plotted to kill Jesus on account of this sign, seems less likely.

Feeding the Crowd
John 6: 1–15

1.	After these things, Jesus went away to the other side of the sea of Galilee, which is also called the Sea of Tiberias.
2.	A great multitude followed him, because they saw the signs which he did on those who were sick.
3.	Jesus went up into the mountain, and he sat there with his disciples.
4.	Now the Passover, the feast of the Jews, was at hand.

---

[158] Biblical Archaeology Societ, "The Bethesda Pool."

5.	Jesus therefore lifting up his eyes, and seeing that a great multitude was coming to him, said to Philip, "Where are we to buy bread, that these may eat?"
6.	This he said to test him, for he himself knew what he would do.
7.	Philip answered him, "Two hundred denarii worth of bread is not sufficient for them, that everyone of them may receive a little."
8.	One of his disciples, Andrew, Simon Peter's brother, said to him,
9.	"There is a boy here who has five barley loaves and two fish, but what are these among so many?"
10.	Jesus said, "Have the people sit down." Now there was much grass in that place. So the men sat down, in number about five thousand.
11.	Jesus took the loaves; and having given thanks, he distributed to the disciples, and the disciples to those who were sitting down; likewise also of the fish as much as they desired.
12.	When they were filled, he said to his disciples, "Gather up the .broken pieces which are left over, that nothing be lost."
13.	So they gathered them up, and filled twelve baskets with broken pieces from the five barley loaves, which were left over by those who had eaten.
14.	When therefore the people saw the sign which Jesus did, they said, "This is truly the prophet who comes into the world."

> 15. Jesus therefore, perceiving that they were about to come and take him by force, to make him king, withdrew again into the mountain by himself.

This story ends with the crowd that wanted to proclaim Jesus as their king, which shows that his campaign to recruit followers was bearing fruit. He, though, thought that it was too early to claim the throne and he departed into the mountain.

His "sign", by feeding the crowd, convinced the people that he was "the prophet who comes into the world". With "world" (κόσμος – kosmos), the gospel meant the "country" or "nation" of Israel.

Two details need clarification: did Jesus simply confiscate or steal the boy's loaves and fishes? What type of magic did Jesus perform to feed a big crowd with only five loaves of bread and two fishes – unless the crowd brought their own lunches along, with the result that no real miracle occurred?

Jesus Walks on the Water
John 6: 16–24

> 16. When evening came, his disciples went down to the sea,
> 17. and they entered into the boat, and were going over the sea to Capernaum. It was now dark, and Jesus had not come to them.
> 18. The sea was rising by reason of a great wind that blew.
> 19. When therefore they had rowed about twenty–five or thirty stadia, they saw Jesus walking on the sea, and drawing near to the boat; and they were afraid.
> 20. But he said to them, "It is I. Don't be afraid."

21.	They were willing therefore to receive him into the boat. Immediately the boat was at the land where they were going.
22.	On the next day, the multitude that stood on the other side of the sea saw that there was no other boat there, except the one which his disciples had entered, and that Jesus hadn't entered with his disciples into the boat, but his disciples went away alone.
23.	However boats from Tiberias came near to the place where they ate the bread after the Lord had given thanks.
24.	When the multitude therefore saw that Jesus wasn't there, neither his disciples, they themselves got into the boats, and came to Capernaum, seeking Jesus.

It may have seemed to the disciples on the boat that Jesus was walking on the water. We are told that the boat reached the shore immediately after Jesus joined the disciples, which may mean that Jesus walked along the shore and that it only appeared as if he was walking on the water when it was dark.

Jesus Goes to Jerusalem
John 7: 1–14

1.	After these things, Jesus walked in Galilee, for he would not walk in Judea, because the Jews sought to kill him.
2.	Now the feast of the Jews, the Feast of Booths, was at hand.
3.	His brothers therefore said to him, "Depart from here, and go into Judea, that your disciples also may see your works which you do.
4.	For no man does anything in secret, and himself seeks to be known openly. If you do these things, reveal yourself to the world."

5.	For even his brothers didn't believe in him.
6.	Jesus therefore said to them, "My time has not yet come, but your time is always ready.
7.	The world can't hate you, but it hates me, because I testify about it, that its works are evil.
8.	You go up to the feast. I am not yet going up to this feast, because my time is not yet fulfilled."
9.	Having said these things to them, he stayed in Galilee.
10	But when his brothers had gone up to the feast, then he also went up, not publicly, but as it were in secret.
11.	The Jews therefore sought him at the feast, and said, "Where is he?"
12.	There was much murmuring among the multitudes concerning him. Some said, "He is a good man." Others said, "Not so, but he leads the multitude astray."
13.	Yet no one spoke openly of him for fear of the Jews.
14.	But when it was now the midst of the feast, Jesus went up into the temple and taught.

This story is confusing and it may be due to bad editing. On the one hand, Jesus was unwilling to attend the feast in Jerusalem out of fear that the Judeans might kill him and because the time was not yet right to become king. He declined the invitation of his brothers to accompany them and to perform some signs in Jerusalem so that his disciples may believe in him (which they already did on account of his precious signs).

Somewhat later, he did go to Jerusalem and taught the people at the temple – despite his previous reluctance to do just that.

It is not clear what the point is that John wanted to make with this story, except to show that Jesus had enemies.

Different Opinions about Jesus
John 7: 40–53; 8: 1–2, 22

40.	Many of the multitude therefore, when they heard these words, said, "This is truly the prophet."
41.	Others said, "This is the Christ." But some said, "What, does the Christ come out of Galilee?
42.	Hasn't the scripture said that the Christ comes of the seed of David, and from Bethlehem, the village where David was?"
43.	So there arose a division in the multitude because of him.
44.	Some of them would have taken him, but no one laid hands on him.
45.	The officers therefore came to the chief priests and Pharisees, and they said to them, "Why didn't you bring him?"
46.	The officers answered, "No man ever spoke like this man!"
47.	The Pharisees therefore answered them, "Are you also led astray?
48.	Has any of the rulers believed in him, or of the Pharisees?
49.	But this cursed multitude doesn't know the law."
50.	Nicodemus (he who came to him by night, being one of them) said to them,
51.	"Does our law judge a man, unless it first hears from him personally and knows what he does?"
52.	They answered him, "Are you also from Galilee? Search, and see that no prophet has arisen out of Galilee."

There seems to have been some confusion in Jerusalem about who and what Jesus really was. Some people regarded him as the promised prophet and Messiah, while others doubted whether the Messiah could have come from Galilee and not from Bethlehem. They relied on the prophecies in Ps 132: 11; Isa 11: 1; Jer 23: 5; and Mic 5: 3, where it was promised that a descendant of David – who hailed from Bethlehem – would be the Messiah.

It seems that the Jewish authorities in Jerusalem issued an arrest warrant for him, although it is not clear what the charge was, except that he was purportedly leading the people astray. Such a charge would not have held water since the teachings of Jesus, as reported in the gospels, never amounted to a rejection or contradiction of the Law of Moses or the writings of the prophets.[159]

He was not apprehended, despite the warrant of arrest "because his hour had not yet come".

The Adulterous Woman
John 7: 53–8: 11

53.	Everyone went to his own house,
1.	but Jesus went to the Mount of Olives.
2.	At dawn, he came again into the temple, and all the people came to him. He sat down, and taught them.
3.	The scribes and the Pharisees brought a woman taken in adultery. Having set her in the midst,
4.	they told him, "Teacher, we found this woman in adultery, in the very act.
5.	Now in our law, Moses commanded us to stone such. What then do you say about her?"

---

[159] Cohn, *The Trial and Death of Jesus*, 53–54.

> 6. They said this testing him, that they might have something to accuse him of. But Jesus stooped down, and wrote on the ground with his finger, as if he didn't hear.
> 7. But when they continued asking him, he lifted himself up, and said to them, "He who is without sin among you, let him throw the first stone at her."
> 8. Again he stooped down, and with his finger wrote on the ground.
> 9. They, when they heard it, being convicted by their conscience, went out one by one, beginning from the oldest, even to the last. Jesus was left alone with the woman where she was, in the midst.
> 10. Jesus lifted himself up, and seeing no one but the woman, said to her, "Woman, where are they? Did no one condemn you?"
> 11. She said, "No one, Lord." Jesus said, "Neither do I condemn you. Go your way. From now on, sin no more."

This passage is obviously a later addition to the gospel because it doesn't appear in the oldest manuscripts. Since it was not part of the original Proto-Gospel of John, it is repeated here with a different letter type. It does, yet, seem to rest on an old tradition and at one point a scribe inserted it while making a new copy of the gospel. It is in accordance with our knowledge about Jesus as recorded in the gospels and may well be a genuine recollection of Jesus.

Bible students have always wondered what Jesus wrote on the ground. A good guess would be: "Where is the man with whom this woman was caught in the act?"

Jesus Opens the Eyes of a Blind Man
John 9: 1–30 & 10: 19–21

> 1. As he passed by, he saw a man blind from his birth.
> 2. His disciples asked him, "Rabbi, who sinned, this man or his parents, that he was born blind?"

3.	Jesus answered, "Neither did this man sin, nor his parents. But, that the works of God might be revealed in him.
6.	When he had said this, he spat on the ground, made mud with the saliva, anointed the blind man's eyes with the mud,
7.	and said to him, "Go, wash in the pool of Siloam" (which means "Sent"). So he went away, washed, and came seeing.
8.	The neighbors therefore, and those who saw that he was blind, before, said, "Isn't this he who sat and begged?"
9.	Others said, "It is he." Still others said, "He is like him." He said, "I am he."
10.	They said therefore to him, "How were your eyes opened?"
11.	He answered, "A man called Jesus made mud, anointed my eyes, and said to me, "Go to the pool of Siloam, and wash." So I went away and washed, and I received sight."
12.	Then they asked him, "Where is he?" He said, "I don't know."
13.	They brought him who before was blind to the Pharisees.
14.	It was a Sabbath when Jesus made the mud and opened his eyes.
15.	Again therefore the Pharisees also asked him how he received his sight. He said to them, "He put mud on my eyes, I washed, and I see."
16.	Some therefore of the Pharisees said, "This man is not from God, because he doesn't keep the Sabbath." Others said, "How can a man who is a sinner do such signs?" There was division among them.
17.	Therefore they asked the blind man again, "What do you say about him, in that he opened your eyes?" He said, "He is a prophet."

18. The Jews therefore did not believe concerning him, that he had been blind, and had received his sight, until they called the parents of him who had received his sight,
19. and asked them, "Is this your son, who you say was born blind? How then does he now see?"
20. His parents answered them, "We know that this is our son, and that he was born blind;
21. but how he now sees, we don't know; or who opened his eyes, we don't know. He is of age. Ask him. He will speak for himself."
22. His parents said these things because they feared the Jews; for the Jews had already agreed that if any man would confess him as Christ, he would be put out of the synagogue.
23. Therefore his parents said, "He is of age. Ask him."
24. So they called the man who was blind a second time, and said to him, "Give glory to God. We know that this man is a sinner."
25. He therefore answered, "I don't know if he is a sinner. One thing I know: that though I was blind, now I see."
26. They said to him again, "What did he do to you? How did he open your eyes?"
27. He answered them, "I told you already, and you didn't listen. Why do you want to hear it again? Do you also want to become his disciples?"
28. They became abusive towards him and said, "You are his disciple, but we are disciples of Moses.
29. We know that God has spoken to Moses. But as for this man, we don't know where he comes from."

30.	The man answered them, "How amazing! You don't know where he comes from, yet he opened my eyes.
19.	Therefore a division arose again among the Jews because of these words.
20.	Many of them said, "He has a demon, and is mad! Why do you listen to him?"
21.	Others said, "These are not the sayings of one possessed with a demon. Can a demon open the eyes of the blind?"

This lengthy passage starts with an important question: "Rabbi, who sinned, this man or his parents, that he was born blind?" Jesus told his disciples that this condition was not to be seen as the punishment by God, but "that the works of God might be revealed in him" – whatever that means. Perhaps Jesus thought that God had made this man blind to give him an opportunity to perform a miracle by restoring the man's sight.

The rest of the story deals with two themes: Jesus repairing the sight of a blind man and the interrogation of the previously blind man and his parents by the Jewish religious leaders because the miracle took place on a Sabbath.

This healing miracle is yet another case of magic. The science of neurology teaches us that if somebody has been born blind, it won't help to treat that person's eyes when he is grown-up because the brain centers for sight never got an opportunity to develop.[160]

People of previous centuries who read this story would have found this astounding tale to be a confirmation that Jesus was indeed a prophet and the Messiah. People of our age will find it difficult to swallow this story. There is simply no way that a little bit of mud

---

[160] Kolb & Wishaw, *Fundamentals*, 480–81.

could have had these healing powers.

It is possible that Jesus did something to help this man, who might have become blind due to a traumatic shock and that Jesus helped him to overcome the trauma,[161] but that the story acquired legendary aspects after some time.

The result of the debate by the religious authorities was that certain Judeans believed in Jesus.

Jesus Escapes Across the Jordan
John 10: 22–23 & 39–42

22.	It was the Feast of the Dedication at Jerusalem.
23.	It was winter, and Jesus was walking in the temple, in Solomon's porch.
39.	They sought again to seize him, and he went forth out of their hand.
40.	He went away again beyond the Jordan into the place where John was at the first baptizing, and there he stayed.
41.	Many came to him. They said, "John indeed did no sign, but everything whatever that John said about this man is true."
42.	Many believed in him there.

Jesus must have gotten wind of the plan of the religious leaders to question him, but he escaped and retired to a quiet spot across the Jordan. Some of his followers also went there and they confirmed that John the Baptist was right about Jesus with the result that they believed in him.

The Raising of Lazarus
John 11: 1–45

---

[161] Kolb & Wishaw, *Fundamentals*, 563.

1.	Now a certain man was sick, Lazarus of Bethany, of the village of Mary and her sister, Martha.
2.	It was that Mary who anointed the Lord with ointment, and wiped his feet with her hair, whose brother, Lazarus, was sick.
3.	The sisters therefore sent to him, saying, "Lord, behold, he for whom you have great affection is sick."
5.	Now Jesus loved Martha, and her sister, and Lazarus.
6.	When therefore he heard that he was sick, he stayed at that time two days in the place where he was.
7.	Then after this he said to the disciples, "Let's go into Judea again."
17.	So when Jesus came, he found that he had been in the tomb four days already.
18.	Now Bethany was near Jerusalem, about fifteen stadia away.
19.	Many of the Jews had come to Martha and Mary, to console them concerning their brother.
20.	Therefore Martha, when she heard that Jesus was coming, went and met him, but Mary stayed in the house.
21.	Therefore Martha said to Jesus, "Lord, if you would have been here, my brother wouldn't have died.
22.	Even now I know that, whatever you ask of God, God will give you."
28.	When she had said this, she went away, and called Mary, her sister, secretly, saying, "The Teacher is here, and is calling you."
29.	She, when she heard this, arose quickly, and went to him.

30. Now Jesus had not yet come into the village, but was in the place where Martha met him.

31. Then the Jews who were with her in the house, and were consoling her, when they saw Mary, that she rose up quickly and went out, followed her, saying, "She is going to the tomb to weep there."

32. Mary therefore, when she came to where Jesus was, and saw him, fell down at his feet, saying to him, "Lord, if you would have been here, my brother wouldn't have died."

33. When Jesus therefore saw her weeping, and the Jews weeping who came with her, he groaned in the spirit, and was troubled,

34. and said, "Where have you laid him?" They told him, "Lord, come and see."

35. Jesus wept.

36. The Jews therefore said, "See how much affection he had for him!"

37. Some of them said, "Couldn't this man, who opened the eyes of him who was blind, have also caused that this man wouldn't die?"

38. Jesus therefore, again groaning in himself, came to the tomb. Now it was a cave, and a stone lay against it.

39. Jesus said, "Take away the stone." Martha, the sister of him who was dead, said to him, "Lord, by this time there is a stench, for he has been dead four days."

40. Jesus said to her, "Didn't I tell you that if you believed, you would see God's glory?"

41. So they took away the stone from the place where the dead man was lying. Jesus lifted up his eyes, and said,

43.	"Lazarus, come out!"
44.	He who was dead came out, bound hand and foot with wrappings, and his face was wrapped around with a cloth. Jesus said to them, "Free him, and let him go."
45.	Therefore many of the Jews, who came to Mary and saw that which Jesus did, believed in him.

There are some curious and inexplicable aspects to this story.

First of all: the episode mentioned in verse 2 of Mary anointing the feet of Jesus, is repeated in John 12: 3. However, according to Matthew 26: 6–7 and Mark 14: 3, this happened in the house of Simon the Leper in Bethany, not the home of Lazarus and his sisters.

The Raising of Lazarus – Mosaic, Church of San Apolinar Nuovo. 530's. Ravenna, Italy

Secondly: why did Jesus wait two days before starting his journey to Judea after getting the news of Lazarus' illness? Why did he not rush off immediately? No reason for this delay is given, although it might have been that Jesus was wary of the fact that the religious authorities were plotting to have him arrested and questioned.

Although the whole story emphasizes the point that Lazarus was already very much dead and that he was laid up in a tomb, Jesus managed to revive him magically by just calling out. This is another "sign" of Jesus, which caused the bystanders to believe in him as the Messiah.

The only rational explanation for this miracle is that Lazarus was not really dead and that he recovered on his own after falling into a coma or a state of unconsciousness, which was interpreted as death. When Jesus peered into the tomb, he may have seen that Lazarus was moving and called upon him to come out.

The fact that this story contains many irrelevant details may be a sign that something really happened in Bethany, but that it acquired legendary and even mythological aspects after many years before being written down.

The Jews Plot to Kill Jesus
John 11: 46–54

46.	But some of them went away to the Pharisees, and told them the things which Jesus had done.
47.	The chief priests therefore and the Pharisees gathered a council, and said, "What are we doing? For this man does many signs.
48.	If we leave him alone like this, everyone will believe in him, and the Romans will come and take away both our place and our nation."
49.	But a certain one of them, Caiaphas, being high priest that year, said to them, "You know nothing at all,

> 50. nor do you take account that it is advantageous for us that one man should die for the people, and that the whole nation not perish."
> 51. Now he didn't say this of himself, but being high priest that year, he prophesied that Jesus would die for the nation,
> 52. and not for the nation only, but that he might also gather together into one the children of God who are scattered abroad.
> 53. So from that day forth they took counsel that they might put him to death.
> 54. Jesus therefore walked no more openly among the Jews, but departed from there into the country near the wilderness, into a city called Ephraim. He stayed there with his disciples.

The only explanation for the attitude of the religious authorities for getting rid of Jesus, was that his campaign to recruit followers in his bid to become the king of Israel, caused some grave concerns and alarm. These Judeans were afraid that a rebellion by Jesus and his followers would cause the Romans to crush the revolt with dire consequences for all the Jews.

Jesus seemed to have heard of this plot against him and decided to stay away from Judea for the time being.

John's source for what was discussed at this meeting must have been some of Jesus' friends who were present and told Jesus and his disciples about it afterwards. These friends may have been Joseph of Arimathea and Nicodemus who laid Jesus in a tomb after his crucifixion (John 19: 39–40).

Jesus is Missed during the Passover
John 11: 55–57

55.	Now the Passover of the Jews was at hand. Many went up to Jerusalem out of the country before the Passover, to purify themselves.
56.	Then they sought for Jesus and spoke one with another, as they stood in the temple, "What do you think? Isn't he coming to the feast?"
57.	Now the chief priests and the Pharisees had commanded that if anyone knew where he was, he should report it, that they might seize him.

The chief priests and other Jewish leaders seemed to have panicked about the success of Jesus' efforts to gather support and they issued an order that people should report Jesus' whereabouts so that his campaign could be stopped.

Jesus Visits Lazarus' Home Again
John 12: 1–11

1.	Therefore six days before the Passover, Jesus came to Bethany, where Lazarus was, who had been dead, whom he raised from the dead.
2.	So they made him a supper there. Martha served, but Lazarus was one of those who sat at the table with him.
3.	Mary, therefore, took a pound of ointment of pure nard, very precious, and anointed the feet of Jesus, and wiped his feet with her hair. The house was filled with the fragrance of the ointment.
4.	Then Judas Iscariot, Simon's son, one of his disciples, who would betray him, said,
5.	"Why wasn't this ointment sold for three hundred denarii, and given to the poor?"

6.	Now he said this, not because he cared for the poor, but because he was a thief, and having the money box, used to steal what was put into it.
7.	But Jesus said, "Leave her alone. She has kept this for the day of my burial.
8.	For you always have the poor with you, but you don't always have me."
9.	A large crowd therefore of the Jews learned that he was there, and they came, not for Jesus' sake only, but that they might see Lazarus also, whom he had raised from the dead.
10.	But the chief priests conspired to also put Lazarus to death,
11.	because on account of him many of the Jews went away and believed in Jesus.

The reason given by John for the pouring of the ointment on Jesus' feet, is that it was done in anticipation of his coming funeral. There is the possibility that Jesus anticipated his crucifixion by the Romans on account of his campaign to restore the Israelite monarchy.

Mary, a close friend of Jesus (if not his wife as some have speculated), anointed his feet to demonstrate her belief in him as Messiah and future monarch. Judas, the treasurer of Jesus' campaign, complained about the wastage of this expensive ointment. Jesus rebuked him and defended the loving gesture of Mary.

People flocked to Lazarus' home to see him and Jesus, the Messiah, in whom they believed.

Jesus' Triumphant Entry into Jerusalem
John 12: 12–19

12.	On the next day a great multitude had come to the feast when they heard that Jesus was coming to Jerusalem,

> 13. they took the branches of the palm trees, and went out to meet him, and cried out, "Hosanna! Blessed is he who comes in the name of the Lord, the King of Israel!"
> 14. Jesus, having found a young donkey, sat on it. As it is written,
> 15. "Don't be afraid, daughter of Zion. Behold, your King comes, sitting on a donkey's colt."
> 16. His disciples didn't understand these things at first, but when Jesus was glorified, then they remembered that these things were written about him, and that they had done these things to him.
> 17. The multitude therefore that was with him when he called Lazarus out of the tomb, and raised him from the dead, was testifying.
> 18. For this cause also the multitude went and met him, because they heard that he had done this sign.
> 19. The Pharisees therefore said among themselves, "See how you accomplish nothing. Behold, the world has gone after him."

Jesus certainly thought that the time was ripe for him to claim the throne in Jerusalem. In order to fulfill a prophecy of Zechariah (9: 9–10) that the Messiah would enter Jerusalem on a donkey, Jesus deliberately procured an ass to sit on as he went along, instead of entering the city on foot as in the past.

The crowds were jubilant, waved palm branches and were yelling: "Hosanna! Blessed is he who comes in the name of the Lord, the King of Israel!" The religious authorities were understandably alarmed by this development.

No information was given on how the crowds knew that Jesus was to enter Jerusalem. The news of his imminent entry into the city must have been spread by his disciples and other supporters on his request. That was, of course before the time of TV announcements and communication through social media. Jesus' followers did a good job with the result that the crowds lined the road along which Jesus was expected to arrive from Bethany to the southeast of the city.

Albrecht Dürer: Jesus enters Jerusalem

There can be no doubt that John recorded a real event. His description agrees with the reports of the Synoptic Gospels.

Some Greeks Seek Jesus
John 12: 20–23, 36–43

20.	Now there were certain Greeks among those that went up to worship at the feast.
21.	These, therefore, came to Philip, who was from Bethsaida of Galilee, and asked him, saying, "Sir, we want to see Jesus."
22.	Philip came and told Andrew, and in turn, Andrew came with Philip, and they told Jesus.
23.	Jesus answered them, "The time has come for the Son of Man to be glorified."

36.	Jesus said these things, and he departed and hid himself from them.
37.	But though he had done so many signs before them, yet they didn't believe in him,
38.	that the word of Isaiah the prophet might be fulfilled, which he spoke, "Lord, who has believed our report? To whom has the arm of the Lord been revealed?"
39.	For this cause they couldn't believe, for Isaiah said again,
40.	"He has blinded their eyes and he hardened their heart, Lest they should see with their eyes, And perceive with their heart, And would turn, And I would heal them."
41.	Isaiah said these things when he saw his glory, and he spoke of him.
42.	Nevertheless even of the rulers many believed in him, but because of the Pharisees they didn't confess it, so that they wouldn't be put out of the synagogue,
43.	for they loved men's approval more than God's approval.

Jesus was suddenly a celebrity, with the result that some Greeks sought an interview with him. It is not clear whether they were Greek-speaking Jews who attended the Passover feast, or were Greek tourists or businessmen visiting Palestine. They, nevertheless, approached Philip and Andrew, two of Jesus disciples with Greek names and who probably knew some Greek.

Jesus – who probably also knew some Greek – assured them that the time had come for him to be "glorified" – that is, to become the king of Israel.

We are told that some unnamed people did not believe in Jesus – probably the Jewish leaders in Jerusalem. John explained that as the fulfillment of Old Testament prophecies (Isa 53: 1; 40:

10–11; 51: 5 and 9; and 44: 8–10).

Jesus Washes his Disciples' Feet
John 13: 2–17 & 21–30

2.	After supper, the devil having already put into the heart of Judas Iscariot, Simon's son, to betray him,
4.	Jesus arose from supper, and laid aside his outer garments. He took a towel, and wrapped a towel around his waist.
5.	Then he poured water into the basin, and began to wash the disciples' feet, and to wipe them with the towel that was wrapped around him.
6.	Then he came to Simon Peter. He said to him, "Lord, do you wash my feet?"
7.	Jesus answered him, "You don't know what I am doing now, but you will understand later."
8.	Peter said to him, "You will never wash my feet!" Jesus answered him, "If I don't wash you, you have no part with me."
9.	Simon Peter said to him, "Lord, not my feet only, but also my hands and my head!"
10.	Jesus said to him, "Someone who has bathed only needs to have their feet washed, but is completely clean. You are clean, but not all of you."
11.	For he knew him who would betray him, therefore he said, "You are not all clean."
12.	So when he had washed their feet, put his outer garment back on, and sat down again, he said to them, "Do you know what I have done to you?

13.	You call me, `Teacher` and `Lord.` You say so correctly, for so I am.
14.	If I then, the Lord and the Teacher, have washed your feet, you also ought to wash one another's feet.
15.	For I have given you an example, that you also should do as I have done to you.
16.	Most assuredly I tell you, a servant is not greater than his lord, neither one who is sent greater than he who sent him.
17.	If you know these things, blessed are you if you do them.
21.	When Jesus had said this, he was troubled in the spirit, and testified, "Most assuredly I tell you that one of you will betray me."
22.	The disciples looked at one another, perplexed about whom he spoke.
23.	One of his disciples, whom Jesus loved, was at the table, leaning against Jesus' breast.
24.	Simon Peter therefore beckoned to him, and said to him, "Tell us who it is of whom he speaks."
25.	He, leaning back, as he was, on Jesus' breast, asked him, "Lord, who is it?"
26.	Jesus therefore answered, "It is he who I will give this morsel to when I have dipped it." So when he had dipped the morsel, he gave it to Judas, the son of Simon Iscariot.
27.	After the morsel, then Satan entered into him. Jesus therefore said to him, "What you do, do quickly."
28.	Now no man at the table knew why he said this to him.
29.	For some thought, because Judas had the money box, that Jesus said to him, "Buy what things we need for the feast," or that he should give something to the poor.

> 30. Therefore, having received that morsel, he went out immediately. It was night.

Jesus, as an Essene, believed in humility and a simple lifestyle, as well as in cleanliness, despite regarding himself as die king-in-waiting of Israel. He performed a servant's task, by washing his disciples' feet during his last meal with them. He did this to teach them humility and to see themselves as servants of the people when the monarchy was restored and they received important and influential positions as Jesus' councilors and cabinet ministers.

Albrecht Dürer: Jesus washes Peter's feet (1514)

The disciple who sat next to Jesus and leaned against him, was always regarded as John, the "beloved disciple" and author of this gospel – or the person whose memories were written down by somebody else.

It is inconceivable that one of Jesus' disciples, Judas, would betray him to the authorities. Cohn is of the opinion that Judas was made a scapegoat to vilify the Jews as the killers of Jesus.[162] However, the fact that the gospels are unanimous about Judas' treachery must be an indication that there must be some truth in this story. It also must be remembered that the Proto-Gospel of John was written before the Jewish War – that is, before the Jews became unpopular throughout the Roman Empire.

---

[162] Cohn, *The Trial and Death of Jesus*, 64–67.

Jesus Warns Simon Peter
John 13: 34–38

34.	A new commandment I give to you, that you love one another, just like I have loved you; that you also love one another.
35.	By this everyone will know that you are my disciples, if you have love for one another."
36.	Simon Peter said to him, "Lord, where are you going?" Jesus answered, "Where I am going, you can't follow now, but you will follow afterwards."
37.	Peter said to him, "Lord, why can't I follow you even now? I will lay down my life for you."
38.	Jesus answered him, "Will you lay down your life for me? Most assuredly I tell you, the rooster won't crow until you have denied me three times.

Jesus told his disciples that they should love another and that others would recognize them as his disciples by their love for each other. In other words: he urged them to continue to help each other with their belongings and practice hospitality, as the Essenes did.

Peter wanted to know what Jesus planned for the future, but Jesus told him that the disciples could not follow him immediately – only later. Most probably, Jesus expected the Roman authorities to clamp down on him after his triumphant entry into Jerusalem where he encouraged the crowds to greet him as their king.

Peter promised to defend him and even lay down his life for Jesus. However, Jesus knew Peter's rash personality and warned him that he would deny knowing him before the night was over and the roosters greeted daybreak with their crowing.

The Arrest of Jesus
John 18: 1–3 & 7–14

1.	When Jesus had spoken these words, he went forth with his disciples over the brook Kidron, where was a garden, into which he entered, himself and his disciples.
2.	Now Judas, who betrayed him, also knew the place, for Jesus often resorted there with his disciples.
3.	Judas then, having taken a detachment of soldiers and officers from the chief priests and the Pharisees, came there with lanterns, torches, and weapons.
7.	Again therefore he asked them, "Who are you looking for?" They said, "Jesus of Nazareth."
8.	Jesus answered, "I told you that I am. If therefore you seek me, let these go their way,"
9.	that the word might be fulfilled which he spoke, "Of those whom you have given me, I have lost none."
10.	Simon Peter therefore, having a sword, drew it, and struck the high priest's servant, and cut off his right ear. The servant's name was Malchus.
11.	Jesus therefore said to Peter, "Put up the sword into its sheath. The cup which the Father has given me, shall I not drink it?"
12.	So the detachment, the commanding officer, and the officers of the Jews, seized Jesus and bound him,
13.	and led him to Annas first, for he was father–in–law to Caiaphas, who was high priest that year.
14.	Now it was Caiaphas who gave counsel to the Jews, that it was expedient that one man should die for the people.

Although John had made it quite clear on various occasions that the Jewish authorities wanted to get rid of Jesus, it was, in fact, the Roman authorities, with the aid of the high priest, who arrested Jesus.

The raiding party is called in Greek a σπεῖρα (*speira*, verses 3 and 12) – in other words, a cohort (the equivalent of a battalion) or any other type of detachment of Roman soldiers, commanded by a χιλίαρχος (*chiliarchos* – a Roman officer with the rank of tribune, verse 12), together with a number of officials of the temple police (ὑπηρέται – *hyperetai*, verses 3 and 12).

The Roman authorities took notice of Jesus' triumphant entry into Jerusalem and the reception by the crowds who hailed him as their king. He was, therefore, rounded up to prevent any rebellion or uprising against Roman rule.

According to Cohn, the Jewish authorities must have heard of the plan of Pontius Pilate, the Roman governor, to catch Jesus. It may even be that Pilate requested the Jewish leaders to help his soldiers to locate Jesus. The Jewish leaders convinced him to allow them to hold Jesus till the next day in an effort to convince Jesus to relinquish his royal aspirations. Jesus was, after all, a popular figure and they could not afford to lose the support of the population. They also did not want a fellow-Jew to be executed by the hated Romans – although they did not regard him as the Messiah and only wanted to stop his campaign to restore the monarchy.[163]

Simon Peter, the leader of the disciples and apparently head of Jesus' bodyguard, defended Jesus with his sword and chopped off the ear of a certain Malchus.[164] Jesus, the Essene pacifist, ordered Peter to put his sword away. He evidently expected an army of

---

[163] Cohn, *The Trial and Death of Jesus*, 90–93.
[164] Some older people in South Africa used to call a chamber pot a "Malchus" because this pot had only one ear or handle.

angels to drive the Romans away and, therefore, armed resistance would be unnecessary.

Most translations of vs 7 mention that "Jesus of Nazareth" was taken into custody. A more correct translation would be "Jesus the Nazorean" (or Essene).

This story of Jesus' arrest has all the hallmarks of being trustworthy – especially the fact that Jesus was taken by a company of Roman soldiers under the command of a Roman officer.

Peter Denies that he Knows Jesus
John 18: 15–27

15.	Simon Peter followed Jesus, as did another disciple. Now that disciple was known to the high priest, and entered in with Jesus into the court of the high priest;
16.	but Peter was standing at the door outside. So the other disciple, who was known to the high priest, went out and spoke to her who kept the door, and brought in Peter.
17.	Then the maid who kept the door said to Peter, "Are you also one of this man's disciples?" He said, "I am not."
18.	Now the servants and the officers were standing there, having made a fire of coals, for it was cold. They were warming themselves. Peter was with them, standing and warming himself.
19.	The high priest therefore asked Jesus of his disciples, and of his teaching.
20.	Jesus answered him, "I spoke openly to the world. I always taught in synagogues, and in the temple, where the Jews always meet. I said nothing in secret.
21.	Why do you ask me? Ask those who have heard me what I said to them. Behold, these know the things which I said."

22.	When he had said this, one of the officers standing by slapped Jesus with his hand, saying, "Do you answer the high priest like that?"
23.	Jesus answered him, "If I have spoken evil, testify of the evil; but if well, why do you beat me?"
24.	Annas sent him bound to Caiaphas, the high priest.
25.	Now Simon Peter was standing and warming himself. They said therefore to him, "Are you also one of his disciples?" He denied it, and said, "I am not."
26.	One of the servants of the high priest, being a relative of him whose ear Peter cut off, said, "Didn't I see you in the garden with him?"
27.	Peter therefore denied again, and immediately the rooster crowed.

Peter and another disciple, probably John, followed Jesus when he was taken to the residence of the retired high priest, Annas. John was known there and he could enter the building and witness the proceedings inside.

Jesus was being interrogated by Annas before being sent to Caiaphas, the incumbent high priest and Annas' son-in-law. When Jesus answered the questions full of self-confidence and defended himself, one of the guards slapped him in the face for being disrespectful. It is possible that Jesus showed his contempt and lack of regard for these religious leaders in Jerusalem, which prompted this assault.

In the meantime, Peter was standing next to a coal fire to warm himself during the cold night. He was probably afraid of what would happen to him if he was recognized as one of Jesus' followers and denied knowing him three times before daybreak when a cock started crowing.

Jesus before Pontius Pilate
John 18: 28–40

28.	They led Jesus therefore from Caiaphas into the Praetorium. It was early, and they themselves didn't enter into the Praetorium, that they might not be defiled, but might eat the Passover.
29.	Pilate therefore went out to them, and said, "What accusation do you bring against this man?"
30.	They answered him, "If this man weren't an evildoer, we wouldn't have delivered him up to you."
31.	Pilate therefore said to them, "Take him yourselves, and judge him according to your law." Therefore the Jews said to him, "It is not lawful for us to put anyone to death,"
32.	that the word of Jesus might be fulfilled, which he spoke, signifying by what kind of death he should die.
33.	Pilate therefore entered again into the Praetorium, called Jesus, and said to him, "Are you the King of the Jews?"
34.	Jesus answered him, "Do you say this of yourself, or did others tell it to you concerning me?"
35.	Pilate answered, "Am I a Jew? Your own nation and the chief priests delivered you to me. What have you done?"
36.	Jesus answered, "My kingdom is not of this world. If my kingdom were of this world, then my servants would fight, that I wouldn't be delivered to the Jews. But now my kingdom is not from here."
37.	Pilate therefore said to him, "Are you a king then?" Jesus answered, "You say that I am a king. To this end have I

> been born, and to this end I have come into the world, that I should testify to the truth. Everyone who is of the truth listens to my voice."
>
> 38. Pilate said to him, "What is truth?" When he had said this, he went out again to the Jews, and said to them, "I find no basis for a charge against him.
>
> 39. But you have a custom, that I should release to you one at the Passover. Therefore do you desire that I release to you the King of the Jews?"
>
> 40. Then they all cried out again, saying, "Not this man, but Barabbas!" Now Barabbas was a robber.

The historical value of this description of Jesus' trial before Pontius Pilate is dubious and shaky.

It may be regarded as correct that Jesus appeared at the Praetorium or court house of Pontius Pilate, but the report about what transpired there amounts to speculation and pious fiction. There are just too many unanswered questions and impossible or improbable aspects in this report for it to be accepted as it stands.

Who were the "they" who led Jesus to the Praetorium? The readers of this report are not informed, but it was presumably the Jewish leaders and the temple guards who kept Jesus prisoner.

Why would the Jews ask Pilate to crucify Jesus? This does not make any sense. Their own laws stipulated death by stoning for blasphemers (Ex 20: 7; Lev 24: 16; Deut 13:10 and 17: 5) – not death by crucifixion.

Which Jewish laws did Jesus break? The Proto-Gospel of John is silent on this subject at this point. The only reason why the religious authorities wanted to get rid of Jesus was to prevent him from starting a rebellion, which would have led to a harsh retaliation by the Romans (John 11: 46–54).

It is not true that the Jews did not have the authority to put anybody to death for transgressing their religious laws. The gospels and Acts contain examples where that did happen (John 8: 3–4, Acts 8: 58–60).

According to Israeli Judge Chaim Cohn, there was no reason why these Jews could not enter Pilate's residence. No purity law prevented them from doing that. Cohn explains that the trial of Jesus must have been held in camera and that was the reason why no Jews attended the trial and John had to invent a story about what happened inside. Cohn also finds it unbelievable that the haughty and cruel Pilate, who had no respect for the Jews and their religion, would have given the Jewish leaders an audience by meeting them outside. It is also impossible that Pilate would have found Jesus innocent after Jesus had openly declared himself king of the Jews and challenged the might and authority of Rome.[165]

It may be assumed that Jesus went on trial for declaring himself king of Israel and the conversation between Jesus and Pilate would certainly have dealt with this topic. There is, however, no reliable record of what transpired between Jesus and Pilate.

According to Judge Cohn, there is no independent indication that Pilate ever gave the Jews the choice of releasing one of his prisoners during Passover.[166]

It is anybody's guess what Jesus thought and felt when he was interrogated by Pilate. The Roman governor's Praetorium was previously the palace of Herod the Great[167] and Jesus may have visualized himself sitting on Herod's throne, which was occupied by the Roman governor on that day. That would happen when the

---

[165] Cohn, *The Trial and Death of Jesus*, 147–49.
[166] Cohn, *The Trial and Death of Jesus*, 151–55, 161.
[167] **Windle.** "Behold the Man: Where Did Pilate Sentence Jesus?"

angels from heaven miraculously intervened as he expected.

The Crown of Thorns
John 19: 1–3

1.	Then Pilate therefore took Jesus, and flogged him.
2.	The soldiers twisted thorns into a crown, and put it on his head, and dressed him in a purple garment.
3.	They said, "Hail, King of the Jews!" and they struck him with their hands.

That report that Jesus was mocked by the Roman soldiers as the king of the Jews and was given a crown of thorn, may be regarded as trustworthy. After all, Jesus was later crucified in public with this cruel and humiliating crown on his head.

Pilate Sentences Jesus to Death
John 19: 4–15

4.	Then Pilate went out again, and said to them, "Behold, I bring him out to you, that you may know that I find no baa charge against him."
5.	Jesus therefore came out, wearing the crown of thorns and the purple garment. Pilate said to them, "Behold, the man!"
6.	When therefore the chief priests and the officers saw him, they cried out, saying, "Crucify! Crucify!" Pilate said to them, "Take him yourselves, and crucify him, for I find no basis for a charge against him."
7.	The Jews answered him, "We have a law, and by our law he ought to die, because he made himself the Son of God."
8.	When therefore Pilate heard this, he was more afraid.

9.	He entered into the Praetorium again, and said to Jesus, "Where are you from?" But Jesus gave him no answer.
10.	Pilate therefore said to him, "Aren`t you speaking to me? Don`t you know that I have power to release you, and have power to crucify you?"
11.	Jesus answered, "You would have no power at all against me, unless it were given to you from above. Therefore he who delivered me to you has greater sin."
12.	At this, Pilate sought to release him, but the Jews cried out, saying, "If you release this man, you aren`t Caesar`s friend! Everyone who makes himself a king speaks against Caesar!"
13.	When Pilate therefore heard these words, he brought Jesus out, and sat down on the judgment seat at a place called "The Pavement," but in Hebrew, "Gabbatha."
14.	Now it was the Preparation of the Passover, at about the sixth hour. He said to the Jews, "Behold, your King!"
15.	They cried out, "Away with him! Away with him! Crucify him!" Pilate said to them, "Shall I crucify your King?" The chief priests answered, "We have no king but Caesar!"

This part of the report regarding Jesus' trial before Pontius Pilate is also historically unreliable.

The first question that comes to mind, is: why did Pilate not release Jesus if he really found him innocent? He had the authority to do just that and it would have out of character to be intimidated by the Jews, whom he despised, to allow Jesus to be crucified.

One may also ask: why did the Jews allegedly found it the grave sin of blasphemy when Jesus called himself the Son of God? That was, after all, a title given to the kings of Israel, like David. A few days earlier, the crowds greeted Jesus when he entered Jerusalem with the words: "Hosanna! Blessed is he who comes in the name of the Lord, the King of Israel!" (John 12: 13).

Since this trial was held in camera, there was nobody to report on what transpired between Jesus and Pilate. It is also highly unlikely that Pilate would have consulted a rowdy mob outside his court building. It is also unthinkable that the crowd, that hailed Jesus a few days earlier as their king, would have suddenly clamored for the death penalty.

The trial must have taken up some time because Jesus was led to Pilate early in the morning and sentence was only passed at "the sixth hour" – at midday. It might be that Pilate also heard other cases during that time, perhaps also the other two villains who were crucified together with Jesus.

John also reported that Jesus was sentenced and crucified on the "Preparation of the Passover". Since the synoptic gospels state that Jesus was crucified on the day of the Passover, a Friday (Mark 15: 42 *etcetera*.),

John's report places this event on the day before the Passover, in other words, on the Thursday.

The Execution of Jesus
John 19: 16–24

16.	Then therefore he delivered him to them to be crucified. So they took Jesus and led him away.
17.	He went out, bearing his cross, to the place called "The place of a skull," which is called in Hebrew, "Golgotha,"
18.	where they crucified him, and with him two others, on either side one, and Jesus in the middle.

> 19. Pilate wrote a title also, and put it on the cross. There was written, "JESUS OF NAZARETH, THE KING OF THE JEWS."
> 20. Therefore many of the Jews read this title, for the place where Jesus was crucified was near the city; and it was written in Hebrew, in Latin, and in Greek.
> 21. The chief priests of the Jews therefore said to Pilate, "Don't write, 'The King of the Jews,' but that, 'he said, I am King of the Jews.'"
> 22. Pilate answered, "What I have written, I have written."
> 23. Then the soldiers, when they had crucified Jesus, took his garments and made four parts, to every soldier a part; and also the coat. Now the coat was without seam, woven from the top throughout.
> 24. Then they said to one another, "Let's not tear it, but cast lots for it, whose it will be," that the scripture might be fulfilled, which says, "They parted my garments among them, For my cloak they cast lots." Therefore the soldiers did these things.

One may ask: Who were the "them" to whom Jesus was delivered to be crucified and who were the "they" who led him away? According to the context, the Jews who accused Jesus of breaking their laws were meant (verse 16). This is a case of careless editing, because Jesus was actually crucified by the Roman soldiers.

The inscription of the cross, that was visible to all, gave the reason for Jesus' execution, namely that he was "the King of the Jews." If he had received the death penalty for breaking any other laws, Jewish or Roman, the inscription would have indicated that. In other words: Jesus was guilty of proclaiming himself king of the Jews, which implied that he rejected the authority of the Roman emperor. That war-ranted the death penalty by crucifixion.

Most translations or the inscription have it wrong. It was not "Jesus of Nazareth" who was crucified, but "Jesus the Nazorean" (Greek: Ἰησοῦς ὁ Ναζωραῖος – *Iesous ho Nazoraios*).

That means that Pilate – or the official who wrote the inscription on his behalf – knew that Jesus was a Nazorean or an Essene.

The Jewish leaders were allegedly dissatisfied with the wording of the notice. It is, though, highly unlikely that John would have overheard such an exchange, if any. If the trial was held in camera, no Jewish leaders would have been allowed to be present.[168]

The soldiers, who crucified Jesus, robbed him of his clothes with the result that he hung there totally naked and humiliated.

Albrecht Dürer: Jesus on the Cross (1511)

The Disciple and Women at the Cross
John 19: 25–37

25.	But there were standing by the cross of Jesus his mother, and his mother's sister, Mary the wife of Clopas, and Mary Magdalene.

---

[168] Cohn. *The Trial and Death of Jesus*, 138.

26.	Therefore when Jesus saw his mother, and the disciple whom he loved standing there, he said to his mother, "Woman, behold your son!"
27.	Then he said to the disciple, "Behold, your mother!" From that hour, the disciple took her to his own home.
28.	After this, Jesus, seeing that all things were now finished, that the scripture might be fulfilled, said, "I am thirsty."
29.	Now a vessel full of vinegar was there; so they put a sponge full of the vinegar on hyssop, and brought it to his mouth.
30.	When Jesus therefore had received the vinegar, he said, "It is finished." He bowed his head, and gave up his spirit.
31.	Therefore the Jews, because it was the Preparation, so that the bodies wouldn't remain on the cross on the Sabbath (for that Sabbath was a special one), asked of Pilate that their legs might be broken, and that they might be taken away.
32.	Therefore the soldiers came, and broke the legs of the first, and of the other who was crucified with him;
33.	but when they came to Jesus, and saw that he was already dead, they didn't break his legs.
34.	However one of the soldiers pierced his side with a spear, and immediately blood and water came out.
35.	He who has seen has testified, and his testimony is true. He knows that he tells the truth, that you also may believe.
36.	For these things happened, that the scripture might be fulfilled, "A bone of him will not be broken."
37.	Again another scripture says, "They will look on him whom they pierced."

The description of this scene can be regarded as the recollection of an eye-witness – most probably of John himself and perhaps related to the person who wrote it down afterwards.

Only one of Jesus' disciples, his best friend in the group of twelve, had the courage to watch the crucifixion and talk to the helpless Jesus who was nailed to the cross, together with Mary, Jesus' mother, and other women. This disciple is mentioned as the source of this information – not necessarily as the author of the gospel.

Flavius Josephus, the Jewish historian, wrote that the women of Jerusalem regularly gave the crucified criminals some drugged wine or vinegar to lessen their pain and to hasten their demise.[169] That also happened in the case of Jesus, but the gospel is silent on who exactly gave the drugged vinegar to Jesus – presumably somebody who believed in him and wanted to aid him.

The Jews, who purportedly clamored for Jesus' death, did not want corpses to hang on the cross during Passover and the following Sabbath. Therefore, they urged Pilate that the legs of the crucified men be broken to end their misery. Because Jesus seemed to be dead already, he was spared this treatment.

The Burial of Jesus
John 19: 38–42

38.	After these things, Joseph of Arimathaea, being a disciple of Jesus, but secretly for fear of the Jews, asked of Pilate that he might take away Jesus' body. Pilate gave him permission. He came therefore, and took away his body.
39.	Nicodemus also came, he who at first came to Jesus by night, bringing a mixture of myrrh and aloes, about a hundred Roman pounds.

---

[169] Cohn. *The Trial and Death of Jesus*, 222.

> 40. So they took Jesus' body, and bound it in linen cloths with the spices, as the custom of the Jews is to bury.
> 41. Now in the place where he was crucified there was a garden. In the garden a new tomb in which no man had ever yet been laid.
> 42. Then because of the Jews' Preparation (for the tomb was near at hand) they laid Jesus there.

Two of Jesus' friends, Joseph of Arimathaea and Nicodemus, got permission from Pilate to take Jesus from the cross and bury him in a nearby tomb. Nicodemus provided spices and botanical extracts, aloe and myrrh, to apply to Jesus' body, which they also wrapped in linen bandages. He brought a huge amount, one hundred Roman pounds or litras (Greek: λίτρα – *litra,* a weight of 340 gm), which adds up to 34 kg.

The ossuary of Caiaphas who was high priest in Jesus' time

This amount was probably only an estimate to convey the idea that there was more than enough of this mixture. This formula of aloe and myrrh is usually explain-ed as an effort by these men to give Jesus a royal burial. In Ps 45: 8 it is said of the messianic king: "All your garments smell like myrrh, aloes, and cassia." On account of that – so it is argued – they wanted to demonstrate their devotion and their faith in Jesus.

It is also often said that these sweet-smelling spices were meant to mask the smell of Jesus' decomposing body and to embalm his body. However, embalming is something the Jews never practiced with their dead – except for Joseph and Jacob who were mummified, according to Egyptian practices (Gen 50: 2 and 26).

The Jews usually left their dead on a shelf in a tomb and after the corpse had been decomposed, the bones of the skeleton were placed in an ossuary, a small coffin of stone or durable wood.[170]

What commentators usually overlook is that aloe and myrrh are potent antiseptics with the ability to heal wounds. The medicinal value of these spices was well-known in Antiquity. It was, for instance, used by the ancient Greeks who provided their soldiers with portions thereof to apply to their injuries sustained in battle.[171]

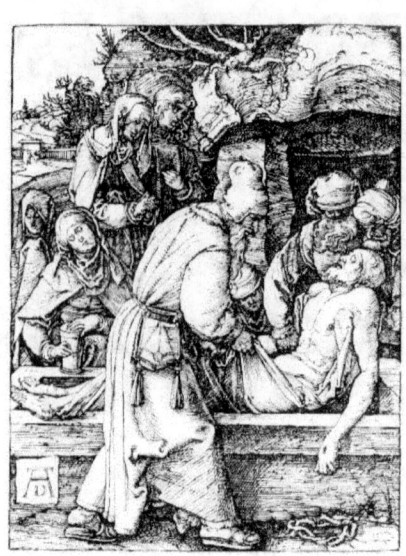

Albrecht Dürer: The Entombment of Jesus, 1510

One may ask: why on earth did Joseph of Arimathea and Nicodemus go overboard with so much of this expensive stuff? They would have needed far less to cover Jesus' body from head to toe if they only wanted to anoint it. The only rational answer is that they needed so much to dress Jesus' body more than once, perhaps daily, on the Thursday, Friday, and the Saturday after the crucifixion. That only makes sense if Jesus was still alive, despite his serious injuries.

---

[170] Jewish Virtual Library, "Death & Bereavement in Judaism."
[171] Akaberi *et al.*, "Therapeutic Effects of *Aloe*"; Medical News Today, "Health Benefits and Risks of Myrrh"; Pace Health, "Aloe"; Pace Health. "Myrrh." Hadhrat Mirza Ghulam Ahmad provides a long list of Arabian medical texts in which this recipe was explained (*Jesus in India*, 67–68).

He had wounds on his head from the crown of thorns, a swollen face due to the blows against his head, lashes all over his body when he was whipped, the wounds where the nails were hammered through his wrists and feet, and the gash on his side where the soldier struck him with his spear.

It is possible that Jesus, a trained Essene healer, gave them the recipe. With these copious amounts of medicinal substances, they must have managed to nurse Jesus back to relative health. It would certainly not have made any sense to apply so much of the expensive stuff to a totally dead corpse.

Mary Magdalene Discovers the Empty Tomb
John 20: 1–10

1.	Now on the first day of the week, Mary Magdalene came early, while it was yet dark, to the tomb, and saw the stone taken away from the tomb.
2.	She ran therefore, and came to Simon Peter, and to the other disciple whom Jesus loved, and said to them, "They have taken away the Lord out of the tomb, and we don't know where they have laid him!"
3.	Peter therefore went forth, and the other disciple, and they went toward the tomb.
4.	They both ran together. The other disciple outran Peter, and came to the tomb first.
5.	Stooping and looking in, he saw the linen cloths lying, yet he didn't enter in.
6.	Then Simon Peter came, following him, and entered into the tomb. He saw the linen cloths lying,
7.	and the cloth that was on his head, not lying with the linen cloths, but rolled up in a place by itself.

8.	Then the other disciple also entered in therefore, who came first to the tomb, and he saw, and believed.
9.	For as yet they didn't know the scripture, that he must rise from the dead.
10.	So the disciples went away again to their own homes.

When Mary Magdalene found an empty tomb her first reaction was to think that Jesus had been removed somewhere else. John and Peter later came to the same conclusion. They saw the linen bandages with which Jesus' body had been covered, lying in the tomb.

The only rational explanation must be that Joseph of Arimathea, Nicodemus, and perhaps some of Jesus' brothers removed him to a better place where he could be cared for.

Verses 8 and 9 contain a contradiction. Verse 8 tells us that John believed, while verse 9 informs us that the disciples did not understand the Scriptures about Jesus' death and resurrection. It has been demonstrated in Chapter 4 that the Old Testament does not contain any predictions or promises in this regard. Paul, as well as John, held this belief on account of wishful thinking and the legendary traits the memories about Jesus obtained as time passed.

Jesus Appears to Mary Magdalene
John 20: 11–16, 18

11.	But Mary was standing outside at the tomb weeping. So, as she wept, she stooped and looked into the tomb,
12.	and she saw two angels in white sitting, one at the head, and one at the feet, where the body of Jesus had lain.
13.	They told her, "Woman, why are you weeping?" She said to them, "Because they have taken away my Lord, and I don't know where they have laid him."

14.	When she had said this, she turned herself back, and saw Jesus standing, and didn't know that it was Jesus.
15.	Jesus said to her, "Woman, why are you weeping? Who are you looking for?" She, supposing him to be the gardener, said to him, "Sir, if you have carried him away, tell me where you have laid him, and I will take him away."
16.	Jesus said to her, "Mary." She turned herself, and said to him, "Rhabbouni!" which is to say, "Teacher!"
18.	Mary Magdalene came and told the disciples that she had seen the Lord, and that he had said these things to her.

Mary Magdalene remained at the empty tomb after the two disciples had left. She suddenly found two men clothed in white sitting on the shelf where Jesus had lain. The text calls them angels, but that must be due to the legendary character this story had acquired after two or three decades. These men probably came to collect the linen bandages. Their white clothes may be a sign that they were Essenes, who mostly wore white clothes.

Jesus also appeared and Mary could not recognize him at first, perhaps due to his swollen face on account of the blows against his head and the wounds caused by the crown of thorns. His body was also probably covered with new bandages. She, nevertheless, recognized his voice when he called her name.

We are not told what Jesus and Mary discussed during this episode. She ran back to tell the disciples that she had seen Jesus.

Jesus Appears to his Disciples
John 20: 19–29

19.	When therefore it was evening, on that day, the first day of the week, and when the doors were locked where the

> disciples were assembled, for fear of the Jews, Jesus came and stood in the midst, and said to them, "Peace be to you."
>
> 20. When he had said this, he showed to them his hands and his side. The disciples therefore were glad when they saw the Lord.
>
> 24. But Thomas, one of the twelve, called Didymus, wasn't with them when Jesus came.
>
> 25. The other disciples therefore said to him, "We have seen the Lord!" But he said to them, "Unless I see in his hands the print of the nails, and put my hand into his side, I will not believe."
>
> 26. After eight days again his disciples were within, and Thomas with them. Jesus came, the doors being locked, and stood in the midst, and said, "Peace be to you."
>
> 27. Then he said to Thomas, "Reach here your finger, and see my hands. Reach here your hand, and put it into my side. Don't be faithless, but believing."
>
> 28. **Thomas answered him, "My Lord and my God!"**
>
> 29. Jesus said to him, "Because you have seen me, you have believed. Blessed are those who have not seen, and have believed."

This story makes it clear that Jesus was bodily present when he met his disciples on two occasions. He showed them his wounds. Thomas, who was absent the first time, was skeptical. When he was present during the second meeting, he was immediately convinced that Jesus was, after all, still alive.

    This appearance of Jesus differed fundamentally from Paul's conception of Jesus' resurrection. Paul taught that Jesus was raised from the grave with a "heavenly body" or a "spiritual body", with which he ascended to the heavens (1 Cor 15).

These reports of Jesus' appearances to his disciples and Mary Magdalene ring true. John gave enough details to provide a lively story, which seems to be the result of personal experience.

Thomas' exclamation, "My Lord and my God!", is certainly a later addition to the text, possibly a small part of the discourse source of John (see Chapter 10). It must have been added when Domitian was emperor in Rome during the eighties or nineties of the first century AD and when the final edition of John's Gospel appeared. He was the first emperor to claim divine status during his lifetime. His predecessors were only elevated to divine status after they had died. According to the Roman historian Suetonius, a grave source of offense to his contemporaries was his insistence on being addressed as "dominus et deus" (master and god)[172] – precisely the exclamation of Thomas. The ancient Latin translation of the Bible, the Vulgate, renders these words of Thomas as: "Dominus meus, et Deus meus" – the exact words that Domitian expected from his subjects. This addition to the text of John's narrative had the object of emphasizing the belief during the last part of the first century that Jesus had a divine status as Son of God, while the emperor did not have the right to call himself a god.

The Purpose of the Book
John 20: 30–31

30.	Therefore Jesus did many other signs in the presence of his disciples, which are not written in this book;

---

[172] Chilver, "Domitian"; Anderson, "The John, Jesus, and History Project", 21; Scholtz. *The Prophecies of Revelation,* 18 and 229.

> 31. but these are written, that you may believe that Jesus is the Christ, the Son of God, and that believing you may have life in his name.

The Proto-Gospel of John ends here. There is also a following chapter that was certainly added later.

The author of this gospel declared that he had a purpose with his book: he wanted to present Jesus as the Messiah, the Son of God, the king of Israel, as well as a miracle worker, a prophet, and a figure who was more important than John the Baptist. He wanted his readers to believe in Jesus and accept him for what he was. This belief would lead to a good life.

Jesus Appears at the Sea of Tiberias
John 21: 1–14

> 1. After these things, Jesus revealed himself again to the disciples at the sea of Tiberias. He revealed himself this way.
> 2. Simon Peter, Thomas called Didymus, Nathanael of Cana in Galilee, and the sons of Zebedee, and two others of his disciples were together.
> 3. Simon Peter said to them, "I'm going fishing." They told him, "We are also coming with you." They immediately went forth, and entered into the boat. That night, they caught nothing.
> 4. But when day was now breaking, Jesus stood on the beach, yet the disciples didn't know that it was Jesus.
> 5. Jesus therefore said to them, "Children, have you anything to eat?" They answered him, "No."
> 6. He said to them, "Cast the net on the right side of the boat, and you will find some." They cast therefore, and now they were not able to draw it in for the multitude of fish.
> 7. That disciple therefore whom Jesus loved said to Peter, "It's the Lord!" So when Simon Peter heard that it was the Lord, he wrapped his coat around him (for he was naked), and threw himself into the sea.

> 8. But the other disciples came in the little boat (for they were not far from the land, but about two hundred cubits away), dragging the net full of fish.
> 9. So when they got out on the land, they saw a fire of coals there, and fish laid on it, and bread.
> 10. Jesus said to them, "Bring some of the fish which you have just caught."
> 11. Simon Peter went up, and drew the net to land, full of great fish, one hundred fifty–three; and even though there were so many, the net wasn't torn.
> 12. Jesus said to them, "Come and eat breakfast." None of the disciples dared inquire of him, "Who are you?" knowing that it was the Lord.
> 13. Then Jesus came and took the bread, gave it to them, and the fish likewise.
> 14. This is now the third time that Jesus was revealed to his disciples, after he had risen from the dead.

The whole of Chapter 21 of John's Gospel is a later addition and, therefore, it is printed in another letter type above. It is certainly not part of the discourse source that was also added later to this gospel since it differs in style and message.

It is possible that this story is based on a real event when Jesus, who cheated death on the cross, appeared to some of his disciples again. This must have been a considerable time after the crucifixion because Jesus seems to have recovered sufficiently from his wounds to be able to travel to Galilee and meet with his disciples who reverted to their old occupations of being fishermen.

Jesus must have been in hiding in the meantime to stay out of sight of the religious authorities in Jerusalem and the Romans. He was certainly a very disillusioned and disappointed man since God's angels did not come to his aid while he was hanging on the cross and his dream of becoming king of the Jews was shattered – at least, for the time being.

The Jesus of this scene was not a spiritual or heavenly being as Paul described the resurrected body of Christ, but a man of flesh and blood who had breakfast with his friends.

Jesus and Peter
John 21: 15–19

15.	So when they had eaten their breakfast, Jesus said to Simon Peter, "Simon, son of Jonah, do you love me more than these?" He said to him, "Yes, Lord; you know that I have affection for you." He said to him, "Feed my lambs."
16.	He said to him again a second time, "Simon, son of Jonah, do you love me?" He said to him, "Yes, Lord; you know that I have affection for you." He said to him, "Tend my sheep."
17.	He says to him the third time, "Simon, son of Jonah, do you have affection for me?" Peter was grieved because he asked him the third time, "Do you have affection for me?" He said to him, "Lord, you know everything. You know that I have affection for you." Jesus said to him, "Feed my sheep.
18.	Most assuredly I tell you, when you were young, you dressed yourself, and walked where you wanted to. But when you are old, you will stretch out your hands, and another will dress you, and carry you where you don't want to go."
19.	Now he said this, signifying by what kind of death he would glorify God. When he had said this, he said to him, "Follow me."

It may be concluded from verse 19 that this Chapter was added after the death of Peter, who died about AD 64 as a martyr when Nero reigned as emperor in Rome and persecuted the Christians.[173]

Peter, who was the leader of the disciples and who is traditionally regarded as the first bishop of Rome, received the mission to look after Jesus' sheep, his followers. This is a reference

---

[173] O'Connor. "Peter the Apostle, Saint".

to the parable of the good shepherd (John 10: 1–21). Jesus was, of course, concerned about the welfare of the people who believed in him as the Messiah.

Jesus and the Other Disciples
John 21: 20–25

20.	Then Peter, turning around, saw a disciple following. This was the disciple whom Jesus sincerely loved, the one who had also leaned on Jesus' breast at the supper and asked, "Lord, who is going to betray You?"
21.	Peter seeing him, said to Jesus, "Lord, and what will this man do?"
22.	Jesus said to him, "If I desire that he stay until I come, what is that to you? You follow me."
23.	This saying therefore went forth among the brothers, that that disciple wouldn't die. Yet Jesus didn't say to him that he wouldn't die, but, "If I desire that he stay until I come, what is that to you?"
24.	This is the disciple who testifies about these things, and wrote these things. We know that his witness is true.
25.	There are also many other things which Jesus did, which if they would all be written, I suppose that even the world itself wouldn't contain the books that would be written.

It may be concluded from this passage that John, the apostle, thought it prudent that this Chapter to his existing gospel be added because of a confusion between the other apostles that Jesus would have promised him that we would not die before Jesus' eventual return. He wished to put the record straight that Jesus never made such a promise.

The last verse in this passage is the final ending to this gospel, declaring that there remained much more to tell.

One cannot but wonder: what happened to Jesus after he showed himself to his disciples after surviving his crucifixion against all odds? John is silent on this matter and one can only speculate that Jesus disappeared from the scene and went into hiding or exile as a disappointed and traumatized man because God did not send an army of angels to prevent his execution or to rescue him from the cross and to drive the hated Romans away. He must also have been a broken man physically due to his ordeal on the cross, despite the ministrations of his friends.

Jesus only appeared to his disciples and closest friends – not to the public at large. To protect him from further harm, the story was distributed that he really died on the cross as an explanation for his disappearance

As known from Paul's letters and the book of Acts, the followers of Jesus continued to venerate him as the Messiah and a prophet. His brother James became the leader of his movement. Some of his teachings and sayings were collected and the Q Document was the result (see Chapter 3). The Q Document did not mention his execution and almost miraculous survival because he must have been still alive somewhere at that time.

Eusebius of Caesarea, the first theologian to write about the history of the Christian church during the early fourth century AD, related that Pontius Pilate had sent a report to Emperor Tiberius after he had heard that Jesus had risen from the dead. Tiberius referred the matter to the Senate, but the Senate declined to pursue the issue any further. Tiberius heard from Pilate that Jesus was revered as a god on account of his resurrection.

Tiberius could not convince the Senate of this belief, which he had found acceptable, and he decided to institute "no hostile measures against Christ."[174]

Whether this report by Eusebius is true is impossible to determine today, although there is no reason to distrust Eusebius'

---

[174] Eusebius, *Historia Ecclesiatica.* Liber II/II.

honesty as a historian. He usually copied or quoted his sources faithfully, but then the authenticity of his sources may sometimes be in doubt. Eusebius quoted as his source for this story the early Christian theologian Tertullian. According to Judd, the veracity of Tertullian's version cannot be verified.[175]

However, if this account of Eusebius (and Tertullian) contains some truth, then it suggests that Jesus was still around some time after his resurrection, but that Tiberius did not regard him as a threat to his authority and position as emperor, although he believed him to be a deity, such as other mythological figures. The reports that Jesus was regarded as a god after his resurrection may result from the fact that Jesus was often called the Son of God by himself and his followers.

Summary

The Proto-Gospel of John, the narrative parts of the gospel as we have it today, seems to be a trustworthy document for the most part. There are legendary parts, such as the descriptions of the magical "signs" or miracles performed by Jesus. There may, however, have been a core of truth in these stories.

The report of the trial of Jesus before Pontius Pilate is clearly the result of speculation and invention, but the description of the arrest of Jesus, his crucifixion, burial, and reappearance can be accepted as essentially accurate.

This proto-gospel contains some inconsistencies and was sometimes badly edited. The style is that of a person who was not used to write and who often struggled to express himself.

---

[175] Judd, "Perspectives about Pontius Pilate in the Ante-Nicene Fathers", 166–69.

How is Jesus portrayed in Proto-John? He was certainly not the divine figure as described by Paul. He was seen as a prophet, the Messiah or king of the Jews, as a healer, and a wise teacher.

Albrecht Dürer: The Risen Christ

John often made the remark that people believed in Jesus after he had performed some or other "sign". That simply means that they accepted him as a prophet, as the Messiah, and as the king of

Israel, and accepted his message. This belief did not result in life everlasting in the afterlife in heaven, as Paul taught in his letters.

The concept of the "Kingdom of God" plays an important role in the Proto-Gospel of John. The word "king" is used on 18 occasions in connection with Jesus and he was precisely nailed to the cross for proclaiming himself king of the Jews.

John reported as faithfully as possible what Jesus said and claimed in this regard. At the time of writing this proto-gospel, there seemed to have been still some hope that Jesus would return and miraculously resurrect the old kingdom of David – perhaps two decades after Jesus' departure during AD 33 after his crucifixion and rescue by Joseph of Arimathea. This hope must have been the motive for compiling this proto-gospel to keep Jesus' movement of supporters informed about his words and actions.

This hope seems to have been around when the epistle of James, the brother of Jesus, was written during the fifties of the first century. This letter does not mention Jesus' death, but his return was still expected at that time (Jas 5: 7–8).

Chapter 6
THE EPISTLE OF JAMES

Although the Epistle of James in the New Testament contains no direct biographical information about Jesus, it is nevertheless an important document to consider when the sources about the life of Jesus of Nazareth are being investigated.

Authorship, Intended Readers, and Date
The author of this epistle introduces himself as "James, a servant of God and of the Lord Jesus Christ" (Jas 1: 1).

Experts agree that this letter of James originated in a Jewish "Christian" community. It is, after all, addressed "to the twelve tribes which are in the Dispersion" (Jas 1: 1) – by which the Jewish followers of Jesus inside and outside of Palestine must have been meant. The followers of Jesus, who were mostly recruited from the party of the Essenes, regarded themselves as the true Israel – hence they are called "the twelve tribes which are in the Dispersion".

In Jas 2: 2 an "assembly" is mentioned, where the word "synagogue" (Greek: συναγωγή – *synagoge*) is actually used. That means that James' readers gathered in (Jewish) synagogues of their own. There are many allusions to the Old Testament and the author seems to have assumed that his readers knew the Hebrew Scriptures.

All this point to the Ebionites as the intended recipients.

There is no agreement as to who the author was and when it was written. Some experts date it late in the first century AD or even later when James, the brother of Jesus and leader of the Ebionites in Jerusalem, was already deceased. According to Josephus, he was killed in AD 62.[176]

There are also those who believe that the author was, in fact, James, Jesus' brother. The book of Acts presents James as the leader of the Jerusalem congregation and as the successor of Jesus as leader of the Jesus Movement (Acts 12: 17; 15: 13–21; 21: 18). Paul mentions "James and Cephas and John, they who were reputed to be pillars" of the community in Jerusalem (Gal 2: 9). According to Eusebius, he was called "James the Just" on account of his piety.[177]

The fact that the epistle was clearly addressed to the Ebionites, certainly points to James, Jesus' brother, as the author. This letter, which deals mainly with ethical issues, often referred to poverty and riches – which agrees with the idea that it originated within an Ebionite community, the Jewish followers of Jesus.[178]

In this letter, no mention is made of the destruction of the Jerusalem temple. The social situation also seems to mirror the period before the Jewish War with the destruction of Jerusalem during AD 66–70 when rich landowners exploited the poor (Jas 1: 10; 2: 1–7; 5: 1–6). Therefore, this letter must have been written before AD 62 when James died.

James uses the imperative mode in fifty-four instances in his letter. That implies that he saw himself as an authoritative leader and teacher – the role that James had in the Jerusalem congregation. Some scholars expressed doubts about James' knowledge of Greek, which was used in this letter.[179] It has already been shown in the

---

[176] Josephus, *Antiquities of the Jews*, Liber XX/IX;

[177] Eusebius, *Histria Ecclesiastica*, Liber II/XXIII.

[178] Enc Brit, "James, The letter of"; Rylaarsdam *et al.*, "Biblical Literature"; Gaum, *Kernensiklopedie*, 510–11.

[179] Encyclopedia of the Bible. "Epistle of James".

previous chapter that Jesus must have known some Greek because he was able to converse with some Greeks and with Pontius Pilate. He may have picked up some Greek when receiving an education at Qumran, the Essene center near the Dead Sea – which may also have been the case with James.

Differences with Paul

It appears that James differed from Paul who taught that one can only be saved from eternal perdition through faith in Jesus Christ who took the eternal punishment of sinners upon himself when he was crucified.

This is certainly not the kind of faith that James had in mind. He argued that faith without actions or works, consisting of obeying the "royal law" is dead and useless (Jas 2: 8, 14–26). In Jas 2: 1 he mentions "the faith of our Lord Jesus Christ, [the Lord] of glory", which seems to be the type of faith or belief found in the gospels, namely the acceptance of Jesus as the Messiah of Israel.

In Jas 2: 5 he wrote: "Didn't God choose those who are poor in this world to be rich in faith, and heirs of the kingdom which he promised to those who love him?" This pronouncement also implies that the earthly "kingdom" envisaged by Jesus, would belong to the poor people who are rich in their faith in Jesus, the Messiah.

However, James does not mention Paul by name or quote from any of his letters. His knowledge of Paul's views could only have come from personal contact at a time before Paul embarked on his travels and started to write letters. The obvious occasion for such an encounter would have been the meeting in Jerusalem of more or less AD 48–50 (Acts 15), where James officiated as chairman. He may have written his epistle shortly after this meeting with the goal of disproving Paul's stance. The date of this letter can, therefore, be placed between AD 48 and 62, which makes it the oldest document in the New Testament, even older than the letters of Paul –at most two decades after the crucifixion of Jesus.

References to the Q Document

A remarkable characteristic of the Epistle of James is the repeated references or allusions to sayings in the Q Document.

It is, of course, possible that these references could have been taken from the canonical gospels of Matthew or Luke, in which case the Epistle of James could not have been written earlier than the end of the first century AD. However, this seems unlikely because all these references are from texts in specifically Q. That may be an indication that Q was a real document that was known and used no later than the fifties of the first century AD.

There is, of course, also the possibility that James remembered some of his elder brother's sayings, which also appeared in Q. One may even wonder: did James perhaps play any role in the compilation of Q by contributing some of his own memories regarding the teachings of his brother?

The following passages in James are clearly dependent upon Q or are parallels of Q:

James 1: 22

22.	But be doers of the word, and not only hearers, deluding your own selves.

Matt 7: 24 – "Everyone therefore who hears these words of mine, and does them, I will liken him to a wise man..."

James 2: 5

Listen, my beloved brothers. Didn't God choose those who are poor in this world to be rich in faith, and heirs of the kingdom which he promised to those who love him?

Luke 6: 20 – "Blessed are you poor, for yours is the kingdom of God.

James 3:12

> Can a fig tree, my brothers, yield olives, or a vine figs? Thus no spring yields both salt water and fresh water.

Matt 7: 16 – By their fruits you will know them. Do you gather grapes from thorns, or figs from thistles?

James 4: 11–12

> 11. Don't speak against one another, brothers. He who speaks against a brother and judges his brother, speaks against the law and judges the law. But if you judge the law, you are not a doer of the law, but a judge.
> 12. Only one is the lawgiver, who is able to save and to destroy. But who are you to judge another?

Matt 7: 1 – Don't judge, so that you won't be judged.

James 5:2

> Your riches are corrupted and your garments are moth-eaten.

Matt 6:19 – Don't lay up treasures for yourselves on the earth, where moth and rust consume, and where thieves break through and steal.

James 5:12

> But above all things, my brothers, don't swear, neither by heaven, nor by the earth, nor by any other oath; but let your yes be yes, and your no, no; so that you don't fall into hypocrisy.

Matt 5: 34–37

34. But I tell you, don't swear at all: neither by heaven, for it is the throne of God;
35. nor by the earth, for it is the footstool of his feet; nor by Jerusalem, for it is the city of the great King.
36. Neither shall you swear by your head, for you can't make one hair white or black.
37. But let your speech be, `Yes, yes; No, no.` Whatever is more than these is of the evil one.

There are at least six places in James that are strikingly similar to sayings in Q. This must be an indication that Q was probably composed during the forties of the first century AD, between ten and fifteen years after the crucifixion – that is to say, if James used ideas from Q in his epistle and did not quote Jesus from memory.

References to Jesus
The name "Jesus" is only mentioned twice in this letter, but he is also referred to as "the Lord". The relevant passages must be commented upon:

Jas 1: 1

James, a servant of God and of the Lord Jesus Christ.

This tells us next to nothing about Jesus, except that he was honored as "the Lord" or "the Master" and had the title of "Christ" or anointed Messiah. It may, perhaps, also mean that Jesus was still alive somewhere in exile or hiding at the time when this letter was written and that James saw himself as a "servant" of a living Jesus.

He regards God and the Lord Jesus Christ evidently as two separate persons or beings. He separates the two with the word "and". If he had regarded Jesus to be God Himself, he would not have used the word "and" as he did.

The word for "Lord" in Greek is κύριος (*kyrios*), a word often used in the New Testament for The Lord (God). Its literal meaning is a title of honor expressive of respect and reverence, with which servants greeted their masters. Thiede and D'Ancona note: "The word 'Lord', *kyrios,* for instance, could be applied to persons far removed from the holy Trinity...."[180]

If Jesus Christ, the Messiah, is named "the Lord", it does not necessarily mean that he is regarded as a divine being; it may simply mean that he was held in high regard as a master or teacher.

Jas 1: 12

Blessed is the man who endures temptation, for when he has been approved, he will receive the crown of life, which the Lord promised to those who love him.

This verse reminds one of the Beatitudes, as well as Matt 19: 28 – "Jesus said to them, 'Most assuredly I tell you, that you who have followed me, in the regeneration when the Son of Man will sit on the throne of his glory, you also will sit on twelve thrones, judging the twelve tribes of Israel.'"

Jas 2: 1

My brothers, don't hold the faith of our Lord Jesus Christ, [the Lord] of glory, with respect of persons.

The translation in Jas 2: 1 of "[the Lord] of glory" is an indication that the word "Lord" does not occur in the original, but was inserted by the translators for the sake of clarity. The expression may also be

---

[180] Thiede and D'Ancona, *The Jesus Papyrus,* 162.

translated as "our master Jesus Christ who is to be regarded as honorable (or: with a good reputation)."

When Jas 2: 1 mentioned "the faith of our Lord Jesus Christ" it cannot mean faith *in* Jesus Christ – it can only point to the teachings of Jesus and the acceptance of Jesus as the Messiah, as this expression is also used in especially the Proto-Gospel of John.

Jas 4: 10

Humble yourselves in the sight of the Lord, and he will exalt you.

It is not quite clear whether this reference to "the Lord" is connected to God, or to Jesus.

If Jesus is meant, then it is an exhortation to honor him when he returns. The word for "in the sight of" in Greek is ἐνώπιος (*enopios*) and it implies a physical presence.

Jas 5: 7–8

7.	Be patient therefore, brothers, until the coming of the Lord. Behold, the farmer waits for the precious fruit of the earth, being patient over it, until it receives the early and late rain.
8.	You also be patient. Establish your hearts, for the coming of the Lord is at hand.

The Greek word for "coming" is παρουσία (*parousia*) and it means "coming, arrival, or advent". This word is sometimes used in the letters of Paul to refer to the return of Christ on Judgment Day. However, this cannot be what James meant since his letter is silent on Jesus' crucifixion, resurrection, ascension into heaven, and eventual return. It can only mean that Jesus was hiding somewhere and waited to return to Jerusalem, where James assumed the (temporary) leadership of the Ebionites, the supporters of Jesus.

Jesus could only have been alive because Joseph of Arimathea and Nicodemus nursed him back to life after they had taken his body from the cross and used a medicinal mixture to treat his wounds (John 19: 38–40).

The word for "at hand" is derived from the verb ἐγγίζω (*engizo*), which means "to bring near, to join one thing to another, to draw or come near to, to approach." With this expression, James reminded his readers that the return of Jesus was imminent. That can only mean that Jesus was still alive at that time and he must have been in his late fifties or early sixties – not too old to have another go at the establishment of the promised "kingdom" (Jas 2: 5).

James also advised his readers twice to be "patient" while awaiting the coming of the Lord. Paul warned his readers that they had to be vigilant – not patient – because the second coming and Judgment Day could come suddenly (Rom 13: 11–12; 1 Thess 5: 1–8. This patience implies that the imminent return of Jesus was a certainty for James.

A Last Word
The epistle of James seems to be the oldest "Christan" document, written more or less twenty years after Jesus' crucifixion. For this reason, much value must be placed on the historical accuracy and relevance of its references to Jesus.

Jesus is certainly not portrayed as a divine personage, as in the letters of Paul and in the discourses and sermons of the Gospel of John. He was almost certainly still alive at the time of writing of this letter because the readers were explicitly warned to be ready for his imminent physical return (which, by the way, did not happen). No religious meaning was attached to his crucifixion and resurrection. He was merely to be honored as a Master, as the founder of a new religious sect in the Jewish world.

Chapter 7
MARK, MATTHEW, AND LUKE

Authorship and Date of Mark
Many biblical scholars date the Gospel of Mark to the sixties of the first century AD. It is, however, a simple matter to date this gospel to the seventies of the first century AD, as will be shown below.

The Spanish scholar, Jose O"Callghan, wrote in 1972 that a papyrus fragment found in Cave 7 near Qumran, where the Essenes hid their library during the Jewish War of AD 66–70, named 7Q5, contains a part of the text of Mark 6: 52–53. That would mean that this gospel must have been written before AD 66. However, the German scholar, Stefan Enste, demonstrated in 2000 that this identification cannot be supported and that the origin of 7Q5 cannot be determined. There are just too few legible Greek letters on this scrap of papyrus to reconstruct the original text.[181]

The Synoptic Gospels, Mark, Matthew, and Luke, all contain purported predictions of Jesus that Jerusalem with its temple would be destroyed, that great hardships and tribulations had to be expected, that false messiahs and false prophets would lead the people astray and that unusual celestial phenomena would occur.

These predictions were linked to Jesus' teachings about Judgment Day in which he warned his followers to expect this terrible day to arrive at any time soon and to be ready to flee from Judea when they hear of "wars and rumors of wars" (Mark 13: 1–19; Matt 23: 37–39; Matt 24: 1–22; Luke 21: 5–24).

---

[181] Enste, *Kein Markustext in Qumran.*

There are two reasons why it can be stated that Jesus never made these predictions and that the author of Mark made it all up:

- The first reason is that when it is kept in mind that Jesus was convinced that he was God's chosen Messiah to restore a theocracy in Israel, it does indeed seem strange that he would warn his followers that the destruction of the temple and the city of Jerusalem was imminent. After all, Jerusalem was supposed to be the capital of the restored kingdom of Israel.
- The second reason is that it is clear from Mark 13: 20 that the author of this gospel actually described history – and not a genuine prediction about the future – since in his carelessness, he used the past tense instead of the future tense in this verse: "And if the Lord *had* not made the time short, no flesh would *have been kept* from destruction; but because of the saints he *has made* the time short" (*emphasis added*). Matthew, who copied these words, changed the past tense to the future tense to fit the pretense that Jesus had predicted these events – instead of describing an event from the past (Matt 24: 22).

The only possible conclusion is that the author of Mark put these words in Jesus' mouth after the temple had been destroyed during the Jewish War in August AD 70 and he then presented Jesus as a prophet who had foreseen it all. The destruction of the temple did happen as Jesus purportedly had predicted: there was indeed a bloody war, the temple was destroyed and not one stone was left standing on the other, while Jesus' followers in Jerusalem and Judea really did flee.[182]

Flavius Josephus, the Jewish historian, gave a detailed de-

---

[182] Eusebius, *Historia Ecclesiastica,* Liber III/VIII/2); Enc Brit, "Jewish Revolt, First".

scription of the Jewish War of AD 66–70. He wrote especially in Book VI of his work *The Wars of the Jews* (completed about AD 78) about conditions within Jerusalem during the siege, how the city was taken by the Roman legions and how the temple went up in flames. The Romans crucified thousands of prisoners, while others were taken into slavery. Before the fall of the city, there were various prophets and "deceivers" proclaiming that God would never allow his holy city to be taken by pagans. When famine broke out after the city had been encircled by the Roman legions, civil war broke out within the city and looters terrorized the trapped population. The leaders were at loggerheads with each other and some hotheads even denounced their own family members as traitors. In the end, the defenders of the city were so weakened by infighting and famine that the Roman soldiers easily breached the last defenses and razed the city. Only three towers of the whole city were left standing.

Josephus' description tallies to a remarkable extent with Jesus' "predictions". The only explanation is that the author of Mark drew on his own knowledge of events to fabricate a prophecy attributed to Jesus, which Matthew and Luke repeated, with some embellishments of their own.

The gospels mention that Jesus allegedly also predicted:

> "But in those days, after that oppression, the sun will be darkened, the moon will not give her light, the stars will be falling from the sky, and the powers that are in the heavens will be shaken" (Mark 13: 24–25).

Josephus and Eusebius of Caesarea both reported that a comet was seen in the sky for almost a whole year during the war.[183] There were

---

[183] Josephus, *War*, Liber VI/V/3; Eusebius, *Historia Ecclesiastica*, Liber III/VIII/2

two almost total lunar eclipses a few months before the siege of Jerusalem started in March AD 70 – as shown on the illustrations below.

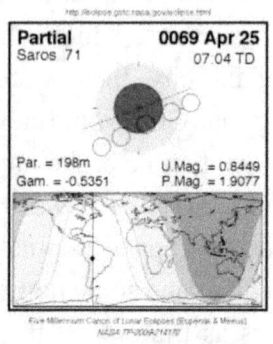 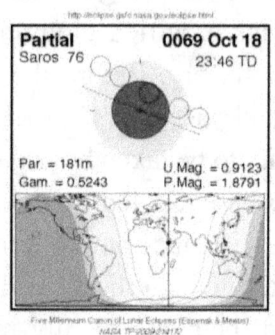

The white parts on these maps show the parts of the earth where two near–total lunar eclipses occurred during the Jewish War. The maximum extent of the first eclipse occurred shortly before sunrise and the second eclipse happened at about 23:00 local time, as seen from Jerusalem.

In addition, several meteor showers (shooting stars) were visible during the second lunar eclipse, as shown on the simulation of the night sky over Jerusalem at the height of the lunar eclipse in October AD 69 when the glare of the full moon was greatly diminished. Meteor showers are caused by the earth moving through the debris left by passing comets and when bits of this debris burn out when they hit the earth's atmosphere.

During the early morning before the destruction of the temple on 30 August AD 70, the planets Venus, Jupiter, and Mercury (regarded as pagan deities) lay in a straight line within the constellation of Leo [the Lion – the sign of the tribe of Judah (Gen 49: 9 and Rev 5: 5)][184] on the eastern horizon, as seen from Jerusalem. In addition, the planet Mars, the pagan god of war, was a

---

[184] Allen, *Star Names*, 253.

threat in Cancer (the Crab), that was ready to pounce upon the Lion with its claws.

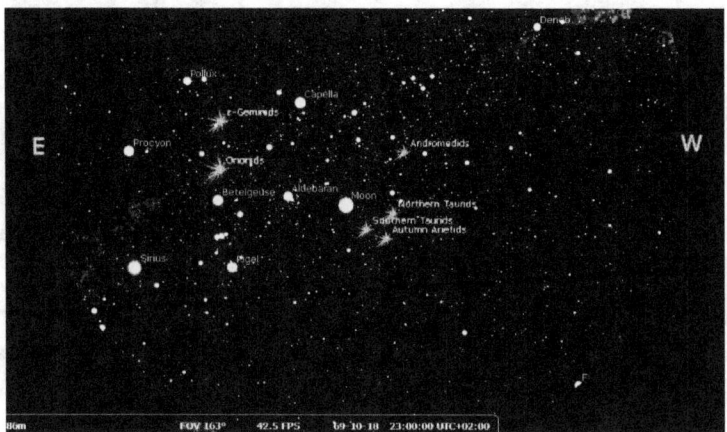

A computerized recreation of the night sky over Jerusalem on 18 October AD 69 at 23:00 when the full moon was almost totally eclipsed. Several meteor showers (shown as dots with spikes) were observed at that time, namely the ε–Geminids, the Orionids, the Andromedids, the Northern Taurids, the Southern Taurids and the Autumn Arietids.

A conjunction between Venus and Jupiter occurred four days earlier when they formed a single bright object in the sky just before dawn. The last few defenders of Jerusalem, as well as their Roman attackers, must have noticed these unusual alignments and concluded that the fate of Jerusalem and Judea was sealed.

From their knowledge of astrology – which was widespread in those days[185] – they would have drawn the conclusion that the gods of Rome were poised to deal the Lion of Judah a fatal blow. Mark 13: 25 also referred to "the powers that are in the heavens"; that must have been an allusion to these celestial phenomena (see

---

[185] Malina, *On the Genre and Message of Revelation*; Jacobus, "The Zodiac"; Scholtz, *The Prophecies of Revelation.*

also Matt 24: 29 and Luke 21: 26).

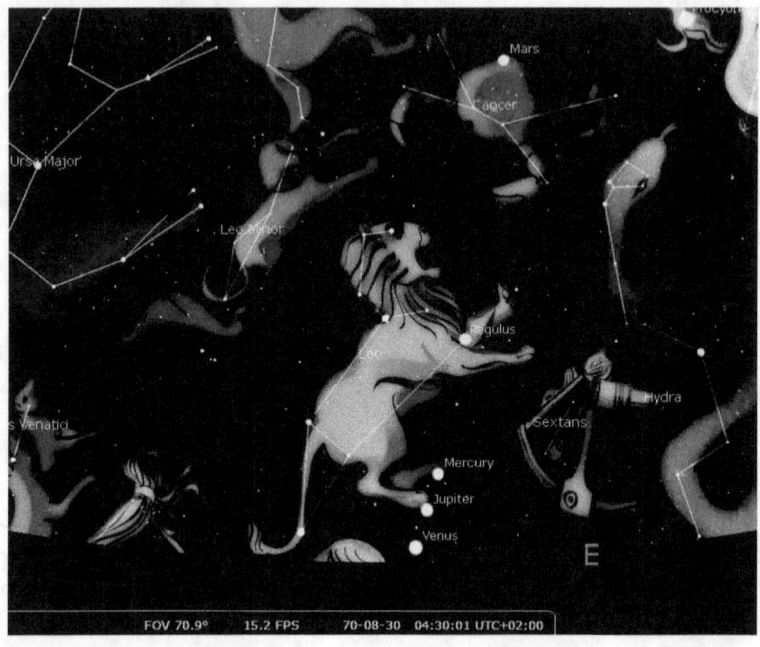

A computerized recreation of the stars, planets, and constellations just above the eastern horizon during the early morning of 30 August AD 70 at 04:30, as seen from Jerusalem, the day on which Jerusalem was conquered by the Romans.

To complicate matters, a partial solar eclipse was visible from Judea on 20 March AD 71, a few months after the destruction of Jerusalem, which occurred on 30 August AD 70 – just as Mark 13: 24 proclaimed that *"after* that oppression [the destruction of Jerusalem], the sun will be darkened..." *(emphasis added)*.

With the total lack of knowledge of celestial mechanics in those days, it is understandable that the superstitious people of those times, who were all convinced of the "truths" of astrology, would have seen these signs in the heavens as evil omens linked to the destruction of Jerusalem and the defeat of the Jews.

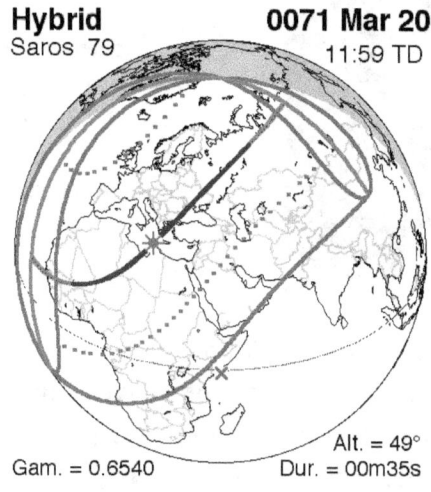

Five Millennium Canon of Solar Eclipses (Espenak & Meeus)

Solar eclipse, 20 March AD 71. The path of the shadow of the moon, eclipsing the sun, is shown where it started in Siberia and ended in West Africa. Totality could have been seen in Greece, but only a partial eclipse was visible in Judea. Totality was reached at 11:24 local time in Athens.

Stephenson noted: "Eclipses of the Sun and Moon are often quite spectacular, and in ancient and medieval times they were frequently recorded as portents – usually of disaster." [186]

Delsemme added: "In ancient times, without interference from streetlights or urban pollution, comets could be seen by everyone. Their sudden appearance – their erratic behavior against the harmonious order of the heavenly motions – was interpreted as an omen of nature that awed people and was used by astrologers to predict flood, famine, pestilence, or the death of kings."[187]

---

[186] Stephenson, "Eclipse."
[187] Delsemme, "Comet".

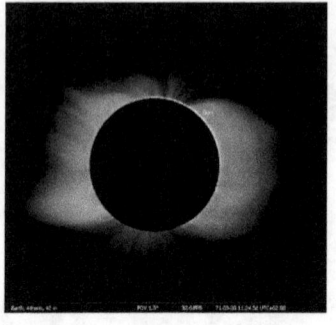 A computerized reconstruction of the total solar eclipse over Athens in Greece on 20 March AD 71 at 11:24 local time when 99,9% of the sun's surface was hidden behind the moon.

The author of the Gospel of Mark, who must have been writing during the seventies of the first century AD – in other words, after the destruction of Jerusalem – would have had knowledge of these frightening celestial phenomena and he included them in the purported predictions of Jesus in order to portray him as a great prophet and to enhance his reputation.

One may even speculate that the author of the Gospel of Mark was in Greece at the time of the solar eclipse of 20 March AD 71 at a location where the eclipse was total and that prompted him to write that "the sun will be darkened" – not realizing that the destroyed Jerusalem experienced only a partial eclipse on that date.

The fact that Mark could have been in Greece (perhaps Athens or Thessalonica) when he composed his gospel, may have contributed to his decision to write his book in Greek for a Greek–speaking readership – and not in Hebrew, Aramaic, or Latin. It is also obvious that he was unaware of the Proto-Gospel of John, which was written a few years previously.

Mark must have thought that it was not possible for Jesus not to have foreseen all these disasters and celestial signs and, therefore, he invented the words ascribed to Jesus in the light of the known history of the Jewish War and his own observations of the eclipses and other celestial phenomena.

The fact that Mark mentioned the solar eclipse of 20 March AD 71 is a clear indication that the final version of this gospel could not have been completed earlier than this date.

Who exactly was the author of the Gospel of Mark? The author does not name himself – in contrast with Paul who introduced himself as author of his letters and John of Patmos whose name is mentioned in the text as the author of Revelation.

The authorship of this gospel was traditionally attributed to a man with the name of Mark (Latin: Marcus).

The first historian of the Christian church, Eusebius, wrote:

> "This also the presbyter said: Mark, having become the interpreter of Peter, wrote down accurately, though not in order, whatsoever he remembered of the things said or done by Christ. For he neither heard the Lord nor followed him, but afterward, as I said, he followed Peter, who adapted his teaching to the needs of his hearers, but with no intention of giving a connected account of the Lord's discourses, so that Mark committed no error while he thus wrote some things as he remembered them. For he was careful of one thing, not to omit any of the things which he had heard, and not to state any of them falsely. These things are related by Papias concerning Mark."[188]

A man named Mark is often mentioned in the New Testament and several commentators regard him as the author of the gospel:

- The disciples met in Jerusalem at the home of Mary, the mother of John Mark (Acts 12: 12).

---

[188] Eusebius. *Historis Ecclesiastica*, Liber III/XXIX/15.

- Mark was a relative of Barnabas (Col 4: 10). He helped Paul and Barnabas on their first journey to preach in Asia Minor (Acts 13: 5). He turned back at Perga and went home (Acts 13: 13). Paul, therefore, refused to take him along on the next journey. Mark then went with Barnabas to Cyprus (Acts 15: 37–39).
- Mark was a co-worker of Paul when Paul was a prisoner in Rome (Philemon 24; Col 4: 10). He had been a help to Paul and Paul requested Timothy to bring Mark to him (2 Tim 4: 11).
- Peter 5: 13 mentions 'Mark, my son'.

Nobody knows whether all these scriptural texts had the same person in mind. There could have been more than one person with the name of Mark. It was, after all, a well-known name in the Roman world. The name means "warlike" and is derived from Mars, the Roman god of war.

Some ancient Roman notables also had the name of Marcus:

- Crassus (Marcus Licinius Crassus: 115–53 BC) – a noble and rich Roman and friend of Sulla;
- Mark Antony (Marcus Antonius: 82–30 BC) – a famous general;
- Agrippa (Marcus Vispanius Agrippa: 63–12 BC) – son-in-law of Emperor Augustus;
- Trajan (Marcus Ulpius Traianus: 53–117 AD) – Roman emperor; and
- Marcus Aurelius (Marcus Aurelius Antoninus: 121–180 AD) – Roman emperor and philosopher.[189]

Whether the person named Mark in the New Testament and by Eusebius was really the author of the gospel bearing his name, will

---

[189] Anon. "Famous People of Ancient Rome."

certainly never be known with certainty.

However, it is necessary to investigate this gospel to ascertain how much of it can be regarded as historically reliable and relevant. It will also be compared with parallel parts in the other Synoptic Gospels to demonstrate how they changed the information in Mark or added to it and how the chronology of Mark was scrambled.

Albrecht Dürer: An Evangelist

It will appear that Matthew and Luke interspersed the parts they copied from Mark with their own comments and embellishments, often taken from Q. These passages from Q have already been discussed in Chapter 3. The unique material utilized by Matthew (M) and Luke (L) will receive attention in the next two chapters. Where Matthew and Luke threw in short comments on the words from Mark, these will be pointed out where the text of Mark is discussed in the paragraphs that follow.

Preamble
Mark 1: 1

> The beginning of the gospel of Jesus Christ, the Son of God.

Some old manuscripts lack the words "the Son of God" and it may safely be regarded as a later addition.

This preamble states the theme of the book: the good news about Jesus, the Messiah. The expression "Son of God" – if it is genuine – may either mean that he was the king of Israel (see Chapter 2), or the second Person of the Divine Trinity.

The Preaching of John the Baptist
Mark 1: 2–12 (Matt 3: 1–12; Luke 3: 1–18)

> 2. As it is written in the prophets, "Behold, I send my messenger before your face, Who will prepare your way before you.
> 3. The voice of one crying in the wilderness, `Make ready the way of the Lord, Make his paths straight.`"
> 4. John came baptizing in the wilderness and preaching the baptism of repentance for forgiveness of sins.
> 5. There went out to him all the country of Judea, and all those of Jerusalem. They were baptized by him in the Jordan river, confessing their sins.
> 6. John was clothed with camel's hair and a leather belt around his loins. He ate locusts and wild honey.
> 7. He preached, saying, "After me comes he who is mightier than I, the thong of whose sandals I am not worthy to stoop down and loosen.
> 8. I baptized you in water, but he will baptize you in the Holy Spirit."

The prophecy mentioned in this passage is to be found in Isa 40: 3 – "The voice of one who cries, prepare you in the wilderness the way of YHWH; make level in the desert a highway for our God."

This prophecy was spoken to the people of God after their exile in Babylonia and it was meant to comfort the people of that time. Isaiah certainly did not have John the Baptist in mind when he wrote his prophecy, but Mark interpreted it as pertaining to John.

John lived as a hermit in the wilderness and wore very basic clothing and lived off the land. He was most probably connected to the Essene community on the shores of the Dead Sea (see Chapter 2). Just as the Essenes, he called the Jews to repent and to worship God according to the prescriptions of the Old Testament.

John is introduced as a herald for Jesus, who appears somewhat later in this gospel.

Matthew and Luke added a few verses from Q to describe John's message to the Pharisees and scribes from Jerusalem and the temptation of Jesus in greater detail.

The Baptism and Temptation of Jesus
Mark 1: 9–13 (Matt 3: 13 – 14: 11; Luke 3: 21–22; 4: 1–13)

9.	It happened in those days, that Jesus came from Nazareth of Galilee, and was baptized by John in the Jordan.
10.	Immediately coming up from the water, he saw the heavens parting, and the Spirit descending on him like a dove.
11.	A voice came out of the sky, "You are my beloved Son, in whom I am well pleased."
12.	Immediately the Spirit drove him out into the wilderness.
13.	He was there in the wilderness forty days tempted by Satan. He was with the wild animals. The angels ministered to him.

It has already been shown in Chapter 2 that the baptism of Jesus probably took place on 24 November AD 29, during a total solar eclipse over Galilee. The unexpected darkness that was caused by the eclipse, the starry heavens that became visible, and a mysterious wind that was interpreted as God's Spirit, gave Jesus the message that he was called by God to be the Messiah, the savior of his people and to be the king of Israel or the son of God.

Mark mentioned the temptation of Jesus in a single sentence. Matthew and Luke added many more details. The ultimate source for this story could only have been Jesus himself, who told his disciples and friends later of his experiences. It has been mentioned in Chapter 2 that the dehydrated and famished Jesus must have been hallucinating, during which time he struggled with Satan in his temporarily malfunctioning mind.

Jesus Calls four Fishermen
Mark 1: 14–20 (Matt 4: 12–22; Luke 4: 14–15; 5: 1–11)

14.	Now after John was taken into custody, Jesus came into Galilee, preaching the gospel of the kingdom of God,
15.	and saying, "The time is fulfilled, and the kingdom of God is at hand! Repent, and believe in the gospel."
16.	Passing along by the sea of Galilee, he saw Simon and Andrew, the brother of Simon, casting a net in the sea, for they were fishermen.
17.	Jesus said to them, "Come after me, and I will make you into fishers for men."
18.	Immediately they left their nets, and followed him.
19.	Going on a little further from there, he saw James, the son of Zebedee, and John, his brother, who also were in the boat mending the nets.

> 20. Immediately he called them, and they left their father, Zebedee, in the boat with the hired servants, and went after him.

After Jesus had been baptized, John was arrested by Herod Antipas, ruler or tetrarch of Galilee, due to John's criticism of his incestuous marriage. Herod could only have captured John if he was baptizing in Galilee at that time, where Jesus was also baptized.

After his experiences during his baptism and his stay in the desert, Jesus started his campaign of recruiting followers for his campaign to establish the kingdom of God, the Israelite monarchy that was due to be realized soon.

He recruited his first four disciples, Simon, Andrew, James, and John – all of them Galilean fishermen. Matthew added that Jesus made Capernaum his headquarters, while Luke tells us that Jesus helped Simon and Andrew to catch a huge harvest of fish.

A Man with an Evil Spirit
Mark 1: 21–28 (Luke 4: 31–37)

> 21. They went into Capernaum, and immediately on the Sabbath day he entered into the synagogue and taught.
> 22. They were astonished at his teaching, for he taught them as having authority, and not as the scribes.
> 23. Immediately there was in their synagogue a man with an unclean spirit, and he cried out,
> 24. saying, "Ha! What do we have to do with you, Jesus, you Nazarene? Have you come to destroy us? I know you who you are: the Holy One of God."
> 25. Jesus rebuked him, saying, "Be quiet, and come out of him!"

26.	The unclean spirit, convulsing him and crying with a loud voice, came out of him.
27.	They were all amazed, so that they questioned among themselves, saying, "What is this? A new teaching? For with authority he commands even the unclean spirits, and they obey him."
28.	The report of him went out immediately everywhere into all the region of Galilee and its surrounding area.

Jesus proved to be a capable preacher in the synagogue of Capernaum, speaking with more authority than the scribes the congregants usually heard. It must be concluded that Jesus had received a thorough training in the Scriptures, probably at the Essene center at Qumran.

A man with a psychiatric disorder disrupted a meeting and he quietened down after Jesus dealt with him. With the lack of medical knowledge in those days, this disorder was seen as being caused by an evil spirit.

Luke repeated this report without any additions.

Jesus Heals Many People
Mark 1: 29–34 (Matt 8: 14–17; Luke 4: 38–41)

29.	Immediately, when they had come out of the synagogue, they came into the house of Simon and Andrew, with James and John.
30.	Now Simon's wife's mother lay sick with a fever, and immediately they told him about her.
31.	He came and took her by the hand, and raised her up. The fever left her, and she served them.

32.	At evening, when the sun had set, they brought to him all who were sick, and those who were possessed with demons.
33.	All the city was gathered together at the door.
34.	He healed many who were sick with various diseases, and cast out many demons. He didn't allow the demons to speak, because they knew him.

Jesus' reputation as a healer grew rapidly as he helped Simon's mother-in-law to get better and he healed some other people from the town. Some were supposedly possessed of evil spirits because the causes of their maladies were unknown, due to the lack of medical knowledge in those days. Jesus must have had some training in the healing arts as a student at the Essene school at Qumran. According to the Jewish philosopher, Philo of Alexandria, some Essenes were known as the "Therapeutae" (Healers) in those days. They were especially known for praying twice a day and their studies of the Scriptures.[190]

Matthew and Luke copied this story essentially unchanged.

Jesus Preaches in Galilee
Mark 1: 35–39 (Luke 4: 42–44)

35.	Early in the night, he rose up and went out, and departed into a desert place, and there prayed.
36.	Simon and those who were with him followed after him;
37.	and they found him, and told him, "All are seeking you."
38.	He said to them, "Let's go elsewhere into the next towns, that I may preach there also, for to this end I came forth."

---

[190] Enc Brit, "Therapeutae".

> 39. He went into their synagogues throughout all Galilee, preaching and casting out demons.

Jesus extended his recruiting and healing campaign into other parts of Galilee and took his disciples along with him, after spending a night in prayer on a mountain.

Luke repeated this report unaltered.

Jesus Heals a Man with Leprosy
Mark 1: 40–45 (Matt 8: 1–4; Luke 5: 12–16)

> 40. There came to him a leper, begging him, kneeling down to him, and saying to him, "If you want to, you can make me clean."
>
> 41. Being moved with compassion, he stretched forth his hand, and touched him, and said to him, "I want to. Be made clean."
>
> 42. When he had said this, immediately the leprosy departed from him, and he was made clean.
>
> 43. He strictly charged him, and immediately sent him out,
>
> 44. and said to him, "See you say nothing to anybody, but go show yourself to the priest, and offer for your cleansing the things which Moses commanded, for a testimony to them."
>
> 45. But he went out, and began to proclaim it much, and to spread about the matter, so that Jesus could no more openly enter into a city, but was outside in desert places: and they came to him from everywhere.

After Jesus had healed a man with leprosy, his reputation as a healer continued to grow, although he asked the man not to tell everybody about his healing because his campaign to recruit supporters was an underground campaign.

Matthew and Luke repeated the story essentially unaltered.

Jesus Heals a Paralyzed Man
Mark 2: 1–12 (Matt 9: 1–8; Luke 5: 17–26)

1.	When he entered again into Capernaum after some days, it was heard that he was in the house.
2.	Immediately many were gathered together, so that there was no more room, not even around the door; and he spoke the word to them.
3.	Four people came, carrying a paralytic to him.
4.	When they could not come near to him for the crowd, they removed the roof where he was. When they had broken it up, they let down the mat that the paralytic was laying on.
5.	Jesus, seeing their faith, said to the paralytic, "Son, your sins are forgiven you."
6.	But there were some of the scribes sitting there, and reasoning in their hearts,
7.	"Why does this man speak blasphemies like that? He blasphemes! Who can forgive sins but one – God?"
8.	Immediately Jesus, perceiving in his spirit that they so reasoned within themselves, said to them, "Why do you reason these things in your hearts?
9.	Which is easier, to tell the paralytic, `Your sins are forgiven;` or to say, `Arise, and take up your bed, and walk?`
10.	But that you may know that the Son of Man has authority on earth to forgive sins" — he said to the paralytic,
11.	"I tell you, arise, take up your mat, and go to your house."

> 12. He arose, and immediately took up the mat, and went out in front of them all; so that they were all amazed, and glorified God, saying, "We never saw anything like this!"

Jesus healed a paralyzed man whose friends lowered him down to Jesus through the roof of the house where Jesus was because they could not reach him otherwise on account of the throng of people packed into that house. Some scribes or teachers of the Law criticized Jesus for declaring that the man's sins were forgiven.

Matthew shortened the story somewhat, while Luke added some Pharisees to the teachers of the Law who doubted Jesus' authority to forgive sins.

Jesus Calls Levi
Mark 2: 13–17 (Matt 9: 9–13; Luke 5: 27–32)

> 13. He went out again by the seaside. All the multitude came to him, and he taught them.
> 14. As he passed by, he saw Levi, the son of Alphaeus, sitting at the place of toll, and he said to him, "Follow me." And he arose and followed him.
> 15. It happened, that he was reclining at the table in his house, and many tax collectors and sinners sat down with Jesus and his disciples, for there were many, and they followed him.
> 16. The scribes and the Pharisees, when they saw that he was eating with the sinners and tax collectors, said to his disciples, "Why is it that he eats and drinks with tax collectors and sinners?"
> 17. When Jesus heard it, he said to them, "Those who are healthy have no need for a physician, but those who are

> sick. I came not to call the righteous, but sinners to repentance."

Jesus recruited a tax collector called Levi to follow him and he enlisted more supporters from some strange circles – other tax collectors, who were hated for their cooperation with the Roman authorities, and sinners or people with blemished reputations. The Pharisees, who saw themselves as respectable people, criticized Jesus for this behavior. Jesus retorted that he was leading these people to repentance, something the Pharisees were incapable of.

Matthew changed the name of the tax collector from Levi to Matthew, while Luke added that Levi invited Jesus and some of his colleagues to a lunch in his house.

The Question about Fasting
Mark2: 18–22 (Matt 9: 14–17; Luke 5: 33–39)

18.	John's disciples and the Pharisees were fasting, and they came and asked him, "Why do John's disciples and the disciples of the Pharisees fast, but your disciples don't fast?"
19.	Jesus said to them, "Can the sons of the bride chamber fast, while the bridegroom is with them? As long as they have the bridegroom with them, they can't fast.
20.	But the days will come, when the bridegroom will be taken away from them, and then will they fast in that day.
21.	No one sews a piece of unshrunk cloth on an old garment, or else the patch shrinks and the new tears away from the old, and a worse hole is made.
22.	No one puts new wine into old wineskins, or else the new wine will burst the skins, and the wine pours out, and the

> skins will be destroyed; but they put new wine into fresh wineskins."

Jesus seemed to have had little time to waste on fasting. He defended himself by comparing himself to a bridegroom in whose presence his friends, the wedding guests, are merry. He added, though, that the day would come when he, the bridegroom, will not be around anymore and then his friends can start fasting and praying.

Mark added two parables that seemingly don't have any bearing on the need to fast – the parable of a new patch on an old cloth and the parable of new wine in old wine bags. However, the new patch and the new wine symbolized the new Israel that Jesus wanted to establish when the monarchy was restored. The old cloth and the old wine bag symbolized the old-fashioned Pharisees and teachers of the Law who did not agree with Jesus' vision of the coming kingdom as a theocracy.

Matthew and Luke gave essentially the same story, but Luke added the following sentence (5: 39) – "No man having drunk old wine immediately desires new, for he says, 'The old is better.'" This seems to contradict the two parables in Mark.

The Question about the Sabbath
Mark 2: 23–28 (Matt 12: 1–8; Luke 6: 1–5)

> 23. It happened, that he was going on the Sabbath day through the grain fields, and his disciples began, as they went, to pluck the ears of grain.
>
> 24. The Pharisees said to him, "Behold, why do they do that which is not lawful on the Sabbath day?"

25.	He said to them, "Did you never read what David did, when he had need, and was hungry, he, and they who were with him?
26.	How he entered into the house of God when Abiathar was high priest, and ate the show bread, which it is not lawful to eat except for the priests, and gave also to those who were with him?"
27.	He said to them, "The Sabbath was made for man, not man for the Sabbath.
28.	Therefore the Son of Man is lord even of the Sabbath."

Jesus seems to have had a less than strict or legalistic view of the Sabbath and thought that the rest on the Sabbath must not be a burden, but something to benefit man.

Matthew and Luke omitted the reference to Abiathar, the high priest, since he wasn't the high priest during the episode mentioned by Jesus; his father Ahimelech was the high priest at that time (1 Sam 21: 3–6).

The Man with a Paralyzed Hand
Mark 3: 1–6 (Matt 12: 9–14; Luke 6: 6–11)

1.	He entered again into the synagogue, and there was a man there who had his hand withered.
2.	They watched him, whether he would heal him on the Sabbath day, that they might accuse him.
3.	He said to the man who had his hand withered, "Stand up."
4.	He said to them, "Is it lawful on the Sabbath day to do good, or to do harm? To save a life, or to kill?" But they were silent.

5.	When he had looked around at them with anger, being grieved at the hardening of their hearts, he said to the man, "Stretch out your hand." He stretched it out, and his hand was restored as healthy as the other.
6.	The Pharisees went out, and immediately took counsel with the Herodians against him, how they might destroy him.

Jesus was angry at the Pharisees who thought that observance of the Sabbath was more important than doing good by helping somebody who suffered.

Matthe added the following: "He said to them, 'What man is there among you, who has one sheep, and if this one falls into a pit on the Sabbath day, will he not grab on to it, and lift it out?'"

A Crowd by the Lake
Mark 3: 7–12 (Luke 6: 12–17)

7.	Jesus withdrew to the sea with his disciples, and a great multitude followed him from Galilee, from Judea,
8.	from Jerusalem, from Idumaea, beyond the Jordan, and those from around Tyre and Sidon. A great multitude, hearing what great things he did, came to him.
9.	He spoke to his disciples, that a little boat should stay near him because of the crowd, so that they wouldn't press on him.
10.	For he had healed many, so that as many as had diseases pressed on him that they might touch him.
11.	The unclean spirits, whenever they saw him, fell down before him, and cried, "You are the Son of God!"

12.	He sternly warned them that they should not make him known.

Jesus drew crowds from various regions to the south, east and north of Galilee to hear his message.

Luke has essentially the same information, but he rearranged the wording.

Jesus Chooses the Twelve Apostles
Mark 3: 13–19 (Matt 10: 1–4; Luke 6: 12–16)

13.	He went up into the mountain, and called to himself whom he wanted, and they went to him.
14.	He appointed twelve, that they might be with him, and that he might send them out to preach,
15.	and to have authority to heal sicknesses and to cast out demons:
16.	Simon, to whom he gave the name Peter;
17.	James the son of Zebedee; John, the brother of James, and them he surnamed Boanerges, which is, Sons of thunder;
18.	Andrew; Philip; Bartholomew; Matthew; Thomas; James, the son of Alphaeus; Thaddaeus; Simon the Zealot;
19.	and Judas Iscariot, who also betrayed him. He came into a house.

Jesus chose exactly twelve disciples or apostles (envoys or missionaries) to symbolize the new Israel that he wanted to create with the restoration of the monarchy. The twelve had to symbolize the twelve patriarchs and the twelve tribes of Israel – just as James addressed his letter to the "twelve tribes which are in the Dispersion" (Jas 1: 1).

The other two Synoptic Gospels contain the same names. Mark exchanged Levi with Matthew.

Jesus and Beelzebul
Mark 3: 20–30 (Matt 12: 22–32; Luke 11: 14 – 12:10)

20.	The multitude came together again, so that they could not so much as eat bread.
21.	When his friends heard it, they went out to lay hold on him: for they said, "He is insane."
22.	The scribes who came down from Jerusalem said, "He has Beelzebul," and, "By the prince of the demons he casts out the demons."
23.	He called them to him, and said to them in parables, "How can Satan cast out Satan?
24.	If a kingdom is divided against itself, that kingdom cannot stand.
25.	If a house is divided against itself, that house cannot stand.
26.	If Satan has risen up against himself, and is divided, he can't stand, but has an end.
27.	But no one can enter into the house of the strong man to plunder, unless he first binds the strong man; and then he will plunder his house.
28.	Most assuredly I tell you, all their sins will be forgiven to the sons of men, and their blasphemies with which they may blaspheme;
29.	but whoever may blaspheme against the Holy Spirit never has forgiveness, but is guilty of an eternal sin"
30.	— because they said, "He has an unclean spirit."

> 31. His mother and his brothers came, and standing outside, they sent to him, calling him.
> 32. A multitude was sitting around him, and they told him, "Behold, your mother, your brothers, and your sisters are outside looking for you."
> 33. He answered them, "Who are my mother and my brothers?"
> 34. Looking around at those who sat around him, he said, "Behold, my mother and my brothers!
> 35. For whoever may do the will of God, the same is my brother, and my sister, and mother."

A somewhat similar episode is narrated in Matt 12: 22–32 and Luke 11: 14 – 12:10, which is part of the Q Document. The differences between Mark and the other two Synoptic Gospels are big enough to warrant the conclusion that they come from different sources, which seems to confirm the veracity of both versions.

This is another example where Jesus was maligned, when he was accused of casting out demons with the power of Beelzebul (Greek: Βεελζεβούλ – *Beelzeboul*), the prince or ruler of the demons. Jesus easily pointed out the logical flaw in this accusation by arguing that it is impossible that Satan (Beelzebul) would be willing to get rid of his helpers, the lesser little devils.

Jesus also compared himself with a strong man who overpowered another strong man (Satan) and looted his treasures.

The name Beelzebul is derived from the name of a Philistine deity, mentioned in 2 Kgs 1: 2–3, 6 & 16) where he is called Beelzebub (Baal or Lord of the Flies) (Hebrew: בַּעַל זְבוּב – *Baal–Zebub*). Those who accused Jesus of using the power of Beelzebul tried to discredit him as an imposter, somebody allied to Satan or a pagan god.

Jesus also declared that it was an unforgivable sin, a sin against the Holy Spirit (the mind of God or God himself) to accuse Jesus, the Messiah and anointed of God, of making use of dark and evil powers.

When confronted by the fact that his family members were looking for him, he answered that all those who were obedient to God can be regarded as his family members since they are also children of God.

Parable of the Sower
Mark 4: 1–9 (Matt 13: 1–9; Luke 8: 4–8)

1.	Again he began to teach by the seaside. A great multitude was gathered to him, so that he entered into a boat in the sea, and sat down. All the multitude were on the land by the sea.
2.	He taught them many things in parables, and told them in his teaching,
3.	"Listen! Behold, the farmer went forth to sow,
4.	and it happened, as he sowed, some seed fell by the road, and the birds came and devoured it.
5.	Others fell on the rocky ground, where it had little soil, and immediately it sprang up, because it had no depth of soil.
6.	When the sun had risen, it was scorched; and because it had no root, it withered away.
7.	Others fell among the thorns, and the thorns grew up, and choked it, and it yielded no fruit.

> 8. Others fell into the good ground, and yielded fruit, growing up and increasing. Some brought forth thirty times, some sixty times, and some one hundred times as much."
> 9. He said, "Whoever has ears to hear, let him hear."

The seed in this parable is a symbol of Jesus' message, which caused different reactions from different sections of society. There were those who reacted positively, but soon forgot about it. Others easily dismissed it. Some more people had so many worries that they could not be bothered. But then there were also those who accepted his message and the number of his supporters grew day by day.

Matthew copied this parable almost word for word, while Luke shortened it somewhat.

The Purpose of the Parables
Mark 4: 10–12 (Matt 13: 10–17; Luke 8: 9–10)

> 10. When he was alone, those who were around him with the twelve asked him about the parables.
> 11. He said to them, "To you is given the mystery of the kingdom of God, but to those who are outside, all things are done in parables,
> 12. that `seeing they may see, and not perceive; and hearing they may hear, and not understand; lest perhaps they should turn again, and their sins should be forgiven them.`"

Jesus explained to his disciples that he could not speak about the "mystery" or secret of the coming kingdom of God too openly and, therefore, he used parables when addressing outsiders.

Matthew added that this was the fulfillment of a prophecy of Isaiah (6: 9–10) and he also quoted a saying from Q to support this.

The Parable of the Sower Explained
Mark 4: 13–20 (Matt 13: 18–23; Luke 8: 11–15)

13.	He said to them, "Don't you understand this parable? How will you understand all of the parables?
14.	The farmer sows the word.
15.	These are they by the road, where the word is sown; and when they have heard, immediately Satan comes, and takes away the word which has been sown in them.
16.	These in like manner are those who are sown on the rocky places, who, when they have heard the word, immediately receive it with joy.
17.	They have no root in themselves, but endure for a while, then, when oppression or persecution arises because of the word, immediately they stumble.
18.	Others are those who are sown among the thorns. These are those who have heard the word,
19.	and the cares of this age, and the deceitfulness of riches, and the lusts of other things entering in choke the word, and it becomes unfruitful.
20.	These are those who were sown on the good ground: such as hear the word, and accept it, and bear fruit, some thirty times, some sixty times, and some one hundred times."

Jesus explained the Parable of the Sower to his disciples. Jesus compared the seed sown onto the hard road surface, where the birds ate the seed, with the Pharisees and teachers of the Law who heard his message, but did not accept it.

Matthew and Luke essentially repeated the passage in Mark unaltered.

A Lamp under a Basket
Mark 4: 21–25 (Luke 8: 16–18)

21.	He said to them, "Is the lamp brought to be put under a basket or under the bed? Isn't it put on the lampstand?
22.	For there is nothing hidden, except that it should be made known; neither was anything made secret, but that it should come to light.
23.	If any man has ears to hear, let him hear."
25.	For whoever has, to him will more be given, and he who has not, from him will be taken away even that which he has."

Jesus was confident that the light or truth about the coming kingdom would be revealed for all to see. Those who opposed his campaign, the wealthy and influential elite in Jerusalem, would lose everything when the kingdom was established.

Luke copied this passage almost unaltered.

The Parable of the Growing Seed
Mark 4: 26–29

26.	He said, "So is the kingdom of God, as if a man should cast seed on the earth,
27.	and should sleep and rise night and day, and the seed should spring up and grow, he doesn't know how.
28.	For the earth bears fruit: first the blade, then the ear, then the full grain in the ear.
29.	But when the fruit is ripe, immediately he puts forth the sickle, because the harvest has come."

According to Jesus, it was inevitable that the kingdom of God, the Israelite theocracy, would gain support and be established – just as it is inevitable that seed that was sown in good soil would yield a good harvest.

The Parable of the Mustard Seed
Mark 4: 30–34 (Matt 13: 31–32; Luke 13: 18–19)

30.	He said, "How will we liken the kingdom of God? Or by what parable will we compare it?
31.	It is like a grain of mustard seed, which, when it is sown in the earth, though it is less than all the seeds that are on the earth,
32.	yet when it is sown, grows up, and becomes greater than all the herbs, and puts out great branches, so that the birds of the sky can lodge under its shadow."
33.	With many such parables he spoke the word to them, as they were able to hear it.
34.	Without a parable he didn't speak to them; but privately to his own disciples he explained all things.

The parable of the mustard seed was used by Jesus to explain that the kingdom of God, of which he was due to become the monarch, would grow from a small beginning to become a strong institution – just as a small mustard seed could grow into a big plant.

Matthew's version of this parable is much shorter and was taken from Q. Luke's version in Q adds that birds nest in the big mustard tree. The fact that there are two independent sources for this parable may be a sign of its authenticity.

Jesus Calms a Storm
Mark 4: 35–41 (Matt 8: 23–27; Luke 8: 22–25)

> 35. On that day, when evening had come, he said to them, "Let's go over to the other side."
> 36. Leaving the multitude, they took him with them, even as he was, in the boat. Other small boats were also with him.
> 37. There arose a great wind storm, and the waves beat into the boat, so much that the boat was already filled.
> 38. He himself was in the stern, asleep on the cushion, and they woke him up, and told him, "Teacher, don't you care that we are dying?"
> 39. He awoke, and rebuked the wind, and said to the sea, "Peace. Be still." The wind ceased, and there was a great calm.
> 40. He said to them, "Why are you so afraid? How is it that you have no faith?"
> 41. They were greatly afraid, and said to one another, "Who then is this, that even the wind and the sea obey him?"

The Sea of Galilee, a fresh water lake about 200 meters below sea level in the Great Rift Valley of Palestine, often experiences sudden storms, especially when cold air from the Mediterranean Sea blows over the hot air on the surface of the lake.[191] It is likely that Jesus and the disciples got caught in such a storm, which occurred suddenly and blew over after some time. The calming of the storm was attributed to Jesus who is said to have scolded the storm.

Matthew and Luke copied the story without major changes.

Jesus Heals a Man with Evil Spirits
Mark 5:1–20 (Matt 8: 28–34; Luke 8: 26–39)

---

[191] Deseret News. "Storms are Common on the Sea of Galilee".

1. They came to the other side of the sea, into the country of the Gadarenes.
2. When he had come out of the boat, immediately there met him out of the tombs a man with an unclean spirit,
3. who had his dwelling in the tombs. Nobody could bind him any more, not even with chains,
4. because he had been often bound with fetters and chains, and the chains had been torn apart by him, and the fetters broken in pieces. Nobody had the strength to tame him.
5. Always, night and day, in the tombs and in the mountains, he was crying out, and cutting himself with stones.
6. When he saw Jesus from afar, he ran and bowed down to him,
7. and crying out with a loud voice, he said, "What have I to do with you, Jesus, you Son of the Most High God? I adjure you by God, don`t torment me."
8. For he said to him, "Come out of the man, you unclean spirit!"
9. He asked him, "What is your name?" He said to him, "My name is Legion, for we are many."
10. He begged him much that he would not send them away out of the country.
11. Now there was there on the mountainside a great herd of pigs feeding.
12. All the demons begged him, saying, "Send us into the pigs, that we may enter into them."
13. At once Jesus gave them permission. The unclean spirits came out, and got hold of the pigs. The herd of about two

> 14. Those who fed them fled, and told it in the city, and in the country. The people came to see what it was that had happened.
> 15. They came to Jesus, and saw him who was possessed by demons sitting, clothed and in his right mind, even him who had the legion; and they were afraid.
> 16. Those who saw it declared to them how it happened to him who was possessed by demons, and about the pigs.
> 17. They began to beg him to depart from their borders.
> 18. As he was entering into the boat, he who had been possessed by demons begged him that he might be with him.
> 19. He didn't allow him, but said to him, "Go to your house, to your friends, and tell them how the Lord has done great things for you, and how he had mercy on you."
> 20. He went his way, and began to proclaim in Decapolis how Jesus had done great things for him, and everyone marveled.

When Jesus and the disciples reached the eastern shore of the lake a man with a serious psychiatric disorder – probably a bipolar (manic-depressive) disorder with psychotic features – confronted Jesus. It is doubtful that he addressed Jesus as the Son of God or king of Israel because Jesus was certainly not known in those parts. Mark or his source must have added this exclamation because he thought the demons would recognize Jesus for whom and what he was.

Jesus, somehow, calmed the man down. If he had a bipolar disorder with psychotic tendencies, he could have entered a more normal phase after having been in an extreme manic phase previously.[192]

A herd of pigs somehow got a fright and rushed into the water where they drowned. This event was linked to Jesus who was thought to have driven the demons in this poor suffering man's mind away and that they invaded the unfortunate swine.

The people of that town became afraid of Jesus, taking him for a magician, and begged him to leave – too afraid of his powers to throw him out.

Matthew and Luke copied the story faithfully, although Matthew wrote that two men, instead of one man, were healed from their evil spirits. In Luke's account, the demons begged Jesus not to banish them to "the Abyss," evidently a place of captivity where some dangerous demons were being kept.

Jairus' Daughter and the Woman who Touched Jesus' Cloak
Mark 5: 21–43 (Matt 9: 18–26; Luke 8: 40–56)

21.	When Jesus had crossed back over in the boat to the other side, a great multitude was gathered to him; and he was by the sea.
22.	Behold, one of the rulers of the synagogue, Jairus by name, came; and seeing him, he fell at his feet,
23.	and begged him much, saying, "My little daughter is at the point of death. Please come and lay your hands on her, that she may be made healthy, and live."
24.	He went with him, and a great multitude followed him, and they pressed upon him on all sides.

---

[192] American Psychiatric Association, *DSM-5*, 149–52.

25. A certain woman, who had an issue of blood for twelve years,
26. and had suffered many things by many physicians, and had spent all that she had, and was no better, but rather grew worse,
27. having heard the things concerning Jesus, came up behind him in the crowd, and touched his clothes.
28. For she said, "If I just touch his clothes, I will be made well."
29. Immediately the fountain of her blood was dried up, and she felt in her body that she was healed of her plague.
30. Immediately Jesus, perceiving in himself that the power had gone forth from him, turned around in the crowd, and asked, "Who touched my clothes?"
31. His disciples said to him, "You see the multitude pressing against you, and you say, `Who touched me?'"
32. He looked around to see her who had done this thing.
33. But the woman, fearing and trembling, knowing what had been done to her, came and fell down before him, and told him all the truth.
34. He said to her, "Daughter, your faith has made you well. Go in peace, and be cured of your disease."
35. While he was still speaking, they came from the synagogue ruler's house saying, "Your daughter is dead. Why bother the Teacher any more?"
36. But Jesus, not heeding the word spoken, immediately said to the ruler of the synagogue, "Don't be afraid, only believe."

37.	He allowed no one to follow him, except Peter, James, and John, the brother of James.
38.	He came to the synagogue ruler's house, and he saw an uproar, weeping, and great wailing.
39.	When he had entered in, he said to them, "Why do you make an uproar and weep? The child is not dead, but is asleep."
40.	They laughed him to scorn. But he, having put them all out, took the father of the child and her mother and those who were with him, and went in where the child was lying.
41.	Taking the child by the hand, he said to her, "Talitha cumi;" which means, being interpreted, "Young lady, I tell you, get up."
42.	Immediately the young lady rose up, and walked, for she was twelve years old. They were amazed with great amazement.
43.	He charged them much that no one should know this. He commanded that something should be given to her to eat

The original readers of the Gospel of Mark, who lived in a world where people believed in magic and miracles, would have found this story credible where Jesus healed a woman with a flow of blood without doing anything and reviving a girl of the age of twelve after she had died. There may be a kernel of truth in these stories, but it is impossible to determine today what really happened, except that some unexplained healings were connected to the presence of Jesus, who was a well-known healer in Galilee and Judea.

The possibility exists that the girl was only in a coma and when Jesus saw her, she was on the point of regaining her consciousness spontaneously. This recovery was then attributed to Jesus' healing powers.

Luke copied the story without any real alterations, except for dropping the negative reference to physicians, but Matthew shortened it and changed the dying girl at the beginning into a girl who was already very dead.

Jesus is Rejected at Nazareth
Mark 6: 1–6 (Matt 13: 53–58; Luke 4: 16–30)

1.	He went out from there. He came into his own country, and his disciples followed him.
2.	When the Sabbath had come, he began to teach in the synagogue, and many hearing him were astonished, saying, "Where did this man get these things?" and, "What is the wisdom that is given to this man, that such mighty works come about by his hands?
3.	Isn't this the carpenter, the son of Mary, and brother of James, Joses, Judas, and Simon? Aren't his sisters here with us?" They were offended by him.
4.	Jesus said to them, "A prophet is not without honor, except in his own country, and among his own relatives, and in his own house."
5.	He could do no mighty work there, except that he laid his hands on a few sick folk, and healed them.
6.	He marveled because of their unbelief. He went around the villages teaching.

Jesus did not find an appreciative audience in the synagogue of his home town, Nazareth. He explained this situation by stating that prophets are not appreciated in their own towns.

Matthew reproduced this story faithfully, but Luke added a lengthy passage from L, according to which Jesus read a part of

Isaiah (11: 2–5) in the synagogue and the folks there threatened to push him over a cliff. Since Nazareth is built in a rugged part of Galilee, there are more than one spot where Jesus could have been thrown over a precipice.[193]

The Mission of the Twelve Disciples
Mark 6: 7–13 (Matt 10: 5–15; Luke 9: 1–6)

7.	He called to himself the twelve, and began to send them out two by two; and he gave them authority over the unclean spirits.
8.	He charged them that they should take nothing for their journey, except a staff only: no bread, no wallet, no money in their purse,
9.	but to wear sandals, and not put on two tunics.
10.	He said to them, "Wherever you enter into a house, stay there until you depart from there.
11.	Whoever will not receive you nor hear you, as you depart from there, shake off the dust that is under your feet for a testimony against them. Assuredly, I tell you, it will be more tolerable for Sodom and Gomorrah in the day of judgment than for that city!"
12.	They went out, and preached that people should repent.
13.	They cast out many demons, and anointed many with oil who were sick, and healed them.

Jesus sent his disciples out in pairs to spread his message and to heal the sick. They had to rely on the hospitality and generosity of their hosts – as was the custom in Essene communities.

---

[193] Anon, "Mount Precipice."

Luke copied the story with the addition that the disciples had to spread the message about the coming kingdom. Matthew added a lengthy passage from Q in which it was succinctly stated that they had to teach the people that the Kingdom of Heaven was at hand.

The Death of John the Baptist
Mark 6: 14–29 (Matt 14: 1–12; Luke 9: 7–9)

14.	King Herod heard this, for his name had become known, and he said, "John the Baptizer has risen from the dead, and therefore these powers work in him."
15.	But others said, "It is Elijah." Others said, "It is the Prophet, or like one of the prophets."
16.	But Herod, when he heard this, said, "This is John, whom I beheaded. He has risen from the dead."
17.	For Herod himself had sent out and laid hold on John, and bound him in prison for the sake of Herodias, his brother Philip's wife, for he had married her.
18.	For John said to Herod, "It is not lawful for you to have your brother's wife."
19.	Herodias set herself against him, and desired to kill him, but she couldn't,
20.	for Herod feared John, knowing that he was a righteous and holy man, and kept him safe. When he heard him, he did many things, and he heard him gladly.
21.	When a convenient day had come, that Herod on his birthday made a supper for his lords, and the high captains, and the chief men of Galilee;
22.	and when the daughter of Herodias herself came in and danced, she pleased Herod and those reclining with him.

	The king said to the young lady, "Ask me whatever you want, and I will give it to you."
23.	He swore to her, "Whatever you shall ask of me, I will give you, up to half of my kingdom."
24.	She went out, and said to her mother, "What shall I ask?" She said, "The head of John the Baptizer."
25.	She came in immediately with haste to the king, and asked, "I want you to give me right now the head of John the Baptizer on a platter."
26.	The king was exceedingly sorry, but for the sake of his oaths, and of his dinner guests, he didn't wish to refuse her.
27.	Immediately the king sent forth a soldier of his guard, and commanded to bring John's head, and he went and beheaded him in the prison,
28.	and brought his head on a platter, and gave it to the young lady; and the young lady gave it to her mother.
29.	When his disciples heard this, they came and took up his corpse, and laid it in a tomb.

Mark 6: 17 records that Herod Antipas, the tetrarch or ruler of Galilee, married his sister-in-law, Herodias, the divorced wife of his half-brother Philip. We are also told that John the Baptist criticized him for this sin. However, Herodias was not the ex-wife of Philip, but of Herod Archelaus, another half-brother and ruler of Judea after the death of their father, Herod the Great. Archelaus was removed from his position by the Romans due to his incompetence and mismanagement.[194]

The superstitious Herod Antipas believed that Jesus was a

---

[194] Josephus, *Antiquities*, XVIII/v/4.

revived or resurrected John the Baptist, although he had him beheaded to please his wife and step-daughter. He had made a rash promise after having ingested too much Palestinian wine, which made him reckless.

Matthew repeated Mark' story but Luke summarized it.

Albrecht Dürer: The Beheading of John the Baptist (1510)

Jesus Feeds Five Thousand Men
Mark 6: 30–44 (Matt 14: 13–21; Luke 9: 10–17)

30.	The apostles gathered themselves together to Jesus, and they told him all things, whatever they had done, and whatever they had taught.
31.	He said to them, "You come apart into a desert place, and rest awhile." For there were many coming and going, and they had no leisure so much as to eat.
32.	They went away in the boat to a desert place by themselves.
33.	They saw them going, and many recognized him and ran there on foot from all the cities. They arrived before them and came together to him.
34.	Jesus came out, saw a great multitude, and he had compassion on them, because they were like sheep without a shepherd, and he began to teach them many things.
35.	When it was late in the day, his disciples came to him, and said, "This place is a desert, and it is late in the day.
36.	Send them away, that they may go into the surrounding country and villages, and buy themselves bread, for they have nothing to eat."
37.	But he answered them, "You give them something to eat." They asked him, "Shall we go and buy two hundred denarii worth of bread, and give them something to eat?"
38.	He said to them, "How many loaves do you have? Go see." When they knew, they said, "Five, and two fish."
39.	He commanded those that all should sit down by companies on the green grass.
40.	They sat down in ranks, by hundreds and by fifties.
41.	He took the five loaves and the two fish, and looking up to heaven, he blessed, and broke the loaves, and he gave to

	his disciples to set before them, and he divided the two fish among them all.
42.	They all ate, and were filled.
43.	They took up twelve baskets full of broken pieces and also of the fish.
44.	Those who ate the loaves were five thousand men.

This story must have acquired a few legendary details after it had been retold many times before Mark eventually wrote it down. Mark informed his readers that Jesus taught a crowd of five thousand men "many things" while they were assembled on an open field. Jesus' voice would only have been audible to those nearest to him, while those further away would not have able to hear a thing without modern sound systems. Therefore, the number of five thousand men must be an exaggeration.

The only way a big crowd could have been fed from five loaves of bread and two fishes – which would not even have been enough for Jesus and his disciples – was that these people brought their own lunch packets along.

The fact that John 6: 1–14 reported something similar, but with some different details, seems to be an indication that there is a nucleus of truth in these stories.

Jesus Walks on the Water
Mark 6: 45–52 (Matt 14: 22–33)

45.	Immediately he made his disciples enter into the boat, and to go ahead to the other side, to Bethsaida, while he himself sent the multitude away.
46.	After he had taken leave of them, he departed into the mountain to pray.

47.	When evening had come, the boat was in the midst of the sea, and he was alone on the land.
48.	Seeing them distressed in rowing, for the wind was contrary to them; and about the fourth watch of the night he came to them, walking on the sea, and he would have passed by them,
49.	but they, when they saw him walking on the sea, supposed that it was a ghost, and cried out;
50.	for they all saw him, and were troubled. But he immediately spoke with them, and said to them, "Cheer up! It is I! Don't be afraid."
51.	He went up to them into the boat; and the wind ceased, and they were very amazed among themselves, and marveled.
52.	for they hadn't understood about the loaves, but their hearts were hardened.

After Jesus had sent the crowd away, he went to pray in the mountain. The disciples took their rowing boat to return home. A strong wind started blowing and that slowed them down.

Jesus went on foot around the lake to await the disciples at their destination. They saw him walking along the shore and it seemed as if he was walking on the water.

Matthew added (from M) that Peter started to walk on the water, just as he saw what Jesus was doing, but he almost drowned.

The Proto-Gospel of John (6: 15–21) reported a similar story, but left out the part of Peter trying to walk on the water. The fact that all four gospels contain the same story is an indication that such an incident must have taken place.

Jesus Heals the Sick in Gennesaret
Mark 6: 53–56 (Matt 14: 34–36)

53.	When they had crossed over, they came to the land to Gennesaret, and moored to the shore.
54.	When they had come out of the boat, immediately the people recognized him,
55.	and ran around that whole region, and began to carry around those who were sick, on their mats, to where they heard he was.
56.	Wherever he entered, into villages, or into cities, or into the country, they laid the sick in the marketplaces, and begged him that they might touch just the fringe of his garment; and as many as touched him were made well.

Gennesaret was a place on the western shore of the Sea of Galilee. When Jesus and his party arrived there, he was recognized and people flocked to him to be healed from their maladies and ailments.

Matthew repeated this story almost exactly.

The Teachings of the Ancestors
Mark 7: 1–13 (Matt 15: 1–9)

1.	Then the Pharisees, and some of the scribes gathered together to him, having come from Jerusalem.
2.	Now when they saw some of his disciples eating bread with defiled, that is, unwashed, hands, they found fault.
3.	(For the Pharisees, and all the Jews, don't eat unless they wash their hands and forearms, holding to the tradition of the elders.
4.	They don't eat when they come from the marketplace, unless they bathe themselves, and there are many other things, which they have received to hold to: washings of cups, pitchers, bronze vessels, and couches.)

5.	The Pharisees and the scribes asked him, "Why don't your disciples walk according to the tradition of the elders, but eat their bread with unwashed hands?"
6.	He answered them, "Well did Isaiah prophesy of you hypocrites, as it is written, 'This people honors me with their lips, But their heart is far from me.
7.	But in vain do they worship me, Teaching as doctrines the commandments of men.'
8.	"For you set aside the commandment of God, and hold tightly to the tradition of men — the washing of pitchers and cups, and you do many other such things."
9.	He said to them, "Full well do you reject the commandment of God, that you may keep your tradition.
10.	For Moses said, 'Honor your father and your mother;' and, 'He who speaks evil of father or mother, let him be put to death.'
11.	But you say, 'If a man will tell his father or his mother, "Whatever you might have been profited by me is Corban, that is to say, given to God;"'
12.	and you no longer allow him to do anything for his father or his mother,
13.	making void the word of God by your tradition, which you have handed down. You do many things like this."

Jesus clashed with the Pharisees and teachers of the Law who came from Jerusalem to investigate his activities. They complained that his disciples didn't wash their hands before eating, as required by their traditions. Jesus condemned them as hypocrites for regarding certain traditions to be more important than the requirement to honor their parents. Jesus quoted from Isaiah (29: 13) to support his words.

Matthew copied this story faithfully.

Things that Make a Person Unclean
Mark 7: 14–23 (Matt 15: 10–20)

14.	He called all the multitude to himself, and said to them, "Hear me, all of you, and understand.
15.	There is nothing from outside of the man, that going into him can defile him; but the things which proceed out of the man are those that defile the man.
16.	If anyone has ears to hear, let him hear!"
17.	When he had entered into the house from the multitude, his disciples asked him about the parable.
18.	He said to them, "Are you so without understanding also? Don't you perceive that whatever goes into the man from outside can't defile him,
19.	because it doesn't go into his heart, but into his belly, and into the latrine, thus making all foods clean?"
20.	He said, "That which proceeds out of the man, that defiles the man.
21.	For from within, out of the hearts of men, proceed evil thoughts, adulteries, sexual sins, murders, thefts,
22.	covetings, wickedness, deceit, lustful desires, an evil eye, blasphemy, pride, and foolishness.
23.	All these evil things proceed from within, and defile the man."

Jesus taught his disciples that real purity does not stem from outward actions and rituals, but from people's thoughts, attitudes, and words, which come from within. When people commit sins they defile themselves.

Matthew expanded this passage and added a saying from Q.

A Woman's Faith
Mark 7: 24–30 (Matt 15: 21–28)

> 24. From there he arose, and went away into the borders of Tyre and Sidon. He entered into a house, and wanted no one to know it, but he couldn't escape detection.
> 25. For a woman, whose little daughter had an unclean spirit, having heard of him, came and fell down at his feet.
> 26. Now the woman was a Greek, a Syrophoenician by race. She begged him that he would cast the demon out of her daughter.
> 27. But Jesus said to her, "Let the children be filled first, for it is not appropriate to take the children's bread and throw it to the dogs."
> 28. But she answered him, "Yes, Lord. For even the dogs under the table eat the children's crumbs."
> 29. He said to her, "For this saying, go your way. The demon has gone out of your daughter."
> 30. She went away to her house, and found the child laying on the bed, with the demon gone out.

Jesus took his disciples to Phoenicia to escape the crowds in Galilee. However, a local Greek-speaking woman recognized him and asked him to heal her daughter. Jesus insulted her initially – probably in Greek – by comparing the pagans to dogs, but relented when she refused to be insulted and he freed the child from the demon.

Matthew added a saying of Jesus, namely that he was only interested in helping "the lost sheep of the house of Israel."

Jesus Heals a Deaf-Mute
Mark 7: 31–37

31.	Again he departed from the borders of Tyre and Sidon, and came to the sea of Galilee, through the midst of the borders of Decapolis.
32.	They brought to him one who was deaf and had an impediment in his speech. They begged him to lay his hand on him.
33.	He took him aside from the multitude, privately, and put his fingers into his ears, and he spat, and touched his tongue.
34.	Looking up to heaven, he sighed, and said to him, "Ephphatha!" that is, "Be opened!"
35.	Immediately his ears were opened, and the bond of his tongue was loosed, and he spoke clearly.
36.	He charged them that they should tell no one, but the more he charged them, so much the more widely they proclaimed it.
37.	They were astonished beyond measure, saying, "He has done all things well. He makes even the deaf hear, and the mute speak!"

After his departure from Phoenicia, Jesus traversed Decapolis on the eastern side of the Sea of Galilea. There he healed a deaf-mute by opening his ears with the command: "Ephphatha! (Greek: ἐφφαθα), which means: "Be opened!" It is the Greek transcription of an Aramaic word, פְּתַח (*phetach*).

Jesus Feeds Four Thousand People
Mark 8: 1–10 (Matt 15: 32–39)

> 1. In those days, when there was a very great multitude, and they had nothing to eat, Jesus called his disciples to himself, and said to them,
> 2. "I have compassion on the multitude, because they continue with me now three days, and have nothing to eat.
> 3. If I send them away fasting to their home, they will faint on the way, for some of them have come a long way."
> 4. His disciples answered him, "From where will one be able to fill these men with bread here in a desert place?"
> 5. He asked them, "How many loaves do you have?" They said, "Seven."
> 6. He commanded the multitude to sit down on the ground, and he took the seven loaves. Having given thanks, he broke them, and gave them to his disciples to serve, and they served the multitude.
> 7. They had a few small fish. Having blessed them, he said to serve these also.
> 8. They ate, and were filled. They took up seven baskets of broken pieces that were left over.
> 9. Those who had eaten were about four thousand. Then he sent them away.
> 10. Immediately he entered into the boat with his disciples, and came into the region of Dalmanutha.

This story seems to be a doublet of the previous feeding of the five thousand men (Mark 6: 30–44), although certain details differ. It is possible that Mark heard the story from two different sources, each one slightly different from the other, and concluded that there were two occasions where such a miracle happened. If both stories actually describe a single event, it is a demonstration of how stories could have become distorted after four decades.

Only Matthew repeated this story.

The Pharisees Ask for a Sign
Mark 8: 11–13 (Matt 16: 1–4)

11.	The Pharisees came out and began to question him, seeking a sign from heaven from him, and tempting him.
12.	He sighed deeply in his spirit, and said, "Why does this generation seek a sign? Most assuredly I tell you, there will no sign be given to this generation."
13.	He left them, and again entering into the boat, departed to the other side.

Jesus refused to perform a miracle on demand to satisfy the curiosity of the Pharisees or to prove himself – as if he hadn't performed many miracles in the past by healing sick people.

Matthew inserted a saying from Q and added that Jesus would only give the Pharisees the sign of Jonah who spent three days in the belly of a big fish, but survived – just as Jesus expected to survive the destiny planned for him by his enemies.

The Yeast of the Pharisees and Herod
Mark 8: 14–21 (Matt 16: 5–12; Luke 12: 1)

14.	They forgot to take bread; and they didn't have more than one loaf in the boat with them.
15.	He charged them, saying, "Take heed: beware of the yeast of the Pharisees and the yeast of Herod."
16.	They reasoned with one another, saying, "It's because we have no bread."

17.	Jesus, perceiving it, said to them, "Why do you reason that it's because you have no bread? Don't you perceive yet, neither understand? Is your heart still hardened?
18.	Having eyes, don't you see? Having ears, don't you hear? Don't you remember?
19.	When I broke the five loaves among the five thousand, how many baskets full of broken pieces did you take up?" They told him, "Twelve."
20.	"When the seven loaves fed the four thousand, how many baskets full of broken pieces did you take up?" They told him, "Seven."
21.	He asked them, "Don't you understand, yet?"

No explanation is given for the expression "the yeast of the Pharisees and the yeast of Herod." Jesus merely reminded the disciples of how the multitudes had been fed and how much left-over were collected afterwards.

Matthew exchanged the name of Herod with "Sadducees" and he explained that Jesus warned his disciples against the teachings of the Pharisees and Sadducees. Luke declared that this yeast amounted to "hypocrisy".

Something of the sort may have been the meaning of the passage in Mark. Herod Antipas was the ruler of Galilee who had John the Baptist executed and his "yeast" may have been the invisible influence he exerted by trying to stamp out the Essenes like John and Jesus who were critical of him.

The Blind Man at Bethsaida
Mark 8: 22–26

22.	He came to Bethsaida. They brought a blind man to him, and begged him to touch him.

23.	He took hold of the blind man by the hand, and brought him out of the village. When he had spit on his eyes, and laid his hands on him, he asked him if he saw anything.
24.	He looked up, and said, "I see men; for I see them like trees walking."
25.	Then again he laid his hands on his eyes. He looked intently, and was restored, and saw everyone clearly.
26.	He sent him away to his house, saying, "Don't enter into the village, nor tell anyone in the village."

Bethsaida was not a city in Galilee and lay on the eastern shore of the Sea of Galilee in the country of Decapolis, mostly inhabited by Greek-speaking people who were inimical towards the Jews.[195]

That must be the reason why Jesus requested his disciples not to talk about his healing of a blind man in Bethsaida.

Peter's Declaration about Jesus
Mark 8: 27–30 (Matt 16: 13–20; Luke 9: 18–21).

27.	Jesus went forth, with his disciples, into the villages of Caesarea Philippi. On the way he asked his disciples, "Who do men say that I am?"
28.	They told him, "John the Baptizer, and others, Elijah, but others, one of the prophets."
29.	He asked them, "But who do you say that I am?" Peter answered, "You are the Christ."
30.	He charged them that they should tell no one about him.

---

[195] Enc com. "Decapolis".

Caesarea Philippi was the capital of the country of Galilee in Jesus' time. While travelling in this area, Jesus asked his disciples what they heard from other people about him. Various answers were given: people mistook him for John the Baptist, a resurrected Elijah, or another prophet. Peter, though, admitted that Jesus was indeed the Christ, the promised Messiah.

Jesus asked his disciples to stay silent about this because his drive to recruit supporters for his campaign was an underground and secret operation at that time.

According to Matthew, Peter said that he was "the Christ, the Son of the living God." Matthew also added that Jesus gave Peter the keys of the kingdom of heaven (part of M).

Jesus Speaks about his Suffering and Death
Mark 8: 31–38; 9: 1 (Matt 16: 21–28; Luke 9: 22–27).

31.	He began to teach them that the Son of Man must suffer many things, and be rejected by the elders, the chief priests, and the scribes, and be killed, and after three days rise again.
32.	He spoke to them openly. Peter took him, and began to rebuke him.
33.	But he, turning around, and seeing his disciples, rebuked Peter, and said, "Get behind me, Satan! For you have in mind not the things of God, but the things of men."
34.	He called the multitude to himself with his disciples, and said to them, "Whoever wants to come after me, let him deny himself, and take up his cross, and follow me.
35.	For whoever wants to save his life will lose it; and whoever will lose his life for my sake and the gospel's will save it.

> 36. For what does it profit a man, to gain the whole world, and forfeit his life?
> 37. For what should a man give in exchange for his life?
> 38. For whoever will be ashamed of me and of my words in this adulterous and sinful generation, the Son of Man also will be ashamed of him, when he comes in the glory of his Father with the holy angels."
> 1. He said to them, "Most assuredly I tell you, there are some standing here who will in no way taste death, until they see the kingdom of God come with power."

Traditional commentators of the Bible have always struggled with Jesus' promise that his followers would see the kingdom of God before they died. When one remembers that Jesus was campaigning to restore the Israelite monarchy with him on the throne in Jerusalem – and that he did not refer to a heavenly and future spiritual kingdom – this promise makes sense. Jesus expected that he would be aided by a host of holy angels.

Mark (as well as Matthew and Luke) inserted this story in his gospel to prepare his readers for the crucifixion at a later stage. But there was more than just that in this story.

Jesus knew very well that his actions were being watched by the Jewish religious authorities and the Roman overlords. It happened regularly that the Romans crucified dangerous criminals and rebels who tried to assassinate Roman soldiers. Therefore, he warned his disciples that such a fate may await him and them. If they really wanted to follow Jesus, they had to be prepared to deny themselves and their own selfish interests, but take up their crosses and be prepared to suffer. Luke added that they had to take up their crosses "daily".

Jesus seems to have had a plan for such an eventuality and he predicted or promised his resurrection after three days.

The Transfiguration
Mark 9: 2–13 (Matt 17: 1–13; Luke 9: 28–38)

2.	After six days Jesus took with him Peter, James, and John, and brought them up onto a high mountain privately by themselves, and he was changed into another form in front of them.
3.	His clothing became glistening, exceedingly white, like snow, such as no launderer on earth can whiten them.
4.	Elijah and Moses appeared to them, and they were talking with Jesus.
5.	Peter answered Jesus, "Rabbi, it is good for us to be here. Let's make three tents: one for you, one for Moses, and one for Elijah."
6.	For he didn't know what to say, for they were very afraid.
7.	A cloud came, overshadowing them, and a voice came out of the cloud, "This is my beloved Son. Listen to him."
8.	Suddenly looking around, they saw no one with them any more, except Jesus only.
9.	As they were coming down from the mountain, he charged them that they should tell no one what things they had seen, until the Son of Man had risen again from the dead.
10.	They kept the saying, questioning among themselves what the rising again from the dead should mean.
11.	They asked him, saying, "Why do the scribes say that Elijah must come first?"

12.	He said to them, "Elijah indeed comes first, and restores all things. How is it written about the Son of Man, that he should suffer many things and be despised?
13.	But I tell you, that Elijah has come, and they have also done to him whatever they wanted to, even as it is written about him."

Conventional explanations of this episode are that Jesus had acquired his glorified body for a brief period, the body with which he was to be resurrected from the grave and ascend to heaven later. This explanation does not hold water since none of the gospels described Jesus' body after his resurrection as anything but an ordinary body of flesh and blood. The idea of a glorified body is only found in the letters of Paull (see, for instance, 1 Cor 15).

There is, however, a more mundane and simpler explanation. This story depends on only three witnesses: Peter, James, and John, of which James died early (Acts 12: 2). Jesus asked them not to talk about what they were seeing until after his resurrection from the grave. It must be noted that John, who probably helped with the writing of his proto-gospel (see Chapter 5), did not include this remarkable episode in his book. This story was only written down four decades after the event and it may have passed through any number of people who heard it and retold it to others – with all the fantastic details added as time went on.

The high mountain onto which Jesus took his three most trusted disciples must have been Mount Hermon, north east of Caesarea Philippi (see the map of Palestine in Chapter 2).

Who were the two men conversing in secret with Jesus on the mountain? The text says that they were Moses and Elijah – two totally and perfectly dead prophets from the Old Testament. It is quite possible that the disciples asked Jesus afterwards who the two men with him were and he could have told them that it was Moses and Elijah, just to protect the identity of his two visitors.

One is compelled to ask: did these prophets really rise from the dead for this occasion? Did Jesus have a meeting with their spirits? According to Jesus' parable of the rich man and Lazarus, it is not possible that somebody can rise from the dead and visit the living (Luke 16: 31). Therefore, it could not have been these completely dead prophets from earlier centuries – although it was reported in Deut 34: 6 that nobody knows where Moses was buried and that Elijah was taken bodily into heaven without really dying (2 Kgs 2: 3–9).

The only explanation is that Jesus was plotting with two unknown accomplices who were very much alive (perhaps Joseph of Arimathea and Nicodemus – see John 19: 39–40) regarding his possible execution by the Romans and how he could survive such an ordeal. It was, somehow, stressed that Jesus had to remember that he was the Son of God, the future king of Israel, who could expect help from heaven.

Jesus, as an Essene, was certainly clothed in white. When the bright sun was shining on his clothes, they shined brightly and looked transparent.

Jesus Heals a Boy with an Evil Spirit
Mark 9: 14–29 (Matt 17: 14–21; Luke 9: 37–43a)

14.	Coming to the disciples, he saw a great multitude around them, and scribes questioning them.
15.	Immediately all the multitude, when they saw him, were greatly amazed, and running to him greeted him.
16.	He asked the scribes, "What are you asking them?"

17. One of the multitude answered, "Teacher, I brought to you my son, who has a mute spirit;
18. and wherever it seizes him, it dashes him down, and he foams at the mouth, and grinds his teeth, and wastes away. I asked your disciples to cast it out, and they weren't able."
19. He answered them, "Unbelieving generation, how long will I be with you? How long will I bear with you? Bring him to me."
20. They brought him to him, and when he saw him, immediately the spirit convulsed him, and he fell on the ground, wallowing and foaming at the mouth.
21. He asked his father, "How long has it been since this has come to him?" He said, "From childhood.
22. Often it has cast him both into the fire and into the water, to destroy him. But if you can do anything, have compassion on us, and help us."
23. Jesus said to him, "If you can believe? All things are possible to him who believes."
24. Immediately the father of the child cried out with tears, "I believe. Help my unbelief!"
25. When Jesus saw that a multitude came running together, he rebuked the unclean spirit, saying to him, "You mute and deaf spirit, I command you, come out of him, and enter no more into him!"
26. Having cried out, and convulsed him greatly, it came out. The boy became like one dead; so much that most of them said, "He is dead."
27. But Jesus took him by the hand, and raised him up; and he arose.

> 28. When he had come into the house, his disciples asked him privately, "Why couldn't we cast it out?"
> 29. He said to them, "This kind can come out by nothing, except by prayer and fasting."

The description of the disorder from which this boy was ailing, makes it clear that he suffered from severe epileptic fits.

Matthew and Luke copied this story faithfully, but Matthew inserted a saying from Q.

Jesus Speaks again about his Death
Mark 9: 30–32 (Matt 17: 22–23; Luke 9: 43b–45)

> 30. They went forth from there, and passed through Galilee. He didn't want anyone to know it.
> 31. For he taught his disciples, and said to them, "The Son of Man is delivered up into the hands of men, and they will kill him; and when he is killed, on the third day he will rise again."
> 32. But they didn't understand the saying, and were afraid to ask him.

Jesus again prepared his disciples for the possibility that he could be executed, but that he also had an escape plan.

Mark and Luke wrote that the disciples didn't understand Jesus' announcement, while Matthew reported that they were sad.

Who is the Greatest?
Mark 9: 33–37 (Matt 18: 1–5; Luke 9: 46–48)

> 33. He came to Capernaum, and when he was in the house he asked them, "What were you arguing among yourselves on the way?"
> 34. But they were silent, for they had disputed one with another on the way about who was the greatest.
> 35. He sat down, and called the twelve; and he said to them, "If any man wants to be first, he will be last of all, and servant of all."
> 36. He took a little child, and set him in the midst of them. Taking him in his arms, he said to them,
> 37. "Whoever receives one such little child in my name, receives me, and whoever receives me, doesn't receive me, but him who sent me."

When Jesus and his disciples returned to their homes in Capernaum, the disciples started arguing about who was the most important amongst them – perhaps because Jesus took only three of them onto the mountain for his secret meeting with two co-conspirators. Each disciple, evidently, wanted to receive a place of honor when Jesus ascended the throne in Jerusalem.

Jesus, however, gave them a lecture about humility by telling them to acquire the attitude of a young child.

Whoever is not against Us is for Us
Mark 9: 38–41 (Luke 9: 49–50)

> 38. John said to him, "Teacher, we saw someone who doesn't follow us casting out demons in your name; and we forbade him, because he doesn't follow us."

39.	But Jesus said, "Don't forbid him, for there is no one who will do a mighty work in my name, and be able quickly to speak evil of me.
40.	For whoever is not against us is on our side.
41.	For whoever will give you a cup of water to drink in my name, because you are Christ's, most assuredly I tell you, he will in no way lose his reward.

The disciples were dismayed because other people copied Jesus by casting out demons – probably other Essenes who practiced their healing skills. However, Jesus regarded them as allies.

Causing Others to Stumble
Mark 9: 42 (Matt 18: 6)

> Whoever will cause one of these little ones who believe in me to stumble, it would be better for him if a millstone were hanged about his neck, and he were cast into the sea.

The "little ones" are those ordinary folks who believe in Jesus as the Messiah. If anybody caused them to "stumble", to have doubts about Jesus, it would be better for that person to be drowned into the sea.

Stumbling
Mark 9: 43–50 (Matt 18: 7–9)

43.	If your hand causes you to stumble, cut it off. It is better for you to enter into life maimed, rather than having your two hands to go into Gehenna, into the unquenchable fire,
44.	'where their worm doesn't die, and the fire is not quenched.'

> 45. If your foot causes you to stumble, cut it off. It is better for you to enter into life lame, rather than having your two feet to be cast into Gehenna, into the fire that will never be quenched —
> 46. `where their worm doesn't die, and the fire is not quenched.`
> 47. If your eye causes you to stumble, cast it out. It is better for you to enter into the kingdom of God with one eye, rather than having two eyes to be cast into the Gehenna of fire,
> 48. `where their worm doesn't die, and the fire is not quenched.`
> 49. For everyone will be salted with fire, and every sacrifice will be seasoned with salt.
> 50. Salt is good, but if the salt has lost its saltiness, with what will you season it? Have salt in yourselves, and be at peace with one another."

The conventional explanation of this passage is that one ought to be wary of anything that could cause one to stumble into committing sins and to reach hell after death because it would be better to arrive maimed and crippled in the heavenly kingdom than to have a whole body and to descend into hell "where their worm doesn't die, and the fire is not quenched."

This explanation does not satisfy, because Jesus nowhere taught that one reaches the afterlife with his earthly body – either intact or with missing body parts. The gospels rather explain that the *soul* or *spirit* of the faithful will reach heavenly bliss after death. For example:

- In the parable of the rich man, we read: "But God said to him, 'You foolish one, tonight your *soul* is required of you. The things which you have prepared – whose will they be?'" (Luke 12: 20).
- Matt16: 26 tells us: "For what will it profit a man, if he will gain the whole world, and forfeit his *soul*? Or what will a man give in exchange for his *soul*?"
- According to Luke 23: 46, Jesus cried out with a loud voice while hanging on the cross: "Father, into your hands I commit my *spirit*."
- Acts 7: 59 – "They stoned Stephen, as he called on the Lord, saying, 'Lord Jesus, receive my *spirit*!'" (*emphasis added*).

Jesus also said explicitly that is would be better "to enter into life maimed". This "life" clearly refers to life of earth – not eternal life in heaven after death.

The kingdom mentioned in this passage must, therefore, be the earthly kingdom Jesus wished to establish and it is equated with "life" on earth. When he mentioned the "kingdom" in other contexts he always meant the Israelite monarchy. The only exception in the Synoptic Gospels is Matt 23: 34 – "Then the King will say to those on his right, 'Come, you who are blessed by my Father; take your inheritance, the kingdom prepared for you since the creation of the world.'"

It is clear that Jesus contrasted "life" and his earthly kingdom with "Gehenna", the garbish dump of Jerusalem that served as a symbol of hell. This expression is usually used in the sense of the eternal hell that awaits all godless people after death (Matt 5: 22; 23: 15; Luke 12: 5), but it must be seen in this case as the opposite of Jesus' Israelite kingdom, namely the "hell" of the Roman domination and suppression of the Jews.

This saying of Jesus must have gone through a process of transformation during the four decades between Jesus' time and the recording thereof in Mark. The source from which Mark gathered this saying, clearly thought that Jesus' reference to "Gehenna" must have meant the eternal hell and he added the words "where their worm doesn't die, and the fire is not quenched" for greater clarity. This rendering of Jesus' saying is clearly a distortion of Jesus' original words.

Jesus warned his followers not to "stumble", that is, not to have doubts about him as the Messiah. One should remove everything from one's life that could lead to this stumbling, even if it may cause some hardship, but that is preferable above living as in the past and enduring the "hell" of the pagan occupiers of their country.

Jesus added that his followers would "be salted with fire" and should be prepared to make sacrifices. Salt was used as a preservative in those times because refrigerators were not yet invented to preserve food. The Greek word for "salted" (ἁλίζω – *halizo*) can also be translated as "preserved".

Matthew gave a summary of this lesson of Jesus and added a part of Q to it.

Divorce
Mark 10: 1–12 (Matt 19: 1–12)

1.	He arose from there and came into the borders of Judea and beyond the Jordan. Multitudes came together to him again. As he usually did, he taught them again.
2.	There came to him Pharisees testing him, and asked him, "Is it lawful for a man to divorce his wife?"
3.	He answered, "What did Moses command you?"

4.	They said, "Moses allowed a bill of divorce to be written, and to divorce her."
5.	But Jesus said to them, "For your hardness of heart, he wrote you this commandment.
6.	But from the beginning of the creation, `God made them male and female.
7.	For this cause will a man leave his father and mother, and will join to his wife,
8.	and the two will become one flesh,` so that they are no longer two, but one flesh.
9.	What therefore God has joined together, let no man separate."
10.	In the house, his disciples asked him again about the same matter.
11.	He said to them, "Whoever will divorce his wife, and marry another, commits adultery against her.
12.	If a woman herself divorces her husband, and marries another, she commits adultery."

Jesus had to cross the Jordan from the region of Capernaum to go to Jericho in the south.

As an Essene or Nazorean, Jesus was totally opposed to divorce, despite laws in the Old Testament regulating the possibility of divorce. He quoted texts to demonstrate that marriage was supposed to be a permanent bond between a man and his wife.

Matthew added that divorce was permitted in cases of adultery.

Jesus Blesses the Children
Mark 10: 13–16 (Matt 19: 13–15; Luke 18: 15–17)

13.	They were bringing to him little children, that he should touch them, but the disciples rebuked those who were bringing them.
14.	But when Jesus saw it, he was moved with indignation, and said to them, "Allow the little children to come to me! Don`t forbid them, for to such belong the kingdom of God.
15.	Most assuredly I tell you, whoever will not receive the kingdom of God as a little child, he will in no way enter therein."
16.	He took them in his arms, and blessed them, laying his hands on them.

Jesus became angry when his disciples chased mothers with their children away when they wanted to see Jesus. He blessed the children and declared that those who wanted to become part of the coming kingdom of God must practice humility and become like children.

Matthew and Luke omitted that Jesus became angry because they didn't want to associate Jesus with such a negative attitude, but they copied the rest of the story.

The Rich Man
Mark 10: 17–31 (Matt 19: 16–30; Luke 18: 18–30)

17.	As he was going forth into the way, one ran to him, kneeled to him, and asked him, "Good Teacher, what shall I do that I may inherit eternal life?"
18.	Jesus said to him, "Why do you call me good? No one is good except one — God.
19.	You know the commandments: `Do not murder,` `Do not commit adultery,` `Do not steal,` `Do not give false

testimony,' 'Do not defraud,' 'Honor your father and mother.'"

20. He said to him, "Teacher, all these things have I observed from my youth."

21. Jesus looking at him loved him, and said to him, "One thing you lack. Go, sell whatever you have, and give to the poor, and you will have treasure in heaven; and come, follow me, taking up the cross."

22. But his face fell at that saying, and he went away sorrowful, for he was one who had great possessions.

23. Jesus looked around, and said to his disciples, "How difficult it is for those who have riches to enter into the kingdom of God!"

24. The disciples were amazed at his words. But Jesus answered again, "Children, how hard is it for those who trust in riches to enter into the kingdom of God!

25. It is easier for a camel to go through the needle's eye, than for a rich man to enter into the kingdom of God."

26. They were exceedingly astonished, saying to him, "Then who can be saved?"

27. Jesus, looking at them, said, "With men it is impossible, but not with God, for all things are possible with God."

28. Peter began to tell him, "Behold, we have left all, and have followed you."

29. Jesus said, "Most assuredly I tell you, there is no one who has left house, or brothers, or sisters, or father, or mother, or wife, or children, or land, for my sake, and for the gospel's sake,

> 30. but he will receive one hundred times now in this time, houses, brothers, sisters, mothers, children, and land, with persecutions; and in the age to come eternal life.
> 31. But many who are first will be last; and the last first."

According to Jesus, one could find eternal life by obeying all God's commandments. As a good Essene, Jesus also thought that opulence led one away from God and, therefore, he advised the rich man who consulted him to get rid of his belongings and follow him, even to the cross, which awaited him. In effect, he invited the rich man to become an Essene himself.

Thereupon, Jesus told a joke. He asked his audience to imagine an absurd situation, namely a camel crawling through the eye of a needle, to demonstrate how impossible it was for a rich man to join his kingdom.

According to Matthew, this rich man was a young man, while Luke calls him a "ruler" (Greek: ἄρχων – *archon*, which means a chief or a leader) – perhaps a member of the Sanhedrin.

Jesus Speaks the Third Time about his Death
Mark 10: 32–34 (Matt 20: 17–19; Luke 18: 31–34)

> 32. They were on the way, going up to Jerusalem; and Jesus was going in front of them, and they were amazed; and those who followed were afraid. He again took the twelve, and began to tell them the things that were going to happen to him.
> 33. "Behold, we are going up to Jerusalem. The Son of Man will be delivered to the chief priests and the scribes. They will condemn him to death, and will deliver him to the Gentiles.

> 34. They will mock him, spit on him, scourge him, and kill him. On the third day he will rise again."

Jesus expected a show-down with the Jewish religious authorities and the pagan Romans, with whom the priestly class was cooperating, when he went to Jerusalem. He was, though, ready with his own plan to cheat death. This passage is a good summary of what happened in the end, but it is also possible that Jesus had a good idea of what awaited him.

Luke added that Jesus told his disciples that his fate was supposed to have been foretold by the prophets – without providing any details – and that the disciples didn't understand what he was telling them.

The Request of James and John
Mark 10: 35–45 (Matt 20: 20–28)

> 35. James and John, the sons of Zebedee, came near to him, saying, "Teacher, we want you to do for us whatever we will ask."
> 36. He said to them, "What do you want me to do for you?"
> 37. They said to him, "Grant to us that we may sit, one at your right hand, and one at your left hand, in your glory."
> 38. But Jesus said to them, "You don`t know what you ask. Are you able to drink the cup that I drink, and to be baptized with the baptism that I am baptized with?"
> 39. They said to him, "We are able." Jesus said to them, "You shall indeed drink the cup that I drink, and you shall be baptized with the baptism that I am baptized with;
> 40. but to sit at my right hand and at my left hand is not mine to give, but for whom it has been prepared."

41.	When the ten heard it, they began to be moved with indignation towards James and John.
42.	Jesus called them to him, and said to them, "You know that they who are recognized as rulers over the Gentiles lord it over them, and their great ones exercise authority over them.
43.	But it shall not be so among you, but whoever wants to become great among you, will be your servant.
44.	Whoever of you wants to become first among you, shall be servant of all.
45.	For the Son of Man also came not to be served, but to serve, and to give his life as a ransom for many."

James and John, who often heard Jesus' message regarding the imminent restoration of the monarchy of Israel, wanted to become his councilors, sitting on both sides of his throne in "glory". Jesus reminded them that he could face the death penalty as a rebel or a terrorist and that they could also fall prey to the might of Rome. He also admonished them for thinking about the coming kingdom as an opportunity to gain power and honor. As a humble Essene, Jesus told them that he saw his position as future king as an opportunity to serve his people, not to lord over them.

Matthew repeated the story with the addition that the request that the sons of Zebedee may sit next to Jesus when he became king, came from their mother on their behalf. She bowed before Jesus, as if he was already crowned as king.

The Blind Bartimaeus
Mark 10: 46–52 (Matt 20: 29–34; Luke 18: 35–43)

46.	They came to Jericho. As he went out from Jericho, with his disciples and a great multitude, the son of Timaeus, Bartimaeus, a blind beggar, was sitting by the road.
47.	When he heard that it was Jesus, the Nazarene, he began to cry out, and say, "Jesus, you son of David, have mercy on me!"
48.	Many rebuked him, that he should be quiet, but he cried out the more a great deal, "You son of David, have mercy on me!"
49.	Jesus stood still, and said, "Call him." They called the blind man, saying to him, "Cheer up! Get up. He is calling you."
50.	He, casting away his cloak, sprang up, and came to Jesus.
51.	Jesus answered him, "What do you want me to do for you?" The blind man said to him, "Rhabboni, that I may see again."
52.	Jesus said to him, "Go your way. Your faith has made you well." Immediately he received his sight, and followed Jesus in the way.

Jesus and his party crossed the Jordan at Jericho, where he restored the eyesight of a blind man. This man called to him as the son of David. In other words, even this blind man knew that Jesus was a descendant of the great king and who hoped to restore the Israelite monarchy.

Matthew and Luke tell the same story, but Matthew changed the single blind man into two blind men.

The Triumphant Entry int Jerusalem
Mark 11: 1–11 (Matt21: 1–11; Luke 19: 28–40)

1. When they drew near to Jerusalem, to Bethsphage and Bethany, at the Mount of Olives, he sent two of his disciples,
2. and said to them, "Go your way into the village that is opposite you. Immediately as you enter into it, you will find a colt tied, on which no one has sat. Untie him, and bring him.
3. If anyone asks you, 'Why are you doing this?' say, 'The Lord needs him;' and immediately he will send him back here."
4. They went away, and found a colt tied at the door outside in the open street, and they untied him.
5. Some of those who stood there asked them, "What are you doing, untying the colt?"
6. They said to them just as Jesus had said, and they let them go.
7. They brought the colt to Jesus, and threw their garments on him, and Jesus sat on him.
8. Many spread their garments on the way, and others were cutting down branches from the trees, and spreading them on the road.
9. Those who went in front, and those who followed, cried, "Hosanna! Blessed is he who comes in the name of the Lord!
10. Blessed is the kingdom of our father David that is coming in the name of the Lord! Hosanna in the highest!"
11. Jesus entered into the temple in Jerusalem. When he had looked around at everything, it being now evening, he went out to Bethany with the twelve.

The young donkey on which Jesus planned to arrive at Jerusalem was placed at a certain spot for the disciples to find. This points to a choreographed entry into Jerusalem for Jesus. He rode on this colt to play the part of the Messiah in accordance with a prophecy in Zecheriah:

> "Rejoice greatly, daughter of Zion; shout, daughter of Jerusalem: behold, your king comes to you; he is just, and having salvation; lowly, and riding on a donkey, even on a colt the foal of a donkey" (Zech 9: 9).

A crowd followed Jesus into Jerusalem, spreading their clothes on the road and waving branches broken from the trees. They must have been informed before the time to be ready when Jesus appeared. They cheered Jesus on as the son of David and the next king of Israel. Luke 19:38 has: "Blessed is *the King who comes ...*"

Certainly, for Mark's readers, who have just seen that Bartimaeus called out to Jesus as the "Son of David," there was no doubt that Jesus was entering Jerusalem as the Messiah from David's line.

Jesus ended his triumphant entry into the city at the temple. Matthew and Luke told essentially the same story. Matthew added the words from Zecheriah, while Luke mentioned that some Pharisees asked Jesus to silence his shouting followers, but he refused.

Jesus Curses a Fig Tree
Mark 11: 12–14 (Matt 21: 18–19)

12.	The next day, when they had come out from Bethany, he was hungry.

1.3.	Seeing a fig tree afar off having leaves, he came to see if perhaps he might find anything on it. When he came to it, he found nothing but leaves, for it was not the season for figs.
14.	Jesus told it, "May no one ever eat fruit from you again!" and his disciples heard it.

The cursing of the fig tree seems to have been pointless because Jesus didn't benefit anybody. Jesus knew that he would not find any figs on the tree because it was just after the end of the winter. Perhaps the tree was diseased in any case and Jesus' presence was seen as the cause of it getting withered.

Mark may have intended to portray the fig tree as a symbol of the Jews in Jerusalem whose religious ceremonies were just for the show, but without any substance, the same as the leaves on the empty fig tree.

Jesus Goes to the Temple
Mark 11: 15–19 (Matt 21: 12–17; Luke 19: 45–48)

15.	They came to Jerusalem, and Jesus entered into the temple, and began to throw out those who sold and those who bought in the temple, and overthrew the tables of the money–changers, and the seats of those who sold the doves.
16.	He would not allow anyone to carry a container through the temple.
17.	He taught, saying to them, "Isn't it written, 'My house will be called a house of prayer for all the nations?' But you have made it a den of robbers!"

18.	The chief priests and the scribes heard it, and sought how they might destroy him. For they feared him, for all the multitude was astonished at his teaching.
19.	When evening came, he went forth out of the city.

The episode of Jesus getting rid of dishonest traders at the temple also appears in John, but there it is placed at the beginning of Jesus' ministry.

Mark mentioned that the chief priests were disturbed by this event, but they were afraid of stopping Jesus because he was so popular.

Cohn pointed out that the Sanhedrin did not have jurisdiction over these traders because they put up their stalls and tables outside the temple, only somewhere on the temple mount. Therefore, they did not interfere.[196]

The Lesson of the Fig Tree
Mark 11: 20–26 (Matt 21: 20–22)

20.	As they passed by in the morning, they saw the fig tree withered away from the roots.
21.	Peter, remembering, said to him, "Rabbi, look! The fig tree which you cursed has withered away."
22.	Jesus answering said to them, "Have faith in God.
23.	For most assuredly I tell you, whoever may tell this mountain, `Be taken up and cast into the sea,` and doesn't doubt in his heart, but believes that what he says happens; he shall have whatever he says.

---

[196] Cohn, *The Trial and Death of Jesus*, 54–59.

24.	Therefore I tell you, all things whatever you pray and ask for, believe that you receive them, and you shall have them.
25.	Whenever you stand praying, forgive, if you have anything against anyone; so that your Father, who is in heaven, may also forgive you your transgressions.
26.	But if you do not forgive, neither will your Father in heaven forgive your transgressions."

When Jesus and the disciples passed the dried fig tree later, Jesus is reported as telling them that this miracle was the result of a strong faith – the type of faith that can even move mountains. This faith must not be confused with a magical fulfillment of earnest prayers, but a faith or confidence in the justness of a good cause, such as the kingdom of God.

Matthew had essentially the same message, although he added it directly after the description of how Jesus cursed the tree.

The Question about Jesus' Authority
Mark 11: 27–33 (Matt 21: 23–27; Luke 20: 1–8)

27.	They came again to Jerusalem, and as he was walking in the temple, the chief priests, and the scribes, and the elders came to him,
28.	and they were asking him, "By what authority do you these things? Or who gave you this authority to do these things?"
29.	Jesus said to them, "I will ask you one question. Answer me, and I will tell you by what authority I do these things.
30.	The baptism of John, was it from heaven, or from men? Answer me."

31.	They reasoned with themselves, saying, "If we should say, 'From heaven;' he will say, 'Why then did you not believe him?'
32.	If we should say, 'From men'"—they feared the people, for all held John to really be a prophet.
33.	They answered Jesus, "We don't know." Jesus said to them, "Neither do I tell you by what authority I do these things."

All three Synoptic Gospels report that the religious authorities wanted to know from Jesus who gave him the authority to do what he was doing. Jesus was, no doubt, aware of their animosity and he asked them to explain to him where John the Baptist got his authority from to perform his baptism. They were trapped because they did not dare to say that he got his authority from God, but also did not dare to say that he got his authority from men.

In this manner, Jesus indirectly told the religious authorities that he was the successor of John the Baptist, but also that he acted on the authority God gave him.

The Parable of the Tenants in the Vineyard
Mark 12: 1–12 (Matt 21: 33–48; Luke 20: 9–19)

1.	He began to speak to them in parables. "A man planted a vineyard, set a hedge around it, dug a pit for the winepress, built a tower, rented it out to a farmer, and went into another country.
2.	When it was time, he sent a servant to the farmer to get from the farmer his share of the fruit of the vineyard.
3.	They took him, beat him, and sent him away empty.

4.	Again, he sent another servant to them; and they threw stones at him, wounded him in the head, and sent him away shamefully treated.
5.	Again he sent another; and they killed him; and many others, beating some, and killing some.
6.	Therefore he had yet one, a beloved son, he sent him last to them, saying, `They will respect my son.`
7.	But those farmers said among themselves, `This is the heir. Come, let`s kill him, and the inheritance will be ours.`
8.	They took him, killed him, and cast him forth out of the vineyard.
9.	What therefore will the lord of the vineyard do? He will come and destroy the farmers, and will give the vineyard to others.
10.	Haven`t you even read this scripture: `The stone which the builders rejected, The same was made the head of the corner.
11.	This was from the Lord, It is marvelous in our eyes`?"
12.	They tried to seize him, but they feared the multitude; for they perceived that he spoke the parable against them. They left him, and went away.

The chief priests and the teachers of the Law didn't like this parable of Jesus. He told them about the servants of the landlord who were sent to collect the rent from the tenants of his wine farm – the prophets of the Old Testament. According to Jesus, the chief priests and teachers of the Law disregarded their messages. In the end, the landlord sent his son (Jesus) who was killed by the tenants. The landlord took vengeance – a warning directed against the Jerusalem elite.

Jesus also quoted from Isa 28: 16 and applied it to himself, identifying himself as the corner stone of Israel.

Luke reproduced the parable almost unchanged, but Matthew added that the chief priests and teachers of the Law understood that Jesus referred to them as the evil tenants.

The Question about Paying Taxes
Mark 12: 13–17 (Matt 22: 15–22; Luke 20: 20–26)

13.	They sent some of the Pharisees and of the Herodians to him, that they might catch him in words.
14.	When they had come, they asked him, "Teacher, we know that you are honest, and don't defer to anyone; for you aren't partial to anyone, but truly teach the way of God. Is it lawful to pay taxes to Caesar, or not?
15.	Shall we give, or shall we not give?" But he, knowing their hypocrisy, said to them, "Why do you test me? Bring me a denarius, that I may see it."
16.	They brought it. He said to them, "Whose is this image and inscription?" They said to him, "Caesar's."
17.	Jesus answered them, "Render to Caesar the things that are Caesar's, and to God the things that are God's." They marveled greatly at him.

Some Pharisees and Herodians (supporters of the royal house of Herod) tried to trap Jesus with the question whether they ought to pay taxes to the Roman emperor. Jesus asked them to show him a coin and they produced one with the face of the emperor on it – something they ought not to have had in their purses or pockets because it depicted a pagan deity, Emperor Tiberius.

Jesus sidestepped their trap by answering that they should pay what is due to Caesar and also what is due to God – thereby acknowledging that Tiberius got his authority from God.

Matthew and Luke repeated this passage with minor changes.

Denarius of Emperor Tiberiu

The Question about Rising from Death
Mark 12: 18–27 (Matt 22: 23–33; Luke 20: 27–40)

18.	There came to him Sadducees, who say that there is no resurrection. They asked him, saying,
19.	"Teacher, Moses wrote to us, `If a man's brother dies, and leaves a wife behind him, and leaves no child, that his brother should take his wife, and raise up children to his brother.`
20.	There were seven brothers. The first took a wife, and dying left no children.
21.	The second took her, and died, leaving no children behind him. The third likewise;
22.	and the seven took her and left no children. Last of all the woman also died.
23.	In the resurrection, when they rise, whose wife will she be of them? For the seven had her as a wife."

> 24. Jesus answered them, "Isn't this because you are mistaken, not knowing the scriptures, nor the power of God?
> 25. For when they will rise from the dead, they neither marry, nor are given in marriage, but are like angels in heaven.
> 26. But about the dead, that they are raised; haven't you read in the book of Moses, at the Bush, how God spoke to him, saying, 'I am the God of Abraham, the God of Isaac, and the God of Jacob?'
> 27. He is not the God of the dead, but of the living. You are therefore badly mistaken."

The Sadducees, a liberal group of Jews, accepted only the Torah as divinely inspired. Since this collection of books doesn't mention the resurrection of the dead, they rejected such a notion.

They tried to trap Jesus with an absurd scenario of seven brothers who all married their eldest brother's widow in a row, without producing any heirs as provided for in Moses' laws. They wanted to know whose wife she would be in the resurrection.

Jesus firstly pointed out that gender differences disappear in the afterlife. He also reminded them that God is not the God of dead people but of the still living ancestors who are in heaven with Him.

Matthew and Luke took over this passage with minor changes.

The Greatest Commandment
Mark 12: 28–34 (Matt 22: 34–40)

> 28. One of the scribes came, and heard them questioning together. Knowing that he had answered them well, asked him, "What commandment is the greatest of all?"

> 29. Jesus answered, "The greatest is, `Hear, Israel, the Lord our God, the Lord is one:
> 30. you shall love the Lord your God with all your heart, and with all your soul, and with all your mind, and with all your strength.` This is the primary commandment.
> 31. The second is like this, `You shall love your neighbor as yourself.` There is no other commandment greater than these."
> 32. The scribe said to him, "Truly, teacher, you have said well that he is one, and there is none other but he,
> 33. and to love him with all the heart, and with all the understanding, with all the soul, and with all the strength, and to love his neighbor as himself, is more than all whole burnt offerings and sacrifices."
> 34. When Jesus saw that he answered wisely, he said to him, "You are not far from the kingdom of God." No one dared ask him any question after that.

When Jesus was asked by teachers of the Law which commandment was the most important, he quoted from the Torah (Deut 6: 4–5 and Lev 19: 18) and thereby gave a summary of the whole Ten Commandments – in effect telling them that all the commandments were equally important.

Matthew copied this passage with some minor changes.

The Question about the Messiah
Mark 12: 35–37 (Matt 22: 41–46; Luke 20: 41–44)

> 35. Jesus responded, as he taught in the temple, "How is it that the scribes say that the Christ is the son of David?

> 36. For David himself said in the Holy Spirit, `The Lord said to my Lord, Sit at my right hand, Until I make your enemies the footstool of your feet.`
> 37. Therefore David himself calls him Lord, so how can he be his son?" The common people heard him gladly.

The Jewish teachers of the Law expected of the Messiah to be a descendant of King David, who was a mighty warrior. The Messiah was, therefore, supposed to be a warrior as well. Jesus tried to demonstrate, though, with a quotation from Ps 110: 1 that the Messiah would be more than David's son because David called him "Lord" or "Master", somebody who would conquer all evil forces.[197]

This meant that Jesus saw it as his task not only to restore David's kingdom, but also to deliver his people from all evil forces, including evil spirits and false leaders. Jesus never denied that he was David's son (Mark 10: 47 and 11: 10).

Matthew and Luke provided their readers with more or less the same report.

The use by Jesus of Ps 110 is, though, questionable (if reported correctly). The "lord" mentioned in the first verse of this Psalm is none other than the Israelite king from the time of David, who received the promise that he would prevail over all Israel's enemies. This king is also called "a priest forever in the order of Melchizedek" (verse 4) This Melchizedek was the king of Salem (Jerusalem) in the time of Abraham, as well as a priest of the High God of the Canaanites (Gen 14: 18–20). His name means "King of Righteousness". Melchizedek's priesthood had nothing to do with the Israelite priesthood of the temple in Jerusalem. David, therefore,

---

[197] Ps 110: 1 – "[A Psalm] of David. The Lord said to my lord, Be seated at my right hand, till I put all those who are against you under your feet."

saw himself in his capacity of the Israelite king as a successor of Melchizedek of earlier centuries and he certainly never had Jesus as Messiah in mind when composing this Psalm.

Jesus' words: "Therefore David himself calls him Lord, so how can he be his [own] son?", does not make sense because David didn't mention a descendant or the Messiah in Ps 110.

Jesus Warns against the Teachers of the Law
Mark 12: 38–40 (Luke 20: 45–47)

38.	In his teaching he said to them, "Beware of the scribes, who desire to walk in long robes, and to get greetings in the marketplaces,
39.	and chief seats in the synagogues, and chief places at feasts:
40.	those who devour widows' houses, and for a pretense make long prayers. These will receive greater condemnation."

Jesus – in a true Essene spirit – condemned the false piety of some teachers of the Law whose religious practices were only for the show so that they could pass themselves off as important people, while showing no empathy with poor widows.

Luke copied this passage with minor changes.

The Widow's Offering
Mark 12: 41–44 (Luke 21: 1–4)

41.	Jesus sat down opposite the treasury, and saw how the multitude cast money into the treasury. Many who were rich cast in much.
42.	There came a poor widow, and she cast in two lepta, which make a quadrans.

> 43. He called his disciples to himself, and said to them, "Most assuredly I tell you, this poor widow gave more than all those who are giving into the treasury,
> 44. for they all gave out of their abundance, but she, out of her poverty, gave all that she had to live on."

There were receptacles in the temple for the collection of money for the upkeep of the temple. Jesus praised a poor widow who deposited two small coins, which was evidently all she had, while condemning the rich people who donated money out of their abundance. With this episode, Jesus demonstrated his Essene background by condemning well-to-do people.

Luke expanded somewhat on this story, but kept the essence.

Jesus Speaks about the Destruction of the Temple
Luke 13: 1–2 (Matt 24: 1–2; Luke 21: 5–6)

> 1. As he went forth out of the temple, one of his disciples said to him, "Teacher, see what kind of stones and what kind of buildings!"
> 2. Jesus said to him, "Do you see these great buildings? There will not be left here one stone on another, which will not be thrown down."

According to Mark, Matthew, and Luke, Jesus predicted the destruction of the temple, which did occur during the Jewish War against Rome during AD 66–70.

It is highly improbable that Jesus would have spoken these words since the restored kingdom of David, of which he was to become the sovereign, was meant to have Jerusalem as its capital with an intact temple. This issue was discussed at the beginning of this chapter where it was used to date the Gospel of Mark.

Troubles and Persecutions
Mark 13: 2–13 (Matt 24: 3–14; Luke 21: 7–19)

3.	As he sat on the Mount of Olives opposite the temple, Peter, James, John, and Andrew asked him privately,
4.	"Tell us, when will these things be? What is the sign that these things are all about to be accomplished?"
5.	Jesus, answering, began to tell them, "Be careful that no one leads you astray.
6.	For many will come in my name, saying, 'I am he!' and will lead many astray.
7.	When you hear of wars and rumors of wars, don't be troubled. For those must happen, but the end is not yet.
8.	For nation will rise against nation, and kingdom against kingdom. There will be earthquakes in various places. There will be famines and troubles. These things are the beginning of birth pains.
9.	But watch yourselves, for they will deliver you up to councils. You will be beaten in synagogues. Before governors and kings will you stand for my sake, for a testimony to them.
10.	The gospel must first be preached to all the nations.
11.	When they lead you away and deliver you up, don't be anxious beforehand, or premeditate what you will say, but say whatever will be given you in that hour. For it is not you who speak, but the Holy Spirit.
12.	"Brother will deliver up brother to death, and the father his child. Children will rise up against parents, and cause them to be put to death.

13.	You will be hated by all men for my name's sake, but he who endures to the end, the same will be saved.

These "predictions" or "prophecies" of Jesus actually describe history, as seen from the time when Mark wrote his gospel during the seventies AD. There was a war when Jerusalem was razed, there were various false messiahs, the message of Jesus' teachings (the gospel) was proclaimed in other countries around the Mediterranean Sea where the Jesus people fled, and the followers of Jesus endured resistance and even persecution.

Matthew and Luke omitted that Jesus told only four of his disciples about the expected destruction of the temple. According to Luke, Jesus spoke to all his disciples while still in the temple – not on the Mount of Olives outside Jerusalem.

The Awful Horror
Mark 13: 14–23 (Matt 24: 15–28; Luke 21: 20–24)

14.	But when you see the abomination of desolation, spoken of by Daniel the prophet, standing where it ought not (let the reader understand), then let those who are in Judea flee to the mountains,
15.	and let him who is on the housetop not go down, nor enter in, to take anything out of his house.
16.	Let him who is in the field not return back to take his cloak.
17.	But woe to those who are with child and to those who nurse babies in those days!
18.	Pray that your flight won't be in the winter.
19.	For in those days there will be oppression, such as there has not been the like from the beginning of the creation which God created until now, and never will be.

> 20. Unless the Lord had shortened the days, no flesh would have been saved; but for the elect's sake, whom he chose, he shortened the days.
> 21. Then if anyone tells you, 'Look, here is the Christ!' or, 'Look, there!' don't believe it.
> 22. For there will arise false christs and false prophets, and will show signs and wonders, that they may lead astray, if possible, also the elect.
> 23. But you watch. "Behold, I have told you all things beforehand.

That Mark described history is clear from verse 20 where he used the past tense, indicating that God had already shortened the days of hardship. Matthew 24: 22 changed the past tense to future tense to preserve the pretense that Jesus predicted all these calamities at least four decades earlier.

According to Mark, Jesus purportedly warned his followers to flee and to hope that they would not have to get away with small children or during winter. It really happened that Jesus' followers, the Ebionites, fled from Galilee and Judea to Pella across the Jordan, Egypt, and Asia Minor when the Roman Army under Vespasian and Titus started to besiege the fortress of Jotapata in Galilee during December AD 67 – at the height of winter.[198]

Luke added that Jerusalem would be surrounded by a pagan army that would trample the city and that many men would be taken captive – which did happen on 30 August AD 70 when Jerusalem fell. Luke would certainly have known about it – as almost everybody else in the Roman Empire at that time.

---

[198] History Today, "Jewish Roman Wars"; Goldberg, "A Chronology of the First Jewish Revolt".

Mark evidently thought that Jesus, a great prophet, must have foreseen the Jewish War and warned his followers to be ready for such an event and., therefore, he invented a prophecy by Jesus to insert into his narrative. Matthew and Luke expanded on it by adding details from known history.

The Coming of the Son of Man
Mark 13: 24–27 (Matt 24: 29–31; Luke21: 25–28)

24.	But in those days, after that oppression, the sun will be darkened, the moon will not give her light,
25.	the stars will be falling from the sky, and the powers that are in the heavens will be shaken.
26.	Then will they see the Son of Man coming in clouds with great power and glory.
27.	Then will he send forth his angels, and will gather together his elect from the four winds, from the ends of the earth to the ends of the sky.

Jesus often told his disciples that he expected to be crucified, but that he would survive and return. Mark changed this return date in the near future to Judgment Day and implied that the destruction of the temple would happen shortly before Judgment Day – which never happened that way because Judgment Day has not arrived yet, while Jerusalem fell centuries ago..

Mark connected the astronomical phenomena during the time of the siege of Jerusalem and thereafter as signs of Jesus' return and Judgment Day. The dates of these phenomena were explained in the first part of this chapter where the date of the compilation of Mark was discussed.

Jesus expected twelve brigades of battle-ready angels to aid him in securing the throne in Jerusalem. Mark changed the appearance of these angels to Jesus' return on Judgment Day.

Matthew and Luke added some drama to Mark's description by adding trumpets – no doubt a memory of the Roman war trumpets that sounded during the war and the siege of Jerusalem – and the appearance of Jesus on the clouds.

The Lesson of the Fig Tree
Mark 13: 28–31 (Matt 24: 32–33; Luke 21: 29–33)

28.	"Now from the fig tree, learn this parable. When the branch has now become tender, and puts forth its leaves, you know that the summer is near;
29.	even so you also, when you see these things coming to pass, know that it is near, at the doors.
30.	Most assuredly I say to you, this generation will not pass away until all these things are accomplished.
31.	Heaven and earth will pass away, but my words will not pass away.

Jesus told the parable of the fig tree that started producing small figs and new leaves when Spring arrived. He used this as an example that his followers would have to be ready for his return and victory with the aid of an army of angels.

Jesus also said that the present generation would experience his return. With that, he had his resurrection after his possible crucifixion and his victory over the enemies of the people of God in mind – not a far-way Judgment Day.

No One Knows the Day or Hour
Mark 13: 32–37 (Matt 24: 36–44)

> 32. But of that day or that hour no one knows, not even the angels in heaven, neither the Son, but only the Father.
> 33. Watch, keep alert, and pray; for you don't know when the time is.
> 34. "It is like a man, traveling to another country, having left his house, and given authority to his servants, and to each one his work, and also commanded the doorkeeper to keep watch.
> 35. Watch therefore, for you don't know when the lord of the house is coming, whether at evening, or at midnight, or when the rooster crows, or in the morning;
> 36. lest coming suddenly he might find you sleeping.
> 37. What I tell you, I tell all: Watch."

Jesus warned his disciples to be ready at any moment for the coming of the kingdom of God. He illustrated that with the parable of the owner of the house who left everything in the hands of his servants who had to be ready for his return at any moment.

One often hears the argument that Jesus, as the Son of God and the Second Person in the Divine Trinity, must have been all-knowing, also as a human being, and that is why he could make all these predictions about the future. In this passage, however, Jesus explicitly said that the Son didn't know when all these hardships, calamities, and his return would occur. Therefore, he could not have been all-knowing or omniscient.

The Plot against Jesus
Mark 14: 1–2 (Matt 26: 1–5; Luke 22: 1–2)

1.	was now two days before the feast of the Passover and the ıleavened bread, and the chief priests and the scribes sought)w they might seize him by deception, and kill him.
2.	)r they said, "Not during the feast, because there might be a ɔt of the people."

There can be little doubt that the religious leaders in Jerusalem felt threatened by Jesus who drew large crowds with his teaching in the temple courtyards. They were afraid that he could start a rebellion to get himself proclaimed king, which the Romans would never allow. They decided not to do anything during the Passover for fear of the crowds that followed Jesus. In the end, Jesus was indeed apprehended just before Pass-over.

Matthew and Luke told essentially the same story, although Matthew added that Jesus predicted that he would be crucified. The evangelists did not disclose their source(s) for this information, but it might have been supporters of Jesus who were also members of the Council.

Jesus is Anointed in Bethany
Mark 14: 3–9 (Matt 26: 6–13)

3.	While he was at Bethany, in the house of Simon the leper, as he sat at the table, there came a woman having an alabaster jar of ointment of pure nard — very costly. She broke the jar, and poured it over his head.
4.	But there were some who had indignation among themselves, saying, "Why has this ointment been wasted?
5.	For this might have been sold for more than three hundred denarii, and given to the poor." They grumbled against her.

> 6. But Jesus said, "Leave her alone. Why do you trouble her? She has done a good work for me.
> 7. For you always have the poor with you, and whenever you want to, you can do them good; but you will not always have me.
> 8. She has done what she could. She has anointed my body beforehand for the burying.
> 9. Most assuredly I tell you, wherever this gospel may be preached throughout the whole world, that also which this woman has done will be spoken of for a memorial of her."

Mark – as well as Matthew who tells the same story – places this episode, where Jesus was anointed with an expensive ointment, in the house of a certain Simon the Leper in Bethany. The disciples grumbled about the waste of an expensive perfume.

The same story is told in John 14: 1–8, but there it happened in the house of Lazarus. Mary Magdalene is named as the woman who anointed Jesus, while it was Judas who complained about the wastage.

The version of John may be regarded as more reliable since the Proto-Gospel of John predated the Gospel of Mark by at least a decade and was nearer in time to the event described. One may, nevertheless, conclude that John and Mark heard of this event from different sources, which may serve as an indication that something like this really happened.

Judas Agrees to Betray Jesus
Mark 14: 10–11 (Matt 26: 14–16; Luke 22: 3–6)

> 10. Judas Iscariot, who was one of the twelve, went away to the chief priests, that he might deliver him to them.

> 11. They, when they heard it, were glad, and promised to give him money. He sought how he might conveniently deliver him.

Judas Iscariot, one of Jesus disciples, was bribed by the religious authorities to deliver Jesus to them. Matthew adds that he was given thirty pieces of silver and Luke relates that Satan drove him to this despicable deed.

Cohn is of the opinion that the authors of the gospels made Judas a scape goat in order to vilify the Jews who were very unpopular after the fall of Jerusalem in AD 70 and to exonerate the Roman governor who sentenced Jesus to death. The story of his treachery must, therefore, be an invention.[199]

However, the Proto-Gospel of John, written before the Jewish War and before the time when the Jews became pariahs, mentions the treachery by Judas in John 13: 21–30. Paul, writing even earlier during the fifties AD, mentions that Jesus instituted the Eucharist "on the night in which he was betrayed" (1 Cor 11: 23). All this is an indication that Judas indeed betrayed Jesus.

Jesus Celebrates the Passover with his Disciples
Mark 14: 12–21 (Matt 26: 17–25; Luke 22: 7–14; 21–23)

> 12. On the first day of unleavened bread, when they sacrificed the Passover, his disciples asked him, "Where do you want us to go and make ready that you may eat the Passover?"
>
> 13. He sent two of his disciples, and said to them, "Go into the city, and there you will meet a man carrying a pitcher of water. Follow him,

---

[199] Cohn, *The Trial and Death of Jesus,* 80.

> 14. and wherever he enters in, tell the master of the house, 'The Teacher says, "Where is the guest room, where I may eat the Passover with my disciples?"'
> 15. He will himself show you a large upper room furnished and ready. Make ready for us there."
> 16. His disciples went out, and came into the city, and found things as he had said to them, and they prepared the Passover.
> 17. When it was evening he came with the twelve.
> 18. As they sat and were eating, Jesus said, "Most assuredly I tell you, one of you will betray me – he who eats with me."
> 19. They began to be sorrowful, and to ask him one by one, "Surely not I?" And another said, "Surely not I?"
> 20. He answered them, "It is one of the twelve, he who dips with me in the dish.
> 21. For the Son of Man goes, even as it is written about him, but woe to that man through whom the Son of Man is betrayed! It would be better for that man if he had not been born."

The man carrying a pitcher of water must have been an unknown or unnamed accomplice of Jesus with whom he agreed earlier to find a secret venue where he and his disciples could celebrate the Passover in peace, out of sight of the religious leaders.

Jesus seems to have had some secret helpers – the men with whom he had a meeting on Mount Hermon (Mark 9: 2–8), Joseph or Arimathea and Nicodemus who provided a tomb after his crucifixion and nursed his wounds (John 19: 39–40), the men in white clothes who sat in the tomb when Mary Magdalene went to anoint Jesus' body (Mark 16: 5–7; John 20: 12), and the men dressed in white who promised the disciples that Jesus would return when he took leave of them in n the Mount of Olives (Acts 1: 10–12). All these men must have been Essenes, belonging to a secret group that worked behind the scenes and who were not members of his group of twelve disciples. The venue that this unnamed man found for Jesus and his disciples or their celebration may have been located in the Essene quarter of Jerusalem.

Matthew and Luke tell essentially the same story about the Passover meal.

The Lord's Supper
Mark14:22–26 (Matt 26: 26–30; Luke 22: 14–20; 1 Cor 11: 23–25))

22.	As they were eating, Jesus took bread, and when he had blessed, he broke it, and gave to them, and said, "Take, eat. This is my body."
23.	He took the cup, and when he had given thanks, he gave to them. They all drank of it.
24.	He said to them, "This is my blood of the new covenant, which is poured out for many.
25.	Most assuredly I tell you, I will no more drink of the fruit of the vine, until that day when I drink it anew in the kingdom of God."
26.	When they had sung a hymn, they went out to the Mount of Olives.

All three Synoptic Gospel tell the same story about Jesus' last meal with his disciples, although Luke added some superfluous details. They also agree with Paul's version in 1 Cor 11: 23–25. Jesus declared that the broken bread and the wine represented his broken body and blood since he expected to be crucified soon.

It is also mentioned in all three gospels – if reported correctly – that Jesus proclaimed that this was the last occasion on which he would drink wine before he drank it in the kingdom of God. He evidently thought that a miracle would occur very soon when the kingdom would be miraculously established with him on the throne after he had survived his crucifixion. His miraculous survival was expected to convince all the Jews that he was indeed the Messiah.

Jesus Predicts Peter's Denial
Mark 14: 27–31 (Matt 26: 31–35; Luke 22: 31–34; John 13: 36–38)

27.	Jesus said to them, "All of you will be made to stumble because of me tonight, for it is written, 'I will strike the shepherd, and the sheep will be scattered.'
28.	However, after I am raised up, I will go before you into Galilee."
29.	But Peter said to him, "Although all will be offended, yet I will not."
30.	Jesus said to him, "Most assuredly I tell you, that you today, even this night, before the cock crows twice, you will deny me three times."
31.	But he spoke all the more, "If I must die with you, I will not deny you." Likewise, they all said so.

Jesus evidently knew Peter with his compulsive personality well enough and predicted that he would deny knowing Jesus during the following night before daybreak when events would come to a head and Jesus was arrested. The prediction of the denial of Peter is also mentioned in John.

According to the synoptics, Jesus based his prediction of Zech 13: 7 – although this verse never had the denial of Peter in mind when it was written.

Jesus certainly had a plan to survive the expected crucifixion and he announced that he would go to Galilee after that.

Jesus Prays in Gethsemane
Mark 14: 32–42 (Matt 26: 36–46; Luke 22: 39–46)

32.	They came to a place which was named Gethsemane. He said to his disciples, "Sit here, while I pray."
33.	He took with him Peter, James, and John, and began to be greatly alarmed and distressed.
34.	He said to them, "My soul is exceedingly sorrowful, even to death. Stay here, and watch."
35.	He went forward a little, and fell on the ground, and prayed that, if it were possible, the hour might pass away from him.
36.	He said, "Abba, Father, all things are possible to you. Please remove this cup from me. However, not what I want, but what you want."
37.	He came and found them sleeping, and said to Peter, "Simon, are you sleeping? Couldn`t you watch one hour?
38.	Watch and pray, that you not enter into temptation. The spirit indeed is willing, but the flesh is weak."
39.	Again he went away, and prayed, saying the same words.
40.	Again he returned, and found them sleeping, for their eyes were very heavy, and they didn`t know what to answer him.
41.	He came the third time, and said to them, "Sleep on now, and take your rest. It is enough. The hour has come. Behold, the Son of Man is betrayed into the hands of sinners.
42.	Arise, let us be going. Behold, he who betrays me is at hand."

After celebrating the Passover, Jesus took his three most trusted disciples with him to the garden of Gethsemane to pray. According to Luke, they camped out on the Mount of Olives during the Passover. There were certainly no lodgings available in the crowded city. This garden was certainly not a suitable spot to celebrate the feast and, therefore, Jesus had to ask a friend to find an appropriate space inside the city. The name "Gethsemane" (Aramaic: גת שמן – *Gath Shaman*) means "olive/oil press". This press must have stood within a grove of olive trees. This was also the spot from where Jesus ascended to heaven, as told in Acts 1: 10–12.

Jesus was evidently under great stress and expressed his fear to his friends. Luke added that he was sweating profusely.

Albrecht Dürer: Christ on the Mount of Olives (1510)

It is understandable that he was afraid that his plans would not work out as he had wished. All three synoptic gospels reported the words that Jesus prayed. How Mark – and the other two evangelists – knew what Jesus said is a mystery because Jesus found his disciples asleep every time where he left them to pray on his own. The contents of his prayers must, therefore, be an invention. It is possible that he prayed that God would indeed send the expected swarms of angels.

The Arrest of Jesus
Mark 14: 43–52 (Matt 26: 47–56; Luke 22: 47–53; John 18: 3–12)

43. Immediately, while he was still speaking, Judas, one of the twelve, came — and with him a multitude with swords and clubs, from the chief priests, the scribes, and the elders.
44. Now he who betrayed him had given them a sign, saying, "Whoever I will kiss, that is he. Take him, and lead him away safely."
45. When he had come, immediately he came to him, and said, "Rabbi! Rabbi!" and kissed him.
46. They laid their hands on him, and took him.
47. But a certain one of those who stood by drew his sword, and struck the servant of the high priest, and cut off his ear.
48. Jesus answered them, "Have you come out, as against a robber, with swords and clubs to seize me?
49. I was daily with you in the temple teaching, and you didn't arrest me. But this is so that the scriptures might be fulfilled."
50. They all left him, and fled.
51. A certain young man followed with him, having a linen cloth thrown around him, over his naked body. The young men grabbed him,
52. but he left the linen cloth, and fled from them naked.

The account of John 18: 3–12 about the arrest of Jesus contains more details, including the fact that the arresting party was composed of Roman soldiers under the command of an officer. Mark – and the other two synoptics – merely state that a multitude, armed with swords and clubs, came from the religious authorities to arrest Jesus. The swords may imply Roman soldiers because the temple police would not have been allowed by the Roman overlords to use military hardware.

Judas identified Jesus with a kiss. He knew where to find Jesus because Jesus and his disciples used the olive grove as a camping spot. Jesus was surprised by this because he was well-known, having taught daily in the temple.

The readers of the gospels are told that one of Jesus' disciples tried to defend him with his sword by slashing off the ear of the servant of the high priest. John mentions that it was Peter who did it and that the servant was called Malchus. According to Luke, Jesus miraculously and magically re-attached the severed ear.

Luke added that Jesus told his disciple to put away his sword because he expected twelve legions of angels to nosedive upon his enemies.

Mark's remark that a certain young man fled when Jesus was arrested, leaving his clothes behind when somebody grabbed him, is usually taken as a description of an adventure that Mark himself experienced.

Jesus Before the Council
Mark 14: 53–65 (Matt 26:57–68; Luke 22: 54–56, 63–71; John 18: 13–24)

53.	They led Jesus away to the high priest. There came together with him all the chief priests, the elders, and the scribes.
54.	Peter had followed him afar off, until he came into the court of the high priest. He was sitting with the officers, and warming himself in the light of the fire.
55.	Now the chief priests and the whole council sought witnesses against Jesus to put him to death, and found none.
56.	For many gave false testimony against him, and their testimony didn't agree with each other.

> 57. Some stood up, and gave false testimony against him, saying,
> 58. "We heard him say, 'I will destroy this temple that is made with hands, and in three days I will build another made without hands.'"
> 59. Even so their testimony did not agree.
> 60. The high priest stood up in the midst, and asked Jesus, "Have you no answer? What is it which these testify against you?"
> 61. But he stayed quiet, and answered nothing. Again, the high priest asked him, "Are you the Christ, the Son of the Blessed?"
> 62. Jesus said, "I AM. You will see the Son of Man sitting at the right hand of Power, and coming with the clouds of the sky."
> 63. The high priest tore his clothes, and said, "What further need have we of witnesses?
> 64. You have heard the blasphemy! What do you think?" They all condemned him to be worthy of death.
> 65. Some began to spit on him, and to cover his face, and to beat him with fists, and to tell him, "Prophesy!" The officers struck him with the palms of their hands.

According to all three synoptics, Jesus was taken to the residence of the high priest, Caiaphas. Peter followed and sat in the courtyard where he joined others around a fire.

We are told that the members of the Council who tried Jesus endeavored to find evidence against him to convict him of blasphemy, but the witnesses contradicted each other. This part of the report must have been an invention of Mark – as well as Matthew and Luke who copied him – because the hearing was behind closed doors, unless some of the Council members told the story afterwards to Jesus' supporters who told Mark later when he gathered information for his gospel.

The Proto-Gospel of John, though, does have a more credible version of what happened in the Council chamber because John was known there and was allowed to observe the meeting.

Judge Cohn believed the Council could not have held an official meeting in a private dwelling at night. Such meetings had to take place in the temple complex during day-time according to the laws in force at that time. There was also nothing in Jesus' teachings, as reported, that warranted the death penalty by stoning for the crime of blasphemy. It is more probable that they tried to convince Jesus to plead innocent when tried later by Pontius Pilate, the Roman governor, on the charge of insurrection because they did not want a popular Jewish teacher to be executed by the Romans. Jesus, however, refused to deny his calling to be the Messiah, the king of Israel (see Chapter 2).[200]

Peter Denies Jesus
Mark 14: 66–72 (Matt 26: 69–75; Luke22: 56–62; John 18: 15–27)

66.	As Peter was beneath in the court, one of the maids of the high priest came,
67.	and seeing Peter warming himself, she looked at him, and said, "You were also with the Nazarene, Jesus."
68.	But he denied it, saying, "I neither know, nor understand what you are saying." He went out into the porch, and the cock crowed.

---

[200] Cohn, *The Trial and Death of Jesus*, 27–31.

69.	The maid saw him, and began again to tell those who stood by, "This is one of them."
70.	But he again denied it. After a little while again those who stood by said to Peter, "You truly are one of them, for you are a Galilean, and your speech shows it."
71.	But he began to curse, and to swear, "I don't know this man of whom you speak!"
72.	The cock crowed the second time. Peter remembered the word, how that Jesus said to him, "Before the cock crows twice, you will deny me three times." When he thought about that, he wept.

All four gospels report that Peter denied knowing Jesus before daybreak when a rooster started crowing. Luke added that Jesus looked at him when he denied him and that caused Peter to leave the courtyard and shed some tears of shame. If Jesus was being interrogated behind closed doors, it would not have been possible for him to hear Peter's words and to look at him.

Jesus is Brought Before Pilate
Mark 15: 1–5 (Matt 27:1–2; Luke 23: 1–3)

1.	Immediately in the morning the chief priests, with the elders and scribes, and the whole council, held a consultation, and bound Jesus, and carried him away, and delivered him up to Pilate.
2.	Pilate asked him, "Are you the King of the Jews?" He answered, "So you say."
3.	The chief priests accused him of many things.
4.	Pilate again asked him, "Have you no answer? See how many things they testify against you!"

5.	But Jesus made no further answer, so Pilate marveled.

Judge Cohn is sure that this report of Mark, Matthew, and Luke must be pious fiction since the hearing in Pontius Pilate's court house was held in camera and no Roman judge would ever have consulted with outsiders before passing sentence. Mark invented a conversation between Pilate and the Jewish leaders. Apart from the hearing in camera, these leaders could not have been present because their presence was needed during the Passover celebrations at the temple at that time.[201]

Both Mark and Luke wrote that Pilate asked Jesus straightaway whether he was the king of the Jews. Jesus did not deny that being the case. Whether this exchange ever took place cannot be determined anymore, but it is clear that Mark and Luke both thought that this topic must have been dealt with while Jesus was in Pilate's court room or Praetorium.

The Jews Wish the Release of Barabbas
Mark 15: 6–15 (Matt 27: 15–26; Luke 23: 13–25)

6.	Now at the feast he used to release to them one prisoner, whom they asked of him.
7.	There was one called Barabbas, bound with those who had made insurrection, men who in the insurrection had committed murder.
8.	The multitude, crying aloud, began to ask him to do as he always did for them.
9.	Pilate answered them, saying, "Do you want me to release to you the King of the Jews?"

---

[201] Cohn, *The Trial and Death of Jesus*, 151–55, 165.

> 10. For he perceived that for envy the chief priests had delivered him up.
> 11. But the chief priests stirred up the multitude, that he should release Barabbas to them instead.
> 12. Pilate again asked them, "What then should I do to him whom you call the King of the Jews?"
> 13. They cried out again, "Crucify him!"
> 14. Pilate said to them, "Why, what evil has he done?" But they cried out exceedingly, "Crucify him!"
> 15. Pilate, wishing to please the multitude, released Barabbas to them, and delivered Jesus, when he had flogged him, to be crucified.

According to Judge Cohn, the haughty and arrogant Pilate would never have consulted with a clamorous and cheeky and cocky crowd outside his court building and tried to please them. There is also no evidence, apart from this report, that Pilate had the custom of releasing any prisoner during the Passover.[202]

Matthew and Luke added that Pilate found Jesus innocent, which cannot be accepted since Jesus was arrested by Roman soldiers precisely because he aspired to become the king of Israel and throw the Roman yoke off, while being cheered on by the crowds. That was a capital offence. It is unthinkable that Pilate would have wasted any time to deal with purported violations of the Jewish religious laws and find Jesus innocent in this regard. Jesus was found guilty of the crime of insurrection or rebellion, according to the notice placed on his cross.

The question must be asked: why didn't Pilate just release

---

[202] Cohn, *The Trial and Death of Jesus,* 164–66.

Jesus if he had indeed found him innocent? He had, after all, the power to do exactly that. Instead, he sentenced Jesus to death.

The Soldiers Mock Jesus
Mark 15: 16–20 (Matt 27: 27–31)

16.	The soldiers led him away within the court, which is the Praetorium; and they called together the whole cohort.
17.	They clothed him with purple, and weaving a crown of thorns, they put it on him.
18.	They began to salute him, "Hail, King of the Jews!"
19.	They struck his head with a reed, and spat on him, and bowing their knees, did homage to him.
20.	When they had mocked him, they took the purple off of him, and put his own garments on him. They led him out to crucify him.

Mark and Matthew both report that after having condemned Jesus to be crucified, Pilate assembled "the whole cohort" – a military unit usually consisting of about 600 soldiers, a whole battalion – to take Jesus away. A squad of a dozen soldiers would usually have been enough to execute a condemned criminal and, therefore, one has to ask: why were so many soldiers necessary?

There can only be one answer: Pilate feared a revolt. Jesus was a popular figure with a large following and the possibility existed that people would try to rescue their king and Messiah – and that had to be prevented.

The soldiers mocked Jesus as the king of the Jews by placing a crown of thorns on his head and temporarily clothing him in a purple cloak.

Jesus is Crucified
Mark 15: 21–32 (Matt 27: 32–44; Luke 23: 26–43)

21.	They compelled one passing by, coming from the country, Simon of Cyrene, the father of Alexander and Rufus, to go with them, that he might bear his cross.
22.	They brought him to the place called Golgotha, which is, being interpreted, "The place of a skull."
23.	They offered him wine mixed with myrrh to drink, but he didn't take it.
24.	Crucifying him, they parted his garments among them, casting lots on them, what each should take.
25.	It was the third hour, and they crucified him.
26.	The superscription of his accusation was written over him, "THE KING OF THE JEWS."
27.	With him they crucified two robbers; one on his right hand, and one on his left.
28.	The scripture was fulfilled, which says, "He was numbered with transgressors."
29.	Those who passed by blasphemed him, wagging their heads, and saying, "Ha! You who destroy the temple, and build it in three days,
30.	save yourself, and come down from the cross!"
31.	Likewise, also the chief priests mocking among themselves with the scribes said, "He saved others. He can't save himself.
32.	Let the Christ, the King of Israel, now come down from the cross, that we may see and believe him." Those who were crucified with him reproached him.

All three Synoptic Gospels relate that the soldiers grabbed a bystander, a certain Simon of Cyrene, to carry Jesus' cross. Jesus was evidently very tired after having had no sleep the previous night and being subjected to torture by the soldiers.

Mark and Matthew wrote that the people mocked Jesus while he was hanging on the cross. Both brigands who were also crucified with him, joined in with the mocking.

Luke differed from the other two evangelists by stating that a crowd of people followed the procession to the place of execution, Golgotha, and that the women wailed and showed their sympathy with Jesus. He managed to console them and warn them that they could expect hardship. According to Luke, the only people who made fun of Jesus were the religious leaders – who were actually needed at the temple to officiate at the feast at that time.

Luke also added that only one bandit joined the people who taunted Jesus, while the other one rebuked him and asked Jesus to remember him when he became king. Jesus promised him that he would be in "Paradise" – the kingdom – with him on that same day.

The soldiers are reported as offering Jesus drugged vinegar, which he refused, probably because he wanted to be fully conscious when the twelve legions of angels suddenly struck.

The inscription on the cross proclaimed Jesus' crime. He was sentenced to death for being the king of the Jews and thereby defying and challenging the authority of the Roman emperor.

Jesus Dies
Mark 15: 33–41 (Matt 27: 45–56; Luke 23: 44–49)

33.	When the sixth hour had come, there was darkness over the whole land until the ninth hour.

34.	At the ninth hour Jesus cried with a loud voice, saying, "Eloi, Eloi, lama sabachthani?" which is, being interpreted, "My God, my God, why have you forsaken me?"
35.	Some of those who stood by, when they heard it, said, "Behold, he calls Elijah."
36.	One ran, and filling a sponge full of vinegar, put it on a reed, and gave it to him to drink, saying, "Let him be. Let's see whether Elijah comes to take him down."
37.	Jesus cried out with a loud voice, and gave up the spirit.
38.	The veil of the temple was torn in two from the top to the bottom.
39.	When the centurion, who stood by opposite him, saw that he cried out like this and breathed his last, he said, "Truly this man was the Son of God!"
40.	There were also women watching from afar, among whom were both Mary Magdalene, and Mary the mother of James the less and of Joses, and Salome;
41.	who, when he was in Galilee, followed him, and served him; and many other women who came up with him to Jerusalem.

All three Synoptic Gospels reported that darkness of three hours descended upon Jerusalem while Jesus hang on the cross. It could not have been a solar eclipse, which takes only a few minutes. Moreover, the Passover was always celebrated at full moon when a solar eclipse is totally out of the question. One explanation is that a fierce dust storm blew from the desert to the east of Jerusalem – something that often happens in Jerusalem.[203]

---

[203] Jerusalem Post Staff, "Dust Storm Coats Jerusalem".

There is also a possibility that the ash and dust clouds of volcanic or seismic activity in the region may have obscured the sun. Matthew (27: 51) mentioned: "The earth quaked and the rocks were split," while Jesus hang on the cross, which may point to volcanic activity. The countries around the eastern Mediterranean are known for frequent seismic and volcanic activity. It is known that seismic activity occurred in the Jordan Valley during AD 33.[204]

After the dust or ash clouds had dissipated, a disappointed and disillusioned Jesus cried out, as described by Mark and Matthew: "My God, my God, why have you forsaken me?" The expected angelic horde never appeared to rescue him and drive the Romans away as he had expected. Luke changed these words into something different: "Father, into your hands I commit my spirit!"

Mark does not explain how the centurion, the officer commanding the team of executioners, got the insight that Jesus was "the Son of God". It is possible that he heard from the Jewish religious leaders or bystanders that Jesus proclaimed himself as the son of God. With his pagan background, this expression must have had the meaning for him of a demi-god, such as the many sons of Jupiter, Zeus, and Osiris of which the mythology of those days had many examples.[205] The darkness caused by the dust storm and/or volcanic activity that followed immediately after Jesus had been crucified could have given this superstitious Roman this insight.

This is, incidentally, the second time when the exact expression "Son of God" was applied to Jesus in Mark's Gospel – the other being Mark 3: 11 when an evil spirit also said something of the sort. Apart from that, according to Mark 1: 11 a voice from the heaven said at Jesus' baptism: "You are my beloved Son…"

---

[204] Earthquake Track, "Recent Earthquakes near Jerusalem"; Wikipedia, "List of Earthquakes in the Levant."
[205] Bible Hub, "Mark 15: 39".

Mark 5: 7 tells of an evil spirit that called Jesus "Son of the Most High God". When Jesus had a secret meeting on the mountain with two men, a voice was reportedly heard: "This is my beloved Son" (Mark 9: 5).

Mark wanted to emphasize with all these expressions that Jesus was, after all, in fact the legitimate king of Israel.

Matthew added some miraculous details to emphasize the importance of the death of Jesus: a curtain in the temple was torn from top to bottom, an earthquake occurred and tombs were opened with the result that corpses inside them became visible or fell out, which he interpreted and magnified as dead people becoming magically alive again.

Jesus is Buried
Mark 15: 42–47 (Matt 27: 57–61; Luke 23: 50–56)

42.	When evening had now come, because it was the Preparation, that is, the day before the Sabbath,
43.	Joseph of Arimathaea, a member of the council of honorable estate, who also himself was looking for the kingdom of God, came. He boldly went in to Pilate, and asked for Jesus' body.
44.	Pilate marveled if he were already dead: and calling to him the centurion, he asked him whether he had been dead for a while.
45.	When he learned it from the centurion, he granted the body to Joseph.
46.	He bought a linen cloth, and taking him down, wound him in the linen cloth, and laid him in a tomb which had been cut out of a rock. He rolled a stone against the door of the tomb.

> 47. Mary Magdalene and Mary, the mother of Joses, saw where he was laid.

Joseph of Arimathea, a follower of Jesus who also expected the coming of the kingdom of God and who was a member of the Council, convinced Pilate to allow him to take Jesus' body from the cross. The centurion in command of the execution team affirmed that Jesus was indeed dead. He laid Jesus in a tomb as the custom of the Jews was. Two women, including Mary Magdalene, watched the entombment. Matthew and Luke added that it was Joseph's own unused tomb.

Luke mentioned that the women went straightaway to the tomb with various spices and ointments to administer those on Jesus' body. The Greek word for "ointment" (μύρον – *myron*) suggests an oily substance with medicinal uses. This implies that they possibly wanted to nurse Jesus back to health because he did not really die on the cross from his wounds. It often happened that crucified men hang more than a day before they eventually died. Jesus did not hang so long – at most six hours – and his chances of survival were, therefore, better than most.

It is not clear on which day of the week Jesus was buried. Joseph laid Jesus in the tomb during the evening on the day before the Sabath. For the Jews, a new day began when it became dark and the stars appeared.[206] If Jesus was buried during the evening after dark, it was already Friday, the day before the Sabath, and that means that he was crucified on a Thursday. If Jesus was put in the grave before the next day started during the evening, he must have been crucified on a Friday. It seems that it was not quite dark yet when Jesus was placed in the tomb because the women could ob-

---

[206] Anon., "Hebrew Days of the Week".

serve what happened.

If Jesus was indeed crucified and buried on a Friday, the day on which the Passover feast was celebrated, the crucifixion likely happened on 3 April AD 33. On that date, the full moon rose above Jerusalem partly eclipsed – as has been shown in Chapter 2.

The Women Find an Empty Tomb
Mark 16: 1–8 (Matt 28: 1–8; Luke 24: 1–12)

1.	When the Sabbath was past, Mary Magdalene, and Mary the mother of James, and Salome, bought spices, that they might come and anoint him.
2.	Very early on the first day of the week, they came to the tomb when the sun had risen.
3.	They were saying among themselves, "Who will roll away the stone from the door of the tomb for us?"
4.	for it was very big. Looking up, they saw that the stone was rolled back
5.	Entering into the tomb, they saw a young man sitting on the right side, dressed in a white robe, and they were amazed.
6.	He said to them, "Don't be amazed. You seek Jesus, the Nazarene, who has been crucified. He has risen. He is not here. Behold, the place where they laid him!
7.	But go, tell his disciples and Peter, `He goes before you into Galilee. There you will see him, as he said to you.`"
8.	They went out, and fled from the tomb, for trembling and astonishment had come on them. They said nothing to anyone; for they were afraid.

The oldest manuscripts of Mark end at this point. Many commentators found it a strange ending with the remark that the three women who found the empty tomb decided to flee because "they were afraid". It was theorized that a last page of the original gospel manuscript perhaps got lost, a page on which the resurrection of Jesus was described in more detail.[207] Such a purported lost last page has never been found and this supposition remains mere speculation.

Chenoweth pointed out that the Greek word for "being afraid" (φοβέω – *phobeo*) is often followed by a noun in the accusative and that suggests that the women must have been afraid of either the Jewish authorities or the Romans – and that suggests a last page that got lost.[208]

Some scribes copying the gospel may also have felt the same and added summaries of the endings of Matthew, Luke, and John to Mark. These summaries are certainly later additions and not authentic parts of the original gospel.

On the other hand, the Greek word for "were afraid" may also be translated simply as "fled", without a noun in the accusative following it. That could mean that the gospel really ended at 16: 8.

The expression used in Greek for "being afraid" may also be translated as "being amazed". Mark, therefore, pointed out that the women were amazed and surprised to find an empty tomb because they did not expect Jesus to be removed somewhere else – perhaps to a safer spot where he could receive better medical attention. The man in the tomb was probably one of those who removed Jesus to be cared for somewhere else.

We are told the women hastened to tell the disciples. "They said nothing to anyone; for they were afraid" – which may also mean that they thought it prudent not to spread the news that Jesus survived the crucifixion because they were afraid of what could

---

[207] Burkitt, "The Historical Character of the Gospel of Mark", 171–73.
[208] Chenoweth, "Oral History", 28.

happen to the resurrected Jesus if the authorities should find him. This explanation also suggests that Mark ended at this point.

It seems as if the controversy regarding the ending of Mark remains unresolved. Nonetheless, Mark tells how the three women went to the grave on the Sunday morning early with spices to anoint Jesus' body. The Greek word for "anoint" is ἀλείψω (*aleipso*). According the Greek dictionary of Arndt and Gingrich, this word could also mean that the spices were being used as a "(household) remedy". This only makes sense if they wanted to heal Jesus from his wounds because he did not really die on the cross.

To their astonishment, they found a man dressed in white inside the tomb – most probably a member of the Essene sect, the members of which usually wore white clothes. He assured them that Jesus has risen and that he went to Galilee, his home province, where he will wait for his followers. That makes sense because he would have been safer in the kingdom of Galilee where Pilate did not have jurisdiction.

Matthew changed the man in white clothes into an angel who caused another earthquake, while Luke wrote that two men in dazzling clothes waited at the tomb.

The author of Mark was unaware of the report in the Proto-Gospel of John that Joseph of Arimathea and Nicodemus had already applied antiseptics and a healing formula to the body of Jesus to help him to get healed from his wounds (John 19: 38–39). Mark's source could have told him a garbled version of the same story in which the women – and not the two men – brought spices to apply to Jesus' body.

A LATER ENDING TO THE GOSPEL OF MARK

Jesus Appears to Mary Magdalene
Mark 16: 9–12 (Matt 28: 9–10)

9.	Now when he had risen early on the first day of the week, he appeared first to Mary Magdalene, from whom he had cast out seven demons.
10.	She went and told those who had been with him, as they mourned and wept.
11.	When they heard that he was alive, and had been seen by her, they disbelieved.

These few verses are clearly a summary of the reports in the Gospels of John and Matthew and must have been added after the completion of these documents.

Jesus Appears to Two Disciples
Mark 16: 12 (Luke 24: 13–35)

12.	After these things he was revealed in another form to two of them, as they walked, on their way into the country.

This verse is a summary of the passage found in Luke where Jesus conversed with two disciples on their way to Emmaus and it does not belong to the original Gospel of Mark.

ANOTHER ADDITION TO THE ORIGINAL GOSPEL OF MARK

Jesus Appears to the Eleven
Mark 16: 13–20 (Matt 28: 16–20; Luke 24: 36–49)

13.	They went away and told it to the rest. They didn't believe them, either.
14.	Afterward he was revealed to the eleven themselves as they sat at the table, and he rebuked them for their unbelief and hardness of heart, because they didn't believe those who had seen him after he had risen.
15.	He said to them, "Go into all the world, and preach the gospel to the whole creation.

16.	He who believes and is baptized will be saved; but he who disbelieves will be condemned.
17..	These signs will accompany those who believe: in my name they will cast out demons; they will speak with new languages;
18.	they will take up serpents, and if they drink any deadly thing, it will in no way hurt them; they will lay hands on the sick, and they will recover."
19.	So then the Lord Jesus, after he had spoken to them, was received up into heaven, and sat down at the right hand of God.
20.	They went forth, and preached everywhere, the Lord working with them, and confirming the word by the signs that followed. Amen.

This is, yet, anther summary of the resurrection stories in the other three gospels. It was only added after the other gospels were completed a decade or more after Mark's completion and cannot be regarded as part of the original Gospel of Mark.

Concluding Remarks

How much can we accept as historical in the Gospel of Mark and how much of it must be regarded as mythological or pious inventions?

The main theme of the Gospel of Mark is Jesus' campaign to become king of Israel and his endeavors to be a reformer who wanted the Jews to turn to God. The kingdom he envisaged was a theocracy in which he would rule as God's representative and as the descendant of David. This ideal of Jesus was never realized, but Jesus, nevertheless, made a huge impact on his fellow-Jews, so much that Mark (or an anonymous author) thought it worthwhile to collect memories about him and include those in a gospel.

It seems that the reports of most of Jesus' sayings and movements, as reported in Mark, can be accepted as accurate. Jesus was, indeed, an inspiring teacher and story-teller who drew crowds to his sermons.

Jesus is also portrayed as a gifted healer. It seems that he did, in fact, healed some sick people, although the miracles attributed to him must be regarded as part of the magical world view of those times. Many of his healings cam, no doubt, be attributed to the placebo effect, where people with psycho-somatic and other complaints got rid of their symptoms simply because their immune systems and minds reacted positively after having had an encounter with the miracle healer, Jesus of Nazareth.

Jesus was not presented as a divine figure and he never used the expression "Son of God" for himself in the Gospel of Mark. That type of expression was used by others. In all cases, that can be regarded as references to his aspirations to become the king of Israel.

Jesus often called himself "the Son of Man" – fourteen times in Mark. This expression is taken from Dan 7: 13–14 –

> "I saw in the night–visions, and, behold, there came with the clouds of the sky one like a *son of man*, and he came even to *the ancient of days*, and they brought him near before him. There was given him dominion, and glory, and a *kingdom*, that all the peoples, nations, and languages should serve him: his dominion is an everlasting dominion, which shall not pass away, and his *kingdom* that which shall not be destroyed" (*emphasis added*).

This passage in Daniel is clearly a prophecy regarding the expected Messiah, who would be a king. When Jesus called himself "the Son of Man" he conveyed the message that he was the promised Messiah and appointed by God, "the Ancient of Days", to be the king of Israel.

John often accused the "Jews" or Judeans of being Jesus' enemies. Mark always portrayed the Pharisees and often the teachers of the Law and the priests as Jesus' enemies who refused to accept him as the Messiah.

Albrecht Dürer: Jesus Placed in the Tomb

Where did Jesus go after his resurrection? Mark is silent on this topic and it was left to Matthew and Luke to gather or invent stories regarding Jesus' appearances and ascension into heaven. Mark seemed to have left open the possibility that Jesus did not really die and survived the ordeal. On the other hand, Matthew and Luke who wrote their gospels some years later, were convinced that Jesus did really die and that his resurrection was a supernatural event.

In any case, wherever Jesus went, he must have been a broken man due to all his injuries and wounds. He was also a disappointed man who did not play any further direct role in the lives of his followers.

There are no signs that Mark was influenced by Paul's depiction of Jesus as a divine personage who was resurrected from the grave with a glorified or spiritual body, with which he ascended into heaven. When Mark wrote his gospel during the seventies of the first century AD the letters of Paul were probably not yet collected in a bundle and regarded as Scripture. That only happened later and the other Synoptic Gospels, the letter to the Hebrews, the letters of Peter, Revelation, and Clement's letter to the Corinthians (see Chapter 12) all show the influence of Paul's message about the cosmic and mythologic Christ.

Chapter 8

MATTHEW'S UNIQUE MATERIAL

Matthew's Sources

It was demonstrated in Chapter 3 that the Gospel of Matthew was composed of three main sources:

- The Q Document – the contents of which were discussed in Chapter 3 and the use made of it by Matthew was pointed out; Matthew contains 235 verses from the reconstructed Q;
- The Gospel of Mark – which was discussed in the previous Chapter and where it was mentioned how Matthew treated the text of Mark; Mark's text has 661 verses, 606 of which appear in Matthew (92%); and
- Some material unique to Matthew – not found in any other gospel; this material is contained in 350 verses.

This Chapter deals with the unique material found only in Matthew – usually called the M Source. Matthew's unique material consists of the following elements:

- Short comments and additions to the text of Mark – which have been mentioned in the previous Chapter;
- Sayings of Jesus and other stories collected from unknown sources – maybe parts of Q not used by Luke or oral traditions based on eye-witness reports;
- The nativity stories; and
- Stories about Jesus' trial and his appearances after his resurrection.

Authorship and Date of Composition

The first Christian theologian to attribute the Gospel of Matthew to specifically this apostle of Jesus, was Irenaeus, bishop of Lyons in Gaul, who wrote about AD 180:[209]

> "Matthew also issued a written Gospel among the Hebrews in their own dialect, while Peter and Paul were preaching at Rome, and laying the foundations of the Church. After their departure, Mark, the disciple and interpreter of Peter, did also hand down to us in writing what had been preached by Peter. Luke also, the companion of Paul, recorded in a book the Gospel preached by him. Afterwards, John, the disciple of the Lord, who also had leaned upon His breast, did himself publish a Gospel during his residence at Ephesus in."

The historian Eusebius confirmed during the early fourth century Irenaeus' identification of the authorship of Matthew:

> "Nevertheless, of all the disciples of the Lord, only Matthew and John have left us written memorials, and they, tradition says, were led to write only under the pressure of necessity. For Matthew, who had at first preached to the Hebrews, when he was about to go to other peoples, committed his Gospel to writing in his native tongue, and thus compensated those whom he was obliged to leave for the loss of his presence."[210]

Eusebius added:

> "But concerning Matthew he [Papias, an earlier author whose works are lost] writes as follows: 'So then Matthew

---

[209] Irenaeus, *Adversus Haereses*, Liber III/I/1.
[210] Eusebius, *Historia Ecclesiastica*, Liber 111/ XXIV/5–6.

wrote the oracles in the Hebrew language, and every one interpreted them as he was able."[211]

It is no longer possible to regard the apostle Matthew as the author of the gospel bearing his name for the simple reason that this gospel must have been composed at the earliest during the eighties of the first century AD, some time after the Gospel of Mark, which was written during the seventies (see Chapter 7).

By that time, the apostle Matthew could either not have been alive anymore, or unable to undertake the arduous task of interviewing numerous eye-witnesses at various locations and writing the gospel due to an advanced age. If he was as old as Jesus and still alive at that time, he must have been at least in his late eighties or even nineties when the gospel was finalized.

Besides – according to legend – Matthew died in Ethiopia where he did missionary work, far from any possible place where the gospel was written.[212]

It is possible that the author was indeed somehow associated with the apostle Matthew. In the list of disciples in Mark, a certain Levi, a tax collector, is named. Matthew changed his name to Matthew (Matt 9: 9 and 10: 3), probably with the idea of establishing apostolic authority for his gospel.[213]

This gospel has a distinct Jewish flavor. Certain prophecies in the Old Testament are often referred to as having been fulfilled in the life of Jesus. Although he wrote a better Greek than Mark, there are certain Hebraisms in his book. For instance, the word "behold" is used 66 times in Matthew. The Greek word is ἰδού (*idou*), which is a translation of the Hebrew הִנֵּה (*hinneh*), which is a very common

---

[211] Eusebius, *Historia Ecclesiastice*. Liber III/XXXIX/16.
[212] Enc Brit, "Matthew (the Evangelist), Saint".
[213] Rylaarsdam *et al.*, "Biblical Literature."

expression in the Old Testament.

The intended readers seem to have been Greek-speaking Jewish Christians, somewhere in Syria, where many Jewish Christians fled during the Jewish War of AD 66–70. There were sizable Jewish and Christian communities in Antioch and Damascus. The opponents of Jesus are not "the Jews" as such, but the Pharisees and teachers of the Law or scribes, who are pictured as the adherents of the outdated Jewish religion, which was abolished after the catastrophic destruction of the temple and supplanted by Christianity.[214]

A comparison of Matthew (and Mark) with the Proto-Gospel of John, which was written at least two decades earlier, shows that Matthew was certainly not aware of John and influenced by this book. Where they described the same episodes – for instance, the cleansing of the temple, the feeding of the multitude, the arrest, trial and crucifixion of Jesus, they use very different words and expressions, with the result that they sometimes contradict each other. Their chronologies of Jesus' ministry differ, as well.

In the following pages, the unique parts of Matthew's Gospel, the M Document, are discussed and analyzed for their historical value.

The Ancestors of Jesus
Matt 1: 1–17

1.	The book of the generation of Jesus Christ, the son of David, the son of Abraham.
2.	Abraham became the father of Isaac. Isaac became the father of Jacob. Jacob became the father of Judah and his brothers.

---

[214] Mullins, *The Gospel of Matthew*.

3.	Judah became the father of Perez and Zerah by Tamar. Perez became the father of Hezron. Hezron became the father of Ram.
4.	Ram became the father of Amminadab. Amminadab became the father of Nahshon. Nahshon became the father of Salmon.
5.	Salmon became the father of Boaz by Rahab. Boaz became the father of Obed by Ruth. Obed became the father of Jesse.
6.	Jesse became the father of David the king. David became the father of Solomon by her who had been the wife of Uriah.
7.	Solomon became the father of Rehoboam. Rehoboam became the father of Abijah. Abijah became the father of Asa.
8.	Asa became the father of Jehoshaphat. Jehoshaphat became the father of Joram. Joram became the father of Uzziah.
9.	Uzziah became the father of Jotham. Jotham became the father of Ahaz. Ahaz became the father of Hezekiah.
10.	Hezekiah became the father of Manasseh. Manasseh became the father of Amon. Amon became the father of Josiah.
11.	Josiah became the father of Jechoniah and his brothers, at the time of the exile to Babylon.
12.	After the exile to Babylon, Jechoniah became the father of Shealtiel. Shealtiel became the father of Zerubbabel.
13.	Zerubbabel became the father of Abiud. Abiud became the father of Eliakim. Eliakim became the father of Azor.
14.	Azor became the father of Sadoc. Sadoc became the father of Achim. Achim became the father of Eliud.

> 15. Eliud became the father of Eleazar. Eleazar became the father of Matthan. Matthan became the father of Jacob.
> 16. Jacob became the father of Joseph, the husband of Mary, from whom was born Jesus, who is called Christ.
> 17. So all the generations from Abraham to David are fourteen generations; from David to the exile to Babylon fourteen generations; and from the carrying away to Babylon to the Christ, fourteen generations.

In biblical times, many families preserved their genealogies carefully. Several genealogic lists are to be found in the Old Testament. Matthew could have gotten his information in this regard from relatives of Jesus, of which some were still available during the last half of the first century AD, according to Eusebius.[215]

Jesus' genealogy is presented in a neat package consisting of three sets of fourteen generations each. Fourteen is the sum of seven plus seven – a symbolic number connected to God's work in his creation. There were, for instance, seven days of creation in Genesis 1 and seven days in a working week. The ancients knew seven planets or moving bodies in the sky – the Sun, the Moon, Mercury, Venus, Mars, Jupiter, and Saturn. The purpose of Matthew with this scheme was to explain that the birth of Jesus, the Christ or Messiah, a true Israelite and a descendant of King David, was the outcome of a plan by God.

This genealogy differs in many respects from that found in the Gospel of Luke. For instance, Joseph, Jesus' father, has two different fathers in the two lists of ancestors. Eusebius explains that Matthew provided the biological descent of Joseph, Jesus' father. Luke provides the name of Joseph's stepfather who married his

---

[215] Eusebius, *Historia Ecclesiastica*, Liber III/XIX–XX.

mother after the death of her first husband.[216]

That Jesus was a descendant of King David, may be regarded as historically confirmed. All four canonical gospels, as well as the letters of Paul, repeatedly testified to this fact.

The Birth of Jesus
Matt 1: 18–25

18.	Now the birth of Jesus Christ was like this; because when his mother, Mary, had been engaged to Joseph, before they came together, she was found pregnant by the Holy Spirit.
19.	Joseph, her husband, being a righteous man, and not willing to make her a public example, intended to put her away secretly.
20.	But when he thought about these things, behold, an angel of the Lord appeared to him in a dream, saying, "Joseph, you son of David, don't be afraid to take to yourself Mary, your wife, for that which is conceived in her is of the Holy Spirit.
21.	She shall bring forth a son. You shall call his name JESUS, for it is he who shall save his people from their sins."
22.	Now all this has happened, that it might be fulfilled which was spoken by the Lord through the prophet, saying,
23.	"Behold, the virgin shall be with child, and shall bring forth a son. They shall call his name Immanuel;" which is, being interpreted, "God with us."
24.	Joseph arose from his sleep, and did as the angel of the Lord commanded him, and took his wife to himself;

---

[216] Eusebius, *Historia Ecclesiastica*, Liber I/VII.

> 25. and didn't know her sexually until she had brought forth her firstborn son. He named him JESUS.

Matthew wrote that a heavenly messenger appeared in a dream to Joseph, the betrothed of Mary, to tell him that his virgin bride was pregnant from the Holy Spirit and that he should not end the engagement. In this respect, one must ask: where did Matthew get this information about Joseph's dream? If Joseph told others of the dream, then one may also ask: is there any independent proof that he really had this dream?

A passage from Isaiah was quoted to explain this virgin birth of Jesus. The quotation from Isaiah rests on a misunderstanding. Isaiah mentioned in chapter 7: 14 of his book that a certain unnamed young woman of his time – not a virgin – would become pregnant. The ancient Greek translation of the Old Testament made a mistake by altering "young woman" or "maiden" to "virgin". This passage in Isaiah can, therefore, in no way be seen as a prediction that Jesus would be born from a virgin.

Matthew evidently also thought that the Messiah must have been born in exceptional circumstances, just as other mythological heroic figures from Antiquity. There are the following examples:

- The Egyptian god Horus was born from a virgin, Isis. He was visited after his birth by wise men;
- The Greek god Adonis was born of the virgin Myrrha;
- Perseus, the Greek god, also had a virgin for a mother;
- Herakles (Hercules), the Greek hero and demi-god, had the king of the gods, Zeus, and a virgin mother as parents;
- The Persian god, Mithras, was born of a virgin; he was later venerated by many Roman soldiers;
- The Persian prophet, Zoroaster, claimed a virgin for a mother;

- The mother of the Greek philosopher Plato was reputedly impregnated by Apollo before she and her husband could have had intercourse;
- The Greek conqueror, Alexander the Great, was born after his mother was reputedly impregnated by either a divine snake or a thunderbolt, sent by Zeus;
- The legendary founders of the city of Rome, Romulus and Remus, were born from a vestal virgin, Rhea Sylvia, and their father was the war god Mars; and
- The first Roman emperor, Augustus, was allegedly sired by the sun god, Apollo.[217]

It may be added that the Ebionites, the Jewish followers of Jesus of which his brother, James, was the leader, rejected the notion of a virgin birth. They declared that Jesus was the biological son of Joseph and Mary (see Chapter 2). It may be argued that the Ebionites were in a better position to know the truth than anybody else.

Matt 1: 24–25 reports that Joseph got married to Mary before Jesus was born, but that they refrained from sexual intercourse. It is, though, a mystery how Matthew – or anybody else, for that matter – knew exactly what had happened or did not happen on or in the matrimonial bed of this couple.

The Wise Men from the East
Matt 2: 1–12

1.	Now when Jesus was born in Bethlehem of Judea in the days of Herod, the king, behold, wise men from the east came to Jerusalem, saying,

---

[217] Ontario Consultants on Religious Tolerance, "The Virgin Birth"; Hitchens, *God is not Great*, 23; Wolmarans, "Jesus", 196–224.

2.	"Where is he who is born King of the Jews? For we saw his star in the east, and have come to worship him."
3.	When Herod the king heard it, he was troubled, and all Jerusalem with him.
4.	Gathering together all the chief priests and scribes of the people, he asked them where the Christ would be born.
5.	They said to him, "In Bethlehem of Judea, for thus it is written through the prophet,
6.	\`You Bethlehem, land of Judah, Are in no way least among the princes of Judah: For out of you shall come forth a governor, Who shall shepherd my people, Israel\`".
7.	Then Herod secretly called the wise men, and learned from them exactly what time the star appeared.
8.	He sent them to Bethlehem, and said, "Go and search diligently for the young child. When you have found him, bring me word, so that I also may come and worship him."
9.	They, having heard the king, went their way; and behold, the star, which they saw in the east, went before them, until it came and stood over where the young child was.
10.	When they saw the star, they rejoiced with exceedingly great joy.
11.	They came into the house and saw the young child with Mary, his mother, and they fell down and worshipped him. Opening their treasures, they offered to him gifts: gold, frankincense, and myrrh.
12.	Being warned in a dream that they shouldn't return to Herod, they went back to their own country another way.

Matthew reported that Jesus was born in specifically Bethlehem as the supposed fulfillment of another prophecy of the Old Testament (Mic 5: 2). How and why his parents travelled there was not disclosed. It is uncertain if he was really born there.

Star gazers or astrologers from the east, probably Babylon or Persia, visited the baby Jesus in Bethlehem on account of a star they saw. This star gave them the message that a king was born in Judea and they wanted to pay homage to him. The logical place to look for this royal baby was in Jerusalem at the court of King Herod the Great.

Albrecht Dürer: The Nativity (1502–1504)

Herod – as well the whole of Jerusalem – was purportedly shocked by this news. Herod asked them to return to him after having visited the baby in Bethlehem where he was supposed to have been born, according to the prophecy, because he wanted to get rid of a possible rival. Another heavenly messenger warned the wise men not to return to Jerusalem.

In a mysterious way, the star led them to the house where the baby Jesus was to be found.

There are so many supernatural and improbable elements to this story that most of it may safely be relegated to the realm of myths. However, there is a possibility that a phenomenon in the sky could have held a message that a king was being born in Judea and many efforts were made to identify this astronomical or astrological event, including an appearance of the comet of Halley.

The most likely explanation is a conjunction of the planets Jupiter and Saturn in the constellation of Pisces (the Fishes) on 23 September, 6 BC.

A computerized recreation of the conjunction between the planets Jupiter and Saturn within the constellation of Pisces (the Fishes) on 23 September 6 BC at 22:00 local time. The two planets were so near to each other as seen from Earth that they created the appearance of a single very bright object.

Jupiter was regarded as the royal star, seen as Jupiter or Zeus, the king of the gods in Roman and Greek mythology. Saturn was the star of specifically Israel. Saturday, the Jewish Sabbath, was named after this seventh planet, Saturn (see Chapter 2). The constellation of Pisces suggested the direction of the Mediterranean Sea to the west of Babylonia.[218] This occurrence may, perhaps, have given some stargazers the message that a king was born in Judea.

The Gospel of Matthew doesn't name these wise men, but they were later given the legendary names of Balthasar, Melchior,

---

[218] Allen. *Star Names*, 337.

and Gaspar and they were regarded as kings and saints.[219]

The three Magi from the East with their gifts for the baby Jesus, together with the star they followed (Matt 2: 1). Their traditional names are written above their heads (Balthassar, Melchior, and Gaspar) and they were declared to be saints by the prefix SCS – the abbreviation for "Sanctus" (*saint*) – before each of their names (mosaic from the church of S Apollinare Nuovo in Ravenna, Italy, 6th century).

The Flight to Egypt
Matt 2: 13–15

> 13. Now when they had departed, behold, an angel of the Lord appeared to Joseph in a dream, saying, "Arise and take the young child and his mother, and flee into Egypt, and stay there until I tell you, for Herod will seek the young child to destroy him."

---

[219] Enc. Brit. "Magi".

> 14. He arose and took the young child and his mother by night, and departed into Egypt,
> 15. and was there until the death of Herod; that it might be fulfilled which was spoken by the Lord through the prophet, saying, "Out of Egypt I called my son."

Albrecht Dürer: The Flight to Egypt

When King Herod heard that a new king was born, he ordered that all boys below the age of two in Bethlehem be killed. Joseph was, though, again warned by an angel in a dream to escape to Egypt where he and his family had to stay until Herod had died. Matthew supplies no details about where they lived and how Joseph was able to support his family.

There was, however, a large Jewish community in Egypt at that time. It is estimated that more or less 40% of the inhabitants of Alexandria were Jews.[220] Many of them must have been Essenes, where Joseph and his family could have received hospitality.

There are some improbable and impossible and implausible elements in this tale. First of all, it was not necessary to flee to Egypt to save the baby Jesus. Joseph resided in Nazareth, a village in Galilee in the north of Palestine (Matt 2: 23) and he could simply have returned home to escape Herod's gang of killers that

---

[220] Enc Brit, "Diaspora".

concentrated their efforts on Bethlehem, which lies south of Jerusalem – that is, if Jesus was really born in Bethlehem.

Messages sent through the medium of dreams are, by definition, subjective and impossible to verify. The other gospels do not have any reports of this purported flight to Egypt. This vanishing act to Egypt was supposedly the outcome of another prophecy. Matthew quoted from Hos 11: 1 –

> "When Israel was a child, then I loved him, and called my son out of Egypt."

There can be no doubt that this sentence certainly did not have the Messiah in mind because the "son" of God in this instance was clearly the nation of Israel, that broke free from Egypt during the time of Moses.

The Massacre in Bethlehem
Matt 2L 16–23

16.	Then Herod, when he saw that he was mocked by the wise men, was exceedingly angry, and sent forth, and killed all the male children who were in Bethlehem, and in all the surrounding countryside, from two years old and under, according to the exact time which he had learned from the wise men.
17.	Then that which was spoken by Jeremiah the prophet was fulfilled, saying,
18.	"A voice was heard in Ramah, Lamentation, weeping and great mourning, Rachel weeping for her children; She wouldn't be comforted, because they are no more."
19.	But when Herod was dead, behold, an angel of the Lord appeared in a dream to Joseph in Egypt, saying,

> 20. "Arise and take the young child and his mother, and go into the land of Israel, for those who sought the young child's life are dead."
> 21. He arose and took the young child and his mother, and came into the land of Israel.
> 22. But when he heard that Archelaus was reigning over Judea in the place of his father, Herod, he was afraid to go there. Being warned in a dream, he withdrew into the region of Galilee,
> 23. and came and lived in a city called Nazareth; that it might be fulfilled which was spoken through the prophets: "He will be called a Nazorean."

Matthew believed that Jer 31: 15 foretold that King Herod the Great would have all boys below two years of age in Bethlehem slaughtered. No independent record of this campaign of extermination exists and it is certainly a piece of fiction, although Herod was notorious for his cruelty and paranoia. For instance, he murdering his wife and some of his children when he distrusted their loyalty.[221]

Nevertheless, in Jer 31: 15 we read the following (and it is quoted by Matthew as proof for his story):

> "A voice is heard in Ramah, lamentation, and bitter weeping, Rachel weeping for her children; she refuses to be comforted for her children, because they are no more."

When one reads the whole chapter in Jeremiah, it appears that he

---

[221] Enc Brit, "Herod".

referred to the laments after the Babylonians had sacked Jerusalem in 586 BC. Jeremiah never intended his words to be applied to the time of Herod the Great, centuries later.

It must be concluded that Matthew invented stories about Jesus to fit his interpretation of certain prophecies or statements from the Old Testament. He seems to have argued that since certain prophecies were to be found in the Scriptures, they simply must have been fulfilled during Jesus' life.

Matthew's statement that there was another prophecy that the Messiah would reside in Nazareth and be called a Nazorean, is unfounded. No such prophecy exists. The fact that Jesus is called a Nazorean in this passage, means that his family belonged to the sect of the Essenes – as has been pointed out in Chapter 2.

The Baptism of Jesus
Matt 3: 13–17

13.	Then Jesus came from Galilee to the Jordan to John, to be baptized by him.
14.	But John would have hindered him, saying, "I need to be baptized by you, and you come to me?"
15.	But Jesus, answering, said to him, "Allow it now, for this is the fitting way for us to fulfill all righteousness." Then he allowed him.
16.	Jesus, when he was baptized, went up directly from the water: and behold, the heavens were opened to him. He saw the Spirit of God descending as a dove, and coming on him.
17.	Behold, a voice out of the heavens said, "This is my beloved Son, in whom I am well pleased."

This passage by Matthew is an expanded version of Mark 1: 9–11. Where Mark stated that the Spirit (or the wind) descended upon Jesus "like a dove", Matthew changed it to the "Spirit [or breath] of God" that took the form of a real dove.

Matthew also added that John purportedly initially refused to baptize Jesus. There is no way to determine whether that really happened.

The Temptation of Jesus
Matthew: 4: 7–8

7.	Jesus said to him, "Again, it is written, `You shall not test the Lord, your God.`"
8.	Again, the devil took him to an exceedingly high mountain, and showed him all the kingdoms of the world, and their glory.

Matthew attached these two verses to the account in Q about the temptation of Jesus. There is a possibility that they originally belonged to Q and that Luke omitted them, while Matthew kept them. It has already been mentioned in the previous Chapter, where this episode was briefly described, that Jesus must have been dehydrated and famished during his stay in the desert, which may have led to hallucinations.

The Multitudes Seek Jesus
Matthew 4: 23–25

23.	Jesus went about in all Galilee, teaching in their synagogues, preaching the gospel of the kingdom, and healing every disease and every sickness among the people.

24.	The report about him went forth into all Syria. They brought to him all who were sick, afflicted with various diseases and torments, possessed with demons, epileptics, and paralytics; and he healed them.
25.	Great multitudes from Galilee, Decapolis, Jerusalem, Judea and from beyond the Jordan followed him.

A similar story is told in Luke 6: 17–19, but there are also some differences. It must be concluded that these passages probably do not come from Q.

Both passages, nevertheless, demonstrate that Jesus was a popular teacher and healer and that people flocked to see and hear him. He must have been a charismatic figure and people felt drawn to him. He somehow managed to heal people with psycho-somatic ailments, caused by the stress caused by poverty and the repression by the Romans.

Jesus preached the gospel (good news) of the kingdom, in which the people would be freed from foreign domination.

Some Beatitudes
Matt 5: 7–10

7.	"Blessed are the merciful, for they shall obtain mercy.
8.	"Blessed are the pure in heart, for they shall see God.
9.	"Blessed are the peacemakers, for they shall be called sons of God.
10.	"Blessed are those who have been persecuted for righteousness' sake, for theirs is the Kingdom of Heaven.

Matthew inserted these verses into a passage taken from Q. It is possible that they were part of the original Q, which were ignored by Luke and, therefore, were not included in the reconstructed Q.

Wherever the Q Document mentioned the "Kingdom of God", Matthew changed it to the "Kingdom of Heaven". That may be a sign of the author's Jewish background, which inhibited him from using the name of God. It is, nevertheless, clear that this kingdom was due to be established soon on earth.

Part of the Sermon on the Mount
Matt 5: 14–24

14.	You are the light of the world. A city set on a hill can't be hid.
15.	*Neither do you light a lamp, and put it under a bushel basket, but on a stand; and it shines to all who are in the house.*
16.	Even so, let your light shine before men; that they may see your good works, and glorify your Father who is in heaven.
17.	Don't think that I came to destroy the law or the prophets. I didn't come to destroy, but to fulfill.
18.	*For most assuredly, I tell you, until heaven and earth pass away, not even one smallest letter or one tiny pen stroke shall in any way pass away from the law, until all things are accomplished.*
19.	Whoever, therefore, shall break one of these least commandments, and teach others to do so, shall be called least in the Kingdom of Heaven; but whoever shall do and teach them shall be called great in the Kingdom of Heaven.
20.	For I tell you, that unless your righteousness exceeds that of the scribes and Pharisees, there is no way you shall enter into the Kingdom of Heaven.

> 21. "You have heard that it was said to them of old time, 'You shall not murder;' and 'Whoever shall murder shall be in danger of the judgment.'
> 22. But I tell you, that everyone who is angry with his brother without a cause shall be in danger of the judgment; and whoever shall say to his brother, 'Raca,' shall be in danger of the council; and whoever shall say, 'You fool,' shall be in danger of the fire of Gehenna.
> 23. If therefore you are offering your gift at the altar, and there remember that your brother has anything against you,
> 24. leave your gift there before the altar, and go your way. First be reconciled to your brother, and then come and offer your gift.

Two verses that appear in the reconstructed Q Document are printed in italics above. They fit in neatly with the rest of the passage in Matthew and it may be assumed that the whole passage was originally part of Q and that Luke did not make use of the rest.

It may also be assumed that these sayings came from Jesus, although they may have been spoken on different occasions. Jesus taught that he expected his supporters, who longed for the kingdom of Heaven to be established, to adhere to the Law of Moses – not only in their overt actions, but also in the covert attitudes and wishes. Jesus was, therefore, not only a throne pretender, but also a religious reformer.

Explanation of the Ten Commandments
Matt 5: 27–38

> 27. "You have heard that it was said, 'You shall not commit adultery;'

28. but I tell you that everyone who gazes at a woman to lust after her has committed adultery with her already in his heart.
29. If your right eye causes you to stumble, pluck it out and cast it from you. For it is profitable for you that one of your members should perish, than for your whole body to be cast into Gehenna.
30. If your right hand causes you to stumble, cut it off, and cast it from you: for it is profitable for you that one of your members should perish, and not your whole body be cast into Gehenna.
31. "It was also said, `Whoever shall put away his wife, let him give her a writing of divorce,`
32. *but I tell you that whoever who puts away his wife, except for the cause of sexual immorality, makes her an adulteress; and whoever shall marry her when she is put away commits adultery.*
33. "Again you have heard that it was said to them of old time, `You shall not make false vows, but shall perform to the Lord your vows,`
34. but I tell you, don`t swear at all: neither by heaven, for it is the throne of God;
35. nor by the earth, for it is the footstool of his feet; nor by Jerusalem, for it is the city of the great King.
36. Neither shall you swear by your head, for you can`t make one hair white or black.
37. But let your speech be, `Yes, yes; No, no.` Whatever is more than these is of the evil one.
38. You have heard that it was said, `An eye for an eye, and a tooth for a tooth.`
39. *But I tell you, don`t resist him who is evil; but whoever strikes you on your right cheek, turn to him the other also.*

Verses 32 and 39, which are printed in italics, appear in the Q Document as reconstructed. They fit in perfectly with the rest of this passage and it may be theorized that the whole passage was copied by Matthew from Q, while Luke ignored the whole passage, save for verses 32 and 39.

In this passage, Jesus explained some of the Ten Commandments and emphasized that one's thoughts and desires should also be pure.

Love for Enemies
Matt 5: 43–44

43.	"You have heard that it was said, `You shall love your neighbor, and hate your enemy.`
44.	*But I tell you, love your enemies, bless those who curse you, do good to those who hate you, and pray for those who spitefully use you and persecute you,*

This is yet another case where a verse in the reconstructed Q Document fits in perfectly with a part of M – which may imply that this part of M was originally part of Q.

Jesus, the Essene or Nazorean, was a pacifist and preached love and tolerance between enemies.

False and Genuine Piety
Matthew 6: 1–18

1.	"Be careful that you don't do your charitable giving before men, to be seen by them, or else you have no reward with your Father who is in heaven.
2.	Therefore when you do merciful deeds, don't sound a trumpet before you, as the hypocrites do in the synagogues

	and in the streets, that they may get glory from men. Most assuredly, I tell you, they have received their reward.
3.	But when you do merciful deeds, don't let your left hand know what your right hand does,
4.	so that your merciful deeds may be in secret, then your Father who sees in secret will reward you openly.
5.	"When you pray, you shall not be as the hypocrites, for they love to stand and pray in the synagogues and in the corners of the streets, that they may be seen by men. Most assuredly, I tell you, they have received their reward.
6.	But you, when you pray, enter into your inner chamber, and having shut your door, pray to your Father who is in secret, and your Father who sees in secret will reward you openly.
7.	In praying, don't use vain repetitions, as the Gentiles do; for they think that they will be heard for their much speaking.
8.	Therefore don't be like them, for your Father knows what things you need, before you ask him.

Jesus taught that his supporters ought not to be religious or pious just to seek the admiration of others.

Forgiveness and Fasting
Matt 6: 14–18

14.	For if you forgive men their trespasses, your heavenly Father will also forgive you.
15.	But if you don't forgive men their trespasses, neither will your Father forgive your trespasses.

16.	"Moreover when you fast, don't be, as the hypocrites, with sad faces. For they disfigure their faces, that they may be seen by men to be fasting. Most assuredly I tell you, they have received their reward.
17.	But you, when you fast, anoint your head, and wash your face;
18.	that you are not seen by men to be fasting, but by your Father who is in secret, and your Father, who sees in secret, will reward you.

Jesus made a distinction between religious observances like fasting for the show and a genuine inner need to serve God with rituals. He also advocates a forgiving spirit and tolerance.

These sayings are in accordance with the teachings of Jesus as found in Q and may well be genuine memories of what he taught.

Serving Two Masters
Matt 6: 24

24.	"No one can serve two masters, for either he will hate the one, and love the other; or else he will hold to one, and despise the other. You can't serve both God and Mammon.

This part of M is found embedded in a series of sayings from Q in Matthew, although it stands on its own without any connection to the preceding and following sayings. It may well have been part of Q, all along.

Jesus warned in this saying that one cannot serve both God and the god of money – in accordance with his Essene background and abhorrence of opulence.

Anxiety about the Future
Matt 6; 33–34

33.	*But seek first God's Kingdom, and his righteousness; and all these things will be added to you.*
34.	Therefore don't be anxious for tomorrow, for tomorrow will be anxious for itself. Each day's own evil is sufficient.

Verse 34 can only be understood in context with the previous verse, which is part of Q (printed in italics). This means that verse 34 is probably also part of Q, but not used by Luke and, therefore, not included in the reconstruction of Q.

Jesus taught that his supporters had to seek the kingdom of God, while doing God's will at the same time, and when all that has been achieved, their worries about the future would be gone.

Jesus Opponents Compared to Dogs and Pigs
Matt 7: 6

6.	"Don't give that which is holy to the dogs, neither cast your pearls before the pigs, lest perhaps they trample them under their feet, and turn and tear you to pieces.

Jesus seems to have compared the rich priests, Pharisees, and teachers of the Law who opposed him, with dogs and pigs. "That which is holy" and the precious pearls are his message regarding his calling from God to be the Messiah and a reformer. He didn't want to waste his time by trying to convince these hostile people of his message.

False Prophets
Matt 7: 15

> 15. "Beware of false prophets, who come to you in sheep's clothing, but inwardly are ravening wolves.

In Jesus' eyes, the false prophets were the false priests and teachers of the Law who refused to accept his message about the kingdom of Heaven, but made the impression of being pious.

Jesus Heals Peter's Mother-in-Law
Matt 8: 14–18

> 14. When Jesus came into Peter's house, he saw his wife's mother lying sick of a fever.
> 15. He touched her hand, and the fever left her. She got up and served him.
> 16. When evening came, they brought to him many possessed with demons. He cast out the spirits with a word, and healed all who were sick;
> 17. that it might be fulfilled which was spoken through Isaiah the prophet, saying: "He took our infirmities, and bore our diseases."
> 18. Now when Jesus saw great multitudes about him, he gave the order to depart to the other side.

This passage records some healings performed by Jesus, including the mother-in-law of Peter. Matthew regarded this as the fulfillment of Isaiah 53: 4 where it is said of the suffering servant of God – "Surely he has borne our infirmities, and carried our sorrows; yet we esteemed him stricken, struck of God, and afflicted."

The "suffering servant of God" of Isa 53 was not the Messiah but the nation of Israel, as has been pointed out in Chapter 5.

Two Blind Men and a Mute Man
Matt 9: 27–36

27.	As Jesus passed by from there, two blind men followed him, calling out and saying, "Have mercy on us, son of David!"
28.	When he had come into the house, the blind men came to him. Jesus said to them, "Do you believe that I am able to do this?" They told him, "Yes, Lord."
29.	Then he touched their eyes, saying, "According to your faith be it done to you."
30.	Their eyes were opened. Jesus strictly charged them, saying, "See that no one knows about this."
31.	But they went out and spread abroad his fame in all that land.
32.	As they went forth, behold, there was brought to him a mute man who was demon possessed.
33.	When the demon was cast out, the mute man spoke. The multitudes marveled, saying, "Nothing like this has ever been seen in Israel!"
34.	But the Pharisees said, "By the prince of the demons, he casts out demons."
35.	Jesus went about all the cities and the villages, teaching in their synagogues, and preaching the gospel of the kingdom, and healing every disease and every sickness among the people.
36.	But when he saw the multitudes, he was moved with compassion for them, because they were weary and scattered, as sheep without a shepherd.

Jesus' fame as a healer spread far and wide. He used the opportunity where he helped people to preach the message of the imminent restoration of the Israelite kingdom. He initially forbade the two blind men to talk about him because his movement was an underground and secret operation at that time.

Receiving Prophets
Matt 10: 41–11: 1

41.	He who receives a prophet in the name of a prophet will receive a prophet's reward: and he who receives a righteous man in the name of a righteous man will receive a righteous man's reward.
42.	Whoever gives one of these little ones just a cup of cold water to drink, in the name of a disciple, most assuredly I tell you he will in no way lose his reward."
1.	It happened that when Jesus had finished directing his twelve disciples, he departed there to teach and preach in their cities.

The last two verses of Matt 10 are attached to a long passage from Q. These verses flow seamlessly from the preceding verses and must, therefore, be regarded as being taken from Q as well, although they don't appear in the reconstructed Q Document.

With these two verses, Jesus advised his followers to practice generosity. The reference to prophets may have its origin in the apostolic age, after Jesus' disappearance, when various prophets were active in spreading the gospel (see Acts 11: 25–27; Acts 13: 1; 1 Cor 14: 2–3; Eph 2: 20; Eph 4: 11; Rev 22: 9).

Matt 11: 1 is merely a casual editorial remark inserted by Matthew to connect two passages.

Remarks about John the Baptist
Matt 11: 14–15

> 14. If you are willing to receive it, this is Elijah, who is to come.
> 15. He who has ears to hear, let him hear.

These two verses also seem to come from Q. In the preceding verses, Jesus was discussing John the Baptist and Matt 11: 14 flows smoothly from them. According to Jesus, John was a resurrected Elijah or his successor.

Jesus' Style of Government
Matt 11: 28–30

> 11:28 "Come to me, all you who labor and are heavily burdened, and I will give you rest.
> 11:29 Take my yoke on you, and learn from me, for I am humble and lowly in heart; and you will find rest for your souls.
> 11:30 For my yoke is easy, and my burden is light."

These three verses do not follow directly from the preceding passage in Matthew 11 and they seem to be a saying that Matthew collected from another source.

This saying makes most sense when interpreted from the perspective of Jesus' teachings about the imminent kingdom of Heaven. This is a declaration of the style of government he would implement as successor of King David. He promised to rule in a benevolent manner and make life as easy as possible for his subjects, in contrast with their current circumstances where they suffered under Roman taxation and repression.

Isaiah's Prophecy
Matt 12: 15–21

15.	Jesus, perceiving that, withdrew from there. Great multitudes followed him; and he healed them all,
16.	and charged them that they should not make him known:
17.	that it might be fulfilled which was spoken through Isaiah the prophet, saying,
18.	"Behold, my servant whom I have chosen; My beloved in whom my soul is well pleased: I will put my Spirit on him, He will declare judgment to the Gentiles.
19.	He will not strive, nor shout; Neither will anyone hear his voice in the streets.
20.	He won't break a bruised reed, He won't quench a smoking flax, Until he sends forth judgment to victory.
21.	In his name, the Gentiles will hope."

As was his custom, Matthew found pronouncements in the Old Testament to apply to Jesus. In this case, he quoted extensively and freely from Isa 42: 1–4.

When one reads the whole Chapter 42 in Isaiah, it becomes clear that the servant of the Lord mentioned in the first verse, is the people of Israel and certainly not the promised Messiah.

Good and Bad Words Come from Within
Matt 12: 33–37

33.	"Either make the tree good, and its fruit good, or make the tree corrupt, and its fruit corrupt; for the tree is known by its fruit.
34.	You offspring of vipers, how can you, being evil, speak good things? For out of the abundance of the heart, the mouth speaks.

35.	The good man out of his good treasure brings forth good things, and the evil man out of his evil treasure brings forth evil things.
36.	I tell you that every idle word that men speak, they will give account of it in the day of judgment.
37.	For by your words you will be justified, and by your words you will be condemned."

These verses do not seem to flow logically from the preceding passage in Matt 12 and they must be regarded as sayings that Matthew found in another source than Q or Mark, although the style is that of Q. It may well be a part of Q not used by Luke.

The message of Jesus is in this case that the language somebody uses is a sign of the type of person he is.

The Parable of the Weeds
Matt 13: 24–30

24.	He set another parable before them, saying, "The Kingdom of Heaven is like a man who sowed good seed in his field,
25.	but while people slept, his enemy came and sowed darnel also among the wheat, and went away.
26.	But when the blade sprang up and brought forth fruit, then the darnel appeared also.
27.	The servants of the householder came and said to him, `Sir, didn't you sow good seed in your field? Where did this darnel come from?`
28.	He said to them, `An enemy has done this.` The servants asked him, `Do you want us to go and gather them up?`
29.	But he said, `No, lest perhaps while you gather up the darnel, you root up the wheat with them.

> 30. Let both grow together until the harvest, and in the harvest time I will tell the reapers, "First, gather up the darnel, and bind them in bundles to burn them; but gather the wheat into my barn."''"

This parable to explain the kingdom appears only in Matthew and must, therefore, be part of M (unless it was, in fact, part of Q, which Luke didn't use).

The farmer in this story represents Jesus and his enemies are the Pharisees and teachers of the Law who contradicted his message, the good seed. They sowed weeds, their false messages. When it is time for the harvest, the time when the kingdom is to be established, the works of the enemies will be exposed and condemned.

That Jesus regarded the Pharisees as his enemies is evident, for instance, from Mark 8: 15 where he explicitly warned his followers against the "yeast" of the Pharisees.

Jesus' Use of Parables
Matt 13: 34–35

> 34. Jesus spoke all these things in parables to the multitudes; and without a parable, he didn't speak to them,
> 35. that it might be fulfilled which was spoken through the prophet, saying, "I will open my mouth in parables; I will utter things hidden from the foundation of the world."

This passage is an adaptation of Mark 4: 33–34, but with the addition of a purported prophecy from Ps 78: 2 – which was never intended as a prophecy, but was a sermon in verse form by an unknown poet who addressed the people of Israel. Matthew apparently scoured the Old Testament to find "prophecies" that he could apply to the ministry of Jesus.

Jesus Explains the Parable of the Weeds
Matt 13: 36–43

36.	Then Jesus sent the multitudes away, and went into the house. His disciples came to him, saying, "Explain to us the parable of the darnel of the field."
37.	He answered them, "He who sows the good seed is the Son of Man,
38.	the field is the world; and the good seed, these are the sons of the kingdom; and the darnel are the sons of the evil one.
39.	The enemy who sowed them is the devil. The harvest is the end of the age, and the reapers are angels.
40.	As therefore the darnel is gathered up and burned with fire; so will it be in the end of this age.
41.	The Son of Man will send forth his angels, and they will gather out of his kingdom all things that cause stumbling, and those who do iniquity,
42.	and will cast them into the furnace of fire. There will be weeping and the gnashing of teeth.
43.	Then the righteous will shine forth as the sun in the kingdom of their Father. He who has ears to hear, let him hear.

The explanation of the Parable of the Weeds given by Matthew is evidently his own invention, which does not agree with the parable as he recorded it from an old tradition.

Matthew's explanation changes Jesus' enemies from the Pharisees and teachers of the Law into the Devil. The harvest is to take place on Judgment Day – not when the Israelite kingdom is restored – and the angels will gather the souls of those who belong to the spiritual Kingdom of Heaven.

Three Parables
Matt 13: 44–52

44.	"The Kingdom of Heaven is like a treasure hidden in the field, which a man found, and hid. In his joy, he goes and sells all that he has, and buys that field.
45.	"Again, the Kingdom of Heaven is like a man who is a merchant seeking fine pearls,
46.	who having found one pearl of great price, he went and sold all that he had, and bought it.
47.	"Again, the Kingdom of Heaven is like a dragnet, that was cast into the sea, and gathered some fish of every kind,
48.	which, when it was filled, they drew up on the beach. They sat down, and gathered the good into containers, but the bad they threw away.
49.	So will it be in the end of the world. The angels will come forth, and separate the wicked from among the righteous,
50.	and will cast them into the furnace of fire. There will be the weeping and the gnashing of teeth."
51.	Jesus said to them, "Have you understood all these things?" They answered him, "Yes, Lord."
52.	He said to them, "Therefore, every scribe who has been made a disciple to the Kingdom of Heaven is like a man who is a householder, who brings forth out of his treasure new and old things."

These three parables taught that the kingdom of Heaven could be compared with something very valuable – a treasure hidden in a field, an exceptionally valuable pearl, or the good fishes caught in a net. Jesus' ministry consisted of a campaign to recruit supporters for his lofty ideal of rebuilding the longed-for Israelite monarchy.

However, Matthew, who wrote his gospel fifty years or more after the time of Jesus, lost sight of this vision of Jesus because the idea of an Israelite kingdom was finally shattered and abandoned with the destruction of Jerusalem more than a decade earlier. Therefore, he explained these parables as if they dealt with Judgment Day in the far future.

Peter Walks on the Water
Matt 14: 28–33

28.	Peter answered him and said, "Lord, if it is you, command me to come to you on the waters."
29.	He said, "Come!" Peter went down from the boat, and walked on the waters to come to Jesus.
30.	But when he saw that the wind was strong, he was afraid, and beginning to sink, he cried out, saying, "Lord, save me!"
31.	Immediately Jesus stretched forth his hand, and took hold of him, and said to him, "You of little faith, why did you doubt?"
32.	When they got up into the boat, the wind ceased.
33.	Those who were in the boat came and worshipped him, saying, "You are truly the Son of God!"

This passage was added by Matthew to the miracle of Jesus who walked on the water, as told in the preceding verses, as taken from Mark 6: 47–51. If it can be explained that Jesus did not really walk on water but only appeared to do so, while walking on the shore next to the lake, then one can also explain Peter's effort to walk on the water as well as merely a case where he fell into the water or tripped and lost his balance by tumbling into the water. A quite ordinary incident was transformed into a miracle by repeated retelling through the decades separating the event from the eventual recording of it in writing. Matthew used this incident to draw the attention again to the idea that Jesus was the Son of God, the Messiah.

Jesus Heals Many People
Matt 15: 29–31

29.	Jesus departed there, and came near to the sea of Galilee; and he went up into the mountain, and sat there.
30.	There came to him great multitudes, having with them the lame, blind, mute, maimed, and many others, and they put them down at his feet. He healed them,
31.	so that the multitude wondered, when they saw the mute speaking, the injured whole, lame walking, and the blind seeing – and they glorified the God of Israel.

Jesus departed from Tyre and Sidon where he healed the daughter of a Canaanite woman and he returned to Galilee. This passage is a repetition of earlier reports of how Jesus healed people with all sorts of ailments, maladies, disorders, and illnesses.

Peter's Testimony
Matt 16: 13–19

13.	Now when Jesus came into the parts of Caesarea Philippi, he asked his disciples, saying, "Who do men say that I, the Son of Man, am ?"
14.	They said, "Some say John the Baptizer, some, Elijah, and others, Jeremiah, or one of the prophets."
15.	He said to them, "But who do you say that I am?"
16.	Simon Peter answered, "You are the Christ, the Son of the living God."

> 17. Jesus answered him, "Blessed are you, Simon Bar–Jonah, for flesh and blood has not revealed this to you, but my Father who is in heaven.
> 18. I also tell you, that you are Peter, and on this rock I will build my assembly, and the gates of Hades will not prevail against it.
> 19. I will give to you the keys of the Kingdom of Heaven, and whatever you will bind on earth will be bound in heaven; and whatever you will loose on earth will be loosed in heaven."

This is an expanded version of Mark 8: 27–30. This passage has been interpreted in different ways by Catholics and Protestants. Catholics see this as Jesus' appointment of Peter – whose name is derived from the Greek word for "rock" – as the rock or leader of his "assembly" or "church", while holding the keys of the spiritual kingdom of Heaven.

Albrecht Dürer: Saint Peter

Peter, though, was not the "rock" he was supposed to be by denying Jesus and criticizing Jesus more than once. Protestants, however, regard Peter's testimony that Jesus was the Son of the living God as the rock on which the church would be built. The keys to the kingdom of Heaven were to be entrusted to the whole church.

Membership of the church was based on having faith in Jesus and that unlocked the spiritual kingdom of Heaven for them.

That the spiritual or heavenly kingdom – and not the restored kingdom of David – is meant becomes clear where Jesus added that all the evil forces of Hades or hell would never be able to overpower this kingdom. That the spiritual or heavenly kingdom is used in this passage betrays its late date, some time after the destruction of Jerusalem when all hope for the realization of the political kingdom of Israel was lost.

The original version of Mark of this passage seems to be a reliable account, but Matthew's additions about the keys of the kingdom of Heaven must be a piece of fiction.

Payment of the Temple Tax
Matt 17: 24–27

24.	When they were come to Capernaum, those who collected the didrachmas came to Peter, and said, "Doesn't your teacher pay the didrachma?"
25.	He said, "Yes." When he came into the house, Jesus anticipated him, saying, "What do you think, Simon? From whom do the kings of the earth receive toll or tribute? From their sons, or from strangers?"
26.	Peter said to him, "From strangers." Jesus said to him, "Therefore the sons are exempt.
27.	But, lest we cause them to stumble, go to the sea, and cast a hook, and take up the first fish that comes up. When you have opened his mouth, you will find a stater. Take that, and give it to them for me and you."

This story sounds like a fairy tale with all sorts of impossible things happening – a fish with some money in its mouth and Jesus knowing that it was just waiting to be caught.

The didrachma that had to be paid as tax is a double drachma [Greek: Δίδραχμον (δ*idrachmon*)]. The coin in the mouth of the magic fish was a stater (Greek: Στατήρ) – a silver coin equal to four Attic or two Alexandrian drachmas, a Jewish shekel.

There may, perhaps, be a nucleus of truth in this story when Peter or one of the other disciples picked up a stater with which Jesus and his disciples could satisfy their tax obligations. It might even be that one of them caught a fish with a coin in its stomach or that the fish was sold to get money.

Parable of the Lost Sheep
Matt 18: 10–14

10.	See that you don't despise one of these little ones, for I tell you that in heaven their angels always see the face of my Father who is in heaven.
11.	For the Son of Man came to save that which was lost.
12.	*"What do you think? If a man has one hundred sheep, and one of them goes astray, doesn't he leave the ninety–nine, go to the mountains, and seek that which has gone astray?*
13.	*If he happens to find it, most assuredly I tell you, he rejoices over it more than over the ninety–nine which have not gone astray.*
14.	Even so it is not the will of your Father who is in heaven that one of these little ones should perish.

This passage seems to be the original version in Q of the Parable of the Lost Sheep, of which Luke only used the two verses printed in italics and were included in the reconstructed Q.

Jesus showed interest in "these little ones", the ordinary Jews who lived in poverty and suffered under foreign domination –

probably mostly his fellow-Essenes. These were the people from whom he recruited most of his supporters. They flocked to him because he treated them differently than the haughty rich priests at the temple and the proud and important teachers of the Law who looked down upon them in the synagogues.

The Parable of the Unforgiving Servant
Matt 18: 23–35

23.	Therefore the Kingdom of Heaven is like a certain king, who wanted to reconcile accounts with his servants.
24.	When he had begun to reconcile, one was brought to him who owed him ten thousand talents.
25.	But because he couldn't pay, his lord commanded him to be sold, with his wife, his children, and all that he had, and payment to be made.
26.	The servant therefore fell down and kneeled before him, saying, 'Lord, have patience with me, and I will repay you all.'
27.	The lord of that servant, being moved with compassion, released him, and forgave him the debt.
28.	But that servant went out, and found one of his fellow–servants, who owed him one hundred denarii, and he laid hold on him, and took him by the throat, saying, `Pay me what you owe!`
29.	So his fellow–servant fell down at his feet and begged him, saying, `Have patience with me, and I will repay you.`
30.	He would not, but went and cast him into prison, until he should pay back that which was due.

> 31. So when his fellow-servants saw what was done, they were exceedingly sorry, and came and told to their lord all that was done.
> 32. Then his lord called him in, and said to him, `You wicked servant! I forgave you all that debt, because you begged me.
> 33. Shouldn`t you also have had mercy on your fellow-servant, even as I had mercy on you?`
> 34. His lord was angry, and delivered him to the tormentors, until he should pay all that was due to him.
> 35. So will my heavenly Father also do to you, if you don`t each forgive his brother from your hearts for his misdeeds."

The moral of this story is that we ought to forgive others who have wronged us since God is willing to show us mercy and patience.

The source of this story is unknown. It may have been an independent tradition that Matthew happened to record, but it may also have been part of the Q Document that Luke left out of his gospel with the result that it was never included in the reconstructed Q.

The Workers in the Vineyard
Matt 20: 1–15

> 1. "For the Kingdom of Heaven is like a man who was the master of a household, who went out early in the morning to hire laborers for his vineyard.
> 2. When he had agreed with the laborers for a denarius a day, he sent them into his vineyard.
> 3. He went out about the third hour, and saw others standing idle in the marketplace.

4.	To them he said, `You also go into the vineyard, and whatever is right I will give you.` So they went their way.
5.	Again he went out about the sixth and the ninth hour, and did likewise.
6.	About the eleventh hour he went out, and found others standing idle. He said to them, `Why do you stand here all day idle?`
7.	They said to him, `Because no one has hired us.` He said to them, `You also go into the vineyard, and you will receive whatever is right.`
8.	When evening had come, the lord of the vineyard said to his steward, `Call the laborers and pay them their hire, beginning from the last to the first.`
9.	When they who were hired at about the eleventh hour came, they each received a denarius.
10.	When the first came, they supposed that they would receive more; and they likewise each received a denarius.
11.	When they received it, they murmured against the master of the household,
12.	saying, `These last have spent one hour, and you have made them equal to us, who have borne the burden of the day and the scorching heat!`
13.	But he answered one of them, `Friend, I am doing you no wrong. Didn`t you agree with me for a denarius?
14.	Take that which is yours, and go your way. It is my will to give to this last just as much as to you.
15.	Isn`t it lawful for me to do what I want to with what I own? Or is your eye evil, because I am good?`

With this parable, Jesus explained how he intended dealing with his followers when the kingdom of Israel was eventually rebuilt. He didn't want to make any difference between early supporters and later supporters of his movement. All that counted was that they were all willing to serve and follow him.

The Parable of the two Sons
Matt 21: 28–32

28.	But what do you think? A man had two sons, and he came to the first, and said, `Son, go work today in my vineyard.`
29.	He answered, `I will not,` but afterward he repented himself, and went.
30.	He came to the second, and said likewise. He answered, `I go, sir,` but he didn`t go.
31.	Which of the two did the will of his father?" They said to him, "The first." Jesus says to them, "Most assuredly I tell you, that the tax collectors and the prostitutes are entering into the kingdom of God before you.
32.	For John came to you in the way of righteousness, and you didn`t believe him, but the tax collectors and the prostitutes believed him. When you saw it, you didn`t even repent afterward, that you might believe him.

We are not told who the audience of Jesus on this occasion was, but it seems to have been ordinary folks, including Pharisees and teachers of the Law – not his disciples. The point he wished to make is that it is required from those who wanted to belong to the kingdom of Heaven is that they have to repent from their sins and believe the message they heard from John the Baptist and from Jesus, even if they were hated tax collectors or despised prostitutes.

The fact that Jesus mentioned the kingdom of God – and not of Heaven as he usually did – may be an indication that he copied this parable with its application from Q.

The Parable of the Wedding Guests
Matt 22: 11–14

11.	But when the king came in to see the guests, he saw there a man who didn't have on wedding–clothing,
12.	and he said to him, 'Friend, how did you come in here not having wedding–clothing?' He was speechless.
13.	Then the king said to the servants, 'Bind him hand and foot, take him away, and throw him into the outer darkness; there is where the weeping and grinding of teeth will be.'
14.	For many are called, but few chosen."

These four verses form part of the Parable of the Wedding Guests of which only the first part appears in Luke 20:20–26. This part was discussed in Chapter 3 where the Q Document was analyzed.

It may be assumed that the four verses quoted above also belonged to Q, but were disregarded by Luke and, therefore, not included in the reconstruction of Q.

The first part of the parable tells of the king who invited guests to his son's wedding. The invited people never turned up and the king ordered his servants to fill the wedding venue with people from the streets.

The proper wedding clothes would have been presented to all those who attended before they entered the hall, but this man who gate-crashed the wedding feast spoiled the event by refusing to get dressed properly. He must be seen as somebody who rejected Jesus as the Messiah and who didn't believe in his message. He was thrown out into the dark night.

Jesus Warns against the Pharisees and Teacher of the Law
Matt 23: 1–12

1. Then Jesus spoke to the multitudes and to his disciples,
2. saying, "The scribes and the Pharisees sat on Moses' seat.
3. All things therefore whatever they tell you to observe, observe and do, but don't do their works; for they say, and don't do.
4. *For they bind heavy burdens that are grievous to be borne, and lay them on men's shoulders; but they themselves will not lift a finger to help them.*
5. But all their works they do to be seen by men. They make their phylacteries broad, enlarge the fringes of their garments,
6. *and love the chief place at feasts, the chief seats in the synagogues,*
7. the salutations in the marketplaces, and to be called 'Rabbi, Rabbi' by men.
8. But don't you be called 'Rabbi,' for one is your teacher, the Christ, and all of you are brothers.
9. Call no man on the earth your father, for one is your Father, he who is in heaven.
10. Neither be called masters, for one is your master, the Christ.
11. But he who is greatest among you will be your servant.
12. Whoever will exalt himself will be humbled, and whoever will humble himself will be exalted.

The two verses printed in italics above appear in Luke and in the reconstructed Q. Matthew seems to have copied the whole passage in Q in which these two verses were embedded. The rest of this passage cannot, therefore, be regarded as part of M, but as part of Q.

That Jesus warned his followers against the Pharisees and teachers of the Law who wanted to be regarded as very important people, is certainly historically correct. After all, Jesus came from an Essene background, where a simple, egalitarian, and humble lifestyle was regarded as desirable.

Jesus claimed for himself the title of teacher since he was called by God to lead his people back to God. The Greek word for "teacher" is διδάσκαλος (*didaskalos*) – a person who was trained to teach the Hebrew Scriptures, as Jesus evidently was.

Jesus Condemns their Hypocrisy
Matt 23: 13–28

13.	*"Woe to you, scribes and Pharisees, hypocrites! For you devour widows' houses, and as a pretense you make long prayers. Therefore you will receive greater condemnation.*
14.	"But woe to you, scribes and Pharisees, hypocrites! Because you shut up the Kingdom of Heaven against men; for you don't enter in yourselves, neither do you allow those who are entering in to enter.
15.	Woe to you, scribes and Pharisees, hypocrites! For you travel around by sea and land to make one proselyte; and when he becomes one, you make him twice as much of a son of Gehenna as yourselves.
16.	Woe to you, you blind guides, who say, `Whoever swears by the temple, it is nothing; but whoever swears by the gold of the temple, he is a debtor.`
17.	You blind fools! For which is greater, the gold, or the temple that sanctifies the gold?

18. 'Whoever will swear by the altar, it is nothing; but whoever will swear by the gift that is on it, he is a debtor.'
19. You blind fools! For which is greater, the gift, or the altar that sanctifies the gift?
20. He therefore who swears by the altar, swears by it, and by everything on it.
21. He who swears by the temple, swears by it, and by him who is living in it.
22. He who swears by the heaven, swears by the throne of God, and by him who sits on it.
23. *Woe to you, scribes and Pharisees, hypocrites! For you tithe mint, dill, and cumin, and have left undone the weightier matters of the law – justice, mercy, and faith. But you ought to have done these, and not to have left the other undone.*
24. You blind guides, who strain out a gnat, and swallow a camel!
25. *Woe to you, scribes and Pharisees, hypocrites! For you clean the outside of the cup and of the platter, but within they are full of extortion and unrighteousness.*
26. *You blind Pharisee, first clean the inside of the cup and of the platter, that the outside of it may become clean also.*
27. *Woe to you, scribes and Pharisees, hypocrites! For you are like whitened tombs, which outwardly appear beautiful, but inwardly are full of dead men's bones, and of all uncleanness.*
28. *Even so you also outwardly appear righteous to men, but inwardly you are full of hypocrisy and iniquity.*

Matthew seems to have replicated a bigger part of the Q Document than Luke (Luke's parts are printed in italics above).

In true Essene or Nazorean tradition, Jesus had little patience with those Pharisees and teachers of the Law who lured proselytes into perdition with their false teachings and hypocritical lifestyle. He condemned their habit of swearing oaths on any conceivable holy object. For him, inner purity of heart was more important than empty pious public ceremonies.

Hypocritical Scribes and Pharisees
Matt 23: 33

33.	You serpents, you offspring of vipers, how will you escape the judgment of Gehenna?

This single verse is part of a longer passage, Matt 24: 29–39. The rest of the passage occurs in the reconstructed Q. For some or other reason Luke left it out, while Matthew retained it.

By calling the Pharisees and scribes serpents and the offspring of vipers he meant to express the idea that they were children of Satan. John the Baptist also called these people vipers (Matt 3: 7 and Luke 3: 7).

Jesus' Words to Endure for Ever
Matt 24: 34–35

34.	Most assuredly I tell you, this generation will not pass away, until all these things are accomplished.
35.	Heaven and earth will pass away, but my words will not pass away.

These two sentences seem to be unrelated. With the first sentence Jesus repeated his promise that the kingdom would arrive before the present generation had died. He also taught that his words would endure since they were spoken on behalf of God.

Parable of the Wise and the Foolish Virgins
Matt 25: 1–13

1.	Then the Kingdom of Heaven will be like ten virgins, who took their lamps, and went forth to meet the bridegroom.
2.	Five of them were foolish, and five were wise.
3.	Those who were foolish, when they took their lamps, took no oil with them,
4.	but the wise took oil in their vessels with their lamps.
5.	Now while the bridegroom delayed, they all slumbered and slept.
6.	But at midnight there was a cry, "Behold! The bridegroom is coming! Come out to meet him!"
7.	Then all those virgins arose, and trimmed their lamps.
8.	The foolish said to the wise, "Give us some of your oil, for our lamps are going out."
9.	But the wise answered, saying, "What if there will not be enough for us and you? You go rather to those who sell, and buy for yourselves."
10.	While they went away to buy, the bridegroom came, and those who were ready went in with him to the marriage feast, and the door was shut.
11.	Afterward the other virgins also came, saying, "Lord, Lord, open to us."
12.	But he answered, "Most assuredly I tell you, I don't know you."

13.	Watch therefore, for you don't know the day nor the hour in which the Son of Man is coming.

The well-known Parable of the Wise and Foolish Virgins is traditionally interpreted as a story to illustrate the unexpected second coming of Jesus on Judgment Day when the heavenly kingdom will be established. A more plausible explanation would be to see it as a story Jesus told to make the point that his earthly kingdom of Israel would be brought into being when nobody expected it.

In this parable, the wedding feast is a symbol of the coming kingdom. Jesus is the bridegroom who arrives unexpectedly. The wise virgins, who were to be part of the wedding procession, represent his followers who accepted his message and awaited the coming of the kingdom. The foolish virgins are those people who rejected him as Messiah and who would not be allowed to attend the wedding feast or benefit from the new dispensation when the Israelite kingdom was eventually created.

The Judgment
Matt 25: 31–46

31.	"But when the Son of Man comes in his glory, and all the holy angels with him, then will he sit on the throne of his glory.
32.	Before him all the nations will be gathered, and he will separate them one from another, as the shepherd separates the sheep from the goats.
33.	He will set the sheep on his right hand, but the goats on the left.

34. Then the King will tell them on his right hand, 'Come, blessed of my Father, inherit the kingdom prepared for you from the foundation of the world;
35. for I was hungry, and you gave me food to eat; I was thirsty, and you gave me drink; I was a stranger, and you took me in;
36. naked, and you clothed me; I was sick, and you visited me; I was in prison, and you came to me.'
37. Then the righteous will answer him, saying, 'Lord, when did we see you hungry, and feed you; or thirsty, and give you a drink?
38. When did we see you as a stranger, and take you in; or naked, and clothe you?
39. When did we see you sick, or in prison, and come to you?'
40. The King will answer them, 'Most assuredly I tell you, inasmuch as you did it to one of the least of these my brothers, you did it to me.'
41. Then will he say also to them on the left hand, 'Depart from me, you cursed, into the eternal fire which is prepared for the devil and his angels;
42. for I was hungry, and you didn't give me food to eat; I was thirsty, and you gave me no drink;
43. I was a stranger, and you didn't take me in; naked, and you didn't clothe me; sick, and in prison, and you didn't visit me.'
44. Then will they also answer, saying, 'Lord, when did we see you hungry, or thirsty, or a stranger, or naked, or sick, or in prison, and did not help you?'

> 45. Then will he answer them, saying, 'Most assuredly I tell you, inasmuch as you didn't do it to one of these least, you didn't do it to me.'
> 46. These will go away into eternal punishment, but the righteous into eternal life."

Albrecht Dürer: The Last Judgment

This is another well-known parable, the parable of the sheep and the goats that would be separated into two separate herds. The conventional explanation is that it deals exclusively with the Final Judgment when Christ would return to judge the world. It does seem, though, that the original parable as Jesus told it, became jumbled and distorted during the decades before Matthew included it in his gospel.

Jesus expected to become the king of Israel with the help of a horde of holy angels. When he had gained the throne he would make sure that his enemies and the godless would receive their deserved punishment. They will also be judged on how much generosity and charity they had practiced.

When no kingdom in Jerusalem was realized, those who retold the parable shifted the establishment of the kingdom to the far future, at the end of time, when Christ would come back to judge all the nations on earth.

The Suicide of Judas
Matt 27: 3–10

> 3. Then Judas, who betrayed him, when he saw that he was condemned, repented himself, and brought back the thirty pieces of silver to the chief priests and elders,
> 4. saying, "I have sinned in that I betrayed innocent blood." But they said, "What is that to us? You see to it."
> 5. He threw down the pieces of silver in the sanctuary, and departed. He went away and hanged himself.
> 6. The chief priests took the pieces of silver, and said, "It is not lawful to put them into the treasury, since it is the price of blood."
> 7. They took counsel, and bought with them the potter's field, to bury strangers in.
> 8. Therefore that field was called "The Field of Blood" to this day.
> 9. Then that which was spoken through Jeremiah the prophet was fulfilled, saying, "They took the thirty pieces of silver, the price of him who was priced, whom some of the children of Israel did price,
> 10. and they gave them for the potter's field, as the Lord commanded me."

There are two independent reports of the death of Judas: this report in Matthew and Acts 1: 18–19. Both state that he committed suicide in remorse and that a piece of land was bought with the money with which he had been bribed to betray Jesus and which he gave back when he realized what he had done. The reports, though, do not quite agree regarding his method of suicide.

Matthew wrote that the plot was called "'the Field of Blood' to this day," whenever that day was – probably during the eighties of the first century AD.

The prophecy quoted does not appear in Jeremiah, but in Zecheriah 11: 12–13. The original words in Zecheriah certainly did not apply to Judas, centuries later. Matthew could not withstand the temptation to make use of the superficial similarity of the two episodes to declare that Judas' action was foretold by an Old Testament prophet.

Mrs Pontia Pilata's Dream
Matt 27: 19

> While he was sitting on the judgment seat, his wife sent to him, saying, "Have nothing to do with that righteous man, for I have suffered many things this day in a dream because of him."

This paragraph is part of M. One can only wonder how Matthew got hold of this story since the trial of Jesus took place in camera and no Jews were present and witness this incident.[222]

It is also a mystery how Mrs Pontia knew who the prisoner was who was being interrogated and tried by her husband. It is, anyway, highly unlikely that she would have dared to interfere with her husband's work as a judge. It is even possible that she stayed at home in Caesarea when Pilate travelled to Jerusalem to oversee security measures during the feast.

It is, therefore, most probably a piece of fantastic pious fiction, used to convince people that, at least, some Romans were sympathetic towards Jesus and that Christianity is an appropriate religion for Romans.

Pilate Washes his Hands
Matt 27:22–26

---

[222] Cohn, *The Trial and Death of Jesus,* 147–49.

> 22. Pilate said to them, "What then will I do to Jesus, who is called Christ?" They all said to him, "Let him be crucified!"
> 23. But the governor said, "Why? What evil has he done?" But they cried out exceedingly, saying, "Let him be crucified!"
> 24. So when Pilate saw that nothing was gained, but rather that a disturbance was starting, he took water, and washed his hands before the multitude, saying, "I am innocent of the blood of this righteous person. You see to it."
> 25. All the people answered, "May his blood be on us, and on our children!"
> 26. Then he released to them Barabbas, but Jesus he flogged and delivered to be crucified.

Matthew wanted to portray the unpopular Jews after the fall of Jerusalem in as bad a light as possible and exonerate the Roman governor, Pilate, in order to convince Romans that Christianity was a suitable religion for them.

It has already been pointed out that the trial of Jesus took place in camera and that the proud and cruel governor, who despised the Jews and their religion, would never have humiliated himself by consulting the rowdy rabble outside his Praetorium about a sentence he had to pass.

The exclamation of the crowd that the blood of Jesus would be on them and their children was abused through the centuries to justify Antisemitism and to punish the Jews as the "killers of Jesus".

This whole incident, including Pilate washing his hands – with or without a bar of soap – never happened.

The Guard at the Tomb
Matt 27: 62–66

> 62. Now on the next day, which is the day after the Preparation, the chief priests and the Pharisees were gathered together to Pilate,
> 63., saying, "Sir, we remember what that deceiver said while he was still alive: `After three days I will rise again.`
> 64 Command therefore that the tomb be made secure until the third day, lest perhaps his disciples come at night and steal him away, and tell the people, `He is risen from the dead;` and the last deception will be worse than the first."
> 65. Pilate said to them, "You have a guard. Go, make it as secure as you can."
> 66. So they went, and made the tomb secure, sealing the stone, the guard being with them.

This story is unique to Matthew. It tells how the religious leaders asked Pilate to provide a guard at Jesus' tomb to prevent his disciples from removing his body and afterwards declaring that he had risen from the dead. A squad of guards was then provided, as requested. This request only makes sense if these leaders had heard that Jesus had publicly announced that he would be crucified, but would be resurrected three days later (Matt 16: 21;17: 23; 20: 19).

Since only Matthew contains this story it is impossible to determine whether it is true or not. It sounds plausible, although Matthew's source would probably not have known any details about the conversation of the Jewish leaders with Pilate. They would only have noticed the guards at the tomb and made their own deductions.

It may also be that Matthew made this story up to enhance the wonder of the miraculous resurrection of Jesus later.

The Report of the Guards
Matt 28: 9–15

> 9. As they went to tell his disciples, behold, Jesus met them, saying, "Rejoice!" They came and took hold of his feet, and worshiped him.
> 10. Then Jesus said to them, "Don't be afraid. Go tell my brothers that they may go into Galilee, and there they will see me."
> 11. Now while they were going, behold, some of the guards came into the city, and told the chief priests all the things that had happened.
> 12. When they were assembled with the elders, and had taken counsel, they gave a large amount of silver to the soldiers,
> 13. saying, "Say that his disciples came by night, and stole him away while we slept.
> 14. If this comes to the governor's ears, we will persuade him and make you free of worry."
> 15. So they took the money and did as they were told. This saying was spread abroad among the Jews, and continues until this day.

This passage, which is unique to Matthew, starts at the point where the women found an empty tomb. Jesus appeared to them and they worshipped him. That he was resurrected with a physical body – and not a spiritual body – is attested by the fact that they grasped his feet.

The guards witnessed this encounter and reported it to the Jewish authorities, although one would have expected them to go to one of their officers, or even directly to Pilate. They were paid hush money and given the promise that nothing would happen to them if they confirmed the story that Jesus' body was stolen by his disciples during the night while they slept.

According to the details provided by Matthew, Jesus could already have been removed to a place where he could receive more medical help before the soldiers were posted outside the tomb.

The Jesus who is portrayed in this passage is no longer an ordinary human being but a divine personage who is worshipped.

Jesus Appears to his Disciples
Matt 28: 16–20

16.	But the eleven disciples went into Galilee, to the mountain where Jesus had sent them.
17.	When they saw him, they bowed down to him, but some doubted.
18.	Jesus came to them and spoke to them, saying, "All authority has been given to me in heaven and on earth.
19.	Go, and make disciples of all nations, baptizing them in the name of the Father and of the Son and of the Holy Spirit,
20.	teaching them to observe all things which I commanded you. Behold, I am with you always, even to the end of the age."

Although Luke and John contain stories how Jesus appeared to his disciples after his resurrection, they all contain different and even contradictory details.

The Jesus presented here was suddenly a divine figure who possessed all power in the universe – not the king-in-waiting of Israel, the charismatic teacher and healer of the middle parts of the gospel. This was the same supernatural and divine being encountered in the nativity stories.

The implicit doctrine of the Trinitarian God found in Paul's letters, is formulated explicitly in Jesus' command to baptize people in the Name of the Father, the Son, and the Holy Spirit.

This baptismal formula differs from Acts 2: 38; Acts 8: 16; Acts 10: 48; Acts 19: 5; and Rom 6: 3. All these texts affirm that new converts were baptized in the Name of Jesus Christ – not the Trinity. It seems, therefore, that the baptismal formula in Matt 28: 19 must be the invention of Matthew (or the M source).

Albrecht Dürer: Resurrection of Jesus

We do not read of an ascension into heaven and, instead, Jesus promised his disciples to stay with them forever – whatever that means.

The gospels of John and Mark made it clear that Jesus was nursed back to health after having survived the crucifixion. Matthew, on the other hand, transformed his appearance to his disciples and the women as a supernatural, miraculous, and inexplicable series of events.

Deductions

Matthew reported extensively about Jesus' teachings regarding the kingdom of Heaven. The word "kingdom" occurs 56 times in this gospel.

Where Matthew quoted from Q, he obviously preserved earlier memories of the sayings of Jesus where Jesus mentioned the political kingdom that he expected to be restored in his lifetime with himself occupying the throne. However, by the time Matthew finalized his gospel, at least five decades after Jesus' time and more than a decade after the destruction of Jerusalem, all hopes regarding this kingdom had been dashed. Matthew had no choice but to reinterpret the expected kingdom as a condition in the far future, after Judgment Day. In this, he followed the example of Mark who invented prophecies of Jesus about the destruction of the temple and combined those with Judgment Day and the return of Jesus at the end of time.

The picture drawn of Jesus by Matthew's Gospel is varied. Matthew seems to have copied the parts taken from the Q Document and Mark fairly accurately. There are some instances where material, which would be classified as M, can really be regarded as coming from the original Q.

Those parts borrowed from Mark and Q, as well as the sayings of M, portray Jesus as the king-in-waiting of Israel, the Messiah who regarded it as his God-given task to resurrect the old monarchy of his ancestor, King David. He is also presented as a religious reformer who wanted to lead his people to greater obedience towards God, as a charismatic teacher and story-teller, an inspiring leader, and a gifted healer. This Jesus was an ordinary mortal.

It will not be wrong to conclude that most of the material quoted from Mark and Q, as well as the saying in M, have a historical basis when the supernatural, mythological, and legendary elements are stripped away.

The Jesus we meet in the nativity stories is a miracle child who was born from a virgin and whose birth was announced by an angel and a miraculous star. He was an exceptional human being, more than a mere mortal. Very little of the nativity stories can be regarded as being trustworthy and historical.

When we meet the Jesus of the passion story, we also find an ordinary mortal who managed to survive a horrible execution. The details of Jesus' trial are mostly fantasy. But then he is transformed into a supernatural figure who was not bound to natural laws. Paul's influence with his visions and revelations about a deified Jesus and a Trinitarian God becomes evident at the end where Matthew presents his own resurrection stories.

Chapter 9
LUKE'S UNIQUE MATERIAL

Sources of the Gospel of Luke and Acts
It has been explained in Chapter 3 that the Gospel of Luke made use of mainly three sources:

- The Q Document, a collection of mainly sayings of Jesus – probably compiled during the forties or fifties of the first century AD in Galilee;
- The Gospel of Mark, most probably written during the seventies of the first century AD; and
- Material unique to this gospel – usually called L.[223]

It was shown in Chapter 7 that the text of Luke is independent of that of Matthew. They both reworked the text of Mark's Gospel in different ways and Luke did not copy Matthew's changes and additions to Mark, and vice versa.

Approximately one-third of Luke is from Mark (about 60% of Mark), 20% of Luke is derived from Q (sometimes arranged with parts of L), and almost 50% is from Luke's special source (L).[224]

The first two chapters of the Acts of the Apostles – evidently written by the same author as the Gospel of Luke – deals with the aftermath of Jesus' resurrection and it must be discussed together with the unique material contained in the Gospel of Luke.

The book of Acts is also based on more than one source:

---

[223] The United States Conference of Catholic Bishops, "Luke".
[224] Rylaarsdam *et al.*, "Biblical Literature".

- Unique material – eye-witness reports and other memories of early followers of Jesus; and
- Notes about the travels of Paul, probably written by a companion of Paul, in which the first person plural ("we") was often used, namely in Acts 16:10–17; 20:5–15; 21:1–18; 27:1–37; 28:1–16.[225]

Authorship and Date

Both the Gospels of Matthew and Luke were written independently, perhaps more or less at the same time and at different locations, probably during the eighties of the first century AD – in any case, at least a few years after the Gospel of Mark, from which they copied large parts. The book of Acts was presumably written shortly after the Gospel of Luke was completed.

Both parts of this two-volume work of Luke-Acts are anonymous. However, the earliest Christian author who attributed the third gospel to Luke was Irenaeus, who wrote during the late second century AD:

> "If Paul had known any mysteries unrevealed to the other apostles, Luke, his constant companion and fellow-traveler, could not have been ignorant of them; neither could the truth have possibly lain hid from him, through whom alone we learn many and most important particulars of the Gospel history."[226]

Eusebius of Caesarea noted:

> "Bu Luke, who was of Antiochian parentage and a physician by profession, and who was especially intimate

---

[225] Rylaarsdam *et al.*, "Biblical Literature".
[226] Irenaeus, *Adversus Haereses*, Liber III/I/1.

with Paul and well acquainted with the rest of the apostles, has left us, in two inspired books, proofs of that spiritual healing art which he learned from them. One of these books is the Gospel, which he testifies that he wrote as those who were from the beginning eyewitnesses and ministers of the word delivered unto him, all of whom, as he says, he followed accurately from the first. The other book is the Acts of the Apostles which he composed not from the accounts of others, but from what he had seen himself."[227]

The oldest manuscript containing the start of the gospel, from about AD 200 – a little more than a century after the completion of the gospel – has the title: "The Gospel According to Luke".[228]

The name of the traditional author of this gospel, Luke, means "light-giving". In Greek it is Λουκᾶς (*Loukas*) and in Latin it is Lucas. It is derived from the Latin word for light, namely "lux".

If Luke was indeed the author of the gospel and the book of Acts, he must be the person mentioned three times in Paul's letters. Paul called both Mark and Luke his co-workers in Philemon 1: 24 and 2 Tim 4: 11 while he was in prison. If these names are those of the authors of two of the gospels it may explain how Luke had access to the Gospel of Mark and expanded upon it.

Paul also calls Luke "the beloved physician" in Col 4: 14.

Luke's Gospel and Acts were written in good Greek and the author must have been an educated person – which can be expected of Luke the physician.[229]

If Luke was indeed the author of both the gospel and Acts and he was a travelling companion of Paul, he would have had the

---

[227] Eusebius, *Historia Ecclesiastica,* Liber III/IV/7.
[228] New World Encyclopedia. "Gospel of Luke".
[229] New World Encyclopedia. "Gospel of Luke".

opportunity to interview the apostles and other eye-witnesses regarding the life of Jesus and the deeds of the apostles, especially during a visit to Jerusalem and Caesarea (Acts 21: 8 – 27: 2). He would also have had the opportunity of experiencing the work and travels of Paul personally. That may explain the parts of Acts where the first personal pronoun in the plural ('we") was employed.

However, the historical reliability of Acts and Luke is suspect. There are some contradictions between Acts and Paul's letters, for instance the accounts of Paul's conversion (Acts 9: 1–30; Gal 1: 13–24) and the meeting in Jerusalem (Acts 15; Gal.1: 1–10).

Acts creates the impression that there was unity of faith between all the early followers of Jesus who were to be found in the congregations in Jerusalem and Palestine and in the churches founded later by Paul in the Greek–speaking world. There are, though enough evidence that this was not the case – Paul created Christianity in Syria, Asia Minor and Greece, while the followers of Jesus in Jerusalem and Judea stayed Jews who upheld the laws of Moses (see Chapters 2 and 4).

On account of the preceding, most scholars now doubt that Luke was really the author of the gospel and Acts and that these books are, in fact, anonymous. It is clear that the author's unique sources (L and the accounts in Acts) suffered from a long period between the events described and the eventual recording thereof. The author must have collected most parts of L and his information about the apostles only long after the death of Paul during the early sixties of the first century. He only gathered his unique information during the seventies or eighties of the first century, which rules out a companion of Paul as author.[230]

The author of the gospel and Acts does not, in addition, seem

---

[230] Rylaarsdam *et al.,* "Biblical Literature".

to have been familiar with the finer points of the theology of Paul or with the writings of Paul. That also rules out a travelling companion of Paul as author of these two books.[231]

Paul seems to be an unlikely source of information about the life of Jesus as found in the Gospel of Luke because he creates the impression in his letters that he was not very interested in the life and teachings of Jesus. All that mattered for him was Jesus' death and resurrection (see Chapter 4).

The good Greek of the gospel and Acts betrays a Greek-speaking Gentile author. He was not familiar with the geography of Palestine and his intended readers were obviously also Greek-speaking Gentiles. He presupposed a certain level of knowledge of the Old Testament from them because he often referred to the Greek translation of the Old Testament.

It is impossible to determine where the author was located and it may well have been anywhere in the Greek-speaking world.[232]

The passages from Luke discussed below, consist of the L Source, the parts that remain after Q and excerpts from Mark have been removed. Only the first two Chapters of Acts will be analyzed, the only parts of that book that have any bearing on the life of Jesus.

Prologue
Luke 1: 1–4

1.	Because many have undertaken to draw up a narrative con-cerning those matters which have been fulfilled among us,
2.	even as they delivered them to us, who from the beginning were eyewitnesses and ministers of the word,

---

[231] New World Encyclopedia, "The Gospel of Luke".
[232] Rylaarsdam *et al*., "Biblical Literature"; New World Encyclopedia, "The Gospel of Luke".

> 3. it seemed good to me also, having traced the course of all things accurately from the first, to write to you in order, most excellent Theophilus;
> 4. that you might know the certainty concerning the things in which you were instructed.

Right at the start of the Gospel of Luke, the reader is informed about the method the author employed to write his book. He explained that he was familiar with previous efforts to describe the life and teachings of Jesus – with which he most probably referred to the Q Document and the Gospel of Mark of which he copied large sections into his gospel. It is not impossible that he was also informed about the existence of the Proto-Gospel of John but that he has not seen a copy of it. According to him, these previous efforts were based on the information from eye-witnesses.

In addition, he also did some research of his own by interviewing people who could provide him with valuable memories.

Both the Gospel of Luke and Acts were dedicated to a certain Theophilus, an important person who is addressed as "most excellent". This expression may also be translated as "most noble". There has been much speculation about his identity and his relationship to the author of Luke's books. The name means "friend of God" and it was a common name in the Roman Empire.

There were even Jews who had this name. The most well-known was Theophilus, son of Annas and brother–in–law of Caiaphas, who were both high priests during Jesus' lifetime. Theophilus succeeded Caiaphas as high priest and occupied this position during AD 37–41. His name in Hebrew or Aramaic was found on the funerary casket of his granddaughter, Johanna. He was called תפלוס בר חנן (*Thephilos Bar Chanan*). It is unlikely that he was the Theophilus mentioned in Luke and Acts because it is doubtful that he would still have been alive when the gospel and Acts were written. Somebody else, who was entitled to be addressed as "Your Excellency" must have been meant – whoever he was.[233]

The Birth of John the Baptist is Announced
Luke 1: 5–25

5.	There was in the days of Herod, the king of Judea, a certain priest named Zacharias, of the priestly division of Abijah. He had a wife of the daughters of Aaron, and her name was Elizabeth.
6.	They were both righteous before God, walking blamelessly in all the commandments and ordinances of the Lord.
7.	But they had no child, because Elizabeth was barren, and they both were well advanced in years.
8.	Now it happened, while he executed the priest's office before God in the order of his division,
9.	according to the custom of the priest's office, his lot was to enter into the temple of the Lord and burn incense.
10.	The whole multitude of the people were praying outside at the hour of incense.
11.	An angel of the Lord appeared to him, standing on the right side of the altar of incense.
12.	Zacharias was troubled when he saw him, and fear fell on him.
13.	But the angel said to him, "Don't be afraid, Zacharias, because your request has been heard, and your wife, Elizabeth, will bear you a son, and you shall call his name John.

---

[233] Josephus, *Antuquities*, Liber XIX/VI/2; Bolt, *Luke, a Commentary*.

14. You will have joy and gladness; and many will rejoice at his birth.
15. For he will be great in the sight of the Lord, and he will drink no wine nor strong drink. He will be filled with the Holy Spirit, even from his mother's womb.
16. He will turn many of the children of Israel to the Lord, their God.
17. He will go before his face in the spirit and power of Elijah, 'to turn the hearts of the fathers to the children,' and the disobedient to the wisdom of the just; to make ready a people prepared for the Lord."
18. Zacharias said to the angel, "How can I be sure of this? For I am an old man, and my wife is well advanced in years."
19. The angel answered him, "I am Gabriel, who stands in the presence of God. I was sent to speak to you, and to bring you this good news.
20. Behold, you will be silent and not able to speak, until the day that these things will happen, because you didn't believe my words, which will be fulfilled in their proper time."
21. The people were waiting for Zacharias, and they marveled while he delayed in the temple.
22. When he came out, he could not speak to them, and they perceived that he had seen a vision in the temple. He continued making signs to them, and remained mute.
23. It happened, when the days of his service were fulfilled, he departed to his house.
24. After these days Elizabeth, his wife, conceived, and she hid herself five months, saying,

> 25. "Thus has the Lord done to me in the days in which he looked at me, to take away my reproach among men."

The only person who experienced the purported appearance of the angel, the messenger from God, was Zacharias, the priest. He may have told other people afterwards of his experience and that may be how Luke heard of it. The supernatural elements of an angel and the sudden muteness of Zacharias place some strain on the credibility of this incident.

However, there may be some historical elements in this tale. The parents of John the Baptist may have been named Zacharias and Elizabeth. Their piety and steadfastness may be a sign that they were Essenes.

The name Elizabeth is a Hebrew name (אֱלִישֶׁבַע – *Elisheba*), meaning "My God is an oath" or "My God is abundance". The wife of Aaron, the brother of Moses, had this name (Ex 6: 23).

The prophecy of the angel about the unborn son of Zacharias amounts to a good summary of John the Baptist's career as a Nazarite prophet, written after his death.

The Birth of Jesus is Announced
Luke 1: 26–38

> 26. Now in the sixth month, the angel Gabriel was sent from God to a city of Galilee, named Nazareth,
> 27. to a virgin pledged to be married to a man whose name was Joseph, of the house of David. The virgin's name was Mary.

28. Having come in to her, the angel said, "Rejoice, you highly favored one! The Lord is with you. Blessed are you among women!"
29. But when she saw him, she was greatly troubled at the saying, and considered what kind of salutation this might be.
30. The angel said to her, "Don`t be afraid, Mary, for you have found favor with God.
31. Behold, you will conceive in your womb, and bring forth a son, and will call his name JESUS.
32. He will be great, and will be called the Son of the Most High. The Lord God will give to him the throne of his father, David,
33. and he will reign over the house of Jacob forever. There will be no end of his kingdom."
34. Mary said to the angel, "How will this be, seeing I am a virgin?"
35. The angel answered her, "The Holy Spirit will come on you, and the power of the Most High will overshadow you. Therefore also the holy one which is born from you will be called the Son of God.
36. Behold, Elizabeth, your relative, also has conceived a son in her old age; and this is the sixth month with her who was called barren.
37. For no word from God will be void of power."
38. Mary said, "Behold, the handmaid of the Lord; be it to me according to your word." The angel departed from her.

This scene is part of the Christmas story, which is told and retold every year during December. The question is, however: how much of it is historically reliable? The only source for information about this encounter with the archangel Gabriel was Mary herself. She was given the promise that she would stay a virgin while becoming pregnant – which is a biological impossibility. The virgin birth became a corner stone of traditional Christian beliefs.

It must be reiterated that the Ebionites, the original Jewish followers of Jesus, denied the virgin birth and declared that Joseph was his biological father (see Chapter 2). Joseph is also called Jesus' father on various occasions in the gospels (Matt 1: 17; 13: 55; Luke 3: 23; 4: 22; John 1: 45; 6: 42), but orthodox scholars usually explain those passages as referring to Joseph as Jesus' adopted father, although those texts do not allow such an interpretation.

Albrecht Dürer: The Annunciation (ca 1510)

The fact that Jesus became a popular teacher and that the crowds greeted him as their king when he entered Jerusalem on the back of an ass a few days before his execution, suggest that he could not have been born out of wedlock and that his parents must have been legally married. After all, we read in Deut 23: 2 –

> "One whose father and mother are not married may not come into the meeting of the Lord's people, or any of his family to the tenth generation."

If Jesus was really born out of wedlock, as reported by Luke and Matthew, he would have been treated as a social outcast, a pariah. Instead, he was regarded as a charismatic preacher, an authoritative teacher and a gifted healer who drew large crowds.

According to legend, Mary also had a miraculous birth. Her elderly and barren parents, Joachim and Anne, vowed to devote any child they may have to the service of Gd. Mary was purportedly born without original sin to prepare her to become the virgin mother of Jesus.[234]

Gabriel is one of the four traditional archangels or chief angels (Dan 8: 16; 9: 21). The other are Michael (Jud 1: 9; Rev12: 7), Raphael (in the apocryphal books of 1 Enoch 9: 1 and Tobit 12: 11–15), and Uriel (in II Esdras 4: 1; 5: 20; 10: 28).

Mary Visits Elizabeth
Luke 1: 39–45

39.	Mary arose in those days and went into the hill country with haste, into a city of Judah,
40.	and entered into the house of Zacharias and greeted Elizabeth.
41.	It happened, when Elizabeth heard Mary's greeting, the baby leaped in her womb, and Elizabeth was filled with the Holy Spirit.
42.	She called out with a loud voice, and said, "Blessed are you among women, and blessed is the fruit of your womb!
43.	Why am I so favored, that the mother of my Lord should come to me?

---

[234] Enc Brit. "Anne and Joachim, Saints".

> 44. For behold, when the voice of your greeting came into my ears, the baby leaped in my womb for joy!
> 45. Blessed is she who believed, for there will be a fulfillment of the things which have been spoken to her from the Lord!"

There can be no doubt that this story is fictitious. There were certainly no eye-witnesses who could inform Luke after eight decades or more of what had transpired in a private home in the hilly countryside of Judea. It is also extremely unlikely that any one of these two women would have told others about Mary's visit, if it had really happened as reported.

The Song of Mary
Luke 1: 546–56

> 46. Mary said, "My soul magnifies the Lord.
> 47. My spirit has rejoiced in God my Savior,
> 48. For he has looked at the humble state of his handmaid. For behold, from now on, all generations will call me blessed.
> 49. For he who is mighty has done to me great things; Holy is his name.
> 50. His mercy is for generations of generations on those who fear him.
> 51. He has shown strength with his arm. He has scattered the proud in the imagination of their heart.
> 52. He has put down princes from their thrones. Has exalted the lowly.
> 53. He has filled the hungry with good things. He has sent the rich away empty.

LUKE'S UNIQUE MATERIAL

> 54. He has given help to Israel, his servant, that he might remember mercy
>
> 55. (As he spoke to our fathers) Toward Abraham and his seed forever."
>
> 56. Mary stayed with her about three months, and returned to her house.

This Psalm, attributed to Mary, is evidently modelled on the song of Hannah, the mother of Samuel (1 Sam 2: 1–10). It is uncertain who composed it and how Luke got hold of it. It may even have been written by Luke himself.

The Birth of John the Baptist
Luke 1: 57–66

> 57. Now the time that Elizabeth should give birth was fulfilled, and she brought forth a son.
>
> 58. Her neighbors and her relatives heard that the Lord had magnified his mercy towards her; and they rejoiced with her.
>
> 59. It happened on the eighth day, that they came to circumcise the child; and they would have called him Zacharias, after the name of the father.
>
> 60. His mother answered, "Not so; but he will be called John."
>
> 61. They said to her, "There is no one among your relatives who is called by this name."
>
> 62. They made signs to his father, what he would have him called.
>
> 63. He asked for a writing tablet, and wrote, "His name is John." They all marveled.

64.	His mouth was opened immediately, and his tongue freed, and he spoke, blessing God.
65.	Fear came on all who lived around them, and all these sayings were talked about throughout all the hill country of Judea.
66.	All who heard them laid them up in their heart, saying, "What then will this child be?" The hand of the Lord was with him.

This is another story filled with miraculous and magical elements and most of it may be regarded as fictitious.

There can be no doubt, though, that the son of Zacharias was called John. The name of John (Greek: Ἰωάννης – *Ioannes*), was a common name in those days. Apart from John the Baptist, one of Jesus' apostles and the author of Revelation also had this name. The name *John* is of Hebrew origin and it is derived from the Hebrew name יְהוֹחָנָן or יוֹחָנָן (*Yehochanan* or *Yochanan*) meaning "YHWH is gracious" and it appears in 2 Chr 17: 17, 2 Chr 23: 1, Neh 12: 22–23, and Jer 42: 8.

Zecheriah's Prophecy
Luke 1: 67–80

67.	His father, Zacharias, was filled with the Holy Spirit, and prophesied, saying,
68.	"Blessed be the Lord, the God of Israel, For he has visited and worked redemption for his people;
69.	Has raised up a horn of salvation for us in the house of his servant David
70.	(As he spoke by the mouth of his holy prophets who have been from of old),

71.	Salvation from our enemies, and from the hand of all who hate us;
72.	To show mercy towards our fathers, To remember his holy covenant,
73.	The oath which he spoke to Abraham, our father,
74.	To grant to us that we, being delivered out of the hand of our enemies, should serve him without fear,
75.	In holiness and righteousness before him all the days of our life.
76.	And you, child, will be called a prophet of the Most High, For you will go before the face of the Lord to make ready his ways,
77.	To give knowledge of salvation to his people by the remission of their sins,
78.	Because of the tender mercy of our God, Whereby the dawn from on high will visit us,
79.	To shine on those who sit in darkness and the shadow of death; To guide our feet into the way of peace."
80.	The child grew, and grew strong in spirit, and was in the desert until the day of his public appearance

It is noteworthy that Luke reported that John grew up in the desert while his parents lived in a town in the hilly countryside of Judea. Thia may mean that John received his education at Qumran, the headquarters of the Essene sect near the Dead Sea. That would explain his lifestyle as an adult, his message of repentance, and his criticism of the rich religious authorities in Jerusalem.

The Psalm attributed to Zacharias is presented by Luke as a prophecy, although it actually described history. John became a prophet in a time when the Jews longed for a Messiah, somebody who would free them from their oppressors. This song retains some memories of Jesus' campaign to restore the kingdom of David and get rid of the hated Romans.

The Birth of Jesus
Luke 2: 1–7

1.	Now it happened in those days, that a decree went out from Caesar Augustus that all the world should be enrolled.
2.	This was the first enrollment made when Quirinius was governor of Syria.
3.	All went to enroll themselves, everyone to his own city.
4.	Joseph also went up from Galilee, out of the city of Nazareth, into Judea, to the city of David, which is called Bethlehem, because he was of the house and family of David;
5.	to enroll himself with Mary, who was pledged to be married to him as wife, being great with child.
6.	It happened, while they were there, that the day had come that she should give birth.
7.	She brought forth her firstborn son, and she wrapped him in bands of cloth, and laid him in a feeding trough, because there was no room for them in the inn.

Most of this story is contradicted by known history. The census during the time when Quirinius was governor of Syria, only took place a decade after Jesus must have been born – that is, if he was born before Herod the Great's death.

There was no need for Joseph and Mary to travel from Nazareth in Galilee to Bethlehem in Judea for the census. People were counted in their place of residence so that the authorities could calculate how much taxes could be extracted from those regions.[235]

It is not impossible that Jesus was born in Bethlehem, although it is unlikely. Matthew also reported that Jesus was born there, but provided no explanation why he was born there and only stated that it was the fulfillment of a prophecy.

That Joseph was a descendent of King David may be accepted as fact. That also applies to Jesus.

The Shepherds and the Angels
Luke 2: 8–20

8.	There were shepherds in the same country staying in the field, and keeping watch by night over their flock.
9.	Behold, an angel of the Lord stood by them, and the glory of the Lord shone around them, and they were terrified.
10.	The angel said to them, "Don't be afraid, for behold, I bring you good news of great joy which will be to all the people.
11.	For there is born to you, this day, in the city of David, a Savior, who is Christ the Lord.
12.	This is the sign to you: you will find a baby wrapped in strips of cloth, lying in a feeding trough."
13.	Suddenly, there was with the angel a multitude of the heavenly host praising God, and saying,
14.	"Glory to God in the highest, On earth peace, good will toward men."
15.	It happened, when the angels went away from them into the sky, that the shepherds said one to another, "Let's go to

---

[235] Gertoux, "Herod the Great and Jesus", 28; Enc Brit, "Census".

	Bethlehem, now, and see this thing that has happened, which the Lord has made known to us."
16.	They came with haste, and found both Mary and Joseph, and the baby lying in the feeding trough.
17.	When they saw it, they publicized widely the saying which was spoken to them about this child.
18.	All who heard it wondered at the things which were spoken to them by the shepherds.
19.	But Mary kept all these sayings, pondering them in her heart.
20.	The shepherds returned, glorifying and praising God for all the things that they had heard and seen, even as it was spoken to them.

According to Matthew, the Baby Jesus was visited by star gazers from the East. Luke knew nothing of them, but he told a story of shepherds near Bethlehem who found the Jesus infant after a choir of Aramaic-speaking (or Greek-speaking) angels had informed them of his arrival. Matthew was silent regarding this event.

Although both stories of visitors who worshipped the divine child are part-and-parcel of the traditional Christmas stories told to children, both may be regarded as pious inventions to convince readers in the ancient world that Jesus was no ordinary mortal human being, but a divine being and the savior of mankind.

Jesus is Named
Luke 2: 21

21.	When eight days were fulfilled for the circumcision of the child, his name was called JESUS, which was given by the angel before he was conceived in the womb.

Adoration of the Shepherds (Albrecht Dürer)

In the Greek New Testament Jesus' name is Ἰησοῦς (*Iesous*). Most languages, including English, use the Latin transcription of this name, namely Jesus. His name in Hebrew or Aramaic – the home language of the Jews at the time – was *Yehoshua* (יְהוֹשֻׁעַ), which means: "YHVH is salvation or deliverance," the same name of Joshua, the successor of Moses as leader of the Israelites.

Jesus is Presented in the Temple
Luke 2: 22–38

22.	When the days of their purification according to the law of Moses were fulfilled, they brought him up to Jerusalem, to present him to the Lord

23. (as it is written in the law of the Lord, "Every male who opens the womb shall be called holy to the Lord"),
24. and to offer a sacrifice according to that which is said in the law of the Lord, "A pair of turtledoves, or two young pigeons."
25. Behold, there was a man in Jerusalem whose name was Simeon; and this man was righteous and devout, looking for the consolation of Israel, and the Holy Spirit was on him.
26. It had been revealed to him by the Holy Spirit that he should not see death, before he had seen the Lord's Christ.
27. He came in the Spirit into the temple. When the parents brought in the child, Jesus, that they might do concerning him according to the custom of the law,
28. then he received him into his arms, and blessed God, and said,
29. "Now let you your servant depart, Lord, According to your word, in peace;
30. For my eyes have seen your salvation,
31. Which you have prepared before the face of all peoples;
32. A light for revelation to the Gentiles, The glory of your people Israel."
33. Joseph and his mother were marveling at the things which were spoken concerning him,
34. and Simeon blessed them, and said to Mary, his mother, "Behold, this child is set for the falling and the rising of many in Israel, and for a sign which is spoken against.
35. Yes, a sword will pierce through your own soul, that thoughts out of many hearts may be revealed."

> 36. There was one Anna, a prophetess, the daughter of Phanuel, of the tribe of Asher (she was of a great age, having lived with a husband seven years from her virginity,
> 37. and she had been a widow for about eighty–four years), who didn't depart from the temple, worshipping with fasting and petitions night and day.
> 38. Coming up at that very hour, she gave thanks to the Lord, and spoke of him to all those who were looking for redemption in Jerusalem.

Luke seems to be unaware of the massacre in Bethlehem and the flight of the Holy Family to Egypt, just as Matthew did not know anything about the presentation of the baby Jesus at the temple and the encounter with two elderly prophets.

The presentation of Jesus at the temple was in accordance with Ex 13: 2, where it is stipulated that all firstborn boys had to be sanctified. The sacrifices that were to be brought after a child's birth are described in Lev 12: 2.

The purported prophecy spoken by the elderly Simeon amounts to a description of the agony that Mary must have felt when Jesus was hanging on the cross, more than three decades later.

The prophetess Anna must have been very ancient. If she married at the age of fifteen, lived with her husband for seven years, and survived him by 84 years, she must have been about 105 years old when she saw the baby Jesus at the temple.

The Return to Nazareth
Luke 2: 39–40

> 39. When they had accomplished all things that were according to the law of the Lord, they returned into Galilee, to their

	own city, Nazareth.
40.	The child grew, and grew strong in spirit, filled with wisdom, and the grace of God was on him.

The village of Nazareth seems to have been an insignificant settlement in Jesus' time because it was not mentioned in ancient sources – only in the gospels.[236]

The Young Jesus in the Temple
Luke 2: 41–52

41.	His parents went every year to Jerusalem at the feast of the Passover.
42.	When he was twelve years old, they went up to Jerusalem according to the custom of the feast,
43.	and when they had fulfilled the days, as they were returning, the boy, Jesus, stayed behind in Jerusalem. Joseph and his mother didn't know it,
44.	but supposing him to be in the company, they went a day's journey, and they looked for him among their relatives and acquaintances.
45.	When they didn't find him, they returned to Jerusalem, looking for him.
46.	It happened, after three days they found him in the temple, sitting in the midst of the teachers, both listening to them, and asking them questions.
47.	All who heard him were amazed at his understanding and his answers.

---

[236] Enc Brit, "Nazareth".

48.	When they saw him, they were astonished, and his mother said to him, "Son, why have you treated us this way? Behold, your father and I were anxiously looking for you."
49.	He said to them, "Why were you looking for me? Didn't you know that I must be in my Father's house?"
50.	They didn't understand the saying which he spoke to them.
51.	He went down with them, and came to Nazareth. He was subject to them, and his mother kept all these sayings in her heart.
52.	Jesus advanced in wisdom and stature, and in favor with God and men.

It is quite possible that Jesus somehow got separated from his family during the feast. A kind teacher of the Law must have looked after the lonely abandoned boy for three days before his parents came back to find him. This teacher of the Law must have taken him along to the temple where Jesus was talking to some learned men. He must have been exceptionally intelligent because he asked meaningful questions. It is possible that he was able to read and write at that age.

It is unknown how Luke got hold of this story, but it could have been an eye-witness who told him about this incident.. It is the only report about Jesus' childhood in the Bible. Whether Jesus knew at that stage that he was meant to be God's Son, is impossible to determine, but it is unlikely.

The Preaching of John the Baptist
Luke 3: 1–18

1.	Now in the fifteenth year of the reign of Tiberius Caesar, Pontius Pilate being governor of Judea, and Herod being tetrarch of Galilee, and his brother Philip tetrarch of the

2. region of Ituraea and Trachonitis, and Lysanias tetrarch of Abilene,
2. in the high priesthood of Annas and Caiaphas, the word of God came to John, the son of Zacharias, in the wilderness.
3. He came into all the region around the Jordan, preaching the baptism of repentance to remission of sins.
4. As it is written in the book of the words of Isaiah the prophet, "The voice of one crying in the wilderness, `Make ready the way of the Lord. Make his paths straight.
5. Every valley will be filled. Every mountain and hill will be brought low. The crooked will become straight, And the rough ways smooth.
6. All flesh will see God`s salvation.`"
7. *He said therefore to the multitudes who went out to be baptized by him, "You offspring of vipers, who warned you to flee from the wrath to come?*
8. *Bring forth therefore fruits worthy of repentance, and don`t begin to say among yourselves, `We have Abraham for our father;` for I tell you that God is able to raise up children to Abraham from these stones!*
9. *Even now the ax also lies at the root of the trees. Every tree therefore that doesn`t bring forth good fruit is cut down, and thrown into the fire."*
10. The multitudes asked him, "What then must we do?"
11. He answered them, "He who has two coats, let him give to him who has none. He who has food, let him do likewise."

12.	Tax collectors also came to be baptized, and they said to him, "Teacher, what must we do?"
13.	He said to them, "Extort no more than that which is appointed you."
14.	Soldiers also asked him, saying, "What about us? What must we do?" He said to them, "Extort from no one by violence, neither accuse anyone wrongfully. Be content with your wages."
15.	As the people were in expectation, and all men reasoned in their hearts concerning John, whether perhaps he was the Christ,
16.	*John answered them all, "I indeed baptize you with water, but he comes who is mightier than I, the latchet of whose sandals I am not worthy to loosen. He will baptize you in the Holy Spirit and fire,*
17.	*whose fan is in his hand, and he will thoroughly cleanse his threshing floor, and will gather the wheat into his barn; but he will burn up the chaff with unquenchable fire."*
18.	Then with many other exhortations he preached good news to the people,
19.	but Herod the tetrarch, being reproved by him for Herodias, his brother`s wife, and for all the evil things which Herod had done,
20.	added this also to them all, that he shut up John in prison.

This passage in Luke is an expanded version of Mark 1: 1–8, together with two passages taken from Q (printed in italics).

Luke started this part of his narrative with an indication of when John the Baptist started his work as a prophet in Palestine, namely during the fifteenth year of the reign of Caesar Tiberius.

Tiberius succeeded his adopted father, Augustus, as emperor on 17 September AD 14. His fifteenth year as emperor started in September AD 28 and John appeared on the scene during the following months.

Luke also listed the most important people in Palestine at that time – the three sons of Herod the Great who each inherited a portion of his kingdom after his death in 4 BC, as well as the retired high priest Annas and the incumbent high priest, Caiaphas, his son-in-law. Pontius Pilate became governor of Judea after Herod Archelaus was dethroned due to maladministration in AD 26.[237]

It has been explained in chapter 2 that Jesus was probably baptized on 24 November AD 29 when a total solar eclipse in Galilee occurred. This fits in neatly with Luke's dating of John's ministry. Luke's effort to date the start of John's career precisely creates the impression that his description of Jesus' ministry from this point onwards contains reliable information.

John came out of the "wilderness" – possibly the headquarters of the Essenes at Qumran near the Dead Sea and he started baptizing people in the Jordan further north after they have declared their repentance of their sins. Luke regarded his work as the fulfillment of a prophecy in from Isa 42: 1–4   People thronged to listen to his sermons, even if he insulted them by calling them venomous vipers – that is, the offspring of Satan, the sly speaking serpent that seduced Eve in the Paradise. He advocated the Essene lifestyle of sharing and hospitality, pacifism, and honesty.

---

[237] Enc. Brit. "Tiberius"; Bolt, *Luke, a Commentary*.

John did not spare Herod Antipas, the ruler of Galilee, who married his divorced sister-in-law, which was regarded as an incestuous union. As an Essene, he disapproved of divorce.

The Ancestors of Jesus
Luke 3: 23–38

23.	Jesus himself, when he began to teach, was about thirty years old, being the son (as was supposed) of Joseph, the son of Heli,
24.	the son of Matthat, the son of Levi, the son of Melchi, the son of Jannai, the son of Joseph,
25.	the son of Mattathias, the son of Amos, the son of Nahum, the son of Esli, the son of Naggai,
26.	the son of Maath, the son of Mattathias, the son of Semein, the son of Joseph, the son of Judah,
27.	the son of Joanan, the son of Rhesa, the son of Zerubbabel, the son of Shealtiel, the son of Neri,
28.	the son of Melchi, the son of Addi, the son of Cosam, the son of Elmodam, the son of Er,
29.	the son of Josa, the son of Eliezer, the son of Jorim, the son of Matthat, the son of Levi,
30.	the son of Simeon, the son of Judah, the son of Joseph, the son of Jonan, the son of Eliakim,
31.	the son of Melea, the son of Menan, the son of Mattatha, the son of Nathan, the son of David,
32.	the son of Jesse, the son of Obed, the son of Boaz, the son of Salmon, the son of Nahshon,
33.	the son of Amminadab, the son of Aram, the son of Joram, the son of Hezron, the son of Perez, the son of Judah,

34.	the son of Jacob, the son of Isaac, the son of Abraham, the son of Terah, the son of Nahor,
35.	the son of Serug, the son of Reu, the son of Peleg, the son of Eber, the son of Shelah
36.	the son of Cainan, the son of Arphaxad, the son of Shem, the son of Noah, the son of Lamech,
37.	the son of Methuselah, the son of Enoch, the son of Jared, the son of Mahalaleel, the son of Cainan,
38.	the son of Enos, the son of Seth, the son of Adam, the son of God.

This genealogy of Jesus differs from the list of ancestors found in Matthew. The church historian Eusebius explained that Matthew listed the biological father of Joseph, Jesus' father, while Luke mentioned Joseph's step-father, the man who married his mother after his father's death (see Chapter 8). Matthew took the list only as far back as Abraham, but Luke included generations back to Adam, perhaps with the object of showing that Jesus was the savior of all mankind.

Luke wrote that Jesus started his teaching career when he was about thirty years old. That must be an approximate age. If Jesus was born before the death of Herod the Great, who died in 4 BC, then Jesus may have been born between 6 and 4 BC. If he started his career after his baptism at the end of AD 29, he may have been at least 33 years old at that stage.

The Bible is silent about what happened to Jesus between his appearance at the temple at the age of twelve and the start of his public ministry at the age of at least 33. These so-called lost years have been the subject of much speculation, but no solid evidence exists about these years. Most likely, Jesus spent a part of these years quietly at the Essene center near the Dead Sea to be educated in the

Hebrew Scriptures and to receive training in the healing arts and other subjects, including Greek, which was the language of learning, politics, and commerce in the eastern parts of the Roman Empire. He may also have spent some time working as a craftsman in Nazareth, perhaps continuing his father's business after his death.

Jesus is Rejected at Nazareth
Luke 4: 16–30

16.	He came to Nazareth, where he had been brought up. He entered, as was his custom, into the synagogue on the Sabbath day, and stood up to read.
17.	The book of the prophet Isaiah was handed to him. He opened the book, and found the place where it was written,
18.	"The Spirit of the Lord is on me, Because he anointed me to preach good news to the poor. He has sent me to heal the brokenhearted, To proclaim release to the captives, Recovering of sight to the blind, To deliver those who are crushed,
19.	And to proclaim the acceptable year of the Lord."
20.	He closed the book, gave it back to the attendant, and sat down. The eyes of all in the synagogue were fastened on him.
21.	He began to tell them, "Today, this scripture has been fulfilled in your hearing."
22.	All testified about him, and wondered at the words of grace which proceeded out of his mouth, and they said, "Isn't this Joseph's son?"
23.	He said to them, "Doubtless you will tell me this parable, 'Physician, heal yourself. Whatever we have heard done at Capernaum, do also here in your hometown.'"

> 24. He said, "Most assuredly I tell you, no prophet is acceptable in his hometown.
> 25. But truly I tell you, there were many widows in Israel in the days of Elijah, when the sky was shut up three years and six months, when a great famine came over all the land.
> 26. Elijah was sent to none of them, except only to Zarephath, in the land of Sidon, to a woman who was a widow.
> 27. There were many lepers in Israel in the time of Elisha the prophet, yet not one of them was cleansed, except Naaman, the Syrian."
> 28. They were all filled with wrath in the synagogue, as they heard these things;
> 29. and they rose up, and threw him out of the city, and led him to the brow of the hill that their city was built on, that they might throw him off the cliff.
> 30. But he, passing through the midst of them, went his way.

This passage was adapted from Mark 6: 1–6 and expanded with material unique to Luke. In Mark this episode was placed at a later stage in Jesus' career, but Luke chose to describe it as the start of Jesus' ministry after his baptism and temptation in the desert, although he mentioned that Jesus had already healed sick people in Capernaum.

According to Luke, Jesus held a sermon in the synagogue after having read a passage from Isaiah 61: 1–3, which he applied to himself. This passage is, indeed, an apt description of how Jesus saw his own career. It is impossible to determine whether Jesus really read this part of Isaiah or whether Luke made this story up as an introduction to his description of Jesus' ministry from that point onwards.

Luke copied from Mark the part where the villagers of Nazareth threatened to push Jesus over a cliff.

Jesus Teaches and Heals
Luke 6: 17–19

17.	He came down with them, and stood on a level place, with a crowd of his disciples, and a great number of the people from all Judea and Jerusalem, and the sea coast of Tyre and Sidon, who came to hear him, and to be healed of their diseases;
18.	also those who were troubled with unclean spirits, and they were being healed.
19.	All the multitude sought to touch him, for power came forth from him, and healed them all.

This passage merely relates that people came from far and wide, even from outside Palestine, to see and hear Jesus. He healed many who were ill. He became a celebrity and a star.

Jesus Raises a Widow's Son
Luke 7: 11–17

11.	It happened soon afterwards, that he went to a city called Nain. Many of his disciples went with him, along with a great multitude.
12.	Now when he drew near to the gate of the city, behold, one who was dead was carried out, the only son of his mother, and she was a widow. Many people of the city were with her.
13.	When the Lord saw her, he had compassion on her, and said to her, "Don`t cry."

14.	He came near and touched the pallet, and the bearers stood still. He said, "Young man, I tell you, arise!"
15.	He who was dead sat up, and began to speak. He gave him to his mother.
16.	Fear took hold on all, and they glorified God, saying, "A great prophet has arisen among us," and, "God has visited his people."
17.	This report went out concerning him in the whole of Judea, and in all the surrounding region.

The only rational explanation for this miracle is that the boy was not really dead – only in a coma and erroneously diagnosed as deceased. He showed signs of life when Jesus saw him and Jesus helped him to get off his litter or pallet with which he was taken away for burial.[238]

Women who Accompanied Jesus
Luke 8: 1–3

1.	It happened soon afterwards, that he went about through cities and villages, preaching and bringing the good news of the kingdom of God, and with him the twelve,
2.	and certain women who had been healed of evil spirits and infirmities: Mary who was called Magdalene, from whom seven demons had gone out;

---

[238] Jewish Virtual Library. "Death & Bereavement in Judaism: Ancient Burial Practices".

LUKE'S UNIQUE MATERIAL

> 3. and Joanna, the wife of Chuzas, Herod's steward, Susanna; and many others; who ministered to them from their possessions.

Jesus had several companions who accompanied him during his campaign to recruit supporters while preaching his message about the coming kingdom of God of which he was to be the sovereign. This group included his twelve disciples, as well as several women who shared their wealth with Jesus in the Essene tradition.

Jesus Mother and Brothers
Luke 8: 19–21

> 19. His mother and brothers came to him, and they could not come near him for the crowd.
> 20. It was told him by some saying, "Your mother and your brothers stand outside, desiring to see you."
> 21. But he answered them, "My mother and my brothers are these who hear the word of God, and do it."

There was an occasion when Jesus' mother and brothers wished to speak to him but it was impossible to reach him due to the crowd that surrounded him. Jesus declared that all those who do the will of God – that is, accepting his message about the kingdom – can also be regarded as his family. In other words: he addressed an elderly woman who believed in him as "Mother" and any adult male who followed him as "Brother".

A Samaritan Village Rejects Jesus
Luke 9: 51–56

51.	It came to pass, when the days were near that he should be taken up, he intently set his face to go to Jerusalem,
52.	and sent messengers before his face. They went, and entered a village of the Samaritans, to prepare for him.
53.	They didn't receive him, because he was traveling with his face set towards Jerusalem.
54.	When his disciples, James and John, saw this, they said, "Lord, do you want us to command fire to come down from the sky, and destroy them, just as Elijah did?"
55.	But he turned and rebuked them, "You don't know what kind of spirit you are of.
56.	For the Son of Man didn't come to destroy men's lives, but to save them." They went to another village.

The Samaritans and the Jews had no love for each other, with the result that the party of the Essenes did not find any adherents in Samaria. When Jesus was travelling through Samaria from Galilee to Jerusalem, the Samaritans were not prepared to offer him the hospitality that he could expect from Jewish Essenes. Despite this, he refused to condemn these Samaritans.

Return of the Seventy-Two
Luke 10: 17–20

17.	The seventy returned with joy, saying, "Lord, even the demons are subject to us in your name."
18.	He said to them, "I saw Satan having fall like lightning from heaven.
19.	Behold, I give you authority to tread on serpents and

> scorpions, and over all the power of the enemy. Nothing will in any way hurt you.
> 20. Nevertheless, don't rejoice in this, that the spirits are subject to you, but rejoice that your names are written in heaven."

In a preceding passage, Luke 10: 1–12 (which is part of Q and corresponds with Matt 9: 37–38; 10: 7–16), Jesus sent out seventy-two of his supporters to spread his message regarding the coming kingdom. Since this passage is part of the Q Document, it is not repeated here.

Only Luke relates how these messengers reported back, telling Jesus that they were able to drive demons out of people. Jesus replied that he had seen Satan fall like a thunderbolt from heaven.

That must be what he had seen in the stars on the day when he was baptized and a solar eclipse occurred, which made the stars in the heaven visible during day-time. Jesus must have regarded the constellation of Serpens, the Serpent, where the occulted sun was situated, as a symbol of Satan. This serpent was held by the constellation of Ophiuchus or Serpenatarius, the Snake Catcher. This figure was also trampling upon the constellation of Scorpius, the Scorpion, another depiction of Satan. That prompted Jesus to tell his supporters that they were given the power to trample upon serpents and scorpions, symbols of evil spirits.

They also got the promise that their names were written in heaven, somewhere between the stars. That guaranteed their immunity from attacks by the evil powers in the sky.

The episode of Jesus' baptism is explained in more detail in Chapter 2 where a computerized recreation of the starry skies on 24 November AD 29 during the total solar eclipse is given.

It is possible that the followers of Jesus who were able to drive evil spirits from ill people were either fellow-Essenes who received some training at Qumran in the healing arts, or men trained by Jesus himself in these skills.

The Parable of the Good Samaritan
Luke 10: 25–37

25.	Behold, a certain lawyer stood up and tested him, saying, "Teacher, what will I do to inherit eternal life?"
26.	He said to him, "What is written in the law? How do you read it?"
27.	He answered, "You shall love the Lord your God with all your heart, with all your soul, with all your strength, and with all your mind; and your neighbor as yourself."
28.	He said to him, "You have answered correctly. Do this, and you will live."
29.	But he, desiring to justify himself, asked Jesus, "Who is my neighbor?"
30.	Jesus answered, "A certain man was going down from Jerusalem to Jericho, and he fell among robbers, who both stripped him and beat him, and departed, leaving him half dead.
31.	By chance a certain priest was going down that way. When he saw him, he passed by on the other side.
32.	In the same way a Levite also, when he came to the place, and saw him, passed by on the other side.
33.	But a certain Samaritan, as he journeyed, came where he was. When he saw him, he was moved with compassion,

> 34. came to him, and bound up his wounds, pouring on oil and wine. He set him on his own animal, and brought him to an inn, and took care of him.
> 35. On the next day, when he departed, he took out two denarii, and gave them to the host, and said to him, `Take care of him. Whatever you spend beyond that, I will repay you when I return.`
> 36. Now which of these three do you think seemed to be a neighbor to him who fell among the robbers?"
> 37. He said, "He who showed mercy on him." Then Jesus said to him, "Go and do likewise."

Jesus told the lawyer or teacher of the Law who engaged him in a conversation that the way to inherit eternal life was to love Gd and to love one's neighbor. This is in stark contrast with the stance of Paul who propagated the view that one should have faith in Christ as the savior of the world to enter eternal life.

This explanation by Jesus led to the well-known Parable of the Good Samaritan, which is part of the L Source.

It must be remembered that a certain Samaritan town refused to provide hospitality to Jesus a short while ago, according to Luke's time scale (Luke 9: 51–56). It is clear that Jesus made a Samaritan the hero of his story on purpose. He wanted to expose the pomposity and arrogance and lack of concern for ordinary and suffering folks shown by the religious authorities in Jerusalem and contrast their attitude with that of this despised Samaritan.

This parable tells the story of this man who was bleeding in the dust and dirt after he had been hijacked by a gang of highway robbers. The Samaritan did more than enough to help this victim of violent crime. According to Jesus, this Samaritan demonstrated the lifestyle of the generous Essenes, which he cherished.

Jesus Visits Martha and Mary
Luke 10: 38–42

> 38. It happened as they went on their way, he entered into a certain village, and a certain woman named Martha received him into her house.
> 39. She had a sister called Mary, who also sat at Jesus' feet, and heard his word.
> 40. But Martha was distracted with much serving, and she came up to him, and said, "Lord, don't you care that my sister left me to serve alone? Ask her therefore to help me."
> 41. Jesus answered her, "Martha, Martha, you are anxious and troubled about many things,
> 42. but one thing is needed. Mary has chosen the good part, which will not be taken away from her."

Luke didn't tell his readers much about these two sisters, Mary and Martha. Somebody who only knew the Gospel of Luke would have concluded that this Mary could not have been the same Mary mentioned in Luke 8: 2, namely Mary Magdalene.

However, John 11 mentions these two sisters who lived in Bethany, together with their brother Lazarus. Although that Mary is not explicitly named Mary Magdalene in John 11, it is clear from the context that that was who she was.

In other words, the Mary mentioned in this passage in Luke was none other than Mary Magdalene. Luke must have gathered his information about Mary Magdalene and Mary the sister of Martha from different sources who were not aware of each other.

The fact that Jesus enjoyed hospitality in the home of these sisters is a sign that they must have been Essenes, who were known for their hospitality towards other members of their sect.

When Martha complained that Mary did not help her with her preparations but sat with Jesus, he gave an enigmatic answer: "Mary has chosen the good part, which will not be taken away from her." It may simply mean that she has chosen to be educated by Jesus regarding his message, but it may also be a hint of a romantic relationship and that her love for Jesus would not be taken from her. If that is the case, it may explain the anointment of Jesus' feet by Mary, as described in John 11. A romantic relationship, though, seems rather less likely because Jesus, as an Essene and Nazirite, may have chosen to stay celibate.

Jesus' Teaching on Prayer
Luke 11: 5–8

5.	He said to them, "Which of you, if you go to a friend at midnight, and tell him, `Friend, lend me three loaves of bread,
6.	for a friend of mine has come to me from a journey, and I have nothing to set before him,`
7.	and he from within will answer and say, `Don`t bother me. The door is now shut, and my children are with me in bed. I can`t get up and give it to you`?
8.	I tell you, although he will not rise and give it to him because he is his friend, yet because of his persistence, he will get up and give him as many as he needs.

The moral of this story is that one should not give up praying to God. We can trust our Creator to be more willing to help us than this lousy neighbor who initially could not be bothered to help his friend.

Jesus, as a good Essene, cherished the virtues of hospitality and generosity.

The Plot of the Pharisees and Scribes
Luke 11: 53–54; 12: 1

53.	As he said these things to them, the scribes and the Pharisees began to be terribly angry, and to draw many things out of him;
54.	laying in wait for him, and seeking to catch him in something he might say, that they might accuse him.
1.	Meanwhile, when a multitude of many thousands had gathered together, so much so that they trampled on each other, he began to tell his disciples first of all, "Beware of the yeast of the Pharisees, which is hypocrisy.

This is, yet again, a report of members of the religious elite in Jerusalem who sought to undermine Jesus and his propagation of the kingdom of God.

That prompted Jesus to warn his audience against "the yeast of the Pharisees". This expression is mentioned in another context in Matt 16:6 and Mark 8:15. Here, Jesus equates their bad influence (the yeast) with their hypocrisy – their tendency to behave very piously, but without real love for God.

It is not clear where this crowd of thousands of people gathered to hear Jesus. One can only wonder how he made himself heard without a public address system.

Turn from Your Sins
Luke 13: 1–5

1.	Now there were some present at the same time who told him about the Galileans, whose blood Pilate had mixed with their sacrifices.

2.	Jesus answered them, "Do you think that these Galileans were worse sinners than all the other Galileans, because they suffered such things?
3.	I tell you, no, but, unless you repent, you will all perish in the same way.
4.	Or those eighteen, on whom the tower in Siloam fell, and killed them; do you think that they were worse offenders than all the men who dwell in Jerusalem?
5.	I tell you, no, but, unless you repent, you will all perish in the same way."

Jesus evidently saw the killing of some Galileans while they were bringing sacrifices and the deaths of the people on whom the tower of Siloam collapsed as a punishment from God. The only way to escape from such a fate is to repent and obey God's laws.

Parable of the Fig Tree
Luke 13: 6–9

6.	He spoke this parable. "A certain man had a fig tree planted in his vineyard, and he came seeking fruit on it, and found none.
7.	He said to the vine dresser, `Behold, these three years I came seeking fruit on this fig tree, and found none. Cut it down. Why does it waste the soil?`
8.	He answered, `Lord, leave it alone this year also, until I dig around it, and fertilize it.
9.	If it bears fruit, fine; but if not, after that, you can cut it down.`"

For Jesus, this fig tree was a symbol of the corrupt and luxury-loving Jerusalem elite who opposed him and refused to take his message seriously. He was willing to give these men some more time to repent but they had to know that he would deal with them when he became king.

Jesus Heals a Woman on the Sabbath
Luke 13: 10–17

10.	He was teaching in one of the synagogues on the Sabbath day.
11.	Behold, there was a woman who had a spirit of infirmity eighteen years, and she was bent over, and could in no way lift herself up.
12.	When Jesus saw her, he called her, and said to her, "Woman, you are freed from your infirmity."
13.	He laid his hands on her, and immediately she stood up straight, and glorified God.
14.	The ruler of the synagogue, being moved with indignation because Jesus had healed on the Sabbath, answered to the multitude, "There are six days in which men ought to work. Therefore come on those days and be healed, and not on the Sabbath day!"
15.	Therefore the Lord answered him, "You hypocrites! Doesn't each one of you free his ox or his donkey from the stall on the Sabbath, and lead him away to water?
16.	Ought not this woman, being a daughter of Abraham, whom Satan had bound eighteen long years, to have been freed from this bondage on the Sabbath day?"

> 17. As he said these things, all his adversaries were put to shame, and all the multitude rejoiced for all the glorious things that were done by him.

Jesus, as an Essene, thought that charity and compassion was more important than observing all sorts of ceremonial laws, like doing nothing at all on the Sabbath.

Jesus Laments Jerusalem
Luke 13: 31–35

> 31. On that same day, some Pharisees came, saying to him, "Get out of here, and go away, for Herod wants to kill you."
> 32. He said to them, "Go and tell that fox, 'Behold, I cast out demons and perform cures today and tomorrow, and the third day I complete my mission.
> 33. Nevertheless I must go on my way today and tomorrow and the next day, for it can't be that a prophet perish out of Jerusalem.'
> 34. *"Jerusalem, Jerusalem, that kills the prophets, and stones those who are sent to her! How often I wanted to gather your children together, like a hen gathers her own brood under her wings, and you refused!*
> 35. *Behold, your house is left to you desolate. I tell you, you will not see me, until you say, 'Blessed is he who comes in the name of the Lord!'"*

A part of Q, printed here in italics, was incorporated by Luke into a longer narrative.

There were some Pharisees who were well disposed towards Jesus since they warned him against Herod Antipas, the superstitious ruler of Galilee, who regarded him as a resurrected John the Baptist and wanted to get rid of him. It may also be that Herod took Jesus' campaign to resurrect the Davidic dynasty seriously and he wanted to stop that to save his own position.

Jesus sent a cheeky message to Herod, calling him a fox and declaring that he still has work to do in Galilee, like casting out demons like Herod, before he had to go as a prophet to Jerusalem. Luke added to this disrespectful message from one king to another king a description of Jesus' lament over the elite in Jerusalem, the place where prophets, like him, were killed.

Jesus Heals a Sick Man on the Sabbath
Luke 14: 1–6

1.	It happened, when he went into the house of one of the rulers of the Pharisees on a Sabbath to eat bread, that they were watching him.
2.	Behold, a certain man who had dropsy was in front of him.
3.	Jesus, answering, spoke to the lawyers and Pharisees, saying, "Is it lawful to heal on the Sabbath?"
4.	But they were silent. He took him, and healed him, and let him go.
5.	He answered them, "Which of you, if your son or an ox fell into a well, wouldn't immediately pull him out on a Sabbath day?"
6.	They couldn't answer him regarding these things.

Jesus was a guest on the Sabbath in the home of an important Pharisee. A sick man was healed by Jesus and he explained this action on the Sabbath as an act of mercy, just as when anybody would rescue his son or an animal who had fallen into a well on the

Sabbath. The Pharisees and lawyers who were present could not refute his argument.

Humility and Hospitality
Luke 14: 7–15

7.	He spoke a parable to those who were invited, when he noticed how they chose the best seats, and said to them,
8.	"When you are invited by anyone to a marriage feast, don't sit in the best seat, since perhaps a more honorable man than you might be invited by him,
9.	and he who invited both of you would come and tell you, `Make room for this man.` Then you would begin, with shame, to take the lowest place.
10.	But when you are invited, go and sit in the lowest place, so that when he who invited you comes, he may tell you, `Friend, move up higher.` Then you will have glory in the presence of all who sit at the table with you.
11.	*For everyone who exalts himself will be humbled, and whoever humbles himself will be exalted."*
12.	He also said to the one who had invited him, "When you make a dinner or a supper, don't call your friends, nor your brothers, nor your kinsmen, nor rich neighbors, or perhaps they might also return the favor, and pay you back.
13.	But when you make a feast, ask the poor, the maimed, the lame, or the blind;
14.	and you will be blessed, because they don't have the resources to repay you. For you will be repaid in the resurrection of the righteous."

> 15. When one of those who sat at the table with him heard these things, he said to him, "Blessed is he who will feast in the kingdom of God!"

As an Essene, Jesus entertained a simple lifestyle, believed in hospitality, and he disapproved of the arrogance of rich and powerful people.

Luke incorporated a saying from Q (printed in italics) into this story of how Jesus taught people about humility and humbleness. One of those who listened to him, concluded that the poor (the Essenes) and the outcasts would receive seats of honor in the coming kingdom of God.

The Cost of Being a Disciple
Luke 14: 25–33

> 25. Now great multitudes went with him. He turned and said to them,
> 26. "If any man comes to me, and doesn't hate his own father, mother, wife, children, brothers, and sisters, yes, and his own life also, he can't be my disciple.
> 27. Whoever doesn't bear his own cross, and come after me, can't be my disciple.
> 28. For which of you, desiring to build a tower, doesn't first sit down and count the cost, to see if he has enough to complete it?
> 29. Or perhaps, when he has laid a foundation, and is not able to finish, everyone who sees begins to mock him,
> 30. saying, 'This man began to build, and wasn't able to finish.'
> 31. Or what king, as he goes to encounter another king in war, will not sit down first and consider whether he is able with

> ten thousand to meet him who comes against him with twenty thousand?
> 32. Or else, while the other is yet a great way off, he sends an envoy, and asks for conditions of peace.
> 33. So therefore whoever of you who doesn't renounce all that he has, he can't be my disciple.

The second part of this passage, which is technically part of L, seems to be a continuation of the first part, which comes from Q (printed in italics). It is, therefore, likely that the whole passage was taken by Luke from Q, while Matthew used only the first part.

The point that Jesus wanted to make is that one should consider the costs of following him. It could even lead to rifts in families and hardship. He illustrated the process of considering the costs of discipleship with somebody who had to calculate the costs he would incur when he planned to build a tower, or how a king would calculate his chances of success in a war if his adversary had a larger army.

The Friends of Jesus
Luke 15: 1–2

> 1. Now all the tax collectors and sinners were coming close to him to hear him.
> 2. The Pharisees and the scribes murmured, saying, "This man welcomes sinners, and eats with them."

Jesus lived as a simple man, true to his Essene background, even if he was a descendant of King David and aspired to the throne in Jerusalem. The result was that ordinary folk, even outcasts, such as tax collectors and people with tainted reputations, flocked to him.

His message, that places of honor would be given to the humble people in his kingdom certainly also played a role.

It was to be expected that some influential Pharisees and teachers of the Law would disapprove of this behavior of Jesus.

The Lost Son
Luke 15: 11–32

11.	He said, "A certain man had two sons.
12.	The younger of them said to his father, `Father, give me my share of your property.` He divided his living to them.
13.	Not many days after, the younger son gathered all of this together and took his journey into a far country. There he wasted his property with riotous living.
14.	When he had spent all of it, there arose a severe famine in that country, and he began to be in need.
15.	He went and joined himself to one of the citizens of that country, and he sent him into his fields to feed pigs.
16.	He wanted to fill his belly with the husks that the pigs ate, but no one gave him any.
17.	But when he came to himself he said, `How many hired servants of my father's have bread enough to spare, and I'm dying with hunger!
18.	I will get up and go to my father, and will tell him, "Father, I have sinned against heaven, and in your sight.
19.	I am no more worthy to be called your son. Make me as one of your hired servants."`
20.	He arose, and came to his father. But while he was still far off, his father saw him, and was moved with compassion, and ran, and fell on his neck, and kissed him.

21.	The son said to him, `Father, I have sinned against heaven, and in your sight. I am no more worthy to be called your son.`
22.	But the father said to his servants, `Bring out the best robe, and put it on him. Put a ring on his hand, and shoes on his feet.
23.	Bring the fattened calf, kill it, and let us eat, and celebrate;
24.	for this, my son, was dead, and is alive again. He was lost, and is found.` They began to be merry.
25.	Now his elder son was in the field. As he came and drew near to the house, he heard music and dancing.
26.	He called one of the servants to him, and asked what was going on.
27.	He said to him, `Your brother has come, and your father has killed the fattened calf, because he has received him safe and sound.`
28.	But he was angry, and would not go in. Therefore his father came out, and begged him.
29.	But he answered his father, 'Behold, these many years I served you, and I never disobeyed a commandment of yours, and you never gave me a goat, that I might celebrate with my friends.
30.	But when this, your son, came, who has devoured your living with prostitutes, you killed the fattened calf for him.`
31.	He said to him, `Son, you are always with me, and all that is mine is yours.
32.	But it was appropriate to celebrate and be glad, for this, your brother, was dead, and is alive again. He was lost, and is found.`"

This parable of the Lost Son, is one of the best-known stories that Jesus told, although only Luke included it in his gospel.

Jesus made more than one point with this tale:

- The lost son is a symbol of a repentant sinner who returned to God.
- The father in this story symbolizes God, who is willing to forgive and accept repentant sinners.
- The elder brother, who was dissatisfied with the reception his younger brother got, is a representative of the proud and haughty Pharisees and teachers of the Law who disapproved of Jesus who made friends with outcasts and other undesirable elements.

Albrecht Dürer: The Prodigal Son

The Shrewd Manager
Luke 16:1–13

1.	He said also to his disciples, "There was a certain rich man, who had a manager. The same was accused to him of wasting his possessions.
2.	He called him, and said to him, 'What is this that I hear about you? Give an accounting of your management, for you can no longer be manager.'
3.	The steward said within himself, 'What will I do, seeing

	that my lord is taking away the management position from me? I don't have strength to dig. I am ashamed to beg.
4.	I know what I will do, so that when I am removed from management, they may receive me into their houses.'
5.	Calling each one of his lord's debtors to him, he said to the first, 'How much do you owe to my lord?'
6.	He said, 'A hundred batos of oil.' He said to him, 'Take your bill, and sit down quickly and write fifty.'
7.	Then said he to another, 'How much do you owe?' He said, 'A hundred cors of wheat.' He said to him, 'Take your bill, and write eighty.'
8.	His lord commended the unrighteous steward because he had done wisely, for the sons of this world are, in their own generation, wiser than the sons of the light.
9.	I tell you, make for yourselves friends by means of unrighteous mammon, so that when you fail, they may receive you into the eternal tents.
10.	He who is faithful in a very little is faithful also in much. He who is unrighteous in a very little is also unrighteous in much.
11.	If therefore you have not been faithful in the unrighteous mammon, who will commit to your trust the true riches?
12.	If you have not been faithful in that which is another's, who will give you that which is your own?
13.	*No servant can serve two masters, for either he will hate the one, and love the other; or else he will hold to one, and despise the other. You aren't able to serve God and mammon."*

Jesus told this story about this manager who was guilty of maladministration and was fired by his employer. The manager abused his position as manager for the last time by reducing the debts of some debtors of his boss by coking the books and thereby won their gratitude and friendship. His boss, who was not so honest himself, praised his ex-manager for his cleverness, although he had lost some income.

Jesus told this story to illustrate how people bought themselves friends through dishonest deals, which was certainly aimed at the rotten and rich religious leaders in Jerusalem who used their money to win friends and influence people.

According to Jesus, honesty is always preferable. It is not possible to worship the god of money (Μαμωνᾶς – *Mamonas*) and also serve the Gd of Israel – something the false priests in Jerusalem tried to accomplish. Luke attached a saying from Q into this story as the punchline.

Jesus Criticizes the Rich Pharisees
Luke 16: 14–15

14.	The Pharisees, who were lovers of money, also heard all these things, and they scoffed at him.
15.	He said to them, "You are those who justify yourselves in the sight of men, but God knows your hearts. For that which is exalted among men is an abomination in the sight of God.

There were some rich Pharisees who felt offended by Jesus' condemnation of their love of money. He retorted that God knows what is in the hearts of men, although these men may seem to be honorable people superficially.

The Rich Man and Lazarus
Luke 16: 19–31

19.	"Now there was a certain rich man, and he was clothed in purple and fine linen, living in luxury every day.
20.	A certain beggar, named Lazarus, was laid at his gate, full of sores,
21.	and desiring to be fed with the crumbs that fell from the rich man's table. Yes, even the dogs came and licked his sores.
22.	It happened that the beggar died, and that he was carried away by the angels to Abraham's bosom. The rich man also died, and was buried.
23.	In Hades, he lifted up his eyes, being in torment, and saw Abraham far off, and Lazarus at his bosom.
24.	He cried and said, Father Abraham, have mercy on me, and send Lazarus, that he may dip the tip of his finger in water, and cool my tongue! For I am in anguish in this flame.
25.	But Abraham said, Son, remember that you, in your lifetime, received your good things, and Lazarus, in like manner, bad things. But now here he is comforted and you are in anguish.
26.	Besides all this, between us and you there is a great gulf fixed, that those who want to pass from here to you are not able, and that none may cross over from there to us.
27.	He said, I ask you therefore, father, that you would send him to my father's house;
28.	for I have five brothers, that he may testify to them, lest they also come into this place of torment.
29.	But Abraham said to him, They have Moses and the prophets. Let them listen to them.

30.	He said, No, father Abraham, but if one goes to them from the dead, they will repent.
31.	He said to him, If they don't listen to Moses and the prophets, neither will they be persuaded if one rises from the dead."

The story of the rich man and Lazarus is another famous story that Jesus told to his listeners.

As could be expected from an Essene, he depicted the rich man in the darkest colors possible. He was without generosity, lived in luxury, but ended up in Hades, in hell, after his death and a beautiful and expensive funeral. On the other hand, Jesus' sympathy lay with the poor beggar, Lazarus, who lived in the greatest misery, but was taken by the angels after his death to Abraham's bosom, another name for heaven.

Jesus taught that a wide unbridgeable canyon separates heaven and hell, which made it impossible to move from one side to the other.

Jesus advised his listeners to pay attention to the commandments, warnings, and promises contained in the Scriptures to prevent eternal torture after death.

Faith
Luke 17: 5–10

5.	The apostles said to the Lord, "Increase our faith."
6.	*The Lord said, "If you had faith as a grain of mustard seed, you would tell this sycamore tree, Be uprooted, and be planted in the sea, and it would obey you.*

> 7. But who is there of you, having a servant plowing or keeping sheep, that will say, when he comes in from the field, Come immediately and sit down at the table,
> 8. and will not rather tell him, Prepare my supper, clothe yourself properly, and serve me, while I eat and drink. Afterward you will eat and drink?
> 9. Does he thank that servant because he did the things that were commanded? I think not.
> 10. Even so you also, when you have done all the things that are commanded you, say, We are unworthy servants. We have done our duty."

The disciples wished to have more faith. Jesus made it clear that they must see themselves as servants of God. Their service will automatically increase their faith, a faith that could even command a tree to be uprooted and plunge into the sea. As a good Essene, Jesus required of his followers to serve God dutifully and to adhere to all the commandments and laws of God.

Luke built this passage around a saying from Q (printed in italics).

Jesus Heals Ten Men
Luke 17: 11–19

> 11. It happened, as he was on his way to Jerusalem, that he was passing along the borders of Samaria and Galilee.
> 12. As he entered into a certain village, ten men who were lepers met him, who stood far away.
> 13. They lifted up their voices, saying, "Jesus, Master, have mercy on us!"
> 14. When he saw them, he said to them, "Go and show yourselves

> to the priests." It happened, as they went, they were cleansed.
> 15. One of them, when he saw that he was healed, turned back, glorifying God with a loud voice.
> 16. He fell on his face at his feet, giving him thanks. He was a Samaritan.
> 17. Jesus answered, "Weren't the ten cleansed? But where are the nine?
> 18. Were there none found who returned to give glory to God, except this stranger?"
> 19. He said to him, "Get up, and go your way. Your faith has healed you."

Jesus told this story of the ten lepers of Samaria who were healed to emphasize the importance of gratitude towards God for all the good things in life, which are signs of his grace.

The Coming of the Kingdom
Luke 17: 20–22

> 20. Being asked by the Pharisees when the kingdom of God would come, he answered them, "The kingdom of God doesn't come with observation;
> 21. neither will they say, Look, here! or, Look, there! for behold, the kingdom of God is within you."
> 22. He said to the disciples, "The days will come, when you will desire to see one of the days of the Son of Man, and you will not see it.

Some Pharisees wanted to know from Jesus when the promised kingdom of God could be expected. He answered that the kingdom was already "within" them. An alternative and more meaningful translation of the words used for "within you" (ἐντός ὑμῶν – *entos humon*) would be: "in your midst". With that, he indicated that the kingdom had already arrived in his person, the king-in-waiting.

The Widow and the Judge
Luke 18: 1–8

1.	He also spoke a parable to them that they must always pray, and not give up,
2.	saying, "A certain judge was in a city, who didn't fear God, and didn't respect man.
3.	A widow was in that city, and she came often to him, saying, Defend me from my adversary!
4.	He wouldn't for a while, but afterward he said to himself, Though I don't fear God, nor respect man,
5.	yet because this widow bothers me, I will defend her, or else she will wear me out by her continual coming."
6.	The Lord said, "Listen to what the unrighteous judge says.
7.	Wont God avenge his elect, who are crying out to him day and night, and yet he exercises patience with them?
8.	I tell you that he will avenge them quickly. Nevertheless, when the Son of Man comes, will he find faith on the earth?"

Jesus contrasted God with a lazy, cynical, and unsympathetic judge. This judge had to prepare a judgment in favor of this poor widow and did it at last because she kept on enquiring about the outcome of her case and he eventually gave his verdict because he wanted to get rid of her. According to Jesus, God is different and He is always willing to grant us our prayers.

The Pharisee and the Tax Collector
Luke 18: 9–14

9.	He spoke also this parable to certain people who were convinced of their own righteousness, and who despised all others.
10.	"Two men went up into the temple to pray; one was a Pharisee, and the other was a tax collector.
11.	The Pharisee stood and prayed to himself like this: God, I thank you, that I am not like the rest of men, extortioners, unrighteous, adulterers, or even like this tax collector.
12.	I fast twice in the week. I give tithes of all that I get.
13.	But the tax collector, standing far away, wouldn't even lift up as his eyes to heaven, but beat his breast, saying, God, be merciful to me, a sinner!
14.	*I tell you, this man went down to his house justified rather than the other; for everyone who exalts himself will be humbled, but he who humbles himself will be exalted."*

The last verse in this passage comes from the reconstructed Q Document. It is, however, clear that the preceding verses are connected to this verse and that leads to the conclusion that the whole passage came from Q.

In this parable, Jesus draws a contrast between a self–righteous, proud, and hypocritical Pharisee and a despised tax collector. The Pharisee wanted to impress God with his wonderful qualities, admirable activities, and meritorious achievements, while the tax collector only begged for mercy from God.

With this parable, Jesus wanted to teach his followers the Essene virtues of humility and modesty.

Jesus and Zacchaeus
Luke 19: 1–10

1.	He entered and was passing through Jericho.
2.	There was a man named Zacchaeus. He was a chief tax collector, and he was rich.
3.	He was trying to see who Jesus was, and couldn't because of the crowd, because he was short.
4.	He ran on ahead, and climbed up into a sycamore tree to see him, for he was to pass that way.
5.	When Jesus came to the place, he looked up and saw him, and said to him, "Zacchaeus, hurry and come down, for today I must stay at your house."
6.	He hurried, came down, and received him joyfully.
7.	When they saw it, they all murmured, saying, "He has gone in to lodge with a man who is a sinner."
8.	Zacchaeus stood and said to the Lord, "Behold, Lord, half of my goods I give to the poor. If I have wrongfully exacted anything of anyone, I restore four times as much."
9.	Jesus said to him, "Today, salvation has come to this house, because he also is a son of Abraham.
10.	For the Son of Man came to seek and to save that which was lost."

Tax collectors were detested and loathed in those days because they were regarded as traitors and collaborators of the hated pagan Roman authorities and because they were often dishonest by collecting more taxes than were due and keeping some of the surplus for themselves.

This incident tells of a rich tax collector in Jericho with the name of Zacchaeus (Greek: Ζακχαῖος – *Zakchaîos*; Hebrew: זכי – *Zaki*) and whose name, ironically, meant "pure, innocent".

He wished to meet Jesus and he got into a sycamore tree to see better due to the crowd that surrounded Jesus. Jesus must have noticed the man and asked the bystanders who he was. Thereupon, Jesus announced that he would visit him in his home.

This visit had such a profound influence upon him that he announced that he would change his ways and perform restitution to those he had wronged to prove his repentance. Jesus declared that it was his task to reach out to those who were lost in sin.

Jesus Weeps over Jerusalem
Luke 19: 41–44

41.	When he drew near, he saw the city and wept over it,
42.	saying, "If you, even you, had known today the things which belong to your peace! But now, they are hidden from your eyes.
43.	For the days will come on you, when your enemies will throw up a barricade against you, surround you, hem you in on every side,
44.	and will dash you and your children within you to the ground. They will not leave in you one stone on another, because you didn't know the time of your visitation."

Luke presented these words of lament over Jerusalem by Jesus as a prophecy regarding the destruction of the city by the Romans, four decades later. It is unlikely that Jesus ever spoke these words because they are a description of what happened much later. Jesus saw himself as the legitimate king of Israel and Jerusalem was supposed to be his capital.

The Need to be Watchful
Luke 21: 34–38

34.	"So be careful, or your hearts will be loaded down with carousing, drunkenness, and cares of this life, and that day will come on you suddenly.
35.	For it will come like a snare on all those who dwell on the surface of all the earth.
36.	Therefore be watchful all the time, asking that you may be counted worthy to escape all these things that will happen, and to stand before the Son of Man."
37.	Every day Jesus was teaching in the temple, and every night he went out, and spent the night on the mountain that is called Olivet.
38.	All the people came early in the morning to him in the temple, to hear him.

The first part of this passage was again presented as a prophecy by Jesus regarding the destruction of Jerusalem, which amounts to a description of what happened decades later. It follows Luke's variation of the purported prophecy by Jesus of the destruction of the temple and the fall of Jerusalem, which was taken from Mark.

Luke also reported that Jesus and his disciples slept on the Mount of Olives, outside Jerusalem. There were olive groves where they could camp out. Jesus taught in one of the temple courtyards during the day.

The Argument about Greatness
Luke 22: 24–30

24.	There arose also a contention among them, which of them was considered to be greatest.
25.	He said to them, "The kings of the Gentiles lord it over them, and those who have authority over them are called benefactors.
26.	But not so with you. But one who is the greater among you, let him become as the lesser, and one who is governing, as one who serves.
27.	For who is greater, one who sits at the table, or one who serves? Isn't it he who sits at the table? But I am in the midst of you as one who serves.
28.	But you are those who have continued with me in my temptations.
29.	I appoint to you a kingdom, even as my Father appointed to me,
30.	that you may eat and drink at my table in my kingdom. You will sit on thrones, judging the twelve tribes of Israel."

Jesus, the Essene, gave his disciples a lesson in humility and meekness after they started arguing about who would be regarded as the most important in Jesus' coming kingdom.

Jesus, though, promised them that they would be appointed as his councilors who would judge the twelve tribes of Israel, the restored nation of which Jesus would become the king.

Purse, Bag, and Sword
Luke 22: 35–38

35.	He said to them, "When I sent you out without purse, and wallet, and shoes, did you lack anything?" They said, "Nothing."

36.	Then he said to them, "But now, whoever has a purse, let him take it, and likewise a wallet. Whoever has none, let him sell his cloak, and buy a sword.
37.	For I tell you that this which is written must still be fulfilled in me: He was counted with the lawless. For that which concerns me has an end."
38.	They said, "Lord, behold, here are two swords." He said to them, "That is enough."

Luke 9: 1–6 contains the report of how Jesus sent his twelve disciples out to recruit supporters for his campaign to prepare the coming of the kingdom of God. He ordered them to rely on the hospitality of their hosts as was the custom in Essene communities. Here, the disciples confirmed that they lacked nothing when they went out because their hosts provided in all their needs.

Jesus advised them at this stage, though, to be prepared for a crisis because he was confident that the kingdom would be established soon. For that purpose, they had to have money of their own and swords to defend themselves, if necessary.

Jesus is Sent to Herod
Luke 23: 6–12

6.	But when Pilate heard Galilee mentioned, he asked if the man was a Galilean.
7.	When he found out that he was in Herod's jurisdiction, he sent him to Herod, who was also in Jerusalem in those days.
8.	Now when Herod saw Jesus, he was exceedingly glad, for he had wanted to see him for a long time, because he had heard many things about him. He hoped to see some miracle done by him.

9.	He questioned him with many words, but he gave no answers.
10.	The chief priests and the scribes stood, vehemently accusing him.
11.	Herod with his soldiers humiliated him and mocked him. Dressing him in curious clothing, they sent him back to Pilate.
12.	Herod and Pilate became friends with each other that very day, for before that they were enemies with each other.

Luke is the only gospel to contain this story of how Jesus was sent to Herod Antipas after he had been arrested and delivered to Pilate.

It is possible to wonder how Luke got hold of this story because none of Jesus' followers seemed to have been present on this occasion and to report on it at a later stage.

Judge Cohn pointed out that there was little time according to Luke's own time frame for this meeting with Herod. Luke wrote that the Sanhedrin only met in the morning (Luke 22: 66). After having found Jesus ostensibly guilty of blasphemy, Jesus was passed on to Pilate. It would have been at least 10:00 before Pilate was finished with Jesus. Jesus was already hanging for a considerable time on the cross at noon when darkness ascended onto the land. That means that there would have been very little time, if any, to go to Herod and to return to Pilate for the final death sentence.[239]

Jesus Talks to the Women of Jerusalem
Luke 23: 27–31

27.	A great multitude of the people followed him, including women who also mourned and lamented him.

---
[239] Cohn, *The Trial and Death of Jesus,* 180–81.

28.	But Jesus, turning to them, said, "Daughters of Jerusalem, don't weep for me, but weep for yourselves and for your children.
29.	For behold, the days are coming in which they will say, Blessed are the barren, the wombs that never bore, and the breasts that never nursed.
30.	Then will they begin to tell the mountains, Fall on us! and to the hills, Cover us.
31.	For if they do these things in the green tree, what will be done in the dry?"

It is hard to imagine how Jesus could have been able to address the women of Jerusalem with a rather lengthy speech while he was led away to be crucified and he was guarded by a company of soldiers and he was carrying his cross.

His words to them amounted to a prophecy about the destruction of Jerusalem decades later, which Jesus certainly never foresaw. This episode must be an invention, either of Luke or one of his sources. It seems to be an embellishment of Mark's story that Jesus, the great prophet, must have predicted the destruction of Jerusalem and its temple.

The Two Crucified Criminals
Luke 23: 40–43

40.	But the other answered, and rebuking him said, "Don't you even fear God, seeing you are in the same condemnation?
41.	And we indeed justly, for we receive the due reward for our deeds, but this man has done nothing wrong."
42.	He said to Jesus, "Lord, remember me when you come into your kingdom."

> 43. He said to him, "Most assuredly I tell you, today you will be with me in Paradise."

Luke copied Mark's narrative that two bandits were crucified with Jesus. It was reported that both mocked Jesus, just as the crowd of onlookers did. Luke changed – or corrected – this by writing that one of these crooked scoundrels repented and begged Jesus to remember him when his kingdom came.

If this story is true, which is possible, it demonstrates that Jesus still believed at that stage while hanging on the cross that an army of angels with wonder weapons would sweep down from the sky onto Jerusalem to rescue him and to vanquish all the enemies of the Jews. Jesus, therefore, promised this man that he would be with him in Paradise – the glorious kingdom – that very same day.

Peter Visits the Tomb
Luke 24: 11 –12

> 11. These words seemed to them to be nonsense, and they didn't believe them.
> 12. But Peter got up and ran to the tomb. Stooping and looking in, he saw the strips of linen lying by themselves, and he departed to his home, wondering what had happened.

Luke added these two verses to Mark's story that the women found an empty tomb where Jesus had been placed after his body was taken from the cross. It seems that the apostles wouldn't believe them but that Peter wanted confirmation that the tomb was indeed empty.

The statement that Peter went to his home is a mistranslation. It is merely said in Greek that he went away on his own.

The Walk to Emmaus
Luke 24–13–35

13.	Behold, two of them were going that very day a village named Emmaus, which was sixty stadia from Jerusalem.
14.	They talked with each other about all of these things which had happened.
15.	It happened, while they talked and questioned together, that Jesus himself came near, and went with them.
16.	But their eyes were kept from recognizing him.
17.	He said to them, "What are you talking about as you walk, and are sad?"
18.	One of them, named Cleopas, answered him, "Are you the only one travelling in Jerusalem who doesn't know the things which have happened there in these days?"
19.	He said to them, "What things?" They said to him, "The things concerning Jesus, the Nazarene, who was a prophet mighty in deed and word before God and all the people;
20.	and how the chief priests and our rulers delivered him up to be condemned to death, and crucified him.
21.	But we hoped that it was he who would redeem Israel. Yes, and besides all this, it is now the third day since these things happened.
22.	Also, certain women of our company amazed us, having been early at the tomb;
23.	and when they didn't find his body, they came saying that they had also seen a vision of angels, who said that he was alive.
24.	Some of us went to the tomb, and found it just like the women had said, but they didn't see him."

25.	He said to them, "Foolish men, and slow of heart to believe in all that the prophets have spoken!
26.	Didn't the Christ have to suffer these things, and to enter into his glory?"
27.	Beginning from Moses and from all the prophets, he interpreted to them in all the scriptures the things concerning himself.
28.	They drew near to the village, where they were going, and he acted like he would go further.
29.	They urged him, saying, "Stay with us, for it is almost evening, and the day is almost over." He went in to stay with them.
30.	It happened, when he had sat down at the table with them, he took the bread and gave thanks. Breaking it, he gave to them.
31.	Their eyes were opened, and they recognized him, and he vanished out of their sight.
32.	They said one to another, "Wasn't our heart burning within us, while he spoke to us along the way, and while he opened the scriptures to us?"
33.	They rose up that very hour, and returned to Jerusalem, and found the eleven gathered together, and those who were with them,
34.	saying, "The Lord is risen indeed, and has appeared to Simon!"
35.	They related the things that happened along the way, and how he was recognized by them in the breaking of the bread.

This story, as it is written, seems to be improbable, especially due to the supernatural element of Jesus just disappearing into thin air – despite the next passage where Jesus told his disciples that he was not a spirit or a ghost but a man of flesh and blood (Luke 24: 39).

There may, nevertheless, be an element of truth in this story. It was established in the analysis of the Proto-Gospel of John and Mark's Gospel that Jesus had indeed survived the crucifixion.

It is, however, unlikely that somebody who was recovering from severe wounds, especially to his feet, would have been able to walk from Jerusalem to Emmaus – unless this incident took place a considerable time after Jesus had survived the cross – months or years later.

The purpose of this story was obviously to demonstrate that Jesus' crucifixion and resurrection was supposed to have been foretold in the Old Testament – which is not the case, as has been pointed out on different occasions in this book.

Albrecht Durer: Christ and the Disciples at Emmaus (1511)

Jesus Appears to his Disciples
Luke 24: 36–49

36.	As they said these things, Jesus himself stood in the midst of them, and said to them, "Peace be to you."
37.	But they were terrified and filled with fear, and supposed that they saw a spirit.

38.	He said to them, "Why are you troubled? Why do questionings arise in your hearts?
39.	See my hands and my feet, that it is I myself. Touch me and see, for a spirit doesn't have flesh and bones, as you see that I have."
40.	When he had said this, he showed them his hands and his feet.
41.	While they still didn't believe for joy, and wondered, he said to them, "Do you have anything here to eat?"
42.	They gave him a piece of a broiled fish and some honeycomb.
43.	He took it, and ate in front of them.
44.	He said to them, "This is what I told you, while I was still with you, that all things must be fulfilled, which are written in the law of Moses, the prophets, and the psalms, concerning me."
45.	Then he opened their minds, that they might understand the scriptures.
46.	He said to them, "Thus it is written, and thus it was necessary for the Christ to suffer and to rise from the dead the third day,
47.	and that repentance and remission of sins should be preached in his name to all the nations, beginning at Jerusalem.
48.	You are witnesses of these things.
49.	Behold, I send forth the promise of my Father on you. But wait in the city of Jerusalem until you are clothed with power from on high."

It may be accepted as fact that Jesus survived the crucifixion and that he had meetings with his disciples afterwards.

That he was a man of flesh and bones – and not somebody with a spiritual or heavenly body as Paul argued in 1 Cor 15 – is borne out by the fact that Jesus confirmed that he was not a spirit or a phantom, that he invited his disciples to inspect his limbs and that he begged for something to eat. They served him some fish – perhaps an indication that all this happened in Gallie, at the lake..

The object of this story was to emphasize, yet again, that the Old Testament was supposed to contain prophecies regarding Jesus' crucifixion and resurrection. It has been shown that the Old Testament nowhere predicted that the Messiah would be executed. If there are no prophecies in this regard, then his resurrecting would also not have been predicted.[240]

How Jesus managed to move around and visit his disciples is a mystery – unless this meeting took place a considerable time after Jesus' resurrection. This report may contain some legendary and mythological elements.

The Ascension
Luke 24: 50–53

50.	He led them out as far as to Bethany, and he lifted up his hands, and blessed them.
51.	It happened, while he blessed them, that he withdrew from them, and was carried up into heaven.
52.	They worshipped him, and returned to Jerusalem with great joy,

---

[240] Wright, *The Self-Revelation of God"*, 199.

53.	and were continually in the temple, praising and blessing God. Amen.

According to Luke's Gospel, Jesus appeared to his disciples in Jerusalem and ascended to heaven from Bethany, a village not far from Jerusalem. All three other gospels mentioned explicitly that Jesus met the disciples in Galilee, either on a mountain or next to the Sea of Galilee – far from Jerusalem. These discrepancies place question marks over the accuracy of all these stories.

Jesus left the earth in a similar manner as the prophets Moses and Elijah by being taken up into heaven with his earthly body. This places this passage in the sphere of mythology and certainly not confirmed history.

Introduction to Acts
Acts 1: 1–5

1.	The first book I wrote, Theophilus, concerned all that Jesus began both to do and to teach,
2.	until the day in which he was received up, after he had given commandment through the Holy Spirit to the apostles whom he had chosen.
3.	To these he also showed himself alive after his suffering by many proofs, appearing to them over a period of forty days, and spoke about Gods kingdom.
4.	Being assembled together with them, he charged them, "Don't depart from Jerusalem, but wait for the promise of the Father, which you heard from me.
5.	For John indeed baptized with water, but you will be baptized in the Holy Spirit not many days from now."

Luke's second book, the Acts of the Apostles, was dedicated to Theophilus, just as the gospel earlier. It was meant to take the story of Jesus and his followers further.

Jesus ordered his apostles not to leave Jerusalem. He appeared to them repeatedly during a period of forty days. This must be a symbolic number. The Israelites spent forty years in the desert after clearing out from Egypt. Moses stayed forty days on the mountain while receiving the Ten Commandments and Jesus fasted forty days while in the desert after his baptism.

Jesus is Taken up into Heaven
Acts 1: 6–11

6.	Therefore, when they had come together, they asked him, "Lord, are you now restoring the kingdom to Israel?"
7.	He said to them, "It isn't for you to know times or seasons which the Father has set within His own authority.
8.	But you will receive power when the Holy Spirit has come on you. You will be witnesses to me in Jerusalem, in all Judea and Samaria, and to the uttermost parts of the earth."
9.	When he had said these things, as they were looking, he was taken up, and a cloud received him out of their sight.
10.	While they were looking steadfastly into the sky as he went, behold, two men stood by them in white clothing,
11.	who also said, "You men of Galilee, why do you stand looking into the sky? This Jesus, who was received up from you into the sky will come back in the same way as you saw him going into the sky."

This passage starts with a very pertinent question from the disciples who wanted to know when Jesus planned to restore the kingdom of

Israel – something he often promised during his ministry. His answer boiled down to more or less the following: "Heaven alone knows."

It is clear that Luke (and the other evangelists) did not know what happened to Jesus after he had appeared to his disciples and then disappeared. Luke invented a fantastic story with a mythological slant of Jesus levitating towards the sky and disappearing behind the clouds. Two men in white suddenly materialized and announced that the disciples could expect the return of Jesus.

Albrecht Dürer: The Ascension

It is possible that these men clothed in white could have been Essenes and secret accomplices of Jesus who helped to spirit him away. Since Luke's sources could not tell him what had happened after that, he devised the story of the miraculous ascent.

This promised return never happened and Luke (and the other evangelists) had to invent stories to explain Jesus' disappearance. Luke borrowed from Paul the idea that Jesus was taken up into heaven. Paul concluded that Jesus must be in heaven as a divine being on account of his visions and revelations (see Chapter 4). Luke provided a tale to explain how Jesus got there.

The Successor of Judas Iscariot
Acts 1: 12–26

12.	Then they returned to Jerusalem from the mountain called Olivet, which is near Jerusalem, a Sabbath day's journey away.
13.	When they had come in, they went up into the upper chamber, where they were staying; that is Peter, John, James, Andrew, Philip, Thomas, Bartholomew, Matthew, James the son of Alphaeus, Simon the Zealot, and Judas the son of James.
14.	All these with one accord continued steadfastly in prayer and supplication, with the women, and Mary, the mother of Jesus, and with his brothers.
15.	In these days, Peter stood up in the midst of the disciples (and there was a multitude of persons gathered together, about one hundred twenty), and said,
16.	"Brothers, it was necessary that this Scripture should be fulfilled, which the Holy Spirit spoke before by the mouth of David concerning Judas, who was guide to those who took Jesus.
17.	For he was numbered with us, and received his portion in this ministry.
18.	Now this man obtained a field with the reward for his wickedness, and falling headlong, his body burst open, and all his intestines gushed out.
19.	It became known to everyone who lived in Jerusalem that in their language that field was called Akeldama, that is, The field of blood.
20.	For it is written in the book of Psalms, Let his habitation be made desolate, Let no one dwell therein, and, Let another take his office.

21.	Of the men therefore who have accompanied us all the time that the Lord Jesus went in and went out among us,
22.	beginning from the baptism of John, to the day that he was received up from us, of these must one become a witness with us of his resurrection."
23.	They put forward two, Joseph called Barsabbas, who was surnamed Justus, and Matthias.
24.	They prayed, and said, "You, Lord, who know the hearts of all men, show which one of these two you have chosen
25.	to take part in this ministry and apostleship from which Judas fell away, that he might go to his own place."
26.	They drew lots for them, and the lot fell on Matthias, and he was numbered with the eleven apostles.

This passage informed its readers that Jesus flew up into heaven from the Mount of Olives, just outside Jerusalem. According to Luke's Gospel (24: 50–51), he took off from the village of Bethany, some distance away from Jerusalem.

We are, furthermore, informed who the remaining eleven apostles were. They gathered with other disciples, as well as with the mother and brothers of Jesus. Peter announced how Judas Iscariot met his death. He had an accident, fell and his body burst open. With the money with which he had been bribed to betray Jesus, he bought a piece of land.

These details differ from Matt 27: 3–10, however. According to Matthew, he committed suicide by hanging himself and the Sanhedrin used the money he had returned to buy a plot.

It was decided to choose a replacement for him to keep the number of apostles at twelve to symbolize the twelve tribes of Israel.

They evidently still expected to become Jesus' team of twelve councilors when he returned from wherever and restored the kingdom.

The Coming of the Holy Spirit
Acts 2: 1–13

1.	Now when the day of Pentecost had come, they were all with one accord in one place.
2.	Suddenly there came from the sky a sound like the rushing of a mighty wind, and it filled all the house where they were sitting.
3.	Tongues like fire appeared and were distributed to them, and it sat on each one of them.
4.	They were all filled with the Holy Spirit, and began to speak with other languages, as the Spirit gave them the ability to speak.
5.	Now there were dwelling at Jerusalem Jews, devout men, from every nation under the sky.
6.	When this sound was heard, the multitude came together, and were bewildered, because everyone heard them speaking in his own language.
7.	They were all amazed and marveled, saying to one another, "Behold, aren't all these who speak Galileans?
8.	How do we hear, everyone in our own native language?
9.	Parthians, Medes, Elamites, and people from Mesopotamia, Judea, Cappadocia, Pontus, Asia,
10.	Phrygia, Pamphylia, Egypt, the parts of Libya around Cyrene, visitors from Rome, both Jews and proselytes,
11.	Cretans and Arabians: we hear them speaking in our languages the mighty works of God!"

LUKE'S UNIQUE MATERIAL

> 12. They were all amazed, and were perplexed, saying one to another, "What does this mean?"
> 13. Others, mocking, said, "They are filled with new wine."

Albrecht Dürer: Outpouring of the Holy Spiri

There is a perfectly natural explanation for the strange and seemingly mysterious events on that day of Pentecost. Luke wrote that a strong wind was heard and that "tongues like fire" were seen on all those present, which caused them to speak in strange languages.

The explanation is simple: those "tongues like fire" were sparks of static electricity, caused by a very dry desert wind and a dust storm blowing over Jerusalem from the east.

A professor in physics explains: "The dry winter months are high season for an annoying downside of static electricity – electric discharges like tiny lightning zaps whenever you touch door knobs..."[241]

When two objects are rubbed together, especially if the surrounding air is dry, the objects acquire equal and opposite electrical charges and an attractive force develops between them. The object that loses electrons becomes positively charged, and the other becomes negatively charged, which causes sparks to fly be-

---

[241] Deffner, "Static Electricity's Tiny Sparks".

tween them when the opposite charges are neutralized.[242]

Phenomena like this are not strange in the country of Israel. The Jerusalem Post published a report a few years ago of the owner of a motor vehicle who was filling the vehicle with fuel at a filling station when sparks of static electricity, caused by a strong dry wind, ignited the fumes of the fuel, which caused the vehicle to go up in flames. A photo showed the wrecked motor car. [243]

If Jesus was crucified on 3 April AD 33, this incident of static electricity sparks must have taken place fifty days later, namely on 23 May – right in the middle of the season for dry easterly or southerly desert winds with dust storms – and the resulting static electricity.[244]

Those who were affected on the day of Pentecost found this experience strange and even magical and they must have called out their amazement and surprise. Some of them may have been pilgrims in Jerusalem from other countries and they used their home languages – creating the impression of a language miracle. Outsiders thought they were under the influence of too much wine. These bystanders, who also were pilgrims from other countries, heard those hysterical people speaking in their own languages.

The strong wind was interpreted as the Spirit or breath of God that took hold of these people. After all, the Greek language uses the same word for "wind", "breath", and "spirit", namely πνευμα (*pneuma*).

Peter's Sermon
Acts 2: 14–42

---

[242] Enc Brit, "Static Electricity".
[243] Jerusalem Post, 28 November 2016.
[244] Weatherspark, "Climate and Average Weather Year Round in Jerusalem Israel".

14. But Peter, standing up with the eleven, lifted up his voice, and spoke out to them, "You men of Judea, and all you who dwell at Jerusalem, let this be known to you, and listen to my words.
15. For these aren't drunken, as you suppose, seeing it is only the third hour of the day.
16. But this is what has been spoken through the prophet Joel:
17. It will be in the last days, says God, I will pour forth of my Spirit on all flesh. Your sons and your daughters will prophesy. Your young men will see visions. Your old men will dream dreams.
18. Yes, and on my servants and on my handmaidens in those days, I will pour out my Spirit, and they will prophesy.
19. I will show wonders in the sky above, And signs on the earth beneath; Blood, and fire, and billows of smoke.
20. The sun will be turned into darkness, And the moon into blood, Before the great and glorious day of the Lord comes.
21. It will be, that whoever will call on the name of the Lord will be saved.
22. "You men of Israel, hear these words. Jesus of Nazareth, a man approved by God to you by mighty works and wonders and signs which God did by him in the midst of you, even as you yourselves know,
23. him, being delivered up by the determined counsel and foreknowledge of God, you have taken by the hand of lawless men, crucified and killed;
24. whom God raised up, having freed him from the agony of death, because it was not possible that he should be held by it.

25. For David says concerning him, I saw the Lord always before my face, For he is on my right hand, that I should not be moved.
26. Therefore my heart was glad, and my tongue rejoiced. Moreover my flesh also will dwell in hope;
27. Because you will not leave my soul in Hades, Neither will you allow your Holy One to see decay.
28. You made known to me the ways of life. You will make me full of gladness with your presence.
29. "Brothers, I may tell you freely of the patriarch David, that he both died and was buried, and his tomb is with us to this day.
30. Therefore, being a prophet, and knowing that God had sworn with an oath to him that of the fruit of his body, according to the flesh, he would raise up the Christ to sit on his throne,
31. he foreseeing this spoke about the resurrection of the Christ, that neither was his soul left in Hades, nor did his flesh see decay.
32. This Jesus God raised up, whereof we all are witnesses.
33. Being therefore exalted by the right hand of God, and having received from the Father the promise of the Holy Spirit, he has poured forth this, which you now see and hear.
34. For David didn't ascend into the heavens, but he says himself, The Lord said to my Lord, "Sit by my right hand,
35. Until I make your enemies the footstool of your feet."
36. "Let all the house of Israel therefore know assuredly that God has made him both Lord and Christ, this Jesus whom you crucified."

37.	Now when they heard this, they were cut to the heart, and said to Peter and the rest of the apostles, "Brothers, what will we do?"
38.	Peter said to them, "Repent, and be baptized, everyone of you, in the name of Jesus Christ for the forgiveness of sins, and you will receive the gift of the Holy Spirit.
39.	For to you is the promise, and to your children, and to all who are far off, even as many as the Lord our God will call to himself."
40.	With many other words he testified, and exhorted them, saying, "Save yourselves from this crooked generation!"
41.	Then those who gladly received his word were baptized. There were added that day about three thousand souls.
42.	They continued steadfastly in the apostles teaching and fellowship, in the breaking of bread, and prayer.

It is highly unlikely that Luke was able to repeat Peter's address accurately – that is, if Peter spoke at all to the people who assembled outside the building where the followers of Jesus were experiencing sparks of static electricity. Luke may simply have followed the example of ancient historians who invented speeches by famous people to fit certain occasions.

If Peter delivered a sermon on that day, it would only have been possible after the dust storm had died down. The impression is created that he addressed a large crowd because it was reported that 3 000 people were baptized on that day – an impossible figure if all of them had to be immersed in a pool or a bath somewhere in Jerusalem on the same day. Those who were baptized were most probably people who already believed in Jesus as the Messiah.

According to Luke, Peter quoted from Joel 2: 28–32. This prophecy was never meant to describe events on that day of Pentecost, but it is, nevertheless, an apt description of certain aspects of that occasion. It mentions a darkened sun and a red moon – events that happened on the day Jesus was crucified.

Peter described Jesus' ascension as the fulfillment of a prophecy by David in Ps 15: 8–11. David merely described how God preserved him and he never the Messiah in mind with his words.

These words can certainly not be regarded as a prophecy that the Messiah would be resurrected. There is also a quotation from Ps 110: 1 to prove that Jesus was meant to ascend into heaven – although this Psalm was never meant to be applied to the Messiah.

Peter ended his address by telling the people that Jesus was declared the Christ or Messiah after his crucifixion and resurrection, which does not agree with the rest of the gospels. Luke 1: 30–35, for instance, reported that the angel told the virgin Mary that her unborn son would be the Son of God and the king of Israel.

It must be pointed out that Peter failed to mention in his address that Jesus' death on the cross was meant as a sacrifice to free sinners from eternal damnation in hell – as taught by Paul. He merely exhorted his audience to be baptized in the name of Jesus and confess their sins.

The Believers
Acts 2: 43–47

43.	Fear came on every soul, and many wonders and signs were done through the apostles.
44.	All who believed were together, and had all things common.
45.	They sold their possessions and goods, and distributed them to all, according as anyone had need.

46.	Day by day, continuing steadfastly with one accord in the temple, and breaking bread at home, they took their food with gladness and singleness of heart,
47.	praising God, and having favor with all the people. The Lord added to the assembly day by day those who were being saved.

This passage is simply a description of the lifestyle of the Essene community in Jerusalem. They lived in the Essene quarter in southwestern Jerusalem where they shared their belongings with each other (see the map of Jerusalem in Chapter 2).

Deductions

The overall impression of the unique parts of Luke is that their historical value is variable.

Where Luke followed Q and Mark, most of his reports may be accepted as more or less valid. He also reported some otherwise unknown sayings and parables of Jesus and most of them may be accepted as accurate.

However, the stories of how John the Baptist and Jesus were born are doubtlessly sacred inventions. Luke wanted to fill up gaps about unknown aspects of the life of Jesus – his birth and his fate after his crucifixion. Luke's fantasy took over by constructing stories to provide in this need. The last few chapters of Luke, together with much of Acts 1–2, must be approached with caution, although there may be some ingredients of truth.

One should not judge Luke too harshly for presenting fiction as fact. His motive, first of all, was to convince his readers that Jesus was the savior of the world, the Messiah, the eternal Son of God. In the process, he included much genuine information about the ministry and life of Jesus, but embellished that with mythological elements. After all, he wrote his gospel at least five decades after the time of Jesus and the details that reached him from various sources got distorted through the years and acquired some legendary aspects.

Even though Luke's accuracy is often suspect, he preserved enough memories of Jesus as the throne-pretender and as an Essene.

When Jesus mentioned the kingdom of Gd, as reported by Luke, he meant the earthly kingdom of which he was meant to be the monarch. This notion was later interpreted as referring to the heavenly kingdom of God, but that interpretation would distort much of Jesus' reported words.

The lifestyle and morals Jesus' preached – as reported in L – were consistent with his Essene background and they can only be understood from this perspective. It is clear that he drew most of his supporters from the party of the Essenes or Nazoreans (Acts 24: 5). The people who gathered around the apostles after Jesus' disappearance were certainly mostly Essenes.

At the time when Luke's Gospel was written, there was no chance that Jesus' hopes of a restored monarchy of Israel could ever be realized. Jesus also disappeared and nobody seemed to have known what happened to him – apart from occasional appearances some time after his resurrection. Luke, nevertheless, wanted to preserve his legacy and convince people that Jesus was taken up into heaven – as Paul believed – from where he guided his flock through the invisible Holy Spirit who took over from him.

Luke often asserted that certain prophecies of the Old Testament were fulfilled in the life of Jesus. This proved to be misguided. These passages in the Old Testament mostly did not have the future Messiah in mind and they can't even be regarded as prophecies in most cases, but merely as the descriptions of the experiences of certain ancient Israelite characters. The execution and death of the Messiah was never foreseen, with the result that his resurrection was also never envisaged. Jesus certainly planned to act in accordance with a prophecy in Zechariah when he arrived in Jerusalem on a donkey while being hailed as the king of Israel by the crowds.

Chapter 10
JOHNS SERMONS, DIALOGUES, AND DISCOURSES

Background

It has been shown in Chapter 5 that the Gospel of John consists of two main ingredients: a sober narrative part and later additions of a philosophical or theological nature. The difference in style between these elements cannot be missed and, therefore, it is possible to divide this gospel into its main components. There are also a few minor parts that have been added at different stages and these have been discussed in Chapter 5, together with the narrative parts.

According to Gilbert van Belle, research has shown that the ultimate version of Johns Gospel was only completed after the final separation of main-stream Christianity from Judaism – a process that started with the missionary work of Paul.[245] The divorce only took effect after the destruction of Jerusalem in AD 70, but the eventual gospel may only have been completed much later, perhaps even during the early second century AD.[246]

A likely place of origin for the Johannine discourses and dialogues is Ephesus, where John the apostle settled, according to Eusebius.[247] Ephesus was an important cultural and academic center in the Greek world, only eclipsed by Alexandria, and there was a

---

[245] Van Belle, "The Signs Source". 51.
[246] Rylaarsdam *et al.*, "Biblical Literature."
[247] Eusebius, *Historia Ecclesiastica*, Liber III/XVIII/1–5; XX/10–11; & XXIII/5; Liber V/XXIV/3

Christian community of which John of Patmos, the author of Revelation, was the leader during the nineties of the first century.[248] John, the apostle, seems to have established a school there and the additions to his gospel may have been written by his pupils.[249]

This school may have been the successor of Paul's work when he taught at the school of Tyrhannus in Ephesus for a period of two years (Acts 19: 9–10).

It is probable that John took the manuscript of his Proto-Gospel to Ephesus at the start of the Jewish War of AD 66–70 when many followers of Jesus fled to Pella, Syria, Egypt. and Asia Minor. This proto-gospel must have stayed unknown until it was incorporated into the final edition of John's Gospel because the Synoptic Gospels and other documents in the New Testament show no signs of having been influenced by it or quoted from it.

Another prominent Christian in Ephesus was Timothy, the pupil of Paul. Eusebius wrote that he was the first bishop of Ephesus.[250]

Various possible sources for the ideas in the discourses and dialogues in John have been identified, such as the Essene literature found at Qumran (also known as the Dead Sea Scrolls), various Greek philosophers such as Plato and Philo of Alexandria, Gnosticism, and the Hebrew Scriptures.[251]

In the paragraphs that follow, some verses of the narrative sections of the gospel will be included in italics to provide the context used by the author(s) of the philosophical and theological parts of the gospel.

---

[248] Scholtz. *The Prophecies of Revelation,* 19–26.
[249] Anderson. "The John, Jesus, and History Project", 21.
[250] Eusebius. *Historia Ecclesiastice,* Liber III/IV/6.
[251] Rylaarsdam *et al.* "Biblical Literature."

Prologue
John 1: 1–14

1.	In the beginning was the Word, and the Word was with God, and the Word was God.
2.	The same was in the beginning with God.
3.	All things were made through him. Without him was not anything made that has been made.
4.	In him was life, and the life was the light of men.
5.	The light shines in the darkness, and the darkness hasn't overcome it.
6.	*There came a man, sent from God, whose name was John.*
7.	The same came as a witness, that he might testify about the light, that all might believe through him.
8.	He was not the light, but was sent that he might testify about the light.
9.	The true light that enlightens everyone was coming into the world.
10.	He was in the world, and the world was made through him, and the world didn't recognize him.
11.	He came to his own, and those who were his own didn't receive him.
12.	But as many as received him, to them he gave the right to become Gods children, to those who believe in his name:
13.	who were born, not of blood, nor of the will of the flesh, nor of the will of man, but of God.
14.	The Word became flesh, and lived among us. We saw his glory, such glory as of the only Son of the Father, full of grace and truth.

Reams of paper have been filled with explanations of the Prologue to the Gospel of John and it has been quoted every so often by theologians who used it to support certain Christian dogmas. Only a few remarks will suffice here.

This passage clearly refers to the creation story of Genesis 1. Both begin with the words: "In the beginning..." The Genesis story tells how God called the world into being by commanding it to exist. John mentions this creative word of God – but also concludes that this creative word, which is actually God himself, became flesh or a human being in Jesus Christ.

The term "word" (Greek: λόγος – *logos*) has a rich meaning. Strong's Dictionary explains:

> "In John, [it] denotes the essential Word of God, Jesus Christ, the personal wisdom, and power in union with God, his minister in creation and government of the universe, the cause of all the worlds life both physical and ethical, which for the procurement of man's salvation put on human nature in the person of Jesus the Messiah, the second person in the Godhead, and shone forth conspicuously from His words and deeds. A Greek philosopher named Heraclitus first used the term Logos around 600 B.C. to designate the divine reason or plan which coordinates a changing universe. This word was well suited to John's purpose in John 1."

It has been asserted that the author(s) of the final version of John's Gospel, and especially of this Prologue, were inspired by ideas of the Jewish philosopher and theologian, Philo of Alexandria, a somewhat older contemporary of Jesus. Philo saw the world as a chain of beings, presided over by the Logos, the mediator between God and his creation.

Philo departed from Plato's philosophy principally in using the term Logos for the Idea of the realm of Ideas or immaterial prototypes of objects and their characteristics and the template of the intelligible world. He anticipated the Christian doctrine when he called the Logos the first-begotten Son of God and even the image of God.[252]

This philosophical introduction to the gospel was often quoted by theologians in support of the doctrine of Jesus Christ's dual nature: a divine or celestial nature and a human or mundane nature, combined in one person. This doctrine is a foundation stone of orthodox or conventional Christianity and was introduced by Paul who had various unverifiable visions and revelations about the metaphysical or mythological Christ.

This doctrine cannot be proved or disproved by historical research because it reaches into the supernatural sphere and it is, therefore, purely a matter of faith that cannot be objectively established or demolished. The earliest Christian documents at our disposal, the Q–Document, the Proto-Gospel of John, the letter of James, and the Didaché (see Chapter 11) contain no signs of this belief and it only appeared a few decades after Jesus' time and found its culmination in the book of Revelation[253] and the discourses and dialogues of Johns Gospel.

It is also a historical fact, as was demonstrated in Chapter 2, that Jesus Jewish followers, the Ebionites, rejected this doctrine and regarded Paul as an apostate.

The Testimony of John the Baptist
John 1: 15–18

---

[252] Enc. Brit. "Philo Judaeu"; Hillar, "Philo of Alexandria"; Lévy. "Philo of Alexandria".
[253] Scholtz. *The Prophecies of Revelation*, 309–11.

15.	John testified about him. He cried out, saying, "This was he of whom I said, He who comes after me has surpassed me, for he was before me."
16.	From his fullness we all received grace upon grace.
17.	For the law was given through Moses. Grace and truth came through Jesus Christ.
18.	No one has seen God at any time. The only conceived Son, who is in the bosom of the Father, he has declared him.

These words, placed in the mouth of John the Baptist, were meant to show that Jesus Christ, the only Son of the Father, made the invisible God visible during his life on earth. Moses and Jesus Christ are contrasted: Moses was merely the law-giver, but Jesus was the source of grace and truth – the truth of the "Word".

John the Baptist on Jesus
John 1: 28–34

28.	*These things were done in Bethany beyond the Jordan, where John was baptizing.*
29.	On the next day, he saw Jesus coming to him, and said, "Behold, the Lamb of God, who takes away the sin of the world!
30.	This is he of whom I said, After me comes a man who is preferred before me, for he was before me.
31.	I didn't know him, but for this reason I came baptizing in water: that he would be revealed to Israel."
32.	John testified, saying, "I have seen the Spirit descending like a dove out of heaven, and it remained on him.

33.	I didn't recognize him, but he who sent me to baptize in water, he said to me, On whoever you will see the Spirit descending, and remaining on him, the same is he who baptizes in the Holy Spirit.
34.	I have seen, and have testified that this is the Son of God."

The person of Jesus presented by this testimony of John the Baptist is almost unrecognizable in comparison with the Jesus portrayed in the narrative parts of the gospel. Here he is introduced as a divine being, the eternal Son of God. His status was confirmed by the Spirit descending upon him like a dove.

John referred indirectly to the baptism of Jesus by John the Baptist when the Spirit took hold of Jesus. It is clear that a greatly garbled version of Jesus' baptism reached the author of this passage.

The calling of Jesus to become the king of Israel at the time of his baptism is absent in this passage.

Nicodemus Visits Jesus
John 3: 1–2, 22–24

1.	*Now there was a man of the Pharisees named Nicodemus, a ruler of the Jews.*
2.	*The same came to him by night, and said to him, "Rabbi, we know that you are a teacher come from God, for no one can do these signs that you do, unless God is with him."*
3.	*Jesus answered him, "Most assuredly, I tell you, unless one is born anew, he can't see the kingdom of God."*
4.	*Nicodemus said to him, "How can a man be born when he is old? Can he enter a second time into his mother's womb, and be born?"*

5.	Jesus answered, "Most assuredly I tell you, unless one is born of water and the Spirit, he can't enter into the kingdom of God!
6.	That which is born of the flesh is flesh. That which is born of the Spirit is spirit.
7.	Don't marvel that I said to you, You must be born anew.
8.	The wind blows where it wants to, and you hear its sound, but don't know where it comes from and where it is going. So is everyone who is born of the Spirit."
9.	Nicodemus answered him, "How can these things be?"
10.	Jesus answered him, "Are you the teacher of Israel, and don't understand these things?
11.	Most assuredly I tell you, we speak that which we know, and testify of that which we have seen, and you don't receive our witness.
12.	If I told you earthly things and you don't believe, how will you believe if I tell you heavenly things?
13.	No one has ascended into heaven, but he who descended out of heaven, the Son of Man, who is in heaven.
14.	As Moses lifted up the serpent in the wilderness, even so must the Son of Man be lifted up,
15.	that whoever believes in him should not perish, but have eternal life.
16.	For God so loved the world, that he gave his one and only Son, that whoever believes in him should not perish, but have eternal life.
17.	For God didn't send his Son into the world to judge the world, but that the world should be saved through him.

> 18. He who believes in him is not judged. He who doesn't believe has been judged already, because he has not believed in the name of the only born Son of God.
> 19. This is the judgment, that the light has come into the world, and men loved the darkness rather than the light; for their works were evil.
> 20. For everyone who does evil hates the light, and doesn't come to the light, for fear that his works would be reproved.
> 21. But he who does the truth comes to the light, that his works may be revealed, that they have been done with God."

The author(s) of the philosophical parts of the gospel used the visit of Nicodemus to Jesus as the context for a discourse on the spiritual kingdom of God and the need to be reborn spiritually in order to be able to enter this kingdom and receive eternal life. Belief in Jesus as savior of the world is necessary to be saved – in contrast with Jesus who taught elsewhere that one could gain eternal life by obeying God's laws.

It is highly unlikely that Jesus ever uttered these words and they are the musings of second-generation or even third-generation Christians who used Jesus as their mouthpiece. This is not the historical Jesus whose words are quoted, but the metaphysical Christ of faith.

Jesus and John
John 3: 25–36

> 25. There arose therefore a questioning on the part of Johns disciples with some Jews about purification.

> 26. They came to John, and said to him, "Rabbi, he who was with you beyond the Jordan, to whom you have testified, behold, the same baptizes, and all men come to him."
> 27. John answered, "A man can receive nothing, unless it has been given him from heaven.
> 28. You yourselves testify about me, that I said, I am not the Christ, but, I have been sent before him.
> 29. He who has the bride is the bridegroom; but the friend of the bridegroom, who stands and hears him, rejoices greatly because of the bridegroom's voice. This, my joy, therefore is made full.
> 30. He must increase, but I must decrease.
> 31. He who comes from above is above all. He who is from the Earth belongs to the Earth, and speaks of the Earth. He who comes from heaven is above all.
> 32. What he has seen and heard, of that he testifies; and no one receives his witness.
> 33. He who has received his witness has set his seal to this, that God is true.
> 34. For he whom God has sent speaks the words of God; for God gives the Spirit without measure.
> 35. The Father loves the Son, and has given all things into his hand.
> 36. He who believes in the Son has eternal life, but he who disobeys the Son won't see life, but the wrath of God remains on him."

The words ascribed to John the Baptist are meant to convey two points:

- John the Baptist was not the Messiah and he rejoiced at the fact that he could aid Jesus as the Messiah; and
- Jesus, who is really a heavenly being, was sent by God as his representative.

The Samaritan Woman
John 4: 10–15

9.	*The Samaritan woman therefore said to him, "How is it that you, being a Jew, ask for a drink from me, a Samaritan woman?" (For Jews have no dealings with Samaritans.)*
10.	Jesus answered her, "If you knew the gift of God, and who it is who says to you, Give me a drink, you would have asked him, and he would have given you living water."
11.	The woman said to him, "Sir, you have nothing to draw with, and the well is deep. From where then have you that living water?
12.	Are you greater than our father, Jacob, who gave us the well, and drank of it himself, as did his sons, and his cattle?"
13.	Jesus answered her, "Everyone who drinks of this water will thirst again,
14.	but whoever drinks of the water that I will give him will never thirst; but the water that I will give him will become in him a well of water springing up to eternal life."
15.	The woman said to him, "Sir, give me this water, so that I don't get thirsty, neither come all the way here to draw."

In this passage, Jesus is reported as telling the Samaritan woman that he is the source of spiritual and life-supporting water and eternal life, just as the well is the source of ordinary water that sustains ordinary life.

John 4: 19–26, 31–38

19.	The woman said to him, "Sir, I perceive that you are a prophet.
20.	Our fathers worshipped in this mountain, and you Jews say that in Jerusalem is the place where people ought to worship."
21.	Jesus said to her, "Woman, believe me, the hour comes, when neither in this mountain, nor in Jerusalem, will you worship the Father.
22.	You worship that which you don't know. We worship that which we know; for salvation is from the Jews.
23.	But the hour comes, and now is, when the true worshippers will worship the Father in spirit and truth, for the Father seeks such to be his worshippers.
24.	God is a Spirit, and those who worship him must worship in spirit and truth."
25.	The woman said to him, "I know that Messiah comes," (he who is called Christ). "When he has come, he will declare to us all things."
26.	Jesus said to her, "I who speak to you am he."

Jesus confirmed to this woman that he was indeed the Messiah and a prophet. Because God is a spirit, He can be worshipped at any place, provided it is done in spirit and truth, as the Jews did it.

31.	*In the meanwhile, the disciples urged him, saying, "Rabbi, eat."*
32.	But he said to them, "I have food to eat that you don't know about."
33.	The disciples therefore said one to another, "Has anyone brought him something to eat?"
34.	Jesus said to them, "My food is to do the will of him who sent me, and to accomplish his work.
35.	Don't you say, There are yet four months until the harvest? Behold, I tell you, lift up your eyes, and look at the fields, that they are white already to harvest.
36.	He who reaps receives wages, and gathers fruit to eternal life; that both he who sows and he who reaps may rejoice together.
37.	For in this the saying is true, One sows, and another reaps.
38.	I sent you to reap that for which you haven't labored. Others have labored, and you have entered into their labor."

The sentence in italics is taken from the narrative parts and is included to provide the context for this passage. This conversation of Jesus with his disciples deals with two unrelated topics:

- He was spiritually nourished by doing the will of his Father; and
- Jesus has sent his disciples out to gather the harvest of followers or believers.

The Paralyzed Man at the Pool of Bethesda
John 5: 17–45

16.	*For this cause the Jews persecuted Jesus, and sought to kill him, because he did these things [healing a paralyzed man] on the Sabbath.*
17.	But Jesus answered them, "My Father is still working, so I am working, too."
18.	For this cause therefore the Jews sought the more to kill him, because he not only broke the Sabbath, but also called God his own Father, making himself equal with God.
19.	Jesus therefore answered them, "Most assuredly, I tell you, the Son can do nothing of himself, but what he sees the Father doing. For whatever things he does, these the Son also does likewise.
20.	For the Father loves the Son, and shows him all things that he himself does. He will show him greater works than these, that you may marvel.
21.	For as the Father raises the dead and gives them life, even so the Son also gives life to whom he desires.
22.	For neither does the Father judge any man, but he has given all judgment to the Son,
23.	that all may honor the Son, even as they honor the Father. He who doesn't honor the Son doesn't honor the Father who sent him.
24.	Most assuredly I tell you, he who hears my word, and believes him who sent me, has eternal life, and doesn't come into judgment, but has passed out of death into life.
25.	Most assuredly, I tell you, the hour comes, and now is, when the dead will hear the Son of Gods voice; and those who hear will live.

26.	For as the Father has life in himself, even so he gave to the Son also to have life in himself.
27.	He also gave him authority to execute judgment, because he is a son of man.
28.	Don't marvel at this, for the hour comes, in which all that are in the tombs will hear his voice,
29.	and will come forth; those who have done good, to the resurrection of life; and those who have done evil, to the resurrection of judgment.
30.	I can of myself do nothing. As I hear, I judge, and my judgment is righteous; because I don't seek my own will, but the will of my Father who sent me.
31.	"If I testify about myself, my witness is not valid.
32.	It is another who testifies about me. I know that the testimony which he testifies about me is true.
33.	You have sent to John, and he has testified to the truth.
34.	But the testimony which I receive is not from man. However, I say these things that you may be saved.
35.	He was the lamp that burns and shines, and you were willing to rejoice for a while in his light.
36.	But the testimony which I have is greater than that of John, for the works which the Father has given me to accomplish, the very works that I do, testify about me, that the Father has sent me.
37.	The Father himself, who sent me, has testified about me. You have neither heard his voice at any time, nor seen his form.
38.	You don't have his word living in you; for whom he sent, him you don't believe.

> 39. You search the scriptures, because you think that in them you have eternal life; and these are they which testify about me.
> 40. Yet you will not come to me, that you may have life.
> 41. I don't receive glory from men.
> 42. But I know you, that you don't have Gods love in yourselves.
> 43. I have come in my Father's name, and you don't receive me. If another comes in his own name, you will receive him.
> 44. How can you believe, who receive glory from one another, and you don't seek the glory that comes from the only God?
> 45. "Don't think that I will accuse you to the Father. There is one who accuses you, even Moses, on whom you have set your hope.
> 46. For if you believed Moses, you would believe me; for he wrote about me.
> 47. But if you don't believe his writings, how will you believe my words?"

Jesus' long lecture to the Jews, as presented in this passage, has no connection to the Jews' anger towards Jesus because he healed somebody on the Sabbath. Neither was it wrong of Jesus to call God his Father, because the kings of Israel from the house of David were deemed to be the sons of God (2 Sam 7: 14; 1 Chr 17: 13, and Ps 2: 7) . God is also called the Father of the Israelites, his people. in Ex 4: 22; Deut 32: 8; Ps 68: 6; Ps 69: 27; Isa 63:16; and Jer 2: 22 and 3: 4.

However – according to this passage – Jesus claimed for himself certain functions of God, including being the judge on Judgment Day, being the giver of life, and being the source of truth.

Jesus the Bread of Life
John 6: 26–71

25.	*When they found him on the other side of the sea, they asked him, "Rabbi, when did you come here?"*
26.	Jesus answered them, "Most assuredly I tell you, you seek me, not because you saw signs, but because you ate of the loaves, and were filled.
27.	Don't work for the food which perishes, but for the food which remains to eternal life, which the Son of Man will give to you. For the Father, even God, has sealed him."
28.	They said therefore to him, "What must we do, that we may work the works of God?"
29.	Jesus answered them, "This is the work of God, that you believe in him whom he has sent."
30.	They said therefore to him, "What then do you do for a sign, that we may see, and believe you? What work do you do?
31.	Our fathers ate the manna in the wilderness. As it is written, He gave them bread out of the sky to eat."
32.	Jesus therefore said to them, "Most assuredly, I tell you, it wasn't Moses who gave you the bread out of heaven, but my Father gives you the true bread out of heaven.
33.	For the bread of God is that which comes down out of heaven, and gives life to the world."

34.	They said therefore to him, "Lord, always give us this bread."
35.	Jesus said to them. "I am the bread of life. He who comes to me will not be hungry, and he who believes in me will never be thirsty.
36.	But I told you that you have seen me, and yet don't believe.
37.	All that which the Father gives me will come to me. Him who comes to me I will in no way throw out.
38.	For I have come down from heaven, not to do my own will, but the will of him who sent me.
39.	This is the will of my Father who sent me, that of all who he has given to me I should lose nothing, but should raise them up at the last day.
40.	This is the will of the one who sent me, that everyone who sees the Son, and believes in him, should have eternal life; and I will raise him up at the last day."
41.	The Jews therefore murmured concerning him, because he said, "I am the bread which came down out of heaven."
42.	They said, "Isn't this Jesus, the son of Joseph, whose father and mother we know? How then does he say, I have come down out of heaven?"
43.	Therefore Jesus answered them, "Don't murmur among yourselves.
44.	No one can come to me unless the Father who sent me draws him, and I will raise him up in the last day.
45.	It is written in the prophets, They will all be taught by God. Everyone who hears from the Father, and has learned, comes to me.

46. Not that any man has seen the Father, except he who is from God. He has seen the Father.
47. Most assuredly, I tell you, he who believes in me has eternal life.
48. I am the bread of life.
49. Your fathers ate the manna in the wilderness, and they died.
50. This is the bread which comes down out of heaven, that a man may eat of it, and not die.
51. I am the living bread which came down out of heaven. If anyone eats of this bread, he will live forever. Yes, the bread which I will give is my flesh, for the life of the world."
52. The Jews therefore contended with one another, saying, "How can this man give us his flesh to eat?"
53. Jesus therefore said to them, "Most assuredly I tell you, unless you eat the flesh of the Son of Man and drink his blood, you don't have life in yourselves.
54. He who eats my flesh and drinks my blood has eternal life, and I will raise him up at the last day.
55. For my flesh is food indeed, and my blood is drink indeed.
56. He who eats my flesh and drinks my blood lives in me, and I in him.
57. As the living Father sent me, and I live because of the Father; so he who feeds on me, he will also live because of me.
58. This is the bread which came down out of heaven — not as our fathers ate the manna, and died. He who eats this bread will live forever."

59.	These things he said in the synagogue, as he taught in Capernaum.
60.	Therefore many of his disciples, when they heard this, said, "This is a hard saying! Who can hear it?"
61.	But Jesus knowing in himself that his disciples murmured at this, said to them, "Does this cause you to stumble?
62.	What if you would see the Son of Man ascending to where he was before?
63.	It is the spirit who gives life. The flesh profits nothing. The words that I speak to you are spirit, and are life.
64.	But there are some of you who don't believe." For Jesus knew from the beginning who they were who didn't believe, and who it was who would betray him.
65.	He said, "For this cause have I said to you that no one can come to me, except it be given to him by my Father."
66.	At this, many of his disciples went back, and walked no more with him.
67.	Jesus said therefore to the twelve, "You don't also want to go away, do you?"
68.	Simon Peter answered him, "Lord, to whom would we go? You have the words of eternal life.
69.	We have come to believe and know that you are the Christ, the Son of the living God."
70.	Jesus answered them, "Didn't I choose you, the twelve, and one of you is a devil?"
71.	Now he spoke of Judas, the son of Simon Iscariot, for it was he who would betray him, being one of the twelve.

This long and rather incoherent conversation Jesus had with his disciples, and some Jews, presents Jesus as "the bread of life" – spiritual nourishment – which can only be attained when people believe in Jesus as the Christ, the eternal Son of God, who will raise the dead from their graves at the end of the world.

Jesus used the words "I am the bread of life." The words "I am..." (ἐγώ εἰμι – *ego eimi*) are emphasized in the Greek. This is a hidden way to give the message that Jesus is the same God who revealed his name to Moses as "I AM WHO I AM , and he said, You shall tell the children of Israel this: I AM has sent me to you" (Ex 3: 14). This emphasis upon "I am..." occurs several times in John.

This conversation contains an anachronism because it also explains the meaning of the eucharist, which was not yet instituted at that time – it only happened shortly before Jesus' execution.

It is also asserted that Jesus knew that Judas would betray him. One can only wonder: why did Jesus recruit him as one of the twelve chosen disciples at all if he had known in advance that Judas would prove to be a disappointment and a two-faced traitor?

This passage tells us more about the beliefs of the author(s) of the discourse source in this gospel than of who and what Jesus really was and what he thought and taught. The differences in style and contents between this passage and the earlier sources of Jesus life, the Q Document and the Proto-Gospel of John, is very visible.

Jesus Goes to Jerusalem
John 7: 15–36

15.	The Jews therefore marveled, saying, "How does this man know letters, having never been educated?"
16.	Jesus therefore answered them, "My teaching is not mine, but his who sent me.
17.	If anyone desires to do his will, he will know of the teaching, whether it is from God, or if I speak from myself.

18.	He who speaks from himself seeks his own glory, but he who seeks the glory of him who sent him, the same is true, and no unrighteousness is in him.
19.	Didn't Moses give you the law, and yet none of you keeps the law? Why do you seek to kill me?"
20.	The multitude answered, "You have a demon! Who seeks to kill you?"
21.	Jesus answered them, "I did one work, and you all marvel because of it.
22.	Moses has given you circumcision (not that it is of Moses, but of the fathers), and on the Sabbath you circumcise a boy.
23.	If a boy receives circumcision on the Sabbath, that the law of Moses may not be broken, are you angry with me, because I made a man every bit whole on the Sabbath?
24.	Don't judge according to appearance, but judge righteous judgment."
25.	Some therefore of them of Jerusalem said, "Isn't this he whom they seek to kill?
26.	Behold, he speaks openly, and they say nothing to him. Can it be that the rulers indeed know that this is truly the Christ?
27.	However we know where this man comes from, but when the Christ comes, no one will know where he comes from."
28.	Jesus therefore cried out in the temple, teaching and saying, "You both know me, and know where I am from. I have not come of myself, but he who sent me is true, whom you don't know.
29.	I know him, because I am from him, and he sent me."

> 30. They sought therefore to take him. No one laid a hand on him, because his hour was not yet come.
> 31. But of the multitude, many believed in him. They said, "When the Christ comes, will he do more signs than those which this man has done?"
> 32. The Pharisees heard the multitude murmuring these things concerning him, and the chief priests and the Pharisees sent officers to take him.
> 33. Then Jesus said, "Yet a little while, am I with you, then I go to him who sent me.
> 34. You will seek me, and won't find me; and where I am, you can't come."
> 35. The Jews therefore said among themselves, "Where will this man go that we won't find him? Will he go to the Dispersion among the Greeks, and teach the Greeks?
> 36. What is this word that he said, You will seek me, and won't find me; and where I am, you can't come?"

This conversation Jesus had with a crowd contains signs of being influenced by Gnosticism. This movement or philosophy incorporated some influences from early Christianity, and vice versa, and it taught that man could be saved from this sinful and evil and amoral material world by obtaining esoteric knowledge of his eternal origin and his eternal destiny, as well as gaining self-knowledge.[254] According to this passage, Jesus had knowledge of whence he came, namely from him who had sent him, and he wanted to teach that to his audience.

Jesus is presented here as an envoy of the source of true

---

[254] Enc. Brit. "Gnosticism".

knowledge, of God, and he has the task of teaching the multitudes. He contrasts his message with the Law of Moses.

Jesus the Living Water
John 7: 37–39

37.	Now on the last and greatest day of the feast, Jesus stood and cried out, "If anyone is thirsty, let him come to me and drink!
38.	He who believes in me, as the scripture has said, from within him will flow rivers of living water."
39.	But he said this about the Spirit, which those believing in him were to receive. For the Holy Spirit was not yet given, because Jesus wasn't yet glorified

Jesus gave no clear explanation of what he meant by "living water", except to hint that it has something to do with the outpouring of the Holy Spirit, somewhere in the future. It is probably meant to convey the idea that those who have the Spirit in their lives will feel refreshed and will reach the afterlife.

There are various allusions to "living water" in the Scriptures, as asserted in this passage, for instance in Job 32: 18–19; Prov 10: 11; 18: 4; Isa 12: 3; 44: 3; 58: 11; 59: 21; Ezek 47: 1–12; and Zech 14: 8. However, none has any bearing on the Messiah.

Jesus Opens the Eyes of a Blind Man
John 9: 31–41

30.	*The man answered them, "How amazing! You don't know where he comes from, yet he opened my eyes.*
31.	We know that God doesn't listen to sinners, but if anyone is a worshipper of God, and does his will, he listens to him.

32.	Since the world began it has never been heard of that anyone opened the eyes of a man born blind.
33.	If this man were not from God, he could do nothing."
34.	They answered him, "You were altogether born in sins, and do you teach us?" They threw him out.
35.	Jesus heard that they had thrown him out, and finding him, he said, "Do you believe in the Son of God?"
36.	He answered, "Who is he, Lord, that I may believe in him?"
37.	Jesus said to him, "You have both seen him, and it is he who speaks with you."
38.	He said, "Lord, I believe!" and he worshipped him.
39.	Jesus said, "I came into this world for judgment, that those who don't see may see; and that those who see may become blind."
40.	Those of the Pharisees who were with him heard these things, and said to him, "Are we also blind?"
41.	Jesus said to them, "If you were blind, you would have no sin; but now you say, We see. Therefore your sin remains

The words ascribed to Jesus deals with spiritual blindness – a lack of knowledge of God and man's eternal origin and destiny. People suffering from this condition cannot recognize Jesus as the Son of God. It was made clear that the man who was born blind and whose eyes were opened, also got rid his spiritual blindness and believed in Jesus as the Son of God.

Parable of the Shepherd
John 10: 1–21

1.	"Most assuredly, I tell you, he who doesn't enter by the door into the sheep fold, but climbs up some other way, the same is a thief and a robber.
2.	But he who enters in by the door is the shepherd of the sheep.
3.	The gatekeeper opens the gate for him, and the sheep listen to his voice. He calls his own sheep by name, and leads them out.
4.	Whenever he brings out his own sheep, he goes before them, and the sheep follow him, for they know his voice.
5.	They will by no means follow a stranger, but will flee from him; for they don't know the voice of strangers."
6.	Jesus spoke this parable to them, but they didn't understand what he was telling them.
7.	Jesus therefore said to them again, "Most assuredly, I tell you, I am the sheep's door.
8.	All who came before me are thieves and robbers, but the sheep didn't listen to them.
9.	I am the door. If anyone enters in by me, he will be saved, and will go in and go out, and will find pasture.
10.	The thief only comes to steal, kill, and destroy. I came that they may have life, and may have it abundantly.
11.	I am the good shepherd. The good shepherd lays down his life for the sheep.
12.	He who is a hired hand, and not a shepherd, who doesn't own the sheep, sees the wolf coming, leaves the sheep, and flees. The wolf snatches the sheep, and scatters them.
13.	The hired hand flees because he is a hired hand, and doesn't care for the sheep.

14.	I am the good shepherd. I know my own, and I'm known by my own;
15.	even as the Father knows me, and I know the Father. I lay down my life for the sheep.
16.	I have other sheep, which are not of this fold. I must bring them also, and they will hear my voice. They will become one flock with one shepherd.
17.	Therefore the Father loves me, because I lay down my life, that I may take it again.
18.	No one takes it away from me, but I lay it down by myself. I have power to lay it down, and I have power to take it again. I received this commandment from my Father."
19.	Therefore a division arose again among the Jews because of these words.
20.	Many of them said, "He has a demon, and is mad! Why do you listen to him?"
21.	Others said, "These are not the sayings of one possessed with a demon. Can a demon open the eyes of the blind?"

This well-known parable of the Good Shepherd reminds one of the parables contained in the other gospels. It is more coherent than many other discourses in John's Gospel and has a clear message: the flock of sheep consists of Jesus followers, those who believe in him, and he saved them by dying for them, although he was resurrected again. Jesus is both the entrance to the sheep stockade, as well as the shepherd. The thieves who plunder and the wolves that ravish are the false prophets and apostles.

In true gnostic style, Jesus declares that he and the Father know each other.

Jesus used the words "I am..." (ἐγώ εἰμι – *ego eimi*) four times: "I am the door..." and "I am the good shepherd..." This is again a hidden way to communicate that Jesus is the same God who revealed his name to Moses as "I AM WHO I AM" (Ex 3: 14).

It is possible that Jesus really told this parable, but that it has been added to during the decades after his time to become the parable as we know it today – for instance the parts dealing with Jesus losing his life for the sake of the sheep to save them and his resurrection afterwards. Of course, Jesus would have had a god idea what awaited him when the Roman authorities clamped down on him, but it is unlikely that he would have included that in his parable, especially if he had the expectation of becoming the king of Israel with the help of a pack of angelic warriors.

Jesus Speaks about his Death
John 12: 24–35

22.	*Philip came and told Andrew, and in turn, Andrew came with Philip, and they told Jesus.*
23.	*Jesus answered them, "The time has come for the Son of Man to be glorified.*
24.	*Most assuredly I tell you, unless a grain of wheat falls into the earth and dies, it remains by itself alone. But if it dies, it bears much fruit.*
25.	*He who loves his life will lose it. He who hates his life in this world will keep it to eternal life.*
26.	*If anyone serves me, let him follow me. Where I am, there will my servant also be. If anyone serves me, the Father will honor him.*
27.	*"Now my soul is troubled. What will I say? Father, save me from this time? But for this cause I came to this time.*

JOHN'S SERMNS, DIALOGUES, AND DISCOURSES

28.	Father, glorify your name!" Then there came a voice out of the sky, saying, "I have both glorified it, and will glorify it again."
29.	The multitude therefore, who stood by and heard it, said that it had thundered. Others said, "An angel has spoken to him."
30.	Jesus answered, "This voice hasn't come for my sake, but for your sakes.
31.	Now is the judgment of this world. Now the prince of this world will be cast out.
32.	I, if I am lifted up from the earth, will draw all men to myself."
33.	But he said this, signifying by what kind of death he should die.
34.	The multitude answered him, "We have heard out of the law that the Christ remains forever. How do you say, The Son of Man must be lifted up? Who is this Son of Man?"
35.	Jesus therefore said to them, "Yet a little while the light is with you. Walk while you have the light, that darkness doesn't overtake you. He who walks in the darkness doesn't know where he is going.

This is another example of a rambling sermon and dialogue with no clear theme. The author(s) who invented this passage and inserted it into the narrative gospel of John, used the occasion when some Greeks wanted to meet Jesus (printed in italics).

We read of a voice from the sky that answered Jesus' prayer and a sudden crowd that eavesdropped on Jesus' interview with the Greek visitors.

Jesus' simile or parable of spiritual rebirth by stating that a seed must die before it can bear fruit, is misleading. Dead seeds are just dead, lifeless, expired, and they won't and can't produce a crop.

Jesus also hinted about the type of death awaiting him, by being lifted up – certainly a reference to his crucifixion.

Jesus Washes his Disciples Feet
John 13: 18–20

18.	I speak not of you all. I know whom I have chosen. But that the scripture may be fulfilled, He who eats bread with me has lifted up his heel against me.
19.	From now on, I tell you before it happens, that when it happens, you may believe that I AM.
20.	Most assuredly I tell you, he who receives whoever I send, receives me; and he who receives me, receives him who sent me."

This short sermon by Jesus was inserted into the narrative of the washing of the disciples' feet. Jesus was made to say that Judas treason was foretold by a scripture, namely Ps 41: 9. This Psalm contains the following sentence:

> "Yes, my own familiar friend, in whom I trusted, who ate bread with me, has lifted up his heel against me."

There is no possibility that the poet of this ancient song would have had specifically Judas' treachery in mind when he wrote these words. The author(s) of this passage wanted to prove that Judas' action was predicted in the Old Testament and nothing better than this sentence could be found. One may, on the other hand, see a parallel between the experience of the poet and Jesus, although Jesus certainly never delivered this short sermon as it was reported.

This is also one of the seven occasions in John where Jesus is reported as saying "I AM" in such a manner that it reminds one of Ex 3: 14 – "God said to Moses, I AM WHO I AM, and he said, You shall tell the children of Israel this: I AM has sent me to you." With this expression, the gospel conveyed the conviction that Jesus was really God who assumed a human form – an idea introduced by Paul on account of his unverifiable visions and revelations.

The Unbelief of the People
John 18: 31–38

30.	Therefore, having received that morsel, he went out immediately. It was night.
31.	When he had gone out, Jesus said, "Now the Son of Man is glorified, and God is glorified in him.
32.	If God is glorified in him, God will also glorify him in himself, and he will glorify him immediately.
33.	Little children, yet a little while I am with you. You will seek me, and as I said to the Jews, Where I am going, you can't come, so now I tell you.
34.	A new commandment I give to you, that you love one another, just like I have loved you; that you also love one another.
35.	By this everyone will know that you are my disciples, if you have love for one another."
36.	Simon Peter said to him, "Lord, where are you going?" Jesus answered, "Where I am going, you can't follow now, but you will follow afterwards."
37.	Peter said to him, "Lord, why can't I follow you even now? I will lay down my life for you."

38.	Jesus answered him, "Will you lay down your life for me? Most assuredly I tell you, the rooster wont crow until you have denied me three times.

The advice to Jesus followers to love one another, may well have been given by Jesus. This love would prove to others that they belong to Jesus because he gave them the example of being a loving, generous, and forgiving person.

Jesus' announcement that he has already been glorified directly after Judas had left to betray him, amounts to an anachronism. According to the Gospels of Matthew and Luke, his glorification would only happen when he was resurrected from the tomb and ascended into heaven. This passage hints at this ascension, which has not yet happened at this junction.

The prediction that Peter would deny knowing Jesus is inserted at this point to prepare the reader for this action by Peter during Jesus' trial later.

Jesus is the Way to the Father
John 14: 1–14

1.	"Don't let your heart be troubled. Believe in God. Believe also in me.
2.	In my Father's house are many mansions. If it weren't so, I would have told you. I am going to prepare a place for you.
3.	If I go and prepare a place for you, I will come again, and will receive you to myself; that where I am, you may be there also.
4.	Where I go, you know, and you know the way."
5.	Thomas says to him, "Lord, we don't know where you are going. How can we know the way?"

6.	Jesus said to him, "I am the way, the truth, and the life. No one comes to the Father, but by me.
7.	If you had known me, you would have known my Father also. From now on, you know him, and have seen him."
8.	Philip said to him, "Lord, show us the Father, and that will be enough for us."
9.	Jesus said to him, "Have I been with you such a long time, and do you not know me, Philip? He who has seen me has seen the Father. How do you say, Show us the Father?
10.	Don't you believe that I am in the Father, and the Father in me? The words that I tell you, I speak not from myself; but the Father living in me does his works.
11.	Believe me that I am in the Father, and the Father in me; or else believe me for the very works sake.
12.	Most assuredly I tell you, he who believes in me, the works that I do, he will do also; and greater works than these will he do; because I am going to my Father.
13.	Whatever you will ask in my name, that will I do, that the Father may be glorified in the Son.
14.	If you will ask anything in my name, that will I do.

It is doubtful whether the historical Jesus would have recognized himself in this passage. The Jesus who talked to his disciples in this scene was a mythological or metaphysical being, almost indistinguishable from God, his Father, of whom he is an embodiment. The following words are placed in his mouth: "I am the way…" – which reminds the reader of God's name in Exodus, "I AM WHO I AM".

The promise that any prayer will be granted, provided it is spoken in the name of Jesus, sounds unrealistic, over-optimistic, and disproved by the experiences of untold numbers of people who prayed in vain.

The statement of Jesus that nobody can reach his Father without him, boils down to arrogance. One may ask: how on earth did the prophets of the Old Testament reach God before Jesus' time?

We find in this passage the promise by Jesus that he would return. That may have been the case after Jesus had survived his crucifixion and went into hiding for some time. In this passage, the return of Jesus is quite a different matter. He would only return after he had prepared place for his disciples and followers in heaven.

The Promise of the Holy Spirit
John 14: 15–31

15.	If you love me, keep my commandments.
16.	I will pray to the Father, and he will give you another Counselor, that he may be with you forever,
17.	– the Spirit of truth, whom the world can't receive; for it doesn't see him, neither knows him. You know him, for he lives with you, and will be in you.
18.	I will not leave you orphans. I will come to you.
19.	Yet a little while, and the world will see me no more; but you will see me. Because I live, you will live also.
20.	In that day you will know that I am in my Father, and you in me, and I in you.
21.	Someone who has my commandments, and keeps them, that person is one who loves me. One who loves me will be loved by my Father, and I will love him, and will reveal myself to him."
22.	Judas (not Iscariot) said to him, "Lord, what will happen that you will reveal yourself to us, and not to the world?"

JOHN'S SERMNS, DIALOGUES, AND DISCOURSES

> 23. Jesus answered him, "If a man loves me, he will keep my word. My Father will love him, and we will come to him, and make our home with him.
>
> 24. He who doesn't love me doesn't keep my words. The word which you hear isn't mine, but the Fathers who sent me.
>
> 25. I have said these things to you, while still living with you.
>
> 26. But the Counselor, the Holy Spirit, whom the Father will send in my name, he will teach you all things, and bring to your memory all that I said to you.
>
> 27. Peace I leave with you. My peace I give to you; not as the world gives, give I to you. Don't let your heart be troubled, neither let it be fearful.
>
> 28. You heard how I told you, I go away, and I come to you. If you loved me, you would have rejoiced, because I said I am going to my Father; for the Father is greater than I.
>
> 29. Now I have told you before it happens so that, when it happens, you may believe.
>
> 30. I will no more speak much with you, for the prince of the world comes, and he has nothing in me.
>
> 31. But that the world may know that I love the Father, and as the Father commanded me, even so I do. Arise, let us go from here.

It is difficult to make sense of this conversation of Jesus with his disciples, due to the contradictions and unclear expressions it contains.

In a previous passage, Jesus called himself "I AM" – the name of God in Exodus, thereby expressing the idea that he is God himself. Here he says that the Father is greater than he is. That means that he is less than God, a lesser deity., a less important divine person

In a single sentence he says that the Holy Spirit is already with his disciples but that he will also come to them sometime in the future. These two statements contradict each other.

It is also not clear how Jesus and his Father would live inside the people whom they love and who love them. Will they take possession of that person's personality and make a puppet of him?

The Holy Spirit is mentioned in this passage as a third divine person who will take Jesus' place after his imminent departure to heaven. This Spirit differs from the Spirit of YHWH of the Old Testament, which was merely the mind or breath of God, or simply God himself.

The esoteric Jesus portrayed in this passage is very far removed from the Jesus who entered Jerusalem on a donkey and who was greeted by the crowds as the son of David and as their king.

Jesus the Real Vine
John 15: 1–15

1.	"I am the true vine, and my Father is the farmer.
2.	Every branch in me that doesn't bear fruit, he takes away. Every branch that bears fruit, he prunes, that it may bear more fruit.
3.	You are already pruned clean because of the word which I have spoken to you.
4.	Remain in me, and I in you. As the branch can't bear fruit by itself, unless it remains in the vine, so neither can you, unless you remain in me.
5.	I am the vine. You are the branches. He who remains in me, and I in him, the same bears much fruit, for apart from me you can do nothing.

6. If a man doesn't remain in me, he is thrown out as a branch, and is withered; and they gather them, throw them into the fire, and they are burned.
7. If you remain in me, and my words remain in you, you will ask whatever you desire, and it will be done to you.
8. In this is my Father glorified, that you bear much fruit; and so you will be my disciples.
9. Even as the Father has loved me, I also have loved you. Remain in my love.
10. If you keep my commandments, you will remain in my love; even as I have kept my Fathers commandments, and remain in his love.
11. I have spoken these things to you, that my joy may be in you, and that your joy may be made full.
12. This is my commandment, that you love one another, even as I have loved you.
13. Greater love has no one than this, that a man lay down his life for his friends.
14. You are my friends, if you do whatever I command you.
15. No longer do I call you servants, for the servant doesn't know what his lord does. But I have called you friends, for everything that I heard from my Father, I have made known to you.
16. You didn't choose me, but I chose you, and appointed you, that you should go and bear fruit, and that your fruit should remain; that whatever you will ask of the Father in my name, he may give it to you.
17. I command these things to you, that you may love one another.

This passage starts with the words" I am the true vine…" with the emphasis on "I AM" The author(s) of the discourse source of John's Gospel wanted, yet again, to make sure that the readers of this gospel get the message that Jesus is identical with the God who called Moses and revealed his name as "I AM WHO I AM".

It is possible that the nucleus of this parable was spoken by Jesus and that some additions accrued through the decades before it was eventually written down. It is probable that Jesus urged his disciples to love each other and to love him and his Father – as occurred elsewhere in this gospel. He may have used the simile of a vine with its branches that bear fruit as an example how they belong together. The fruit that was expected of them would become visible by their actions when they proclaim his message of love, hospitality, and generosity and put it into practice.

This passage displays a gnostic flavor when Jesus tells his disciples that he has given them the knowledge and the commandments from his Father for them to attain joy and be his friends.

We read again of the spurious promise that all prayers will be heard and granted when they are prayed in Jesus' name.

What does Jesus mean when he says that his disciples can't do anything without him? No answer to this question is given.

The World's Hatred
John 15: 18–27

18.	If the world hates you, you know that it has hated me before it hated you.
19.	If you were of the world, the world would love its own. But because you are not of the world, since I chose you out of the world, therefore the world hates you.

20.	Remember the word that I said to you: A servant is not greater than his lord. If they persecuted me, they will also persecute you. If they kept my word, they will keep yours also.
21.	But all these things will they do to you for my name's sake, because they don't know him who sent me.
22.	If I had not come and spoken to them, they would not have had sin; but now they have no excuse for their sin.
23.	He who hates me, hates my Father also.
24.	If I hadn't done among them the works which none other did, they wouldn't have had sin. But now have they seen and also hated both me and my Father.
25.	But that the word may be fulfilled that is written in their law, They hated me without a cause.
26.	When the Counselor has come, whom I will send to you from the Father, the Spirit of truth, who proceeds from the Father, he will testify about me.
27.	You will also testify, because you have been with me from the beginning.

John 16: 1–4

1.	"These things have I spoken to you, so that you wouldn't be caused to stumble.
2.	They will put you out of the synagogues. Yes, the time comes that whoever kills you will think that he offers service to God.
3.	They will do these things because they have not known the Father, nor me.

> 4. But I have told you these things, so that when the time comes, you may remember that I told you about them.

Jesus ostensibly warned his disciples that the world would hate and persecute them. The word for "world" is κόσμος (*kosmos*), which often has the meaning of "nation" (of Israel) in John. That the Jews, and not other nations were meant by using the word "world" becomes clear when the disciples are warned that they would be thrown out of the synagogues.

The situation described in this passage is a description of the animosity that arose between the Jews and the Christians after the Jewish War against Rome during AD 66–70. The Jews could not forgive the Ebionite followers of Jesus and the Christians for refusing to help with the defense of Jerusalem. The Christians, on the other hand, thought of the Jews as the killers of Jesus and regarded the destruction of Jerusalem as God's punishment for this deed. This bad relationship between Christians and Jews was clearly expressed in the book of Revelation – written during AD 96–97 – especially in Rev 11: 8.[255]

This passage must, therefore, have been written several years after the Jewish War, in contrast with the Proto-Gospel of John that was written before the war.

The Work of the Holy Spirit
John 16: 5–15

> 5. I didn't tell you these things from the beginning, because I was with you. But now I am going to him who sent me, and none of you asks me, Where are you going?

---

[255] Scholtz, *The Prophecies of Revelation*, 17, 80–82, 172–75, 309.

> 6. But because I have told you these things, sorrow has filled your heart.
> 7. Nevertheless I tell you the truth: It is to your advantage that I go away, for if I don't go away, the Counselor won't come to you. But if I go, I will send him to you.
> 8. When he has come, he will convict the world in respect to sin, and righteousness, and judgment;
> 9. of sin, because they don't believe in me;
> 10. of righteousness, because I am going to my Father, and you see me no more;
> 11. of judgment, because the prince of this world has been judged.
> 12. I have yet many things to tell you, but you can't bear them now.
> 13. However when he, the Spirit of truth, has come, he will guide you into all the truth, for he will not speak from himself; but whatever things he hears, he will speak. He will declare to you the things that are to come.
> 14. He will glorify me, for he will take from what is mine, and will declare it to you.
> 15. All things whatever the Father has are mine; therefore I said that he takes of mine, and will declare it to you.

The Jesus speaking in this passage is certainly not the Jesus who aspired to restore the Israelite monarchy. This Jesus is telling his disciples that he is ready to leave them and return to his Father in heaven. In his place the Spirit of truth, the Holy Spirit, is to come.

This Spirit differs from the Spirit of YHWH in the Old Testament, which was merely the mind or breath of God. For John it is a separate divine person, apart from the Father and the Son. He deliberately made a grammatical error by calling this Spirit "he" and "him" – the male personal pronoun, instead of the neutral personal pronoun, "it", that would have fitted the word "spirit", which is an impersonal or neutral noun.

The introduction of the Holy Spirit as a separate divine person in the discourse source of John is a continuation of Paul's teachings in this regard. It is, however, noticeable that the Spirit played no part in earlier documents, such as the Q Document, the Proto-Gospel of John, the letter of James, or the Didaché.

Sadness and Gladness
John 16: 16–24

16.	A little while, and you will not see me. Again a little while, and you will see me."
17.	Some of his disciples therefore said to one another, "What is this that he says to us, A little while, and you won't see me, and again a little while, and you will see me; and, Because I go to the Father?"
18.	They said therefore, "What is this that he says, A little while? We don't know what he is saying."
19.	Therefore Jesus perceived that they wanted to ask him, and he said to them, "Do you inquire among yourselves concerning this, that I said, A little while, and you won't see me, and again a little while, and you will see me?
20.	Most assuredly I tell you, that you will weep and lament, but the world will rejoice. You will be sorrowful, but your sorrow will be turned into joy.
21.	A woman, when she is in travail, has sorrow, because her time has come. But when she has delivered the child, she doesn't remember the anguish any more, for the joy that a

	child is born into the world.
22.	You therefore now have sorrow, but I will see you again, and your heart will rejoice, and no one will take your joy away from you.
23.	In that day you will ask me no question. Most assuredly I tell you, whatever you may ask of the Father, he will give it to you in my name.
24.	Until now, you have asked nothing in my name. Ask, and you will receive, that your joy may be made full.

This passage is anything but clear. The reader is repeatedly told that Jesus announced his departure and his return. There is, however, no indication when this departure would occur. Will it be when Jesus is crucified and buried or when he ascends into heaven? Is his return meant to be his resurrection or his return on Judgment Day?

The reader is, once again, reminded that his prayers will be heard if he asks in Jesus' name – something that runs counter to the experience of all believers through the ages.

Victory over the World
John 16: 25–33

25.	I have spoken these things to you in figures of speech. But the time comes when I will no more speak to you in figures of speech, but will tell you plainly about the Father.
26.	In that day you will ask in my name; and I don't say to you, that I will pray to the Father for you,
27.	for the Father himself loves you, because you have loved me, and have believed that I came forth from God.
28.	I came out from the Father, and have come into the world. Again, I leave the world, and go to the Father."

29.	His disciples said to him, "Behold, now you speak plainly, and speak no figures of speech.
30.	Now we know that you know all things, and don't need for anyone to question you. By this we believe that you came forth from God."
31.	Jesus answered them, "Do you now believe?
32.	Behold, the time comes, yes, has now come, that you will be scattered, everyone to his own place, and will leave me alone. Yet I am not alone, because the Father is with me.
33.	I have told you these things, that in me you may have peace. In the world you have oppression; but cheer up! I have overcome the world."

In this passage, Jesus told his disciples that he would talk in plain language from that moment onwards (as if he hadn't done so many times in the past). Because of that, they may believe in him.

The disciples were also warned that they would be scattered and persecuted, which did happen especially during the reigns of Emperor Nero (AD 54–68) and Emperor Domitian (AD 81–96). Because this part of John was written towards the end of the first century AD or even later, those predicted hardships were already history.

Jesus Prays for his Disciples
John 17: 1–26

1.	Jesus said these things, and lifting up his eyes to heaven, he said, "Father, the time has come. Glorify your Son, that your Son may also glorify you;
2.	even as you gave him authority over all flesh, that to all whom you have given him, he will give eternal life.

3.	This is eternal life, that they should know you, the only true God, and him whom you sent, Jesus Christ.
4.	I glorified you on the earth. I have accomplished the work which you have given me to do.
5.	Now, Father, glorify me with your own self with the glory which I had with you before the world existed.
6.	I revealed your name to the people whom you have given me out of the world. They were yours, and you have given them to me. They have kept your word.
7.	Now they know that all things whatever you have given me are from you,
8.	for the words which you have given me I have given to them, and they received them, and knew for sure that I came forth from you, and they believed that you sent me.
9.	I pray for them. I don't pray for the world, but for those whom you have given me, for they are yours.
10.	All things that are mine are yours, and yours are mine, and I am glorified in them.
11.	I am no more in the world, and these are in the world, and I am coming to you. Holy Father, keep them through your name which you have given me, that they may be one, even as we are.
12.	While I was with them in the world, I kept them in your name. Those whom you have given me I have kept. None of them is lost, except the son of perdition, that the Scripture might be fulfilled.
13.	But now I come to you, and I say these things in the world, that they may have my joy made full in themselves.

14.	I have given them your word. The world hated them, because they are not of the world, even as I am not of the world.
15.	I pray not that you would take them from the world, but that you would keep them from the evil one.
16.	They are not of the world even as I am not of the world.
17.	Sanctify them in your truth. Your word is truth.
18.	As you sent me into the world, even so I sent them into the world.
19.	For their sakes I sanctify myself, that they themselves also may be sanctified in truth.
20.	Neither for these only do I pray, but for those also who believe in me through their word,
21.	that they may all be one; even as you, Father, are in me, and I in you, that they also may be one in us; that the world may believe that you sent me.
22.	The glory which you have given me, I have given to them; that they may be one, even as we are one;
23.	I in them, and you in me, that they may be perfected into one; that the world may know that you sent me, and loved them, even as you loved me.
24.	Father, I desire that they also whom you have given me be with me where I am, that they may see my glory, which you have given me, for you loved me before the foundation of the world.
25.	Righteous Father, the world didn't know you, but I knew you; and these knew that you sent me.

> 26. I made known to them your name, and will make it known; that the love with which you loved me may be in them, and I in them."

The Jesus who was speaking in this passage, was certainly not the historical Jesus, a man of flesh and blood, but a glorified, exalted, and metaphysical being who had already left this world and resided in heaven after having accomplished the task given him by the Father. It is clear that this passage contains the musings of John's students or followers who added the discourse source to his proto-gospel long afterwards – and not anything that Jesus ever said or prayed.

When Jesus announced in this prayer that the work given to him by his Father had been completed, one is tempted to ask: was it then necessary that he be crucified and raised from the dead to save sinners from hell if he had already succeeded in his task of being the savior of mankind?

The repeated prayer that Jesus disciples and followers stay united never resulted in anything resembling unity. The book of Acts and Paul's letters testify of the opposite. The history of Christianity tells the story of how Christians liquidated and slaughtered each other and condemned each other to the everlasting flames and sparks of hell due to their differences regarding doctrinal issues.

The Arrest of Jesus
John 18: 4–6

> 4. Jesus therefore, knowing all the things that were coming on him, went forth, and said to them, "Who are you looking for?"

5.	They answered him, "Jesus of Nazareth." Jesus said to them, "I AM." Judas also, who betrayed him, was standing with them.
6.	When therefore he said to them, "I AM," they went backward, and fell to the ground.

These paragraphs were later added to John's Proto-Gospel at the point where Jesus' arrest was described to find a place where the author(s) of the discourse source could, once again, proclaim that Jesus is actually the same God who appeared to Moses (Ex 3: 14). It is no surprise that this story adds that his captors fell on their backs from the shock they got – although Jesus was, nevertheless and in spite of this shock, arrested.

Comments
Several conclusions can be drawn regarding the later additions and insertions into the Proto-Gospel of John.

It is apparent that this discourse source was never a single and coherent document. It consists of a loose collection of dialogues, speeches, and philosophical or theological arguments. They differ regarding style and contents and different hands may even be detected. There may have been a final editor who oversaw the final edition and who may even have made some corrections. These author(s) and editor must have thought that the Proto-Gospel of John was incomplete and needed to be enhanced. Out of respect for the apostle John, the contents of his proto-gospel were usually kept intact and unaltered.

The contents and style of this collection of documents is very different from earlier sources about Jesus' ministry, such as the Q Document and Johns Proto-Gospel – and even the Didaché (see Chapter 10). The final gospel must have been finalized during the time of Emperor Domitian between AD 81 and 96 (or even later) – more than 50 or 60 years after Jesus' crucifixion.

This late date explains why the image of Jesus differs so much from earlier descriptions because the story of Jesus acquired many legendary and even mythological accretions as the decades rolled by. One can safely say that the Jesus of the discourse source in John is not the same person encountered in the earliest documents.

Albrecht Dürer: Jesus and his Mother (1503)

It may also be argued that the Jesus presented in these sources has acquired more legendary and even mythological traits than found in the Synoptic Gospels, which can be dated to the seventies and eighties of the first century AD – at least a decade or two earlier than the discourse sources in John.

The earlier documents describe Jesus' campaign to convince people that he was the Messiah, the king of Israel who would restore the monarchy of King David. His message was that the arrival of the kingdom of God, a theocracy on earth, was imminent. When the discourse sources mentioned the kingdom of God it was exclusively a spiritual kingdom, far removed from a political kingdom on earth with Jerusalem as its capital.

The discourse sources contain the doctrine of the trinitarian God in embryonic form more clearly than the letters of Paul.

The three divine persons, Father, Son, and Holy Spirit, united in one Godhead, are clearly distinguished from each other in this source.

The historical value of this source is that it is a record of how the students and followers of John regarded Jesus. We find very little of the historical Jesus in this source. There may have been some genuine sayings and parables in a distorted form, interpreted from a vantage point of several decades later, but it is difficult to reconstruct them.

The theology of this source corresponds to a remarkable degree with the theology of the book of Revelation, which also had its origin in Ephesus towards the end of the first century AD, although its style and method of presentation of the message is very different. Revelation also presents Jesus as a celestial being who shares the heavenly throne with God, while the seven-fold Spirit is situated next to this throne.[256]

---

[256] Scholtz. *The Prophecies of Revelation.*

Chapter 11
THE DIDACHE

Introductory Notes

A document known as the "Didache" and of which the full translated title is "The Teaching of the Lord through the Twelve Apostles" (Διδαχὴ Κυρίου διὰ τῶν δώδεκα ἀποστόλων – *Didache Kuriou dia ton dodeka apostolon*), was only rediscovered in 1873 and immediately caused a stir after its publication in 1883 by Philotheos Bryennios, Metropolitan of Nicomedia, since it proved to be the oldest Christian document not contained in the New Testament.

Luschnig and Luschnig, who published the Greek text with a commentary, describe it as "a manual of early church discipline and church practices probably from the church in Syria, near Antioch, where the new believers were first called Christians." The author's name is unknown and the title is only a description of its contents. It is clear, though, that the author (or editor), who addresses his readers as "my children", was a Jewish believer who knew the Old Testament well, although he often quoted sayings of Jesus known from oral traditions or taken from written sources later incorporated into the gospels, like Q – which agree remarkably well with the reports of Jesus teachings in the gospels.[257]

The author(s) could have known some of the apostles of Jesus, who passed on Jesus' teachings to his other followers – hence the title of the document.[258]

---

[257] Luschnig and Luschnig. *The Teaching of the Twelve*, 1–3.
[258] Luschnig and Luschnig. *The Teaching of the Twelve*, 12–13.

The following topics are dealt with in the Didache:

- The two ways: the way of life and the way of death;
- Baptism;
- Fasting and prayer;
- The Eucharist and Eucharist prayer;
- Wandering teachers;
- Prophets, true and false;
- Christian wayfarers and immigrants;
- Payment of prophets and teachers;
- Worship n the Lords Day;
- Choosing bishops and deacons from the community; and
- The last days.

The document makes the impression of being a compilation of diverse unrelated elements. Chapters 1–6 give ethical instruction concerning the two ways, the way of life and the way of death, and reflect early Jewish-Christian ethical instructions for new converts before being baptized. Chapters 7–15 is the earliest example of a church order and it discusses baptism, fasting, prayer, the Eucharist, how to receive and test traveling apostles and prophets, and the appointment of bishops and deacons. Chapter 16 considers the signs of the expected coming of the Lord.[259]

The way in which Jesus is treated in this document is interesting. He is four times referred to as "Jesus thy child/son or servant" – that is, Gods child/son or servant (Did 9: 2; 9: 3; 10: 2; and 10: 3). The Greek word used, παιδὸς (*paidos*), is often translated with "servant" (Luke 1: 54, for example). This expression does not mean that Jesus is regarded as the only-begotten Son of God and of the same substance as God, for we also

---

[259] Enc. Brit. "Didaché".

read of "David thy child/son or servant" (Did 9: 2). When Jesus and David are both called sons of God it is an expression to emphasize their royal status as Israelite kings.

The title "Christ" is used twice, once in conjunction with the name Jesus. That may only mean that Jesus was regarded as a messiah, an anointed of God.

Luschnig and Luschnig concluded: "But to the earliest one or two generations of followers of Jesus, his religion seemed not to be different from Judaism but, rather, reformed and perfected Judaism."[260] This reformed Judaism – which may be equated with Ebionism – had no place for a deified Christ. Jesus is portrayed in the Didache merely as a wise teacher, not the eternal divine Son of God.

That these early Jewish followers of Jesus did not see themselves as anything but Jews is borne out by the archaeological record. Excavations of sites in Judea and Galilee dating from the first century AD demonstrate that no site can be regarded as specific Christian. Meyers and Chancey noted: "The material culture of the earliest followers of Jesus is extremely difficult to identify, precisely because it was largely indistinguishable from that of other Jews."[261]

Date and Place of Origin
There is uncertainty amongst scholars regarding the date and place of origin of the Didaché. Some authorities place it in the early second century AD, either in Egypt or Syria[262] while experts such as Luschnig and Luschnig found that at least certain parts were

---

[260] Luschnig and Luschnig,.*The Teaching of the Twelve,* 4.
[261] Meyers and Chancey. *Alexander to Constatine,* 177.
[262] Enc Brit, "Didache".

written during the forties and fifties of the first century AD, perhaps in Syria – contemporary with the letters of Paul, or even earlier.[263]

A thorough analysis of the contents of this document and its relationship with the gospels and Paul's letters, will show that one can indeed date this document – or its oldest parts, if it was a composite document with later additions – with confidence to the fifties of the first century AD, or even earlier. One encounters a situation like that described in Acts with itinerant apostles or missionaries, prophets, and teachers and no fixed ecclesiastical structures or hierarchies yet. There is no hint of the destruction of Jerusalem and the temple during the Jewish War of AD 66–70 as can be found in Mark, Matthew, and Luke. That means that it was compiled more or less two decades after Jesus' execution when many eye-witnesses of Jesus ministry were still available to be consulted.

The place of origin may well have been Syria. We read in Acts 9: 1–19 of followers of Jesus in Damascus, including Ananias, one of their leaders, who found the sightless Paul in the house of a certain Jew named Judas and baptized him after his conversion on the Damascus Road. These "disciples" of Jesus must have been Essenes, Nazoreans, or Ebionites, members of the community where the Didaché was likely compiled some years later.

According to Nesbit, there was a sizable Jewish community in Damascus at that time, including some Essenes. On the other hand, many Jews of the Diaspora also lived in Egypt, especially in Alexandria, the cultural and intellectual capital of the Roman Empire, and some of them were Essenes, from whom Jesus drew most of his followers.[264] On account of that, Egypt and Alexandria may be regarded as the place of origin of the Didaché, as well. It

---

[263] Luschnig and Luschnig, *The Teaching of the Twelve*, 1.
[264] Nesbit. *Jesus an Essene*, 5–6.

was certainly not Palestine, otherwise it may have been written in Hebrew or Aramaic, like most of the Dead Sea Scrolls.

An analysis of relevant selections of this document provides some interesting details about the life and teachings of Jesus:[265]

The Two Ways and the First Commandment
Did. 1.

1.	There are two Ways, one of Life and one of Death; but there is a great difference between the two Ways.
2.	Now the Way of Life is this: First, Thou shalt love God who made thee; secondly, thy neighbor as thyself; and all things whatsoever thou wouldst not have done to thee, neither do thou to another.
3.	Now the teaching of these [two] words [of the Lord] is this: Bless those who curse you, and pray for your enemies, and fast for those who persecute you; for what thank is there if ye love those who love you? Do not even Gentiles the same? But love ye those who hate you, and ye shall not have an enemy.
4.	Abstain from fleshly and bodily [worldly] lusts. If any one give thee a blow on the right cheek turn to him the other also, and thou shalt be perfect. If any one press thee to go with him one mile, go with him two; if any one take away thy cloak, give him also thy tunic; if any one take from thee what is thine, ask it not back, as indeed thou canst not.
5.	Give to every one that asketh thee, and ask not back, for the Father wills that from our own blessings we should give to

---

[265] The translation of the Didache used here was done by Philip Schaff and is published on the website of Catholic Planet eBooks.

> all. Blessed is he that gives according to the commandment, for he is guiltless. Woe to him that receives; for if any one receives, having need, he shall be guiltless, but he that has not need shall give account, why he received and for what purpose, and coming into distress he shall be strictly examined concerning his deeds, and he shall not come out thence till he have paid the last farthing.
>
> 6. But concerning this also it hath been said, "Let thine alms sweat (drop like sweat) into thy hands till thou know to whom thou shouldst give."

The idea of two ways come from Jesus who taught in Matt. 7: 13–14 (a part of M, Matthews unique material):

> "Enter in by the narrow gate; for wide is the gate, and broad is the way, that leads to destruction, and many are those who enter in by it. How narrow is the gate, and restricted is the way that leads to life! Few are those who find it."

The "way of life" according to the Didache, differs substantially from the message of salvation given in Paul's epistles and the discourse sources of John. For instance, Paul wrote in Rom 3: 23–25:

> "… for all have sinned, and fall short of the glory of God; being justified freely by his grace through the redemption that is in Christ Jesus; whom God set forth to be an atoning sacrifice, through faith, in his blood, to show his righteousness because of the passing over of the sins done before, in the forbearance of God."

Nothing of this sort is to be found in the Didache. There is nothing to suggest that one should put one's trust in Jesus Christ to be saved, as Christians are taught by Paul.

Jesus told a rich man that he ought to obey the Ten Commandments and practice charity by selling all his assets, donating the proceeds to the poor and to become a follower of Jesus to gain "eternal life" (Mark 10: 17–23). In effect, Jesus invited him to join the party of the Essenes if he wanted to attain eternal life.

The summary of the law in Did 1: 2 is quoted from Deut 6: 4; 10: 12; and 30: 6. The golden rule also mentioned in Did 1: 2 is an adaptation of Matt 7: 12 and Luke 6: 31, which is part of the Q document.

The command in 1: 3 to love one's enemies is very similar to Matt 5: 43–47, which was taken from Q. Similarly, the advice to be tolerant and generous in Did 1: 4–5 comes from Matt 5: 39–42, which also occurs in Q.

The advice found in Did 1: 4–5 is an adaptation of Matt 5: 39–42 and Luke 6: 29–30 – both of which appear in Q.

The last sentence (1: 6) ["Let thine alms sweat (drop like sweat) into thy hands till thou know to whom thou shouldst give"] also seems to be a saying of Jesus, not recorded anywhere else, although various early church fathers quoted it as if it were Scripture.[266] It may well have been contained in a part of Q not used by Matthew and Luke, or it may have been known from oral tradition.

Other Sins Forbidden
Did. 3: 7

7.	But be thou meek, for the meek shall inherit the earth.

Did 3: 7 is very similar to Matt 5: 5, a unique part of Matthew (part of M), not found in the other gospels: "Blessed are the humble, for they shall inherit the earth."

---

[266] Luschnig & Luschnig, *The Didaché*, 21.

Various Precepts
Did. 4

1.	My child, thou shalt remember night and day him that speaks to thee the word of God, and thou shalt honor him
2.	My child, thou shalt remember night and day him that speaks to thee the word of God, and thou shalt honor him as the Lord, for where the Lordship is spoken of, there is the Lord.
3.	Thou shalt not desire (make) division, but shalt make peace between those at strife. Thou shalt judge justly; thou shalt not respect a person (or, show partiality) in rebuking for transgressions.
4.	Thou shalt not be double–minded (doubtful in thy mind) whether it shall be or not.
5.	Be not one that stretches out his hands for receiving, but draws them in for giving.
6.	If thou hast [anything], thou shalt give with thy hands a ransom for thy sins.
7.	Thou shalt not hesitate to give, nor in giving shalt thou murmur, for thou shalt know who is the good recompenser of the reward.
8.	Thou shalt not turn away him that needeth, but shalt share all things with thy brother, and shalt not say that they are thine own; for if you are fellow–sharers in that which is imperishable (immortal), how much more in perishable (mortal) things?
10.	Thou shalt not in thy bitterness lay commands on thy man–servant (bondman), or thy maid–servant (bondwoman), who hope in the same God, lest they should not fear Him who is God over [you] both; for He comes not to call [men]

> .   according to the outward appearance (condition), but [he comes] on those whom the Spirit has prepared.
> 13. Thou shalt not forsake the commandments of the Lord, but thou shalt keep what thou hast received, neither adding [thereto] nor taking away [therefrom].
> 14. In the congregation (in church) thou shalt confess thy transgressions, and thou shalt not come to thy prayer (or, place of prayer) with an evil conscience. This is the way of life.

Did 4: 1 reminds one of Matt 18: 20 (part of M) where Jesus said: "For where two or three are gathered together in my name, there I am in the midst of them."

It does seem as if Did 4: 3–8 contain sayings of Jesus not known from any other source. Where Did 4: 13 mentions "the commandments of the Lord", that may well refer to the foregoing verses.

The generosity recommended in Did 4: 5–8 is in accordance with the lifestyle of the Essenes, as known from other sources.

It is known that the Essenes did not keep slaves. The command in Did 4: 10 to treat slaves or servants humanely and as fellow-believers may be understood against this background.

Did. 4: 13 is an echo of Jesus who taught:

> "Whoever then goes against the smallest of these laws, teaching men to do the same, will be named least in the kingdom of heaven; but he who keeps the laws, teaching others to keep them, will be named great in the kingdom of heaven" (Matt 5: 19 – part of M).

The original Greek for "the commandments of the Lord" in Did 4: 13 clearly refers to the totality of Jesus teachings available to the compiler(s) of the Didaché at that time, either in oral or written form.

The word for "congregation" or "church" (ἐκκλησία – *ekklesia*) in Did 4: 14 is the word Jesus used in Matt 18: 15–19 (part of M) to describe the body or gathering of his followers and it does not necessarily refer to the churches or congregations founded by Paul in the Greek world, but may refer to the group of "disciples" in Damascus in Acts 9: 19, as well as like-minded groups elsewhere (see the map of Palestine and surrounding areas in Chapter 1).

The Way of Death
Did. 5

1.	But the way of death is this: [A long list of sins is then given.]
2.	Persecutors of the good, hating truth, loving a lie, not knowing the reward of righteousness, not cleaving to that which is good nor to righteous judgment, watchful not for that which is good but for that which is evil; far from whom is meekness and endurance, loving vanity, seeking after reward, not pitying the poor, not toiling with him who is vexed with toil, not knowing Him that made them, murderers of children, destroyers of the handiwork of God, turning away from the needy, vexing the afflicted, advocates of the rich, lawless judges of the poor, wholly sinful.
3.	May ye, children, be delivered from all these.

This Chapter mentions a long list of sins condemned in the Old Testament, which lead to the way of death. Emphasis is placed on helping the poor and condemning the rich – much as Jesus taught in accordance with his Essene background.

Against False Teachers, and Food Offered to Idols
Did. 6

2.	For if indeed thou art able to bear the whole yoke of the Lord thou shalt be perfect; but if thou art not able, do what thou canst.
3.	And as regards food, bear what thou canst, but against idol-offerings be exceedingly on thy guard, for it is a service of dead gods.

The "yoke of the Lord" reminds one of Jesus who said:

> "Take my yoke on you, and learn from me, for I am humble and lowly in heart; and you will find rest for your souls. For my yoke is easy, and my burden is light." (Matt 11: 29–30 – a part of M).

The advice to avoid food sacrificed to idols echoes Paul who gave the same advice to the Corinthians (1 Cor 10: 20). The strong antipathy of the Jews in Jesus time against the Romans and their pagan religion must also have played a role in this verse. Because this issue is raised in two independent documents is an indication that many followers of Jesus – as well as Jews in general – had questions in this regard.

Baptism
Did 7.

1.	Now concerning baptism, baptize thus: Having first taught all these things, baptize ye into the name of the Father, and of the Son, and of the Holy Spirit, in living water.
2.	And if thou hast not living water, baptize into other water; and if thou canst not in cold, then in warm (water).

> 3. But if thou hast neither, pour [water] thrice upon the head in the name of the Father, and of the Son, and of the Holy Spirit.
> 4. But before Baptism let the baptizer and the baptized fast, and any others who can; but thou shalt command the baptized to fast for one or two days before.

This passage mentions twice that baptism must be performed "in the name of the Father, and of the Son, and of the Holy Spirit". This is a quotation from Matt 28: 19. This verse in Matthew is not repeated anywhere in any of the other gospels and is unique to Matthew. Since Matthew was composed long after the Didaché, it must be concluded that this baptismal formula must have been copied and inserted from Matthew by the scribe who produced the only extant copy of the Didache. This baptismal formula is, anyway, quite out of character compared with the rest of the Didache.

In Acts 2: 38; Acts 8: 16; Acts 10: 48; Acts 19: 5; and Rom 6: 3 it is reported that the apostles baptized new converts merely "in the name of Jesus Christ". Similarly, Did 9: 5 mentions "those baptized into the name of the Lord." The formula to baptize in the name of the three divine persons, therefore, seems to be a later addition to the Didaché, done by a scribe or editor who may also have added Chapter 16 at the end of the Didache (*q v*). The baptismal formula of Matt 28: 19 seems to be the invention of the author of Matthew's Gospel, which did not reflect the usual formula in apostolic times.

This baptism was a continuation of the practice of John the Baptist, as well of Jesus and his disciples (John 3: 22– 23 & 26; 4: 1– 2). The Essenes were also known for their ritual baths (see Chapter 2). The baptism described in the Didaché must, therefore, not be confused with the baptism as performed by Paul to converts from paganism into his brand of Christianity (Acts 16: 15 & 33; 18: 8; 1 Cor 1: 14–16).

Fasting and Prayer
Did 8.

1.	Let not your fasts be with the hypocrites, for they fast on the second and fifth day of the week; but ye shall fast on the fourth day, and the preparation day (Friday).
2.	Neither pray ye as the hypocrites, but as the Lord commanded in His Gospel, so pray ye: "Our Father, who art in heaven, hallowed be Thy Name. Thy Kingdom come. Thy will be done, as in heaven, so on earth. Give us this day our daily (needful) bread. And forgive us our debt as we also forgive our debtors. And bring us not into temptation, but deliver us from the evil one (or, from evil). For Thine is the power and the glory for ever."
3.	Pray thus thrice a day.

Jesus condemned the way the hypocrites of his time used to fast and pray in Matt 6: 5 & 16 – just as Did. 8: 1–2 does. These verses are from the M source.

The Didaché provides the text of the Lord's Prayer as it is to be found in Matt 6:9–13 and Luke 11: 2–4 as part of Q, while adding the last phrase of this prayer, which does not occur in the oldest manuscripts of Matthew and never in Luke, but were added later – perhaps taking it from the Didaché.

The Eucharist
Did. 9

1.	Now as regards the Eucharist (the Thank-offering), give thanks after this manner:
2.	First for the cup: "We give thanks to Thee, our Father, for the holy vine of David Thy servant, which thou hast made known to us through Jesus, Thy servant: to Thee be the glory for ever."
3.	And for the broken bread: "We give thanks to Thee, our Father, for the life and knowledge which Thou hast made known to us through Jesus, Thy servant: to Thee be the glory for ever.
4.	"As this broken bread was scattered upon the mountains and gathered together became one, so let Thy church be gathered together from the ends of the earth into Thy kingdom, for Thine is the glory and the power through Jesus Christ for ever."
5.	But let no one eat or drink of your Eucharist, except those baptized into the name of the Lord; for as regards this also the Lord has said: "Give not that which is holy to the dogs."

This Chapter deals with the Lords Supper, here called the Eucharist (Greek: εὐχαριστία – *eucharistia*), a term used a few times by Paul in his letters and which must have been already in widespread use when the Didaché was written. The usual meaning of this word is "thanksgiving"

The description of the Eucharist differs fundamentally from that given in Matt 26:26–28; Mark 14:22–24; Luke 22:17–20, and I Cor 11:23–25. Although the drinking of wine and the breaking of bread, as described in the Didache, are also part of the ceremony as mentioned in the scriptural texts, there is no link with the crucifixion of Jesus as in the other parts of Scripture. It is purely a thanksgiving celebration for God's blessings "through Jesus, Thy servant (or son/child)". It is also a prayer that God bless his church.

Albrecht Dürer: The Last Supper (1523)

Jesus is, though, not the only servant or son of God; David is also called Gods son or servant. This title is meant to point to the royal status of both.

Did 9: 5 contains a quotation from Matt 7: 6, which is also part of the M Document.

Prayer after Communion
Did. 10.

1.	Now after being filled, give thanks after this manner:
2.	"We thank Thee, Holy Father, for Thy Holy Name, which Thou hast caused to dwell (tabernacle) in our hearts, and for the knowledge and faith and immortality which Thou hast made known to us through Jesus Thy Servant, to Thee be the glory for ever.

> 3. "Thou, O, Almighty Sovereign, didst make all things for Thy Names sake; Thou gavest food and drink to men for enjoyment that they might give thanks to Thee; but to us Thou didst freely give spiritual food and drink and eternal life through Thy Servant.
> 4. "Before all things we give thanks to Thee that Thou art mighty; to Thee be the glory for ever.
> 5. "Remember, O Lord, Thy Church to deliver her from all evil and to perfect her in Thy love; and gather her together from the four winds, sanctified for Thy kingdom which Thou didst prepare for her; for Thine is the power and the glory for ever.
> 6. "Let grace come, and let this world pass away. Hosanna to the God of David. If anyone is holy let him come, if any one is not holy let him repent. Maranatha. Amen."
> 7. But permit the Prophets to give thanks as much as [in what words] they wish.

In Did 10: 2 "Jesus Thy Servant" (or child/son) is again mentioned. Thanks is being given to God who gave Jesus as a messenger or teacher regarding "the knowledge and faith and immortality". Jesus is certainly not seen as Gods eternal divine Son or the savior of believers by dying on the cross.

According to Did 10: 3 this message brought "spiritual food and drink and eternal life through Thy Servant" (Jesus).

The prayer in Did 10: 5 that God will gather his church "together from the four winds" is similar to Mark 13: 27 (and Matt 24: 31): "Then will he send forth his angels, and will gather together his elect from the four winds, from the ends of the earth to the ends of the sky."

Of course, the Didaché could not have copied this verse from Mark because this gospel was only written much later. Mark and Did 10: 5 both copied this expression from Zech 6: 5 and Dan 7: 2.

Two strange words are used in Did 10: 6 – "Hosanna" and "Maranatha". The word ὡσαννά (*hosanna*) is found in Mark 11: 9–10 and Matt 21: 9 & 15 when the crowds in Jerusalem shouted this word when welcoming Jesus on the back of an ass as their king. This is the Greek rendering of a Hebrew expression found, for instance, in Ps 118: 25 – הוֹשִׁיעָה נָּא (*hoshiah na*), which may be translated with "help or save (us)!" It was a common expression in the Jewish world and use of it by the Didaché cannot be seen as a quotation from the gospels.[267]

The expression Μαρανα θα (*Marana the*) is also used in 1 Cor 16: 22 and is derived from Aramaic (מרנאתא – *marnata*). It may be translated as "Come, Lord!" It was in common use by the Jews and Jewish Christians.[268]

Teachers, Apostles, and Prophets
Did 11
This Chapter deals with wandering teacher, apostles (missionaries) and prophets and how to discriminate between genuine and false preachers. This situation was typical of the apostolic age when ecclesiastical offices were not yet fully formalized, although bishops and deacons are mentioned in Did 15.

We find in Eph 4:11 a list of all these itinerant preachers during the apostolic age:

---

[267] Luschnif & Luschnig. *The Didache*. 47.
[268] Luschnif & Luschnig. *The Didache*. 47.

"He gave some to be apostles; and some, prophets; and some, evangelists; and some, shepherds and teachers…"

This plethora of holy people are also mentioned in Rom 12: 6, Rom 16: 7. I Cor. 14:1– 33, and 1 Thess 5: 20.

Although this chapter tells us nothing about the life and teachings of Jesus, it helps us to date the Didaché to the apostolic age, the first few decades after Jesus' time.

Reception of Christians
Did 12.
In this Chapter, hospitality towards fellow-Christian is advocated. The way travelling Christians must be treated reminds one of the hospitality and sharing of belongings as practiced by the Essenes and the followers of Jesus in Jerusalem (Acts 2: 44–46).

This Chapter (1: 4) mentions "a Christian" (Χριστιανός – *Christianos*). This name was given to the disciples in Antioch and Herod Agrippa wanted to know from Paul whether he was trying to make a Christian of him (Acts 11: 26; 26: 28). The term is also used in 1 Pet 4: 16 and it seems as if some other followers of Jesus adopted this name during the apostolic age, as happened in the community where the Didaché originated.

Support of Prophets
Did 13.
This Chapter deals with the support of resident prophets and teachers serving in a certain local church. This, again, describes conditions during the apostolic age.

Christian Assembly on the Lords Day
Did 14

> 1. And on the Lords Day of the Lord come together, and break bread, and give thanks, having before confessed your transgressions, that your sacrifice may be pure.
> 2. Let no one who has a dispute with his fellow come together with you until they are reconciled, that your sacrifice may not be defiled.
> 3. For this is that which was spoken by the Lord: "In every place and time offer me a pure sacrifice, for I am a great King, saith the Lord, and my name is wonderful among the Gentiles."

It is not certain what is meant by "the Lords Day of the Lord". The only place in the New Testament where "the Lords Day" is mentioned is Rev. 1: 10. This is usually understood to be a Sunday.

Luschnig & Luschnig also think that the Didaché refers to a Sunday,[269] the day on which the converts of Paul gathered for their meetings (Acts 20:7, 11, 13; 1 Corinthians 16:1– 2).

It has already been shown, on the other hand, that the Didaché was compiled in a Jewish Christian or Ebionite community. These Christians lived according to the Law of Moses (Acts 15: 1– 2) and it may, therefore, be that this chapter refers to worship on the Jewish Sabbath, the Saturday.

The need for reconciliation mentioned in Did 14: 2 is taken from Matt 5: 23– 24 (which is part of M) –

> "If therefore you are offering your gift at the altar, and there remember that your brother has anything against you, leave your gift there before the altar, and go your way. First be reconciled to your brother, and then come and offer your gift."

---

[269] Luschnig & Luschnig, "The Teaching of the Twelve Apostles", 57.

The third verse in this Chapter is quoted from Malachi 1:11.

Bishops and Deacons; Christian Reproof
Did 15

1.	Elect therefore for yourselves Bishops and Deacons worthy of the Lord, men meek, and not lovers of money, and truthful, and approved; for they too minister to you the ministry of the Prophets and Teachers.
2.	Therefore despise them not, for they are those that are the honored [men] among you with the Prophets and Teachers.
3.	And reprove one another not in wrath, but in peace, as ye have [it] in the gospel; and with every one that transgresses against another let no one speak, nor let him hear [a word] from you until he repents.
4.	But so do your prayers and alms and all your actions as ye have [it] in the gospel of our Lord.

The election of office-bearers had to be done by the show of hands, according to the Greek expression used. Bishops or overseers were initially also called elders or presbyters in Acts and the letters of Paul. Deacons were mostly involved with charitable activities (Acts 15: 2; Rom 16: 1; Phil 1:1; I Tim. 3:1– 13; and Titus 1:5– 9).

The conciliation spoken of in 15: 3 refers to Matt 18: 15–17. Of this passage in Matthew, verse 15 is part of Q and verses 16–17 come from M.

Chapter 15: 3–4 mentions "the gospel" twice. This may be the Q document and the M document that the compiler of the Didaché had at his disposal.

Watchfulness: the Coming of the Lord
Did 16.

1. Watch over your life; let not your lamps be quenched and let not your loins be unloosed, but be ye ready; for ye know not the hour in which our Lord comes.
2. But be ye frequently gathered together, seeking the things that are profitable for your souls; for the whole time of your faith shall not profit you except in the last season ye be found perfect.
3. For in the last days the false prophets and destroyers shall be multiplied, and the sheep shall be turned into wolves, and love shall be turned into hate.
4. For when lawlessness increases, they shall hate and persecute, and deliver up one another; and then shall appear the world-deceiver as Son of God, and shall do signs and wonders, and the earth shall be delivered into his hands, and he shall commit iniquities which have never yet come to pass from the beginning of the world.
5. And then shall the race of men come into the fire of trial, and many shall be offended and shall perish; but they who endure in their faith shall be saved from under the curse itself.
6. And then shall appear the signs of the truth: first the sign of opening in heaven; then the sign of the voice of the trumpet; and the third, the resurrection of the dead.
7. Not, however, of all, but as was said, "The Lord shall come, and all the saints with him."
8. Then shall the world see the Lord coming upon the clouds of heaven.

These warnings regarding the coming of the Lord and Judgment Day are evidently a later addition to the document. The following considerations lead to this conclusion:

- There is no logical connection with the preceding chapter, as is the case with the rest of the document. It deals with a totally unrelated topic, namely the coming of the Lord.
- There are various quotations and allusions to the canonical gospels in this Chapter. Some of them occur in Q and M, but also in Mark and Luke. The quotations in the previous chapters all come from Q and M, apart from a few references to the Old Testament. The fact that Mark and Luke are quoted means that this Chapter must have been written a few decades after the rest of the document when the canonical gospels were already in circulation.

In this Chapter, there are many sayings of Jesus known from the gospels. They are all repeated from the gospels in a rather random order.

Summary

A scrutiny of the contents of the Didaché reveals the following:

- The core of this document was drawn up no later than the fifties of the first century AD, at a time when the canonical gospels – including John's Proto-Gospel – have not yet appeared and where the organization of the various churches reflected the conditions prevailing during the apostolic age as described in Paul's letters and the book of Acts.
- The compiler(s) of the Didaché made extensive use of the Q document and the M document. There is nowhere any sign that the L document, the unique parts later incorporated into Luke, as well as the rest of the gospels, were consulted. There is the possibility that certain parts of M could have been a part of Q, which was not quoted by Luke and, therefore, was not included in the reconstructed Q Document (see Chapter 3).

- The Didaché often mentions "the gospel". That expression probably refers to the Q document and the M document, which were known to the author(s) of the Didaché
- The fact that the Q document and the M document were frequently referred to in the Didache confirms the hypothesis that these sources were written documents before they were incorporated into the canonical gospels, after which they were discarded because their contents were anyway preserved in the other gospels (that is, if the parts of M quoted by the Didaché was not a part of Q, which Luke did not use).
- There are signs that the Didaché contains sayings of Jesus not recorded elsewhere, although there is no certainty about which sayings come from Jesus or are the ideas of the compiler(s) of the Didaché.
- Jesus is portrayed in the first fifteen (original) chapters as an ordinary mortal and not as a divine personage who ascended bodily (like Elijah) up to heaven after his death and resurrection and who is expected to return sometime in the future. Where he is called the servant, son, or child of God, it is only to emphasize his royal status as a descendant of David, who is also called the servant, son, or child of God.
- No mention is made of Jesus crucifixion and death as reported in the New Testament – not even in conjunction with the Eucharist, which is usually regarded as a commemoration of Jesus last meal with his disciples before he was crucified.
- The members of the community in which the Didaché originated called themselves "Christians", although not in the sense meant by Paul and his converts. They were mostly Jewish followers of Jesus who lived either in Syria where the appellation "Christian" was used for the first time, or in Egypt.

- The title of this document, "The Teaching of the Lord through the Twelve Apostles", claims that it contained the teachings of Jesus and his group of twelve apostles – who were all Jews who worshipped in the Jerusalem temple and lived according to the Laws of Moses (Acts 2: 40; Acts 15: 1; Gal 2: 11– 14). They were Essenes, Nazoreans, or Ebionites and many of their convictions and practices are reflected in this document.
- The fact that the Didaché never became part of the New Testament, is an indication that it must have had a rather restricted readership and was rejected by the church fathers of the second century AD and later who gathered the documents that became the New Testament, due to its Ebionite ideas that contradicted the teachings of Paul and the canonical gospels.
- The Didache may be regarded as a trustworthy historical source for the life and teachings of Jesus and the conditions under which his followers practiced their religion during the first few decades after his crucifixion.

Chapter 12
CLEMENS ROMANUS

According to Catholic tradition, Saint Clement of Rome, also called Clemens Romanus – to use his Latin name – was the fourth bishop of Rome and a successor of Peter, who is regarded as the first bishop and pope in Rome.

Little is known about his life. He is thought to have died in AD 99, either as a martyr, or of natural causes. Paul mentions a certain Clement in Phil 4: 3 and some ancient authors thought that this Clement was also one of the successors of Peter in Rome.

The only piece of writing that can be attributed to him with some certainty is his letter to the church in Corinth in which he admonished a few hotheads who caused conflict in that church.

Clement probably knew Paul and Peter in Rome before their deaths during the reign of Nero and he would have been familiar with their versions of the gospel message.[270] It is clear from the following passage in Chapter 47 that he knew Paul's writings:

> "Take up the epistle of the blessed Apostle Paul. What did he write to you at the time when the Gospel first began to be preached? Truly, under the inspiration of the Spirit, he wrote to you concerning himself, and Cephas, and Apollos, because even then parties had been formed among you."

---

[270] Cath. Enc. "Pope St. Clement I"; N W Enc. "Pope Clement I"; Peterlin. "Clement's Answer to the Corinthian Conflict".

If he had indeed died in AD 99, this letter must have been written before that time – more or less at the same time as the canonical book of Revelation, which can be accurately dated to AD 96–97.[271] This makes this letter the earliest writing of one of the Church Fathers.

In this letter to the Corinthians, Clement often refers to Jesus Christ. He mostly calls him "our Lord Jesus Christ", "Jesus Christ our Lord", or simply "Christ". He also often calls Christ simply "the Lord" (Greek: ὁ κυρίος – *ho kurios*) but he uses this name also for God, although it is sometimes used in the following combination: "The Lord God" (Greek: κύριος ὁ Θεὸς – *kyrios ho theos*). With this, he followed the usage of the gospels and Paul's letters where Jesus is also often called "the Lord" – which simply means "the Master". When this word is used for God, it is the translation of the Hebrew name for God (יהוה – *YHWH*).

A few snippets of Jesus teachings are quoted. In the paragraphs that follow, Clément's references to Jesus will be analyzed and evaluated for their credibility and value as historical sources.[272]

Salutation
Chapter 1

> The Church of God which sojourns at Rome, to the Church of God sojourning at Corinth, to those who are called and sanctified by the will of God, through our Lord Jesus Christ: Grace to you, and peace, from Almighty God through Jesus Christ, be multiplied.

---

[271] Scholtz. *The Prophecies of Revelation.*
[272] The translation of 1 Clement made by Charles Hoole and published on the website of Early Christian Writings will be used in this examination of this letter.

The salutation of this rather lengthy letter is anonymous. It is written on behalf of the church in Rome, probably by Clement. Jesus is mentioned twice – once as the savior of the faithful. The salutation is more or less in the style of Paul's letters.

Humility
Chapter 13

> Let us therefore, brethren, be of humble mind…, but let him that glories glory in the Lord, in diligently seeking Him, and doing judgment and righteousness", being especially mindful of the words of the Lord Jesus which He spoke, teaching us meekness and long–suffering. For thus He spoke: "Be merciful, that you may obtain mercy; forgive, that it may be forgiven to you; as you do, so shall it be done to you; as you judge, so shall you be judged; as you are kind, so shall kindness be shown to you; with what measure you measure, with the same it shall be measured to you." By this precept and by these rules let us establish ourselves, that we walk with all humility in obedience to His holy words. For the holy word says, "On whom shall I look, but on him that is meek and peaceable, and who trembles at My words?"

The sayings attributed to Jesus in this chapter seem to be a summary of teachings found in the Q Document and the gospels, except for the last sentence. Clement quotes Jesus words from memory and he does not mention where he found them. One may wonder whether he relied on any written source or did he remember what he may have heard from Peter and other sources?

All these sayings are in accordance with Jesus simple and peace-loving lifestyle, as known from Q and the canonical gospels.

Chapter 16

For Christ is of those who are humble–minded, and not of those who exalt themselves over His flock. Our Lord Jesus Christ, the Sceptre of the majesty of God, did not come in the pomp of pride or arrogance, although He might have done so, but in a lowly condition, as the Holy Spirit had declared regarding Him. For He says, "Lord, who has believed our report, and to whom is the arm of the Lord revealed? We have declared [our message] in His presence: He is, as it were, a child, and like a root in thirsty ground; He has no form nor glory, yea, we saw Him, and He had no form nor comeliness; but His form was without eminence, yea, deficient in comparison with the [ordinary] form of men. He is a man exposed to stripes and suffering, and acquainted with the endurance of grief: for His countenance was turned away; He was despised, and not esteemed. He bears our iniquities, and is in sorrow for our sakes; yet we supposed that [on His own account] He was exposed to labour, and stripes, and affliction. But He was wounded for our transgressions, and bruised for our iniquities. The chastisement of our peace was upon Him, and by His stripes we were healed. All we, like sheep, have gone astray; [every] man has wandered in his own way; and the Lord has delivered Him up for our sins, while He in the midst of His sufferings opens not His mouth. He was brought as a sheep to the slaughter, and as a lamb before her shearer is dumb, so He opens not His mouth. In His humiliation His judgment was taken away; who shall declare His generation? For His life is taken from the earth. For the transgressions of my people was He brought down to death. And I will give the wicked for His sepulchre, and the rich for His death, because He did no iniquity, nor was guile found in His mouth. And the Lord is pleased to purify Him by stripes. If you make an offering for sin, your soul shall see a long–lived seed. And the Lord is pleased to relieve Him of the affliction of His soul, to show Him light, and to form Him with understanding, to justify the Just One who ministers well to many; and He Himself shall carry their sins. On this account He shall inherit many, and shall divide the spoil of the strong; because His soul was delivered to death, and He was reckoned among the transgressors, and He bare the sins of many, and for their sins was He delivered." And again He says, "I am a worm, and no man; a reproach of men, and despised of the people. All who see Me have derided Me; they have spoken with their lips; they have wagged their head, [saying] He hoped in God, let Him deliver Him, let Him save Him, since He delights in Him." You see, beloved, what is the example which has been given us; for if the Lord thus humbled Himself, what shall we do who have through Him come under the yoke of His grace?

This lengthy passage contains a free rendering of Isa 52–53, which deals with the suffering servant of God. Clement applied that to Jesus who died to free others from their sins. He also quoted loosely from Ps 22 where the poet calls himself a worm, due to being despised by the people and he also applies that to Jesus.

Clements calls Christ "the Sceptre of the majesty of God" and it seems as if he does not see Christ as a divine being – only somebody declared by the Holy Spirit to be the son of God.

Order in Creation
Chapter 20

The very smallest of living beings meet together in peace and concord. All these the great Creator and Lord of all has appointed to exist in peace and harmony; while He does good to all, but most abundantly to us who have fled for refuge to His compassions

> through Jesus Christ our Lord, to whom be glory and majesty for ever and ever. Amen.

The first part of this Chapter (not quoted) deals with the order to be seen in God's creation. God's care and compassion for his children become most visible through Jesus Christ, who deserved "glory and majesty for ever and ever" (a quote from Heb 2: 9).

Those who must be Honored
Chapter 21

> Let us rather offend those men who are foolish, and inconsiderate, and lifted up, and who glory in the pride of their speech, than [offend] God. Let us reverence the Lord Jesus Christ, whose blood was given for us; let us esteem those who have the rule over us; let us honour the aged among us; let us train up the young men in the fear of God; let us direct our wives to that which is good.

According to this Chapter, Jesus Christ is only one of a list of people who must be honored – rulers, old people, young people, and wives. Clement thinks of him as a special person, but not as a divine being, although he gave his blood for us.

Chapter 22

> Now the faith which is in Christ confirms all these [admonitions]. For He Himself by the Holy Ghost thus addresses us: "Come, you children, listen to Me; I will teach you the fear of the Lord. What man is he that desires life, and loves to see good days? Keep your tongue from evil, and your lips from speaking guile. Depart from evil, and do good; seek peace, and pursue it. The eyes of the Lord are upon the righteous, and His ears are [open] to their prayers.

Clement quotes two otherwise unknown sayings of Jesus. It is impossible to determine whether they are genuine. If Clement served the church of Rome together with Peter – which seems probable from Chapter 5 of this letter – he may have heard these sayings from the apostle.

Resurrection a Natural Process
Chapter 24

> Let us consider, beloved, how the Lord continually proves to us that there shall be a future resurrection, of which He has rendered the Lord Jesus Christ the first-fruits by raising Him from the dead. Let us contemplate, beloved, the resurrection which is at all times taking place. Day and night declare to us a resurrection. The night sinks to sleep, and the day arises; the day [again] departs, and the night comes on. Let us behold the fruits [of the earth], how the sowing of grain takes place. The sower goes forth, and casts it into the ground; and the seed being thus scattered, though dry and naked when it fell upon the earth, is gradually dissolved. Then out of its dissolution the mighty power of the providence of the Lord raises it up again, and from one seed many arise and bring forth fruit.

Chapter 25

> Let us consider that wonderful sign [of the resurrection] which takes place in Eastern lands, that is, in Arabia and the countries round about. There is a certain bird which is called a phoenix. (...)

Clement believed there was nothing unusual about Jesus Christ's resurrection from the grave, since death and rebirth is a natural process throughout creation. He even cites the example of the mythological bird, the Phoenix, that lived 500 years, died and was reborn again, as proof for this assertion.

This explanation of the resurrection is not found anywhere in the New Testament. It is part and parcel of the mythological and magical thinking of the ancient world. It is also noticeable that Clement fails to refer to any gospels description of how Jesus appeared to his disciples after being resurrected. One may ask: did Clement and the church in Rome ever had a copy of one of the gospels at their disposal?

Jesus a Descendant from Jacob
Chapter 32

> Whosoever will candidly consider each particular, will recognise the greatness of the gifts which were given by him [Jacob]. For from him have sprung the priests and all the Levites who minister at the altar of God. From him also [was descended] our Lord Jesus Christ according to the flesh. From him [arose] kings, princes, and rulers of the race of Judah. Nor are his other tribes in small glory, inasmuch as God had promised, "Your seed shall be as the stars of heaven." All these, therefore, were highly honoured...

Jesus Christ was just one of the many descendants of the patriarch Jacob, according to this passage. Clement added that he was a descendant "according to the flesh", which suggests that Jesus was more than a mere mortal.

Christ our High Priest
Chapter 36

> This is the way, beloved, in which we find our Saviour, even Jesus Christ, the High Priest of all our offerings, the defender and helper of our infirmity. By Him we look up to the heights of heaven. By Him we behold, as in a glass, His immaculate and most excellent visage. By Him are the eyes of our hearts opened. By Him

In this chapter, Clement wrote more about his convictions regarding Jesus Christ than anywhere else in this letter to the Corinthians. He loosely follows the train of thoughts in the first Chapter of the Letter to the Hebrews where it is shown with quotations from the Old Testament that Jesus, as son of God, is higher than the angels. Jesus is also called our savior and high priest (Hebr 3).

However, the relationship between God and Jesus Christ, his son, stays nebulous and ambiguous in this chapter.

The Hierarchy in the Church
Chapter 42

> The apostles have preached the Gospel to us from the Lord Jesus Christ; Jesus Christ. Christ therefore was sent forth by God, and the apostles by Christ. Both these appointments, then, were made in an orderly way, according to the will of God. Having therefore received their orders, and being fully assured by the resurrection of our Lord Jesus Christ, and established in the word of God, with full assurance of the Holy Ghost, they went forth proclaiming that the kingdom of God was at hand.

Chapter 44

> Our apostles also knew, through our Lord Jesus Christ, and there would be strife on account of the office of the episcopate. For this reason, therefore, inasmuch as they had obtained a perfect fore–knowledge of this, they appointed those [ministers] already mentioned, and afterwards gave instructions, that when these should fall asleep, other approved men should succeed them in their ministry. We are of opinion, therefore, that those appointed by them, or afterwards by other eminent men, with the consent of
> the whole Church, and who have blamelessly served the flock of Christ in a humble, peaceable, and disinterested spirit, and have for a long time possessed the good opinion of all, cannot be justly dismissed from the ministry.

The kingdom of God, mentioned in Chapter 42, was meant to be a spiritual kingdom with God at the top, Jesus Christ, and the Holy Spirit at a somewhat lower level, and below Jesus Christ are the apostles. Still lower are the bishops who succeeded the apostles after their deaths. This orderly organization of heavenly beings and of the church was taught by Jesus Christ to his apostles, according to Clement. Nothing like that is to be found in any gospel and it is questionable whether Jesus ever said something of the sort.

Chapter 46

> Why are there strifes, and tumults, and divisions, and schisms, and wars among you? Have we not [all] one God and one Christ? Is there not one Spirit of grace poured out upon us? And have we not one calling in Christ? Why do we divide and tear to pieces the members of Christ, and raise up strife against our own body, and have reached such a height of madness as to forget that "we are members one of another?" Remember the words of our Lord Jesus Christ, how He said, "Woe to that man [by whom offences come]! It were better for him that he had never been born, than that he should cast a stumbling–block before one of my elect. Yea, it were better for him that a millstone should be hung about [his neck], and he should be sunk in the depths of the sea, than that he should cast a stumbling–block before one of my little ones.

Clement quotes a saying of Jesus from Luke 17: 1–2. It is unclear whether he took this from the gospel, from Q, or from an oral tradition.

Christ's Love
Chapter 49

> Let him who has love in Christ keep the commandments of Christ. Who can describe the [blessed] bond of the love of God? What man is able to tell the excellence of its beauty, as it ought to be told? The height to which love exalts is unspeakable. Love unites us to God. Love covers a multitude of sins. Love bears all things, is long-suffering in all things. There is nothing base, nothing arrogant in love. Love admits of no schisms: love gives rise to no seditions: love does all things in harmony. By love have all the elect of God been made perfect; without love nothing is well-pleasing to God. In love has the Lord taken us to Himself. On account of the Love he bore us, Jesus Christ our Lord gave His blood for us by the will of God; His flesh for our flesh, and His soul for our souls.

Clement paraphrases 1 Cor 13, Paul's poetical description of brotherly love. For him, the sacrifice by Jesus on the cross is the pinnacle of God's love for us.

Chapter 50

> All the generations from Adam even to this day have passed away; but those who, through the grace of God, have been made perfect in love, now possess a place among the godly, and shall be made manifest at the revelation of the kingdom of Christ. (…) This blessedness comes upon those who have been chosen by God through Jesus Christ our Lord; to whom be glory for ever and ever. Amen.

The kingdom of Christ, mentioned here, is not an earthly monarchy, but a spiritual realm to which all believers belong. This rendering of the kingdom of God is understandable because there was no possibility during the nineties of the first century AD that the monarchy of Israel could be resurrected as Jesus had hoped. The subjects of this kingdom have been chosen by God, through Christ (or on account of Christ). In this passage, the reader encounters the mythological Christ of Paul's letters, not a historical person of flesh and blood.

Conclusions

Although Clement probably knew the apostles Peter and Paul and must have heard from them much about Jesus, he provides very little biographical details about Jesus. It is unclear whether he had access to any of the gospels, although he clearly knew some of Paul's letters and the letter to the Hebrews. His goal was to convince a few trouble makers in Corinth to accept the authority of the bishops and presbyters – not on teaching his readers about Jesus Christ, although he often refers to him as "the Lord".

For Clement, Jesus seems to be on a somewhat lower level than God, although he is on a higher level than the angels.

When Jesus lived as a man and descendant of the patriarch Jacob, he acted as a teacher and a few otherwise unknown sayings of Jesus were quoted.

If an early Christian had only this letter to guide him about who Jesus of Nazareth was, then he would have found rather little of substance – although that which is told about Jesus' teachings and his execution seem to be historically useful and valid.

This letter shows, however, that an important bishop in the early church had not yet developed a clear idea about the person of Jesus and his relationship with God, as later theologians did. He absorbed both the teachings of Peter, who represented the Ebionite stance that Jesus was an ordinary mortal, and the teachings of Paul, who thought of Christ as the divine and eternal Son of God, and failed to reconcile these opposing lines of thought.

Chapter 13
THE GOSPEL OF THOMAS

Background

There are several apocryphal gospels known – dating mostly from the second and third centuries AD. Of some, the full text is available and of others only fragments are known – mostly from quotations by early Christian theologians. They were all rejected by mainstream or orthodox Christianity during those times and were only used by fringe groups. Only the four gospels of Matthew, Mark, Luke, and John were regarded as Scripture and inspired by the Holy Spirit. These apocryphal gospels differed so much from the canonical gospels that it is understandable that they were rejected.

Due to their late date, it is highly unlikely that they contain any accurate information about Jesus and they will, therefore, not be discussed in this book.

However, in 1945 a hoard of Coptic[273] gnostic books was discovered by farmers near the Egyptian town of Nag Hamadi, including a sayings gospel, purportedly written by the apostle Thomas. It was not so easy to dismiss this gospel as spurious since many of the sayings it contains are also to be found in the biblical gospels.

This gospel of Thomas spurred new interest in the theoretical Q Document, which also contains nothing but sayings of Jesus and

---

[273] Coptic – the Egyptian language spoken in Egypt during early Christian times and written in the Greek alphabet, instead of the old Egyptian hieroglyphs.

the hope was rekindled that a copy of Q would also turn up, sooner or later.

Scholars connected a few Greek papyrus fragments containing sayings of Jesus, also found in Egypt at the town of Oxyrhynchus, with the Coptic Gospel of Thomas, proving that the Coptic version must have been translated from the original Greek.

The existence of the Gospel of Thomas was known from references and quotations by early Christian authors who condemned the contents of this document as heretical. The Nag Hamadi document gave scholars the whole text of this long-lost gospel.

There is no indication of the identity of the author(s) or compiler(s) of this document, although it is certain that it could not have been Thomas, the apostle of Jesus. Saying 27, which expects of those who seek the kingdom of heaven to fast and to keep the Sabbath, may point to a community of gnostic Jewish Christians where this document originated.

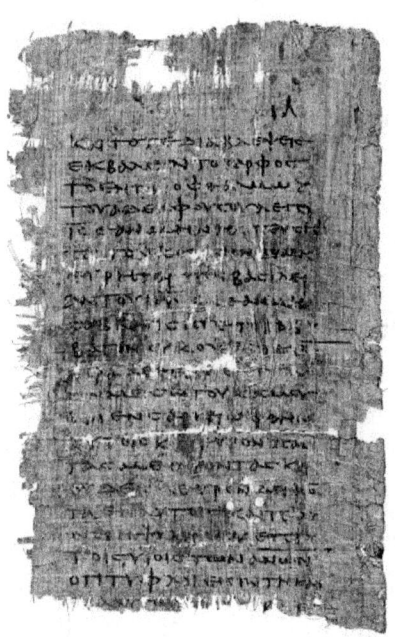

P. Oxy. 1 – A papyrus fragment of the Greek Gospel of Thomas, found at Oxyrhynchus

Some scholars think that this gospel went through a few stages before it was finalized – just as Mack has identified three strata in the development of Q. It is, therefore, possible that the oldest parts of Thomas, containing sayings of Jesus that also occur in the New Testament, could be older than the rest of this document.

Researchers cannot agree on a date of origin for this gospel and dates between AD 50 and the middle of the second century AD were proposed. The single Coptic copy of this gospel can be dated to the early fourth century, but that does not tell us anything about the date of the original document. A few expressions in Thomas seem to correspond with remarks in the discourse sources of John and the book of Revelation, both of which can be dated to the nineties of the first century AD. These verses must, therefore, have been written later than this. These occasions will be pointed out when the contents of Thomas are commented upon.

Since this gospel was found with other gnostic writings, scholars generally accept that it also contains gnostic beliefs – as will be shown when the different paragraphs are discussed. [274]

Not much is known about the origin of Gnosticism, although one of the early leaders was Simon the Magician (or Simon Magus) of Samaria of whom we read in Acts 8. This amorphous movement seems to have been influenced by various sources: Judaism, early Christianity, the Iranian religion, and Neo-Platonism.

Plato taught that the visible world is the materialization of eternal ideas, which reside in an eternal realm of ideas. These ideas are the templates of material objects and their qualities. A spirit, called a "demiurge", created the material world by impressing these ideas onto unformed matter. Plato also taught a dualism between body and soul. The body is part of the material world, while the soul belongs to the realm of ideas.

The Iranian religion taught that there is an eternal struggle

---

[274] Biblical Archaeology Society Staff. "The Nag Hammadi Codices and Gnostic Christianity'"; Early Christian Writings. *Gospel of Thomas Commentary;* Johnson. "The Gospel of Thomas"; Wikipedia. "Gospel of Thomas".

between the forces of good and evil, personalized as a good god and an evil spirit.

Some gnostic sects or groups claimed Jesus as their own and distorted some of his teachings to fit into their philosophy.

The name "Gnosticism" is derived from the Greek word γνωσις (*gnosis*), which means "(esoteric or secret) knowledge", which a person needs to acquire to connect him to his origin and destiny in the kingdom of heaven or the realm of ideas.[275]

The Gospel of Thomas is a short book, containing only 114 sayings. Most of them start with the words: "Jesus said…"

An intelligent guess as to why this collection of exactly 114 random sayings of Jesus was compiled may be that a weekly sermon was delivered to explain one of the sayings to the congregation. This would imply a cycle of two years, which required 104 sayings. That leaves five extra sermons on special feast days each year to get to the total of 114 sermons.

In the commentary that follows, the translation by Thomas Lambdin will be used. The translations of the Greek Oxyrhynchus fragments by B.P. Grenfell, A.S. Hunt. and Bentley Layton are given in italics at the appropriate spots. It will become clear that the Coptic translation does not follow the Greek text always precisely.

Reliance will be placed on the commentary on Thomas as published by the organization Early Christian Writings, which quotes the comments of various experts after each separate saying, together with references to the canonical gospels.

Commentary

> These are the secret sayings which the living Jesus spoke and which Didymos Judas Thomas wrote down.

---

[275] Enc Brit, "Gnosticism" and "Simon Magus".

> *These are the secret sayings which were spoken by Jesus the Living One, and which Judas, who is called Thomas, wrote down."*

The expression "the living Jesus" in the preamble probably has Jesus before his execution in mind – not the resurrected Jesus, because many of the sayings that also occur in the canonical gospels were spoken by Jesus during his ministry. These sayings are "secret" because they belonged to a gnostic sect that wanted to keep its teachings hidden from outsiders – especially the orthodox or Pauline wing of Christianity that persecuted suspected heretics and the Roman overlords who blamed Judaism and Christianity for the Jewish War of AD 66–70.

The disciple of Jesus, Thomas, is called Didymus on three occasions (John 11: 16; 20: 24; 21: 2). The Greek word Δίδυμος (*Didymos*) means "twin", while the name Thomas is an Aramaic word with the same meaning. The Greek name of Didymus was, therefore, just a translation of Thomas. The compiler(s) of the Gospel of Thomas, somehow, thought that it would be appropriate to use his name as author or collector of Jesus sayings.

> 1.   And he said, "Whoever finds the interpretation of these sayings will not experience death."
> *He said to them: "Whoever hears these words shall never taste death."*

This is an echo of John 8: 51 – "Most assuredly, I tell you, if a person keeps my word, he will never see death."

These words in John are part of the discourse source of John. If Thomas quoted from it, it is an indication of a late date for this document, at least the end of the first century AD.

> 2. Jesus said, "Let him who seeks continue seeking until he finds. When he finds, he will become troubled. When he becomes troubled, he will be astonished, and he will rule over the All."
>
> *[Jesus said]: "Let him who seeks not cease until he finds, and when he finds he shall wonder; wondering he shall reign, and reigning shall rest."*

This saying reminds one of Luke 11: 9–10 (a part of Q).

Thomas meant to teach that the seeker, who eventually finds the truth about his origin and destiny, will be absorbed into the All, the kingdom of heaven, where he will find rest.

> 3. Jesus said, "If those who lead you say to you, See, the kingdom is in the sky, then the birds of the sky will precede you. If they say to you, It is in the sea, then the fish will precede you. Rather, the kingdom is inside of you, and it is outside of you. When you come to know yourselves, then you will become known, and you will realize that it is you who are the sons of the living father. But if you will not know yourselves, you dwell in poverty and it is you who are that poverty."
>
> *Jesus said, "If those who attract you say, See, the Kingdom is in the sky, then the birds of the sky will precede you. If they say to you, It is under the earth, then the fish of the sea will precede you. Rather, the Kingdom of God is inside of you, and it is outside of you. [Those who] become acquainted with [themselves] will find it; [and when you] become acquainted with yourselves, [you will understand that] it is you who are the sons of the living Father. But if you will not*

> *know yourselves, you dwell in poverty and it is you who are that poverty."*

One of the tenets of Gnosticism was that it is necessary to know oneself, as part of the esoteric knowledge about one's eternal origin – as is set out in this passage. This self-knowledge will lead to entry into the spiritual kingdom.

Luke 21: 17 (part of L) declares that "the kingdom of God is within you."

> 4. Jesus said, "The man old in days will not hesitate to ask a small child seven days old about the place of life, and he will live. For many who are first will become last, and they will become one and the same."
>
> *Jesus said: "Let the old man who is full of days not hesitate to ask the child of seven days about the place of life; then he will live. For many that are first will be last, and last, first, and they will become a single one."*

The mention of an infant of seven days seems to refer to a boy who was not yet circumcised – a sign that this gospel may have originated in a Jewish Christian setting with gnostic tendencies. It is assumed that a new-born baby will retain memories of his pre-existence in the kingdom of heaven, the Platonic realm of ideas.

Mark 10: 15 records these words of Jesus: "Most assuredly I tell you, whoever will not receive the kingdom of God as a little child, he will in no way enter therein."

This saying also reminds one of Luke 10: 21 – "In that same hour Jesus rejoiced in the Holy Spirit, and said, I thank you, O Father, Lord of heaven and earth, that you have hidden these things from the wise and understanding, and revealed them to little children."

> 5. Jesus said, "Recognize what is in your sight, and that which is hidden from you will become plain to you. For there is nothing hidden which will not become manifest."
> *Jesus said: "Recognize what is before your face and that which is hidden from the you will be revealed to you. For there is nothing hidden which shall not be made manifest, nor buried which shall not be raised."*

This saying quotes Jesus: "But there is nothing covered up, that will not be revealed, nor hidden, that will not be known" (Luke 12: 2 – part of Q) – meaning that all lies will be exposed in the end. The Greek text added that people who are dead and buried, will be resurrected.

> 6. His disciples questioned him and said to him, "Do you want us to fast? How shall we pray? Shall we give alms? What diet shall we observe?" Jesus said, "Do not tell lies, and do not do what you hate, for all things are plain in the sight of heaven. For nothing hidden will not become manifest, and nothing covered will remain without being uncovered."
> *His disciples asked him and said to him, "How do you want us to fast? And how shall we pray? And how [shall we] give alms? And what kind of diet shall we follow?" Jesus said, "Do not lie, and do not do what you hate, for all things are disclosed before truth. For there is nothing hidden which shall not be shown forth."*

This saying does not seem to quote any canonical gospel.

Jesus answered the disciples' question indirectly by pointing out that it is more important to be honest and not to violate one's principles than to adhere to certain rituals.

> 7. Jesus said, "Blessed is the lion which becomes man when consumed by man; and cursed is the man whom the lion consumes, and the lion becomes man."

The reference to a lion in this rather obscure saying probably refers to the beastly passions in man that must not be allowed to devour a person. It may also be a reference to Satan who is described as a lion in 1 Pet 5: 8.

> 8. And he said, "The man is like a wise fisherman who cast his net into the sea and drew it up from the sea full of small fish. Among them the wise fisherman found a fine large fish. He threw all the small fish back into the sea and chose the large fish without difficulty. Whoever has ears to hear, let him hear."

The most likely explanation of this parable of the wise fisherman is that the gnostic must discard all the teachings, religions, and philosophies of the world and retain the most important teaching regarding the secret knowledge of Gnosticism.

The last sentence ("Whoever has ears to hear, let him hear," which also occurs in Mark 4: 9, Matt 11: 15, Luke 8: 18. and seven times in Rev 2 and 3) is meant to draw the attention of the listener or reader to an important message.

> 9. Jesus said, "Now the sower went out, took a handful (of seeds), and scattered them. Some fell on the road; the birds came and gathered them up. Others fell on the rock, did not take root in the soil, and did not produce ears. And others fell on thorns; they choked the seed(s) and worms ate them. And

> others fell on the good soil and it produced good fruit: it bore sixty per measure and a hundred and twenty per measure."

This is a garbled version of the parable of the Sower (Matt 13: 18–23; Mark 4: 13–20; Luke 8: 11–15). The seed is clearly the message of Gnosticism, which did not receive a positive reception everywhere.

It is not possible to determine whether Thomas got this parable from the canonical gospels or from an oral tradition.

Albrecht Dürer: The Sower

> 10. Jesus said, "I have cast fire upon the world, and see, I am guarding it until it blazes."

This saying is almost the same as Luke 12: 49 (part of Q).

> 11. Jesus said, "This heaven will pass away, and the one above it will pass away. The dead are not alive, and the living will not die. In the days when you consumed what is dead, you made it what is alive. When you come to dwell in the light, what will you do? On the day when you were one you became two. But when you become two, what will you do?"

Paul mentions a "third heaven" in 2 Cor 12: 2 – presumably he dwelling place of God. The two lower heavens, mentioned by

Thomas, are the heaven filled with clouds and the heaven containing stars.[276]

Jesus said something similar in Luk 16: 17 – "But it is easier for heaven and earth to pass away, than for one tiny stroke of a pen in the law to fall."

The saying makes the point that when living people consume dead beings, they turn these dead beings into living parts of themselves.

Humanity started off as a unity, but was later divided into those who live in the light and those who perish.

It is very unlikely that Jesus ever made such a jumbled statement.

---

12. The disciples said to Jesus, "We know that you will depart from us. Who is to be our leader?" Jesus said to them, "Wherever you are, you are to go to James the righteous, for whose sake heaven and earth came into being."

Jesus purportedly told his disciples that he would leave them (see John 14: 2–3 – part of the discourse source). His place as leader of the Jesus movement was later to be taken by his brother James, who is called the "righteous" or "just" in this passage, a name that does not occur in any of the gospels or Acts, but was given to him later according to ancient historians. He was killed in AD 62.

This passage describes a situation that occurred after Jesus' departure from the scene. James is made here into a mythological figure for whose sake the whole of creation came into being as if the exalted status of Jesus was later given to him.

This saying was certainly never spoken by Jesus who expected to become the king of Israel and not to leave his followers.

---

[276] Pretorius. *Who, Where, and What is God?* 31–59.

> 13. Jesus said to his disciples, "Compare me to someone and tell me whom I am like." Simon Peter said to him, "You are like a righteous angel." Matthew said to him, "You are like a wise philosopher." Thomas said to him, "Master, my mouth is wholly incapable of saying whom you are like." Jesus said, "I am not your master. Because you have drunk, you have become intoxicated from the bubbling spring which I have measured out." And he took him and withdrew and told him three things. When Thomas returned to his companions, they asked him, "What did Jesus say to you?" Thomas said to them, "If I tell you one of the things which he told me, you will pick up stones and throw them at me; a fire will come out of the stones and burn you up."

According to Mark 8: 27–29, Matt 16:13–20, and Luke 9:18–20, Jesus asked his disciples what the people said about him. Something similar is described in this passage, although the contents are different. Jesus is compared with an angel or a wise philosopher. However, when Thomas – the purported author of this gospel – calls Jesus his "Master" he is rebuked, but is also given secret knowledge about Jesus real identity, which would have sounded blasphemous to the others who haven't received this secret insight yet.

This secret knowledge is compared with a bubbling spring, which reminds us of John 4:14 (part of the discourse source) where Jesus told the Samaritan woman that "whoever drinks of the water that I will give him will never thirst; but the water that I will give him will become in him a well of water springing up to eternal life."

> 14. Jesus said to them, "If you fast, you will give rise to sin for yourselves; and if you pray, you will be condemned; and if

> you give alms, you will do harm to your spirits. When you go into any land and walk about in the districts, if they receive you, eat what they will set before you, and heal the sick among them. For what goes into your mouth will not defile you, but that which issues from your mouth – it is that which will defile you."

Saying 6 already dealt with fasting, prayer, and alms–giving where these pious activities were declared to be of less importance than the secret knowledge of Gnosticism.

Part of saying 14 seems to be a direct quotation from Luke 10: 7–9 (part of Q), where Jesus told his disciples to eat what their hosts put before them and to heal the sick while they are recruiting supporters for the coming kingdom.

There is a clear allusion to Mark 7: 15 – "There is nothing from outside of the man, that going into him can defile him; but the things which proceed out of the man are those that defile the man." (see also Matt 15: 17–20).

It may be concluded that this passage relies on sayings from the canonical gospels, which are taken out of context and combined.

> 15. Jesus said, "When you see one who was not born of woman, prostrate yourselves on your faces and worship him. That one is your father."

This saying means that God, the Father, has had no beginning and is eternal. He must be worshipped.

> 16. Jesus said, "Men think, perhaps, that it is peace which I have come to cast upon the world. They do not know that it is dissension which I have come to cast upon the earth: fire,

> sword, and war. For there will be five in a house: three will be against two, and two against three, the father against the son, and the son against the father. And they will stand solitary."

This saying contains an almost exact quotation from Luke 12: 52–53 (part of Q), although the original context is ignored. Thomas explains that there can be no peace and unity between gnostic believers and outsiders.

> 17. Jesus said, "I shall give you what no eye has seen and what no ear has heard and what no hand has touched and what has never occurred to the human mind."

Paul quotes a similar saying of Jesus in 1 Cor 2: 9, perhaps known from an oral tradition – where Thomas may have found it as well.

The message of Thomas is that the secret knowledge of Gnosticism is beyond human experience.

> 18. The disciples said to Jesus, "Tell us how our end will be." Jesus said, "Have you discovered, then, the beginning, that you look for the end? For where the beginning is, there will the end be. Blessed is he who will take his place in the beginning; he will know the end and will not experience death."

This saying connects the beginning and the end of the world in a continuous cycle where time does not progress linearly. It is the eternal cycle out of which the gnostic believer with his esoteric knowledge and enlightenment wishes to escape (as in Buddhism).

This passage contains a memory of Rev 1: 8 – "I am the Alpha and the Omega, the Beginning and the End, says the Lord God, who is and who was and who is to come, the Almighty."

> 19. Jesus said, "Blessed is he who came into being before he came into being. If you become my disciples and listen to my words, these stones will minister to you. For there are five trees for you in Paradise which remain undisturbed summer and winter and whose leaves do not fall. Whoever becomes acquainted with them will not experience death."

This saying teaches the pre-existence of the soul or spirit before a human being is born into the material and evil world and the aim of the esoteric gnostic knowledge is to restore the memory of that blessed pre-existence. This dualism between spirit and body is typical of all schools of thought that were inspired by Plato.

This blessed existence is compared with evergreen trees in Paradise, which is reminiscent of Rev 22: 2 – "On this side of the river and on that was the tree of life, bearing twelve kinds of fruits, yielding its fruit every month. The leaves of the tree were for the healing of the nations."

This train of thought would have been totally foreign to Jesus, the Jewish rabbi whose belief system and teachings were based on the Hebrew Scriptures.

> 20. The disciples said to Jesus, "Tell us what the kingdom of heaven is like." He said to them, It is like a mustard seed. It is the smallest of all seeds. But when it falls on tilled soil, it produces a great plant and becomes a shelter for birds of the sky."

This saying is almost a copy of the parable of the mustard seed (Mark 4: 30–32, as well as Luke 13: 18–19 – copied from Q), with the difference that the disciples ask for information regarding the kingdom of heaven, instead of Jesus posing this question himself. For Thomas, this kingdom is the only reality, in contrast with the material world that is evil, filled with suffering, and illusory.

> 21. Mary said to Jesus, "Whom are your disciples like?" He said, "They are like children who have settled in a field which is not theirs. When the owners of the field come, they will say, Let us have back our field. They (will) undress in their presence in order to let them have back their field and to give it back to them. Therefore I say, if the owner of a house knows that the thief is coming, he will begin his vigil before he comes and will not let him dig through into his house of his domain to carry away his goods. You, then, be on your guard against the world. Arm yourselves with great strength lest the robbers find a way to come to you, for the difficulty which you expect will (surely) materialize. Let there be among you a man of understanding. When the grain ripened, he came quickly with his sickle in his hand and reaped it. Whoever has ears to hear, let him hear."

The only way to understand this enigmatic saying is to apply gnostic symbolism and to forget conventional Christian or biblical symbols.

The key sentence in this saying is as follows: "[B]e on your guard against the world." That means that the field on which the children – the gnostic disciples of Jesus – were staying, is this sinful and evil world. The owners of the field are Satan and his demons.

When these "children" die and leave this "field" (the world), it is as if they are shedding their clothes and return to their original or natural state by going back to their own field, the kingdom of heaven.

Satan is compared to a thief who comes unannounced to break in and gnostic believers must be wary of his attacks. The man with the sickle must be Jesus who cuts the grain by taking away his followers.

The last sentence serves to warn the listeners and readers of this saying that they must pay attention to something important (Rev 2 and 3).

The sudden second coming of Christ is often compared in the New Testament with an unexpected thief at night. This parable, however, sees Satan as the thief.

---

22. Jesus saw infants being suckled. He said to his disciples, "These infants being suckled are like those who enter the kingdom." They said to him, "Shall we then, as children, enter the kingdom?" Jesus said to them, "When you make the two one, and when you make the inside like the outside and the outside like the inside, and the above like the below, and when you make the male and the female one and the same, so that the male not be male nor the female; and when you fashion eyes in the place of an eye, and a hand in place of a hand, and a foot in place of a foot, and a likeness in place of a likeness; then will you enter the kingdom."

In a previous saying (Thomas 4), Jesus was made to say that a wise man must ask a baby of seven days about the kingdom. This idea is expanded in this saying and it reminds one of Jesus who said: "Allow the little children to come to me, and don't hinder them, for the kingdom of God belongs to ones like these" (Luke 18: 16). Jesus also said: "Most assuredly I tell you, unless you turn, and become as little children, you will in no way enter into the Kingdom of Heaven" (Matt 18: 3; see also Mark 10: 15).

The rest of the saying conveys the idea in a clumsy manner that a person must shed his earthly body and acquire a heavenly body to be able to enter the kingdom after death.

It is certain that Jesus never taught anything like this.

> 23. Jesus said, "I shall choose you, one out of a thousand, and two out of ten thousand, and they shall stand as a single one."

This is a description of how the gnostic community saw itself – a small exclusive group. When they enter the kingdom later, they will lose their individuality and be dissolved into the All.

> 24. His disciples said to him, "Show us the place where you are, since it is necessary for us to seek it." He said to them, "Whoever has ears, let him hear. There is light within a man of light, and he lights up the whole world. If he does not shine, he is darkness."

This saying reminds one of Luke 11: 34 (part of Q): "The lamp of the body is the eye. Therefore when your eye is good, your whole body also is full of light; but when it is evil, your body also is full of darkness."

The light shining inside a gnostic believer is the secret knowledge he has.

> 25. Jesus said, "Love your brother like your soul, guard him like the pupil of your eye."

This passage reminds one of Jesus who said that we should love our neighbors as we love ourselves (Mark 12: 31). Thomas, however, has a "brother" – a fellow-believer – instead of a neighbor.

> 26. Jesus said, "You see the mote in your brother's eye, but you do not see the beam in your own eye. When you cast the beam out of your own eye, then you will see clearly to cast the mote from your brother's eye."

This saying is very similar to those in Matt 7: 3–5 and Luke 6: 41–42 (part of Q). It is not clear whether Thomas copied it from Q, the canonical gospels, or sourced it from an oral tradition.

> 27. Jesus said, "If you do not fast as regards the world, you will not find the kingdom. If you do not observe the Sabbath as a Sabbath, you will not see the father."
> *Jesus said: "Unless you fast to the world, you shall in no way find the Kingdom of God; and unless you sabbatize the Sabbath, you shall not see the Father."*

Fasting regarding the world would mean, in gnostic terms, abstinence from worldly affairs, due to the evil to be found in the material world.

The insistence that the Sabbath be honored points to a gnostic Jewish Christian origin of this gospel. The rest on the Sabbath would mean resting from committing sin.

> 28. Jesus said, "I took my place in the midst of the world, and I appeared to them in flesh. I found all of them intoxicated; I found none of them thirsty. And my soul became afflicted for the sons of men, because they are blind in their hearts and

> do not have sight; for empty they came into the world, and empty too they seek to leave the world. But for the moment they are intoxicated. When they shake off their wine, then they will repent."
>
> *Jesus said: "I stood in the midst of the world, and in the flesh I was seen by them, and I found all drunken, and I found none among them thirsty. And my soul grieved over the souls of men, because they are blind in their heart and see not. [...]*

This saying reminds one of Luke 21: 34 (part of L) – "So be careful, or your hearts will be loaded down with carousing, drunkenness, and cares of this life, and that day will come on you suddenly."

Drunkenness is equated with ignorance and carelessness in this saying of Thomas. Jesus is portrayed as the savior who came in the flesh to help mankind get rid of this ignorance and carelessness.

> 29. Jesus said, "If the flesh came into being because of spirit, it is a wonder. But if spirit came into being because of the body, it is a wonder of wonders. Indeed, I am amazed at how this great wealth has made its home in this poverty."

"This great wealth" is the spiritual sphere, the kingdom of heaven, the Platonic realm of ideas. Thomas finds it a mystery how the spirit could ever be combined with a material body, which is part of the sinful and evil world of matter.

It is certain that Jesu never uttered this piece of gnostic philosophy.

> 30. Jesus said, "Where there are three gods, they are gods. Where there are two or one, I am with him."

> *Jesus said: "Where there are [two, they are not] without God, and when there is one alone, [I say,] I am with him. Raise the stone, and there you will find me; cleave the wood, and there I am."*

This saying seems to be a jumbled version of Matt 18: 20 (part of M) – "For where two or three are gathered together in my name, there I am in the midst of them."

> 31.   Jesus said, "No prophet is accepted in his own village; no physician heals those who know him."
> *Jesus said: "A prophet is not acceptable in his own country, neither does a physician work cures upon those that know him."*

This saying is a version of Mark 6: 4 – "A prophet is not without honor, except in his own country, and among his own relatives, and in his own house." It is perhaps possible that the version in Thomas may be more original than the one in Mark and the other synoptic gospels.

> 32.   Jesus said, "A city being built on a high mountain and fortified cannot fall, nor can it be hidden."
> *Jesus said: "A city built on the top of a high hill and fortified can neither fall nor be hid." (—) Jesus said: "Thou hearest with one ear, [but the other thou has closed].*

Matthew 5: 14 (part of M) teaches something similar: "You are the light of the world. A city set on a hill can't be hidden."

> 33. Jesus said, "Preach from your housetops that which you will hear in your ear. For no one lights a lamp and puts it under a bushel, nor does he put it in a hidden place, but rather he sets it on a lamp stand so that everyone who enters and leaves will see its light."

This is almost a combination of –

- Luke 12: 3 ("What I tell you in the darkness, speak in the light; and what you hear whispered in the ear, proclaim on the housetops"); and

- Luke 11: 33 ("No man, when he has lit a lamp, puts it in a cellar, nor under a basket, but on the stand, that they which enter in may see the light").

This exhortation to spread the message seems to contradict the stance of the gnostics that their esoteric knowledge and teachings should be kept hidden and secret.
It cannot be determined whether Thomas fount this in Q, or from an old oral tradition.

> 34. Jesus said, "If a blind man leads a blind man, they will both fall into a pit."

This short parable also occurs in Luke 6: 39 (part of Q) – ""Can the blind guide the blind? Wont they both fall into a pit?

> 35. Jesus said, "It is not possible for anyone to enter the house of a strong man and take it by force unless he binds his hands; then he will (be able to) ransack his house."

Luke 11: 21–22 (part of Q) is very similar: "When the strong man, fully armed, guards his own dwelling, his goods are safe. But when someone stronger comes on him, and overcomes him, he takes from him his whole armor in which he trusted, and divides his spoils."

Thomas probably saw the intruder as Satan who aspires to steal the believer's spirit or soul.

36.	Jesus said, "Do not be concerned from morning until evening and from evening until morning about what you will wear." *Jesus said, "Do not worry from dawn to dusk and from dusk to dawn about [what food] you [will] eat, [or] what you will wear. [You are much] better than the [lilies], which [neither] card nor spin. And for your part, what [will you wear] when you have no clothing? Who would add to your stature? It is he who will give you your clothing.*

This saying corresponds with Luke 12: 22 (found in Q) – "He said to his disciples, 'Therefore I tell you, don't be anxious for your life, what you will eat, nor yet for your body, what you will wear.'"

The Coptic text is shorter than the Greek text – perhaps because another copy of the Greek gospel was translated. The Greek contains more of Jesus teaching in the Sermon on the Mount.

37.	His disciples said, "When will you become revealed to us and when shall we see you?" Jesus said, "When you disrobe without being ashamed and take up your garments and place them under your feet like little children and tread on them, then will you see the son of the living one, and you will not be afraid." *His disciples said to him, "When will you be visible to us, and when shall we behold you?" He said, "When you strip naked without being ashamed, and take your garments and*

644

> *put them under your feet like little children and tread upon them, then you will see the child of the Living, and you will not be afraid."*

Just as in Saying 21, the taking off of clothes points to the shedding of the earthly body at death. When the purified spirit enters the kingdom of heaven, Jesus will become visible.

> 38. Jesus said, "Many times have you desired to hear these words which I am saying to you, and you have no one else to hear them from. There will be days when you will look for me and will not find me."

This saying seems to depend on Luke 17: 22 (part of L) – "He said to the disciples, "The days will come, when you will desire to see one of the days of the Son of Man, and you will not see it."

> 39. Jesus said, "The pharisees and the scribes have taken the keys of knowledge [gnosis] and hidden them. They themselves have not entered, nor have they allowed to enter those who wish to. You, however, be as wise as serpents and as innocent as doves."

Luke 11: 52 (part of Q) says something similar: "Woe to you lawyers! For you took away the key of knowledge. You didn't enter in yourselves, and those who were entering in, you hindered."

This is combined with Matt 10: 16 (part of M) – "Behold, I send you forth as sheep in the midst of wolves. Therefore be wise as serpents, and harmless as doves."

Thomas uses the expression "keys of knowledge" in a gnostic sense, meaning that the secret teachings of this movement must be hidden from outsiders, namely that Jesus came to help believers get the liberating knowledge of their origin and ultimate fate.

> 40.   Jesus said, "A grapevine has been planted outside of the father, but being unsound, it will be pulled up by its roots and destroyed."

Saying 40 is certainly dependent upon Matt 15: 13 (part of M) – "But he answered, Every plant which my heavenly Father didn't plant will be uprooted."

Thomas sees the vine as the material world that was "planted outside of the father" (perhaps by the Platonic demiurge or Satan). Since it is an evil entity, it will be destroyed.

> 41.   Jesus said, "Whoever has something in his hand will receive more, and whoever has nothing will be deprived of even the little he has."

This saying sounds much like Luke 8: 18 – "Be careful therefore how you hear. For whoever has, to him will be given; and whoever doesn't have, from him will be taken away even that which he thinks he has" (see also Mark 4: 25 and Matt 13: 12).

The person who "has something in his hand" is somebody who has attained self-knowledge, which is elsewhere compared with a treasure. This person will receive much more, namely entry into the kingdom.

> 42.   Jesus said, "Become passers-by."

Thomas urged his listeners and readers not to be at home in this sinful and wicked world, but to adopt the attitude of "passers-by" or travelers who are on a journey to the kingdom of heaven.

> 43. His disciples said to him, "Who are you, that you should say these things to us?" Jesus said to them, "You do not realize who I am from what I say to you, but you have become like the Jews, for they (either) love the tree and hate its fruit (or) love the fruit and hate the tree."

In this strange saying, the disciples ask a strange question and they want to know who Jesus is – as if they had never heard what he told them. Jesus rebukes them for not understanding him and he compares them with the Jews who thought that good trees can bear bad fruit or that good fruit can come from bad trees.

The implication is that Jesus is the good tree that bears good fruit, his words, and teachings.

> 44. Jesus said, "Whoever blasphemes against the father will be forgiven, and whoever blasphemes against the son will be forgiven, but whoever blasphemes against the holy spirit will not be forgiven either on earth or in heaven."

This saying is an adaptation of Mark 3: 28–29 – "Most assuredly I tell you, all their sins will be forgiven to the sons of men, and their blasphemies with which they may blaspheme; but whoever may blaspheme against the Holy Spirit never has forgiveness, but is guilty of an eternal sin" (see also Matt 12: 31–32 and Luke 12: 10).

The main difference with the canonical gospels is that Thomas adds the Father and the Son as persons against whom one may also blaspheme. With this, Thomas seems to be familiar with the Christian doctrine of the Divine Trinity. The fact that this saying occurs in all the Synoptic Gospels, may be an indication that Thomas copied this saying from at least one of them.

> 45. Jesus said, "Grapes are not harvested from thorns, nor are figs gathered from thistles, for they do not produce fruit. A good man brings forth good from his storehouse; an evil man brings forth evil things from his evil storehouse, which is in his heart, and says evil things. For out of the abundance of the heart he brings forth evil things."

This passage can be explained as a combination of passages from Matthew and Luke (both are part of Q):

- Matt 7: 16–20 – "By their fruits you will know them. Do you gather grapes from thorns, or figs from thistles? Even so, every good tree brings forth good fruit; but the corrupt tree brings forth evil fruit. A good tree can't bring forth evil fruit, neither can a corrupt tree bring forth good fruit. Every tree that doesn't grow good fruit is cut down, and thrown into the fire. Therefore, by their fruits you will know them."
- Luke 6: 44–45 – "For each tree is known by its own fruit. For people don't gather figs from thorns, nor do they gather grapes from a bramble bush. The good man out of the good treasure of his heart brings forth that which is good, and the evil man out of the evil treasure of his heart brings forth that which is evil, for out of the abundance of the heart, his mouth speaks."

> 46. Jesus said, "Among those born of women, from Adam until John the Baptist, there is no one so superior to John the Baptist that his eyes should not be lowered (before him). Yet I have said, whichever one of you comes to be a child will be acquainted with the kingdom and will become superior to John."

Thomas adapted this saying from Luke 7: 28 (part of Q) – "For I tell you, among those who are born of women there is not a greater prophet than John the Baptizer, yet he who is least in the kingdom of God is greater than he."

Thomas changes the meaning though, by stating that the gnostics who become like children and have acquitted an insight about the spiritual kingdom of heaven are greater than John.

47. Jesus said, "It is impossible for a man to mount two horses or to stretch two bows. And it is impossible for a servant to serve two masters; otherwise, he will honor the one and treat the other contemptuously. No man drinks old wine and immediately desires to drink new wine. And new wine is not put into old wineskins, lest they burst; nor is old wine put into a new wineskin, lest it spoil it. An old patch is not sewn onto a new garment, because a tear would result."

This saying is a combination of two texts from the Synoptics:

- Luke 16:13 (part of Q) teaches: "No servant can serve two masters, for either he will hate the one, and love the other; or else he will hold to one, and despise the other. You aren't able to serve God and mammon."
- Luke 5: 36–40 contains the following parable: "No one puts a piece from a new garment on an old garment, or else he will tear the new, and also the piece from the new will not match the old. No one puts new wine into old wineskins, or else the new wine will burst the skins, and it will be spilled, and the skins will be destroyed. But new wine must be put into fresh wineskins, and both are preserved. No man having drunk old wine immediately desires new, for he says, The old is better" (see also Mark 2. 21 f and Matt 9. 16 f.).

Thomas changed the meaning of these texts by implying that the newer teachings of Gnosticism are preferable to the old beliefs.

It is possible that the parable of the two horses and two bows may be a genuine saying of Jesus, taken from an oral tradition or from a part of Q not incorporated into one of the canonical gospels.

> 48. Jesus said, "If two make peace with each other in this one house, they will say to the mountain, Move Away, and it will move away."

This saying is somewhat like saying 103. It is a combination and an adaptation of the following texts:

- Matt 18: 19 (part of M) – "Again, assuredly I tell you, that if two of you will agree on earth concerning anything that they will ask, it will be done for them by my Father who is in heaven."
- Mark 11:23 – "For most assuredly I tell you, whoever may tell this mountain, Be taken up and cast into the sea, and doesn't doubt in his heart, but believes that what he says happens; he shall have whatever he says."

> 49. Jesus said, "Blessed are the solitary and elect, for you will find the kingdom. For you are from it, and to it you will return."

There is a parallel with John 16: 28 (part of the discourse sources), although this saying is not necessarily dependent upon it. This text declares: "I came out from the Father, and have come into the world. Again, I leave the world, and go to the Father."

The saying in Thomas reminds the gnostic reader that he has had a pre-existence in the kingdom and that he will return thither.

50. Jesus said, "If they say to you, Where did you come from?, say to them, We came from the light, the place where the light came into being on its own accord and established itself and became manifest through their image. If they say to you, Is it you?, say, We are its children, we are the elect of the living father. If they ask you, What is the sign of your father in you?, say to them, It is movement and repose."

There is nothing in the canonical gospels corresponding with this.

This saying also teaches the pre-existence of gnostic believers who dwelt in the light and are children of the light, which is identical with their living Father. The sign that they came from this Father is their ability to move and to come to rest in death.

51. His disciples said to him, "When will the repose of the dead come about, and when will the new world come?" He said to them, "What you look forward to has already come, but you do not recognize it."

Thomas reworked Luke 17: 20–21 (part of L), which declares: "Being asked by the Pharisees when the kingdom of God would come, he answered them, The kingdom of God doesn't come with observation; neither will they say, Look, here! or, Look, there! for behold, the kingdom of God is within you."

Thomas wanted to convey the thought that people don't realize that the "new world", the kingdom where the dead can rest, is already present and that people only have to gain knowledge about their eternal origin to come to rest in this life.

52. His disciples said to him, "Twenty-four prophets spoke in Israel, and all of them spoke in you." He said to them, "You

> have omitted the one living in your presence and have spoken (only) of the dead."

The twenty-four prophets of Israel are the twenty-four books of the Old Testament. These dead prophets have been superseded by the gnostic Jesus with a new revelation.

> 53. His disciples said to him, "Is circumcision beneficial or not?" He said to them, "If it were beneficial, their father would beget them already circumcised from their mother. Rather, the true circumcision in spirit has become completely profitable."

The matter of circumcision, or not, was a dividing point between Jewish followers of Jesus and Paul's Christians (Acts 15) and, therefore, this question was also debated in the gnostic community, which could have harbored many Jewish converts. Thomas argued that circumcision is not natural and that a spiritual circumcision – gaining spiritual knowledge – is much better.

> 54. Jesus said, "Blessed are the poor, for yours is the kingdom of heaven."

This is an almost exact repetition of Luke 6: 20 (part of Q). This saying may be a sign that the gnostics did not value earthly possessions, which belong to this horrible and cruel material world.

> 55. Jesus said, "Whoever does not hate his father and his mother cannot become a disciple to me. And whoever does not hate his brothers and sisters and take up his cross in my way will not be worthy of me."

This saying is a version of the following saying in the Q–Document: "If any man comes to me, and doesn't hate his own father, mother, wife, children, brothers, and sisters, yes, and his own life also, he can't be my disciple. Whoever doesn't bear his own cross, and come after me, can't be my disciple" (Luke 14: 26–27).

According to Thomas, it is expected of believers to regard their convictions and the gnostic community as more important than family ties.

> 56. Jesus said, "Whoever has come to understand the world has found (only) a corpse, and whoever has found a corpse is superior to the world."

There is nothing in the canonical gospels that correspond with this saying. It is a typical gnostic idea that the only way to understand this evil and sordid material world, is to realize that it can be compared to a rotting corpse.

> 57. Jesus said, "The kingdom of the father is like a man who had good seed. His enemy came by night and sowed weeds among the good seed. The man did not allow them to pull up the weeds; he said to them, I am afraid that you will go intending to pull up the weeds and pull up the wheat along with them. For on the day of the harvest the weeds will be plainly visible, and they will be pulled up and burned."

This passage is simply a summary of Matt 13: 30–34 (part of M) – the parable of the wheat and the weeds in the same field.

The field is an allegory of the world, which contains believers and unbelievers. They will be separated when the kingdom arrives.

> 58. Jesus said, "Blessed is the man who has suffered and found life."

Although this saying reminds one of the Beatitudes, there is no parallel in the canonical gospels. The word "suffered" may also be translated as "labored". It is not impossible that this is a genuine saying of Jesus, passed on through an oral tradition, or a part of Q not utilized by Matthew and Luke.

> 59. Jesus said, "Take heed of the living one while you are alive, lest you die and seek to see him and be unable to do so."

"The living one" in this passage in none other than Jesus himself (see the prologue where Jesus is called the "living Jesus"). One must find him before death makes this impossible.

> 60. They saw a Samaritan carrying a lamb on his way to Judea. He said to his disciples, "That man is round about the lamb." They said to him, "So that he may kill it and eat it." He said to them, "While it is alive, he will not eat it, but only when he has killed it and it has become a corpse." They said to him, "He cannot do so otherwise." He said to them, "You too, look for a place for yourself within repose, lest you become a corpse and be eaten."

It has been suggested that the Coptic translation misunderstood the original Greek and that it was Jesus who watched the Samaritan with his lamb while Jesus was on his way to Judea. The advice of Jesus to his disciples means that they should secure a place for themselves "within repose", in the kingdom, in heaven, to prevent a bad afterlife and simply become corpses.

> 61. Jesus said, "Two will rest on a bed: the one will die, and the other will live." Salome said, "Who are you, man, that you ... have come up on my couch and eaten from my table?" Jesus said to her, "I am he who exists from the undivided. I was given some of the things of my father." <...> "I am your disciple." <...> "Therefore I say, if he is destroyed, he will be filled with light, but if he is divided, he will be filled with darkness."

The meaning of this passage is unclear, perhaps due to a bad Coptic translation from the Greek. In addition, parts of the text are missing. What may be clear is that death strikes unexpectedly.

We also read in this passage of Salome who was a female disciple of Jesus.

> 62. Jesus said, "It is to those who are worthy of my mysteries that I tell my mysteries. Do not let your left (hand) know what your right (hand) is doing."

This text refers to Matt 13: 11 (part of M) – "To you it is given to know the mysteries of the Kingdom of Heaven, but it is not given to them."

The second part of the text is a garbled version of Matt 6: 3 (part of M) – "But when you do merciful deeds, don't let your left hand know what your right hand does…"

For Thomas, the "mysteries" are evidently the doctrines of the Gnostics, which must not be divulged to outsiders.

> 63. Jesus said, "There was a rich man who had much money. He said, I shall put my money to use so that I may sow, reap, plant, and fill my storehouse with produce, with the Result

> that I shall lack nothing. Such were his intentions, but that same night he died. Let him who has ears hear."

This saying is a summary of the parable in Luke 12: 16–21 (part of Q). The point of this saying in Thomas is that earthly belongings are of no real value – the same point of view of Jesus, the Essene.

> 64. Jesus said, "A man had received visitors. And when he had prepared the dinner, he sent his servant to invite the guests. He went to the first one and said to him, My master invites you. He said, I have claims against some merchants. They are coming to me this evening. I must go and give them my orders. I ask to be excused from the dinner. He went to another and said to him, My master has invited you. He said to him, I have just bought a house and am required for the day. I shall not have any spare time. He went to another and said to him, My master invites you. He said to him, My friend is going to get married, and I am to prepare the banquet. I shall not be able to come. I ask to be excused from the dinner. He went to another and said to him, My master invites you. He said to him, I have just bought a farm, and I am on my way to collect the rent. I shall not be able to come. I ask to be excused. The servant returned and said to his master, Those whom you invited to the dinner have asked to be excused. The master said to his servant, Go outside to the streets and bring back those whom you happen to meet, so that they may dine. Businessmen and merchants will not enter the places of my father."

This rather long passage is also to be found in Luke 14: 16–24, the parable of the banquet, albeit with a few extra twists, which may come from the original in Q.

> 65. He said, "There was a good man who owned a vineyard. He leased it to tenant farmers so that they might work it and he might collect the produce from them. He sent his servant so that the tenants might give him the produce of the vineyard. They seized his servant and beat him, all but killing him. The servant went back and told his master. The master said, Perhaps he did not recognize them. He sent another servant. The tenants beat this one as well. Then the owner sent his son and said, Perhaps they will show respect to my son. Because the tenants knew that it was he who was the heir to the vineyard, they seized him and killed him. Let him who has ears hear."

This passage is clearly dependent upon Mark 12: 1–9 and the corresponding texts in Matthew and Luke – the parable of the owner of the vineyard who sent his son to collect the rent. The tenants are an allegory of Israel and the servants represent the prophets. The son of the owner is obviously Jesus who was rejected by Israel, according to the synoptical gospels, as well as Thomas.

> 66. Jesus said, "Show me the stone which the builders have rejected. That one is the cornerstone."

Mark 12: 10 has something similar: "Haven't you even read this scripture: The stone which the builders rejected, The same was made the head of the corner" (a quotation from Ps 118: 22).
    This cornerstone is obviously Jesus who was rejected by the Jews.

> 67. Jesus said, "If one who knows the all still feels a personal deficiency, he is completely deficient."

Nothing of this sort is to be found in the canonical gospels.

The "All" of which a gnostic may have knowledge is obviously knowledge of his eternal origin and eternal destiny, the kingdom of heaven. If somebody with this knowledge still feels dissatisfied, his dissatisfaction is total because he does not realize the value of his knowledge of the "All".

68.	Jesus said, "Blessed are you when you are hated and persecuted. Wherever you have been persecuted they will find no place."

69.	Jesus said, "Blessed are they who have been persecuted within themselves. It is they who have truly come to know the father. Blessed are the hungry, for the belly of him who desires will be filled."

These two saying seem to be a garbled version of Luke 6: 21–23 (part of Q): "Blessed are you who hunger now, for you will be filled. Blessed are you who weep now, for you will laugh. Blessed are you when men shall hate you, and when they shall separate you from them and reproach you, and throw out your name as evil, for the Son of Mans's sake. Blessed are you when men shall hate you, and when they shall separate you from them and reproach you, and throw out your name as evil, for the Son of Mans's sake."

It may be gathered that the gnostic community where this gospel originated, suffered persecution from the Roman authorities, the Jews, and the Christians.

70.	Jesus said, "That which you have will save you if you bring it forth from yourselves. That which you do not have within you will kill you if you do not have it within you."

This is a typical gnostic statement. That which a believer can bring forth from himself is another way of referring to self–knowledge, the insight regarding the believer's true origin and destiny outside of this evil and cruel world.

> 71. Jesus said, "I shall destroy this house, and no one will be able to build it [...]."

This saying reminds one of Mark 14: 57–58: "Some stood up, and gave false testimony against him, saying, We heard him say, I will destroy this temple that is made with hands, and in three days I will build another made without hands."

The saying is also reminiscent of John 2: 19 (part of the Proto-Gospel of John) – "Jesus answered them, "Destroy this temple, and in three days I will raise it up."

It is noteworthy that Thomas omits the rebuilding of the temple. That may be due to a gnostic rejection of Jesus resurrection, or a reference to the Jerusalem temple that was destroyed in AD 70.

> 72. A man said to him, "Tell my brothers to divide my father's possessions with me." He said to him, "O man, who has made me a divider?" He turned to his disciples and said to them, "I am not a divider, am I?"

This saying is derived from Luke 12: 13–14 (part of Q) – "One of the multitude said to him, Teacher, tell my brother to divide the inheritance with me. But he said to him, Man, who made me a judge or an arbitrator over you?"

> 73. Jesus said, "The harvest is great but the laborers are few. Beseech the Lord, therefore, to send out laborers to the harvest."

This is a quotation from Luke 10: 2 (a part of Q) – "Then he said to them, The harvest is indeed plentiful, but the laborers are few. Pray therefore to the Lord of the harvest, that he may send out laborers into his harvest."

These laborers are those who have to convince people of the truth of the gnostic message.

> 74. He said, "O Lord, there are many around the drinking trough, but there is nothing in the cistern."

It is not clear who the "Lord" is who is being addressed – it may be God, or it may be Jesus who listened to a disciple. The drinking trough or well that is mentioned contains the water of true knowledge. Many people, however, do not take advantage of it.

> 75. Jesus said, "Many are standing at the door, but it is the solitary who will enter the bridal chamber."

The "bridal chamber" is a symbol of the union between the soul of the solitary seeker and his ultimate destiny in the kingdom of heaven. Only a small number of people will achieve that.

> 76. Jesus said, "The kingdom of the father is like a merchant who had a consignment of merchandise and who discovered a pearl. That merchant was shrewd. He sold the merchandise and bought the pearl alone for himself. You too, seek his

> unfailing and enduring treasure where no moth comes near to devour and no worm destroys."

This saying is a combination of the following passages in Matthew:

- "Again, the Kingdom of Heaven is like a man who is a merchant seeking fine pearls, who having found one pearl of great price, he went and sold all that he had, and bought it" (Matt 13: 45–46 – part of M).
- "Don't lay up treasures for yourselves on the earth, where moth and rust consume, and where thieves break through and steal; but lay up for yourselves treasures in heaven, where neither moth nor rust consume, and where thieves don't break through and steal" (Matt 6: 19–20 – also part of M). See also Luke 12: 33–34 (part of Q).

For Thomas, this valuable pearl is a symbol of the esoteric and secret knowledge and teachings of Gnosticism.

> 77. Jesus said, "It is I who am the light which is above them all. It is I who am the all. From me did the all come forth, and unto me did the all extend. Split a piece of wood, and I am there. Lift up the stone, and you will find me there."

The Jesus whose words are quoted here, is not the Jesus who spoke to his disciples while he was still alive, but a metaphysical Jesus, patterned after certain passages in Paul's letters:

- "He put all things in subjection under his feet, and gave him to be head over all things to the assembly, He put all things in subjection under his feet, and gave him to be head over all things to the assembly" (Eph 1: 23–24).

- "... there can't be Greek and Jew, circumcision and uncircumcision, barbarian, Scythian, bondservant, freeman; but Christ is all, and in all (Col 3: 11).
- There is also an allusion to John 8: 12 (part of the discourse source) – "Again, therefore, Jesus spoke to them, saying, "I am the light of the world."

Thomas coveys an almost panentheistic gnostic thought, namely that the All, the universe in its widest sense, partakes in the existence of God and is part of the divine. In the afterlife, the spirit of the believer is also dissolved into the All.

78.	Jesus said, "Why have you come out into the desert? To see a reed shaken by the wind? And to see a man clothed in fine garments like your kings and your great men? Upon them are the fine garments, and they are unable to discern the truth."

This saying reminds one of Luke 7: 24–25 (part of Q) – "When Johns messengers had departed, he began to tell the multitudes about John, What did you go out into the wilderness to see? A reed shaken by the wind? But what did you go out to see? A man clothed in soft clothing? Behold, those who are gorgeously dressed, and live delicately, are in kings' courts."

Thomas quotes some of these words, but fails to apply them to John the Baptist. The point he wished to make is that people wearing luxurious clothes, such as kings and magistrates, are ignorant regarding the teachings of Gnosticism.

79.	A woman from the crowd said to him, "Blessed are the womb which bore you and the breasts which nourished you." He said to her, "Blessed are those who have heard the word

> of the father and have truly kept it. For there will be days when you will say, Blessed are the womb which has not conceived and the breasts which have not given milk."

This saying combines two different statements of Jesus in the gospels:

- Luke 11: 27–28 (part of Q) – "It came to pass, as he said these things, a certain woman out of the multitude lifted up her voice, and said to him, Blessed is the womb that bore you, and the breasts which nursed you! But he said, On the contrary, blessed are those who hear the word of God, and keep it."
- Luke 23: 29 (part of L) – "For behold, the days are coming in which they will say, Blessed are the barren, the wombs that never bore, and the breasts that never nursed."

As he did elsewhere, Thomas changed "God" to "Father". For him, "the word of the Father" can only mean one thing, namely the secret knowledge contained in the teachings of the gnostics.

> 80. Jesus said, "He who has recognized the world has found the body, but he who has found the body is superior to the world."

This saying is very much like number 56, where the world is compared to a corpse.

Here, Thomas teaches that the believer who knows the world as a dead and lifeless place, can appreciate his own living body, the seat of his spirit.

> 81. Jesus said, "Let him who has grown rich be king, and let him who possesses power renounce it."

This saying seems to be paradoxical, until one realizes that the riches mentioned in the first part are a symbol for the valuable knowledge of Gnosticism. The man with this treasure is able to be king over his own life. On the other hand, those who possess worldly power should renounce it.

> 82. Jesus said, "He who is near me is near the fire, and he who is far from me is far from the kingdom."

There is nothing in the New Testament that resembles this saying.

The fire is a symbol of the light of the kingdom. Jesus, the wise teacher of Gnosticism, is the key to enter the kingdom.

> 83. Jesus said, "The images are manifest to man, but the light in them remains concealed in the image of the light of the father. He will become manifest, but his image will remain concealed by his light."

The images that become manifest or visible in man are the perfect Platonic ideas or templates of objects and qualities in the material world. These images or ideas remain invisible due to the overpowering light of the Father.

There are no parallels in any of the gospels of this saying.

> 84. Jesus said, "When you see your likeness, you rejoice. But when you see your images which came into being before you, and which neither did not become manifest, how much you will have to bear!"

When somebody sees his reflection in a mirror, he likes what he sees. His image, his invisible immortal spirit, which existed before he entered the evil and miserable world, will not become visible in this world. Nobody will stay alive if his spirit is liberated.

It is certain that Jesus never taught anything like this Greek philosophical idea.

> 85. Jesus said, "Adam came into being from a great power and a great wealth, but he did not become worthy of you. For had he been worthy, he would not have experienced death."

Adam, who was made in the image of God, had something very valuable, namely his immortal spirit. However, he became unworthy, that is, he sinned and that led to death.

This is a gnostic interpretation of the story of the fall of mankind in Genesis 3.

> 86. Jesus said, "The foxes have their holes and the birds have their nests, but the son of man has no place to lay his head and rest."

This is an almost exact quotation from Luke 9: 58 and Matt 8: 20 (part of Q). The gnostic believer, the son of man, is encouraged not to cling to earthly belongings.

> 87. Jesus said, "Wretched is the body that is dependent upon a body, and wretched is the soul that is dependent on these two."

The body that is dependent upon another body, is another way of saying that children are born from the bodies of their mothers. If a soul or spirit is incarcerated in the material body, as taught by Plato, that person is doomed to suffer in this evil and wretched material world.

Nothing of this sort was certainly ever taught by Jesus of Nazareth, the Jewish rabbi.

> 88. Jesus said, "The angels and the prophets will come to you and give to you those things you (already) have. And you too, give them those things which you have, and say to yourselves, When will they come and take what is theirs?"

The angels and the prophets (of Gnosticism) taught the believers about their true riches, their valuable souls. The angels will, though, take back those immortal souls at death. This reminds one of Luke 12: 20 (part of Q) – "But God said to him [the rich man], You foolish one, tonight your soul is required of you. The things which you have prepared — whose will they be?"

> 89. Jesus said, "Why do you wash the outside of the cup? Do you not realize that he who made the inside is the same one who made the outside?"

This saying is clearly a reference to Luke 11: 39–40 (part of Q) – "The Lord said to him, Now you Pharisees cleanse the outside of the cup and of the platter, but your inward part is full of extortion and wickedness. You foolish ones, didn't he who made the outside make the inside also?"

The point Thomas wished to make, is that one should have a pure soul, not only a clean body.

> 90. Jesus said, "Come unto me, for my yoke is easy and my lordship is mild, and you will find repose for yourselves."

This is a skewed quotation from Matt 11: 28–30 (part of M) – "Come to me, all you who labor and are heavily burdened, and I will give you rest. Take my yoke on you, and learn from me, for I am humble and lowly in heart; and you will find rest for your souls. For my yoke is easy, and my burden is light."

The rest which Thomas mentions is the eternal rest in the kingdom after the liberation of the soul.

> 91. They said to him, "Tell us who you are so that we may believe in you." He said to them, "You read the face of the sky and of the earth, but you have not recognized the one who is before you, and you do not know how to read this moment."

It is strange hat the disciples wanted to know who Jesus was, as if they did not already know it. Jesus rebuked them for not recognizing him for what he was and their lack of self-knowledge.

> 92. Jesus said, "Seek and you will find. Yet, what you asked me about in former times and which I did not tell you then, now I do desire to tell, but you do not inquire after it."

The first part of this saying is quoted from Luke 11: 9 (part of Q) – "I tell you, keep asking, and it will be given you. Keep seeking, and you will find. Keep knocking, and it will be opened to you."

The second part of the saying reminds one of John 16: 25 (part of the discourse source) – "I have spoken these things to you in figures of speech. But the time comes when I will no more speak to you in figures of speech, but will tell you plainly about the Father."

The point Thomas wishes to make is that not many people are ready or able to grasp the teachings of Gnosticism.

> 93. Jesus said, "Do not give what is holy to dogs, lest they throw them on the dung–heap. Do not throw the pearls to swine, lest they [...] it [...]."

Matthew 7: 6 (part of M) says something similar: "Don't give that which is holy to the dogs, neither cast your pearls before the pigs, lest perhaps they trample them under their feet, and turn and tear you to pieces."

That which is holy and the pearls are the secret teachings of Gnosticism. The dogs and the swine are those people who are not able or willing to understand it and persecute the gnostic believers.

> 94. Jesus said, "He who seeks will find, and he who knocks will be let in."

This saying has the same origin and message as saying 92.

> 95. Jesus said, "If you have money, do not lend it at interest, but give it to one from whom you will not get it back."

Something similar is found in Luke 6: 30 (part of Q) – "Give to everyone who asks you, and don't ask him who takes away your goods to give them back again."

Thomas taught generosity, but also told his hearers and readers that money and other worldly possessions are without any real value.

> 96. Jesus said, "The kingdom of the father is like a certain woman. She took a little leaven, concealed it in some dough, and made it into large loaves. Let him who has ears hear."

Luke 13: 20–21 (part of Q) has almost the same wording: "What shall I compare to the kingdom of God? It is like yeast, which a woman took and hid in three sata of flour, until it was all leavened."

Thomas message was that the kingdom is invisible, but has a great influence on those who accept the teachings of Jesus.

> 97. Jesus said, "The kingdom of the father is like a certain woman who was carrying a jar full of meal. While she was walking on the road, still some distance from home, the handle of the jar broke and the meal emptied out behind her on the road. She did not realize it; she had noticed no accident. When she reached her house, she set the jar down and found it empty."

There is nothing like this in the canonical gospels.

This saying seems to be a warning not to be careless with the message of the kingdom because it may be spoilt when it is unknowingly revealed to outsiders.

> 98. Jesus said, "The kingdom of the father is like a certain man who wanted to kill a powerful man. In his own house he drew his sword and stuck it into the wall in order to find out whether his hand could carry through. Then he slew the powerful man."

Nothing like this is to be found in the New Testament.

The "powerful man" seems to be a symbol for the hostile and evil world. Believers must be careful in their encounters with the world and make sure that they can overcome its power.

> 99. The disciples said to him, "Your brothers and your mother are standing outside." He said to them, "Those here who do the will of my father are my brothers and my mother. It is they who will enter the kingdom of my father."

Mark 3: 32 –35 contains the same episode: "A multitude was sitting around him, and they told him, Behold, your mother, your brothers, and your sisters are outside looking for you. He answered them, Who are my mother and my brothers? Looking around at those who sat around him, he said, Behold, my mother and my brothers! For whoever may do the will of God, the same is my brother, and my sister, and mother."

Thomas wished to convey the idea that people with the same spiritual convictions are closer to each other than blood relatives.

> 100. They showed Jesus a gold coin and said to him, "Caesars men demand taxes from us." He said to them, "Give Caesar what belongs to Caesar, give God what belongs to God, and give me what is mine."

This is a summary of the episode described in Mark 12: 13–17 (and the corresponding parts in Matthew and Luke). This is the only instance where Thomas used the word "God" instead of "Father". He seems to have thought of the Old Testament God, the creator and owner of the evil and foul material world or the Platonic demiurge.

Thomas added the last sentence and one may conclude that he regarded Jesus as more important than God. The souls or spirits of the believers belong to him.

> 101. Jesus said, "Whoever does not hate his father and his mother as I do cannot become a disciple to me. And whoever does

> not love his father and his mother as I do cannot become a disciple to me. For my mother [...], but my true mother gave me life."

This saying is an expansion of saying 56 where Jesus urged his followers to hate their relatives.

In this saying, Jesus has two fathers – his earthly father and his heavenly Father, whom his disciples must love. He also has two mothers – a human mother and a true (spiritual) mother, the latter of whom he loves. This must be the All into which the soul is to be dissolved at death.

> 102. Jesus said, "Woe to the pharisees, for they are like a dog sleeping in the manger of oxen, for neither does he eat nor does he let the oxen eat."

This parable is known from the fables of Aesop, but it is not impossible that it was also spoken by Jesus and picked up by Thomas.

The point is that the Pharisees (or people like them) stop others from seeing the light of the gnostic message.

> 103. Jesus said, "Fortunate is the man who knows where the brigands will enter, so that he may get up, muster his domain, and arm himself before they invade."

This saying deals with the same subject as saying 21.

Jesus used this saying in Luke 12: 39 (part of Q) to warn his followers that his return would be unexpected: "But know this, that if the master of the house had known in what hour the thief was coming, he would have watched, and not allowed his house to be broken into."

Thomas' saying does not focus on the time of the robbery, but on the place where it would happen.

> 104. They said to Jesus, "Come, let us pray today and let us fast." Jesus said, "What is the sin that I have committed, or wherein have I been defeated? But when the bridegroom leaves the bridal chamber, then let them fast and pray."

This saying is a reworking of Mark 3: 19–20 – "Jesus said to them, "Can the sons of the bride chamber fast, while the bridegroom is with them? As long as they have the bridegroom with them, they can't fast. But the days will come, when the bridegroom will be taken away from them, and then will they fast in that day."

Jesus sees no need to fast and pray because he hasn't committed any sin to confess. The "bridal chamber" is a symbol of the union of the soul with Jesus and the kingdom (saying 75). Should Jesus as the bridegroom leave the bridal chamber (by ending the union), it is time for people to fast and pray because all will be lost.

> 105. Jesus said, "He who knows the father and the mother will be called the son of a harlot."

This obscure saying is probably a reference to the fact that Jesus was accused of being born out of wedlock, due to an affair between his mother and a Roman soldier (see Quran, surah 19: 27–28).

> 106. Jesus said, "When you make the two one, you will become the sons of man, and when you say, Mountain, move away, it will move away."

The promise that mountains can be moved when a believer prays earnestly enough, is to be found in Mark 11: 23 (and parallel parts in Matthew and Luke).

Believers will become "sons of man", just as Jesus, in the hereafter where the difference between the sexes will disappear. That something like this will happen, must be believed, just as one has to believe that when praying earnestly, a mountain will get moved.

> 107. Jesus said, "The kingdom is like a shepherd who had a hundred sheep. One of them, the largest, went astray. He left the ninety–nine sheep and looked for that one until he found it. When he had gone to such trouble, he said to the sheep, I care for you more than the ninety–nine."

This is a version of the parable of the lost sheep (Luke 15: 3–7 – part of Q). The largest and most valuable sheep that got lost and was found by the shepherd (Jesus), was told that he was more loved than the other sheep. The lost sheep is a symbol of the gnostic believer who has been found.

> 108. Jesus said, "He who will drink from my mouth will become like me. I myself shall become he, and the things that are hidden will be revealed to him."

There is nothing in the biblical gospels corresponding with this saying.

Drinking from Jesus mouth means accepting the message coming from his lips. The believer will be absorbed into Jesus, the kingdom, and the All in the afterlife, where he will receive all hidden knowledge.

> 109. Jesus said, "The kingdom is like a man who had a hidden treasure in his field without knowing it. And after he died, he left it to his son. The son did not know (about the treasure). He inherited the field and sold it. And the one who bought it went plowing and found the treasure. He began to lend money at interest to whomever he wished."

This saying reminds one of Matt 13: 44 (part of M) – "The Kingdom of Heaven is like a treasure hidden in the field, which a man found, and hid. In his joy, he goes and sells all that he has, and buys that field."

The original owner of the land and his son are the people who are unaware of the treasure of Jesus' (gnostic) message. The man who bought the field and discovered the treasure, is the happy gnostic believer who knows his origin and destiny.

> 110. Jesus said, "Whoever finds the world and becomes rich, let him renounce the world."

No parallel of this saying occurs in the Bible. The man who became rich is the man who discovered the treasure of Jesus' (gnostic) message. He ought to withdraw from the corrupt and evil material world with all its distractions and temptations.

> 111. Jesus said, "The heavens and the earth will be rolled up in your presence. And the one who lives from the living one will not see death." Does not Jesus say, "Whoever finds himself is superior to the world?"

The expression about the heavens and the earth being rolled up is taken from Rev 6: 14 – "The sky was removed as a scroll when it is rolled up. Every mountain and island were moved out of their places."

One needs self-knowledge to survive Judgment Day and live forever as Jesus does.

> 112. Jesus said, "Woe to the flesh that depends on the soul; woe to the soul that depends on the flesh."

Human beings were seen by Thomas to be an unholy and catastrophic mixture of body and soul, of the rotting flesh and the pure spirit.

> 113. His disciples said to him, "When will the kingdom come?" Jesus said, "It will not come by waiting for it. It will not be a matter of saying here it is or there it is. Rather, the kingdom of the father is spread out upon the earth, and men do not see it."

Since the kingdom of heaven is a spiritual kingdom, it is not located anywhere on the surface of the earth. It is, rather, ubiquitous.

> 114. Simon Peter said to him, "Let Mary leave us, for women are not worthy of life." Jesus said, "I myself shall lead her in order to make her male, so that she too may become a living spirit resembling you males. For every woman who will make herself male will enter the kingdom of heaven."

Simon Peter seems to have been dissatisfied with Mary Magdalene in their midst, due to his male chauvinism. Jesus, however, told him that the difference between the genders will disappear in the afterlife, in the kingdom of heaven.

Winding Up

The first impression after having perused the Gospel of Thomas is that Jesus is presented as a gnostic sage – very far removed from the Jewish Essene rabbi found in the oldest reports about his life, where he is described as an ordinary mortal who wanted to convince the Jews to follow the Law of Moses strictly and who wanted to claim the throne of David, his ancestor.

A very pertinent question is: which sources were used by the author of the Gospel of Thomas? Did he rely on independent oral traditions, or did he copy and rework sayings from the canonical gospels and even from other parts of the New Testament? Both possibilities may be considered, but it is more probable that Thomas relied for the most part on earlier documents.

Thomas seems to have used the Q Document 74 times – that is 65% of the sayings. M is seemingly referred to on twelve occasions and L is quoted from on 4 occasions. That gives a total of 79% of the sayings in Thomas.

Since Thomas seems to have used the Q Document so frequently and it was clearly his favorite source, one may theorize that M and L were actually also part of Q, but that Matthew or Luke made separate uses of those sayings in their gospels.

Thomas used the Gospel of Mark in 21 of his sayings. The final version of the Gospel of John, into which the discourse sources were incorporated, was used in six sayings. His frequent use of Q, M, and L is an indication that he did not have the final versions of Matthew and Luke at his disposal – only the Gospels of Mark and John, apart from Q, M, and L.

Thomas used expressions from the book of Revelation on more or less eight occasions.

Thomas contains some sayings not found in any canonical gospel. Some of them may have been genuine sayings, preserved in parts of Q not used by Matthew or Luke, or they may have survived in the memories of people who passed them on to Thomas.

Some may even be pious inventions of Thomas or his informants.

The use of the final Gospel of John and Revelation, which can both be dated to the nineties of the first century AD, or even later, is an indication that Thomas cannot be dated earlier than the early second century AD. His extensive use of Q is an indication that this document was still in circulation after the end of the first century AD.

Albrecht Dürer: Jesus Appears to his Disciples

Another possibility that must also be considered is that Thomas relied on sayings of Jesus that were heard from Christians and understood incorrectly – just as Muhammad, the prophet of Islam who was an illiterate man, heard Bible stories from Christians and recited his skewed understanding of these stores to his followers, who wrote them down afterwards (see the next chapter).

The allusions to circumcision, the Sabbath, fasting, and prayer point to a gnostic Jewish group of Jesus people where this gospel originated. It is noteworthy that the Christian rite of baptism is nowhere encountered, although John the Baptist is mentioned twice.

This gospel is also silent about Jesus' crucifixion and resurrection.

Thomas avoided the name of God – perhaps due to the Jewish fear of using Gods name disrespectfully. It is always "the Father" or "the Lord".

The overall impression is that Thomas is certainly not a reliable source of knowledge about the life, message, and execution of Jesus of Nazareth. The time elapsed between the crucifixion of Jesus during AD 33 and the compilation of Thomas – seventy years, at least – must have blurred any possible oral traditions and transformed them into legends. Thomas interpreted the sayings of Jesus he found in all the sources mentioned above in the light of his gnostic beliefs. That skewed and distorted all the information he presented regarding Jesus and his ministry.

Chapter 14
THE QUR'AN

Since Jesus is often mentioned in the holy book of Islam, the Qur'an, this document must also be investigated to see whether it contains any reliable and historically relevant information about Jesus.

Muhammad
The founder of the religion of Islam, the prophet Muhammad (AD 570–632), left an indelible mark on the world's history because his followers, the Muslims, form the second largest religious group in the world, second only to Christianity.

Muhammad lost his father before he was born and his mother died when he was six years old. Family members then took care of the orphan. He could allegedly trace his ancestry back to Ishmael, the son of Abraham. He married a wealthy woman, 15 years his senior, and she bore him two sons (who died young) and four daughters.

He was a religious man who initially adhered to the traditional pagan religion of the Arabs. He often retreated to the desert for prayer and meditation. When he was 40 he had his first vision of the Archangel Gabriel who appeared to him and commanded him to "recite". Muhammad was initially reluctant to recite anything, but then the first verses of the Qur'an started to flow from his lips.

A bewildered Muhammad told his wife about this experience and she called upon a cousin, a Christian, to guide her husband through this spiritual event. He regarded this episode as his calling to become Gods messenger. For the next 23 years Muhammad received many more revelations and visions when the archangel appeared to him or when God spoke directly to him.

He recited the revelations to his family members and friends who learnt them by heart because none of them could read or write. These revelations were later written down and became the Qur'an. More and more people followed him and accepted him as a prophet.

Muhammad often had contact with Jews and Christians during his travels as a merchant, whom he described as the "People of the Book" (the Bible). There were Jewish and Christian communities in Arabia and Syria from whom Muhammad heard stories from the Bible, which convinced him that there is only one God, called Allah in Arabian.

After the death of his first wife, he married other women, including a slave girl Mary, who was a Christian. The Christians with whom he had contact were mostly Nestorians and Monophysites who held heretical views about the relationship between Jesus divine and his human natures.

There is also the possibility that some of these Christians still regarded themselves, even after six centuries, as Nazoreans, the sect to which Jesus also belonged and from which he drew most of his Jewish supporters. The Arab word for Christianity was "Nasraniyah", which seems to be related to or derived from "Nazorean".[277]

It is not impossible that there were still some Nazoreans in Muhammads time. It has been shown in Chapter 2 that bishop Epiphanios wrote during the fourth century that they were still to be found at Pella and elsewhere on the eastern bank of the Jordan.

---

[277] Armstrong. *Muhammad;* Hughes. "Christianity"; Hughes. "Jesus Christ"; Nasr. "Muhammad"; Tisdall. *The Original Sources of the Qur'an,* Chapter IV.

There is evidence that Muhammad visited the monastery of Saint Catherine in the Sinai Peninsula and guaranteed its security.[278] It is reasonable to suppose that he also heard some stories from the Bible from the monks in this monastery.

These are some researchers who assert that Muhammad's visions and revelations were the result of temporal lobe epilepsy. Whether this was really the case cannot be determined with any degree of certainty today. However, he does seem to have displayed the typical symptoms of the so-called Geschwind Syndrome, a variety of a temporal lobe epilepsy, including hyper-religiosity, hallucinations or visions, a quick temper, and verbosity.[279] The Apostle Paul also seemed to have suffered from this condition.[280]

The Qur'an

The revelations of Muhammad were collected after his death into a single document, called the Qur'an. It is the holy book of Islam and it is regarded as the Word of God, dictated by the archangel Gabriel or God himself to Muhammed and, therefore, perfect and without any flaw or mistake.

The Qur'an only got its final form several decades after the death of Muhammad. There were several versions, which were suppressed in favor of the final one we have today. It is much shorter than the New Testament and contains 114 Chapters or surahs of unequal length. They are arranged haphazardly with no rational order or sequence.[281]

---

[278] Anon., " Mohammed and the Holy Monastery of Sinai".
[279] Aziz, "Did Prophet Mohammad (PBUH) have epilepsy?"; Freemon, "A Differential Diagnosis of the Inspirational Spells of Muhammad"; Veronelli et al., "Geschwind Syndrome".
[280] Pretorius, *Jesus of Nazareth,* 132–37.
[281] Jones. *The Koran;* Schimmel. "Islam".

It is only possible to understand the Qur'an adequately with a knowledge of the Bible since this sacred text repeatedly mentions characters from the Bible and their deeds and words. One encounters, for instance, Adam, Abraham, Jacob, Moses, Aaron, David, Solomon, Mary, and especially Jesus. It is clear that Muhammad did not always remember the stories from the Bible told to him correctly and he made mistakes in this regard. For instance, he mistook Jesus' mother Mary for Aaron and Moses' sister, Miriam (Surah 3: 35–36; 19: 28).

The name "Jesus" (Isa in Arabian) is mentioned 28 times, including three occasions when he is named "Jesus Christ" or "Jesus the Messiah". Jesus' mother, "Mary", occurs 38 times and Jesus is named the "son of Mary" on 23 occasions. The combination "Jesus the son of Mary" can be found in 14 places. The title "Christ" or "Messiah" is used eleven times. Other names and titles are, in addition, frequently used for Jesus. It is, therefore, clear that Jesus plays an important role in the Qur'an, although other figures such as Abraham and Moses are mentioned more often.[282]

Gordon Nickel adds: "The total material about Jesus in the Qur'ān is not particularly abundant... Out of some ninety verses related to Jesus in the Qur'ān, sixty-four belong to the stories of his birth in surā s 3 and 19. The remaining twenty-six verses also contain significant repetition, further reducing the basic material on aspects of Jesus' adult life and ministry. This compares to some 500 verses related to the figure of Moses in the Qur'ān and more than 240 about Abraham."[283]

Since the surahs are arranged haphazardly, no clear chronological story of Jesus is presented in the Qur'an. For that reason, the most important verses dealing with his life will be pre-

---

[282] Hughes. "Jesus Christ"; Nickel. "Jesus in the Qur'an".
[283] Nickel. "Jesus in the Qur'an", 289.

sented below in a logical order.

The Immaculate Conception of Mary
Surah 3: 35–36

35.	The wife of Imran said, "My Lord, I have vowed to You what is in my womb, dedicated, so accept from me; You are the Hearer and Knower."
36.	And when she delivered her, she said, "My Lord, I have delivered a female," and Allah was well aware of what she has delivered, "and the male is not like the female, and I have named her Mary, and have commended her and her descendants to Your protection, from Satan the outcast."

The father of Mary, according to these verses, was Imran – known in the Bible as Amram (Ex 6: 20) – the father of Moses, Aaron, and Miriam. This is an anachronism because Amram was not her father.

The Qur'an repeats the extra-biblical legend that Mary was conceived immaculately.

Jesus Birth Announced
Surah 3. 37–43

37.	Her Lord accepted her with a gracious reception, and brought her a beautiful upbringing, and entrusted her to the care of Zechariah. Whenever Zechariah entered upon her in the sanctuary, he found her with provision. He said, "O Mary, where did you get this from?" She said, "It is from Allah; Allah pro–vides to whom He wills without reckoning."
38.	Thereupon Zechariah prayed to his Lord; he said, "My Lord, bestow on me good off–spring from Your presence; You are the Hearer of Prayers."

39.	Then the angels called out to him, as he stood praying in the sanctuary: "Allah gives you good news of John; confirming a Word from Allah, and honorable, and moral, and a prophet; one of the upright."
40.	He said, "My Lord, how will I have a son, when old age has overtaken me, and my wife is barren?" He said, "Even so, Allah does whatever He wills."
41.	He said, "My Lord, give me a sign." He said, "Your sign is that you shall not speak to the people for three days, except by gestures. And remember your Lord much, and praise in the evening and the morning."
42.	The angels said, "O Mary, Allah has chosen you, and has purified you. He has chosen you over all the women of the world.
43.	"O Mary, be devoted to your Lord, and bow down, and kneel with those who kneel."

The Qur'an is clearly confused and mixes the stories about the announcement to the priest Zecharias that his son, John the Baptist, would be born and the story of Mary hearing from an angel that Jesus would be born (Luke 1: 5–45).

The Birth of Jesus
Surah 19. 22–34

21.	So she carried him, and secluded herself with him in a remote place.
22.	The labor–pains came upon her, by the trunk of a palm–tree. She said, "I wish I had died before this, and been completely forgotten."

24.	Whereupon he called her from beneath her: "Do not worry; your Lord has placed a stream beneath you.
25.	And shake the trunk of the palm–tree towards you, and it will drop ripe dates by you."
26.	"So eat, and drink, and be consoled. And if you see any human, say, I have vowed a fast to the Most Gracious, so I will not speak to any human today."
27.	Then she came to her people, carrying him. They said, "O Mary, you have done some–thing terrible.
28.	O sister of Aaron, your father was not an evil man, and your mother was not a whore."
29.	So she pointed to him. They said, "How can we speak to an infant in the crib?"
30.	He said, "I am the servant of Allah. He has given me the Scripture, and made me a prophet.
31.	And has made me blessed wherever I may be; and has enjoined on me prayer and charity, so long as I live.
32.	And kind to my mother, and He did not make me a disobedient rebel.
33.	So Peace is upon me the day I was born, and the day I die, and the Day I get resurrected alive."
34.	That is Jesus son of Mary—the Word of truth about which they doubt.

The "remote place" where Mary sheltered her unborn child may be a case where Muhammad misunderstood the story he heard about the infant Jesus taken by his parents to Egypt to escape the murderous gangs of Herod the Great (Matt 2: 13–15).

Mary's family accused her of having an illegitimate son, but the baby spoke and confirmed that he was destined to be a prophet of Allah. Muhammad repeated the gospels account that Mary was a virgin when Jesus was born.

Albrecht Dürer: Virgin and Child (1503)

The baby's purportedly prophecy about his own death and resurrection seems to contradict surah 4: 157–59 where it is stated that Jesus didn't die on the cross and only appeared to die. This prophecy of his own death seems to repeat Jesus' announcements in the biblical gospels that he expected to be crucified and to get resurrected after three days.

Mary is called the sister of Aaron, which means that she is confused with Miriam – an anachronism.

The Miraculous Birth of Jesus
Surah 3: 43–47

43.	"O Mary, be devoted to your Lord, and bow down, and kneel with those who kneel."
44.	These are accounts from the Unseen, which We reveal to you. You were not with them when they cast their lots as to which of them would take charge of Mary; nor were you with them as they quarreled.
45.	The Angels said, "Oh, Mary, Allah gives you good news of a Word from Him. His name is the Messiah, Jesus, son of Mary, well–esteemed in this world and the next, and one of the nearest.

46.	He will speak to the people from the crib, and in adulthood, and will be one of the righteous."
47.	She said, "My Lord, how can I have a child, when no man has touched me?" He said, "It will be so. Allah creates whatever He wills. To have anything done, He only says to it, Be, and it is."

This passage repeats the virgin birth of Jesus, but also an apocryphal account of the infant being able to speak shortly after birth. The angel announced to Mary that her son, the Messiah and named Jesus, would be a prophet of Allah.

It is noticeable that the Qur'an doesn't mention Joseph, Mary's husband.

Miracles of Jesus
Surah 5: 112–115

112.	"And when the disciples said, O Jesus son of Mary, is your Lord able to bring down for us a feast from heaven? He said, Fear Allah, if you are believers."
113.	They said, "We wish to eat from it, so that our hearts may be reassured, and know that you have told us the truth, and be among those who witness it."
114.	Jesus son of Mary said, "O Allah, our Lord, send down for us a table from heaven, to be a festival for us, for the first of us, and the last of us, and a sign from You; and provide for us; You are the Best of providers."
115.	Allah said, "I will send it down to you. But whoever among you disbelieves thereafter, I will punish him with a punishment the like of which I never punish any other being."

This passage seems to be a garbled variation of the Last Supper of Jesus with his disciples.

Albrecht Dürer: The Last Supper (1523)

The Mission of Jesus
Surah 58: 26, 27

26.	We sent Noah and Abraham, and established in their line Prophethood and the Scripture. Some of them are guided, but many of them are sinners.
27.	Then We sent in their wake Our messengers, and followed up with Jesus son of Mary, and We gave him the Gospel, and instilled in the hearts of those who followed him compassion and mercy. But as for the monasticism which they invented—We did not ordain it for them—only to seek Allah's approval. But they did not observe it with its due observance. So We gave those of them who believed their reward, but many of them are sinful.

Surah 2: 87

87.	We gave Moses the Scripture, and sent a succession of messengers after him. And We gave Jesus son of Mary the clear proofs, and We supported him with the Holy Spirit. Is

it that whenever a messenger comes to you with anything your souls do not desire, you grew arrogant, calling some impostors, and killing others?

Surah 2: 253

253. These messengers: We gave some advantage over others. To some of them Allah spoke directly, and some He raised in rank. We gave Jesus son of Mary the clear miracles, and We strengthened him with the Holy Spirit. Had Allah willed, those who succeeded them would not have fought one another, after the clear signs had come to them; but they disputed; some of them believed, and some of them disbelieved. Had Allah willed, they would not have fought one another; but Allah does whatever He desires.

Surah 61: 6

6. And when Jesus son of Mary said, "O Children of Israel, I am Allah's Messenger to you, confirming what preceded me of the Torah, and announcing good news of a messenger who will come after me, whose name is Ahmad." But when he showed them the miracles, they said, "This is obvious sorcery."

These verses all contain the message that the task of Jesus was to be a servant, messenger, or apostle of Allah to Israel and to spread the gospel.

Surah 2: 87, 136 & 253

87. We gave Moses the Scripture, and sent a succession of messengers after him. And We gave Jesus son of Mary the

> clear proofs, and We supported him with the Holy Spirit. Is it that whenever a messenger comes to you with anything your souls do not desire, you grew arrogant, calling some impostors, and killing others?
>
> 136. Say, "We believe in Allah; and in what was revealed to us; and in what was revealed to Abraham, and Ishmael, and Isaac, and Jacob, and the Patriarchs; and in what was given to Moses and Jesus; and in what was given to the prophets— from their Lord. We make no distinction between any of them, and to Him we surrender."
>
> 253. These messengers: We gave some advantage over others. To some of them Allah spoke directly, and some He raised in rank. We gave Jesus son of Mary the clear miracles, and We strengthened him with the Holy Spirit.

Jesus was strengthened by "the Holy Spirit" – another name used for the archangel Gabriel.

We are told that Jesus, a prophet, received revelations from God – alongside a row of other prophets and apostles.

The Crucifixion of Jesus
Surah 4: 155–59

> 155. But for their [the Jews] violation of their covenant, and their denial of Allah's revelations, and their killing of the prophets unjustly, and their saying, "Our minds are closed." In fact, Allah has sealed them for their disbelief, so they do not believe, except for a few.
> 156. And for their faithlessness, and their saying against Mary a monstrous slander,

> 157. and for their saying, "We have killed the Messiah, Jesus, the son of Mary, the Messenger of Allah." In fact, they did not kill him, nor did they crucify him, but it appeared to them as if they did. Indeed, those who differ about him are in doubt about it. They have no knowledge of it, except the following of assumptions. Certainly, they did not kill him.
> 158. Rather, Allah raised him up to Himself. Allah is Mighty and Wise.
> 159. There is none from the People of the Scripture but will believe in him before his death, and on the Day of Resurrection he will be a witness against them.

According to this passage, the Jews slandered Mary and boasted that they had crucified Jesus. However, Jesus did not die on the cross, although the Jews thought that he did. When he eventually died at a later stage, God took him up into heaven.

This may an old memory of certain Christians with whom Muhammad had contact (Nazoreans?) that Jesus survived the crucifixion. The Qur'an fails to mention the role played by the Roman authorities in Jesus' execution.

The killing of the prophets by the Jews is mentioned in 1 Kgs 18: 4 & 19: 10; Neh 9: 26; Jer 2: 30; and 2 Chr 30: 16.

Jesus Divinity
Surah 5: 15–17

> 15. Oh, People of the Book! Our Messenger has come to you, clarifying for you much of what you kept hidden of the Book, and overlooking much. A light from Allah has come to you, and a clear Book.

16.	Allah guides with it whoever follows His approval to the ways of peace, and He brings them out of darkness into light, by His permission, and He guides them in a straight path.
17.	They disbelieve those who say, "Allah is the Christ, the son of Mary." Say, "Who can prevent Allah, if He willed, from annihilating the Christ son of Mary, and his mother, and everyone on earth?" To Allah belongs the sovereignty of the heavens and the earth and what is between them. He creates whatever He wills, and Allah has power over everything.

This passage makes it clear that Jesus, the Messiah, and son of Mary, was an ordinary mortal without any divine status. This was revealed by Muhammad, the final messenger of God.

The Trinity
Surah 5: 72–75

72.	They [the Jews and Christians] disbelieve those who say, "Allah is the Messiah the son of Mary." But the Messiah himself said, "O Children of Israel, worship Allah, my Lord and your Lord. Whoever associates others with Allah, Allah has forbidden him Paradise, and his dwelling is the Fire. The wrongdoers have no saviors."
73.	They disbelieve those who say, "Allah is the third of three." But there is no deity except the One God. If they do not refrain from what they say, a painful torment will befall those among them who disbelieve.
74.	Will they not repent to Allah and ask His forgiveness? Allah is Forgiving and Merciful.
75.	The Messiah son of Mary was only a messenger, before whom other Messengers had passed away, and his mother was a woman of truth. They both used to eat food. Note how

> We make clear the revelations to them [the Christians]; then note how deluded they are.

The Qur'an asserts that Jesus himself denied the Christian doctrine of the trinitarian God and that he had a divine nature. There is only one God whom he also worshipped. Jesus was just a messenger, a prophet. He died in the end like other prophets before him.

Surah 19: 29–35

29.	So she pointed to him [the baby Jesus]. They said, "How can we speak to an infant in the crib?"
30.	He said, "I am the servant of Allah. He has given me the Scripture, and made me a prophet.
31.	And has made me blessed wherever I may be; and has enjoined on me prayer and charity, so long as I live.
32.	And kind to my mother, and He did not make me a disobedient rebel.
33.	So Peace is upon me the day I was born, and the day I die, and the Day I get resurrected alive."
34.	That is Jesus son of Mary—the Word of truth about which they doubt.
35.	It is not for Allah to have a child—glory be to Him. To have anything done, He says to it, "Be," and it becomes.

The Qur'an, with its strict monotheism, denied that it is possible for Gd to have a son. The infant Jesus is reported as declaring that he is merely the servant of God, a prophet, somebody who will die and be resurrected into eternal life.

Surah 5: 171–172

171.	Oh, People of the Scripture! Do not exaggerate in your religion, and do not say about Allah except the truth. The Messiah, Jesus, the son of Mary, is the Messenger of Allah, and His Word that He conveyed to Mary, and a Spirit from Him. So believe in Allah and His messengers, and do not say, "Three." Refrain — it is better for you. Allah is only one God. Glory be to Him — that He should have a son. To Him belongs everything in the heavens and the earth, and Allah is a sufficient Protector.
172.	The Messiah does not disdain to be a servant of Allah, nor do the favored angels. Whoever disdains His worship, and is too arrogant — He will round them up to Himself altogether.

Christians are admonished not to believe in three gods, but only in one God, Allah, who cannot have a son. Jesus is only a servant and a messenger of God.

Surah 9: 30–31

31.	The Jews said, "Ezra is the son of Allah," and the Christians said, "The Messiah is the son of Allah." These are their statements, out of their mouths. They emulate the statements of those who blasphemed before. May Allah assail them! How deceived they are!
31.	They have taken their rabbis and their priests as lords instead of Allah, as well as the Messiah son of Mary. Although they were commanded to worship none but The One God. There is no god except He. Glory be to Him; High above what they associate with Him.

The Qur'an declares that it amounts to blasphemy when Christians say that Jesus is the son of God.

Deductions

The Qur'an can by no stretch of imagination be regarded as a trustworthy guide to the life, teachings, and trial of Jesus. This book is silent on these matters.[284]

The details about Jesus' birth are partly apocryphal and borders on the miraculous with an infant in the crib who can speak.

There is only one reference to the crucifixion of Jesus and it is declared that the Jews – not the Romans – boasted that they had crucified him, but in reality failed to kill him. This may, perhaps, be a remnant of an old memory held by certain Christian groups that Jesus did not die when he was crucified. On the other hand, the Qur'ans view that Jesus did not die, may also be a skewed memory of the stories of Jesus miraculous resurrection after having died from his horrible wounds as mentioned in the letters of Paul and the Synoptic Gospels.

The insistence that Jesus was an ordinary mortal, only a messenger and prophet of God, was one of the convictions of the Ebionites, the Jewish followers of Jesus after his departure from the scene. If Jesus was not a divine being and not the eternal only–begotten son of God, then the doctrine of the divine Trinity must be abandoned, as the Qur'an also did.

Since Muhammad could not read or write, he never had the opportunity of reading any of the biblical gospels. His knowledge of the Bible was second-hand – stories told to him by Christians who did not always have a good grasp of the contents of the Bible. Some extra-biblical information may perhaps have lingered on in certain Christian groups, six centuries after the time of Jesus, and Muhammad made use of them in his sermons, as recorded in the Qur'an.

---

[284] Nickel. "Jesus".

The final conclusion must be that the Qur'an cannot be used as a trustworthy and reliable source of knowledge about the life of Jesus. All the information about Jesus contained in this book is second-hand, hear-say, and dependent upon Muhammad's unverified and unverifiable revelations and visions.

Chapter 15
CONCLUSION: THE VALUE OF THE GOSPEL NARRATIVES

The Evidence about Jesus as King of the Jews
It is possible that some critics of this book may argue that it amounts to one huge circular argument. They might say that that, which had to be proved by the investigation, was already presupposed at the start as the final outcome. The investigation was, therefore, merely an effort to find confirmation for the initial thesis.

It is granted that this book started off in Chapter 2 with the argument that Jesus of Nazareth must be regarded primarily as a throne-pretender who wanted to re-establish the Israelite monarchy and drive the hated pagan Romans away with the help of a crowd of angels from heaven. The rest of the book is, indeed, an explanation of the contents of the gospel narratives with this supposition in mind.

However, the evidence in the canonical gospels is so overwhelming that Jesus of Nazareth, the historical Jesus – and not the Jesus of faith as invented or introduced or initiated by the Apostle Paul – was indeed the king-in-waiting of Israel. That is how he saw himself. That is how his supporters regarded him. That is how Pontius Pilate viewed him. When this supposition is seen as the key to unlock the gospels, many obscure passages in the gospels become clearer and make sense. The detailed analysis of the contents of the gospels in the preceding chapters confirmed this finding.

It is a mystery why this all-important aspect of the life and work of Jesus was largely overlooked and ignored in literature regarding the historical Jesus. Scholars such as James Tabor and Chaim Cohn, for instance, briefly hinted and commented upon this aspect, without elaborating on it or exploring it further.[285]

The Organization Early Christian Writings published on its website a list of the most important approaches regarding "Historical Jesus Theories" by contemporary scholars. The following theories are listed:

- Jesus the Myth: Heavenly Christ;
- Jesus the Myth: Man of the Indefinite Past;
- Jesus the Hellenistic Hero;
- Jesus the Revolutionary;
- Jesus the Wisdom Sage;
- Jesus the Man of the Spirit;
- Jesus the Prophet of Social Change;
- Jesus the Apocalyptic Prophet; and
- Jesus the Savior.[286]

All these theories, certainly, contain partially valid perspectives and each author cited copious amounts of information from the canonical gospels in support of a certain theory. But not one of them describe Jesus as primarily the king-in-waiting of Israel. There are simply too many indications in the gospels to come to any other conclusion and this book is meant to rectify this neglected and overlooked perspective.

The finding of the Jesus Seminar that Jesus was crucified by the Romans because he was merely a troublemaker and a public nuisance, also cannot be supported in the face of all the evidence.

---

[285] Tabor. *The Jesus Dynasty,* 172–73, 191–93; Cohn. *The Trial and Death of Jesus,* 170–76.
[286] Early Christian Writings. "Historical Jesus Theories".

CONCLUSION: THE VALUE OF THE GOSPEL NARRATIVES

All the literature written by traditional or orthodox Christian authors about Jesus contain the unsupportable view that all the available sources about the life of Jesus must be interpreted from a single perspective, namely the dogma that Jesus had a dual nature – divine and human – and that he is the second person in the Divine Trinity.[287] This approach ignores the clear evidence in the gospels to the contrary. This book has shown that the earliest and most trustworthy sources for knowledge about Jesus portray him as an ordinary mortal human being.

The later sources about the life of Jesus – the Gospels of Mark, the unique material in Matthew and Luke, as well as the discourses and dialogues in John's Gospel, followed Paul in presenting Jesus as a divine being who adopted a human form. This view is the result of Paul's unverifiable visions and revelations, as well as the long time – at least five decades – that elapsed between Jesus' time and the recording of the recollections of eye-witnesses in these documents. That provided enough time for legendary and mythological aspects to creep and seep into the memories of the sources used by these gospels.

We may summarize the very explicit evidence for the thesis that Jesus saw himself above all as the divinely-appointed monarch of Israel in the following points:

- Jesus called God his Father and referred to himself as the Son of God – the title of the Israelite kings from the dynasty of David, as well as of pagan kings and emperors;
- Jesus had King David as an ancestor with two genealogies to prove his ancestry;

---

[287] Good examples of this approach are: König: *Die Helfte is my nooit oor Jesus Vertel nie;* and Simpson: "The Authenticity of the Gospels."

- Jesus' extraordinary experiences during and after his baptism convinced him that he was chosen by God to be his beloved Son, the king of Israel;
- The favorite topic in Jesus' sermons and dialogues was the kingdom of God with him on the throne with the help of battalions of belligerent angels from heaven;
- Jesus told his supporters that they would see this kingdom very soon, during their lifetimes and before they died;
- Jesus was declared on various occasions by his followers to be the next king of Israel and he did not contradict them;
- Jesus deliberately enacted a prophecy about the future king of Israel by entering Jerusalem triumphantly on an ass, while the crowd cheered him as their king; and
- Pontius Pilate had Jesus crucified precisely because he presented himself as the king of the Jews – the serious crime of rebellion – and a notice to that effect was placed on the cross.

Albrecht Dürer: Christ before Pilate (1507)

The analysis and explanation of the canonical gospels from the perspective of Jesus who saw himself as the divinely-appointed king of Israel is, therefore, fully warranted. The evidence is very convincing and compelling when all the metaphysical, mythological, supernatural, magical, and legendary aspects in the gospels have been identified and cleared up.

When the razor of Occam is applied to the sayings of Jesus, namely that the most simple and least complicated explanation of a text is usually the correct or most likely explanation, then it makes sense to interpret Jesus' sayings regarding the coming kingdom in a literal sense. When this principle is applied, it must be concluded that he meant the resurrection of the Israelite monarchy – and not some ethereal, spiritual, and heavenly kngdom of the far future.

Apart from being characterized as the king-in-waiting of the Jews, Jesus can also be described in the following terms on account of the available evidence in the gospels:

- Jesus was a learned Jewish rabbi who knew the Hebrew Scriptures well and often gave an original explanation of their contents;
- Jesus also saw himself as a religious reformer who wanted to lead his people back to God and establish a theocracy;
- Jesus was a member of the sect of the Essenes or Nazoreans and many of his sermons and parables were explanations of typical Essene beliefs and convictions;
- Most of Jesus' followers and supporters were fellow-Essenes;
- As a Jewish rabbi who was educated by the Essenes, he was a skilled healer who helped many people with their ailments and psycho-somatic disorders;
- Jesus was a charismatic leader who attracted people and drew crowds who came to listen to his sermons and stories; and
- Jesus was a master story-teller who illustrated his messages with imaginative and sometimes humorous tales and parables.

The Development of the Gospels

It must be remembered that the gospel narratives, as we have them in the New Testament, went through a process of development. The earliest documents, the Q Document, the Didaché, and the Proto-Gospel of John, together with the Epistle of James, are the oldest sources of knowledge about Jesus. They can all be dated between ten and thirty years after Jesus' time and they must be regarded as the most dependable and accurate descriptions of Jesus' life.

These documents are mostly sober and straightforward narratives, except for the Proto-Gospel of John that contains stories about some supernatural signs or miracles performed by Jesus. This proto-gospel is, nevertheless, more trustworthy than the other gospels. It contains, for instance, the most detailed and convincing description of Jesus' arrest. It is the only gospel that provides a rational and medical explanation for Jesus' survival and resurrection after his crucifixion. Matthew and Luke, on the other hand, presented the resurrection as an unexplainable miracle, while Mark only mentions an empty tomb without giving any explanations.

Another set of relatively early documents, the letters of Paul from the fifties and early sixties of the first century AD, provide very little biographical details of Jesus. Whereas Jesus was described in the earlier documents as an ordinary mortal, Paul transformed him into a divine figure. Jesus' title of Son of God meant for Paul that he was a divine and heavenly figure who appeared to him in visions and revelations. Paul, who grew up in a Greek city, recreated and redesigned Jesus into a figure that almost fitted into a Greek mythological mold – just as there were many sons of Zeus known in Greek mythology.

Paul concluded that Jesus must be in heaven with God after he was resurrected from the grave after his crucifixion. Paul argued that Jesus was resurrected with a glorified or heavenly body – not the ordinary body of brawn and bones and blood with which he appeared to his disciples, according to the gospels. For Paul, this glorified body was composed of the same mysterious stuff as the

CONCLUSION: THE VALUE OF THE GOSPEL NARRATIVES

stars and other heavenly bodies that enabled him to enter heaven beyond the stars.

Paul attached great religious value to Jesus' crucifixion and resurrection. He saw Jesus' death on the cross, as reported to him, as a vicarious sacrifice. He suffered the punishment sinners deserve in hell after death. If anybody believes in him as the savior of the world his place in heaven with a glorified or spiritual body in the afterlife is guaranteed.

This belief in Christ as the savior of sinners differs fundamentally from the belief people had when they believed in Jesus as described in the earlier parts of the gospels. That belief meant that they accepted him as the Messiah, as a healer, and supported him as the liberator and king of Israel. John 20: 31 decclares that this gospel was "written, that you may believe that Jesus is the Christ, the Son of God, and that believing you may have life in his name."

This type of faith in Jesus had nothing to do with the salvation from eternal punishment in hell, which all sinners deserve and the promise of life everlasting in heaven with God, as propagated by Paul. It was a life without suffering and want, an existence in freedom.

It is a Christian article of faith that Jesus definitely and doubtlessly and decidedly died on the cross. This article of faith, however, is not supported by the available evidence. The gospels relate undeniably that Jesus survived the crucifixion with his earthly and physical body and that he had meetings with his disciples and friends after his survival. The Q Document is silent about his purported death on the cross. He was able to survive after he had received medical treatment from his friends after his entombment. The Qur'an may be trusted on this point, namely that Jesus did not die on the cross.

CONCLUSION: THE VALUE OF THE GOSPEL NARRATIVES

The Synoptic Gospels that appeared during the seventies and eighties of the first century AD, were influenced by Paul's theology – especially in their nativity and some resurrection narratives with their supernatural overtones.

Mark, the oldest of the three, is the most down-to-earth in dealing with his material. He started with the work of John the Baptist and continued with the ministry of Jesus. Many miracles were ascribed to Jesus, but the teachings of Jesus also received attention.

Matthew and Luke merged Mark with Q and some material of their own. When they followed Q and Mark, the narratives of Matthew and Luke are mostly restrained and devoid of metaphysical or mythological or legendary elements.

However, Matthew and Luke added conflicting stories about the birth of Jesus and his appearances after his resurrection in which he was pictured as a mythological and magical and miraculous figure. These stories may certainly be regarded as fiction or fantasy or fabrications.

All three Synoptic Gospels contain a long prophecy attributed to Jesus about the destruction of the temple and Judgment Day. This may safely be regarded as an invention and a description of what actually had happened during the Jewish war of AD 66–70.

Albrecht Dürer: Virgin and Child on the Crescent Moon with a Diadem (as described in Rev 12: 1–2)

CONCLUSION: THE VALUE OF THE GOSPEL NARRATIVES

John's Gospel was completed during the nineties by the addition of discourses, dialogues, and debates, which were attributed to Jesus but were very much the thoughts of second-generation or even third-generation Christians who gave the Gospel of John its final form. The Jesus of these discourses was no longer the Jewish rabbi of six decades or more earlier, but a sage, a philosopher, a theologian with profound insights, somebody who equated himself with the God of Moses, and who called Himself "I AM WHO I AM."

Needless to say, these discourses and theological ruminations in the Gospel of John have very little historical and biographical value regarding Jesus' life. They tell us only how certain people thought about him many years after his disappearance. They followed the example of Plato who explained his philosophy in the form of imaginary dialogues and debates of his teacher Socrates with other people.

The authors or compilers of the Proto-Gospel of John and the Synoptic Gospels collected as many reminiscences about Jesus as possible and reproduced them as faithfully as possible, although they did not always fit into the theological framework of some decades after the time of Jesus. The synoptics often interpreted these memories from their theological perspectives, namely that Jesus was simultaneously a divine and a human person and that he was the savior of the world.

This reinterpretation happened most often when the synoptic evangelists reported Jesus' pronouncements about the kingdom of God. There are enough indications that Jesus meant the earthly kingdom, a theocracy in Israel – as is apparent from Q and the Proto-Gospel of John. When the synoptics were written after the disappearance of Jesus and the destruction of Jerusalem, they had no choice but to create the impression that Jesus actually meant the heavenly kingdom of God that would arrive only at Judgment Day and Jesus' second coming on the clouds with legions of angels.

However, in their efforts to preserve as much as possible of Jesus' teachings, they could not totally hide Jesus' campaign to resurrect the Israelite monarchy. There are simply too many instances when he spoke about the kingdom that cannot be seen as references to a spiritual kingdom of the far future.

It transpired that extra-biblical documents, such as the letter of Clement, the Gospel of Thomas, and the Qur'an tell us very little of value about Jesus. They may safely be disregarded as reliable sources of valid information about the historical Jesus. They only tell us how certain groups adopted Jesus as a spokesman of their own ideas.

Clemens Romanus was not quite sure how to approach Jesus' divinity, while the Gospel of Thomas reconstructed him into an enlightened gnostic oracle and a neo-Platonic philosopher. The Qur'an, written a few centuries later, distorted the biblical narratives, described Jesus as a mere prophet, but also denied Jesus' divine status.

A clear trend became apparent as the time between Jesus' life and the description thereof increased. The earliest documents depicted Jesus as an ordinary human being, albeit an exceptionally gifted one. As more and more decades between the time of Jesus and the later gospels elapsed, the more Jesus was presented as a super-human and divine figure. This trend reached its culmination in the discourse sources of the Gospel of John where Jesus was repeatedly presented as God himself who temporarily adopted a human body.

This tendency can also be seen in the book of Revelation, written after AD 96. The author, John of Patmos, regarded the astrological constellations and planets he saw in the night sky as symbols of the celestial Christ and other spiritual beings.[288]

It has been shown that it was Paul who introduced the myth that Jesus was a divine figure. He sometimes contradicted himself, though, by portraying Jesus as a lesser deity, subservient to God, and a personage who would resign or retire or retreat from his elevated position after Judgment Day.

The late Swiss-German theologian, Hans Küng, who wrote a monumental book about Jesus, concluded that Jesus cannot be regarded as a divine figure and the second person of the Divine Trinity. His main argument was that the Old Testament nowhere equated the expected Messiah with God.[289] The Vatican forbade him in 1979 to teach Catholic theology but the University of Tübingen in Germany, where he was employed, kept him on in his position as director of the Institute for Ecumenical Research.[290]

If Jesus was an ordinary mortal who was the biological offspring of Joseph and Mary, then the contention in Heb 7: 26; Heb 9: 14; 1 Pet 1: 19; 1 Pet 2: 22; and 1 John 3:5 that he was without any blemish of sin or wrongdoing, cannot be maintained. He was not a perfect person and he felt the need to confess his sins when he was baptized by John – just as many other Jews who were baptized.

Dates in the Life of Jesus

The Bible provides us with enough details to enable us to calculate certain dates in the life of Jesus with some certainty – especially if they can be coordinated with astronomical phenomena.

---

[288] Scholtz. *The Prophecies of Revelation*.
[289] Küng. *Christ Sein*.
[290] Enc. Brit. "Küng, Hans".

- Jesus was most probably born during *6–4 BC*, while King Herod the Great was still alive.
- If the story of the Wise Men from the east is true and they saw a miraculous star, probably the conjunction of the planets Jupiter and Saturn inside the constellation of Pisces, then that star can be dated to *23 September 6 BC*.
- The ministry of John the Baptist started during the fifteenth year of the reign of Emperor Tiberius. That was during *AD 28 or 29*.
- According to Mark's description of Jesus' baptism by John the Baptist, this event coincided with a total solar eclipse over Galilee on *24 November AD 29*. Jesus started his career as preacher, healer, and leader of a movement in Galilee and Judea shortly after this.
- The crucifixion of Jesus probably happened on *Friday, 3 April AD 33*. A partial lunar eclipse was seen that night.

What Happened to Jesus?
The canonical gospels report that Jesus survived his crucifixion and appeared afterwards repeatedly to his disciples and friends. He wasn't a phantom, a spirit, a specter, a hallucination, a phantasm, or an immaterial celestial being. His disciples and friends could touch him and talk to him and he enjoyed breakfast with them.

There are indications that Jesus and some unnamed and unidentified co-conspirators anticipated his crucifixion by the Roman authorities, but that they also planned his almost miraculous resurrection to enhance and strengthen his claim to the throne of Israel. He expected the help of a heavenly military force armed with deadly flame-throwers – which never happened.

But what happened after that? Nobody knows for sure.

The impression is created in the gospels of Matthew and especially Luke that Jesus appeared to his disciples and friends only

CONCLUSION: THE VALUE OF THE GOSPEL NARRATIVES

in the limited time between his resurrection and his ascension into heaven. Since Luke's two conflicting descriptions of Jesus' ascension certainly amount to a devout fantasy to explain Paul's visions and revelations that Jesus appeared to him as a heavenly being, it may well be that Jesus' appearances happened a long time after his resurrection and recuperation. It may have been some months or even years later that he occasionally visited his old disciples and that Matthew, Luke, and John described some of these occasions without indicating exactly when that happened.

The last chapter of the Gospel of John quotes Jesus who told his disciples after his resurrection at the Sea of Galilee that he would return during the lifetime of the disciple whom he loved (John: 21: 22–24). This return could have had only one goal, namely to restart the campaign to gain the throne in Jerusalem. This promise contradicts the reports about Jesus' ascension into heaven. The Proto-Gospel of John ends at that point – with the promise of Jesus that he would return in the foreseeable future. That did not quite happen that way and no angels swept down from the sky onto the Romans in Palestine.

It does seem from the letter of James that Jesus was still alive at the time when this letter was written, not later than the fifties of the first century AD. This letter also promised his return – which never happened.

The reason for the compilation of the Q Document, containing many sayings of Jesus regarding the imminent resurrection of the kingdom of Israel, was not only to record some recollections about Jesus. This document was most probably written to keep Jesus' followers motivated to disseminate his message about the kingdom, while they awaited his expected return at any moment to complete his planned rebuilding of the Israelite kingdom – which never happened.

CONCLUSION: THE VALUE OF THE GOSPEL NARRATIVES

Mirza Ghulam Ahmad, the founder of a Muslim sect, the Ahmadiyya Movement in 1889, wrote a book in 1899 in which he claimed that Jesus left Palestine after his miraculous survival after his crucifixion and that he travelled to India where he ministered to a lost tribe of Israelites. His tomb is said to be in the town of Srinagar in Kashmir. This book was translated into English from Urdu and several editions were printed, the last one in 2003.[291] The purported tomb of Jesus is a tourist attraction in Srinagar today.[292]

The book of Ahmad makes the impression of a valiant effort to prove its claim, but the evidence provided is not convincing. It was not possible to find any recognized biblical scholar who took this book seriously. The German Norbert Klatt examined in 1988 the evidence that Ahmad quoted in his book and found that an independent evaluation of his sources does not support his findings.[293]

The authors Imcha Jacobovici and Charles Pellegrino caused quite a stir in 2007 with their book, The Jesus Family Tomb. They told the story of the discovery of a rather crude stone ossuary in a Jerusalem museum which purportedly had contained the remains of Jesus. This ossuary was retrieved in 1988 when a previously unknown tomb was discovered during excavations for a new housing project at Talpiot, a Jerusalem suburb.

The ossuary reportedly contained the inscription that it belonged to "Jesus, the son of Joseph". Ossuaries of other members of ostensibly the same family were also taken from the tomb and stored in the museum, until these authors realized their potential

---

[291] Ahmad. *Jesus in India.*
[292] Zachariah. "'Tomb of Jesus' in Kashmir–Roza Bal Shrine."
[293] Klatt. *Lebte Jesus in Indien?*

importance and wrote a book[294] and produced a documentary film about their finds.

Ossuaries of the persons with the following names were found in the Talpiot tomb: Joseph, Mary, Jesus (the son of Joseph), Mariamne (possibly Mary Magdalene and supposedly Jesus' wife) and Judah (the son of Jesus). The remains of these people taken from these ossuaries were buried at an unknown location by Israeli authorities when the ossuaries were stored in a museum.

The names on the ossuaries were common names during the first century AD in Palestine, but the authors calculated the statistical odds that precisely the names of Jesus' family members would appear on ossuaries in the same tomb and concluded that the chances would be very slim for something like that to happen at random.

The inside of the Talpiot Tomb, with author Imcha Jacobovici

---

[294] Jacobovici and Pelegrini, *The Jesus Family Tomb:*

A conference, attended by fifty theologians, archaeologists, and statisticians, was held in January 2008 in Jerusalem to discuss the possibility that the tomb and ossuary of Jesus of Nazareth was indeed found. Some scholars dismissed such a scenario, but others thought that there is a real possibility that the ossuaries of Jesus and his family members have, in fact, been found.[295]

Meanwhile, an ossuary in the possession of the Israeli engineer and collector of antiquities, Oded Golan, which reportedly belonged to Jesus' Brother, James, was introduced to the world in 2002. The following inscription in Aramaic appeared on the outside: יעקוב בר יוסף אחוי דישוע (*Ya'akov bar-Yosef akhui diYeshua* – Jacob [James] the son of Joseph, brother of Jesus). James Tabor suggested that this ossuary originally came from the Talpiot tomb, but that it had disappeared from the museum where the other ossuaries were being kept. According to him, this is an indication of the authenticity of the Talpiot ossuaries.[296]

It does seem, though, as if the consensus has shifted in the direction of rejecting the Talpiot Tomb as that of Jesus of Nazareth and his family. Perhaps the most important consideration is that it would have been unlikely for Jesus' family to have a tomb in Jerusalem, and not in Galilee where they used to live. Joseph, Jesus' father, doesn't seem to have been alive when Jesus started his public ministry and he would certainly have been buried in his home town of Nazareth.[297]

On the other hand, we read in Acts 1: 14 that Jesus' mother, Mary, and his brothers were present on the day of Pentecost in Jerusalem. Jesus' brother, James, became the leader of the Jerusalem

---

[295] McGirk. "Jesus' Tomb Controversy Reopened".
[296] Tabor. *The Jesus Dynasty,* 14–21, 28–9, 276–78.
[297] Evans and Feldman. "The Tomb of Jesus?"

congregation (Acts 15: 13) and he was killed in Jerusalem in AD 62, as has been shown in Chapter 2. It does seem, therefore, that Jesus' family members did settle in Jerusalem – although there is also the tradition that Mary was buried in Ephesus where she moved with the Apostle John after Jesus had entrusted her to the care of the "disciple whom he loved" while he was hanging on the cross (John 19: 26).[298]

In the light of all this, it remains difficult to decide whether the Talpiot Tomb had any connection with Jesus and his family. James Tabor points out that neither traditional Christians, nor orthodox Jews, would be prepared to accept that Jesus was indeed buried with his family in a tomb in Jerusalem due to dogmatic prejudices.[299]

Jesus must have been a damaged, demoralized, and disillusioned man after his crucifixion and almost miraculous recovery. He promised his disciples that he would return – which never happened. Luke invented two conflicting stories of how Jesus was taken up into heaven and disappeared behind the clouds to explain his disappearance.

The only rational conclusion is that Jesus disappeared and went into hiding or even exile. There are no extant records from Antiquity of what happened to him after he had greeted his disciples for the last time in Galilee – apart from the promise in John's Gospel and the letter of James that he would return and the possibility that Pontius Pilate wrote to Emperor Tiberius about him and that Tiberius decided not to do anything about Jesus.

The Secret of Jesus' Success

There can be no doubt that Jesus achieved much success in his campaign to gather supporters for his vision of a revived Israelite

---

[298] Eusebius. *Historia Ecclessiastica,* Liber III/I/1.
[299] Tabor. *The Jesus Dynasty,* 212.

kingdom. Various reasons for this success can be mentioned.

Jesus' recruits were mostly members of the Essene sect. One of their distinguishing characteristics was their abhorrence of opulence and luxury and their opposition to affluent people. The reason for this attitude is simple: they didn't like the rich people precisely because they were the poor ones. Poor people cannot help but to compare themselves with those who are more fortunate in financial terms and they often perceive that as an injustice. Jesus preached a popular theology by condemning the rich and powerful Jews – the influential priestly class and other members of the elite in Jerusalem, as well as the Roman overlords. This message resonated with the poor Jews' aspirations and beliefs.

The gap between the haves and the have-nots in the Jewish society created much tension and Jesus, together with John the Baptist, gave a voice to those who felt that they were left behind, were wronged, and were disadvantaged.

Many people in Jesus' time suffered under the Roman yoke and Jesus promised deliverance from that situation with the help of an army of angry and aggressive angels from above. There was a deep-seated yearning for a messiah, a savior out of this system of oppression, unbearable tax burdens, disrespect for their religious and cultural identity, lack of political independence, and the haughtiness of the Romans. Jesus fitted the expectations of the Jews for somebody to deliver them – he was a descendant of David, he was an excellent orator with a popular message, he had a clear vision for the future, and he had a charismatic personality that drew people to him. Jesus can be described as a populist orator whose message fitted the yearnings, wishes, hopes, and expectations of his audience. He told his supporters exactly what they wanted and needed to hear. The core of his teachings can be summarized with the following slogan: "The time is fulfilled, and the kingdom of God is at hand! Repent, and believe in the gospel" (Mark 1: 15).[300]

It was exactly this frustration with the Roman occupation of their country that led to the Jewish revolt in AD 66 and the bloody war that ended with the destruction of Jerusalem in AD 70.

The Jews of those times also shared the magical and mythological world-view, which Jesus espoused. They could believe in his magical healing powers, they accepted his power over sinister spirits, and they could believe in his promise that the Romans would be driven away by swarms of supernatural spirits, the angelic hordes sent by the God of Israel.

It was probably Jesus' plan to enhance his standing with his people as God's favorite son by seemingly dying on the cross and getting resurrected again, almost as if by magic. It is likely that Jesus sought support in Ps 16: 9–11 and saw it as a promise from God:

> "Therefore my heart is glad, and my tongue rejoices. My body shall also dwell in safety. For you will not leave my soul in Sheol, neither will you allow your holy one to see corruption. You will show me the path of life."

His plans did not work out as well as he had wished and he left the scene as a disappointed and disillusioned and deluded man.

The Legacy of Jesus

Jesus of Nazareth, also known as Jesus Christ, was a most remarkable man in all respects. He created a movement within Judaism, consisting of people who shared his dream of the restoration of the Israelite monarchy as promised by various prophets of Israel.

---

[300] This slogan of Jesus reminds one of the slogan of Ex-President Donald Trump: "Make America Great Again!"

People started collecting his teachings some time after his disappearance and the Q Document was the result. Some of the sayings and parables in the M and L sources were probably also part of Q, but were not included in the reconstructed Q because either Matthew, or Luke, did not make use of these parts.

Four gospels in the New Testament were written to preserve memories about him. A few apocryphal gospels also appeared.

After Jesus' disappearance, his followers branched off into different movements. His Jewish followers, who were mostly Essenes, became known as the Ebionites. Their leader was Jesus' brother, James the Just. The Gentile converts of Paul, who received visions and revelations in which a divine and heavenly Jesus appeared to him, were the first Christians. Christianity split into various factions and sects since the second century AD. The gnostic movement also claimed Jesus as their own and he was regarded as a gnostic teacher who preached a mystery religion.

In addition, there were also those who revered John the Baptist as a prophet and the gospels were written to convince them that Jesus was more important than John.

Of these three movements, Christianity in its orthodox variety won the day, although this religion is today divided into thousands of denominations, sects, movements, cults, associations, and schools. All of them claim to be followers of Jesus. Almost a third of the world's population call themselves Christians.

Because of all this, there can be no doubt that Jesus of Nazareth was the most influential figure in the history of mankind – although that was never his intention because he was only interested in liberating his people, the Jews, the lost sheep of the house of Israel.

Jesus had a clear vision – he wanted to establish a theocracy in Israel where the people would be liberated from foreign rule and be governed according to the principles and laws of the Hebrew Scriptures, as interpreted from an Essene perspective.

He would certainly have been horrified if he had known that he would later be worshipped as the eternal and divine Son of God by millions of Christians through the ensuing centuries. This development would have been totally unacceptable to him. He never envisaged a world-wide movement and his focus was exclusively on his own people, the Jews.

Many stories in the New Testament about him are legendary or even mythological, but there is much material that can be regarded as valid and historically valuable. The extreme skepticism of members of the Jesus Seminar about the reliability of the gospels is not warranted.

In the first chapter of this book, an article by Leopold Scholtz was mentioned. This historian examined the resurrection stories in the gospels, Acts, and 1 Corinthians 15 and concluded that the resurrection really happened, despite some discrepancies and contradictions in these narratives. This book can certainly confirm his finding and add that most of the reports about the teachings, healings, crucifixion, and survival of Jesus in the earliest sources before the start of the Jewish War in AD 66 can be accepted as essentially reliable and credible.

The process of researching and writing of this book is almost compatible with the work of an archaeologist who digs up the past below the surface of the earth and uncovers the signs and remains of the past. This book amounted to a search for signs of the past, the life of Jesus of Nazareth. The top layers of the stories we have about him, especially in the canonical gospels with their familiar texts, had to be cleared away.

These top layers, consisting of legends, mythological speculation, fiction, dogmatic prejudices, and plain superstition resting on a pre-scientific world view, had to be cleared away to uncover clues and signs about what really happened during Jesus' ministry in Palestine during the early thirties of the first century AD. To get to that point, it was necessary to reconstruct the process through which these stories came to be recorded and revised and reworked and added to.

What emerged, was the image of a first century Jewish rabbi who belonged to the party of the Essenes, who wanted to lead his people back to God, who taught a message of tolerance, forgiveness, charity, and hospitality, while he gathered supporters in his bid to rekindle the kingdom of his ancestor, King David. He tragically failed, but then his memory was hi-jacked by Paul and his followers who molded him into the founder of Christianity and the savior of the world, something he never envisaged or intended.

Albrecht Dürer: Christ on the Cross with the Angels

It has been shown that it is possible to interpret the canonical gospels in a rational, scientific, and original way when they are viewed within a wider perspective, with disinterested eyes, with an open mind, and without dogmatic prejudices. Many texts that caused problems for conventional and orthodox Christian scholars, suddenly become clear and make sense when viewed from the perspective presented in this book. A coherent, consistent, convincing, and credible picture of Jesus emerged.

Jesus of Nazareth certainly deserves a place in the history of Israel and the world, neither as a blasphemer, a deceiver, or a false prophet as seen from the viewpoint of conventional Judaism, nor as the savior of repentant and believing sinners and the second person of the Divine Trinity as regarded by Christians, but as a religious reformer and a tragically deluded hero.

BIBLIOGRAPHY

Editions of the Bible
Passages from the Bible are quoted from the *World English Bible* as found on a CD with the title *The Bible Collection, Deluxe Edition*, and published by ValuSoft, a division of THQ Inc, Waconia MN, 2002.

The above-mentioned CD also contains the Hebrew text of the Old Testament and the Greek text of the New Testament, as well as *Strong's Complete Greek & Hebrew Lexicon*. Other lexica utilized are mentioned under the heading of Other Publications.

The text of the Q Document, containing parts of the Gospel of Luke, were taken from the New Revised Standard Version, as corrected by Funk and Miller.

In addition, the following editions of the biblical text in the original languages were consulted:

Elliger, K. and W. Rudolph, eds. *Biblia Hebraica Stuttgartensia*. Stuttgart: Deutsche Bibelgesellschaft, 1997.

Nestle, E. and E. Nestle, eds. *Novum Testamentum Graece*. Stuttgart: Deutsche Bibelstiftung, 1981.

The text of the ancient Greek translation of the Old Testament, the so-called *Septuagint (LXX)*, was downloaded from the following website:

https://www.academic-bible.com/en/online-bibles/septuagint-lxx/read-the-bible-text/

The text of the ancient Latin translation of the New Testament, the Vulgate, was found in the following publication:

Wordsworth, Iohannes et A.M. White, eds. *Novum Testamentum Latine: Secundum Editionem Sancti Hieronymi, ad Codicum Mauscrip-*

torum Fidem Recensuerunt. London: Oxford University Press, 1955.

The Qur'an

Quotations from the Qur'an were taken from the translation by Talal Itani, ed. *Quran in English, Modern English Translation.*
https://blog.clearquran.com/download/

Other Literature

Ahmed, Hadhrat Mirza Ghulam. *Jesus in India: Jesus' Deliverance from the Cross & Journey to India.* (Translated from Urdu by Qasi Abdul Hamid and Chaudfry Mohammed Ali) London: Islam International Publications, 2003.

Akaberi, Maryam *et al.* "Therapeutic Effects of *Aloe* spp. in Traditional and Modern Medicine: A Review." Biomedicine & Pharmacotherapy , Volume 84, December 2016, Pages 759-772

Allen, Richard Hinckley. *Star Names: Their Lore and Meaning.* New York: Dover, 1963.

American Psychiatric Association. *Diagnostic and Statistical Manual of Mental Disorders, Fifth Edition, DSM-5.* Washington DC, American Psychiatric Association, 2013.

Anderson, Paul. *The Christology of the Fourth Gospel: Its Unity and Disunity in the Light of John 6 (With a New Introduction, Outlines, and Epilogue).* Cascade, Eugene, OR, 2010.

-----. "The John, Jesus, and History Project – New Glimpses of Jesus and a Bi-Optic Hypothesis". *Bible and Interpretation,* February 2010:
http://www.bibleinterp.com/articles/john1357917.shtml

Anon. "Famous People of Ancient Rome."
https://www.visionpubl.com/en/cities/rome/famous-people-ancient-rome/

-----. "Hebrew Days of the Week".
https://www.ivritalk.com/hebrew-days-of-the-week/

-----. " Mohammed and the Holy Monastery of Sinai".

http://www.sinaimonastery.com/en/index.php?lid=68
———. "Mount Precipice."
   https://www.israeljerusalem.com/mount-precipice.htm
Armstrong, Karen. *Fields of Blood: Religion and the History of Violence.* London: Vintage, 2014.
———. *Muhammad: a Biography of the Prophet.* London, Phoenix, 2001,
Aziz, Hasan. "Did Prophet Mohammad (PBUH) have epilepsy? A Neurological Analysis."
   https://doi.org/10.1016/j.yebeh.2019.106654Get rights and content
Barrett, C. K. *The Gospel According to St. John: an Introduction With Commentary and Notes on the Greek Text.* Philadelphia, Westminster, 1978.
Ben Sira. *The Wisdom (Ecclesiasticus).* United States Conference of Catholic Bishops.
   https://bible.usccb.org/bible/sirach/0
Ben-Tziyyon, Mordochai. "The "Suffering Servant" in ch.53 of *Y'shayahu".*
   https://mordochai.tripod.com/yshayahu53.html#top
Bible Hub. "Mark 15: 39".
   https://biblehub.com/commentaries/mark/15-39.htm
Biblical Archaeology Society Staff. "The Bethesda Pool, Site of one of Jesus' Miracles." Bible History Today, February 11, 2023.
   https://www.biblicalarchaeology.org/daily/biblical-sites-places/jerusalem/the-bethesda-pool-site-of-one-of-jesus-miracl.
———— "The Nag Hammadi Codices and Gnostic Christianity". Biblical Archaeology Society, February 07, 2023.
   https://www.biblicalarchaeology.org/daily/biblical-artifacts/the-nag-hammadi-codices/
Bolt, Peter G. Luke, a Commentary.
   https://www.thegospelcoalition.org/commentary/luke/
Bright, Hilda. "Letter of Joy: An Easy English Bible Version and Commentary (2800 word vocabulary) on Paul's Letter to the Philippians".

https://www.easyenglish.bible/bible-commentary/philippians-lbw.htm

Bultmann, Rudolf. *Das Evangelium des Johannes (Kritisch-exegetischer Kommentar* Biblical Archaeology Society Staff February 07, 2023*ntar Uber das Neue Testament, 2)*. Göttingen: Vandenhoeck & Ruprecht,1986.

Burkitt, F. Crawford. "The Historical Character of the Gospel of Mark". *The American Journal of Theology,* Vol XV, No 2, April 1911: 169 –93.

Catholic Encyclopedia. "Pope St. Clement 1", New Advent. https://www.newadvent.org/cathen/04012c.htm

Chadwick, H. "John the apostle, saint." Chicago: Encyclopædia Britannica, 2010.

Chenoweth, Ben. "Oral History and the e Beginning and End of the Gospel of Mark". *Evangelical Quarterly,* 90.1 (2019], 24–37.

Chilver, G.E.F. "Domitian". Chicago: Encyclopædia Britannica, 2010.

Clement of Rome. *First Epistle*. English Translation of 1 Clement by Charles Hoole. Early Christian Writings. http://www.earlychristianwritings.com/text/1clement-roberts.html

Cohn, H. *The Trial and Death of Jesus*. Old Saybrook, Ct: Konecky & Konecky, 1980.

Craighead, W.E. and C.B. Nemeroff, eds. *The Corsini Encyclopedia of Psychology and Behavioral Science, Volume 4*. Hoboken, NJ: John Wiley & Sons, 2002.

Dann, Moshe. "The Essenes and the Origins of Christianity: How the Essenes played a part in history". Jerusalem Post: 13 July, 2018. https://www.jpost.com/jerusalem-report/the-essenes-and-the-origins-of-christianity-562442

Deffner, Sebastian. "Static Electricity's Tiny Sparks". *The Conversation,* January 6, 2017. https://theconversation.com/static-electricitys-tiny-sparks-70637

Dolansky, S. "How the Serpent Became Satan : Adam, Eve and the Serpent in the Garden of Eden". *Biblical Archaeology*, 04.08.2016.

http://www.biblicalarchaeology.org/daily/biblical-topics/bible-interpretation/how-the-serpent-became-satan/

Didaché, the. Published on the website of Catholic Planet eBooks and is a reprint of the translation by Philip Schaff from the Jerusalem Manuscript of the Didache, originally published in 1885 by Funk & Wagnalls, New York.

Duling, Dennis. "The Jewish World of Jesus". In *The New Testament: An Introduction.* San Diego, Harcourt Brace Jovanovich, 1982, pp. 4–35.
https://pages.charlotte.edu/james-tabor/the-jewish-world-of-jesus-an-overview/

Early Christian Writings. *Gospel of Thomas Commentary.*
http://www.earlychristianwritings.com/thomas/

––––– "The Existence of Q".
http://www.earlychristianwritings.com/q-exist.html

–––––"Historical Jesus Theories".
https://www.earlychristianwritings.com/theories.html

–––––"The Lost Sayings Gospel Q at a Glance"
http://www.earlychristianwritings.com/q.html

––––– "The Priority of Mark".
http://www.earlychristianwritings.com/mark-prior.html

Earthquake Track. "Recent Earthquakes near Jerusalem, Israel.
https://earthquaketrack.com/il-06-jerusalem/recent

Eisenman, R. *James the Brother of Jesus: The Key to Unlocking the Secrets of Early Christianity and the Dead Sea Scrolls.* Harmondsworth: Penguin, 1997.

Encylopaedia Britannica, 2010. "Anne and Joachim, Saints".

–––––. "Census".

–––––. "Dehydration".

–––––. "Diaspora".

–––––. "Didache".

–––––. "Ebionites".

–––––. "Essenes".

–––––. "Gnosticism".

———. "James, The Letter of".
———. "Jewish Revolt, First".
———. "John The Baptist, Saint"
———. "Judas Iscariot".
———. "Maccabees.".
———. "Matthew Gospel of.".
———. "Matthew (the Evangelist), Saint".
———. "Nazarenes".
———. "Nazareth".
———. "Pantheism".
———. "Philo Judaeus".
———. "Pontius Pilate".
———. "Satan".
———. "Simon Magus".
———. "Simon the Apostle, Saint."
———. "Therapeutae."
———. "Tiberius".
———. "Zealots."
Encyclopedia.com. "Decapolis".
    https://www.encyclopedia.com/history/asia-and-africa/ancient-history-middle-east/decapolis#:~:text=Decapolis%20in%20biblical%20times%2C%20a,Philadelphia%2C%20Canatha%2C%20and%20Damascus.
———., "Spirit of God".
    https://www.encyclopedia.com/religion/encyclopedias-almanacs-transcripts-and-maps/spirit-god
Encyclopedia of the Bible. "Epistle of James".
    https://www.biblegateway.com/resources/encyclopedia-of-the-bible/Epistle-James
Enste, Stefan. *Kein Markustext in Qumran: eine Untersuchung der These: Qumran-Fragment 7Q5*. Paderborn: Universitätsverlag, 2000.
Epiphanios. *Panarion, Liber I*. Translated by Frank Williams.

https://web.archive.org/web/20170916133936/http://www.masseiana.org/panarion_bk1.htm

Eusebius of Caesarea. *Historia Ecclesiastica, Libri I, II, III et V.* http://www.documentacatholicaomnia.eu/03d/0265-0339,_eusebius_caesariensis,_church_history,_en.pdf

---- *Ευσεβιου Καισαρειας, Εκκλησιαστικη Ιστορια.* http://www.documentacatholicaomnia.eu/03d/0265-0339,_Eusebius_Caesariensis,_Historia_Ecclesiastica,_GR.pdf

Evans, Craig and Feldman, Steven. "The Tomb of Jesus? Wrong on Every Count." *Bible History Daily*, 1 February 2023. https://www.biblicalarchaeology.org/daily/archaeology-today/biblical-archaeology-topics/the-tomb-of-jesus-wrong-on-every-count/

Fortna, Robert T. "Jesus Tradition in the Signs Gospel". In Robert T. Fortna – Tom Thatcher (Eds.), *Jesus in Johannine Tradition*, Louisville Ky, Westminster John Knox, 2001, 199-208.

---- *The Fourth Gospel and its Predecessor: From Narrative Source to Present Gospel*, Philadelphia, Pa, Fortress Press, 1988.

Fredriksen, Paula. *Jesus of Nazareth, King of the Jews: A Jewish Life and the Emergence of Christianity.* London: Macmillan. 2000.

Freemon, Frank R. "A Differential Diagnosis of the Inspirational Spells of Muhammad the Prophet of Islam," *Journal of Epilepsia*, 17:4, 23–427, 1976.

Frontline. "The War Scroll". https://www.pbs.org/wgbh/pages/frontline/shows/religion/portrait/scrolltranslation.html

Gertoux, Gérard. *Herod the Great and Jesus : Chronological, Historical and Archaeological Evidence.* 2015. file:///C:/Users/User/Downloads/Herod_the_Great_and_Jesus_Chronological.pdf

Goldberg, G.J. "A Chronology of the First Jewish Revolt against Rome according to Josephus". https://www.josephus.org/warChronologyIntro.htm

Goulder, M. *St. Paul Versus St. Peter: A Tale of two Missions.* Atlanta: John Knox, 1995.

Gray, G.B., transl. "The Psalms of Solomon, Translated from Greek and Syriac Manuscripts". In *The Apocrypha and Pseudepigrapha of the Old Testament in English*, edited by R.H. Charles. Oxford: Clarendon, 1913.
http://wesley.nnu.edu/sermons-essays-books/noncanonical-literature/noncanonical-literature-ot-pseudepigrapha/the-psalms-of-solomon/

Hillar, Marion. "Philo of Alexandria." Internet Encyclopedia of Philosophy. https://iep.utm.edu/philo/

History Today. "Jewish Roman Wars".
https://www.heritage-history.com/index.php?c=resources&s=war-dir&f=wars_romanjewish

Hughes, Thomas Patrick. "Christianity" and "Jesus Christ". In *A Dictionary of Islam*. London, W.H. Allen & co, 1895.

International Standard Bible Encyclopedia. "Essenes".
https://www.internationalstandardbible.com/E/essenes.html

Irenaeus, Saint – of Lyons. *Adversus Haereses, Libri I et III*. Translated by Alexander Roberts and William Rambaut.
http://www.newadvent.org/fathers/0103126.htm
http://www.newadvent.org/fathers/0103314.htm

Jacobovici, Simcha, and Pelegrini, Charles. *The Jesus Family Tomb: The Discovery that will Change History Frever*. London: Harper Element, 2007.

Jacobus, H.R. "The Zodiac Sign Names in the Dead Sea Scrolls (4q318): Features and Questions". *Aram*, 24 (2012) 311–31.
file:///c:/users/user/downloads/the_zodiac_sign_names_in_the_dead_sea_sc.pdf

Jerusalem Post Staff. "Dust Storm Coats Jerusalem in Sand for the Second Time in a Month". May 21, 2022.
https://www.jpost.com/israel-news/article-707318

---- "Static Electricity Fire Engulfs Car in Flames at Israeli Gas Station.", 28 November 2016.

https://www.jpost.com/israel-news/watch-static-electricity-fire-engulfs-car-in-flames-at-israeli-gas-station-473865

Jewish Encyclopedia. "Nazarenes". In *Jewish Encyclopedia*, 1906/2021 https://www.jewishencyclopedia.com/articles/11393-nazarenes#anchor1

Jewish Virtual Library. "Death & Bereavement in Judaism: Ancient Burial Practices."
https://www.jewishvirtuallibrary.org/ancient-burial-practices

Johnson, B.A.. "The Gospel of Thomas: Manuscripts, Texts, and Early Citations".
https://owlcation.com/humanities/what-do-we-know-about-the-gospel-of-thomas

Jones, Arnold Hugh Martin, and Glen Richard Bugh, "Palestine". *Encyclopaedia Britannica*, Chicago, 2010.

Jones. Ron. "The Early Church Fathers on the Authorship of the NT Gospels: Historical Evidence for Matthew, Mark, Luke, and John".
https://www.academia.edu/9269890/Early_Church_Fathers_on_the_Authorship_of_the_NT_Gospels_Updated_5_2023_

Josephus, Flavius. *The Wars of the Jews, or History of the Destruction of Jerusalem*. In *The Genuine Works of Flavius Josephus the Jewish Historian. Translated from the Original Greek, According to Havercamp's Accurate Edition*. Translated by William Whiston, 1737.
http://penelope.uchicago.edu/josephus/ant-18.html

-----. *The Wars of the Jews, or History of the Destruction of Jerusalem*. Translated by W Whiston. Project Gutenberg E-Book, 2009McGrath, James F "He Shall Be Called a Nazorean: Intertextuality without an Intertext?" Paper presented in the Intertextuality in the New Testament consultation at the Society of Biblical Literature annual meeting in Atlanta, November 22nd, 2010).
https://digitalcommons.butler.edu/cgi/viewcontent.cgi?article=1285&context=facsch_papers

Judd, Frank F. Jr. "Perspectives about Pontius Pilate in the Ante-Nicene Fathers," *Studies in the Bible and Antiquity*: Vol. 8 , Article 9, 2016.
https://scholarsarchive.byu.edu/sba/vol8/iss1/9

Justin Martyr. *Dialogue with Trypho*,
http://www.earlychristianwritings.com/text/justinmartyr-dialoguetrypho.html

Kinzig, Wolfram. "The Nazoreans". In Oskar Skarsaune and Reidar Hvalvik, Eds., *Jewish Believers in Jesus*, Peabod, MS, Hendrickson, 2007, 463–87.

Klatt, Norbert. *Lebte Jesus in Indien?* Göttingen: Wallstein-Verlag, 1988.

Kloppenborg, John S. *Q, the Earliest Gospel : An Introduction to the Original Stories and Sayings of Jesus.* Louisville: Westminster John Knox, 2008.

Kohler, K. "Ebionites". In *Jewish Encyclopedia*, 1906/2021.
https://www.jewishencyclopedia.com/articles/5867-essenes#anchor24

Küng, Hans. Christ Sein. München: DTV Verlag, 1976.

McClintock and Strong. Biblical Cyclopedia, "Jessaeans".
https://www.biblicalcyclopedia.com/J/jessaeans.html

Kolb, Bryan and Ian Wishaw. *Fundamentals of Neuropsychology.* New York, Worth, 2009.

König, Adrio. *Die Groot Geloofswoordeboek.* Vereeniging: Christelike Uitgewersmaatskappy. 2006.

———. *Die Helfte is my nooit oor Jesus Vertel nie.* . Wellington: Lux Verbi, 2001.

Lévy, Carkos. "Philo of Alexandria". *Stanford Encyclopedia of Philosophy.*
https://plato.stanford.edu/entries/philo/

Lüdemann, G. *Heretics: The Other Side of Early Christianity.* Atlanta: John Knox, 1996.

Luschnig, C.E. and L.J. Luschnig. "The Teaching of the Twelve Apostles: A Greek Reader with Introduction and Notes."
http://www.worldwidegreek.com/downloads/didache.pdf

MacArthur, John. "Background to Colossians."
https://bible.org/seriespage/background-colossians
Mack, Burton. *The Lost Gospel: the Book of Q &Christian Origins*.
Brisbane: Element, 1994.
McDowell, Josh. "What is the document Q supposed to be?"
Josh McDowell Ministry
https://www.bethinking.org/bible/q-what-is-the-document-q-supposed-to-be
McGirk, Tim. "Jesus' Tomb Controversy Reopened". *Time*, 16 January 2008.
http://www.time.com/time/world/article/0%2C8599%2C1704299%2C00.html
McGrath, James F. "He Shall Be Called a Nazorean."
jfmcgrat@butler.edu
Medical News Today. "Health Benefits and Risks of Myrrh".
https://www.medicalnewstoday.com/articles/267107
Meier, John P. "The Present State of the 'Third Quest' for the Historical Jesus: Loss and Gain". *Biblica* 80 (1999) 459-487.
https://web.archive.org/web/20060827023818/http://www.bsw.org/project/biblica/bibl80/Comm11.htm
Mellowes, Marilyn. "More About Q and the Gospel of Thomas: An Accidental Discovery in Egypt Seems to Confirm the Existence of the 'Lost' Gospel of Q.
https://www.pbs.org/wgbh/pages/frontline/shows/religion/story/qthomas.html
Meyers, E.M. and M.A. Chancey. *Alexander to Constantine: Archaeology of the Land of the Bible*. New Haven: Yale University Press, 2012.
Miller, Robert J. ed. *The Complete Gospels: Annotated Scholars Version*. Sonoma, CA: Polebridge, 1992.
Mullins, Michael. *The Gospel of Matthew: a Commentary*. 30 November 1999.
https://www.catholicireland.net/the-gospel-of-matthew-a-commentary/
NASA. "Eclipse Web Site: Catalog of Solar Eclipses, 0001 To 100 Ce – 0029 Nov 24".

https://eclipse.gsfc.nasa.gov/5mcsemap/0001-0100/29-11-24.gif
——. "Eclipse Web Site: Catalog Of Lunar Eclipses, 0001 To 100 Ce – 0029 Dec 09."
https://eclipse.gsfc.nasa.gov/5mclemap/0001-0100/le0029-12-09p.gif
——. "Eclipse Predictions: Lunar Eclipses from 0001 to 0100, Jerusalem, Israel."
http://eclipse.gsfc.nasa.gov/jlex/jlex-as.html
Nasr, Seyyed Hossein. "Muhammad". Encyclopaedia Britannica, Chicago, 2010.
Nasrai, Abba Yesai. "Cherubic Sword: A Qabbalistic Glossary (With Some Nazorean Terms)".
https://www.faculty.umb.edu/gary_zabel/Courses/Phil%20281b/Philosophy%20of%20Magic/Arcana/Kabbalah/glossary9.htm
Nesbit, E. Planita. *Jesus an Essene.* Evinity Publishing, 2009.
https://www.sacred-texts.com/chr/jae/jae03.htm
New World Encyclopedia. "Pope Clement I."
https://www.newworldencyclopedia.org/entry/Pope_Clement_I
Nickel, Gordon. "Jesus in the Qur'an".
https://www.academia.edu/33310377/Jesus_in_the_Quran
Oakes, L. and L. Gahlin. *Ancient Egypt: An Illustrated Reference to the Myths, Religions, Pyramids and Temples of the Land of the Pharaohs.* London: Hermes, 2004.
O'Connor, Daniel William. "Peter the Apostle, Saint". *Encyclopaedia Britannica*, Chicago, 2010.
Origenes Adamnatios. *Contra Celsum.*
http://www.documentacatholicaomnia.eu/03d/0185-0254,_origenes,_contra_celsus,_en.pdf
Orlov, A. *The Atoning Dyad: The Two Goats of Yom Kippur in the Apocalypse of Abraham.* Studia Judaeoslavica, 8; Leiden: Brill, 2016.
Pace Health. "Aloe".
https://www.peacehealth.org/medical-topics/id/hn-2036003

-----. "Myrrh."
https://www.peacehealth.org/medical-topics/id/hn-2134003#:~:text=Myrrh%20is%20an%20anti%2Dinflammatory, doctors%20for%20people%20with%20UC.

Painter, J. *Just James – The Brother of Jesus in History and Tradition.* Minneapolis: Fortress, 1999.

Peterlin, Davorin. "Clement's Answer to the Corinthian Conflict In Ad 96". *JETS* 39/1 (March 1996) 57–69.

Philo Alexandrinus. *Every Good Man is Free,* XII, 75–87 (as quoted by Lawrence H. Schiffman, *Texts and Traditions*, Ktav, Hoboken 1998, p.282–284).
https://cojs.org/philo–_every_good_man_is_free_xii–_75–87–_description_of_the_essenes/

Pixner, Bargil. "Jerusalem's Essene Gateway: Where the Community Lived in Jesus' Time". *Biblical Archaeological Review,* May/June 1997.
http://www.centuryone.org/essene.html

Pliny. Natural History Liber V, xv. (Trans. H. Rackham, Pliny– Natural History II (Loeb Classical Library; Cambridge, Harvard University Press, 1942), p. 277.

Pocock, Helen. Christ has Everything you Need: An Easy English Commentary (2800 word vocabulary) on Paul's Letter to the Colossians.
https://www.easyenglish.bible/bible-commentary/col-lbw.htm

Pretorius, Albertus. *Jesus of Nazareth: a Deluded Messiah.* Eugene, OR, Wipf & Stock, 2022.

—— *The End of Christianity.* Eugene, OR, Wipf & Stock, 2022.

—— *Who, Where and What is God?* Eugene, OR, Wipf & Stock, 2022.

Ratzon, Eshbal. "The First Jewish Astronomers: Lunar Theory and Reconstruction of a Dead Sea Scroll". *Science in Context* 30(2), 113–139 (2017).
file:///C:/Users/User/Downloads/first_jewish_astronomers_lunar_theory_and_reconstruction_of_a_dead_sea_scroll%20(1).pdf

Robinson, James, *et al. The Critical Edition of Q: Synopsis including the Gospels of Matthew and Luke, Mark and Thomas with English,*

German, and French Translations of Q and Thomas, The International Q Project
Minneapolis, MN: Augsburg Fortress, 2000.
Rylaarsdam, J. Coert *et al.* "Biblical Literature". In *Encyclopædia Britannica*, 2010.
Sanders, E.P. "Paul, the Apostle, Saint." In *Encyclopædia Britannica*, 2010.
Schimmel, Annemarie. "Islam". In *Encyclopædia Britannica*, 2010.
Scholtz, Adelbert. *The Prophecies of Revelation: A Reconstruction of the Visions of John of Patmos*. Mauritius: Lambert Academic, 2017.
Scholtz, Leopold. "Jesus se Kruisiging en Opwekking: 'n Akademies–Historiese Waardering van die Bronne." (Jesus' Crucifixion and Resurrection, an Academic–Histrical Evaluation of the Sources) Tydskrif vir Geesteswetenskappe. vol.61 n.1 Pretoria Mar. 2021.
Sela, Shlomo. "Saturn and the Jews". In *Blog of the Katz Center for Advanced Judaic Studies, University of Pennsylvania*, November 10, 2017.
https://katz.sas.upenn.edu/resources/blog/saturn-and-jews
Simpson, Peter. "The Authenticity of the Gospels."
https://www.academia.edu/39849069/The_Authenticity_of_the_Gospels
Stephenson, F.R. "Eclipse". In *Encyclopaedia Britannica*, 2010.
Swaab, J. *Wij zijn ons Brein: Van Baarmoeder tot Alzheimer*. Amsterdam: Uitgeverij Contact. 2010.
Tabor, James D. *The Jesus Dynasty: Stunning New Evidence about the Hidden History of Jesus*. London: Harper Element, 2006.
Taylor, Joan E. "On Pliny, the Essene Location and Kh. Qumran". *Dead Sea Discoveries, 16 (2009) 1–21*.
The United States Conference of Catholic Bishops. "Luke".
https://bible.usccb.org/bible/luke/0
Thomas, Gospel of. Translated by Thomas O. Lambdin.
https://www.earlychristianwritings.com/text/thomas-lambdin.html

Tisdall, W. St. Clair. *The Original Sources of the Qur'an.* London, Society For Promoting Christian Knowledge, 1905. https://www.answering-islam.org/Books/Tisdall/Sources/index.htm

Toy, C.H. "Psalms of Solomon, The." In *Jewish Encyclopedia.* https://www.jewishencyclopedia.com/articles/12411-psalms-of-solomon-the.

Van Belle, Gilbert. "The Signs Source in the Fourth Gospel, a Critical Evaluation of the Semeia Hypothesis in Recent Research (1994–2013)". https://www.academia.edu/29027959/the_signs_source_in_the_fourth_gospel

Valis, Michel. "The old Nazoreans: A Higher Idea of God" https://www.academia.edu/34528711/The_Nazoreans_a_higher_idea_of_God?email_work_card=view-paper

Veronelli, Laura *et al.* "Geschwind Syndrome in Frontotemporal Lobar Degeneration: Neuroanatomical and Neuropsychological Features over 9 Years". *Cortex,* . 2017 Sep;94:27-38. doi: 10.1016/j.cortex.2017.06.003. Epub 2017 Jun 27.

Weatherspark. "Climate and Average Weather Year Round in Jerusalem, Israel" https://weatherspark.com/y/98866/Average-Weather-in-Jerusalem-Israel-Year-Round

Wikipedia. "Gospel of Thomas." https://en.wikipedia.org/wiki/Gospel_of_Thomas

———, "Jesus Seminar". https://en.wikipedia.org/wiki/Jesus_Seminar

———, "List of Dead Sea Scrolls". https://en.wikipedia.org/wiki/List_of_the_Dead_Sea_Scrolls

———. "List of Earthquakes in the Levant." https://en.wikipedia.org/wiki/List_of_earthquakes_in_the_Levan

Windle, Bryan. "Behold The Man: Where Did Pilate Sentence Jesus?" *Bible Archaeology Report,* 14 April 2022.

https://biblearchaeologyreport.com/2022/04/14/behold-the-man-where-did-pilate-sentence-jesus/

Wise, Michael O., Martin G. Abegg, and Edward M. Cook. *The Dead Sea Scrolls: a new translation.* Harper San Francisco, 1996. Reprinted at: https://www.qumran.org/js/qumran/hss/1qm

Wright, N.T. "The Self-Revelation of God in Human History: A Dialogue on Jesus with N.T. Wright". In Antony Flew. *There is a God: How the World's most Notorious Atheist Changed his Mind.* New York: Harper Collins, 2007.

Young, G.B. "Hyperthermia". In *Encyclopedia of the Neurological Sciences*, edited by M.J. Aminoff. Elsevier Science, 2003, 610–12.

Zachariah, Moby Sara. 'Tomb of Jesus' In Kashmir–Roza Bal Shrine. *India Heritage Walks.* https://www.indiaheritagewalks.org/blog/tomb-jesus-kashmir-roza-bal-shrine

Zeichmann, Christopher B. "Military Forces in Judaea 6–130 CE: The *status quaestionis* and Relevance for New Testament Studies." Currents in Biblical Research 2018, Vol. 17(1) 86–120. https://journals.sagepub.com/doi/pdf/10.1177/1476993X18791425

LIST OF ILLUSTRATIONS

Outside cover
Papyrus Fragment of the New Testament
https://www.christiantoday.com/article/rare.new.testament.fragment.found.on.ebay/71421.htm

Chapter 1
An evangelist writing (anonymous), 17th century
Metropolitan Museum of Art, New York
https://www.metmuseum.org/art/collection/search/397017

Albrecht Dürer: Jesus with the Crown of Thorns
https://za.pinterest.com/pin/290060032221037514/

Chapter 2
Map of Palestine during the First Century AD
https://www.conformingtojesus.com/images/webpages/israel_at_the_time_of_jesus_christ_1.png

Map of Jerusalem during the First Century AD
http://www.centuryone.org/essene.html

Chapter 4
The Apostle Paul' (494-495 AD), ceiling mosaic, Archiepiscopal Chapel of St. Andrew (oratory), Ravenna, Italy
https://www.jesuswalk.com/paul/01_saul.htm

Isaiah 53 in the Great Isaiah Scroll, the best preserved of the biblical scrolls found at Qumran from the second century BC
https://en.wikipedia.org/wiki/Isaiah_53

Part of Paul's Epistle to the Romans in Papyrus, early 3rd century
https://en.wikipedia.org/wiki/Holy_Spirit_in_the_Pauline_epistles

LIST OF ILLUSTRATIONS

Lucas van Leyden: Apostle Paul
https://collections.tepapa.govt.nz/object/38619

Chapter 5
The Raising of Lazarus
    Mosaic. Church of San Apolinar Nuovo. 530's. Ravenna, Italy
    https://pravoslavie.ru/69858.html

The Ossuary of Caiaphas who was High Priest in Jesus' Time
    https://en.wikipedia.org/wiki/Caiaphas_ossuary

Albrecht Dürer: The Entombment of Jesus, 1510
    https://en.wikipedia.org/wiki/List_of_woodcuts_by_Albrecht_D%C3%BCrer#/media/File:Albrecht_D%C3%BCrer,_The_Deposition,_probably_c._1509-1510,_NGA_6778.jpg

Albrecht Dürer: The Risen Christ
    https://en.wikipedia.org/wiki/List_of_woodcuts_by_Albrecht_D%C3%BCrer#/media/File:Albrecht_D%C3%BCrer,_The_Resurrection,_probably_c._1509-1510,_NGA_6779.jpg

Chapter 7
Lunar and Solar Eclipses
    NASA Eclipse Website

Computerized Recreations of the Night Sky with Pictures of Constellations
    https://stellarium.en.softonic.com/

Albrecht Dürer: An Evangelist
    https://smarthistory.org/albrecht-durers-woodcuts-and-engravings/

Albrecht Dürer: The Beheading of John the Baptist
    https://www.metmuseum.org/art/collection/search/388381

Denarius of Caesar Tiberius
    https://en.wikipedia.org/wiki/Tribute_penny

LIST OF ILLUSTRATIONS

Albrecht Dürer: Jesus on the Mount of Olives
https://www.metmuseum.org/art/collection/search/387410

Albrecht Dürer: The Resurrection
https://upload.wikimedia.org/wikipedia/commons/3/3a/The_Resurrection_MET_DP816789.jpg

Albrecht Dürer: Jesus Placed in the Tomb
https://en.wikipedia.org/wiki/List_of_woodcuts_by_Albrecht_D%C3%BCrer#/media/File:Albrecht_D%C3%BCrer,_The_Deposition,_c._1497,_NGA_6688.jpg

Chapter 8
Albrecht Dürer: The Nativity
https://www.kellybagdanov.com/2017/12/15/albrecht-durer/

A computerized recreation of the conjunction between the planets Jupiter and Saturn
www.stellarium.com

The Three Magi from the East
https://www.european-traveler.com/italy/see-the-basilica-of-santapollinare-nuovo-in-ravenna/

Albrecht Dürer: The Flight to Egypt
https://www.nationalgallery.org.uk/exhibitions/past/durers-journeys-travels-of-a-renaissance-artist/durer-the-printmaker

Albrecht Dürer: Saint Peter
https://www.metmuseum.org/art/collection/search/387760

Albrecht Dürer: The Last Judgment
https://www.metmuseum.org/art/collection/search/388072

Albrecht Dürer: Resurrection of Jesus
https://en.wikipedia.org/wiki/List_of_woodcuts_by_Albrecht_D%C3%BCrer#/media/File:Albrecht_D%C3%BCrer,_The_Resurrection,_probably_c._1509-1510,_NGA_6779.jpg

LIST OF ILLUSTRATIONS

Chapter 9

Albrecht Dürer: The Annunciation
https://www.metmuseum.org/art/collection/search/388039

Albrecht Dürer: Adoration of the Shepherds
https://commons.wikimedia.org/wiki/File:Adoration_of_the_Shepherds_%28Albrecht_D%C3%BCrer%29.jpg

Albrecht Dürer: The Prodigal Son
https://commons.wikimedia.org/wiki/File:Albrecht_D%C3%BCrer_-_The_Prodigal_Son_-_WGA7275.jpg

Albrecht Durer: Christ and the Disciples at Emmaus.
https://www.wikiart.org/en/albrecht-durer/christ-and-the-disciples-at-emmaus-1511

Albrecht Dürer: The Ascension
https://commons.wikimedia.org/wiki/File:D%C3%BCrer_-_Ascension_of_Christ.jpg

Albrecht Dürer: Outpouring of the Holy Spirit
https://www.wikiart.org/en/albrecht-durer/the-descent-of-the-holy-spirit-1511

Chapter 10

Albrecht Dürer: Jesus and his Mother
https://artuk.org/discover/stories/ten-things-to-know-about-albrecht-durer

Albrecht Dürer: The Last Supper
https://www.metmuseum.org/art/collection/search/388486

Chapter 13

P. Oxy. 1 – A papyrus fragment of the Greek Gospel of Thomas, found at Oxyrhynchus
https://en.wikipedia.org/wiki/Gospel_of_Thomas

Albrecht Dürer: The Sower

LIST OF ILLUSTRATIONS

https://commons.wikimedia.org/wiki/File:Albrecht-Durer-The-Parable-of-the-Sower.jpg

Albrecht Dürer: Jesus Appears to his Disciples
https://collections.artsmia.org/art/47547/christ-appearing-to-his-disciples-albrecht-duerer

Chapter 14

Albrecht Dürer: Mary with Child
https://www.metmuseum.org/art/collection/search/391214

Albrecht Dürer: The Last Supper (1523)
https://www.wikiart.org/en/albrecht-durer/the-last-supper-1523

Chapter 15

Albrecht Dürer: Christ before Pilate
https://www.metmuseum.org/art/collection/search/387416

The inside of the Talpiot Tomb with Simcha Jacobovici
https://www.nbcnews.com/id/wbna17599355

Albrecht Dürer: Virgin and Child on the Crescent with a Diadem
https://www.metmuseum.org/art/collection/search/391214

Albrecht Dürer: Christ on the Cross with the Angels
https://www.wikiart.org/en/albrecht-durer/christ-on-the-cross-with-three-angels-1525

www.ingramcontent.com/pod-product-compliance
Lightning Source LLC
Chambersburg PA
CBHW052037290426
44111CB00011B/1535